dBASE IV

BEYOND THE BASICS

dBASE IV

BEYOND THE BASICS

Mark Brownstein
Dan D. Gutierrez

John Wiley & Sons, Inc.
New York • Chichester • Brisbane • Toronto • Singapore

Library of Congress Cataloging-in-Publication Data

Brownstein, Mark.
    dBase IV : beyond the basics / Mark Brownstein, Dan Gutierrez.
      p. cm.
    Includes index.
    ISBN 0-471-61748-2 (pbk.)
      1. Data base management.   2. dBASE IV (Computer program)
    I. Gutierrez, Dan.   II. Title.
    QA76.9.D3B784   1991
    005.75′65—dc20   90-29088

Printed in the United States of America

10 9 8 7 6 5 4 3 2 1

Trademarks

Foreword

dBASE was created when one computer user needed a simple, flexible, productive, and functional database tool. It just so happened that the user was a talented programmer at Pasadena's Jet Propulsion Laboratory named Wayne Ratliff. In 1975, when Wayne needed a way to track statistics for the football pool, he created a "scaled-down" version of JPLDIS, a mainframe database language. He put it on his IMSAI 8080 (a 48K computer built from a kit) and called it Vulcan. It was later marketed by Ashton-Tate as dBASE II, the precursor of today's Clipper, FoxBase+, FoxPro, dBXL, Quicksilver, and, of course, dBASE III+ and dBASE IV.

The original Vulcan solved a real-world need, and that's the legacy of all dBASE-related tools. Today, dBASE IV addresses a much greater range of needs, but the intent is the same—to put the power in the user's hands and to get the job done. Whether you manage a mailing list, analyze financial data, or develop custom applications for resale, dBASE IV provides a solution.

Of course, there's a price to pay for all the power. That price is the time and effort it takes to learn and master the tool. dBASE IV is big. It was developed through years of research and development by hundreds of programmers, designers, and testers at Ashton-Tate. So, where do *you* start? Do you use the Query by Example, the application generator, the report generator, the template language, SQL, or the programming language? Can the Control Center meet your needs? Which feature does the job, and what level of skill does it require?

Fortunately, you don't have to face these questions alone. *dBASE IV: Beyond the Basics* guides you carefully through the complexities of dBASE IV. You learn by doing, so you get a feel for what works and what doesn't. The book focuses on dBASE's "automatic" features, so you don't have to become a programming whiz. (If you want to program, the book provides a solid foundation.) In *dBASE IV: Beyond the Basics*, Mark Brownstein and Dan Gutierrez take you under the hood of dBASE IV, and you won't even get grease under your fingernails.

—David M. Kalman
Columnist for DATABASE PROGRAMMING AND DESIGN
Former editor of DATA BASED ADVISOR
President of Kalman Technology/Communications.

Preface

It may be a little known fact, but the Preface to most books, including this one, is written last—thus allowing the luxury of putting afterthoughts first. During the development, concepts for a computer book often change. These changes represent the many modifications of the program from the time the book was started through the time it was completed.

When this book was begun, Version 1.0 of dBase IV had just started receiving criticism from a handful of vocal developers who were finding that (1) the program was slow, and (2) it was buggy. Both indictments were true, but ignored some other important factors. Most of the bugs found were relatively obscure—if you were a developer who was writing original program code, you could occasionally find bugs. If you were comparing performance of dBase IV to compiled applications (such as those created using FoxBase, FoxPro, or Clipper), the speed issue was real.

But the point that was missed by press reports and developer complaints was that real, useful work could still be done using dBASE IV. If you wanted to design and run applications that didn't require you to get into the programming aspects of dBASE IV, you could do so. Many applications have been designed by nonprogrammers, and are actually doing what they were designed to do.

Version 1.1 of dBASE IV is much improved. Most bugs have been exterminated— the ones that remain will be the esoteric ones that were not discovered by the more than 2,300 beta testers and the millions (literally) of internal tests performed by Ashton-Tate. The program runs considerably faster than its predecessor, and it features vastly improved memory management.

For the nonprogrammer, the interface is nearly bulletproof.

Who This Book Is for

When conceived, this book was thought of as a follow-up and enhancement of *USING dBASE IV: Basics for Business*. In many ways it is a much improved successor, just as Version 1.1 is a much improved successor to Version 1.0.

The book had two basic goals. The first was to provide useful examples that would guide nonprogrammers in developing truly useful, effective applications using dBASE IV. If you aren't a programmer, and don't want to learn to program, this book is for you. If you aren't a programmer, but want to learn, the code generated by the many examples in this book will also provide a good set of examples to learn how your design can generate code.

The Control Center in dBASE IV allows you to build complete applications without writing any programming code. The only things approaching programming are the unavoidable descriptions and conditions that you must learn to specify in order to take advantage of special features in dBASE IV. If you are afraid of programming, and merely want to get things done, this book should be easy enough, and provide enough examples that can be copied into your specific applications, to allow you to develop your applications.

Midway through the writing of this book, my excellent technical editor, Dan Gutierrez, became my co-author. The chapters on the Application Generator are his and provide what are among the best explanations of the Application Generator available anywhere. When put into the context of a nonprogrammer's tutorial, the chapters are quite an accomplishment.

My dealings with Dan, a professional developer, confirmed and amplified what I had suspected when I started work on my first book—experienced programmers can also take advantage of the Control Center for developing applications.

Here's why: The Control Center provides an easy to use interface into dBASE IV. You can define the way a form or report should look, and dBASE IV writes the code that makes your definition work. You can easily define a query, pulling data from a number of data files, by simply defining links between records and describing any calculated or other fields, and dBASE IV produces the code to retrieve the desired data.

Although many longtime programmers protest that they've gotten their basic forms and tools already and that they can write better code than dBASE IV can generate, they're missing the point. Although dBASE IV can't replace the tools that have been developed over many years' effort, the Control Center can provide a very rapid way to produce new applications.

Dan recently told me about an application that required rapid development and a low budget. Instead of cranking out his coding tools, he took advantage of the Control Center's features and designed an application that was quickly put into use. The application met the user's specifications, the speed of development made Dan look like a hero, and the time saved kept Dan well under budget.

Another benefit to the programmer is that applications can be quickly prototyped and presented to the client for approval. Once a shell application is developed, the client can suggest changes, and the changes can be rapidly demonstrated. Later, the developer can fine tune the design, if desired.

Thus, this book should be useful for both the nonprogrammer and the experienced developer. The examples included in the book should be general enough to serve as a basis for your application needs. Whenever possible, more than one way to accomplish a particular task is demonstrated.

Why You May Have Bought This Book

You purchased this book because you have dBASE IV or you don't have dBASE IV. This much is obvious. If you already use dBASE IV, this book will be a useful document that will guide you through design and implementation of data management systems. If you don't own dBASE IV, you may be exploring the product as one of a number of potential candidates for meeting your data management needs. A number of powerful PC-based data management packages are available. However, for ease of use and raw power, none compare to dBASE IV, for a number of reasons.

The easy-to-use data managment titles, represented by programs like Professional File, Q&A, Reflex 2, PC:FILE, and other, provide user interfaces that range from elegant to rather difficult. However, these programs do not have the relational capabilities of dBASE IV. In this book you'll see why the relational model is much more powerful than that used by these so-called flat file data managers.

If your data needs don't extend beyond simple mailing lists, perhaps dBASE IV may be more database than you need.

At the other extreme, programs like Clipper can provide high levels of data management power. However, those products require an intimate knowledge of programming and are far from easy to use.

FoxPro and other "fast" data management tools provide relational capabilities. But Dan and I agree that their user interfaces are far from intuitive. It isn't easy to design database systems using these tools.

Which brings us back to dBASE IV. In spite of the warts that certain developers have pointed out, dBASE IV has an extremely good user interface. Using the techniques shown in this book, you can take advantage of the power of dBASE IV without the pain.

Acknowledgments

There are a few people who deserve special acknowledgment for their help in providing the necessary resources or support that was required finally to get this book completed.

To Liz Sidnam-Wright, I offer a large dose of gratitude for her help in steering my requests for assistance through the layers of politics at Ashton-Tate. I also thank Ed Esber, Bill Lyons, David Proctor, and James Neiser for the assistance needed at critical moments.

Thanks also go to Dave Kirkey at Advanced Logic Research for the use of the ALR 386-25, which was used for the writing of the book. And thanks to Pat Meier for arranging the use of the Tandon system for running dBASE IV.

Data Products provided the laser printer that was used to create the output for the first eleven chapters, and Hammermill provided the special laser printer paper. My gratitude also goes to SymSoft for HotShot Graphics, which was used to capture the screens used in this book.

I don't want to leave out thanks to Katherine Schowalter for her patience throughout the development of this book.

And special thanks go to my family: Vonnie, Charles, and Barbara for putting up with me during the years this hellacious project took to complete.

Finally, I'd like to thank the reader of this book for choosing this over the many others. You made the right choice.

Mark Brownstein

Contents

1

The Control Center

dBASE IV was designed by Ashton-Tate to provide the user and developer with most, if not all, of the features of the many competing database products and the wide array of products that have been developed as add-ons for dBASE III and dBASE III + . Among the many important features are an intermediate compiler that converts a program into code that runs more quickly than programs written in earlier versions of dBASE, an applications generator that allows the user to design and build complete applications with a minimal amount of programming, and an entirely new user interface.

Version 1.1 includes a number of enhancements. Most of the enhancements relate to the hardcore developer, who has been asking for them in order to significantly improve his or her programming powers. However, several important enhancements have also been added to the non-programmer-specific components of Version 1.1 that make it more powerful and easier to use than was the original dBase IV Version 1.0.

The new user interface, called the *dBASE IV Control Center*, allows you to interact with the program in most of the areas where such interaction is necessary to design, analyze, and print reports, labels, and other items. The Control Center is the primary user interface used in this book, and, it is hoped, will be the interface of choice for most of the users of this book. Experienced dBASE IV programmers can take advantage of features in the Control Center to ease the development process and speed up the design and implementation of database systems.

Even if you are a veteran dBASE programmer, you will find many elements of the Control Center that will assist you in the development of database management systems by automatically generating program code for the forms, reports, queries, and applications that you will continue to develop.

A Look at the Control Center

The Control Center normally comes up as a default menu item when you have installed dBASE IV using the automatic installation procedures that are included with the program. The Control Center screen is shown in Figure 1-1. If the screen doesn't look like this, it is probably because dBASE IV was installed so that it does not automatically display the Control Center when the program is first started. The change to the program was made in the CONFIG.DB file, by modifying the file with a text editor, a word processor, or SETUPDB, or from within the dBASE IV text editor. The change will remain in effect until the CONFIG.DB file is changed.

If you don't see the Control Center on your screen, there are two ways to activate it. The first way is to Type: *ASSIST Enter*

The command ASSIST is left over from dBASE III+, which used the same command to load its much less capable user interface. When you type the command, and press the **Enter** key, the dBASE IV Control Center is loaded into the system, and you see a screen that looks like Figure 1-1. (Differences in display types and setup may make screens in this book look somewhat different from those on your computer; the general layout of each screen should be substantially similar, however).

The second way to bring up the Control Center is to press the **F2** key. The **F2** key was defined at setup as issuing the ASSIST command. In effect, when you press the **F2** key, the system types *ASSIST Enter* for you.

In fact, when you press the **F2** key, you'll see the word *ASSIST* flash briefly on the screen before the Control Center pops into view.

There is an instance when the **F2** key doesn't automatically load the Control

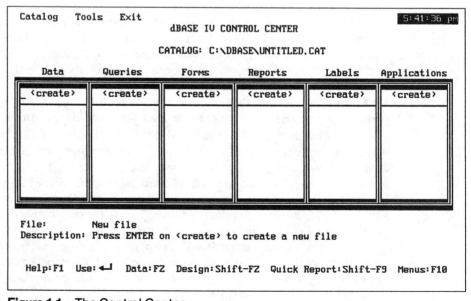

Figure 1-1 The Control Center.

Center—especially if the system didn't automatically bring you there. dBASE IV allows the user to redefine the meaning of the function keys and other keys. The standard definition for the **F2** key is **Assist;** (the semicolon indicates a return (or **Enter**) should be pressed). However, a user can redefine the key to mean something else.

It is remotely possible that the key was redefined by a previous user, or by the person who installed the program, to mean something other than the command to load the Control Center user interface. For now, however, we'll assume that the function keys carry the functional definitions as they are set initially by Ashton-Tate.

The Control Center provides you with a substantial amount of information. The prominent feature of the screen is a series of six connected columns (referred to as *panels*), with the headings for each bar appearing above the box produced by the set of panels. For now, you'll look at the menu from the top down.

At the top left corner of the screen are three menu items; *Catalog*, *Tools*, and *Exit*. These menus will be dealt with in more detail shortly. For now, however, suffice it to say that the menus perform the functions that their titles suggest: the Catalog menu allows you to select and modify data files and other related files (including data input forms, report formats, queries, labels, and other design files) to be used in your application. The Tools menu provides you with useful utilities for data management, for import and export of data, for control of your files through a DOS function, and for the way that you interact with the program. And the Exit menu allows you the option of quitting dBASE IV or jumping to the dot prompt programming interface.

At the right side of the screen, the current time of day may appear. Display of the time of day is an option that can be modified from within DBSETUP or by modifying the CONFIG.DB file. In the examples used in this book, the clock will be displayed.

The top line of this screen, and that of many screens produced by dBASE IV, provides you with command menus that can be pulled down (or opened up) to display additional commands or command options. With the Applications Generator, you will be able to design pull-down menus, like those that are used throughout dBASE IV, in addition to pop-up windows and other types of displays. These will also be covered later in this book.

The next line on the screen is a title line. In this case, it tells the user that he or she is viewing the dBASE IV Control Center screen. Although this may seem obvious, the information is useful, because you can easily design screens that appear similar to the main screen in the Control Center but aren't part of the Control Center. Also, having a title line is especially useful when working inside other panels.

The next line on the screen shows the name and directory path for the catalog currently in use. In the case illustrated in Figure 1-1, the catalog shown is the default catalog that comes onto the screen when you first load dBASE IV. The catalog currently in use here is called UNTITLED.CAT and is located in the C:\DBASE\ directory path.

When a catalog has been selected or created, and you properly exit from dBASE IV, the system will remember which catalog you last used and will bring that catalog up on the screen the next time you use dBASE IV. A proper exit from dBASE IV is one done using the Exit menu from within the Control Center, or by using the QUIT command from within the dot prompt interface. Both types of exit allow the system to close any opened file, and record the active catalog.

An improper exit, which can be performed by turning off the computer while dBASE IV is running, by performing a warm boot (simultaneously pressing the **Ctrl-Alt-Del** keys), or by power failure while running dBASE IV will probably result in loss of any changes made during a worksession. In addition, an improper exit may also result in loss or destruction of the database files in use. You should thus be extremely careful to regularly back up your work, and to be certain to make a proper exit from dBASE IV before shutting the computer off or rebooting it.

The next line shows the panel titles. The area that includes the panel titles and panels is referred to as the *work area*. Data management, retrieval, printing, report generation, analysis, forms creation, programming, and applications development can all be performed using the tools provided by the panels. Each panel will be briefly explained, and navigation will be discussed shortly.

Below the work area is the name of the file currently selected or currently in use. As you move the cursor through the panels, and onto the various entries in each panel, the *File:* line will show the name of the currently highlighted file.

The line below the filename shows a description of the file that you assign to it when it is created or stored. A file can be renamed from within the Catalog menu. In addition, as shown here, when <create> is highlighted from within a panel, the system instructs you how to activate the <create> function. In effect, the description for the <create> file is the instruction to press **Enter** to create a new file.

Remember that the description line can also be used for any relevant comment relating to the file highlighted—and in some cases, you may wish to issue an instruction, rather than a file description, as was done here.

The bottom line displayed indicates keys that can be used to perform certain operations. For example, the first item, *Help:F1*, tells you that if you require help, you should press the **F1** key. To see how it works, press **F1** now.

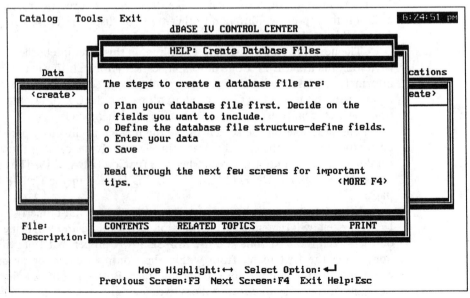

Figure 1-2   A Help screen.

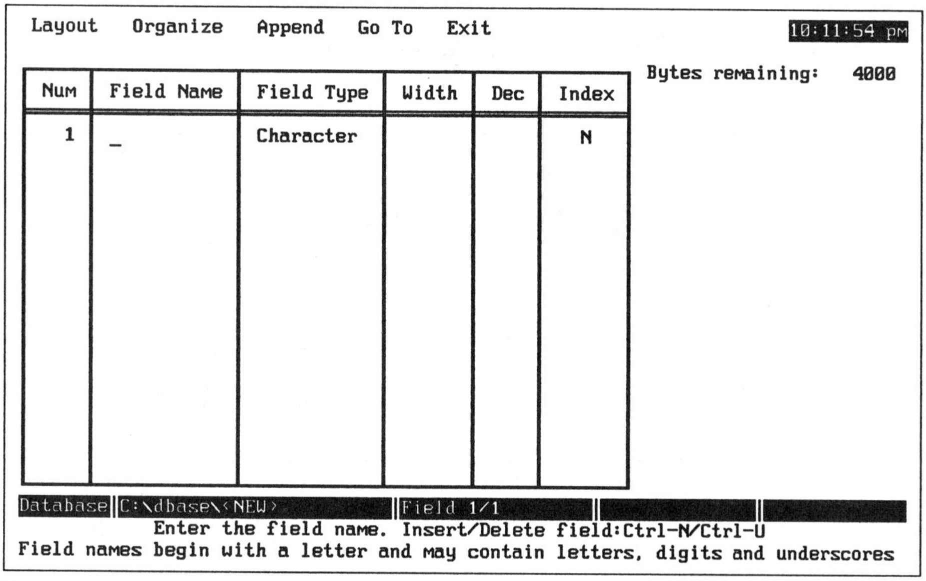

```
   Layout   Organize   Append   Go To   Exit              10:11:54 PM
                                                    Bytes remaining:   4000
  ┌─────┬────────────┬────────────┬───────┬─────┬────────┐
  │ Num │ Field Name │ Field Type │ Width │ Dec │ Index  │
  ├─────┼────────────┼────────────┼───────┼─────┼────────┤
  │  1  │ _          │ Character  │       │     │   N    │
  │     │            │            │       │     │        │
  └─────┴────────────┴────────────┴───────┴─────┴────────┘
  Database│C:\dbase\<NEW>                │Field 1/1
           Enter the field name. Insert/Delete field:Ctrl-N/Ctrl-U
  Field names begin with a letter and may contain letters, digits and underscores
```

Figure 1-3   Two-line message line.

The screen will look like Figure 1-2.

Similarly, pressing the keys indicated on the bottom of the screen will perform the functions indicated on the line. These capabilities will be discussed shortly.

An additional line, not seen on the screen yet, is a message line. The bottom two lines of the screen are used for an instruction, and for a message. Figure 1-3 shows the two message lines in an empty Database design screen.

A Closer Look at the Control Center

Now that you've taken a broad look at the Control Center, a closer look should provide much more detail about the basic features of this screen. It is important to note that the screen is relatively basic—conventions and design features in this screen are emulated in numerous other screens when you are working with dBASE IV. A strong understanding of the basics of navigation from within dBASE IV's Control Center will help you get familiar with the overall feel of the program.

Selecting a Menu

The menu line at the top of the screen shows the title of the pull-down menus available from within that screen. In the case of the main Control Center screen, the three menu items are *Catalog*, *Tools*, and *Exit*. Figure 1-3, the Database design screen, provides you with five menu options: *Layout*, *Organize*, *Append*, *Go To*, and *Exit*.

The menus available will vary, based on which panel you are working in.

There are two ways to select a pull-down menu. The first is to press the **F10** key. Now press **Esc** to close the help screen, and press **F10** to open the pull-down menu.

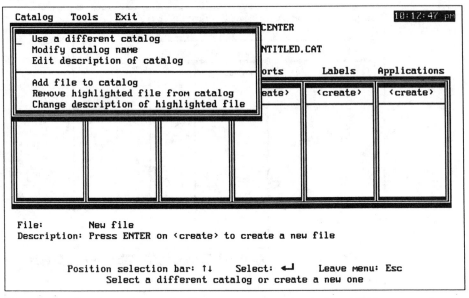

Figure 1-4   Catalog menu—the first menu popped up when **F10** is pressed.

If this is the first time you've pulled down a menu since you started this dBASE IV session, you'll see the screen as shown in Figure 1-4. The system brings up the Catalog menu when you first press **F10**. However, the **F10** key doesn't always bring up the Catalog menu when you press the key—it will bring up the last menu that you used during your session.

To see this, press the **Left Arrow** or the **Right Arrow** key. You will see that pressing the **Right Arrow** moves the highlight to the right, bringing up the Tools menu, and then the Exit menus, before returning to the Catalog menu.

Similarly, the **Left Arrow** key moves to the left, and then begins moving to the left from the rightmost panel. The arrow keys, then, move the highlighted panel in the direction that they are pointing. When they have reached the end of the options available in that direction, they will scroll through, beginning from the first entry available. They move as if the first and last options were somehow connected—that is, as if they were, perhaps, wrapped around a tube, end to end, so that in the case of the Control Center, for example, *Catalog* would naturally occur to the right of *Exit*, and the Exit menu would naturally be to the left of the Catalog menu.

To see how the **F10** key selects the menu last used, move the highlight, using the arrow keys, so that it is on the Tools menu. The Tools menu looks like Figure 1-5. Next, press **Esc** to close the menu and return to the Control Center work area.

To see that **F10** does, indeed, select the menu last used, press **F10** now. As expected, the Tools menu will be on the screen.

There is a simpler way to select a desired menu. This method is especially useful for other screens that may have as many as six or more menu pop-ups. Using **F10** may bring you to the menu last used. But if you want to select another menu, the Arrow keys, while fast, are still somewhat slower than the method about to be discussed.

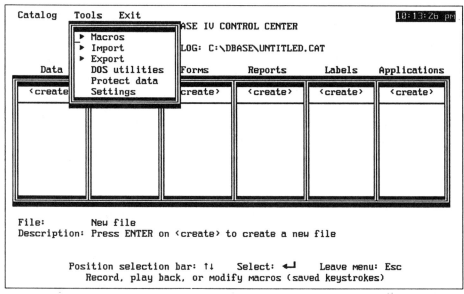

Figure 1-5   Tools menu.

To rapidly pop up a menu window, press **Alt** plus the first letter of the menu's heading. For example, in the current menu, **Alt-C** would bring up the Catalog menu, **Alt-T** would bring up the Tools menu, and **Alt-E** would bring up the Exit menu.

Once you've gotten used to this method, it is doubtful that you'll ever want to go back to using the **F10** key to open a menu window.

The Menu Windows

Now that you've seen how simple it is to open a menu window, you'll learn about the contents of the menu windows and how to select menu items.

Reopen the Catalog window (by pressing **Alt-C**).

You should notice that a colored background bar (if you're using a color monitor) or a shaded background (if you're using a monochrome system) highlights the top line of the menu, *Use a different catalog*. By pressing the **Up Arrow** or **Down Arrow** keys, you can move the highlight to any appropriate option.

It is important to notice that only the top four options are visible in highlighted (or bold) text. The bottom two options, *Remove highlighted file from catalog* and *Change description of highlighted file* are in dimmer type. The dimmer type indicates that the option is not currently available.

In the current example, it's clear why. You haven't highlighted any files yet.

Once you create or select an existing file, those two options will become available. The distinction between available and unavailable options is more important in other screens. This is because many of the menu screens used in dBASE IV are shared by more than one panel, and not all options in the menu are available to or appropriate for all the panels.

For example, the Words menu window includes options for varying the style of the text characters being printed. This menu is used in designing reports, labels, and forms. The text style attribute is not available in all panels, although the menu clearly includes the option.

Options that cannot be selected also cannot be highlighted using the Arrow keys. To see this, press the **Up Arrow** key. You will notice that the system skipped the bottom two items that were not highlighted, and therefore not selectable, and highlighted the first option available in that direction, *Add file to catalog*. Pressing **Down Arrow** will similarly skip the bottom two nonselectable items and return you to the first selectable item in the catalog.

Later, after you've added a database file and selected it, the last two options will become available and will be highlighted by the **Up Arrow** and **Down Arrow** keys.

You will also notice another key component of many of the menu screens—a line dividing the menu window into two or more parts. The line is used to separate component parts that may perform different tasks.

In the case of the Catalog menu, the top three items deal with loading and defining a catalog. The catalog includes all related files, forms, and other design formats that are included in one larger data management catalog.

The bottom three items deal with management of files that are included in the current panel in the catalog. Thus, the lower three items deal with your data at a *file* level, while the upper three deal with the catalog *as a whole*. Other screens will feature menu windows similarly divided by functional grouping. When you use the Applications Generator, you will also have the ability to design panels using lines to separate options into functional groups.

As with the selection of menu windows, there is more than one way to select a menu option. The first way, which you've already seen, is to move the highlight to the desired option using the arrow keys. Once the item is highlighted, pressing the **Enter** key will activate that selection.

A second, somewhat faster method is to type the first letter of the option (or, in some cases, the first capital letter in the option line). When the first letter (or first capital letter) is typed, the desired option will automatically be selected and activated.

To see this, press **U**.

Use a different catalog will be highlighted, and the Catalog menu, which appears something like that seen in Figure 1-6, will appear. Please note that, if you haven't created other catalogs, only the <create> option and UNTITLED.CAT will be displayed.

This screen also shows another capability of dBASE IV. You will notice that one or two new windows popped onto the screen when you selected *Use a different catalog*. At the right of the Catalog menu, slightly below the time, a window has popped up to select a catalog to use. At the lower part of the work area, a second window has popped up, showing the description of the selected catalog, if there is one.

In the case of the list shown in Figure 1-6, a highlight was moved to the catalog called *PERSONEL.CAT*. A description was given to this catalog. When the highlight is moved to this catalog, the description appears in the window.

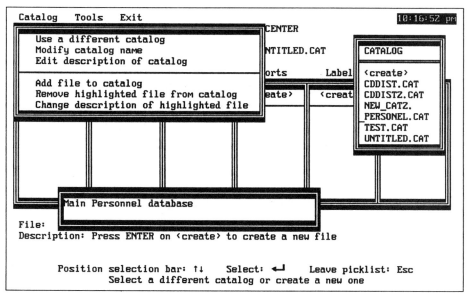

Figure 1-6   Catalog selection pick list.

Selecting from a Pick List

A pick list is a list with a number of choices. As seen in Figure 1-6, a number of catalogs could have been selected, and you could have selected the one you wanted by moving the highlight to the item you wished to pick, and pressing **Enter**.

But there's an easier way.

To show how this is done, the PERSONEL.CAT catalog was loaded into the system. There is no need for you to try to create items now to test this example—in future chapters you'll make good use of the pick lists.

In Figure 1-7, the contents of PERSONEL.CAT are displayed. It is obvious that there are many data files and form files that can be selected. Using the arrow keys will work, but the arrows are slower than the method to be discussed here.

In dBASE IV, you can type the first characters in the name of a pick list item. As you do, the highlight will move to the first entry in the list that exactly matches the letters typed so far. The first letters in those items in the pick list that match all the characters so far typed will change. The change will appear as a change in the color of the first letter(s) of the item name.

For example, assume that you wanted to select EMP_DATA. When *E* is pressed, the highlight will move to the line with EEOC as a file entry. This is shown in Figure 1-8. The first letter in EMP_DATA is not changed, and the highlight is on EEOC.

Now pressing **M,** the second letter of the item you wish to pick, moves the highlight to the EMP_DATA line. Here the first two letters of the item, E and M, are highlighted. Once the desired item is highlighted, press **Enter** to complete the selection.

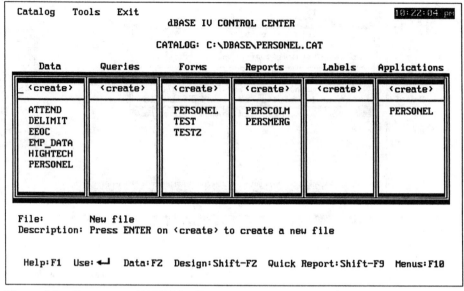

Figure 1-7   Contents of PERSONEL. CAT.

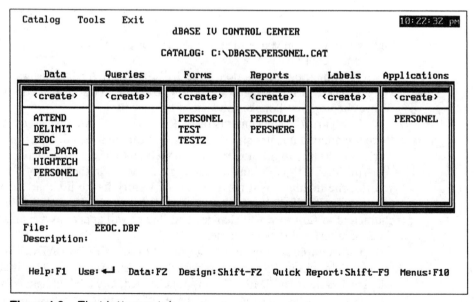

Figure 1-8   First-letter match.

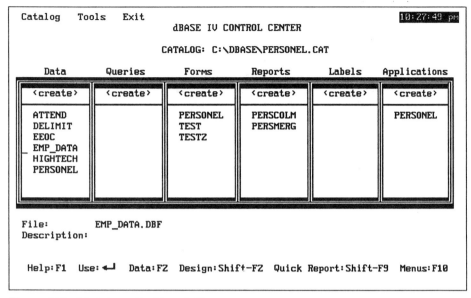

Figure 1·9   Match on first two letters.

Figure 1-9 shows the highlight to be on EMP_DATA and the filename listed below the panels.

If you type a letter that has no match, the system will beep, indicating that an error has been made. However, you will rarely have to type more than the first few letters of a filename, unless you are using a potentially confusing naming convention that uses the same beginning letters, followed by a data or version letter. When you design your systems, you should keep in mind that it is probably best to put the items that differentiate filenames at the front, rather than the rear.

For example, if you were designing a database with monthly bills, your files for consecutive databases could be named BILL0989, BILL1089, and so forth. A more useful way of naming the monthly bills, one which would allow you to easily access the files, would put the variable part of the name (in this case, the date) at the front of the file. For example, 0989BILL, 1089BILL, and so forth, would make it easier to pick the file than the other way around.

The pick method just described is extremely useful—a method that you'll often use. In addition, the method works in any pick list, whether it's found inside a panel, as part of a catalog option, or wherever else it may appear.

Conclusion

This chapter has only scratched the surface of how to work with the dBASE IV Control Center. The Control Center will be shown to be a useful method for both the nonprogrammer and the experienced dBASE IV application developer to quickly create powerful applications. What was shown in this chapter is a basic introduction to the components of the Control Center, and a hint of some of the shortcuts that can be used for navigating the various panels, using the pick lists, and selecting menu options.

Future chapters explore the fine points of database design and the use of all the panels and other design features, and carry you through to the design and implementation of a complete application. Programmers will see the easy way to design forms, reports, and data structures while automatically producing a program code that can be incorporated into custom applications—providing a significant time savings for all users.

2

The Control Center—Part Two

Chapter 1 provided a basic overview of the Control Center: its main screen, some methods for entering and exiting from the panel design and edit screens, and some of the basics of navigation within the screens. In this chapter, the Control Center panels and their functions are further explored, giving you an overview of how the Control Center's components are designed to interact. Later chapters deal with specifics of design and analysis using the various panels.

The goal here is to familiarize you with the overall program. In Chapter 3, the menus selectable from within the Control Center will be explored in more detail, along with more detail about catalog and file management, and a look at using the many tools and utilities available from within the Tools menu.

About the Control Center Panels

The Control Center in dBASE IV allows you to design and perform many of the tasks that are required as parts of a complete database management system. Each panel supports its own aspect of database development and management. The panels allow you to design the type of screen or analytic process that the panel's name suggests and to apply those design elements to your data.

Using the **Shft-F2** key combination, you can easily create or modify the design for a particular function. Menu tools that can be accessed from within the design windows allow you to specify which parameters in the design are the most important. For data input forms, for example, you can set up specific conditions that must be met in order for the data to be acceptable, you can set up specific form designs, or you can use designs that can be automatically generated by dBASE IV.

You will also be shown some of the navigational shortcuts that can be carried through from panel to panel.

How to Get Help

dBASE IV was designed to make data management systems simple both for experienced programmers and for those users not familiar with, or actually avoiding, programming. The Control Center takes over much of the required code generation that was necessary for development of complete systems using earlier versions of dBASE.

For all of the Control Center's added features and intuitive interface capabilities, at times an answer to a particular question or further explanation of a certain prompt is needed. The designers of dBASE IV have created a very good context-sensitive Help facility.

To access Help, simply press the **F1** key. This key causes the system to look at where you are in the program, and to bring up a help file that pertains to the task you are attempting to perform. Although you may not always get the right answer, the Help function is often very useful.

In many cases, the system will bring up a help file that is more than one screenful of data. In this case, the **F4** key is used to move to the next full screen of information. As may be expected, the **F3** key moves you back one screen.

It may be interesting to note that you can continue to move through other topics, and often to related topics, by continuing to press the **F4** key. The information that is contained in the help files is stored sequentially—when you press the **F1** key to get help with a particular subject, the system determines what function you were performing and brings the cursor into the relevant help file. There is nothing that prevents you from moving beyond the relevant topic (by continuing to press **F4**), or even before the topic (by pressing **F3**).

Additionally, you can access a list of contents (this is not actually a table of contents, because the list seems to vary somewhat based on the context from which the listing is accessed), or a list of related topics by pressing **C** for Contents or **R** for Related Topics. You can also print a screen of help information by pressing **P**. The Contents, Related Topics, and Print functions can also be selected by moving the cursor (using the **Left Arrow** or **Right Arrow** keys) so that the desired operation is highlighted, and then pressing **Enter**.

Further, once a list of available topics is loaded in a pop-up window, as seen in Figure 2-1, you can select a desired topic by highlighting the topic and pressing **Enter**. You may also select the topic by typing the first letter or letters of the item's name until the desired item is highlighted, and then pressing **Enter**.

The **F1** key doesn't always bring a Help window onto the screen, however. If a pop-up menu is showing, you may be unable to get Help. You should be able to activate Help at most main menus, and in many of the design and analysis screens.

The Data Panel

The Data panel is the primary panel for data file management. From within this panel, you can design your data files. You can append data (add data at the end of the current data file) to these files using data taken from files created by other database programs or spreadsheets, and can even bring data in from some word processors.

Indexes and sorted versions of your data files can be defined and created from

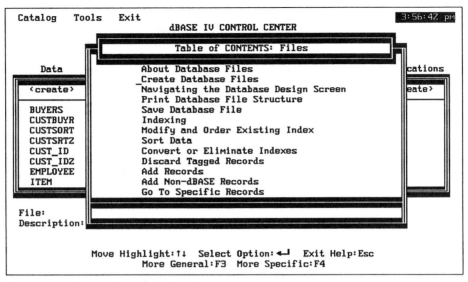

Figure 2-1   Help table of contents.

within this panel. You will also be using the design portion of the panel to delete records that you've previously marked for deletion from your data file.

From within the design screen, you can jump directly to the Browse or Edit screens by pressing **F2**. In order to do this, however, you must close any menus appearing on screen. In other words, if there are *no* menus on the screen, you may go to the Browse or Edit screens by pressing **F2**.

When you have accessed the Browse and Edit screens from within the Design menu, you have the option of viewing your data and returning to the Database design screen. To do this, select the Exit menu (by pressing **Alt-E**). Three options are available in this menu.

The *Transfer to Query Design* option allows you to enter the Query design window. A query is a way of telling the system how you want to retrieve data. Although you can transfer from a Browse or Edit window to the Query design screen, and you may transfer back to the Edit or Browse screens, you will not be able to return to the Database design screen if you exit to Query design from the Browse or Edit menu.

When you are in the Query design window, you may only exit to the Control Center. Thus, when you transfer to the Query design screen from any other panels, you will not be returned to the design panels when you exit from the Query design panel.

The Queries Panel

The Queries panel is an implementation of a data retrieval and analysis technique called *Query by Example*. Query by Example is a model that in many ways simplifies the design of code for retrieving data. In earlier versions of dBASE, the user very frequently had to generate complicated code expressions for evaluating the data in one or more data files.

Although retrieval of data was possible using these earlier versions of dBASE (and, indeed, many consultants made large amounts of money developing such systems), the code was often difficult to produce, and often hard to debug. In theory, Query by Example asks you to tell dBASE IV what kind of data you want to retrieve, and dBASE IV will create an expression to retrieve it from the data files.

Although the implementation of Query by Example (QBE) is not quite as simple as its description makes it sound, the process is actually fairly easy once basic concepts are learned.

You will probably notice that the menu items in this screen differ from those in either of the data screens. This is because the Query screen performs functions that substantially differ from those of the Database design screen.

Another important feature, one that will be used in other panels as well, is the *Zoom* function. When the **F9** key is pressed, a large window opens up, allowing the user to enter more data (or to view longer programs or parameter statements) than could be entered (or seen) in the space of a normal field. The **F9** key is a toggled key— pressing it once enlarges a window; pressing it a second time shrinks the window to its previous size.

In other panels, the **F9** (Zoom) key will place a window the full width of the screen at the bottom of the screen. This allows users to view and edit a command or statement being placed into a particular area, field, or condition box.

A query may be written whether or not a data file is opened by the system. A query previously saved can be implemented by highlighting its name and pressing **F2**. A query may be modified by highlighting the query and pressing **Shft-F2**.

In addition, from within a Query design screen, the user may view the results of a query by pressing the **F2** key. An option on the Exit menu allows the user to return to the Query design screen to further modify or to save the query.

Queries will be covered in significant depth in later chapters.

The Forms Panel

All the panels in dBASE IV's Control Center are important. The Forms panel may be one of the most important (and longest awaited by developers). This panel allows developers (and relatively unsophisticated users) to design custom input and display forms, to define what data should go into each field, to define when *not* to accept data, and to build a system with error messages and user prompts. Custom fields, such as those that are the result of mathematical computations between two or more fields or a field and a constant value, can also be incorporated into a data entry form.

This panel does what many developers have been requesting for many years: It makes the job of designing custom screens much simpler than the task would be if code had to be written.

The Form screen allows a designer to develop a virtually unlimited number of special forms. From within the design window, the developer can modify an existing design, and can even apply it for use with other data files.

If you abandon your changes, the system will return you to the Control Center, and any changes that were made since you last saved your form will be lost.

A third way to exit is through a "back door." You can jump from your design screen directly into Browse or Edit by pressing **F2**. Whichever way you exit from design, dBASE IV will ask you if you want to save your form.

Using the Exit menu allows you to return to the Form design screen from the Edit or Browse screens. In fact, you may evaluate the look of your form by jumping to the Browse/Edit screens, return via the Exit menu to the design screen, and fine tune the form.

Thus, with the ability to quickly see the effect your changes will have on your designed form, you can design a form that provides no surprises when it is actually implemented in your application.

Finally, once you've designed a form, you may load the form and browse the data from within it. When you move to the Data panel, the active form will be used for display and input of the data in the attached data file.

The Reports Panel

The Reports panel in the Control Center is used to design reports. Reports can be placed on your screen, printed to a file that can be printed out to a printer later, or immediately printed to a printer.

Three quick layouts are provided for rapid creation of reports. The Quick layouts menu looks like Figure 2-2.

Three different quick layouts are available. The first, *Column layout*, allows the display of data in a columnar form. In this format, each field defines a column, with the data being displayed below it, with one row used for each record. This format appears very much like the Browse screen.

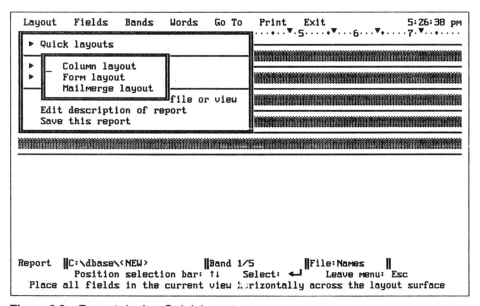

Figure 2-2 Report design Quick layouts menu.

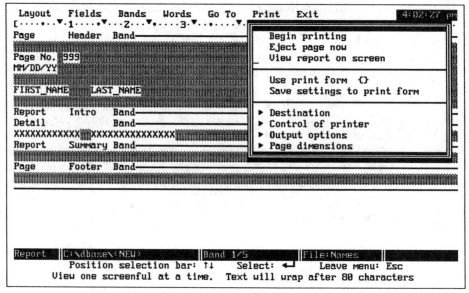

Figure 2-3   The Print menu.

Form layout, on the other hand, looks much like the Edit screen. Each field occupies its own line, and data appears with one screen for each record. At the top of this form is a set of lines that print the date and the page number. This mode is good for printing out the contents of each record, with each record on its own page. (Depending upon the number of fields in each data file, you may be able to print more than one record per page. *Form layout* will allow you to view or print one record (or more) on each page.)

A third layout, *Mailmerge layout*, is designed to allow you to create form letters or other documents, merging the contents of data fields into your letter. There are also two kinds of editing, an important factor when considering mailmerge.

The Print menu is one that is also common in printing panel designs. Figure 2-3 shows the variety of options you have for setting up and controlling your printer and printed output.

The final menu, the Exit menu, is roughly the same in this panel as it is in any of the other panels. Switching to the Browse/Edit screens does not allow you to preview the appearance of the report. Previewing of a report is done through the Print menu.

The Labels Panel

The Labels panel is the last panel that allows you to design forms in the same manner that the Forms and Reports panels did. This Label design screen, shown in Figure 2-4, is quite similar to the Report screen, except that the Bands menu is missing.

The Dimensions menu on this screen allows you to design your printed output so that it fits various predefined formats, as shown in Figure 2-5.

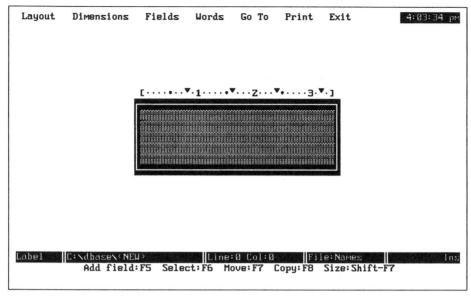

Figure 2-4   The Label design screen.

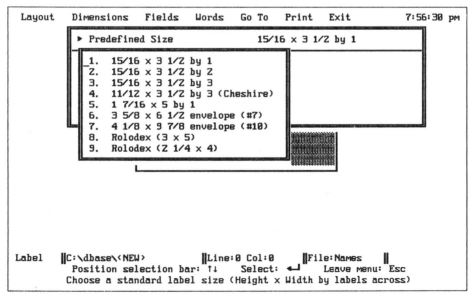

Figure 2-5   Predefined label formats.

And, as with the Report screen, when you switch to Browse or Edit, the data is displayed, but not as it would appear on your label. In order to view how the label will appear, you must print a sample to the screen.

Labels and reports may be printed to a file, rather than directly to a printer. If you plan to print many labels or a long report, it is often best to print to a file because the file, which stores all printer commands on disk, is created more rapidly. When printing to a printer, the data can be generated more rapidly than the printer can print it. Thus, your report or label will ultimately be produced at the speed of the printer, rather than at the speed at which the printer commands can be stored to a hard disk or floppy disk.

Printing a report or form to a file prints the data at the speed of your hard or floppy disk, or as quickly as your computer can process the dBASE IV instructions that will produce the commands for the printer, whichever is slower. Later, when more time is available (perhaps overnight), a file can be printed without keeping you from using the computer for interactive tasks.

The Applications Panel

The final Control Center panel, *Applications*, differs in a number of ways from the other panels. When you invoke it with <create> highlighted, you get a window, as shown in Figure 2-6, that asks whether you want to go to the dBASE programming module or to use the Applications Generator.

The pop-up menu gives you a choice of two options. You may select *dBASE program* or *Applications Generator*.

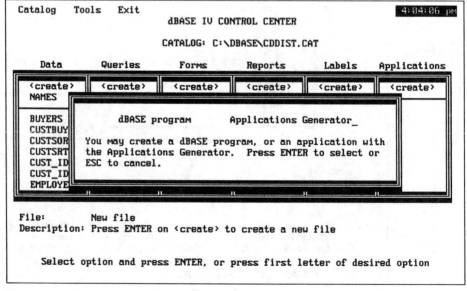

Figure 2-6   Applications selection pop-up.

If you select *dBASE program*, the system loads an edit screen, allowing you to edit or modify a dBASE application.

Additionally, from within this menu you can load a program to modify, and you can modify a "standard" program to suit a specific application, saving it with a new name and description. This option also provides access to the dBASE IV text editor, which allows you to edit programs, in addition to other text files. It is similar to the MODI COMM command from within the dot prompt.

The Exit menu allows you to save or abandon your changes. In addition, it allows you to run your program or to debug the program. The debug process steps you through the program, indicating where problems with the program code have occurred.

The focus of this book is on preparing complete applications without writing code. In truth, you should be able to produce fairly complete applications through the use of the Control Center and the tools provided from within this interface.

The second option in the Applications panel is the Applications Generator. The Applications Generator, a significant part of the new dBASE IV, allows you to design a complete data management system. Further, the generator allows you to run applications that have already been designed.

Using a script that is easily written, you can set up a system that automatically loads dBASE IV, and loads the application that you develop. Thus, using dBASE IV's Applications Generator, a complete turnkey system can be developed.

The Applications Generator uses a programming technique known as *object-oriented programming*. Basically, what you will be doing when you develop your application is developing objects (the windows, menus, and menu items) and assigning certain properties or behaviors to the objects.

The Control Center itself has been developed with an object-oriented approach. The menus in the opening Control Center screen are objects, with additional objects nested inside. Thus, when you select the Catalog object, a menu pops onto the screen that lists those objects that can be selected. Selection of a menu item (actually another object) causes something else to happen—it may be the appearance of another menu screen (in the case of the *Use a different catalog* option) or deletion of a highlighted file from your catalog (if the *Remove highlighted file from catalog* object is chosen).

In the case of dBASE IV, using objects is an effective method of designing complete applications. The Applications Generator provides you with a wide range of tools for customizing the look and operation of your data management systems.

Conclusion

This chapter has provided an overview of the panels, with tips on navigation and some basic procedures that are common to many of the design and maintenance tasks in dBASE IV. Later chapters will explore key concepts in considerably more detail. However, many of the basics covered in this chapter will not be treated in great detail, it being assumed that they were learned in this chapter.

3

The Control Center Menus

The Control Center provides you with nearly all the tools that you need to design and run complete applications. Chapters 1 and 2 introduced the Control Center, exploring its overall layout and navigation, and examining the functions performed by the panels.

This chapter explores the Catalog and Tools menus and their numerous related functions. The Catalog menu brings up the subject of file management and catalog function. The Tools menu includes such concepts as macros, the excellent DOS utilities, data import and export, interface settings, and data security.

The Catalog Menu

The Catalog menu, shown in Figure 3-1, provides you with the basic tools for building a catalog and managing catalog files. Before this can be explored more fully, however, the concept of a catalog should be discussed.

What is a catalog? The answer may seem almost intuitive: A catalog is a list of files that are all related as parts of a catalog. In dBASE IV, a catalog manages all the files that will be used in a particular application. In effect, the catalog contains all the application's files (including data, screen designs, output designs, query designs, and even related applications and program files).

In a particular application, you will typically have one or more data files. You may develop many ways to look at the data—many data input screens, perhaps a variety of label forms (maybe one for printing envelopes and another for printing 3 × 5 file cards), a number of report forms (purchase order, invoice, inventory reports, etc.), and a variety of queries that you use to update your records or prepare new data files based on the contents of many data fields, which may even reside in a number of data

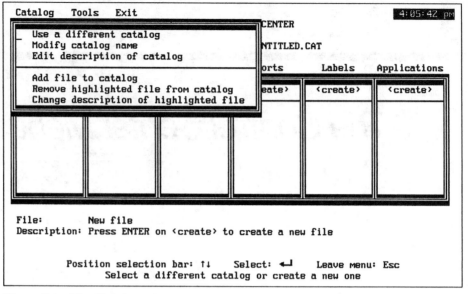

Figure 3-1   The Catalog menu.

files. Such a complete application could conceivably involve dozens of different files, files that perform the separate tasks you've defined as part of your application.

The catalog makes managing all the different forms, queries, and data files simple. The name of each file is shown in the appropriate panel. (The word ''file'' is used generically in this chapter to represent any stored computer file that is used in the catalog—a data file, a query, a data entry or edit form, a report or label design, or a program or application.)

Since dBASE IV's catalog processor keeps track of all the files in a catalog, you no longer have to. This is a valuable feature—especially if you are developing many different applications and have a large number of similarly named files that cover many different applications.

The Catalog menu allows you to add or remove a file from the catalog, or to change catalogs. In addition, you may modify descriptions of the catalog or the files in the catalog.

You will note that there is a line dividing the Catalog menu into two sections. The top half of the menu relates to the catalog, while the bottom part relates to file management. If no file has been selected, the last two options on the menu, *Remove highlighted file from catalog* and *Change description of highlighted file* will not be highlighted, and cannot be selected as options.

In addition, dBASE IV is intelligent—it knows which type of file you are currently selecting. For example, if you open the Catalog menu from within the Data panel, dBASE IV automatically lists the available .DBF (data) files; from within the Queries panel, dBASE IV will list the available .QBF panels.

To change to another catalog, pop up the Catalog menu, and choose *Use a different catalog*, which can easily be done in a number of ways. First, when the

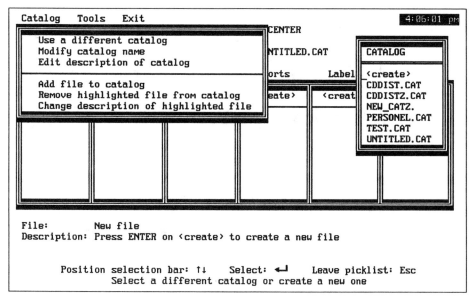

Figure 3-2   Catalog selection menu.

Catalog menu is initially popped up, this option is normally highlighted. If this option is highlighted, simply pressing **Enter** will activate the catalog selection menu.

If this option is not highlighted, you may select it by pressing *U*. The third way, which is actually unnecessary, since pressing the **U** key will normally do the job, is moving the cursor so that *Use a different catalog* is highlighted, and pressing the **Enter** key.

When you have selected *Use a different catalog*, dBASE IV will bring up one or two windows, as seen in Figure 3-2. The window on the right of the screen will list the available catalogs on the currently logged disk drive and directory. A second window, at the middle of the work area, appears when you move the cursor into a named catalog; this box shows a description of the catalog.

The figure shows catalogs that were created during the writing of the first book in this series, *Using dBASE IV: Basics for Business*. If you have developed no catalogs, the screen should show two options: UNTITLED.CAT, the catalog that you are currently using, and <create>, which allows you to create a new catalog. You will create a new catalog soon.

At the bottom third of the screen, approximately in the middle, is a box that shows the description of each catalog, if one was entered when the catalog was last used or modified. For example, in Figure 3-3, the catalog called *PERSONEL.CAT* is highlighted and its description shown in the description window.

When you select a catalog, all the forms, data files, and other related files are loaded into the Control Center panels. Figure 3-4 shows how this works, with PERSONEL.CAT catalog loaded into dBASE IV.

The Control Center now shows that the current catalog is PERSONEL.CAT. When this catalog is loaded, any files that were in the previously active catalog will be saved, and stored with that catalog.

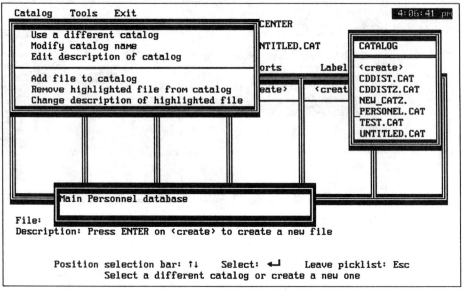

Figure 3-3 Catalog highlighted, with description given.

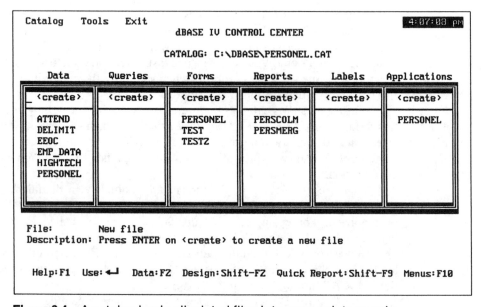

Figure 3-4 A catalog loads all related files into appropriate panels.

Common Files

It is possible for a single file to be used by more than one catalog. For example, you may have a master file listing all of your customers. A company that sells a number of different types of products may have a separate category for each division. For example, a computer company may have a hardware division and a software division. In theory, each division is entirely independent of the other, with the divisional managers reporting to the company's president or CEO. Although the divisions are independent, it is useful to share a clients database, since any of the companies in the database may be a potential customer. Thus, a software catalog and a hardware catalog may both use the same clients data file. This can present a few problems, however. Since both divisions may be using the same catalog, each may be making changes to the shared file. Another, potentially more serious, problem may be the deletion of a file from the computer's disk. Thus, there must be some method or procedure to safeguard a file used in common.

A number of steps can be taken. The first would be to *not* use common files. Instead, a copy of a standard file would be made for use in a second catalog. For example, a standard customer file may be named CUSTOMER.DBF. This file would not be used by either the hardware or software division for standard day-to-day work. Instead, two copies of CUSTOMER.DBF would be made (one might be called HARD-CUST, the other SOFTCUST) and included in the appropriate catalogs.

When a file has been added to HARDCUST or SOFTCUST, the file CUS-TOMER can be changed by an update query that finds those customers who are not already in the CUSTOMER database, and adds them in. Deleting customers can also be done by using an update query.

Password protection of a catalog or database would effectively keep unauthorized users from making any changes in data files. All files and records in a catalog would be protected by requiring a password before dBASE IV can be accessed.

It may be simpler to try to minimize use of a file by more than one catalog. One approach to solving the problem is to build independent catalogs that are based on those already developed. For example, you can create a new catalog, add the necessary files from another catalog into the new one, and then change the names of the files.

Adding Files

When you create many catalogs for different companies or departments, you may be using similar data structures and want to use standard screen, report, query, and form designs. dBASE IV allows you to use files that are used in other catalogs, or that are in other directories on your disk. You can thus create a set of standard forms, add them to your catalog, then modify a form, customizing whatever identifying data may need changing, and give the form a new name. Once the form is copied and renamed, it becomes a different entity, and the problems of a file being used by more than one catalog are avoided.

Two methods could be used to make the copy to the new catalog. The first is to add the original file (the file that you will be using as a model) and modify it, save it

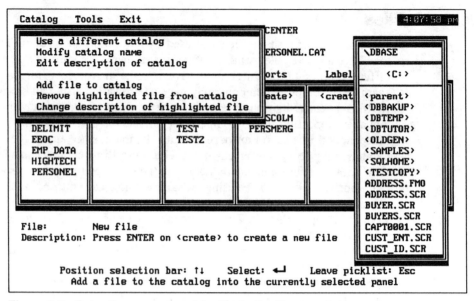

Figure 3-5   Selection menu to add a file to the Forms panel.

with a new name, and then delete the original file from the catalog. This sounds like more work than it actually is, as you'll see in the following example.

In this example, a file will be copied into the UNTITLED. CAT catalog, modified, and deleted. The catalog menu, with only one file, NAMES, will be copied from the disk and placed into the UNTITLED. CAT catalog. To add a file into the catalog, the cursor is moved into the Forms panel, and the Catalog menu is selected. After *Add file to catalog* option is selected, a window pops up showing the available files that can be selected for placement in the active panel.

In our current example, the screen will look like Figure 3-5. Your screen will not show the same files, however, since they have not yet been created.

The file with the extension .scr will be selected. The .fmo extension tells dBASE IV how to display the screen and how it is to filter data (which entries are permitted, when to allow data to be edited, and so on), but its design cannot be altered. The file PERSONEL.SCR will be added to the catalog. When it is selected, dBASE IV asks for a description of the file. The description is saved separately from the one for the same screen in a different catalog.

As shown in Figure 3-6, the PERSONEL.SCR file in the Forms panel for the UNTITLED.CAT catalog has a different description than the same file in Figure 3-7, in the PERSONEL.CAT catalog.

Although the files are identical, the descriptions are different. This does not imply that any changes in the file will not be carried through to whichever catalog calls the file. In fact, any changes to the file, other than the file description, will carry through to *all* other catalogs that use the file or form. Thus, it is important that a file be renamed as soon as possible after it is loaded into a catalog, in order to avoid inadvertently changing forms used by other catalogs.

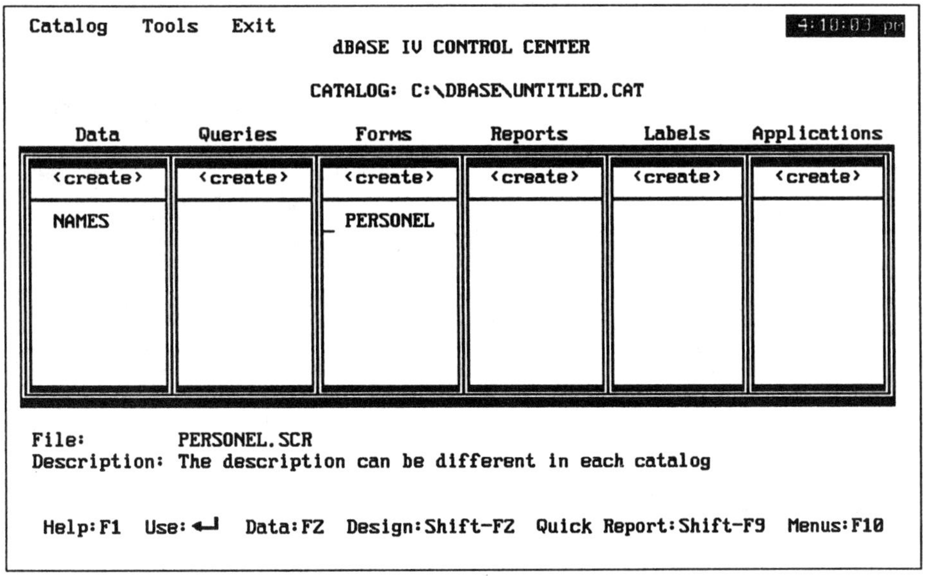

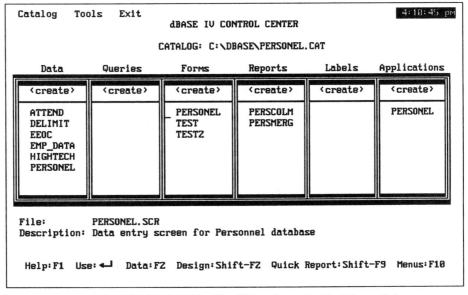

Figure 3-6   The description for this file differs from that in Figure 3-7.

The second way to move a file into your catalog is to copy the file that you wish to use in your catalog, rename it, and then add it to the catalog. This may sound tricky. It isn't. It can be done from within DOS, or using the DOS utilities, which will be covered shortly.

Figure 3-7   The description for this file differs from that in Figure 3-6.

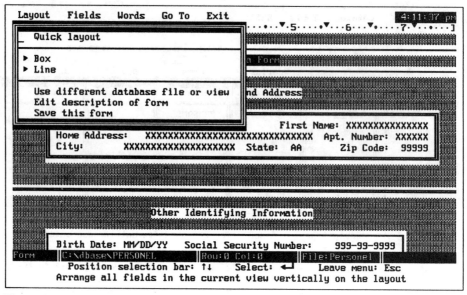

Figure 3-8   Layout menu for Form design.

Renaming Forms

Renaming a form in a catalog is simple. To make a change, highlight the file that you want to change, and press **Shft-F2**.

The system will first check to see that the fields in the selected form match those in the data file that is in use. If not, dBASE IV will tell you that there is not a match, but will display the form, in any case. When the form is displayed, the Layout menu, seen in Figure 3-8, allows you to save the form, giving you the option of using the same name or a new name for the file.

To save the layout with a new name (and thus prevent changing a file that may be used in other catalogs), select *Save this form*. A filename window will appear, prompting you for a name. Changing the name (in this case, changing the name from PERSONEL.SCR to PERSONE2.SCR) provides you with a new copy of the original file, which can now be modified without affecting the original screen file.

The Layout menu also allows you to use a different database or view with the form. Thus, you can tell dBASE IV to use the file that you are currently modifying with a data file that is in the current catalog. In this example, the form has been saved with the new name PERSONE2. Once the file has been saved with the new name, and dBASE IV has been returned to the Control Center, the Forms panel looks like Figure 3-9.

It is clear that the original file, PERSONEL, is still in the catalog, while the copy, PERSONE2, has been added. Since you don't want your original file to remain in the catalog, it should be removed as soon as possible after it is copied.

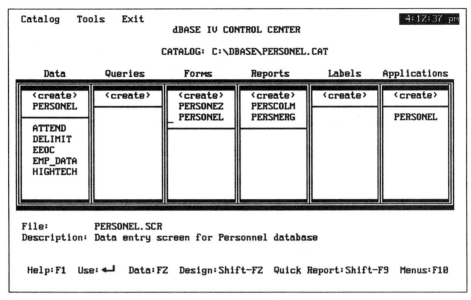

Figure 3-9   Forms panel with a newly named file.

Removing Files

To remove a file from the Catalog menu, simply move the highlight to the file to be removed and press **Del**. The system will prompt you, asking if you want to remove the file from the catalog, and also asking if you want to remove it from the disk. You should be especially careful not to delete the file from the disk, since this will make it unavailable to any catalogs calling it. If you should inadvertently delete the file from the disk you can, obviously, copy the copy (in this case PERSONE2), renaming it PERSONEL and saving it. You can also use a file recovery utility, such as Norton Utilities or Mace Utilities, to reclaim the deleted file, as long as this is done immediately after deleting the file. Copying from the copy is safest, since undelete programs work best when no data has been recorded over the data that has been deleted; quitting dBASE IV may result in changes that make complete recovery impossible.

A second method of removing a file from a catalog is to highlight it, call up the Catalog menu and select *Remove highlighted file from catalog*. Both methods work, although the **Del** key saves you the steps involved in bringing up the Catalog menu.

The options in the top half of the Catalog menu are straightforward. You've seen how to select a catalog; modifying a catalog name is also simple. When you wish to modify a catalog name, dBASE IV brings up a window for renaming your catalog, as seen in Figure 3-10.

At this point, you can backspace over the name displayed in the window, and type the new name. You don't have to type the extension .CAT, since dBASE IV will automatically add that for you. If the name that you've given the catalog is already used

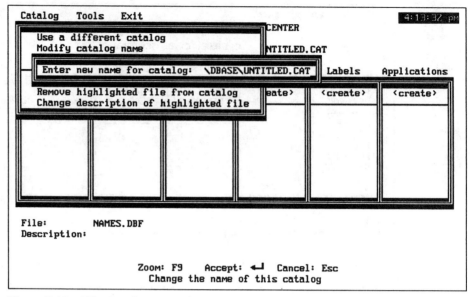

Figure 3-10   Window for renaming a catalog.

for another catalog, dBASE IV will prompt you, asking if you want to overwrite the other catalog. In most cases, you don't want to do this; if you tell dBASE IV that this is what you want to do, dBASE IV will replace the file listings for the catalog already named with those for the new catalog.

This doesn't mean that the files in the catalog are lost—they aren't deleted. However, the catalog will have to be rebuilt by adding the old files into the new catalog. Links between forms and the data file that uses them may also have to be redefined. In short, when renaming a catalog, you should be careful to make your new name different from the names of other catalogs in your database system.

A second point that should be made is that dBASE IV always has an UN-TITLED.CAT catalog. When you name a catalog that was originally built as UN-TITLED.CAT, the files will be transferred to a catalog with the new name, and a blank UNTITLED.CAT will again be created. It should also be pointed out that you can't just copy a catalog by renaming it.

In order to copy a catalog design, you would have to start a new catalog, and add the appropriate files into its panels. A renamed catalog is still the same as the original catalog—it just has a different name.

Navigating File Directories

In many of the screens within dBASE IV, you will be asked to select a file. This is true of *Add file to catalog* window. When this is selected, dBASE IV will bring up a pick list.

This display gives you more information than may be immediately apparent. At the top of the window is the listing of the currently selected subdirectory. Below this is the currently logged drive. To change to another drive, move the highlight onto the drive designation (in this case, the <C:>) and press **Enter**. A new window will pop onto the screen, just to the left of the selection window.

To select a different drive, type the letter for the drive or move the highlight to the drive letter and press **Enter**. Depending on the computer you are using, more or fewer drives may be shown in this menu window. When you select a drive, dBASE IV will then build a file directory. In the file selection window, a listing of directories and subdirectories is shown, with the currently available files listed. The subject of parent and child directories should be discussed briefly here.

dBASE IV is shown here installed on drive C: in its own subdirectory, \DBASE. The \DBASE subdirectory is one of many subdirectories on the C: disk. If you are reading this book, you should be familiar with hard disk file structure. However, suffice it to say that subdirectories can have subdirectories, and these subdirectories can also have subdirectories. In fact, subdirectory structures can go many levels deep. To access any of the subdirectories, simply move the highlight to the appropriate subdirectory (typing the name doesn't select a directory or subdirectory), and press **Enter**.

To move up one directory level, move the highlight to <parent> and press **Enter**. In the example, the parent directory is the root directory. The display shows all subdirectories that can be reached from the root directory. The <parent> option is not highlighted, indicating that there *is no parent* directory at this level. In other words, dBASE IV has reached the root directory, and there is no higher level on the disk.

The file selection window and the simple navigation tools provided make it easy to select any file in any directory or subdirectory on any disk. If you don't want to select a file, pressing **Esc** will cancel the operation.

The Tools menu features a set of tools referred to as *DOS utilities*, which allow you control over many of the DOS functions, including copying, sorting, viewing, and editing files. These are covered in the second part of this chapter.

The Tools Menu

The Tools menu provides you with a number of areas of control and customization of your dBASE system. The menu looks like Figure 3-11.

Macros

The first component of the Tools menu is *Macros*. A macro is a recorded sequence of keystrokes that are automatically entered by dBASE IV when you type a defined key combination. A simple example of a macro is the one that loads the Control Center from within the dot prompt. You may recall that, if you're in the dot prompt (rather than the Control Center) and press **F2**, dBASE IV types the command for loading the Control Center (the command is *ASSIST* **Enter**), and dBASE IV then loads the Control Center.

The macros that you create are stored in what is referred to by dBASE IV as a *macro library*. Each library can hold up to 35 defined macros. Each macro is given a unique name; the names all start with an alphabetic key (such as **A**, **B**, through **Z**,).

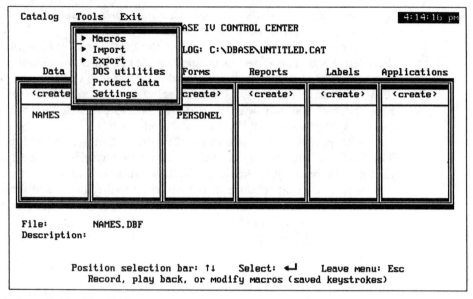

Figure 3-11   The Tools menu.

Macros can also be a combination of the **Alt-F10** key and a function key, thus allowing macros ranging from **Alt-F1** through **Alt-F10**.

Macros may be designed to perform a specific function from within a specific panel or data file. For example, you may want to record a macro that places certain fields on a form that you frequently design. Such a macro may type a field name, then pull down the field selection menu, select a particular field for placement on the form, select various attributes for the field, place the field, and then do the same for additional fields. This can be accomplished with two keystrokes, if the macro is recorded properly.

However, the macro will execute the same keystrokes whenever it is invoked. If you were to press the keys that activate the macro from within another panel, the results could be surprising and might even damage your designs or data. In the instance just described, if you were editing data and accidentally activated the design macro, dBASE IV would likely be confused by the irrelevant and erroneous keystrokes.

We'll create a simple macro to demonstrate how macros work. This macro will load the NAMES data file, transfer to query design, design a query to find all records with a first name of MARK, and then return to the Control Center. Although this is not a particularly useful macro, the principles demonstrated can be easily adapted.

First, select the Macros menu. The menu looks like Figure 3-12. Three options are shown in the menu: *Begin recording, Talk*, and *Load library*. Before designing our macro, it may be useful to explain *Load library* and *Talk*.

When you have designed macros, you are given the option of saving them into a file called a "library." You can have up to 35 macros in a library. While using dBASE IV, you may switch libraries by loading a new library. This may be useful if you have a large number of macros. For example, if you are sending out many different form

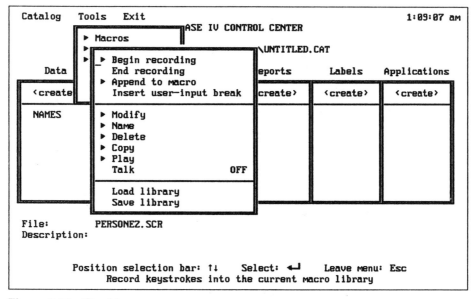

```
 Catalog   Tools   Exit                                    1:09:07 am
                              ┌ASE IV CONTROL CENTER
              ▶ Macros        ┃
              ▶          ┌─────┃──\UNTITLED.CAT
              ▶ │ ▶ Begin recording
      Data    ▶ │   End recording        eports    Labels    Applications
            ┌───│ ▶ Append to macro
   <create  │   │   Insert user-input break  create>  <create>   <create>
            │   │
   NAMES    │ ▶ Modify
            │ ▶ Name
            │ ▶ Delete
            │ ▶ Copy
            │ ▶ Play
            │   Talk                 OFF
            │
            │   Load library
            │   Save library
            └───────────────────────────┘
   File:       PERSONEZ.SCR
   Description:


            Position selection bar: ↑↓    Select: ◄┘    Leave menu: Esc
            Record keystrokes into the current macro library
```

Figure 3-12 The Macros menu.

letters that are written using standard phrases (referred to as "boilerplate"), it may be simpler to use a macro to have the desired paragraphs automatically entered by dBASE IV than it would be to type the letter in. It may be desirable to have a macro library for the boilerplate phrases and a different library for design of other panels or for use in the dot level programming environment. Alternately, you may have a set of macros that is designed for each panel; a Data library, a Query library, a Forms library, and so on. These libraries can be loaded when you are performing the design tasks related to each panel and can speed those tasks.

The Talk function is optional. When Talk is set to ON, each step in the macro is shown on the screen as it is executed. With Talk OFF, the macro executes without displaying the keystrokes.

When you select *Begin recording*, a window like that shown in Figure 3-13 pops onto the screen. The top half of the window shows the name of the macro assigned to each function key, representing **Alt-F1** through **Alt-F9**. **Alt-F10** differs from the other function keys. In order to select (or record a macro for) a letter key, you must first push **Alt-F10**, and then the letter for the macro that you want to execute.

To tell dBASE IV that you want to use a particular key, press that key that you want to assign the macro to. In this case, press **M** to tell dBASE IV that you will be recording a macro that is activated by pressing **Alt-F10-M**.

At the bottom of the screen, dBASE IV will remind you that you are recording a macro, and to press **Shft-F10-E** to end the recording. (Pressing **Shft-F10** returns you to the Macros menu.) Now that dBASE IV is waiting for you to record your macro, type the name of the file that you want to select.

In this case, although you can type the letter *N* to highlight the NAMES database, it is good practice when recording a macro that includes a file name or field name, to

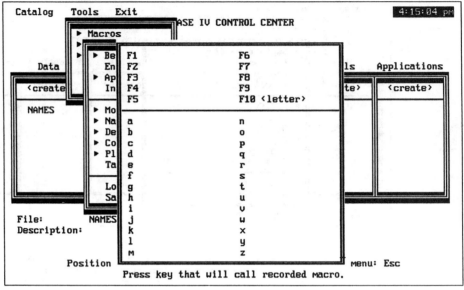

Figure 3-13   Macro selection menu.

type the complete name. A file name may be unique now, but you may later add other files, which could be selected instead of the one you want. For example, if you were to add a data file called NAME, and wrote a macro to select the first file that started with the letters NAM, the NAME data file, and not the NAMES file will be selected and loaded. Thus, for this macro, type *NAMES* **F2**.

This will bring up the Edit screen or the Browse screen. To be sure that dBASE IV is displaying the first file, you can open the Go To menu (by pressing **Alt-G**), and select *Top Record* (by pressing **T**).

Although you could have selected *Top Record* from within the Go To menu by touching the **Enter** key, it is safer to touch the key that selects an option than it is to assume that the cursor will pop up with the desired option highlighted.

Next, select the Exit menu by pressing **Alt-E**. Now, press **T** to *Transfer to Query Design*.

It should be clear by now that dBASE IV is behaving exactly as it would were you not recording a macro. The only difference from normal operation is that dBASE IV reminds you with a prompt at the bottom of the screen that it is recording a macro.

Next, press the **Tab** key to move the highlight into the FIRST_NAME field in the Query design screen. Now type "*Mark*" (being sure to include the quotation marks). The screen, with the simple query designed, will look like Figure 3-14.

Now that the query has been designed, press **F2** to process the query and have dBASE IV display the records that match the parameters. The system will display the first record that matches. This isn't exactly what you want, so press **F2** to switch to the Browse screen. The screen will look like Figure 3-15.

Finally, return to the Control Center by going to the Exit menu (by pressing **Alt-E**), and pressing *E* to initiate the Exit command.

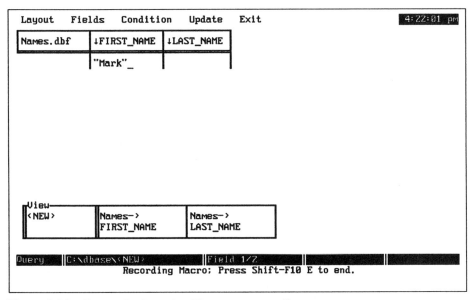

Figure 3-14   Query designed, with macro recording.

The system will prompt, asking if you want to save the query design. *No* will be highlighted. Press **Enter** to tell dBASE IV to return you to the Control Center. Finally, save the macro.

Press **Shft-F10**. The system will bring up a menu that gives you three options. The first option is *End recording*. If you choose this option, the macro will be saved, and

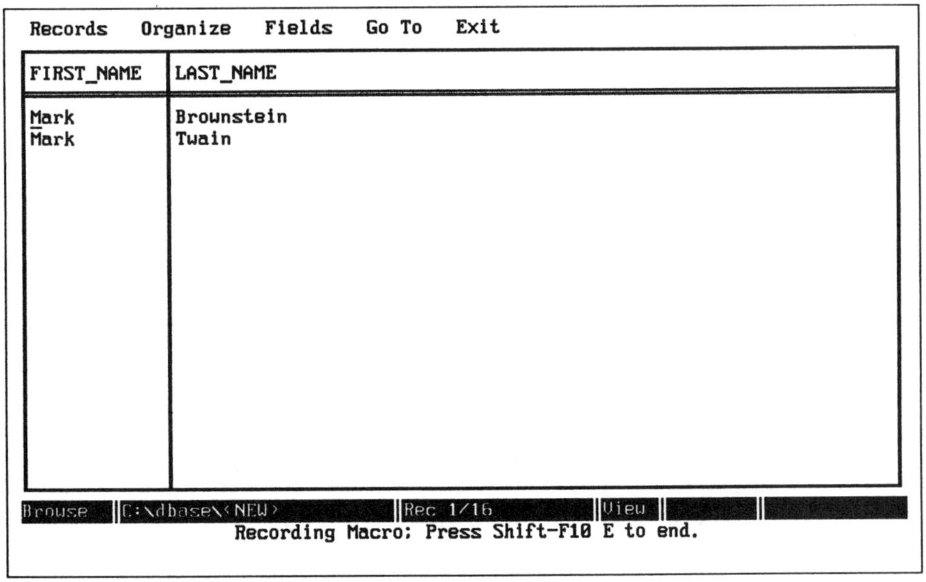

Figure 3-15   Browse screen with query results.

your recording of this macro will be finished. The second option is *Insert user-input break*. The third option, *Continue recording*, lets you recover from the possible error of pressing the **Shft-F10** key when you really didn't want to insert a break or end recording of your macro. In this case, you *do* want to finish recording your macro, so press **E** to end recording.

The system will tell you that it has finished recording the macro by changing the prompt at the bottom of the screen. Now, press **Alt-F10-M** to play back the macro. The entire process performed to create the macro will flash by on the screen very quickly.

In actual practice, you will probably want to write a macro that loads the file and brings up the Query design screen, and then stops once the query is written and the data selected. A second macro can be used to exit to the Control Center.

Macros can also be designed to incorporate pauses for user input. For example, in the macro previously recorded, you may want dBASE IV to stop while in the Query design screen, to allow the user to type in the first name that is to be searched for.

To do this, create a new macro, by opening the Tools menu, selecting *Macros* (by pressing *M*), and pressing **B** (for *Begin recording*). Next, press **A** to assign the macro to the **A** key. Type *NAMES* and press **F2**. Note that if you typed *NAMES* and pressed **Enter**, you would get a different menu than you may have seen previously, since the first option toggles between *Close file* and *Use file*. That is, if the file was already in use, and you assumed while writing your menu that the NAMES database was not already selected, the file would be closed rather than opened. However, by typing the complete name of the file and pressing **F2**, you will open the desired file in either case.

Next, select the Exit menu by pressing **Alt-E**. Press **T** to *Transfer to Query Design*. Now, Press the **Tab** key to move the cursor to the FIRST_NAME field. Type a quotation mark ''.

This is where the procedure changes. You want the user to type the name that he or she wants to search for, in order to produce a list of all records with that particular first name.

Press **Shft-F10** to bring up the macro menu.

Press **I** to select *Insert user-input break*. This tells dBASE IV to pause for the user to type information or to fill in a field. In this case, you're stopping execution of the macro in order to allow the user to type in the first name of the person to be searched for.

When the macro is run, the user types the name of the person to search for, then presses **SHIFT-F10** to cause the macro to continue to execute. When you design your macro, you next enter the keystrokes that are to follow the user-input break. In this example, you will close the quotation marks and look at the data. To do this, type another quotation mark (to enclose the name typed by the user), and press **F2**. dBASE IV will process the query.

Stop recording the macro, since you have had the first name typed in, and have gone out to get the data. Press **Shft-F10-E**.

Now, return to the Control Center, and run the macro, by pressing **Alt-F10-A**. The system will load the file, and bring you to the Query design screen. It will then prompt you to enter data. The prompt looks like Figure 3-16.

To see how the Macro works, Type *John*, and press **Shft-F10**. dBASE IV will then process the query, and return the Browse screen shown in Figure 3-17.

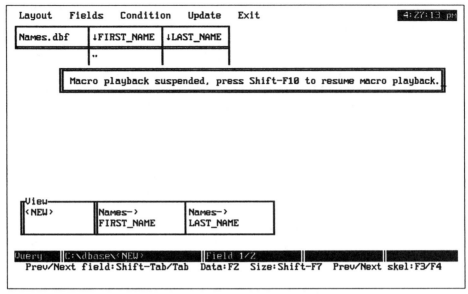

Figure 3-16   Macro playback—waiting for user input.

To see how the Talk function works, reopen the Tools menu, followed by the Macros menu, and press **T** to turn Talk ON (if it was previously set to OFF). The **Enter** key toggles the Talk function on and off—when Talk is on, the macro commands show on the lower left corner of the screen as each command is executed. This is useful for

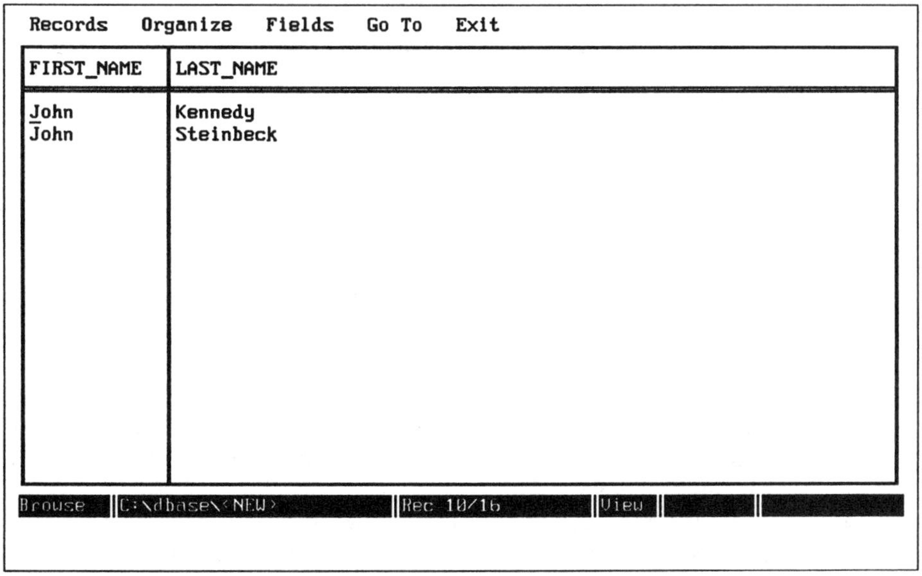

Figure 3-17   Browse screen based on user input.

tracking the progress of a macro to see where it may stop working as expected. In most cases, however, you would probably want the Talk function to be OFF so that the user doesn't see the macro and get confused by it.

It should be clear that macros do, indeed, work. The power of macros to stop and wait for user input is significant. You can design macros that automatically load a data file, bring up the Query design screen, and pause for search parameters to be input. In fact, a number of pauses for user-inserted data can be built into a macro. Such a macro can save many of the routine keystrokes involved in repetitive data management operations.

Modifying Macros   The Macros menu allows you to make modifications to an existing macro, as well as manage the macros in each active library. The top division in the menu provides you options that change, depending upon whether you have macros activated in dBASE IV. When you bring up the menu, you can always record a new macro (if an unused key is available).

Append to macro allows you to add keystrokes to an existing macro. To do this, you must first select *Append to macro* from the menu. This brings up the Macros menu. Next, select a macro that you want to append to.

Once a macro is selected, you can again run through the steps in your addition to the macro that you are appending to. To save the additions, or to insert a user-input break, press **Shft-F10**, followed by the appropriate letter for the next operation (**E** for *End recording,* **I** for *Insert user-input break*, or **C** for *Continue recording*). When you are finished, the entire macro, including the appended keystrokes, will be played whenever it is activated.

The second half of the Macros menu is used to manage your macros. The *Name* option allows you to assign a name to your macro. When you give a macro a name, you are making it easier to remember what the macro's function is. It is important to note that a macro's name must be a single word—no spaces are permitted in a macro name. The *Delete* option allows you to remove a macro from the directory, while *Copy* allows you to copy a macro's design to another key.

You can easily design a new macro that is based on one that has already been written and is known to work properly. Once the macro is copied, you can open the Modify menu and make changes to the copy of the macro, retaining the ability to return to the original, unchanged macro should something go wrong with the macro that you are modifying.

When *Modify* is selected, you are asked to choose a macro from the macros library listing. Once you select a macro to modify, dBASE IV will bring up an edit menu, which lists all the keystrokes used in the macro. The macro that is activated using **Alt-F10-A** looks like Figure 3-18.

The edit screen is a standard screen used for editing programs and memo text. This screen is a simple text editor, allowing you to add or delete characters. Some of the techniques for editing from within an editing screen will be dealt with in more detail later in this book.

One important point to remember when editing a macro is that labelled keys are enclosed in braces {} (such as {**Tab**}, {**Alt-e**}, or {**InpBreak**}, in this example). Regular alphanumeric keys are not enclosed in braces.

You can write a complete macro without first stepping through the program,

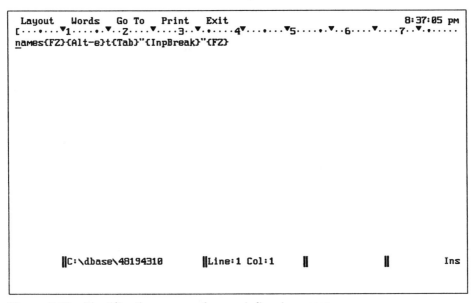

Figure 3-18   Modification screen for predefined macros.

simply by going into the *macro editor*. If you do this, or attempt to make changes to a macro from within the editor, you must remember that special keys or sequences must be enclosed in braces (and must be entered using specific names or abbreviations), while standard characters are not enclosed in braces.

Few options are provided on this screen, since few are needed. The Print menu allows you to print the macro. If you are using a lengthy macro, it may be useful to be able to print the macro, so that it can be debugged from the paper sheet. This is also useful if you wish to create a new macro in a different catalog.

Another capability that is sometimes useful is the ability to call another macro from within a different macro. Thus, if you have a macro that automatically types your company's name and address, you can design a billing macro that calls the name macro at the appropriate location in an invoice being printed and goes on to complete the form.

Remember that the execution of a particular macro may work *only from within a certain panel or certain screen*. When executing a macro, you must be careful that the cursor is in the proper location in the program before executing the macro. Failure to exercise caution in the execution of a macro could result in data loss or failure of the program.

It should also be noted that you can create a new macro without going through the Tools menu. To begin a new macro, press **Shft-F10**, to bring a *dBASE IV macro processing box* onto the screen, and press **B** for *Begin recording*.

Import and Export

The Import and Export utilities allow dBASE IV to bring data files in from other programs—including dBASE II, RapidFile, Lotus 1-2-3, Framework II, and

PFS:File—and to move data out to these programs and most other spreadsheet or word processing programs.

In addition to the two menu items in the Tools menu, however, the data file design screen also allows the importation of data from other versions of dBASE and other programs.

DOS Utilities

The *DOS utilities* menu is selected by pressing the **D** key or by highlighting *DOS utilities* in the Tools menu. The *DOS utilities* menu looks like Figure 3-19. The DOS utilities are rich in features. The most prominent feature of the *DOS utilities* menu is the window that provides information on the files used in the currently logged directory. The menu lines work in conjunction with the Files window to sort files, and mark them for deletion, copying, or moving. The Files window provides information that would seem to be fairly logical, but which deserves elaboration.

The top line of the Files window indicates the name and path information of the currently logged directory. If you have set up your copy of dBASE IV according to the instructions that came with the program, you should have a parent directory and a number of subdirectories shown in the window. Using the **Up Arrow** or **Down Arrow** keys, you can highlight a different directory (the subdirectories are shown below the < parent > directory and above the files in the directory). When you select a subdirectory, dBASE IV will then indicate the complete path information for the subdirectory.

To return to the dBASE subdirectory, you can select < parent > by highlighting and pressing the **Enter** key. The graphical nature of the path display also helps keep track of the structure of the database drive. When the < parent > directory is selected

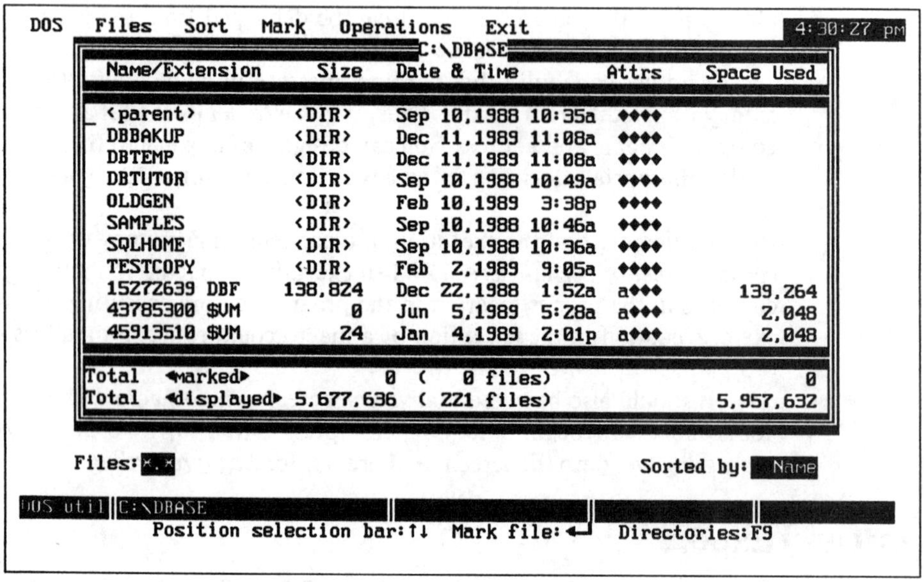

DOS	Files	Sort	Mark	Operations	Exit			4:30:27 pm

C:\DBASE

Name/Extension	Size	Date & Time	Attrs	Space Used
<parent>	<DIR>	Sep 10,1988 10:35a	◆◆◆◆	
DBBAKUP	<DIR>	Dec 11,1989 11:08a	◆◆◆◆	
DBTEMP	<DIR>	Dec 11,1989 11:08a	◆◆◆◆	
DBTUTOR	<DIR>	Sep 10,1988 10:49a	◆◆◆◆	
OLDGEN	<DIR>	Feb 10,1989 3:38p	◆◆◆◆	
SAMPLES	<DIR>	Sep 10,1988 10:46a	◆◆◆◆	
SQLHOME	<DIR>	Sep 10,1988 10:36a	◆◆◆◆	
TESTCOPY	<DIR>	Feb 2,1989 9:05a	◆◆◆◆	
15272639 DBF	138,824	Dec 22,1988 1:52a	a◆◆◆	139,264
43785300 $VM	0	Jun 5,1989 5:28a	a◆◆◆	2,048
45913510 $VM	24	Jan 4,1989 2:01p	a◆◆◆	2,048

Total	◆marked◆	0	(	0 files)	0
Total	◆displayed◆	5,677,636	(	221 files)	5,957,632

Files: *.*   Sorted by: Name

DOS util C:\DBASE

Position selection bar:↑↓   Mark file:↵   Directories:F9

Figure 3-19   The *DOS utilities* menu.

from within the current directory (C:\DBASE), a listing of the root directory and files on the root directory appears.

A few things should be noted. First, the directory information line at the top of the file information screen changes, withdrawing one level (marked by the backslash, \ character). Second, directories are listed in the window with the characters <DIR>, rather than the file size.

The information columns in the file information window are fairly clear. *Name/ Extension* provides the file name and extension for files in the current directory. If a file has no extension, just the first part of the filename is shown (no extension). A file that lacks an extension may appear, looking at this one column only, as if it is a directory listing, rather than a file. But that's taken care of in the next column item, *Size*.

The *Size* column tells the actual number of bytes used by a file. If the listing is for a directory, the characters <DIR> appear in this column.

The next column item, *Date & Time*, gives the time and date when the file or directory entry was created or last updated.

The next column, *Attrs* (for *Attributes*), provides information on the type of file. For example, the files in this screen have an *a* in their attributes listing. This means that the files are *archived*—that is, they have been copied or have backup copies. Normally, when a new data file is created, its archive bit (a single data bit that is recorded into the file's header when it is put onto a disk) is not set to show that it has been archived. However, if the file has been copied or backed up, dBASE IV usually resets the archive bit to show that the file *has* been archived.

Other attributes include *r* for read only, and *h* for hidden. A read-only file can be viewed, but the data in the file cannot be deleted or updated. A hidden file is one that cannot be read from or written to, and that is usually hidden from the user (and not listed in a standard directory listing). MS-DOS, some system software, and some copy-protected software create hidden files. These files normally are not called directly by the computer user. File attributes cannot normally be changed by the user (aside from performing functions that will cause DOS or an application to set an archive bit, or to make a file read only).

The final item, *Space Used*, is very revealing. If you do a lot of word processing, for example, and have a lot of small files, the hard disk drive may fill up with far fewer files than would be expected. For example, a 20-megabyte disk drive could be filled up with 5 or 6 megabytes of small text files. The answer to how and why this happens appears in the Space Used column.

Figure 3-19 shows files that are zero bytes in size or slightly larger, but which take up 2048 bytes of space on the hard disk drive. How and why does this happen? A simple answer is that all hard disks, and also all floppy disks, are divided into *sectors*. When a file is opened, the data in that file, including data that name and describe the file, are recorded onto one or more sectors. The smallest file, even one with a name and no contents, takes up an entire sector—no additional files can be recorded onto the same physical sector.

Depending on the hardware system in use, a physical sector can be 1024, 2048, or even 4096 bytes in size. Thus, although you may have many files that contain just a few hundred bytes each, each file may take up as much as 4 kilobytes of disk storage. The space used by the smallest files indicates the sector size—a number that may otherwise be difficult to get from dBASE IV. All files take a multiple of the minimum sector size. This explains why fewer bytes of data or files can be stored on a drive than is the drive's rated capacity.

At the bottom of the Files window, dBASE IV indicates how many files have been marked, and how many are in the directory being viewed. This window is useful for viewing not only the currently used directory, but also any other directories.

Below the file information box, dBASE IV tells you how the files have been selected (in this case *Files: *.** represents a wildcard telling dBASE IV to show all files in the directory), and the way that the files have been sorted. In the figures, the files were sorted by name.

The DOS Utilities Menus

The first menu on the screen, *DOS*, produces a window like that seen in Figure 3-20.

The top half of the menu gives you two options, *Perform DOS command* and *Go to DOS*. *Perform DOS command* is useful for performing tasks like formatting or copying disks.

When *Perform DOS command* is selected, dBASE IV prompts you to enter the command. Only one command at a time can be executed, although the commands may be repeated in order. This option is designed to allow DOS to execute a single function and return you to the *DOS utilities* menu.

There is one thing you should be careful to avoid in this option. If you type the word **command**, dBASE IV will load up the DOS command processor. In effect, you will be returned to DOS, but with dBASE IV still active. dBASE IV will look as if it is

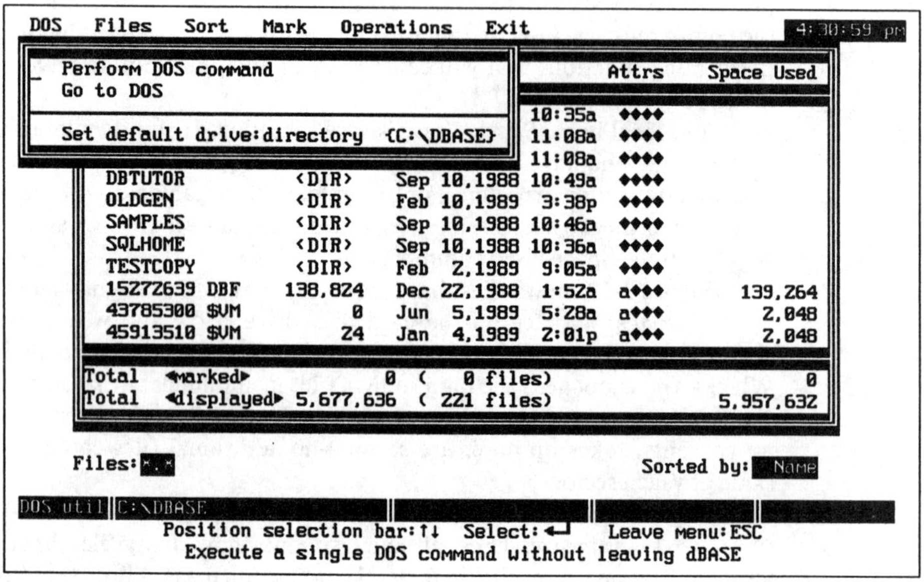

Figure 3-20 The DOS menu.

in DOS, and not actually running dBASE IV. There is a significant danger in this. Since it will look as if you are in DOS, and not actually running dBASE IV, you run the risk of treating your computer system as if you were only running DOS. The real danger here is that you may turn off or reboot the computer from within "DOS," when you really are actually inside a DOS shell, with dBASE IV temporarily suspended, but very much alive. You have shelled to DOS by selecting *Perform DOS command* and typing in *command*, which loaded a command processor and opened a new DOS window. If you turn the computer off or reboot, you stand a very good risk of losing any changes that you made during your dBASE IV session. At worst, such an action could corrupt the program, making reinstallation necessary. Data may also be irretrievably lost.

The point of this discussion is to make a clear warning *not* to type in the DOS command *COMMAND* from within this option unless you are *certain* that you will return to dBASE IV by typing *EXIT* before leaving your computer unattended or forgetting that you are in a shell, with dBASE IV still active.

The second option is *Go to DOS*. This option performs a function much like what typing *COMMAND* from the *Perform DOS command* window does. The major difference between this type of DOS access and the access that resulted from using the *COMMAND* command is that dBASE IV puts a reminder on the screen that you are running in a dBASE DOS window. The warning line helps to alert you that you aren't just in DOS, and that you must return to your application before turning off the computer.

From within a DOS window, you may perform most DOS functions, memory permitting. Many programs can be run from inside a DOS window. The window allows you to perform file management tasks or run programs without quitting dBASE IV or the work that you are doing. For example, if you were working in dBASE IV and had to send or receive a file from another office or a bulletin board, you could open a DOS window, load your telecommunications software, and perform your telecommunications tasks. Once the task was completed, you could then return to dBASE IV.

Running large programs, or programs that have been known to fail before, is not recommended. In fact, you should try running programs within a window with an empty catalog loaded, so that you won't lose any data if dBASE IV locks up on you. The DOS window can be dangerous but usually isn't. It is intended for performing file maintenance tasks. You can format a disk, copy files, maybe view a directory from within this window.

Another item you should watch for is deleting or moving files that dBASE IV may be using. For example, if you are working on a data file and move the file to a different directory, when you close the window and return to dBASE IV, dBASE IV will not know where to find the data file. Care must be taken to assure that you do not perform any file operations that will change any files that you are working on.

In addition, you should not remove "funny" files. A "funny" file may be an intermediate file created by dBASE IV when it allows you to open a DOS window. This file may have an odd-looking name, and may not appear to make much sense. However, the intermediate file contains information telling dBASE IV what files were opened, and where you were in your dBASE session when you opened the DOS window. Without this "funny" information, dBASE IV may not know where to go when you exit from your DOS window.

In addition, you should take care not to load any TSR (terminate-and-stay-resident) programs inside a DOS window. There are many such programs in common use. SideKick is probably one of the most popular, although many more are also in regular use. These programs load into DOS, grabbing certain areas of memory and waiting for you to press a specified key combination to wake them up.

The problem with using a TSR program from inside a DOS session accessed from within the Tools menu is that the TSR takes its own piece of memory out of an environment that will change or disappear. Although a TSR can work well when it is loaded before any other programs, if you load such a program and do not remove it before closing your dBASE IV DOS session, you could lock up dBASE IV, creating a "hole" in memory that is still owned by the nonexistent TSR.

> The key here is this: Don't run TSR programs in a dBASE IV DOS window (or as a DOS command), and don't run any program that doesn't finish running and get out of the way before you can close up the DOS window. If you break either rule, you're asking for trouble.

The third option in the DOS window, *Set default drive:directory* lets you tell dBASE IV where it is to look for (and save) files created during your dBASE session. This is useful if you are developing applications for different clients or departments. If you use a different directory for each account/client, you can then create a new catalog, and new list of files, for each department by changing your default drive:directory to the one for the client for which you are currently developing an application.

Making this change is simply a matter of highlighting the option (or pressing **S**) and pressing **Enter**, and typing the new drive:directory data.

The Files Menu The Files menu allows you to control what is seen in the screen window. This menu allows you to change to a different drive and/or directory that you wish to view or modify from within the DOS utilities window. By selecting the *Change drive:directory* menu option and pressing **Enter**, you will cause dBASE IV to bring up a window to specify the new drive and directory. This window looks like Figure 3-21.

If you don't know the exact name of the directory or subdirectory you wish to change to, make sure that you've set the drive you wish to select, and press *Shft-F1* to bring up a directory selection tree similar to that shown in Figure 3-22.

Move the highlight to the directory you wish to change to, using the **Up Arrow** and **Down Arrow** keys, and press **Enter** to select the directory desired. The system will read the list of files in the directory, and display them in the DOS utilities window.

The second option, *Display only*, allows you to set up filters for the files to be displayed. The default {*.*} displays every file in the directory. By changing this setting, you can tell dBASE IV to show only those files that match a certain parameter. For example, to see only database (.DBF) files, you may type in the parameter ***.DBF**. This setting will show only files with the .DBF file extension. Wildcards are supported. The asterisk * is used to denote all characters at or beyond the asterisk in a filename. The asterisk may be placed in any position: in the filename or extension, or both.

dBASE IV's DOS search parameter *.* uses a wildcard for the filename and extension. Every file in the chosen directory is selected. If you wanted to show only the .DBF files, the keys to define only the .DBF files would be ***.DBF**. The extension .dbf would tell dBASE IV to select only those files whose extensions were .DBF. The * tells

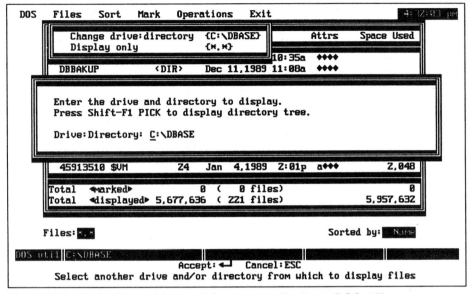

Figure 3-21   Selecting a drive and directory to display in DOS utility.

dBASE IV that you want to select all files that match the selected criterion. The combination of the two selects all files with the .DBF extension.

A second wildcard, the question mark **?** is used to donate a wildcard selection *only* for the character position where the mark is located, and not for all characters beyond that mark. For example, if *.DB? was your parameter, you would get all files

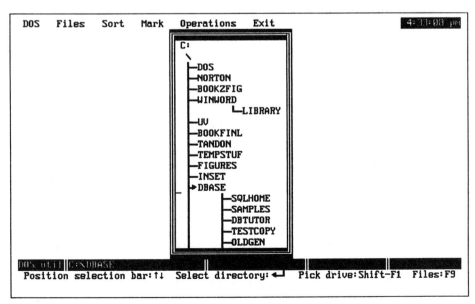

Figure 3-22   Directory selection tree.

with extensions running from .DBA through .DBZ, and .DB0 through .DB9, plus any other legal extensions starting with db. By carefully defining the *Display only* parameter, you can have dBASE IV select and display only those files that you tell it to look for.

The Sort Menu The Sort menu gives you four choices of sort parameters. The four choices—*Name, Extension, Date & Time,* and *Size*—allow you to tell dBASE IV how to group the files that meet the display parameters. Being able to sort the files in a variety of ways can be quite useful. For example, sorting by date and time lets you see which files are newest, and which are oldest. This allows you to quickly find the file(s) that you most recently worked on.

Sorting by extension puts all files of a particular type into one group. Thus, if you wanted to view all .SCR files, for example, a display sorted by extension would allow you to do this easily. Sort parameters are selected by typing the first letter of the parameter you wish to sort by, or by moving the highlight to the desired sort type and pressing **Enter**.

The Mark Menu The Mark menu works in conjunction with the Operations menu. When a file is marked, you can perform a desired operation on that file. Operations include deleting, copying, moving, renaming, viewing, and editing. The Mark menu makes it easy to mark, unmark, or reverse marks on a file or group of files. The *Reverse marks* option marks those files that were unmarked, and unmarks files that were marked.

Individual files are marked by moving the highlight to the file that you want to mark and pressing the **Enter** key. To unmark a file, highlight the marked file and press **Enter**. When a file has been marked, it stays marked until you unmark it, using the *Unmark all* option, unmark it using the **Enter** key, or close the DOS utilities window. A marked file will stay marked even if you go to another drive or directory to mark other files.

The Operations Menu The Operations menu, shown in Figure 3-23, allows you to do *something* to your marked files. The first four options—*Delete, Copy, Move,* and *Rename*—have secondary menus that ask for confirmation (before deleting) or information about new names, or destination directories or names.

The options can be applied to displayed files and single files, as well as to marked files, as can be seen from the Delete menu, shown in Figure 3-24. The menu allows you to delete a single file, all marked files, or all displayed files.

When you select *Single File*, dBASE IV prompts you to confirm that you wish to delete the file that is highlighted on the screen. In order to delete a single file, then, you must first highlight it. Pressing **P** to *P*roceed with the deletion process tells dBASE IV to delete the file. The option works in much the same way in the other file operations.

The *Marked Files* option tells dBASE IV to perform the operation on all marked files. In the Delete menu, choosing to delete marked files will cause dBASE IV to remove all the marked files from your disk.

The *Displayed Files* option is a third method of selecting files. The displayed files can represent those files that have been selected using the *Display only* file criteria from

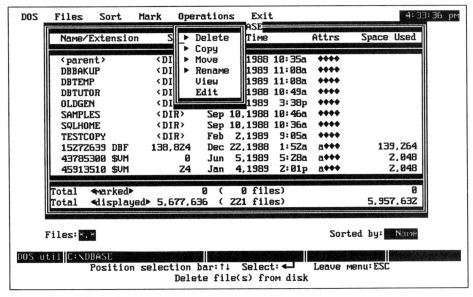

Figure 3-23 Operations menu.

the Files window. For example, if you want to copy all your database files, and only database files, to another directory, this can be done in two steps.

The first step is to define the parameters for displaying a file from within the Files menu. The syntax for displaying only database files is *.DBF. By using this filter, dBASE IV will only display database files (files with the .DBF file extension).

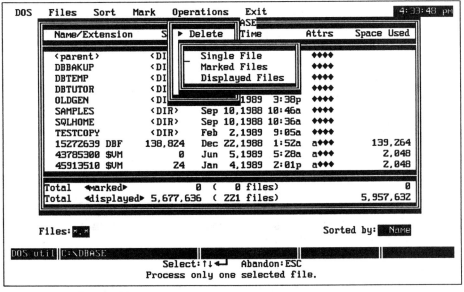

Figure 3-24 Delete files menu.

As long as there are fewer than one screenful of selected files, choosing to delete (or move or copy) displayed files will cause the desired operation to be performed on the selected files. If more files are selected than can be displayed on your screen, the *Mark all* command can be used to mark all the files that have been selected using your selection parameters. Using *Mark all* is faster than selecting and operating on a screen at a time.

The Copy option copies the selected file or files. A copy can be made inside the current directory, allowing you to make a duplicate copy of a file that you want to edit. This is useful if you want to create a new data file, using an existing data file as a common core from which to build.

For example, you may have a data file with all the parts that your company sells. You want to create a specialized data file for a new division. This new file will contain many of the parts listed in your overall company database, but you expect to add some special items that will not be available from the general company database.

In addition, you will be deleting a large percentage of the files from the master database. Clearly, making these changes to your original, company-wide parts database would be inappropriate. However, copying the database file, renaming it, and working on the newly created file should safely accomplish your design goal.

In addition to copying a single or marked file to the current directory, you may often wish to copy files to another directory. If you are developing many applications, this may be done more frequently than copying single files within a directory.

Note that you cannot copy files to a directory that does not exist. Therefore, you may have to perform a DOS command to create the target directory that you wish to copy your files into.

Selecting file destination is performed in two steps. The first step is to establish the target drive and directory for your files to be copied to. A box for defining the destination appears below the Copy window. Once you've typed the directory and path for your files to be copied to, press **Enter**, and dBASE IV will move the highlight into a prompt asking the name of your copied files.

If you wish to copy the selected files to another directory without changing the file names, leave the name field blank. The file naming field, which appears in the destination appears below the Copy window. Once you've typed the directory and path for your files to be copied to, press **Enter** and dBASE IV will move the highlight into a prompt asking the name of your copied files.
the names unchanged. If, however, you want to copy and simultaneously rename the files, this can also be done.

Once you've defined the copy criteria, press **Ctrl-End** to perform the copy. If dBASE IV detects that it will be creating a file with the same name as one already in the target directory, it will prompt you to tell it whether it should overwrite the file already in the directory, or skip copying the file over.

Other types of renamed copies can also be made. For example, you may want to copy your files and give a numeric prefix to those you've modified. This number tells you which revision you last worked on. In this case, you may want to retain as much of the original name of the files as possible. The syntax for this type of copy would use the number that you wish to use for your new revision, followed by *.* (for example, if you wanted to rename your files so that they started with the number 1, the syntax would be 1*.*).

There is one potential problem, however. If your file normally begins with the number you are assigning to your version, the copied file will retain the original name (in this case, you've changed the initial character, 1, to 1, or no change at all).

Using a combination of the * global wildcard and the ? wildcard (which applies only to a single character), you can take advantage of a wide range of copying and renaming options.

The Move command performs two operations. First, it copies the selected files to a new directory. Next, it removes the original files from the original directory. A move made by DOS is different from a physical move, where you pick something up from one place, and put it down in another. In DOS, a move involves grabbing an exact image of a file, placing it somewhere else, and then removing the original. If you watch "Star Trek," such a move is easy to visualize. In fact, if transporters worked like computers, the show has the process all wrong.

Moving, say, Spock would involve two steps, just as DOS would do it. First, Spock would be scanned and digitized, and the scanned Spock would be assembled at the destination. There would initially be two Spocks (and this would be extremely valuable, in case something went wrong during the transfer). Once the Spock that was placed at the destination was confirmed to be an exact copy of the original, the original Spock, still on the *Enterprise*, would be removed by the transporter and deleted. What you'd have, then, is an *exact* copy of Spock, right down to the pointy ears, that looks, feels, acts, and *is* Spock (although the original is, of course, gone).

The same process goes with a DOS move. Two steps are involved, as just outlined. A Move differs from a Copy because in a move the original file is removed from the source directory. Again, as with the Copy option, you may simultaneously move and rename files, using the options and wildcards already described.

The Rename option can be used to rename a single file, marked files, or a screen at a time of displayed files. This option is slightly different from Copy or Move. Although you were able to copy a file or files, and rename them when they were written to their new destination, the original name remained intact. A Move to the same directory is functionally equivalent to a Rename of files in a directory, although the actual DOS processes are slightly different.

Renaming a document involves changing the name information that is associated with the contents of a file. The file is not copied, moved, or physically altered during a Rename, with the exception of the change in the filename in the directory table that tells dBASE IV where to find the associated file.

Again, the wildcards already described can be used during a Rename.

The next two options in the Operations menu, *View* and *Edit*, differ from the file management operations outlined earlier. These options are concerned with the contents of specific files, and can be only used with the files currently highlighted. Where the options previously described dealt with file naming and file management, these options let you explore what's *inside* of a file.

The View option allows you to look at the contents of a highlighted file. The Edit option allows you to go one step further, and make changes to the contents of the selected file. This doesn't make sense for binary (.BIN), compiled (.COM), or executable files (.EXE), since these files are not stored as text and would appear as virtually unusable digital code that could only be understood (perhaps) by experienced assembly language programmers. For other files, however, viewing a document may be useful, on occasion, to get a quick look at the contents of the document (and may be quicker than trying to load from the Control Center).

When you highlight a file and choose to Edit that file, the contents of the file appear in a standard dBASE IV Edit window. The DOS utilities provide a great deal of flexibility and functionality to the user of dBASE IV. In fact, by giving you the ability to do sophisticated file management, plus providing a DOS shell, and the interesting *Space Used* column, the designers of dBASE IV have significantly enhanced the product and have allowed you to perform tasks that you may have had to leave the program to perform in previous versions of dBASE.

To exit from the DOS utilities, press the **Esc** key or **Alt-E**. The system will prompt to see if you really want to return to the Control Center. Providing the appropriate response will return you to the Control Center.

Protect Data

The *Protect data* option in the Tools menu allows you to secure your data files in a number of ways, from inspection or modification by unauthorized users. When used on a network, a complete security system can be developed, with the assignment of a database administrator who controls access to files for the users on the network.

Single-user protection can also be important, if you are working on sensitive data or don't want others to see or alter the work you are doing.

The security system works in much the same way on a single-user installation as it does on a multiuser installation on a network. Three levels of security are provided by dBASE IV.

The first level is *password security*. In order to be able to load dBASE IV, a pre-assigned password is required in a system that has been set up for security. The second level is by *access level*. A group administrator is responsible, in conjunction with appropriate supervisory or management persons, to define access levels for any employees who will be using dBASE IV or any of its files.

Each user can be assigned a particular access level when related to a specific data file. The system can be set to allow a user to have full control of a data file, to read only (and prevent any editing or modification), or can provide no access to the file. In addition, access to particular fields can be controlled, and the system can be set up to not even *show* a file or a field.

The highest access level is level 1, while the lowest level is 8. If the database administrator set access to view files to level 5, an employee with an access level of 6 or above would be unable to view the protected files, but any employees with access levels of 5 or lower could view them.

If level 3 and higher allowed authorized users to edit and modify the files, then it would be clear that, while anyone with an access level of 5 or lower could view the files, only those with access levels of 3, 2, or 1 would be allowed to edit the files.

A fourth type of protection is *encryption*. An encrypted file is one that has been "scrambled," based on an algorithm built around a password "key." Without particular diligence, and perhaps a miracle or two, an unauthorized user would be unable to make any sense out of the data or dBASE IV program files, even if they were to be copied off dBASE IV and attempts were made to decode them.

To reassemble your files, dBASE IV will ask for the decryption key word (the same word that was used to encrypt your file), and the files and dBASE IV programs will be recreated to match the originals before they were encrypted. Thus, a high degree of protection can be provided by dBASE IV.

The system only allows you to protect nine data files at a time. Once nine have been protected, with defined access codes and encryption code words (if desired), the security parameters must be saved before additional files are similarly protected. When security is set up, and saved, dBASE IV will be in effect, and will continue in effect in all subsequent sessions. Although access levels and security for particular files can be changed by the dBASE IV manager, you will be unable to set up dBASE IV to run without the password without a complete reinstallation.

The first step in enacting a security system is to select *Protect data* from the Tools menu (by pressing **P** or by moving the highlight to *Protect data* and pressing the **Enter** key). dBASE IV will then bring up a prompt asking if you really want to permanently assign passwords to dBASE IV and your data.

When you accept the prompt, dBASE IV will bring up a screen asking for you to type your password. dBASE IV allows up to 16 alphabetic or numeric characters for your password, and Ashton-Tate recommends that you use all 16.

You should record your password and store it in a safe place where it can be retrieved when needed. Storing the password in a file on your computer makes little sense; a person who truly wanted to get into your system would probably be able to find a password hidden in a batch or text file on your system.
guesses by anyone who wants to break into dBASE IV. The use of a full 16 characters makes the possible combinations of characters that could be used in a password astronomical. Since dBASE IV freezes dBASE IV after four incorrect password entry attempts, randomly guessing a password would be futile.

You should record your password and store it in a safe place where it can be retrieved when needed. Storing the password in a file on your computer makes little sense—a person who truly wanted to get into your system would probably be able to find a password hidden in a batch or text file on your system.

If you lose or forget your password, you may end up permanently locked out of the protected version of dBASE IV, and may be permanently unable to view, retrieve, or use the data and files that were developed using dBASE IV. Thus it is *essential* that you keep a backup record of your password in a place where, in an emergency, you can retrieve it so that you can restart dBASE IV.

Once you've typed and confirmed your password, dBASE IV will bring up the screen that allows you (or the access administrator) to control access levels, passwords, and groups for your organization. The security system administrator will be responsible for controlling access levels, passwords, and other aspects of dBASE IV's security. As for individual users, simple password security is probably adequate for keeping unauthorized users off of dBASE IV.

It is useful to note, however, that a data file can be assigned to only one group. Multiple groups cannot share a common data file, if the file or users are controlled by a security system. However, a person with a low enough access level can make copies of data files, or produce new data files that include the data needed by a particular group.

If you've brought up the security menu and don't want to proceed, press **Esc** and confirm that you want to *Abandon protect*. (Note: at no other times are you encouraged to exit an operation by escaping out of it. However, since this is the surest way of making sure that your efforts at security *aren't* saved, this method is given, rather than choosing *Abandon* from the Exit menu).

Once you abandon the *Protect data* processes, you will be returned to the Control Center. If, on the other hand, you save your security settings, all subsequent sessions using dBASE IV will implement password security.

Settings

The Settings menu, a subset of the DBSETUP program that you may have run when you installed dBASE IV, allows you to make changes to your system's operational options and the display. To select the Settings menu, bring up the Tools window, and press **S**, or move the cursor to the word *Settings* and press **Enter**.

The Settings Options look like those in Figure 3-25. To choose any of the options that you wish to change, you may move the highlight to the item you wish, or type the first letters of the option name. Once the item is highlighted, pressing **Enter** will toggle through options, or, in the case of items requiring numeric values, bring up a screen asking for a number to be input. The numbers are accepted using the **Enter** key, which closes the window and saves the new value.

The individual options are relatively self-explanatory, and only a few will be discussed here. *Carry* allows dBASE IV to copy the contents from the previous record onto a new record. This option is useful in cases where most of the data from record to record is unchanged.

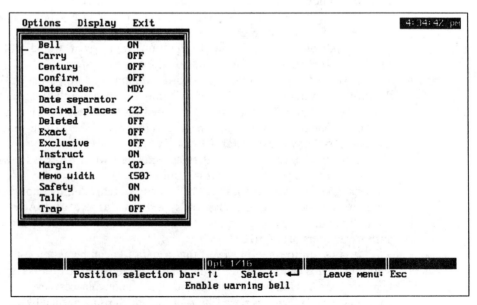

Figure 3-25 Settings Options window.

For example, if you are preparing a data file on all the people who live on a certain street, copying all the information automatically (then changing the street number and identifying information for each individual) will be faster and easier than retyping an entire record. Another example is preparing a directory of employees by department. In this case, the alterations being made may be as minor as a name change. Setting Carry to ON will substantially simplify the task of entering new records.

The *Talk* setting allows dBASE IV to show you what it's doing as it performs operations that you specify. For example, if you've designed a label, when you save the label, dBASE IV will look at your specifications and generate code that it will use to speed up execution when you ask it to print the label.

This may be especially valuable if you have designed a complex report, a complicated query, or a complex application. Being able to monitor the operation of dBASE IV, especially if it is performing a very time-consuming operation, will give you peace of mind, with the assurance that dBASE IV is working (and has not locked up).

The *Display options* menu allows you to make changes to the appearance of your display. These options will be discussed in more detail in later chapters on reports, labels, and the Applications Generator.

It should be noted that any changes in the Settings menu are only temporary—they last only as long as the current dBASE IV worksession. You should feel free to write down the settings, if they are to your liking, so that they can be made to the CONFIG.DB file (either by running DBSETUP or editing the CONFIG.DB file).

To return to the Control Center from the Settings menu, you may select the Exit menu (by pressing **Alt-E**, or by pressing **F10**), and accept the Exit option.

The Exit Menu

The functions of the Exit menu are fairly straightforward. The menu allows you two options—you may exit to the *dot prompt*, which will allow you to interact with dBASE IV using dBASE IV language commands, or you may quit from dBASE IV and return to DOS.

If you exit to the dot prompt and wish to return to the Control Center, you may do so by pressing the **F2** key. To quit from within the dot prompt, type *Quit* **Enter**. To access the Exit menu from within the Control Center, press **Alt-E**, or press the **F10** button and move the cursor to highlight the menu. Highlight the desired option, or type the first letter of the option name. dBASE IV will bring you to the desired level (DOS or dot prompt interface).

Conclusion

In this chapter, the Control Center menu lines were discussed at some length. The Control Center serves as a consistent, relatively intuitive user interface.

From within the Control Center, you should be able to design and run complete data management applications. The specific operations of each Control Center panels were not discussed in this chapter but will be covered in considerable detail through the rest of this book.

The focus of this chapter was the additional tools—macros, navigational keystrokes, DOS utilities, and other basics—that will either be referred to as having been learned already from future chapters or that will be useful to future operations.

The Control Center is designed so that the novice user, as well as the experienced developer, could simply design complete data management systems.

Future chapters will build on the foundations set in this chapter and will show how each component of a database system is designed.

4

Database Design

The first three chapters of this book covered many of the basics of operating dBASE IV. The rest of this book will cover the techniques involved in designing and implementing database systems, and in building and operating complete, functional database applications. In this chapter, you'll learn some of the basics of good database design, and design a number of the database files that will be used to build the sample application developed in this book.

Good Database Design

Much has been written about good database design, and there is much to cover here. dBASE IV is promoted by Ashton-Tate as being a relational database management system. If the rules that must be implemented to be a truly relational product were applied to dBASE IV (or, for that matter, many of the database products that claim to be relational), it would be clear that dBASE IV doesn't meet the requirements. In fact, very few database products do.

What dBASE IV *does* provide is the ability to link data files and to do analysis based on the links established. For example, in the application to be built here for a compact disk distribution company, you can create a report listing the titles purchased by each customer, even though neither data file (customer or title) has information about the other. You will use two files: a customer data file, and a CD titles file. An order file containing the customer number and the CD identification number can be used to process orders. When it's time to complete the order, dBASE IV can retrieve the customer information from the record in the customer file that matches the customer ID on the order form, and can also retrieve the title, price, and other information from the CD titles data file.

In practice, *relations* (the term that will be used throughout this book to mean "the linking of data files in a database system") will probably be used quite frequently to prepare reports or labels, or otherwise get at your data. The ability to relate files is often necessary due to design considerations in developing relational databases.

One of the key rules for designing a database application is to try to keep the number of fields duplicated in more than one file to a minimum. For example, an order entry data file can be designed that includes space for all the identifying information for a customer (company name, address, phone number, and so on). This information would have to be filled in each time an order is taken.

However, the form can also be designed to use only the customer's ID number. When the actual invoice and shipping forms are printed, dBASE IV can match the customer ID number to the ID number in the customer data file, and can automatically retrieve and print the customer's address data onto the appropriate forms.

Not only is it time-consuming for the order entry clerk to have to take down information that you've already gotten securely stored in a customer database, you're also bogging down the system with information that isn't really needed. By putting more data than you need into more than one file, you're creating larger files. For a database with thousands of files, the amount of extraneous data could run into many megabytes of disk storage. In addition, if you are recording the same data in two or more different data files, you may run into a few problems.

First, if you make a change in one file, you'll have to (somehow) make the same changes in any other files that contain the same data. dBASE IV provides no simple way to do this. Further, if you assume that the contents of the same field in multiple files are the same, you may run into trouble when the field's contents have been changed in one file but not in another. Thus, you should take care to duplicate only fields that will be used later to link (or combine) data files. In the example given, an order entry file will be linked to the customer list by means of the customer number (and customer information for the matching customer will be taken from the customer data file), and the file will be linked to the title ordered by the disk number (with pricing and other information pulled out of the titles data file).

The relational capabilities of dBASE IV allow you to make the references you will need to extract data from other data files. To print out an invoice, the system can be told to read the order file. From inside the order file, the customer ID number is read. An instruction in the query form tells the system to go to the customer data file, look up the appropriate customer based on a unique ID number, and retrieve the required address information.

The system may also print out a description of the item(s) ordered. In this case, the order form will have a unique identification number for each item ordered. This number will be related to a file with product identification numbers, and will merge the identifying information into the invoice. Thus, although all the information required to print a complete invoice can be put onto the basic order entry form, it is unnecessary, can possibly cause longer delays in processing your queries or reports, and can easily make your data record system much larger than necessary.

A key to good database design, one that can't be stressed enough, is to take the time required to *carefully* plan your database. Careful planning before building the database, and a test with a small number of records, can help prevent costly changes that may result from a poorly designed database application.

If you are preparing an application for a client, it is useful to examine the forms currently in use. It can be valuable to spend some time watching how the systems you wish to develop applications for are currently being done. One mistake that many programmers (and some consultants) continue to make is designing a system that they *think* the customer wants, without knowing what the customer *really* wants. Time spent with a client detailing what types of information are necessary, how the information is to be used, which forms are being used (with the possibility of developing new forms or deleting current forms), and how the data will be evaluated and implemented will prove to be time well spent.

Try to categorize what types of information are needed. Design the sample data structures, and define the input and output forms. Based on the specifications as outlined by the customer (or client), you should try to envision an entire database application at all levels. You should evaluate your designs to ensure that there is a minimum of redundancy from data file to data file. You should evaluate your designs to make sure that there are adequate (and appropriate) *unique* links between data files in order to make relating data possible.

If the application you are designing is meant to replace an existing system, you should consider trying to provide compatibility with the existing system (without sacrificing performance to do so) in order to lessen the training required for people who will use the system, as well as to lessen the shock and reduce the resistance of some workers who are resistant to change. The amount of difference from the original system that will be tolerated can usually be easily determined by talking to your client. Testing a prototype of the system also helps to determine areas that need fixing, or areas where the client would like changes made.

One feature in dBASE IV that makes it easy to perform a gradual compatibility change is the ease with which screen forms can be designed. The design of a data entry form will be discussed in detail in the next chapter. However, for the purposes of this discussion, it should be noted that form design is an easy process.

You may reduce user resistance by initially designing your data forms so that they resemble or imitate forms that the user is currently familiar with. Later on, you can implement improvements merely by replacing the current forms with more effective input forms that use the same fields and filters as the original. dBASE IV provides you with the tools necessary to easily change the appearance of your forms and documents. A gradual change in a system may involve as little as the redesign of commonly used forms.

Other considerations should be taken into account when developing a database application. Linking between fields to be related is a key consideration. Relating (or linking) data files has already been briefly discussed. The mechanism is simple, but the process is prone to error if not performed carefully.

When a link is made, the system is asked to look at the contents of a designated field in two or more data files. For example, you may wish to match a customer number in an order form with the customer number in a customer identification form. The system will look at the order form, read the customer number, and then search through the customer identification data file until it finds a record with an identical customer number. As long as the two numbers are identical and unique, the relation should work properly. But what if the numbers were slightly different? For example, the order form shows a customer number of 3827 and the customer information file shows the number as 38-27. In such a case, the system will not detect a match. Thus, it is important to standardize the way data is recorded.

This is particularly important if abbreviations or jargon are used in data entry. For example, in the compact disk distributor example to be built in this chapter, one of the fields in the catalog is for the name of the record label. If one input operator abbreviates Columbia with the letters Col, and another abbreviates it Columb, you may end up with two different records for the same title. Even using a routine designed to strip out duplicates, dBASE IV may not detect the two items since they are from "different" publishers.

If you are developing a medical records system, the problem of abbreviations may become more pronounced. Your system may catalog diagnoses by using abbreviations. One person's entry of CA could mean cancer, while another's entry of CA could mean cardiac arrest. Adopting a standard set of abbreviations, and making sure that anyone using the abbreviations understands and uses them consistently, will assure the consistency of your data.

If the number of possible values for a field is small, you may incorporate a multiple-choice data entry design for the field values. However, for fields where there may be a large number of responses, a multiple-choice field is not appropriate. In many cases, a "bible" that lists the approved values for each field should be provided to each input operator and religiously adhered to.

Another important point to discuss is the uniqueness of linking fields. dBASE IV allows you great flexibility in defining fields to be linked. In the order entry example, you could have chosen to link based on the customer name rather than the customer identification number. The system would read the name of the customer as entered on the order form, then look through the customer identification file until it found a match.

This kind of link may work in most cases. But with a large customer list, the chances of finding two *John's Records* is significant, and may result in the order being sent to the wrong John's Records. A related problem arises if the order entry clerk takes an order for Jon's Records (instead of John's Records) and dBASE IV is unable to produce an invoice or shipping documents because there is no link between Jon's Records and John's Records. By linking on a unique value, the customer number, which should be assigned to *only one* person, company, or entity, the likelihood of making correct links increases significantly.

Assigning a unique number to each customer can avoid the problems that arise when links are made on fields that may contain the same data for different records. You should be careful to assure that such unique fields are included in your database design.

An additional consideration helps to reduce the possibility that data belonging in one field ends up in another. If the customer ID field uses six digits, for example, and the item numbers also use six digits, a customer number may be entered into a stock number field, or vice versa.

Thus, the format for your unique fields should differ from that for the other fields. One possible solution to the problem of customer ID and stock numbers would be to give each customer a unique six-digit ID, which would allow for one million customers (or more, if letters were used in addition to numbers), and to use nine-character stock numbers (perhaps a three-letter label abbreviation followed by a six-digit identification number).

The use of letters instead of numbers as part of an identifier allows more possible unique identifiers to be used by the same amount of characters. This should be obvious when you consider that there are 26 available alphabetic characters, any of which can be used, while there are only 10 possible digits.

You should try to plan for reasonable growth when designing your identifiers. Obviously, a three-digit customer identifier may quickly prove inadequate, since it allows for only 999 customers (1000 if 000 is permitted). It should be equally clear that a 12-digit customer identification field would be larger than needed, unless you expect every living person on earth, and his or her dogs or cats, and maybe even some of their fleas, to also become customers.

About Data Management Approaches

The terms "relational" and "link" have been used extensively in the past few pages. The words are an important part of a way of thinking about storing, analyzing, and retrieving your data. It should be clear that everyone uses data. The telephone book is a database with a very large file. Your address book is another data file, containing some of the same types of information as the phone book, but also holding other types of information. It is this way of thinking about data—as a single file that contains all the information you'll need about a subject—that is the most easily understood when you first begin thinking about data. A number of quite good data management products on the market use this basic model for data management.

For example, RapidFile II, Ashton-Tate's "flat file" database program does a very good job of supporting the creation, editing, and use of data files that include all required information in a single file. The approach is called "flat file" because it only has a single dimension. Unlike the data structure type used by dBASE IV, which connects other data files to your single file, the data in a "flat" data file is complete, without any references or linkages to other data files.

In a phone list, you can include such fields as *first name*, *last name*, *street address*, *unit number*, *city*, *state*, *ZIP code*, *home phone*, and *office phone*. These fields may provide all the information you need. If you wish, you may add such fields as *birthdate*, *shirt size*, and *shoe size*. The important point is that if you want to get any information about a particular record, the information can be easily retrieved from that single record. If you need to record more information, you just add a new field for that information.

Flat file database development and management is really quite easy. It's also well suited to a wide range of applications that may require such an approach. However, a flat file approach is also quite limiting. Say, for example, that you want to design an order entry system. With a flat file, this would be tricky and would produce a lot of redundant data. You would probably design a data file that contains the customer's name, address, phone number, and credit card number (if appropriate), and provide four or five fields for the items ordered. This may work for small systems. But what happens if the customer orders fifty different items? Do you fill out five forms? Do you make up ten separate bills or fifty separate bills? If you get one check, how do you post payments? If you get fifty checks, how much trouble will it be to post all fifty?

The problems that arise when using a flat file database arise out of a set of relationships called "one-to-one (1:1)" and "one-to-many (1:M)." In the case of a telephone list, it is reasonable to assume that all the information you need can be recorded in one form. A single individual (with his or her own record) can be expected to have only one address and (usually) only one phone number. The home address and the person's name or Social Security number will have a 1:1 relationship to each other.

In your order entry system, on the other hand, a one-to-many relationship exists. Although there may only be one customer, the customer may order many items. In such a case, a flat file system can't easily handle the data management tasks you wish it to. This is where the relational system used by dBASE IV comes into play. Although you can certainly use dBASE IV as a high-powered flat file data management program, its real strength is in handling the one-to-many and many-to-many types of real life problems encountered by business.

For order entry, a new data file can be used. The order entry data file may be made up of as few as three fields: *customer number*, *item number*, and *quantity ordered*. One record will be made for each item ordered. For an order of ten different items, ten records will be made. Using dBASE IV, you can even have the system copy the previous customer number, quantity, and item code to a new record, since it would be faster to change only the item number and quantities than it would be to have to retype all three fields.

Many items will be ordered by one customer, with a separate record for each item ordered. When the order is to be filled, printed, billed, or otherwise processed, dBASE IV can easily find all items ordered by each customer, and can easily prepare such documents. Using links, or relations, dBASE IV will look at the order entry data files, match the customer number to the appropriate customer name in the customer data file, and find all items ordered by that customer. Similarly, an item number can be linked to a third data file that contains the product information and the product identification number that was placed into the order record.

Thus, using a relational approach, you can link a number of data files together, based on unique fields. You can easily handle a company that has 100 telephone numbers but only one company name, by creating a telephone file that includes only the company name field and the telephone number field, and matching it to the company information file. This is certainly a lot more flexible than creating a flat file with 100 telephone number data fields.

Breaking files into smaller components that will be related through a special, separate file, or through the use of a special query, provides additional power, but also extracts a price when it is used in dBASE IV. The problem in dBASE IV is that you can only view or edit one file at a time.

When you are setting up a new customer, you may want to fill out each of the separate forms required to set up the account: a customer form, a buyer identification form, a billing information/credit form, and possibly other forms. So, to set up a new account, you have to fill out the customer form, close the form, bring up the buyer form and fill it out, close the form, and go to the next form. If you want to fill out an order, it would be useful to be able to get the customer number off the customer file. Unfortunately, to do this, you'd have to close the order entry form and load up the customer record form. To get the number for a product being ordered, you would have to leave the order entry form and open the product directory file. In short, dBASE IV makes the process somewhat difficult by not allowing you to view or retrieve data from forms other than the one you are using. (Programmers are able to work around this, but those approaches are beyond the scope of this book. Future versions of dBASE may address this limitation.)

All is not lost, however. Using macros that you can easily create from within the Control Center, you can close your current data entry task, bring up a desired file and Browse for the information you need, and finally return to the original order entry activity you were performing. Not necessarily the best way to accomplish the task, but *a* way.

When thinking relationally, the goal is to break your data system into logical blocks of related data. In an order entry system, blocks such as customer information, buyer information, product information, and stock information all lend themselves to independent files. Special files, such as the order entry file just described, provide links between the smaller blocks. The goal is to provide flexible support for the many-to-many relationships in your data system, while keeping each block no larger than necessary.

The Application

The application to be developed will be for a distributor of compact discs and digital audio tapes called Discs and DAT.

The Catalog

First, create a new catalog, calling it CDDIST (for *CD DIST*ributor). To do this, bring up the Catalog menu. The Catalog menu can be accessed by pressing **Alt-C** or by pressing **F10** and moving the cursor to open the Catalog menu.

Next, select *Use a different catalog* by highlighting the option and pressing **Enter** or by pressing the **U** key (uppercase or lowercase U). This will bring up the catalog selection menu.

Select < create >, and the system will bring up a window for naming the new catalog, as in Figure 4-1. Type *CDDIST*, the name for your new catalog, and press **Enter.** The screen will show a new catalog name, with no files shown.

Now that you've created your new catalog, the next step is to describe it. If your database system typically uses many different catalogs, having a description of each can aid in determining which catalog you wish to load. This is especially true if you use similar catalog names.

Again, bring up the Catalog menu, and select *Edit description of catalog*. This option may be selected once the Catalog menu is brought onto the screen, either by pressing **E**, or by moving the highlight to highlight *Edit description of catalog* and pressing **Enter**. Now type *CD and DAT distribution Application Catalog*.

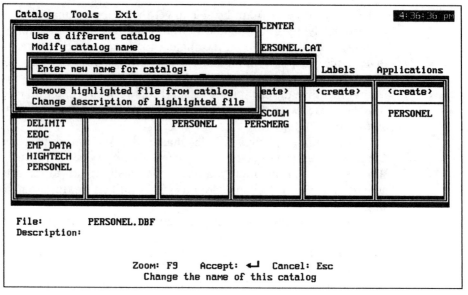

Figure 4-1 Catalog naming window.

Press **Enter**, and the system will return the cursor to its location prior to activating the Catalog menu (in this case, on <create> in the Data panel). To see how the catalog description works, bring up the Catalog menu and select *Use a different catalog*. Next, move the cursor to highlight the CDDIST.CAT catalog listing. A window in the lower third of the screen will display your description of the catalog.

Press **Esc Esc** to return the cursor to the Control Center design screen.

Creating the Files

To build a complete database management application you will need to create a variety of data files. Among the files that you'll need to build are a customer identification file, a stock (or inventory update) file, a list of titles, an order entry file, and a buyers file (listing the buyer names for each store). Other files may be added to this basic core as necessary.

The first step to be taken is to create a new data file in the CDDIST.CAT catalog. To do this, highlight the word <create> in the Data panel, and press **Shft-F2**.

> **Note** The **Shft-F2** key combination is a shortcut that can be used to bring you into the design screen. The same key combination can also bring you into design screens in all other panels but the Applications panel.

Selecting the word <create> also loads a design form. Although accepting the word <create> by pressing the **Enter** key brings up the design menu, it is better to get into the habit of using **Shft-F2** for modifying a file or form, and **F2** for viewing the data on the form.

The system will bring up a blank data file design screen, as shown in Figure 4-2.

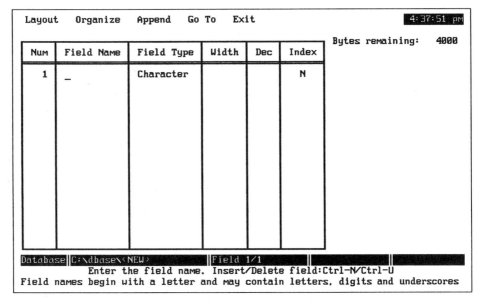

Figure 4-2 Data file design screen.

The first column numbers the fields in the order in which they will be stored in your data file. This order is not necessarily the order that your data input forms will take, nor does it have to be the same order as that your reports will take.

In addition to designing your data file in the order in which the data will most frequently be retrieved, you should also pay close attention to how your data will be used. To illustrate this, consider the matter of a client's name. In some cases, it may be perfectly acceptable to have a single field that consists of first name and last name. In others, this would be completely unacceptable.

If your application for the names in the mailing list, for example, were merely to print envelopes and to print an address at the top of a letter, using a single field for first and last name would probably be more than adequate. However, you might at some time wish to print form letters that use only the last name of the addressee.

For example, an annoying letter "to the Smith household" could be generated easily if first name and last name were separate fields, but not so easily if the two fields were not separated. The other option, a letter "to the John Smith household" could be annoying, and even more obviously a form letter.

The Fields

When designing the fields in your data file, it is well to err by having too many fields rather than too few. Although adding unused fields takes up extra storage and can slow down the system when a lot of records are being sorted, queried, or reported on, the extraneous fields can always be deleted at a later date. But to remove *part* of a field and convert it to a second field is often more trouble than it's worth.

Some common sense in field design, planning for the possible uses of each data field, and perhaps a bit of instinct can assure the creation of the right number (and breakdown) of the fields to be used in a file.

When naming a field, you may use up to ten characters. The naming characters may be alphabetic or numeric. Spaces are not permitted in a field name. A common solution to the problem of creating a field name of two or more words without using a space is to use the underline _ character. Many dBASE programmers use the underline as a conventional separator that means essentially the same thing as a standard space.

You should be careful to create field names that tell about the data field, and that are relatively unique. Figure 4-3 shows a data file designed to keep track of stocks and back orders of each title. The first field in the data file is the internal stock number. This number will be placed onto the order form for this particular title; the same number will be used in the titles data file. The titles data file will include a full description of the compact disk or digital audio tape.

It should be noted that this information could also have been part of a titles data file if this company sold only compact disks, and so had only one stock number for each title. In this case, however, the stock number for a compact disk would differ from that for a digital audio tape of the same title.

But even if this company stocked nothing but compact disks, having two data files (one for stock information and one for a list of titles available) would be preferable to having a single file combining stock information and a description of each title. This is because the two different files will often be used for different purposes. The titles data file will be used to look up each individual title and to print out a monthly catalog. More information about the artist, type of music, and so on, will be included in this data file and the resulting printout than will be necessary in the stock data file.

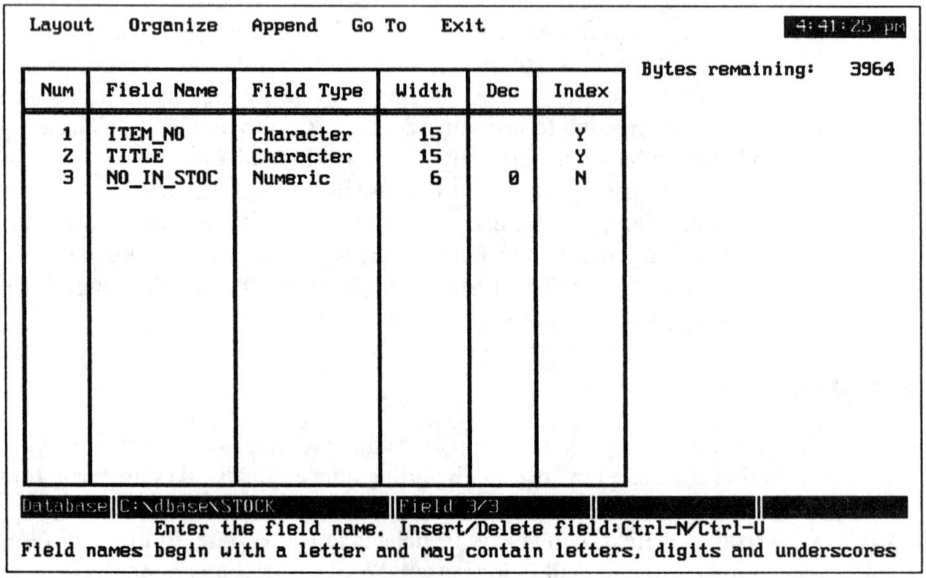

```
 Layout    Organize    Append    Go To    Exit                    4:41:25 pm

                                                        Bytes remaining:   3964
 ┌─────┬────────────┬────────────┬───────┬──────┬─────────┐
 │ Num │ Field Name │ Field Type │ Width │ Dec  │  Index  │
 ├─────┼────────────┼────────────┼───────┼──────┼─────────┤
 │  1  │ ITEM_NO    │ Character  │  15   │      │    Y    │
 │  2  │ TITLE      │ Character  │  15   │      │    Y    │
 │  3  │ NO_IN_STOC │ Numeric    │   6   │  0   │    N    │
 └─────┴────────────┴────────────┴───────┴──────┴─────────┘

 Database C:\dbase\STOCK          Field 3/3
            Enter the field name.  Insert/Delete field:Ctrl-N/Ctrl-U
 Field names begin with a letter and may contain letters, digits and underscores
```

Figure 4-3   Stock tracking data screen.

The stock data file (STOCK) tells how many items are in stock, how many are on order, and when the new orders are expected to arrive. In fact, a concession was made in the stock data file. The third field, TITLE, was unnecessary for the proper design or implementation of a stock tracking system (all that would have been needed to identify the title was the item number). However, to make it easier on the stock clerks, or for general stock searches (and to reduce the chances of pulling the wrong item if an incorrect stock number was entered onto an order), the title of the CD or DAT is included on the data form.

This file is used to keep track of current inventory of each title. When orders are shipped, a report generator automatically updates the number in stock field (NO_IN_STOC) to reflect the new number of units in stock. A second data file is used to place an order for each title. This file shows the number ordered and the due date. When new copies of a title arrive, a third file logs in the arrival (a separate record for each new title received), and a report generator adds the new units to the stock list. Assume that you have 20 units at the beginning of the day and sell 10 units. A stock adjustment query will subtract the number of units sold (10) from the number on hand (20), and change the value of NO_IN_STOC to 10. During the day, you receive a shipment of 30 units. The same query will add in the number of units received (30) and update the NO_IN_STOC field to reflect the actual number in stock (40). Although a number of files are required for maintaining units shipped and received, and a report is needed to update the number of units in stock, using such an approach can maintain regular control of all products in stock.

In most cases, this information should only be entered or changed by the people directly responsible for ordering and updating the stock information.

Field Types

There are six different types of fields.

Character A character field is one composed of alphanumeric characters: either numbers or letters, with some punctuation permitted. Character fields cannot normally be used for calculations. For example, you can't normally add the contents of two character fields, although there are methods in dBASE IV that make this possible.

When you set up the data input screens, you will be able to tell the system which characters are permitted and which are not. For example, you can set up a character field and later define it to only accept numbers.

However, when you use a character field, you should not plan to do any calculation or numerical comparisons on the contents of that field.

Numeric A numeric field is one that contains numbers. Numbers may be positive or negative integers or decimals. As with character fields, you can specify acceptable numbers when you define your data entry screens. As a general rule, a numeric field is one on which you plan to do some calculation or value relations. (A value relation might be: Find all files where the value of a field is greater than some preselected value or the value of some other field.)

In addition to matching values, and finding greater than or less than relationships, dBASE IV also provides commands for finding maximum values, minimum values, averages, and counts of certain values. Statistical functions are also supported.

Float Floating point numbers are a new field type supported by dBASE IV. These numbers are roughly equivalent to the numeric values used in earlier versions of dBASE. The difference between a floating point and a numeric value has to do with the way that the computer calculates numbers, and is roughly related to rounding errors.

In a floating point calculation, the last digits in a number are not stored as an exact number; instead, they are an approximation of the true numeric value. When multiple calculations are made using floating point values, errors can often creep in, giving a result that does not match the actual value that would result from a lengthy, manual calculation with pencil and paper or chalk on blackboard.

An example of how floating point errors creep into a calculation can be demonstrated with a simple pocket calculator. Take the square root of a number that doesn't result in an even answer—for example, the square root of 35. Then square that number. In theory, the product of a squared square root should be *exactly* equal to the original number, but most calculators will give a number like 34.9997 for the squared square root of 35. On a PC, floating point errors occur in much the same way.

Earlier versions of dBASE introduced floating point errors into their calculations because there was no support for a ''real'' number mode that overcame many of the artifacts introduced by floating point calculations. If you are developing a new system that will use numbers produced using earlier versions of dBASE, or that will be used to compare to results obtained using earlier versions of dBASE, you may be required to use floating point fields, rather than the more accurate numeric calculations. The reason for this is that, although the floating point calculations tend to be less accurate than numeric field calculations, they are consistent with the calculations made with earlier versions of dBASE.

There is a story of a top accounting firm that had been using dBASE III for many years and wanted to upgrade to dBASE IV. The firm had to use floating point fields, rather than the more accurate numeric field, so that its clients wouldn't detect inconsistencies between the new and old figures, and (wrongly) suspect errors made by the accounting firm.

The types of calculations described for numeric fields apply equally to floating point fields.

One other point should be raised with regard to floating point versus numeric fields. When designing your data files, you should consider whether or not you'll be doing mathematical procedures in which floating and numeric fields will be combined (added, subtracted, multiplied, divided, etc.). Remember that floating point numbers can introduce inaccuracies into calculations, and that the result of mixed calculations (using floating point and numeric fields) will be subject to possible floating point errors.

Date A date field is predefined by the system. The format for a date is set from within the DBSETUP facility, or through the settings menu in the Tools utility. The standard default setting puts the date into month, day, and year order, with a slash used as a separator character. Thus, August 17, 1989, would be listed as 08/17/89 in a date entry. The width for the date field is eight characters (two characters for the month, one character for a slash, two characters for the day, one character for the slash, and two more characters for the last two numbers in the year). The system automatically enters a setting for the width of the field.

Logical A logical field is by definition a one-character field. The character to be used is usually Y or N (for Yes or No) or T or F (for True or False). You can set the response options to True or False or Yes or No when you design your input forms.

Logical entry fields are answers to questions that can be answered with the True/ False or Yes/No responses. Thus, questions like *Union Member? (Y/N)*, or *In Stock? (Y/N)* can become logical fields, but other items that normally produce one of two responses need some modification.

For example, *Sex? (M/F)* is not a logical field; it is a character field that can be set up to accept either of two answers, but isn't treated as a logical field in this case. However, it can easily be made into a logical field by restating it so that one of the options is true, and the other false. Thus, a field query *Male?* (or *Female?*) could only be answered Y or N and would then become a logical field.

Logical fields are also useful if you want to produce counts on ranges of numeric values, rather than calculations of numerical results. For example, if you were researching cancer survival statistics, and wanted to know survival rates in six-month increments, the following table (made up of logical fields) could produce results for an entire data file simply by counting the Y responses in each field.

Less than 6 months Y/N

6 months–1 year Y/N

12 months–18 months Y/N

18 months–24 months Y/N

24 months–30 months Y/N

and so on.

The results from such a design could be used to provide crude statistics, and might be adequate in cases where exact numbers are not required.

The use of logical fields to get at information that would otherwise require calculation may be an easy way to retrieve certain types of data.

Memo A memo field differs from all the other possible fields because nothing is done to or with the data. A memo field is designed to contain notes, information, or other material that is not to be acted on by the database. For example, a memo field in the current compact disk example could be used for comments about each title. A memo field for the Beatles' "Let It Be" CD could say something like "*The Beatles' last album.*" When the time comes to print out a catalog of available titles, the contents of the memo field could then be printed as a brief description of the title.

> | Note ⟩ You can't do any calculations on the contents of a memo field.

Creating a File Structure

The file structure shown in Figure 4-3 will function as your stock tracking screen. It shows how many copies of each title are in stock. In the Database design screen, the system presents a blank structure, waiting to be filled in with data field names, field types, field widths, and information about decimal places (where appropriate) and indexing.

When you type in a field name, the system automatically capitalizes the name—it doesn't matter whether the names of the field are in uppercase or lowercase when you type them in. However, if you wish to use punctuation, such as the underline character (for separating words), you will have to depress the **Shft** key in order to get the shifted character.

> Note ⟩ Care should be taken to give each field a unique name; one that describes the field unambiguously.

Once a field name is entered, you can move to define the field type in a number of ways. First, if the field name is a full ten characters in length, the system will automatically bring the cursor into the *Field Type* column. You can also move to the next column by pressing the **Enter** key after completing the field name, or you can move the cursor from one field to the next by using the **Tab** key or the **F4** key.

To move back one field, use the **Shft-Tab** or **F3** keys. The **Tab** and **F4** keys and the **Shft-Tab** and **F3** keys are functionally equivalent and can be used in most tabular screens for moving bidirectionally from field to field.

To quickly enter the field type, just press the first letter of the type desired:

C for *C*haracter field

N for *N*umeric field

F for *F*loat(ing) (point) numeric field

D for *D*ate field

L for *L*ogical (Y/N or T/F) field

M for *M*emo field

The system automatically completes the entry of the field type into the *Field Type* column. If the field is a Logical or Date field, the system will automatically enter a width for the data field. Logical fields cannot be indexed, so the system automatically moves the cursor to the next line, so that the next field item may be entered into the data file definition. A Date field may be indexed, so the system will advance the cursor to index assignment field. (Indexing will be discussed a little later in this chapter.)

If the field type that you define is neither Date nor Logical, the system will prompt you for a width that your data field will use. This width measurement should include spaces for any separator characters or other characters that are not actually part of the data, but which can be used to make the data more readable. For example, if you were to specify a field for a phone number, you might define the number as an eight-character field. This field will include the first three numbers (the prefix), a hyphen, and the last four numbers of the phone number. Similarly, a Social Security number field may use eleven characters, including the nine numbers in the Social Security number, plus the two hyphens traditionally used to separate the number into three parts.

When you define the field width, it is important to have a good understanding of the nature of the data that will be used in filling out the field. You should take care not to make a field wider than necessary, while also providing enough width for the widest expected data entry into the field.

Providing a width of 40 characters for a first name is probably excessive for just about any first name. However, in some cultures, a hyphenated first name may be common, and first names could conceivably run close to 30 characters. Thus, knowing the types of data that will be entered into each field can help you to determine appropriate widths for your fields.

A reasonable rule of thumb for planning your field widths is to look at the data that has already been collected for the field of interest. In a few cases, the type of data that you are looking to collect in the data file may not be readily available, but most applications are being built to answer a need for information, and sample data should be readily available.

When you've determined the reasonable maximum width for the chosen field, add a few characters of width to accommodate those field entries that are larger than the expected maximum, and you can be reasonably comfortable that few, if any, records, will exceed the preset widths. It is good practice to try to define your fields as a *reasonable* amount larger than your maximum expected field entry, and not to go overboard to accommodate the rare data file that may have an entry exceeding the predefined width.

You should also take care not to define too small a field width. Although you can go back into the design of your data file, and assign more character width to any field, this change will not be reflected on any fields that were shortened in order to fit the previously small fields. For example, if you had a city field width of ten characters, an entry of LOS ANGELES would have been truncated to LOS ANGELE. Adding five more characters to the database would allow entry of the complete city name in future records, but would do nothing to change the records that say LOS ANGELE to LOS ANGELES. Thus, careful planning of field width is an important consideration for the design of database applications.

The *Dec* column allows you to tell the system how many decimal places are to be used by your numeric or floating point numeric data. This field can only be selected when you have defined a numeric or floating point field. For dollars and cents, you'll probably want to use two decimal places. However, if you're dealing with small parts that may cost tenths or hundredths of a cent, three or four decimal places may be more appropriate. Again, understanding your data is essential in defining your data file and its associated fields. When defining field widths for decimal numbers, you should also add in the decimal point as one character, since it takes up one character width for display and storage. For example, the $1.00 takes up four spaces, not counting the dollar sign.

About Indexing

Indexing is a method used by dBASE IV to allow the user to easily view or retrieve data in a particular order. When a field is indexed, the system sets pointers to each file based on its position in an index order.

A field index is created much the same as is a book index. The system goes through the data files and reads the contents of the field being indexed on. It then puts the contents into the order specified, finally creating an index file that contains pointers to the records having the data in the order desired.

In other words, the system creates a new table—a table that contains the order of records that corresponds to the index order. The data files are still in the same order as they were when they were created. However, when you put your files into indexed order, the system displays them in indexed order, bringing the data files onto the screen in the order that the index indicated. This can be easily seen in an indexed file by looking at the record number, which you'll see shortly.

Indexing is not to be confused with *sorting*. When a file is sorted, the records are put into a particular sort order. For example, a file of first names sorted in ascending alphabetic order (A–Z) would rearrange the records so that the first record in the data file is also the one whose first name is the first one alphabetically in the file, and where the first name in the last file is alphabetically the last name. The actual order of the files is changed when a file is sorted. An indexed file doesn't change the order in which the records are stored. It merely changes the order in which they are displayed. The index refers to the records in order, but does nothing to change the order in which the records are stored.

Although you can index most of the fields in a data file, it is often unwise to do so. Indexing takes time. When you add a record to a large data file, the system attempts to place the new record into its proper position in the index order. With many indexes and many files, this process could take a substantial amount of time. In fact, if you have a very large data file and many indexed fields, the lag between the time you enter a new record and the time the system allows you to enter the next can become disconcerting, and may become a definite annoyance.

Thus, it is important that you index those fields that you expect to want to view or analyze in indexed order. To see some of the options, press **Alt-O** to bring up the Organize menu. This menu, shown in Figure 4-4, will come onto the screen whenever you select the *Modify a Data File* option for this file.

The system assumes, when you bring up the *Modify Design* screen for a data file that has already been designed, that you will want to perform an indexing operation, or will put the files into index order, or do some other file management operation that can only be done from within the Organize menu, or will program from the dot prompt.

The .NDX file is treated differently in dBASE IV than it was in earlier versions of dBASE. Earlier versions of dBASE created individual index files, with the file extension .NDX. Each .NDX file was the order for a particular indexing parameter (or set of parameters).

dBASE IV takes index management further than earlier versions of dBASE. A new structure allows a catalog of specified indexes to be managed as part of a master index, or .MDX, file. The new .MDX file is compatible with the .NDX files created using earlier versions of dBASE. But the new .MDX structure allows .NDX management, in much the same way that data forms, reports, queries, and so forth are managed by dBASE IV's catalog structure. More detailed explanation of indexing, sorting, and .MDX will be provided later.

Complete the STOCK form, filling in the values as shown in Figure 4-3. If an error is made in an entry, remember that **Shft-Tab** or **F3** will move the cursor back a field at a time, and that the **Tab** or **F4** key will move the cursor forward a field at a time. **Up Arrow** moves the cursor up one line, and **Down Arrow** moves the cursor down one line.

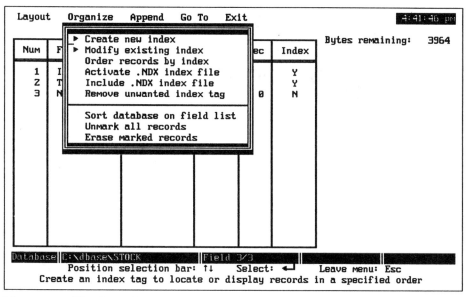

Figure 4-4 The Organize menu.

Other Details

Some other points must be discussed to round out the instructions for creating or modifying a data file design form. Lines can be added to or deleted from your data file form with a few simple keystrokes. To insert a new line so that a data field can be added, move the cursor so that it is on the line where you want to add the field and press **Ctrl-N**. A blank line will appear on the line where the cursor was placed before you pressed **Ctrl-N**, and all data fields below the insertion will move down one line. To delete a line, position the cursor on the line to be deleted, and press **Ctrl-U**.

> **Note** ⟩ You should be careful *not* to duplicate a field name that already exists on your data form. dBASE IV will allow such duplication to be made to the form.

If you want to rearrange a file's order by moving fields on the form, this can be done in a number of ways. The process involves deletion of some fields (if only temporarily), and insertion of others. One way to move a field on your file design is to insert a line at the position to which you want to move your field, and copy the width, data type, decimal and index information, if appropriate, from the field you wish to move. To avoid the error that the system will indicate if you give your new field the name of the one you are copying from, give it a temporary name while you are copying the field definition information (something like COPY1 may do nicely). Once the parameters are copied, you may delete the line with the original field information, and return the cursor to the line where the field data and temporary name were stored, replacing the temporary name with the correct name of the field.

Care should be taken to copy the original field name *exactly*. A difference of a single character or punctuation mark will make the system unable to find any data that

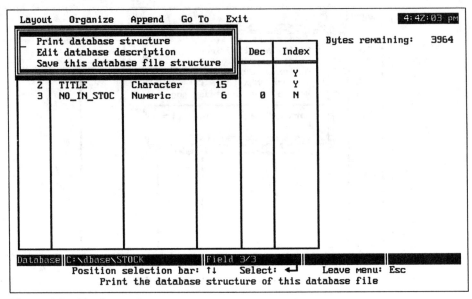

Figure 4-5   The Layout menu.

was stored using your original (and now different) field name. To assure that the field name is exactly copied, a few things can be done. You can carefully write down (or just remember) the exact character sequence used to enter the original field name. Or, for a file structure that has already been saved and for which data has been recorded, you may print the data structure and use the printed structure as a model for any changes. Additionally, you may save your original data file structure, giving it a new name. This creates a copy of your original file structure. You can then modify the copy without fear of damaging your original file structure or file data.

To print your data file structure, pop up the Layout menu, as shown in Figure 4-5, and select *Print database structure*. The system will then print the structure. Until you've saved the current database file, however, the Print option may be unavailable to you.

Saving the database file structure is a different matter. At any stage in your database file design, you can save your structure. To save your database file structure, first bring up the Layout menu, and select *Save this database file structure* by pressing **S** or moving the highlight to the appropriate line, and pressing **Enter**. The system will bring up a window asking what you would like to name the structure. If you've already given a name to your database file design, you can accept the current name by pressing **Enter**.

You want to name this file STOCK.DBF. The system will automatically insert the extension, .DBF, for you, so all you have to do to name the file STOCK is to type *STOCK*. (The system automatically enters the name in uppercase characters, regardless of how you type them in.)

> **Note** ⟩ It is a good practice to regularly save your design files as a protection against loss of your design in the event the system locks up or you make changes that you want to undo. Regularly saving your files, perhaps every few minutes, or whenever you have made a change that you want to incorporate into your design, is to be encouraged.

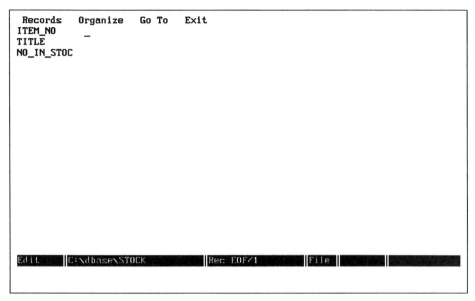

Figure 4-6 Data entry screen.

You can, of course, also rename each revision, so that you have an easily reproduced history of the development of a file, and as a mechanism for going back to any key point in the development of your file, enabling you to make changes from a specific point on. dBASE IV provides a great deal of flexibility in naming your data files (and other files, as well). The only penalty for saving intermediate versions of a design is one of storage space; however, you can free up the usually small amount of space used by the design by deleting from the system any intermediate designs that you no longer need.

Once you tell the system to save a data file design, the system will convert the design into pseudocode that allows more rapid operation than does a standard dBASE program. If you have data already attached to a data file, the system will go through it, creating the index(es) specified in the data file design. Depending on the number and size of your records, this indexing process can be very rapid, or can take hours to complete. You will notice that once a design is saved, the name and path of the screen appears in the information line at the bottom of the form.

If you want to begin entering data immediately after completing your data form, you can do this by moving the cursor into the first blank field after all others have been designated, and pressing **Enter**. The system will issue a prompt, ''Input data records now? (Y/N).'' A Y response will bring up an input screen, based on the new design. (If the design hasn't been saved, the system will save your design first, indexing any data, and then bring up the editing window). You can also view or edit your data from within Database file design by pressing the **F2** key. The data entry screen looks like Figure 4-6.

As soon as you have data entered into your file, you can switch from editing a single record to the Browse screen, which allows you to edit and view a full screen of records. To make the switch between Edit and Browse, press **F2**. The Browse screen looks like Figure 4-7.

If you wish to continue modifying the Database design screen, you may return to

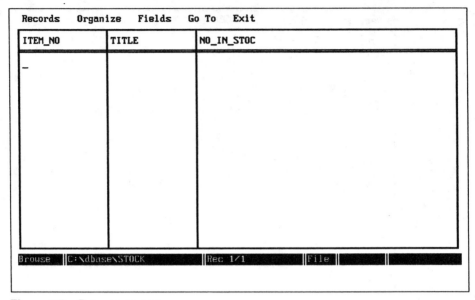

Figure 4-7   Browse screen.

it through the Exit menu available from within Browse or Edit. To return, bring up the Exit menu (by typing **Alt-E**). The Exit menu looks like Figure 4-8.

   Pressing **R** returns you to the Database design window. Pressing **T** will *Transfer to Query Design,* and pressing **E** (or hitting Enter with Exit highlighted) will bring you back to the Control Center, after saving the design and data you've last edited.

   In order to build a complete system for your CD business, you must develop a

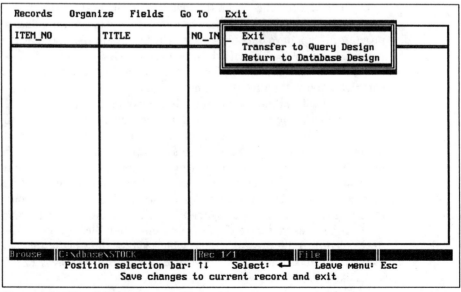

Figure 4-8   The Exit menu.

number of other data files. While it's nice to know about stock on hand, this obviously isn't enough to take and track orders, to track stock, to record salesperson productivity, to generate invoices and packing slips, or to perform many of the other necessary tasks that a complete database application should perform.

Please copy the designs for the additional forms, as seen in Figures 4-9 through 4-15, to provide the basic data file framework for the application that is being built. Notice that Figure 4-9 shows the first 16 fields. Figure 4-10 shows the seventeenth field in the data file design.

Note also that the CUST_ID form deviated slightly from requirements for true relationality by providing for the use of two telephone numbers on the same form. In most cases, for the design to be truly normalized (the term "normal" is used to refer to a database design that meets the rules for relational design), the telephone number field would have to be deleted from the design, and a separate PHONE data file created that could be linked to the customer via the customer number. In this case, you want to specify a maximum of phone numbers to be attached to a particular customer, and don't really have to go to the trouble of linking the two files in order to see a customer's phone numbers. (Additionally, for rapid lookup, having the ability to find both phone numbers in the same file as the customer name and address would be more valuable to many users than knowing that their system is more fully relational).

The basic forms shown in Figures 4-9 through 4-13 should provide a basis for the management of an order entry and stock analysis system. Some files are intentionally sparse—for example, the employee form only has five fields, and is used primarily to identify the employee. It is not intended to be used as a payroll worksheet, or for withholding, or employee development, or for any reason other than easily determining which employee made a particular sale. It is an identification file only, and not intended to take the place of specialized forms that can perform the specialized payroll and employee development tasks.

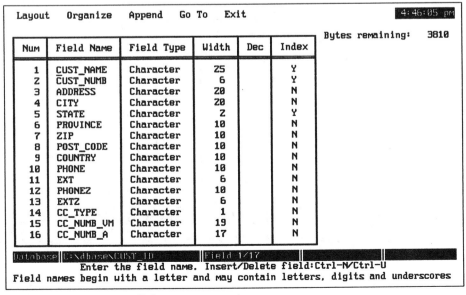

Figure 4-9   Customer ID form—screen 1.

Layout Organize Append Go To Exit 4:46:24 pm

Bytes remaining: 3810

Num	Field Name	Field Type	Width	Dec	Index
17	CC_EXP_DAT	Date	8		N

Database C:\dbase\CUST_ID Field 17/17

Enter the field name. Insert/Delete field:Ctrl-N/Ctrl-U

Field names begin with a letter and may contain letters, digits and underscores

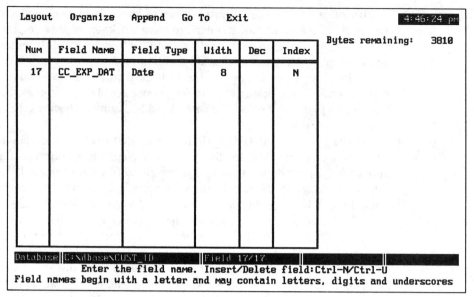

Figure 4-10 Customer ID form—screen 2.

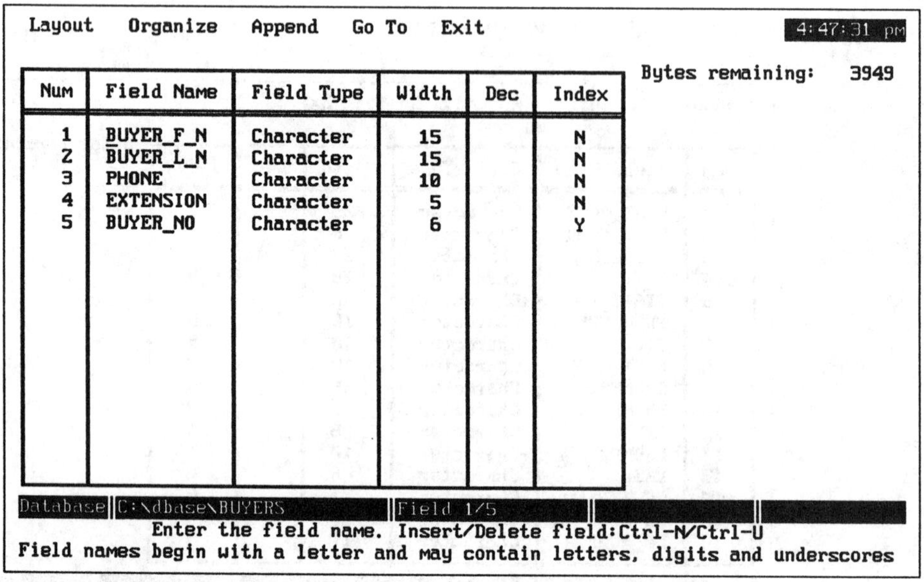

Layout Organize Append Go To Exit 4:47:31 pm

Bytes remaining: 3949

Num	Field Name	Field Type	Width	Dec	Index
1	BUYER_F_N	Character	15		N
2	BUYER_L_N	Character	15		N
3	PHONE	Character	10		N
4	EXTENSION	Character	5		N
5	BUYER_NO	Character	6		Y

Database C:\dbase\BUYERS Field 1/5

Enter the field name. Insert/Delete field:Ctrl-N/Ctrl-U

Field names begin with a letter and may contain letters, digits and underscores

Figure 4-11 TITLES data file.

```
 Layout   Organize   Append   Go To   Exit                      1:18:14 pm
                                                    Bytes remaining:    3811
 ┌─────┬────────────┬────────────┬───────┬─────┬───────┐
 │ Num │ Field Name │ Field Type │ Width │ Dec │ Index │
 ├─────┼────────────┼────────────┼───────┼─────┼───────┤
 │  1  │ CUST_NUMB  │ Character  │   6   │     │   N   │
 │  2  │ CUST_NAME  │ Character  │  20   │     │   Y   │
 │  3  │ ORDER_NO   │ Character  │  15   │     │   N   │
 │  4  │ ORDER_BY   │ Character  │  20   │     │   N   │
 │  5  │ ORDER_DATE │ Date       │   8   │     │   Y   │
 │  6  │ ID_ITEM1   │ Character  │  15   │     │   N   │
 │  7  │ UNITS_ITM1 │ Numeric    │   6   │  0  │   N   │
 │  8  │ ID_ITEM2   │ Character  │  15   │     │   N   │
 │  9  │ UNITS_ITM2 │ Numeric    │   6   │  0  │   N   │
 │ 10  │ ID_ITEM3   │ Character  │  15   │     │   N   │
 │ 11  │ UNITS_ITM3 │ Numeric    │   6   │  0  │   N   │
 │ 12  │ ID_ITEM4   │ Character  │  15   │     │   N   │
 │ 13  │ UNITS_ITM4 │ Numeric    │   6   │  0  │   N   │
 │ 14  │ ID_ITEM5   │ Character  │  15   │     │   N   │
 │ 15  │ UNITS_ITM5 │ Numeric    │   6   │  0  │   N   │
 │ 16  │ TAKEN_BY   │ Character  │  15   │     │   Y   │
 └─────┴────────────┴────────────┴───────┴─────┴───────┘
 Database C:\dbase\<NEW>            Field 1/16                        Ins
            Enter the field name. Insert/Delete field:Ctrl-N/Ctrl-U
 Field names begin with a letter and may contain letters, digits and underscores
```

Figure 4-12   Order form.

```
 Layout   Organize   Append   Go To   Exit                      1:20:58 pm
                                                    Bytes remaining:    3938
 ┌─────┬────────────┬────────────┬───────┬─────┬───────┐
 │ Num │ Field Name │ Field Type │ Width │ Dec │ Index │
 ├─────┼────────────┼────────────┼───────┼─────┼───────┤
 │  1  │ FIRST_NAME │ Character  │  15   │     │   N   │
 │  2  │ LAST_NAME  │ Character  │  20   │     │   Y   │
 │  3  │ SS_NUMBER  │ Numeric    │  11   │  0  │   Y   │
 │  4  │ HIRE_DATE  │ Date       │   8   │     │   Y   │
 │  5  │ EMPLOY_ID  │ Character  │   8   │     │   Y   │
 │     │            │            │       │     │       │
 │     │            │            │       │     │       │
 │     │            │            │       │     │       │
 │     │            │            │       │     │       │
 │     │            │            │       │     │       │
 │     │            │            │       │     │       │
 │     │            │            │       │     │       │
 │     │            │            │       │     │       │
 └─────┴────────────┴────────────┴───────┴─────┴───────┘
 Database C:\dbase\EMPLOYEE         Field 1/5                        Ins
            Enter the field name. Insert/Delete field:Ctrl-N/Ctrl-U
 Field names begin with a letter and may contain letters, digits and underscores
```

Figure 4-13   Employee ID file form.

The TITLES Data File

The structure for the TITLES data file deserves some explanation. In the case of CD or DAT titles, the title of both forms of the recording remains the same. (If you were to include LP records and cassette tapes, you might end up with four different forms of the same title.) To complicate matters, each form of the title may have a different price and a different price code. This appears to be a classic case of a one-to-many relationship, with one title having many different forms (CD, DAT, Cassette, and LP).

Because of this, a relational approach to pricing and ordering CD and DAT recordings is necessary for this system. A titles data file includes information and description of the title, plus a code number that is unique *for the title*. Separate data files are used for pricing codes and unique identification numbers. In other words, the item number for a CD version of a title would differ from the one for the DAT, Cassette, or LP version of the same title. When the CD version is ordered, its unique number is taken by the order clerk. A separate entry is made into the item code database for each format of a recording. When an order is taken, it can be linked by the title number to the titles data file, so that a description of the file can be printed along with the price and code for the format ordered.

Although you could have designed a system that included pricing in the titles data file, while using the individual title's identification number, this would reduce flexibility and future growth, since it would be difficult to add a different format or pricing category to the title. (As sometimes happens, special sales may be run on a particular title. To make this process simple, a new item number is given to each item on sale. You can sell a title at a new price by entering this new item number, without making changes to any other data files or records in the system.) Thus, when designing a data system, you should take into account, and anticipate, future growth needs.

Tying pricing and other information into a description file may work in some instances, but you should be careful when you allow such a structure to be developed, since these structures reduce flexibility and limit the simple growth of a data system.

Some of the fields in the TITLES data file may need explanation. The artist field will contain the name of the group or artist who is on the cover and is the principal artist on the musical title (for example, the artist(s) on "Abbey Road" is The Beatles, while the artist(s) on "Full Sail" is Loggins and Messina). The composer's name is included for titles where the composer is as important as the artist. For example, while The Berlin Philharmonic may be the artist on a recording of "Beethoven's Sixth Symphony," the composer, Beethoven, is an equally important piece of information and description for this title.

REL_DATE is the date that the title was released *in any form*. Since CDs are relatively recent, a large library of recordings that have been made over the past 50 or more years have been brought out in CD format. This field indicates the date that the title was first released, *not* the date it became available as a compact disk. If the date it was first made available as a CD or DAT is important, these items of information can be added to this data file.

SPARS_CODE is a field that is important to some audiophiles. It relates to how the title was recorded, edited, and converted for distribution as a compact disk. The code is a three-letter code. A compact disk that was recorded, edited, and mastered (converted to a master disk, from which all other compact disks are made) using only digital techniques is given a code of **DDD** (for *D*igital *D*igital *D*igital). Older recordings that were recorded on analog equipment (such as nondigital tape recorders or record platters) may carry a label of **AAD** (for *A*nalog *A*nalog *D*igital), indicating that the only step that was performed digitally was converting the old analog recordings to press the compact disks. The code is important to some people, and is thus included in this data file.

The COMMENTS field is used to hold notes and comments about a title. Again, a description can be valuable as a reference to answer a customer inquiry or for inclusion in a catalog that is produced from this data file. It can also contain key words that can be searched for from within a query.

The ITEM data file contains only four fields. ID_NUMBER is the same number that was given to the TITLE field in the TITLES data file. ITEM_CODE is the unique code for the specific version of the title that this record describes (in other words, the CD version of the title will have one unique number, the DAT version will have another unique number, specially discounted versions will have another number, and so on). Extra character space was left in the ITEM_CODE field to allow for a simple method of numbering the products—using the title number and adding up to three letters at the end (*CD, DAT*, or some other abbreviation).

PROD_TYPE can be set up as a multiple-choice field, and is designed to indicate whether the title is a CD or a DAT version. Of course, taking this approach, other choices may be added when appropriate. The data file can function perfectly well without this field; however, it may be helpful, when reviewing this data file, to be able to quickly determine if you're pricing a CD or a DAT, and having this field may make it simpler to make that determination.

Finally, PRICE_CODE is used on the data design. Even though it may *seem* sensible to type in a price, there are some good reasons why, for this application, it isn't. In the record and CD industry, only a small range of price points, usually fewer than 20 or so, are used for all titles. Each price is usually given an alphabet digit that relates to the price point. That is, all titles with a "G" price code sell for the same "G" price. If you want to change the price of "G" recordings, you can easily call "G" a new price, and all products that sell for "G" are automatically changed to the new price.

The coded pricing necessitates another data file, a small one that contains only two data fields: *price code* and *price*. To change a price, you simply go to the related code and enter the new price. This is a lot more efficient than looking through your entire data file (which may contain thousands of items) and changing the appropriate ones. It is also a demonstration of how relational designs (or file linking) can ease the process of the frequent many-to-many real-world data problems. Figure 4-14 shows the PRICE data file.

In addition to the files already designed, you may wish to add one for tracking orders and deliveries of titles that will be coming *in* to your company. A good inventory tracking system tracks not only what's on the shelves and what has been shipped, but also tracks what has been ordered, what has been received, and when orders are expected to arrive.

A file, called SHIPPING, contains information that is produced by the shipping

```
 Layout   Organize   Append   Go To   Exit                      10:18:55 pm

                                               Bytes remaining:    3989
 ┌─────┬─────────────┬─────────────┬───────┬───────┬─────────┐
 │ Num │ Field Name  │ Field Type  │ Width │  Dec  │  Index  │
 ├─────┼─────────────┼─────────────┼───────┼───────┼─────────┤
 │  1  │ PRICE_CODE  │ Character   │   5   │       │    Y    │
 │  2  │ PRICE       │ Numeric     │   6   │   2   │    Y    │
 │     │             │             │       │       │         │
 │     │             │             │       │       │         │
 │     │             │             │       │       │         │
 │     │             │             │       │       │         │
 │     │             │             │       │       │         │
 │     │             │             │       │       │         │
 │     │             │             │       │       │         │
 │     │             │             │       │       │         │
 │     │             │             │       │       │         │
 └─────┴─────────────┴─────────────┴───────┴───────┴─────────┘
 Database║C:\dbase\PRICE           ║Field 2/2       ║          ║
               Enter the field name. Insert/Delete field:Ctrl-N/Ctrl-U
 Field names begin with a letter and may contain letters, digits and underscores
```

Figure 4-14   PRICE data file.

```
 Layout   Organize   Append   Go To   Exit              ▮▮▮▮▮▮▮▮▮

                                               Bytes remaining:    3958
 ┌─────┬─────────────┬─────────────┬───────┬───────┬─────────┐
 │ Num │ Field Name  │ Field Type  │ Width │  Dec  │  Index  │
 ├─────┼─────────────┼─────────────┼───────┼───────┼─────────┤
 │  1  │ ▮▮▮▮▮▮▮▮    │ ▮▮▮▮▮▮▮▮    │ ▮▮▮   │ ▮▮▮   │   ▮     │
 │  2  │ NO_ORDERED  │ Numeric     │   5   │   0   │   N     │
 │  3  │ NO_SHIPPED  │ Numeric     │   5   │   0   │   N     │
 │  4  │ NO_BACKORD  │ Numeric     │   5   │   0   │   N     │
 │  5  │ SHIP_DATE   │ Date        │   8   │       │   Y     │
 │  6  │ WHSE_EMPL   │ Character   │   6   │       │   N     │
 │     │             │             │       │       │         │
 │     │             │             │       │       │         │
 │     │             │             │       │       │         │
 │     │             │             │       │       │         │
 │     │             │             │       │       │         │
 └─────┴─────────────┴─────────────┴───────┴───────┴─────────┘
 ▮▮▮▮▮▮▮▮▮▮▮▮▮▮▮▮▮▮▮▮▮▮▮▮▮▮▮▮▮▮▮▮▮▮▮▮▮▮▮▮▮▮▮▮▮▮▮▮▮
               Enter the field name. Insert/Delete field:Ctrl-N/Ctrl-U
 Field names begin with a letter and may contain letters, digits and underscores
```

Figure 4-15   SHIPPING data file.

department when it receives an order. The file is shown in Figure 4-15. This file uses some familiar fields, and a few new ones. ITEM_NUMBE is the item number that was assigned to each unique item. NO_ORDERED indicates the number of units of the item that were ordered (whether they were shipped or not). NO_SHIPPED is the number of units actually shipped to the customer. The next field, NO_BACKORD, is the number of units that were not available for shipping; since they weren't in stock, they will be considered back ordered. (Technically, they were out of stock, but in this business, any out-of-stock titles are reordered. If they're not in stock, they can be assumed to be on order with the distributor.) The SHIP_DATE field shows the actual date the order was filled and shipped. Finally, the WHSE_EMPL field is for the employee who filled the order to put in his or her employee number.

In practice, one record will be filled out for each item. Although this may seem tedious when one customer orders many different items, dBASE IV can be set to copy the information from one record to the next. Further, forms can be designed to place the information that changes from record to record at the beginning of a form, moving the data that doesn't frequently change (date, employee number, customer ID) further down on the form.

Conclusion

Effective database design is probably the most important component in any data management system. In this chapter, the basics of relational database design have been discussed in detail. In addition, the methods for designing, saving, and modifying data file structures were explored.

The use of a relational, linking structure provides for more flexibility and analytical capabilities than the typical "flat file" database. The concept of relational, or linking, files was explored and, it is hoped, clearly explained.

Indexing was briefly discussed and will be explored in further detail in later chapters.

Basic structures that will be used in future chapters as part of a general data management system were designed in this chapter. Although the structures were designed for a specific application, a Compact Disk Distribution system, the basic forms can be modified to meet the needs of many businesses or other users.

Subsequent chapters will explore the techniques for form design, data validation, data analysis, report generation, and data retrieval. The power of the relational model and of the applications generator will also be fleshed out.

5

Form Design and
Data Validation

In Chapter 4, the files that will be used as the basis for the application to be developed in this book were defined. This chapter explores dBASE IV's form design capabilities. Using dBASE IV, you will design special data entry forms and build data validation, verification, and other capabilities into your data entry forms. As will be demonstrated, dBASE IV contains an extensive set of data entry and validation options.

A Customer Entry Form

Data entry forms and data validation parameters are selected from within the Forms panel. The first example, one that will make use of many of the entry and validation features in dBASE IV, will be a special customer entry form built around the CUST_ID data file.

First, move the cursor into the Data panel and select CUST_ID as the active data file. This can be done in a few ways. You may move the cursor into the Data panel, and press **C** to move the highlight to CUST_ID; you may move the cursor so that the highlight is on CUST_ID; or you can begin typing the first letters of CUST_ID until the data file is highlighted.

Once the CUST_ID data file is highlighted, you may choose to use the data file by pressing **Enter**. This will bring up an option screen that gives you three choices: *Use file*, *Modify structure/order*, or *Display data*. Selecting *Use file* tells the system that this is the file whose data you will be working with.

You could also have highlighted the file and pressed **F2** to load the file and bring up a data entry screen. Pressing **Esc** to close the screen would then make the CUST_ID file active. It is probably best to select the screen, and press **Enter** quickly twice. This has the effect of loading the options screen, and selecting the *Use file* option. It also avoids getting into the bad habit of using the **Esc** key, rather than the Exit menu, to close a data screen.

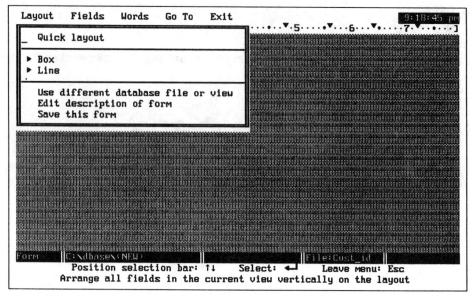

Figure 5-1 Form design screen with Layout menu opened.

When you have selected CUST_ID as the active screen, it will be displayed on the Data panel positioned immediately below <create> and above a horizontal line. The line in the panel separates the active file(s) from those that are not presently in use.

Once CUST_ID has been selected as the active screen, move the cursor to the Forms panel. The form that you will design will provide the data entry interface for your data entry operators. Since there are currently no forms in the catalog, the highlight should be on <create>. If you already have forms in the Forms panel, move the highlight to <create>. Pressing **Enter** loads the Form design screen.

If you were instead planning to modify an existing form, highlighting the form and pressing **Shft-F2** would automatically load the form modification screen. Alternatively, to select an action on a highlighted form, press **Enter** to bring up an option menu that allows you to choose whether to *Display data* or *Modify layout*.

The Form design screen, shown in Figure 5-1, initially appears with the Layout menu opened. The highlighted option *Quick layout* is used to automatically place the field names and field entry areas on the screen.

If *Quick layout* is selected, with CUST_ID as the active file, the screen will look like Figure 5-2. To see how the data entry form will look, press **F2**, and the system will create the data entry form based on the quick layout, and will display the form, as shown in Figure 5-3.

> **Note** You can view the appearance of your form using the **F2** key to compile your form and switch to the data edit screen. To return to the data design screen, use the Exit menu, and select *Return to Form Design*, as seen in Figure 5-4.

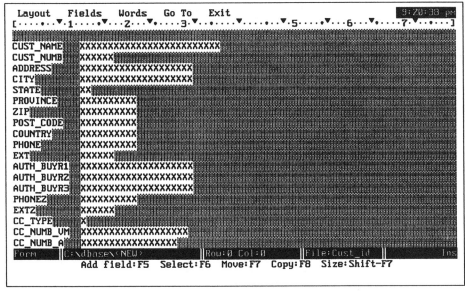

Figure 5-2   Form designed using *Quick layout*.

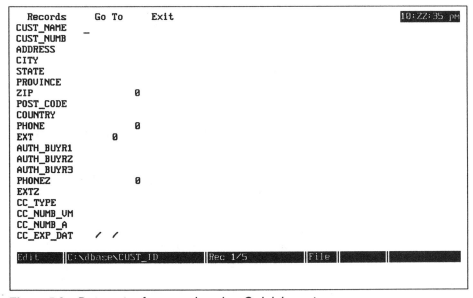

Figure 5-3   Data entry form made using *Quick layout*.

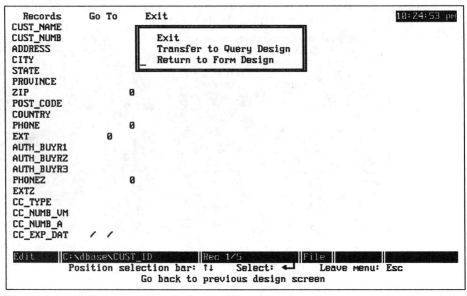

Figure 5-4   Exit menu allows return to Form Design.

It should be obvious that the customer entry form can be made easier to use. This can be done by rearranging the fields on the form, grouping the fields into appropriate clusters, and closing up some of the space by placing more than one data item onto the same line. dBASE IV allows you to design with two basically different types of items: data fields and characters. Data fields represent the actual fields that will be filled in when the form is activated. A data entry field is automatically set to the same width as its definition when the database file was designed.

When you move the cursor into a data field, the entire field is highlighted, and the information about the field appears at the bottom of the screen. In Figure 5-5, the cursor is moved into the CUST_NAME field, with the resulting descriptive information appearing at the bottom of the screen. A variety of controls over the appearance and data validation of data fields will be discussed shortly.

Character fields are essentially anything on the form that is not a data field. This includes field names, lines, boxes, and other text that may be placed on the form. In order to select character fields, you must activate a selection option and outline the boundaries of the area you are selecting. Again, this will be discussed a little later in this chapter.

A final entity that dBASE IV supports is the *box*. This is important when you plan to add or remove lines of text or data fields from your form. Boxes are treated as entities separate from characters or data fields. In Figure 5-6, the CUST_NAME and CUST_NUMB fields have been moved in towards the center of the screen, and a box placed around them.

When you add or delete a line, all character fields move to adjust to the changed number of lines in the form. However, the box does not move, because it is not

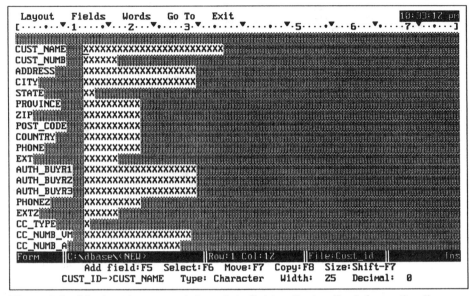

Figure 5-5   Moving the cursor into a data field activates the information line.

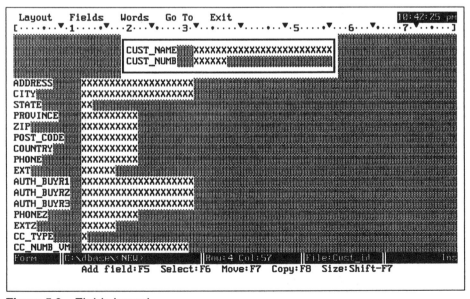

Figure 5-6   Fields boxed.

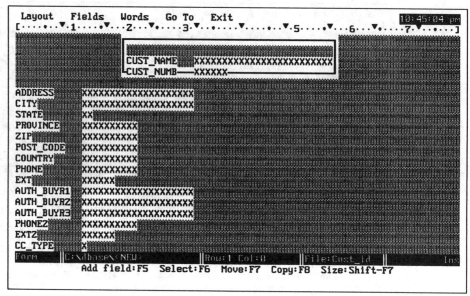

Figure 5-7   Line added moves characters, doesn't affect boxes.

anchored to the character fields. In Figure 5-7, a blank line has been added at the top of the form, demonstrating how adding a line to a character form can affect the appearance of any boxes placed on the form.

Fortunately, boxes can be easily selected by moving the cursor onto any part of the box and pressing **F6-Enter**. The box can then be moved by placing the cursor at the top left corner of the destination and pressing **F7-Enter**. Thus, although boxes do not move along with characters, simple selection and movement reduces the problems involved in redesign when lines are added or removed from a form.

Moving and Copying Characters and Boxes

Although the quick layout produced by dBASE IV may be satisfactory for some simple forms, it is generally desirable to take advantage of the sophisticated copying and editing capabilities built into dBASE IV. In the past, some programmers may have avoided designing the most useful forms because of the difficulties involved in writing the instructions to produce the forms. However, with the design simplicity provided in the Forms panel, this objection has been all but eliminated. Having the system automatically place the fields and field names on the form provides a framework that can be moved or copied while you design a new form. Moving text or a field involves a number of steps.

First, the characters or fields to be moved must be selected. To do this, move the cursor to the beginning of the area that is to be moved. In this example, you want to move all the data fields further to the right, placing them below the tab stop at 2.4″.

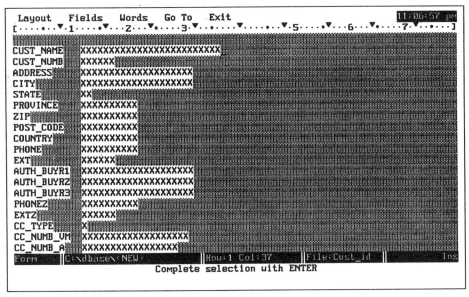

Figure 5-8   Highlight extends to end of field.

Move the cursor to the beginning of the first field—in this case, the beginning of the CUST_NAME data entry field. The field will be highlighted, as seen previously in Figure 5-5.

> **Note** If the cursor was located any distance from the area where you wished to begin your selection, pressing the **PgUp** key would bring the cursor to the top of the current screen. The **Home** key brings the cursor to the left margin.

When the cursor is located at the beginning of the area to be highlighted, press **F6** to begin the highlight. The system now prompts you to *Complete selection with ENTER*. The system is really telling you to highlight the rest of the area you desire to select for the move or copy operation, and *then* to press **Enter**.

dBASE IV allows you a number of options for selecting an area that you wish to highlight. For now, you want to highlight all the data fields on screen. Press **PgDn**, and the system will move the highlight to the bottom of the screen. However, the highlight is only one character wide. This illustrates an important point—to highlight an area, you must select its height and width. The fastest way to do this is to move the cursor into the line with the widest field and press the **End** key. In this case, press **PgUp** to bring the cursor to the top of the screen, and bring the cursor down one line, into the CUST_NAME field. This field is the widest on the form.

A single character is highlighted. Now, press **End**, and the highlight will extend to the end of the field, as seen in Figure 5-8. Now, press **PgDn** to extend the highlight to the bottom of the screen. To be certain no fields are omitted from the move, press the **Down Arrow** until you have selected all the fields. Use the **Up Arrow** key to move the highlight just below the last field. The screen will look like Figure 5-9. Now, complete the selection of the highlighted area by pressing **Enter**.

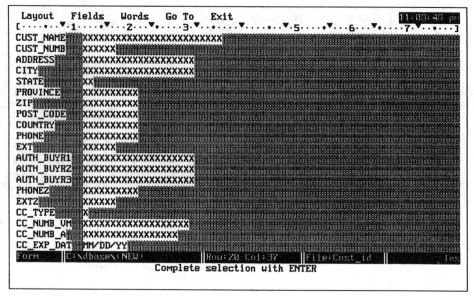

Figure 5-9   Down Arrow extends highlight beyond bottom of screen.

Next, tell the system what you want to do with the highlighted area.

In this case, you want to move, rather than copy, the highlighted fields. (If you chose to copy the fields, you would be duplicating them. Since these are data entry fields, you don't want more than one of each field entry in the same form.)

Move the cursor to the top of the page by pressing **Ctrl-PgUp**. (The **Ctrl-PgUp** combination moves to the top of the form. Similarly, **Ctrl-PgDn** moves to the bottom.) Next, press **F7** to tell the system that you want to move the highlighted text.

Now, place the cursor so that it is in the second line, directly below the arrow at 2.4″, which indicates the tab stop. The screen should look like Figure 5-10. You will note that the entire highlight moves along with the cursor and demonstrates where the highlighted block will be placed if the current position is accepted. To accept the new location for the move, press **Enter**.

In this case, the move isn't automatically completed, because to do so would cover (and delete) existing text on the page. Although you are moving text, and would be upset if the move didn't delete and rewrite text to be moved, dBASE IV asks you to confirm that you will delete covered text as a safeguard against inadvertently deleting data during a move. The confirmation screen looks like Figure 5-11.

Press **Y** to confirm that you wish to make the deletions, and the highlighted areas will be moved. While the area is still highlighted, it may be moved again, if the position of the area is not exactly where you desire it to be. As long as the area is still highlighted, it can be moved. However, once the highlight is removed (by pressing the **Esc** key), it will have to be highlighted again if you wish to move it. Press the **Esc** key now, to remove the highlight.

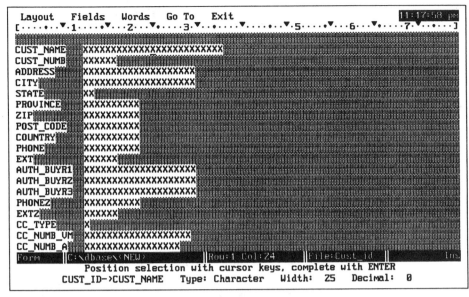

Figure 5-10   Highlight repositioned for move.

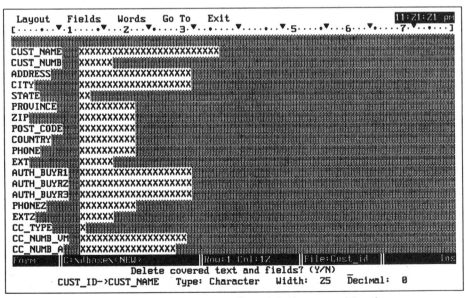

Figure 5-11   The system prompts to confirm deletions resulting from a move.

In addition to the use of the **Home, PgUp, PgDn,** and **End** keys to quickly extend a highlight, the Highlight key **F6** also can be used to extend a highlight. When pressed once, the **F6** key activates the highlighting option. Using the arrow keys or the previously described keypad keys, you may extend the highlight to any location on your form. If you press **F6** a second time, the entire line where the cursor is located is highlighted. To highlight more than one line, you may press the **F6** key once, move the highlight down to include all the lines you wish to select, and then press **F6** a second time. The entire width of the lines will then be selected. To select an entire form, press **F6** a third time. Pressing **Enter** after highlighting the area desired locks in the highlight.

To Copy a field or text, you must similarly highlight the area to be copied, press the **F8** key to activate the Copy function, and place the cursor on the beginning of the area to be copied to. Pressing **Enter** (and confirming deletions, if appropriate) completes the copy. Again, you should carefully consider whether you want to *Copy* or *Move* a highlighted area. The system does not allow entry of data into the same field more than once on a form—it doesn't make sense, and could effectively confuse the system if different values were placed in each entry field. In most cases, you probably want to Move, rather than Copy, a field.

There is one instance where a data field can be used more than once on a form, however. In the case of multipage forms, where data is input into more than one screen, it may be useful to show the contents of a data field. For example, on a two-page order entry form, it may be useful to *show* the order number on the second page. To do this, you must make the order entry number noneditable on the second page. This means that the order entry operator can *see* the number, but can't *change* it.

At this point, it is useful to point out that you should save your design at regular intervals. Although it isn't essential to save your design until it's completed, if your design is complicated or involves much moving of fields and original text or boxes, you would be protected against loss of your design efforts if something should happen to the system during your design session.

Although it may only happen infrequently, the system may fail. Power may go off, the system may run out of memory (with early versions of dBASE IV this was often not an infrequent problem), or some other unpredictable event may result in the loss of whatever work you have done, unless you have saved it.

What if you make changes, but want to go back to an earlier version? The solution to this is simple: While you're creating or modifying a form, save each revision (or at steps along the way), giving each revision a new name. For example, in this CUST_ID form, the first time you save it, you could call it CUST_ID1, the second time, it's CUST_ID2, and so on.

To save the form, open the Layout menu. (Press **Alt-L.**) Next, select *Save this form*. Although you could move the highlight to *Save this form* and press **Enter** to go to the next step, pressing **S** automatically selects the option. A window pops onto the screen, prompting you for a name for your form. The screen will look like Figure 5-12.

Next, type *CUST_ID1*. You aren't required to enter an extension for the form name. In fact, you *shouldn't* enter a name extension, since the system automatically enters the correct extension for you. If you use the wrong extension name, the system will accept it, but may be confused when it comes time to use it, because the extension

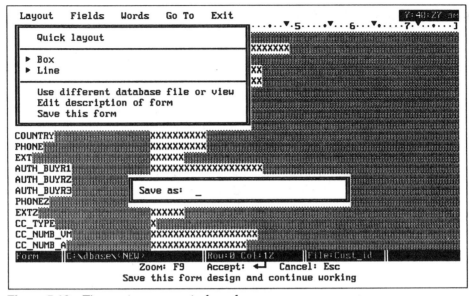

Figure 5-12   The system prompts for a form name.

won't match the one that the system expected. Once you've typed the name of the form into the system, press **Enter** and the system will save your form with its new name (or will tell you if there is already a form with the same name).

It sometimes takes the system a considerable amount of time to save a form. When the system saves your design it does more than simply write it to disk. It evaluates your design, and generates program code that can be quickly loaded into an application. Actually, two files are created. One file includes the program code to describe the screen and all related settings; the other file is partially compiled, resulting in faster operation.

The technique of giving each version of your form a new name can also be applied to copying forms. For example, you may be creating entry forms for some very similar data files. In one instance, you may have two different applications that use a very similar structure. Perhaps you're creating a compact disk distribution system for a number of different distributors. You wish to use the same basic form design, but personalize the forms for each store.

To do this, you can load a form developed for another application into your catalog, customize the form, and save it with the name of the new client for whom you are developing the application. In fact, a series of basic, generic forms that can be customized for specific clients can be very useful and can save considerable design and debugging time.

Once the form has been saved, you can continue designing or modifying it. Although each intermediate version will appear on the Catalog menu, you can later delete those that you no longer need to retain in your catalog, or remove them from your disk.

Insert and Overtype

dBASE IV provides you with two basic modes for adding your text to the design of your forms, or for use within memo design, report design, or other areas where you will be designing various forms—Insert mode and Overtype mode. These are roughly equivalent to those used in many word processing and other text editing programs. The Insert and Overtype modes are alternately toggled by pressing the **Ins** key on the numeric keypad. It is easy to tell which mode is currently active—aside from the difference in the way the characters are placed on the screen, the information bar at the lower right corner of your screen says "Ins" when the Insert mode is active.

The Insert mode places any characters or carriage returns into the page, moving whatever is beyond them. To see how this works, move the cursor into any character field. For example, if you place the cursor on the text that says CUST_NAME on the screen (not inside the actual data field), and type some characters, all characters to the right of the insertion point will move to the right. If you type enough characters, the text will eventually bump into the actual data field, pushing it to the right. To delete inserted text, merely backspace over it, and all text on the line to the right of the insertion point will again scroll back to the left. If you press **Enter** on a blank line, while "Ins" is on the information bar, all lines below the point where you press the **Enter** key will be pushed down on the screen.

The Overtype mode works differently. When this mode is selected, any text or characters typed onto the screen will type over existing text (which is the reason that this mode is called Overtype). For example, if you were to type onto the CUST_NAME text line (and not in the data field), whatever is typed will replace the original CUST_NAME text. If you were to press **Enter** on an empty line, the cursor will move to the next line, rather than inserting a carriage return and pushing text down. Further, from within a line that contains text, the **Enter** key will move the cursor down, rather than inserting a carriage return.

Data Validation

Now that moving fields has been discussed, it's time to take further steps in designing our form. The customer identification form will be used as the primary source of data about each customer. To make it simple to find the information needed, a slight reorganization of the data on the form has been performed. In addition, the data has been grouped into easily handled blocks.

Through the use of simple Move commands, as discussed previously, you can highlight and move fields or lines. Although you should be able to easily create the screen seen in Figure 5-13 using just the Move function already discussed, and pressing **Enter** while in the Insert mode to add blank lines, should you have to delete any lines while reproducing Figure 5-13, this may be done by moving the cursor to the line, and pressing **Alt-Y**.

Now, you can get a bit more fancy, by giving more readable, easily understood descriptions to the fields on your forms. Lining up the descriptions on the left side of the screen so that the rightmost characters in each field description line up one or two

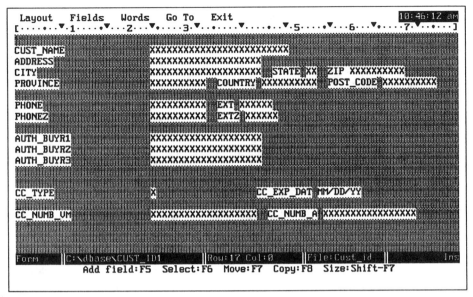

Figure 5-13   Initial steps in redesign of form.

spaces from the data entry field provides a pleasing appearance. This is somewhat tricky—the simplest way to line the characters up is to decide *exactly* what your field description will say, move the cursor to the point where the last character will be typed, and use the **Left Arrow** key to move the cursor one space to the left for each character in the file description. When you have stopped counting out the letters, the cursor should be at the correct position for typing in the field names.

Please make the changes to your form so that it looks like Figure 5-14. The simplest way to make the changes in the left half of the form is to use the Overtype mode. While in Overtype, you can type in the new field description in its correct location, while leaving the original descriptions at the left margin.

> **Note** If you type the complete description in the left margin, you may press the **F6** key to begin a highlight. Pressing the **Home** key brings the highlight to the beginning of the line. Press **Enter** to confirm the area of your highlight. When you press **F7** to begin your move, you can move a block the width of the new description so that the end of your text is exactly the desired number of spaces to the left of your data fields.

To delete the characters from the left margin, merely place the cursor at the margin (by pressing the **Home** key), and hold down the **Del** key until the cursor has moved to the location of the first letter that you wish to display.

If you attempted to delete the characters while in Insert mode, this would have the effect of pulling all the characters to the right of the deletion mark towards the left of the page—correcting this would involve reinserting spaces, and possibly involve moving data fields. Now save the form, renaming it CUST_ID2.

You may have also noticed that there is a difference between blank areas and spaces. When you look at the screen, you can easily see a dotted pattern that is used as

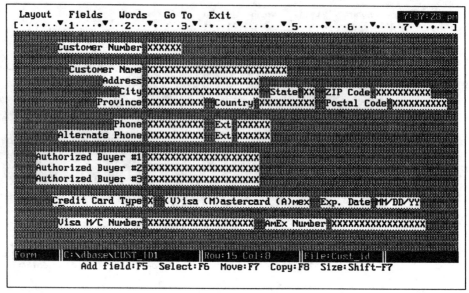

```
 Layout   Fields   Words   Go To   Exit                         7:37:28 pm
[·····•···▼·1·····▼··2···▼·•···▼·····•···▼·5·····▼··6···▼·•····7·•·····]
```

Figure 5-14 Customer ID form, with fields rearranged.

the normal background on your design screen. When you type characters or enter spaces, the background pattern is removed, leaving a solid color behind the characters or spaces.

The system treats spaces differently from blanks. The distinction between the two can be important for a few reasons. If you have assigned a different background color to data description areas than is used for standard background, the appearance of spaces will be different from the appearance of blank areas. For example, the Customer Name block has been given a new colored background, to make it stand out from the rest of the form (and to demonstrate the difference in appearance of blanks and spaces). In Figure 5-15, the data entry form is shown, with blanks used instead of spaces to separate text from data entry fields. In particular, look on the form to see the spaces between the words *Customer* and *Name*, *ZIP* and *Code*, and *Postal* and *Code* to see how spaces appear on the screen.

Figure 5-16 shows the area that was seen in Figure 5-15 as it looked on the design screen. You will easily notice that areas with blanks are not shown with the background color.

Figure 5-17, by contrast, shows the same area with spaces replacing blanks. Thus, a solid background is shown on the screen. Figure 5-18 shows the data design screen with the defined area shown in Figure 5-17. Note that the entire area is shown using the background color, rather than just the areas that use spaces.

We don't want to save the changes to the form at this point, so we can Exit to the Control Center, and reload the CUST_ID2 form to return us to the version of the form that was last saved. To load a form for later modification, highlight the form and press **Shft-F2**. We're not done designing the form. Data validation and some fairly sophisticated filtering will allow the form to be designed with a great degree of functionality.

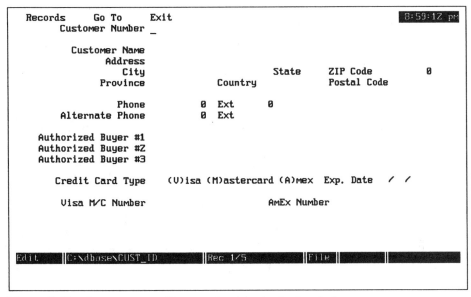

Figure 5-15   Appearance of form using blanks instead of spaces.

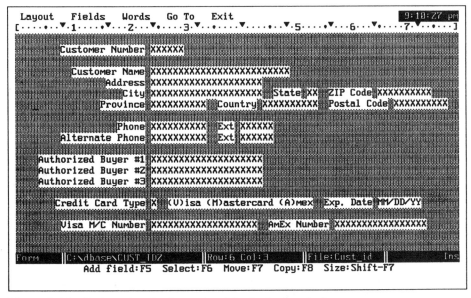

Figure 5-16   Data entry design using blanks instead of spaces.

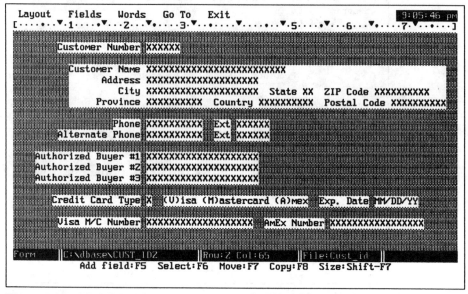

Figure 5-17 Highlighted area using spaces instead of blanks.

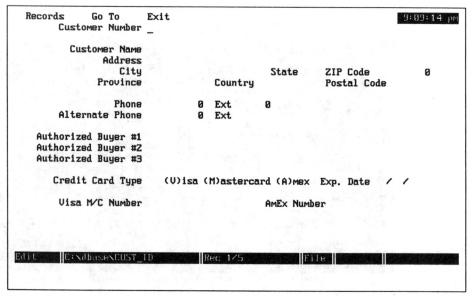

Figure 5-18 Data entry form made from design in Figure 5-17.

Working with Fields

Just as the field is the fundamental unit for storing data, the Fields menu on your Form design screen is the fundamental interface for determining how that data is to be presented in order for it to be accepted as valid data. The Fields menu, seen in Figure 5-19, can be easily opened by pressing the **Alt-F** key combination.

As important as it is, the Fields menu can be considered almost extraneous. This is not to imply that it isn't necessary. dBASE IV allows you to bypass this first-level menu, and quickly jump to the more important second level of the menu, where field selection, definition, and validation parameters are available. To see some of the field management basics, you'll delete a field, and then add it in, using techniques that you will probably use quite frequently. In fact, with these techniques, you may frequently bypass the opening Fields menu entirely.

To delete a field, move the cursor to the field you wish to delete, and press the **Del** key. For the purposes of the current example, we'll delete the Customer Name data entry field. Move the cursor so that the CUST_NAME field is highlighted. The name and description of the field should appear at the bottom of the screen. Now, press the **Del** key. The field will be removed from the screen, leaving a blank area.

Now, you'll add the CUST_NAME field back into its previous location. Although you can do this by going through the Fields menu, and selecting the *Add field* option, it is quicker to go directly to the field addition screen by pressing **F5**. Move the cursor to the position where you want the field to begin, and press **F5** now.

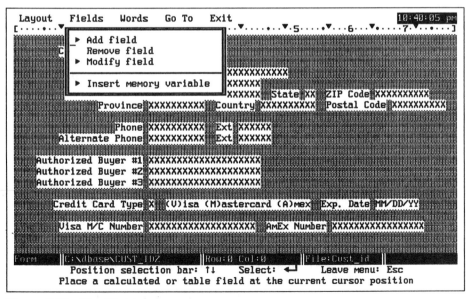

Figure 5-19 The Fields menu.

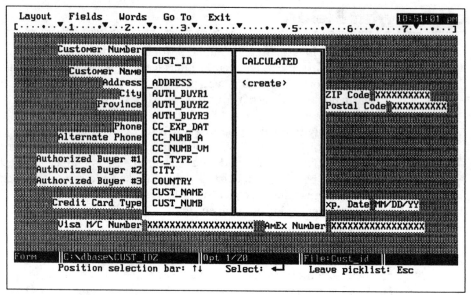

Figure 5-20   Field selection menu.

The menu, shown in Figure 5-20, will appear on screen. The menu shows all fields in the currently active data file. It also allows you to create calculated fields. Calculated fields will be discussed shortly. As with other menus produced by dBASE IV, you are given a variety of methods of selecting fields. You may move the highlight to the field you wish to use, and press **Enter**, or you may type the first letter(s) of the unique field that you wish to select. In this case, typing *CU* is all that is required to move the highlight to the desired field.

Before selecting this field, however, you should be aware of what the two panels presented in this window represent. It should be obvious that the panel on the left, the one in which the cursor is currently located, presents all fields in the current data file. In fact, that's exactly what it is—at the top of the panel, the name of your data file indicates the file that you are extracting fields from.

The panel at the right, CALCULATED, is used for calculated fields. A calculated field is a special field that is calculated by doing mathematical processes on data in one or more fields. Although the current data file doesn't lend itself to the development of a calculated field, others in the application you are developing certainly do. For example, in an order entry data file, you may wish to create a field that shows the total price of each quantity of an item ordered. In this case, you may wish to create a field named TOTAL that represents the product of UNIT_COST and QUANTITY ordered. Even though this isn't a field that is used in your data file, it is a valid field that can be displayed on the form. You'll see how to write and create a calculated field later in this book.

When you have selected a field from your data file (in this case, the CUST_NAME field) press **Enter** to load the next menu. The option menu allows you to

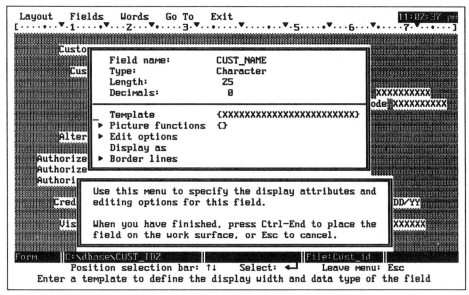

Figure 5-21   Data options and validation window.

specify filtering, and other functions that will be used for data entry and validation. This menu is seen in Figure 5-21.

The top half of the window describes the field as it was defined when you created the current data file. The information in the top half cannot be edited inside this window. The bottom half of the window shows the available options. Not all options are always available. For example, in the current window, you are unable to select the *Display as* or *Border lines* options. These options are used only for memo fields, and apply to the method for displaying the data in the field on the form.

Templates

The Template option is a very useful one—it allows you to tell the system what types of input are acceptable to the system, and when the input must be capitalized. To activate the template definition options, make sure that the Template line is highlighted, and press **Enter**. The highlight will change on the line, as the established template becomes dark, and a list of template symbols appears at the bottom, as in Figure 5-22.

The template symbols are somewhat self-explanatory. It should be obvious that Y is used for logical fields where only a Yes or a No response is appropriate. It should also be obvious that L is used to define data entry in a logical field where Y(es), N(o), T(rue), or F(alse) are the only acceptable responses. X is used where any alphanumeric character is acceptable. This is used primarily for character fields, where letters, numbers, and some punctuation characters may be expected to be used in certain records. For example, you may run across a customer called "3-D CDs." If only alphabetic characters were acceptable, such an entry would not be permitted, and you

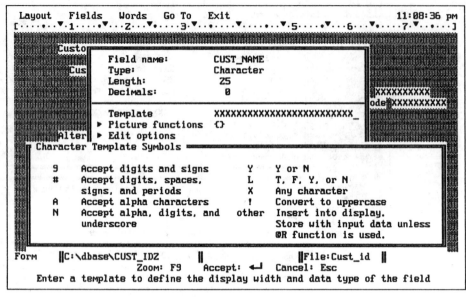

Figure 5-22   Template options displayed.

would have to change the way the name was entered, which would introduce possible errors into the system.

The current field, CUST_NAME, will be defined to allow any character (X), with one exception. Since the name of the customer should always be a proper name, you will signal the system to always capitalize the first letter in the name. This is done using the exclamation mark ! to indicate that the character in that field should always be displayed as an uppercase character. When this character is a number, it is shown as the number, rather than as the uppercase symbol that would normally be typed by capitalizing the number on a keyboard.

The definition for the CUST_NAME field should appear as it does in Figure 5-23. To accept the template, press **Enter**, and the system will return you to the options menu. To accept the changes to the field, and to place the field on the screen (or to modify a field already on the screen), press **Ctrl-End**. Once this is done, the CUST_ NAME field will be placed on the screen. To see how existing fields can be modified, move the cursor to the STATE field. When the data entry field is highlighted, press **F5** to bring up the option window. This window looks like Figure 5-24.

> **Note** It should be obvious that when you position the cursor on an existing field and press **F5**, the system automatically jumps to the field options screen. This saves you the extra steps required using the Fields menu to get to this point.

Since the STATE field will contain two-letter abbreviations for states in the United States, the system should only allow alphabetic characters—no numbers, no punctuation. Thus, for this field, the template AA is most appropriate. Change the

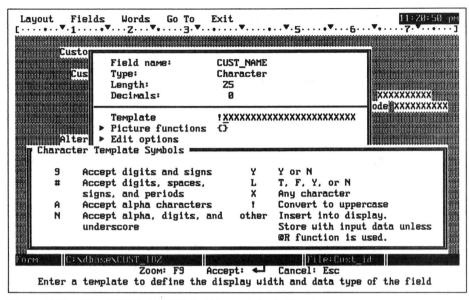

Figure 5-23   The CUST_NAME field template defined.

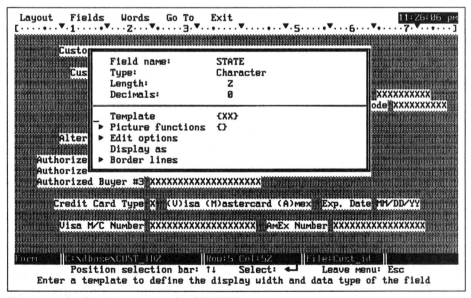

Figure 5-24   Options screen for STATE field.

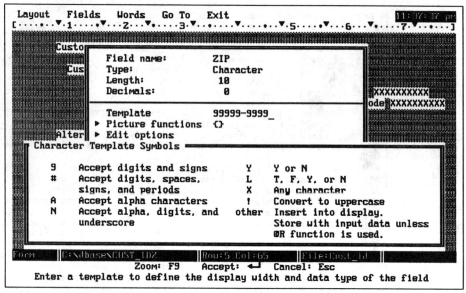

Figure 5-25 ZIP_CODE template—all digits, hyphen inserted in middle.

template to AA, and save the new template. (Press **Enter** with the Template line highlighted, to open the template editing screen. Type *AA* as your template entry and press **Enter** to return to the field design box. Finally, press **Ctrl-End** to save the change and return to the form). The cursor will be placed in the field you just defined (in this case STATE), and the new template will be shown.

Characters that are part of a template, and that are automatically inserted during data entry can also be added into your form design. To see this, move the cursor to the ZIP field and press **F5** to bring up the options menu. In this case, a ZIP code can only be a number. Further, it can be either five numbers long, or a nine-number code with a hyphen placed between the first five and the last four numbers.

Bring up the Template window and type the first five template characters (all **9**s). Next, press the hyphen - key. This will insert the hyphen into the template. When you enter data into this field, the hyphen will always be placed in the data field. As data is entered, the system will skip the data entered from the fifth place, over the hyphen, so that the next number appears as the seventh character entered (the hyphen occupies a space, so is counted as a sixth character). Finally, add the last four **9**s to complete the template. The template should look like Figure 5-25. Accept the changes, and return to the forms design window.

The PHONE fields require slightly different handling. The template seen in Figure 5-26 accomplishes a number of tasks. In this case, it should be clear that the actual template goes beyond the ten digits in the field definition. However, the characters that have been added to the template to improve the appearance and format of the data), (, and -, are not part of the data and are not included (or acted on by the system) as part of the data input. The 9s in the template are obvious—they indicate that only

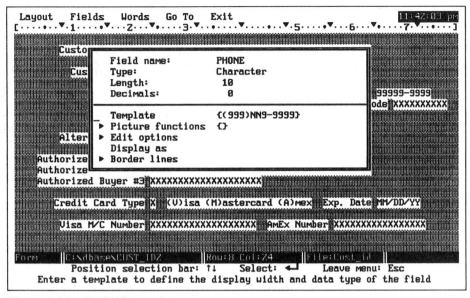

Figure 5-26   PHONE template.

numbers are acceptable to the system. However, the Ns have been used to account for the use of character prefixes, rather than numeric prefixes. An X was not used as part of the definition because it would have accepted any character. Using N accepts only underscores, alphabetic characters or digits. Although the system would accept under-score ＿ characters, it is unlikely that the data entry operator would ever intentionally (and would probably never accidentally) enter this symbol. You will note that the new template pushes the next field and its associated text to the right.

You will use the same template for the second field, PHONE2 (Alternate Phone). When both field templates have been defined, the *Ext* text and associated extension fields will be lined up one on top of the other. To fix the clutter, it is probably easiest to highlight the two fields and the text associated with them and move them all to the right. To do this, move the highlight into the *Ext* field name and press **F6**. Press **End** to move the cursor to the end of the *Ext* field, and move the cursor down one line (using the **Down Arrow**). Both fields and field names will be highlighted.

Accept the highlighted area as the one you wish to move, by pressing **Enter**. Next, move the cursor up one line (using the **Up Arrow**), so that it is positioned in the first *EXT* field.

Now, press **F7** to tell the system that you wish to move the field. Move the cursor so that the indicator on the ruler line is at 4.1″. The highlighted area for the field looks like that seen in Figure 5-27. Press **Enter** to tell the system that you wish to move the highlighted fields to the position indicated. The system will ask if you wish to delete covered text and fields. Respond by pressing **Y**, and the field will be moved to its desired location.

Next, modify the template for the CC_TYPE. Since this can only be an A (for

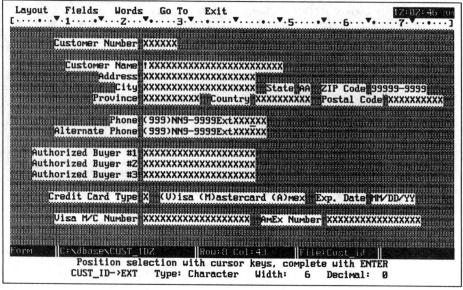

Figure 5-27 Fields to be moved are placed at their target positions.

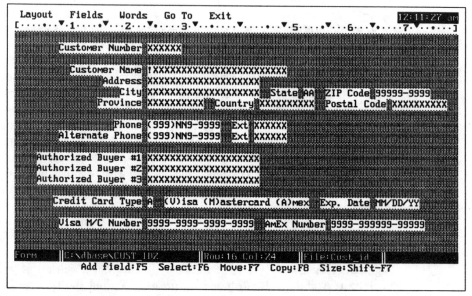

Figure 5-28 Completed screen with templates defined.

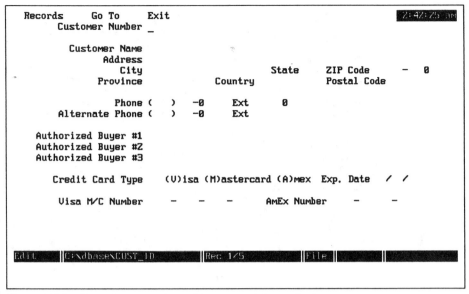

Figure 5-29 Data form produced by current form design.

American Express), a V (for Visa), or an M (for Mastercard), the template A is appropriate, since it will not allow symbols to be used. In addition, this field will be used to demonstrate additional validation functions.

Finally, change the numeric templates for CC_NUMB_VM and CC_NUMB_A to match those shown in Figure 5-28. Before going on, save the form, calling it CUST_ ID3. The completed form, when displayed as a data entry form, looks like Figure 5-29. Note that numeric fields are shown with the number 0 in the field.

Picture Functions and Edit Options

At this point, you've created a data form, and have defined the format for acceptable data. While these skills are useful, they represent only a small portion of dBASE IV's capabilities. Processes referred to as *Picture functions* and *Edit options* provide a significant amount of power and control over your data entry and validation processes. The capabilities provided by dBASE IV's user interface, through the use of the design panels, are equal to, and in some cases surpass, those that were only available through the use of extensive programming.

What Ashton-Tate has done with dBASE IV's Control Center interface and panel design capabilities is to make sophisticated design possible for the nonprogrammer, and to make the process of designing database structures and applications easier for experienced dBASE programmers. Many of these capabilities will be utilized by the applications developed in this book.

The *Picture functions* menu allows you to select a variety of options for displaying or viewing your data. A slightly different set of options and default settings is pre-

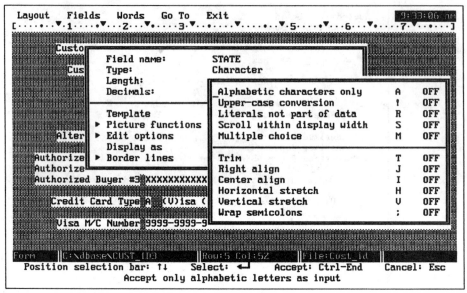

Figure 5-30   Picture functions menu for STATE data field.

sented, depending upon what type of field you are defining. To open the *Picture functions* window, you must first select a data field, and then select *Picture functions*. As with other options in dBASE IV, this may be selected by moving the highlight to *Picture functions* and pressing **Enter**, or by pressing **P** from inside the field options window.

To see how they work, you will select a picture function that can be used in the *State* data field. First, move the cursor so that the *State* data field is highlighted. Next, press **F5**. When the option window opens, press **P** to open the *Picture functions* menu (or move the cursor to the *Picture functions* line and press **Enter**). The *Picture functions* menu for STATE looks like Figure 5-30. (You should recall that you have set the template for this field to only accept alphabetic characters. However, it will accept both uppercase and lowercase characters.)

The field will contain only state abbreviations. These abbreviations should always be capitalized. From within the *Picture functions* menu, selecting *Upper-case conversion* will convert the data input into the field to uppercase letters, regardless of the case used for entering the characters.

To select an option in the *Picture functions* menu, move the cursor to the option you wish to select and press **Enter** or the first letter of the option you wish to select. When either method is used, the system toggles the option ON or OFF.

The options available will vary, depending upon the type of field you are defining. The options that apply to a character field are seen in Figure 5-30. The options in the top half of the *Picture functions* menu perform the following functions.

Alphabetic Characters Only   This option tells the system to only accept alphabetic characters as input to the system in the selected data field. When this option is selected, an A appears in the Picture functions menu.

Uppercase Conversion This option tells the system to convert data to uppercase characters. In the present example, if the data entry operator types *ca*, *Ca*, *CA*, or even *cA*, the system will save the entry as CA. For a data field such as STATE, being able to convert all data entered into uppercase only allows consistency of input for that field from record to record.

In some cases, you may wish to use this option for fields that may not require conversion to all uppercase. This option may be useful for fields where the data entered may be a mixture of uppercase and lowercase. Although the search options allow you to ignore the case of the character strings you will be searching for, it may be as simple to define a field so that it saves text entered as only uppercase.

Literals Not Part of Data This option tells the system that characters, such as the hyphen -, parentheses (), the dollar sign **$**, the number or pound sign **#**, or other symbols that are used to format the appearance of your data will not be stored as part of your data field. For example, when you designed your template for telephone numbers, you added parentheses and hyphens to make the phone number appear in the standard format.

This may be more important in numeric or float fields, where you've used commas or the dollar ($) or British pound (£) sign to format your data. If you don't tell the system to ignore the symbols (referred to by dBASE IV as "literals"), it will attempt to include them when performing calculations. In addition, the literals are used as formatting characters, but are not stored in the data file as a data character.

Thus, if you were to set up the telephone number fields as shown earlier, the digits in a telephone number will be displayed as the template defines them, including the literals that are used to improve the appearance of digits, but when the telephone number is stored, only the characters in the number will be stored in the file. Not storing literals as part of the data also allows you to use smaller data fields than those which include literals. For large data files, this can save considerable storage space.

Scroll within Display Width This option allows the system to display data that includes more characters than the display template allows. For example, if you design a form that only displays 30 characters, and you are using a field with a width of 50 characters, you will not be able to display the full 50 characters of text in your smaller display window.

By setting *Scroll within display width* to ON, you can use a display area smaller than the actual field width, and allow the data to scroll in the display window.

Multiple Choice This option allows you to designate a field as a multiple-choice field. When this is accepted, a prompt, as shown in Figure 5-31, will appear, asking for acceptable choices. Type the choices into the screen, separating each with a comma. When finished entering options, press **Enter** to save your multiple-choice options.

Note that, although you could theoretically have listed each of the 50 states as an acceptable multiple-choice entry, this approach would prove cumbersome, but possible.

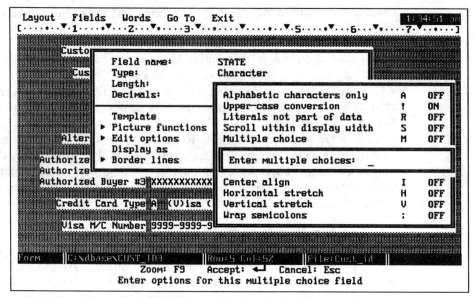

Figure 5-31   *Multiple choice* option window.

Not setting up the STATE field as multiple choice allows the possible entry of illegal state abbreviations—in other words, state abbreviations like AX or CY, or any two letter combination, would be accepted by the system.

If you want to be certain that only legal state abbreviations are entered, you could use a multiple-choice picture function to validate any entries. This might be even more important if you were developing a database for specific regions. Setting up a database for the Pacific Coast states, for example, would be easy—just specify CA, OR, WA, or HI as acceptable choices.

A list of multiple-choice options is automatically displayed by the system at data entry time. Only one of the acceptable choices can be selected from such a multiple-choice menu. Each choice should be typed, separated from other choices by a comma ,.

At the bottom of the Picture functions menu, six options are shown. These options are used to modify the arrangement and alignment of the text displayed in your field. The options are not available in this two-character field. For now, select *Upper-case conversion* to turn the option on for the STATE field. To accept the picture functions, press **Ctrl-End**. The active picture functions (in this case !) will appear on the *Picture functions* line in the field options menu. Save the menu settings for STATE, by pressing **Ctrl-End**. The cursor will return to the data entry field for STATE.

The options at the bottom of the *Picture functions* menu for character fields feature options which are not available in Forms design, but can be selected in Report design.

Picture Functions for Numeric Fields

Numeric fields feature a different set of picture functions. These functions are used for formatting your numeric data. The options are as follows:

Positive Credits Followed by CR When this option is selected, all positive values are followed by the letters CR (for credit). This may be useful for certain financial operations, where simple entry of a positive number is not considered to be an adequate indication of the positive value. If this option is selected, a value of $525.32 will appear as $525.32CR.

Negative Credits Followed by DB This option is a frequent companion to the previous option. In this case, all negative values are followed by the two-letter code DB (for debit). A value of -132.45 will be shown as 132.45DB when this option is active.

Use ( ) Around Negative Numbers This option tells the system to enclose negative numbers in parentheses. Again, this option is valuable for any applications where this format for negative numbers is utilized. A value of -123.45 displayed in this format will be shown as **(123.45)**.

Only one of the two options for displaying negative numbers can be activated at one time. If neither option is selected, the system will use a minus sign $-$ to indicate a negative value.

Show Leading Zeros This option displays zeros in your data fields, rather than leaving the leading zeros blank. For example, if you receive a $500 payment on an invoice that totals $500.85, the system will display the new balance as $000.85 if this option was selected. A $490 payment will display the value as $010.85. Activating this option may be useful as an indicator of how large the field can become. It may also make it slightly easier to scan through columns of numbers.

Blanks for Zero Values This option is essentially the opposite of the previous option. All leading zeros are blanked. Thus, for the previous payment example, values of $ .85 and $ 10.85 would be displayed.

You can only choose one of the two options for a numeric field.

Financial Format This option displays numbers in dollars and cents (and may also display in other decimal currency units in international versions of the program). The option places the dollar sign before the value is displayed.

Exponential Format This option uses scientific notation for displaying numbers in this field. Values of this type are displayed using powers of ten. A value of 60 is the same as 6×10^1, and is displayed as 6E1, where the E means "10 to the power of," and the 1 represents the power that the number is raised to.

This is useful for very large or very small numbers, and is useful when exact numbers are not particularly significant. For example, if you are working with billions of units, it may be easier (and faster) to use the notion 9E9 to represent nine billion, than it would be to enter 9,000,000,000. Although you may actually be working with 9,000,000,050 units, the last few units cease to be significant beyond a point. (If you really wanted to track all units, you could, by representing the value as 9.00000005E9).

The display options at the bottom of both *Picture functions* menus are not available from within the Forms design panel, and will be discussed in a future chapter.

Setting Picture Functions

The current form uses a number of picture function settings. For the STATE field, *Uppercase conversion* is set ON. PHONE and PHONE2 have *Literals not part of data* set ON. CC_TYPE has *Uppercase conversion* set ON. It is also worth noting that picture functions are not available for date fields. This can be seen by opening the field options menu for the CC_EXP_DAT field on this form.

Edit Options

The edit options are among the most useful options in form design, since they allow you to specify parameters for acceptance of data, for editing data, and for allowing data to be input. In short, it is the edit options, more than any other feature available on the Form design screen, that provide intelligent control of the data inputting process.

To see one useful example of the power of *Edit options*, you will set up a system to *automatically* assign a customer number to each new customer. To see how this is done, move the cursor to the CUST_NUMB field and press **F5**. This brings up the field options menu. Select *Edit options* by pressing **E** or moving the highlight to *Edit options* and pressing **Enter**. The *Edit options* menu looks like Figure 5-32.

In this example, you will have the system automatically assign a customer number. The customer number assigned by the system is the same as the record number for that customer. In order to accomplish this, you must do a number of things. First, you must set a default value that tells the system to read the record number, and insert it into the CUST_NUMB field. This number will be read in as a character string, and will be set to display only the numbers, stripping out any blank spaces in the field. (For

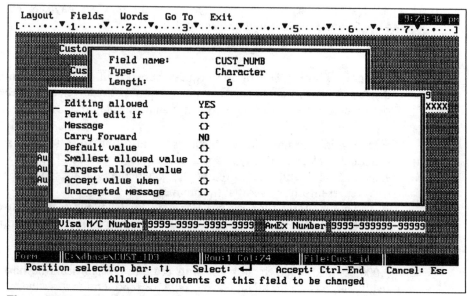

Figure 5-32   *Edit options* menu.

example, the first nine customer numbers will be 1 through 10, rather than 000001 through 000010). Second, you must set the system to prevent users from typing in a customer number. This bears some further discussion.

The *Edit options* menu provides two options which may appear somewhat similar to each other. The first, *Editing allowed*, tells the system whether or not to permit values for the field to be edited. If you set this to NO, you would not be able to add a value to the field—not even if the system is programmed to insert a default value. Thus, the setting for *Editing allowed* should be considered absolute—if YES, editing can be performed, as long as conditions in *Permit edit if* allow editing; if NO, editing is absolutely not allowed.

Permit edit if allows you to set a condition that, if met, allows a value to be entered for that field. You will see shortly a more sophisticated use of this option. For now, however, you will set the value of *Permit edit if* to .f. (which means that *if* the value of the current field in the current record is *FALSE*—that is, if there is no data in the record—editing will be permitted).

To change any option in the menu, select the option by pressing the first letter of its name or by moving the highlight to the option and pressing **Enter**. This action will open the edit area of the desired option. If you need more space than is provided in the *Edit options* window, pressing **F9** opens the currently selected option, bringing it down to the bottom of the screen so that you can use a full line of text to view or edit your expression. A zoomed *Default value* line is shown in Figure 5-33.

After you've entered your expression or value, press **Enter**, and the system stores the value, closes the zoomed window, and returns the highlight to the most recently edited line. If the value or expression is not valid, the system will indicate that the value is unacceptable. In some cases, expressions may be somewhat difficult to write (the edit

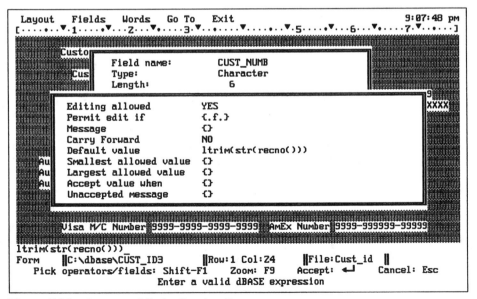

Figure 5-33   A zoomed Default value line.

options are designed primarily for programmers, although nonprogrammers can also make full use of this feature).

Further options in the *Edit options* window should also be explained.

Message This option allows you to enter a message that is displayed at the bottom of the screen. In the current example, you may wish to use a message such as ''Number automatically assigned. Press ENTER to advance.''

Carry Forward This option automatically inserts the value for this field in the previous record into the current record. This can be useful when you are making entries from a list that has already been sorted based on the data in the field you are entering.

For example, if you allow *Carry Forward* in a state field, and have already put the records still to be entered into order by state, the system will automatically insert the state from the previous record into a new record. If the state changes from CA to CO, for example, you would have to change the state data entry to reflect the new value—all future values will be CO, until you change them to reflect another value.

Carry Forward is also useful for fields where you don't expect values to change frequently. Again, a state field is a good example. Similarly, if your list of records to be input into your database was sorted by city, *Carry Forward* could be used to automatically place the city name into each new record.

Default Value This value has already been discussed. In the current example, a default value automatically converts the record number to a character value, and inserts it into the data entry field. To change the value, you would simply edit (if editing is allowed by the other parameter settings in the *Edit options menu*.)

If you are working with a state field, and most of your customers were located in CA, you may wish to enter CA as the default value. For each new record, the value for STATE will automatically be set for CA. For the few records that are outside of CA (or, in general, don't match the default value), you can enter the new values, if editing is allowed by the system's *Edit options* settings.

It should be clear that there is a potential for a carry forward and a default value to conflict. However, since default values can be overwritten by the system or the user, a value carried forward can overwrite a default value. Thus, you should be careful to usually select one or the other option, or neither (but not both), in order to guard against any ''surprise'' or ''illegal'' entries creeping in.

Another point should be made about the current default value for CUST_NUMB. This setting automatically assigns the current record number to any customer who has not yet been assigned a number. However, this assumes that you will not delete *any* customers from your data file. If you delete records from your file and then pack your file (which will remove any deleted records and reassign record numbers to those records that remain), you will then face the possibility of assigning the same number to more than one record (since the default only looks to see if the current record has an assigned number, and doesn't check to see if the value is already used by another record). Thus, although the current default works well, it should only be used for files where records will not be deleted or inserted.

Smallest Allowed Value This option tells the system the minimum size for an acceptable entry in the selected data field. For example, if you were developing a specialized catalog of '60s music, the smallest allowed value for an initial pressing date would be 1960. Any values smaller than 1960 would not be accepted as valid.

Largest Allowed Value This option tells the system the maximum value for an acceptable entry. In the example just given, the largest acceptable value would be 1969.

Accept Value When This option provides somewhat different capabilities. Although you can certainly set the logic to include the maximum or minimum values, with a statement like *DATE > 1959 .AND. < 1970,* this option can also be set to allow comparison of an entry in this field to an entry in another field in this record.

Shortly, you'll see how this option is used to differentiate credit card numbers for American Express, Visa, and Mastercard. In addition to simply relating the value to that in another field, you can relate the value to a date or calculated value. This will be shown in the Expiration Date field's *Edit options* setting.

Unaccepted Message This option allows you to tell the system to display text (instructions, help, or a comment) whenever an unacceptable value is entered. An unacceptable value is one that doesn't meet the *Accept value when* conditions, doesn't match the template, or is not in the range of acceptable values.

If you try to enter a phone number that spells a word (such as 1-800-GETLOST), the message "PLEASE TYPE IN A VALID TELEPHONE NUMBER," or something similar may be displayed, since the system is looking for only numbers for the third through seventh phone number digit.

In the case of the CUST_NUMB field, there should be no unaccepted values, since the system will automatically insert a value if none has been assigned. However, the user may attempt to enter a value, which may trigger the unaccepted message. Thus, you may wish to enter an unaccepted message for this field. An example of such a message is "Please press ENTER to move to next field."

Although the unaccepted message and the message itself are both optional, it is often useful to provide a message for both instances.

When all edit options have been added, press **Ctrl-End** to save the new settings. The system will return the cursor either to the field just modified or to the field options menu. To return to the Form design screen from the field options menu, press **Ctrl-End** a second time.

Edit Options for This Data Form

As with the picture functions, a number of special edit options will be used to provide extra power for data entry evaluation. CUST_NAME, ADDRESS, CITY, STATE, ZIP, PROVINCE, COUNTRY, and POST_CODE require no special edit options, although a message instructing the operator what to enter (although this is obvious) can be added to the edit options. In addition, if you wish, you may consider using a *Permit edit if* statement that would allow PROVINCE, COUNTRY, and POST_CODE to be edited

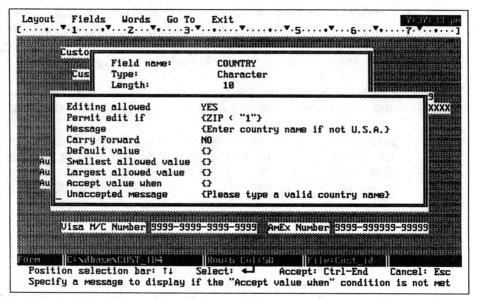

```
Layout  Fields  Words  Go To  Exit                        7:37:33 pm
[·····•···▼·1····▼···2·····▼·····3·▼··•······▼··5·····•···6···▼··•·····7·▼···•·]

      Custo┌─────────────────────────────────────────────────┐
       ┌───│       Field name:        COUNTRY                 │
       │Cus│       Type:              Character               │
       │   │       Length:            10                      │9
       │   ├─────────────────────────────────────────────────┤XXXX
       │   │   Editing allowed        YES                     │
       │   │   Permit edit if         {ZIP < "1"}             │
       │   │   Message                {Enter country name if not U.S.A.}
       │   │   Carry Forward          NO                      │
       │   │   Default value          {}                      │
       │ Au│   Smallest allowed value {}                      │
       │ Au│   Largest allowed value  {}                      │
       │ Au│   Accept value when      {}                      │
       _   │   Unaccepted message     {Please type a valid country name}
       └───└─────────────────────────────────────────────────┘

      ┌Visa M/C Number┬9999-9999-9999-9999┬AmEx Number┬9999-999999-99999┐

 Form     ‖C:\dbase\CUST_ID4       ‖Row:6 Col:50      ‖File:Cust_id‖
   Position selection bar: ↑↓     Select: ↵      Accept: Ctrl-End     Cancel: Esc
   Specify a message to display if the "Accept value when" condition is not met
```

Figure 5-34 Edit options for COUNTRY field.

only if ZIP is less than 1. This way, you can avoid the confusion that may result from entering data in both ZIP and foreign fields. To further clarify your data input field, you may enter a message like *"Type COUNTRY if not U.S.A."* in the message line for COUNTRY. An example of the edit options to do this is shown in Figure 5-34.

It is important to note that the ZIP field will normally not allow you to advance to the next field until a valid entry is made. The user has two choices when getting into any field. He or she may enter a valid value and advance to the next field (or record), or may choose to skip the field entirely (by pressing **F4** or **Enter**). However, in some fields, if an entry is started, the system will not permit advancing to the next field without entry of a valid value. Thus, if you were using the test for ZIP shown in Figure 5-34, you should also include a message in ZIP that says "Type ZIP only for U.S. ZIP CODES" or something similar. A similar setting for *Permit edit if* may be used for PROVINCE and POST_CODE fields, to prevent entries of both ZIP and foreign data.

The next fields, through CC_TYPE, don't require any special edit options, although messages would be helpful, and would help to maintain the consistency of your input form. The credit card and credit card number entries, however, demonstrate some of the power of dBASE IV's edit options. What you want to do is accept only three inputs, **V** (for Visa), **M** (for Mastercard), and **A** (for American Express). The edit option for CC_TYPE, shown in Figure 5-35, shows the settings to accept only those three values.

The important option in this case is *Accept value when*. The expression in that option, {**cc_type $ 'VMA'**}, means to accept the value entered in CC_TYPE if it is contained in the string VMA (the $ in the expression means "is contained in the

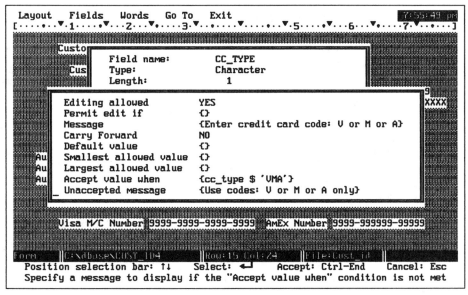

Figure 5-35   CC_TYPE edit options accept only **V** or **M** or **A**.

string''). This means that, if the entered value is V or M or A, the value is valid and can be accepted. Any values not contained in the string VMA will not be accepted.

Now that the system knows only to accept V, M, or A, you must also apply intelligence to recording the account number for the credit card. A problem arises, since the numeric format for American Express differs from the one for Mastercard or Visa. Thus, you want to set *Edit options* to allow editing only for the appropriate field. To accomplish correct number entry, you have two credit card fields, CC_NUMB_VM (for Visa or Mastercard), and CC_NUMB_A (for American Express). The edit options shown in Figures 5-36 and 5-37 show the options for CC_NUMB_VM and CC_ NUMB_A, respectively.

A look at the way the *Permit edit if* options work will show how the system can tell which card type is entered, and allow number entry only on the appropriate form. In the edit options for CC_NUMB_VM, the statement permits editing only if the CC_ TYPE is *either* V (for Visa) *or* M (for Mastercard). The editing conditions specifically call for either Visa or Mastercard. When an American Express code, A, is found in the CC_TYPE field, the system causes the cursor to automatically skip the CC_NUMB_ VM data entry field, since entry for American Express will not be permitted in this field.

Similarly, the CC_NUMB_A option will only allow editing if the CC_NUMB equals A (for American Express). Any other value for CC_TYPE will cause the system to skip this data entry field, since editing would not be permitted. You can also enter the condition *CC_TYPE $ 'A'*, but since the string is a single character, the = works equally well.

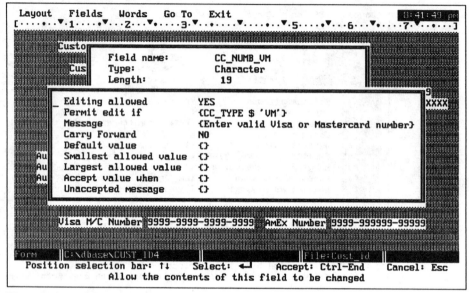

Figure 5-36 CC_NUMB_VM edit options.

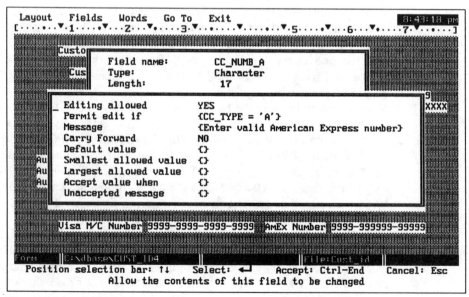

Figure 5-37 CC_NUMB_A edit options.

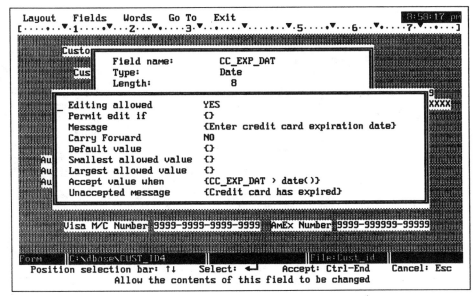

Figure 5-38   CC_EXP_DAT checks expiration against current date.

A final, special edit option is used for CC_EXP_DAT. In this case, you want to have the system only allow expiration dates of cards that are still current. The edit options for CC_EXP_DAT are shown in Figure 5-38.

The expression **CC_EXP_DAT** > **date()**, used in *Accept value when*, can be translated to mean the following: Accept the value when the date shown in CC_EXP_DAT is greater than that shown on the system clock. The **date( )** expression uses a function built into dBASE IV, which tells the system to look at the current date on the computer's internal clock. This command checks the expiration date against today's date, and determines whether or not a card has expired.

Date calculations are relatively easy in dBASE IV. In addition to the simple comparison shown here, you can also perform date mathematics. For example, if you wanted to create a field that would be used to flag accounts that are within 60 days of expiration, you could easily use the expression **CC_EXP_DATE - date()** < **60** to select those cards that will soon expire. Similarly, days past due can be calculated by subtracting the date due from the current date.

The edit options shown here should point to a number of areas where substantial verification and validation power can be easily implemented in a data file. With a little experimentation, you should be able to easily develop your own powerful data validation techniques.

Using the Words Menu

The Words menu allows you to modify the appearance of your form, change the placement of highlighted characters, add or remove lines, and read or write text files.

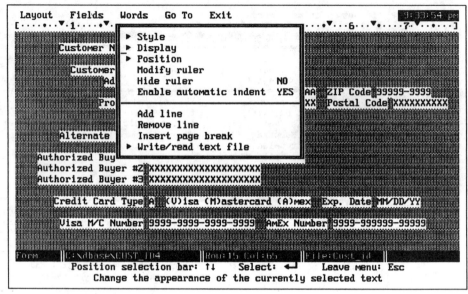

Figure 5-39   The Words menu.

The menu looks like Figure 5-39, and is also available in the Report and Label design screens.

The Style option is not available from within the Form design screen. It is used to modify the types of characters (bold, underlined, italic) used for printing selected blocks of text or text characters. This option will be explored more fully in Chapter 11.

The Display option is used to modify the colors of the characters and background for selected text or blocks. It is useful for producing blocks that stand out from the rest of your design screen. The first step in using the Display option of the Words menu is to select the area that will be effected by the changes you make in the display characteristics. This is done by highlighting the area to be modified.

Once the area is selected, open the Words menu. The quickest way to open the Words menu is to press the **Alt-W** key combination. (You can also press **F10** and move the cursor, using the arrow keys so that the Words menu is displayed.) Next, select the Display options by pressing **D** (or if the highlight is on *Display*, press **Enter**).

The display options should now appear. You will see two columns of colors. The left column is used to select the foreground color, the color of the text; the right column, labelled *Background* allows you to select the background color. In addition, the column indicates whether or not your foreground characters blink.

Although the use of the Display menu was apparently thought to be somewhat intuitive, in actual practice, it takes some getting used to. The selection of foreground and background colors is easy, but seeing what the color is that you've actually selected may be slightly confusing at first. A bar indicates which color is currently selected for background or for foreground. To move the bar from background to foreground, press the **Left Arrow** or the **Right Arrow** keys. The highlight will obviously move from one column to the other. To move the bar inside a column, use the **Up Arrow** and **Down Arrow** keys. The highlight will return to the top (or bottom) of the panel when it scrolls beyond the bottom (or top) of the panel.

An arrow appears in the panel that was not selected for color assignment. Looking at the bar that the arrow points to indicates the color of the selected foreground or background, and indicates how the highlighted text will appear if the current settings are accepted.

The arrow may be somewhat unnecessary. In the Foreground panel, all foreground colors will be shown with the selected background color. In the Background panel, the selected foreground color will likewise appear in all color fields in the column. Thus, to determine what the selected display will look like, simply look at the column that the bar is adjacent to. Although the color of the bar will not change, it isn't the bar that matters, it's the color line that the bar is adjacent to that indicates the appearance of the selected combination.

> **Note** To make the foreground blink (or to turn off a blink), press **B**. The blink attribute is a toggle—it can be alternately turned ON or OFF by pressing the **B** key.

Once you've chosen the color combination you wish to use, press **Ctrl-End** to accept the colors and return to the design screen. To leave without changing the colors, press **Esc**. Pressing **Esc** backs you up to the Words menu.

The next option in the Words menu is the Position menu. This menu automatically places a selected block of text at the left margin, the right margin, or the center of the screen. This is useful for section headings, form headings, and other text items that you want to automatically position on your screen.

The text centering capabilities are probably the most valuable, since it is relatively simple to position text at either the left or right margins. Centering, however, involves calculating the width of the highlighted text, and figuring out where to place the block of text so that it is centered on the page. Using the Position option, you can quickly and accurately center text on your screen or form.

If you are planning to center many text items, the system provides a way to very rapidly do this. Since the system remembers the last used options, you merely have to highlight your block of text, press **Alt-W** to open the Words menu, press **Enter** to select *Position* (which should still be highlighted), and press **Enter** a second time to accept *Center*, which should be your last used option. In actual practice, this is faster than it sounds, requiring a rapid push of **Alt-W**, followed by the **Enter** key quickly pressed two times.

It is also useful to note that most of the menu options also allow repeat selection, since the options used last are normally highlighted when you reopen a menu. This will also be useful for line and box drawing from within the Layout menu.

Modify Ruler This option allows you to change the margins for your screen or data entry form. In the Report or Label design screens, these changes will also determine the margin settings for your printed output. To open the *Modify ruler* screen, press **M** from within the Words menu, or move the highlight to the *Modify ruler* item and press **Enter**.

The cursor will be moved to the ruler line, the line at the top of the edit box. To change the left margin, move the cursor to where you want it placed, and press the **[** key.

You may have to delete the left margin indicator if the system doesn't automatically accomplish the move for you. Similarly, the right margin is indicated using the **]** key.

Tabs are added by pressing the **!** key. Tabs are deleted by pressing the **Del** key. Further, you can delete a tab or margin indicator by moving the cursor to its right and using the backspace key to backspace over the symbol you want removed.

The left margin and initial indent can be set to 0 by pressing the **0** number key. Finally, an option that is more useful for reports allows you to set an indent for the first line of text, with no indent for subsequent lines in a paragraph. To use this option, move the cursor to the location of the first line indent, and mark that location using the **#** key. Once your tab and margin choices have been indicated, you may return to the design screen by pressing the **Enter** key.

Hide Ruler This option allows you to remove the ruler from your design screen, and provides you with a better approximation of the appearance of your form. It is normally set to NO, but can be toggled on and off by moving the highlight to the *Hide ruler* line and pressing **Enter**, or by pressing **H** when the Words menu is opened.

This gives you one more line on screen to view or create your design. In most cases, you'll probably want to retain the ruler line, so that you can tell where natural tab stops and margins occur.

Enable Automatic Indent This is a feature that is not available from within the Form design screen. This tells the system, when creating a report, to automatically indent the first line of a paragraph, as marked by the # on the ruler line.

The next options are listed as a separate group. These options primarily deal with line spacing, page breaks, and writing or reading text files. As you'll see in the next few paragraphs, the first two are options that you'll probably never use, once you learn the shortcuts that accomplish the same thing.

Add Line This option inserts a line at the position of the cursor. This can also be performed by pressing the **Enter** key when you are in Insert mode. Even if you have to toggle from Overtype mode to Insert mode, it's still probably faster and easier to press the **Ins** key (to go from Overtype to Insert), press **Enter** (to insert your line), and press **Ins** (to return to overtype mode) than it is to open the Words menu and press **A**. It is certainly faster and easier if you are already working in the Insert mode.

It should be noted that this function moves text down one line, but doesn't change the position of any lines or boxes on the page. Lines and boxes must be highlighted and moved, to continue to fit text that they are surrounding or enclosing.

Remove Line This is another option that can be performed quickly using a simple keystroke combination. Pressing **Ctrl-Y** deletes the line that the cursor is currently positioned on. This removes any text or data entry fields that are currently positioned on the line. Since there is no Undo function in dBASE IV, you should be certain that you really want to delete the line before actually doing so.

Insert Page Break This option is unavailable from within the Label design screen. When you are preparing reports or labels, this option can be used to force the system to load the next page at this point in your form.

Write/Read Text File This option allows you to save frequently used text to a text file, and to copy it into a different form. For example, if you have developed a title screen, or instruction lines, or some similar block of text, this block can be highlighted and copied to a text file.

If you design a variety of forms, and want to use a consistent form title line, this can be saved, and then copied from the file onto the new form. To activate this option, you must first open the Words menu, and then select *Write/read text file* from the menu. This is done by pressing the **W** key, or moving the cursor down to highlight the option and pressing **Enter**. Once this is selected, the system pops a window onto the screen asking if you want to write your selection to a file, or read text from a file. You will then be prompted to enter a filename for the file.

If you are reading text from a file, you must know the name of the file in order to read it into your form. Unlike other areas in dBASE IV, the system at this point does not provide you with help in finding a file. Therefore, you should be careful to keep track of text files that you plan to read into other forms, so that they can be correctly retrieved.

A file that is read into your form will be placed in your form beginning at the location of the cursor. You should take care to position the cursor at the desired location for the text to be inserted. You should also have the Insert mode ON, to avoid any possibility that inserted text will overwrite (and thus delete) text already on the form.

The Go To menu is most useful for report design or for forms that are many lines long. It is also useful for searching within a file for specific data values.

The Go To menu looks like Figure 5-40.

To activate any of the options in the Go To menu, move the cursor to highlight the

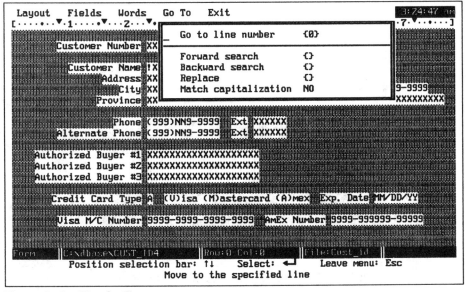

Figure 5-40 The Go To menu.

option desired, and press **Enter**, or type the first letter of the option. When this is done, a window will open, asking you to provide a line number or search text to go to.

The Replace option may be useful if you are modifying forms for different departments or different clients, and merely want to replace one company name or term with another.

The customer entry form is still not quite complete. At this point, you have all the field names and field entry information (template, picture functions, and edit options) specified. However, it would also be useful to have a title graphic or title box to further improve the look of the form.

Box and Line Drawing

Lines and boxes are useful for designating specific areas on your forms, separating one area from another area on your form, and improving the overall appearance of a form. A visually interesting form can reduce the fatigue or boredom that a plain form may help to cause. Lines can also be used effectively to draw graphics or logos.

dBASE IV provides you with a variety of tools for line and box drawing. You can use standard line characters and produce single- or double-spaced lines or boxes. You can also use any standard character (letters, numbers, or symbols) to draw your lines or boxes.

Line and box drawing features can be accessed from the Layout menu. The first level of menus allows you to select a box or a line. Select either option by pressing the first letter of the option (**B** for *Box* or **L** for *Line*). You'll start by drawing a box that completely encloses the form. Press **B** to bring the draw options menu. This menu looks

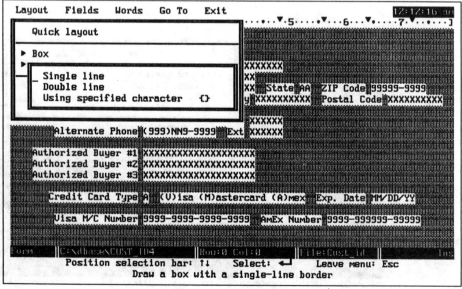

Figure 5-41   Box or line draw options menu.

like Figure 5-41. The first two options are pretty much self-explanatory. The third deserves more explanation.

Using specified character allows you to select an ASCII character that will be used to draw the borders of the box. The first two options (*Single line* and *Double line*) used a predetermined, special, line drawing character provided by ASCII. This third option allows you to use any character. As with other options, *Using specified character* can be selected by pressing **U**. Do that now.

At the right side of the screen, as seen in Figure 5-42, a window with available characters is shown. The left column is the decimal number of the character. The middle column is the hexadecimal number used by the computer to refer to the character. The right column displays the character as it will appear on the box or line. To see more characters a screen at a time, press the **PgDn** key. To scroll up a screen at a time, press the **PgUp** key. You may also scroll through the characters using the **Up Arrow** or **Down Arrow** keys.

Since this application is for a music distribution business, you might select the musical note symbols (number 13 or 14). For this example, 13 has been selected by moving the highlight to the character desired and pressing **Enter**.

To draw a box, you must tell the system where the box will start, and where you want it to end. To indicate the beginning of the box, move the cursor to the point where you wish to start the box. In this case, the box starts at the top left corner of the screen. To quickly move the cursor to that location, press **Home** and press **PgUp**. Now, press **Enter** to mark the beginning of the box.

Once the beginning of the box is marked, use the arrow keys to move the box to the opposite corner. In this case you would be moving the border using the **Right Arrow**

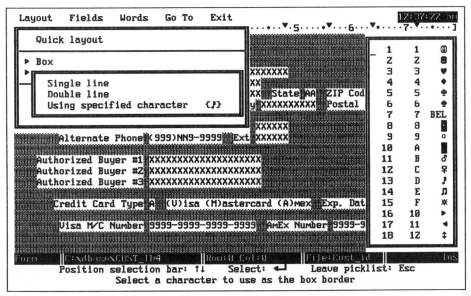

Figure 5-42   Special characters for line or box drawing.

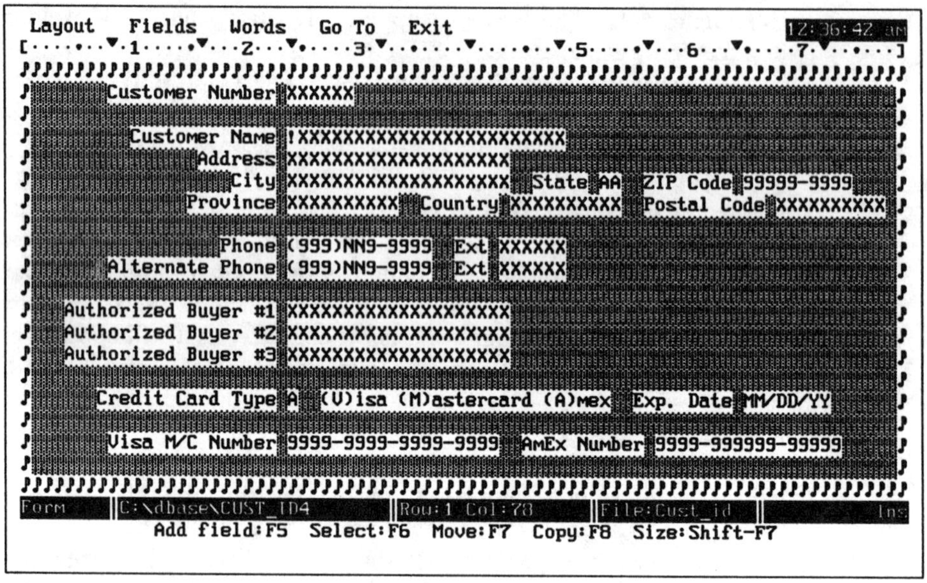

Figure 5-43   Screen with special characters.

and **Down Arrow** keys. You could also have started the box from any corner, and moved the keys to an opposite corner. For this example, however, it was easy to start at the top left corner.

Once you've placed the borders of the box where you want them to be, press **Enter** to complete drawing the box. If you wish to change the foreground or background of the box, this may be done now, by going to the Words menu and selecting Display. With the box drawn using your specified characters, move the cursor out of the box. The screen should look like Figure 5-43.

About the Top Line of a Form

To see how the actual form will appear during data entry, press **F2**. The screen should look like Figure 5-44. You will notice that the top of the form is at the top of your screen. No menu options are shown. Unless the user knows to press the **F10** key or uses the correct **Alt** key combinations to pop up the option windows, the user will not be aware of (or able to use) the Records, Organize, Go To, or Exit menus from within the form. With a menu window popped down onto the screen, the edit form will look like Figure 5-45.

The first line of your form is used to display the keywords used to pop down the Records, Go To, and Exit menus. If you want these visible, your top line should be blank. Bring up the Exit menu, and select *Return to Form design* to bring you back to the design for this form. In order to make the menu options line visible, you must blank the top line. However, the Customer Number data field is already on the second line,

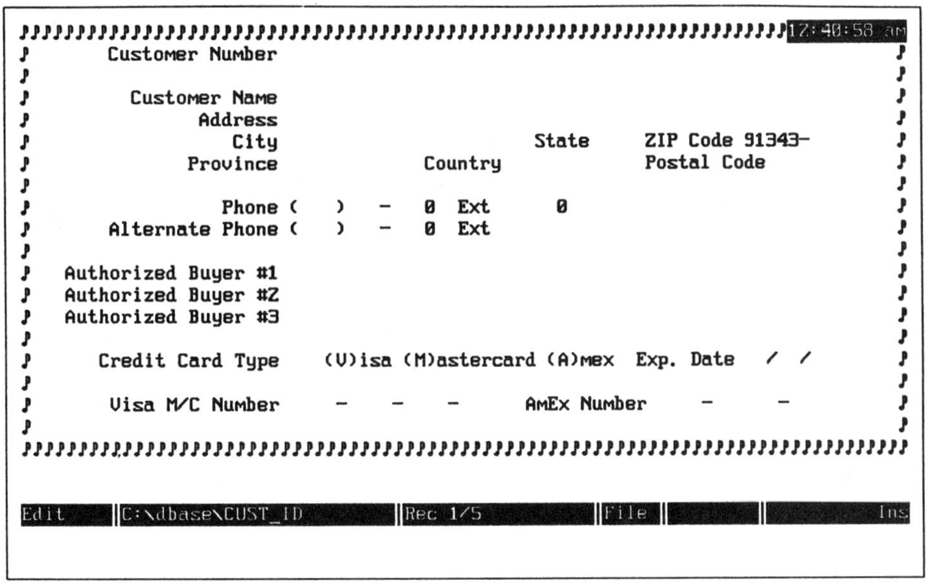

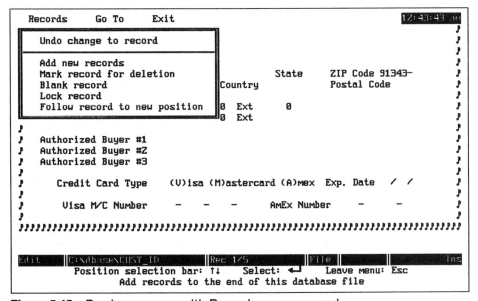

Figure 5-44   Form as saved hides menu options.

Figure 5-45   Previous screen with Records menu opened.

which is where you want the box to start. To move down all the text on the screen, place the cursor onto line two, making sure the system is in Insert mode, and press **Enter**. You will notice that all the text moved one line.

The next step is to fix the box. When you move the cursor to any part of the box, the entire box is highlighted. This allows simple selection of the box for moving and copying. However, you can't easily resize the box. With the box highlighted, press **Del** to erase the box from the screen. Next, select the Layout menu, the Box option, and *Using specified characters*. Select the same character, and press **Enter**.

You are now ready to redraw the box. Move the cursor to the second line of the form (the line above Customer Number), make sure your cursor is at the left margin, and press **Enter** to begin drawing the box. Again, move the box so that it extends to the bottom right corner of your screen, and press **Enter**. If you want the Records, Organize, Go To, and Exit pop-ups visible, you should leave the top line blank when you design your form.

> **Note** > Drawing boxes with single or double lines is done in the same way as it is done with special characters. The same considerations apply to single- or double-line boxes and line drawing, with regard to the top line of a form.

Text can be placed on top of your box. Your box still remains on the form, but it is not displayed because text characters take priority over box characters. To see how this works, move the cursor into the top line of the box, and type *Customer Entry Form*. Add a space at the beginning and end of the typed text. The typed characters will be displayed, replacing the box characters. However, the characters that made up the box are still on the form. To see this, highlight the text, including the spaces.

Next, open the Words menu and select the Position option. Try moving the block to the left, center, and middle of the form (by reopening the Words menu, selecting Position, and choosing the appropriate position). You will see that the box characters fill in any area that is not occupied by text. The form, with the text centered, looks like Figure 5-46.

Next, you'll draw a similar box using the line draw feature, rather than box drawing. First, you should remove the box from the screen. As shown before, you should move the cursor into any area of the box (the box will be highlighted), and press **Del** to remove the box. The box disappears, but the text that is written on top of the box remains.

Although a box can be thought of as made up of four lines, lines are significantly different from boxes. A box is treated as a single entity—if you move the cursor into a box, the entire box is highlighted. For this reason, a box can be easily selected, copied, moved, or deleted.

Lines are treated as a collection of single character elements. As you draw a line, dBASE IV automatically places a character onto the screen for each movement of the cursor. However, if you want to delete, copy, or move any portions of the line, this must be done by highlighting the areas to be moved, using the **F6** key and directional arrow keys.

Line drawing can be used for drawing graphics on your forms. Since the system places a character anywhere the cursor is moved, you can use the line drawing function

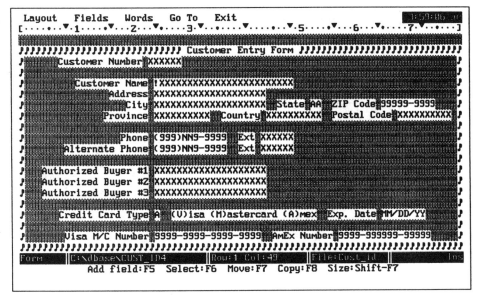

Figure 5-46   Data entry screen with text centered over box.

to place lines, or selected characters, anyplace on your form. Thus, a line drawn logo could be easily drawn. Line drawing can be used much like an "Etch-A-Sketch," with characters placed vertically or horizontally. Although tedious, it is possible to create a logo or graphic that can later be saved to a text file, and read into other forms.

In this example, you'll draw a "box" using Line, rather than Box, mode. To open the Line menu, pop down the Layout window (press **Alt-L**), and press **L** to open the Line menu. This menu looks identical to the one used for box drawing.

In this case, you'll use a different specified character, character number 14. Once you select a draw character, move the cursor to the point where you want to begin drawing your line and press **Enter**. Remember that anyplace you move the cursor places the draw character on the screen. Draw a border like the one shown in Figure 5-47.

Now, save the form, naming it CUST_ID. To do this, open the Layout menu, select *Save this form*, and name the form CUST_ID. Next, open the Exit menu, and select *Save changes and exit*.

This will return you to the Control Center. Now, since you won't be needing the intermediate forms that you saved while you were developing your data entry form, make sure the highlight is on *CUST_ID3*, and press **Alt-C** to open the Catalog menu. Select *Remove highlighted file from catalog*, and confirm that you want to remove the file from the catalog. It may also be removed from the disk; however, unless your disk is nearly full, it would still be useful to retain the file on disk, in case you may want to design another form based on the interim designs. You may wish to remove your intermediate files (CUST_ID1 through CUST_ID4) once you've produced the form you plan to be using for your application.

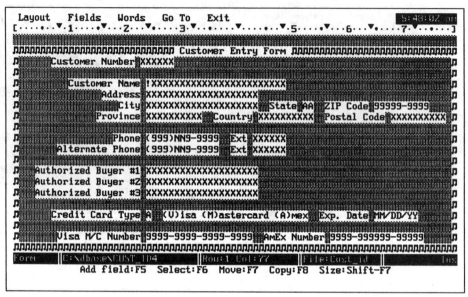

Figure 5-47 Box drawn using the Line drawing mode.

Input Forms

Now that the CUST_ID form has been completed, you should create input forms for the other data files. Although the system does not require that forms be developed in order to edit or modify data files, and will display the data fields as they will appear if you use the *Quick layout* feature of Form design, such an undesigned form will lack any picture functions, template, or edit option information that allows you to verify your data and filter input options.

Note It is usually preferable to create at least one data input form for each data file.

Multiple input forms for the same data file can serve different functions, while still working with the data in a common database. For example, the CUST_ID form, developed previously, is useful for adding a new customer to your database. It stores much of the information that is required when a customer is first signed in to the system. However, you may want to use a different form, which includes fewer items, for performing tasks that don't require gathering as much data. For example, you may want to create a form that is used only to change the address information and does not provide access to credit card data.

In this case, a form like the one shown in Figure 5-48 may be useful. Note that only five fields are shown on the form. This form was designed to display only the customer name and address. Edit options have been included in the field descriptors that do not allow editing of the customer number on this form. (The expression **CUST_NUMB >99999** was used in the *Permit edit if* option, setting a condition that is not possible to be reached with this database, and which will always be false, thus preventing any editing of either field.)

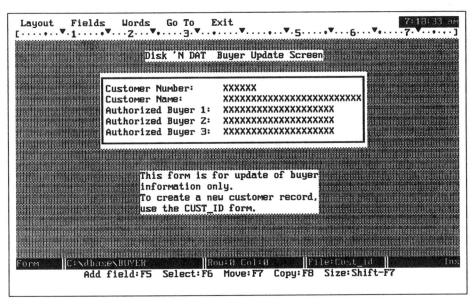

Figure 5-48 Buyer update screen using a subset of the CUST_ID file.

In addition, a further edit option setting only allows editing of an address field on forms that include a valid customer number. In this case, the expression **CUST_ NUMB> "00001"** was used to define the condition in the *Permit edit if* option line. With the edit options set, it should be clear that customer names and numbers cannot be changed and that only addresses can be changed for records that are assigned customer numbers. Further, the edit options will not allow new files to be added to the database—if the user attempts to add a record, the system will be locked, with the "Add New Records <Y/N>?" prompt locked onto the screen. If the system is locked in this manner, the user would have to press the **Esc** key, close the file, and then reopen the file, since the system will attempt to go to the last used record (actually, the end of the last record), and will again end up locked.

> **Note** To avoid a "locked up" condition, at least one field can be set to allow editing. However, this would allow for the creation of erroneous data.

The reasons for using a variety of forms for the same database may not be obvious. In this example, you have prepared a specialized update form that performs a specific function. For this task, a form made up of a subset of the file was designed. If you implement security into your database, you can set up a system that allows the data in this limited screen to be edited. A higher security level would be required for access to the CUST_ID data form, which allows access to credit card numbers and expiration dates.

Thus, you can design special forms for special functions (through the use of passwords and authorization levels, specific forms for specific personnel can be used to update or modify your data files). An added advantage is that when a user is editing data that is controlled by a data form, the Browse view only displays those fields in the form, and not the fields that make up the entire data file.

In theory, you could create one large data file that contains all the information that will be needed by your application. Designing the special forms for each data entry and management task would allow the feel of performing special functions, with the advantage of automatically updating the data in your master file. In fact, more sophisticated databases use what is called a "data dictionary." In essence, this is a list of all fields used by an application. All data manipulation is done through interactions with the data dictionary. For dBASE IV, however, the concept of a data dictionary is not practical. Instead, you have created many files. Later, you'll relate the contents of one data file to other data files.

Other Forms

Before moving on to the next chapter, additional forms should be created. The TITLES form will be made in a slightly different manner from the one used for CUST_ID. In this case, close the file currently displayed in the Data panel. Next, move the cursor into the Forms panel. The cursor should be on the <create> bar. There should be no other titles located above the line under <create>. Press **Enter** to open the Form design window. The Layout menu box will be open, and *Use different database file or view* will be highlighted. *Quick layout* will be dim, indicating that you can't accept the option. This is because no database file has been selected. A quick layout can only be made when there are data fields that can be placed into the layout. When no database file is attached to the Forms design menu, the option makes no sense, and is not available.

From within this menu, even before attaching a file, you can draw lines and boxes, describe the form, and even save the blank design. This may be useful when you want to develop a standard form design for all data forms. Once the blank form is developed, it can be named and saved. To use the custom template, you would later load the blank form (with boxes already designed), and then select *Use different database file or view* to provide the fields that will be added to the form. With *Use different database file or view* highlighted, press **Enter** to bring up a list of all available database files.

Select the TITLES database by highlighting the database (press **T**, then **Enter** to highlight and select this file). The Layout box will close, and the system will display a blank screen, ready for design development. If you were to reopen the Layout menu, you would see that *Quick layout* is now a selectable option. Selecting *Quick layout* gives you a screen like the one shown in Figure 5-49.

The *MISC* field is a memo field. In this field, the user will be able to type notes or comments without having to adhere to specific formats imposed by all the other fields.

Memo Fields

Memo fields can be displayed on the form in two ways. When you move the cursor into the field definition area, and select the field definition window (by pressing **F5** when *MEMO* is highlighted), you will see the current display option shown on screen.

The first option is MARKER. The other option is WINDOW. These two options may be toggled by moving the cursor into the *Display as* line, and pressing **Enter** or touching the **Spacebar**.

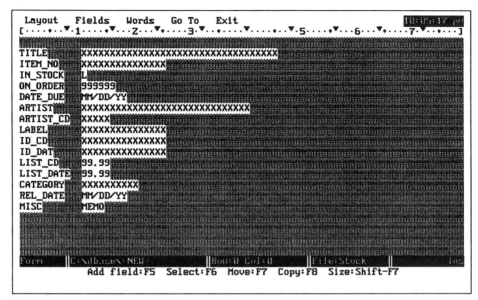

Figure 5-49   Quick layout for STOCK.DBF.

A marker places a box on the entry form. Inside the box, the word MEMO (or memo) appears. With a marker, the contents of the memo field are not shown as part of the form.

When editing a memo field, you must open the memo box in order to view and modify the contents of the field. In the next chapter, you'll see how it's done. If a memo field contains text, the word MEMO will be in all capital letters. If there is no text in the memo field, the word will be in lowercase. The form, as it currently appears, looks like Figure 5-50.

If the memo field is defined as a window field, you will be able to define a window on your form that will allow you to view the first lines of information in the memo field. How much can be viewed depends on the size of the window you specify when you define the form. Editing the contents of the window still requires that it be opened, using the techniques shown in the next chapter.

To create a window memo field, it is best to move the cursor to the position where you want to start the window, and then place the field. (In other words, delete the MEMO entry field from your form, then press **F5** to reopen it at its new position). Select the COMMENTS field, and move the cursor into the *Display as* option line.

Toggle the option to Window by pressing the **Enter** key or **Spacebar**, and select the option by pressing **Ctrl-End**. A line will appear at the position of the cursor. If this is where you wish to start the window, press **Enter**; otherwise, move the cursor to the desired start of your window and press **Enter**. Once the beginning of the window is placed, use the cursor keys to define the size of the memo window. Figure 5-51 shows a memo window four lines high. Once you've defined the window dimensions, accept them by pressing the **Enter** key.

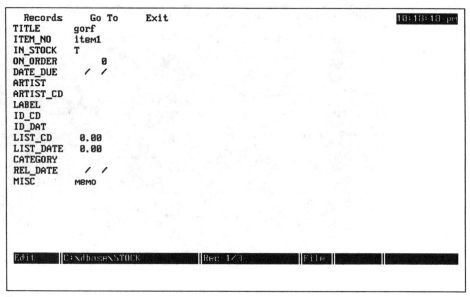

Figure 5-50   Form displayed using a Marker MEMO field.

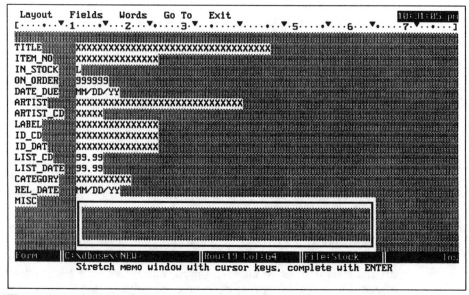

Figure 5-51   Memo window as defined for this example.

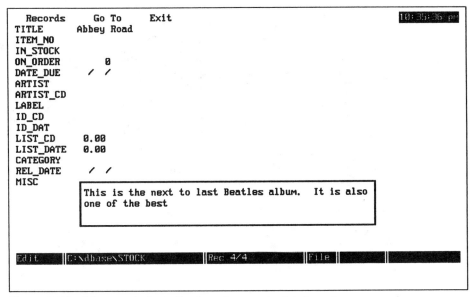

Figure 5-52   Memo window displayed as part of data entry screen.

Once accepted, the window will be filled with the letter **X** to indicate that it has been defined to hold text. Don't be concerned that your memos may run many pages longer than you are able to display in a window. The purpose of the window is to allow you a view of the contents—not to display the entire contents of a memo field. You will still be able to open a memo window, and view and edit the entire contents of a memo field.

Your data form that uses a memo window will look like Figure 5-52. It should be noted that in Version 1.1 of dBASE IV moving a memo marker is not an intuitively easy task. When you move the cursor into a marked memo box, the entire box becomes highlighted. However, you can't mark such a highlighted box simply by pressing **F6**. Instead, to move a marked memo box, you must move the cursor to one corner of the box, press **F6** to begin marking the box, and move the cursor to the opposite corner, pressing **Enter** when you've completed marking the box.

> **Note** Since memo windows are not easily moved, it is best to only create marker windows after the rest of a form has been designed.

To define different display characteristics, the entire window must be highlighted (using the **F6** key and the cursor arrows), and then modified using the Display option in the Words menu.

A new form that takes up two screens has been designed for this application. The first screen, with some fields renamed (or better explained), looks like Figure 5-53. The second screen of the form, which will appear on screen after the first block of data is entered, looks like Figure 5-54.

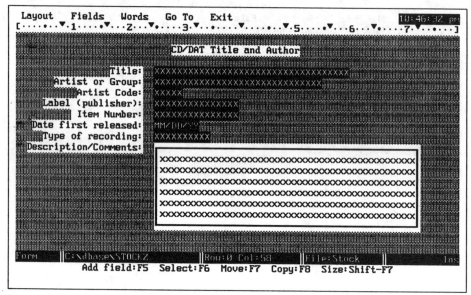

Figure 5-53   First screen of two-screen STOCK form.

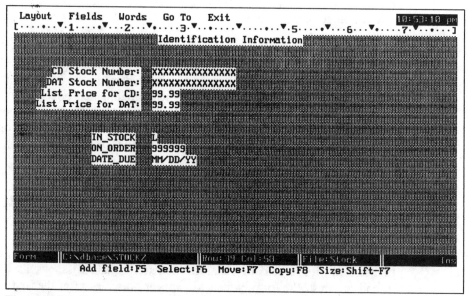

Figure 5-54   Second screen of two-screen STOCK form.

Save this form with the name TITLES, using the Layout menu Save option to name the form. Again, to view the form as it will appear to the data input operator, press **F2** to load the edit form.

By now, it should be clear that you can design forms that may take up many screens (or pages) of space. These forms can replace many of the lengthy forms that you may be replacing with your database application. (In most cases, you may wish to break the data files, and the forms used, into smaller units that can be related to each other during report generation and query updates. While useful on a single form for manual data entry, many times a form can be broken down into logical, easily managed parts, which need only be connected for certain tasks. Additional forms will be shown as they become necessary for the next chapters.

Conclusion

This lengthy chapter has provided you with many of the essential, and quite a few of the less essential but valuable, tools for designing forms and validating your data. In addition, some tricks have been shown to allow data entry only under certain conditions. Many of the capabilities were previously only available to (or easily used by) programmers. With the tools given here, you will be able to perform many of the sophisticated forms design tasks previously relegated only to expert users.

If you are a programmer, or have used prior versions of dBASE, and are convinced that the only *real* way to design a form is to program it, line by line, the examples in this chapter should have shown you an easier (and better) way. There is no disgrace in telling the system to draw a box or line—and avoiding the many lines of code you would otherwise have to write in order to accomplish the same task.

Using the Control Center is not just for wimps. Experienced programmers are also taking advantage of many of the time-saving capabilities provided by this user interface. Although a programmer can certainly take advantage of capabilities that can't be mastered from within the Control Center, the Control Center can still be used to substantially reduce the time required for developing an application.

Although real men may not eat quiche, real programmers (smart programmers) can, and do, use the Control Center.

6

Data Entry

In Chapter 5, data entry forms were shown to be key components of any data acquisition and analysis system. The forms not only allow you to customize the look of your application, they also verify and validate the data as it is entered into your system.

In this chapter and in Chapter 7, a number of topics will be explored. First, you will see how to input data onto your form (with or without the use of a form and validation templates). You'll also see how to bring data in from other sources. These sources include Lotus 1-2-3, other database programs, and other software programs. Moving the data from dBASE IV to other software formats is also explored, and in addition, you will see how the Append menu works, and will add records to the files that are created in this chapter.

Editing a Data File

The data files you built in the earlier chapters will contain the data needed to run your database system. In Chapter 5, you built the data structures that simplify data entry, and that also control and evaluate the data that is entered into the files. The forms that were built can modify the look of the data entry and viewing screens. They can be used to validate data as it is entered. In short, they are important tools for managing the input and viewing of your data—both as it is entered, and when it is edited. But the forms you developed aren't automatically applied to the data files.

To see what is meant here, close any data files that may be active. To do this, move the cursor into the Data panel and press the **Enter** key. This will bring up the option menu. Select *Close file* by pressing **C** (or pressing **Enter** when *Close file* is highlighted). The Control Center should show no active files.

Next, move the highlight to CUST_ID. Press **F2** to tell the system that you want to edit the file. The screen should look something like Figure 6-1.

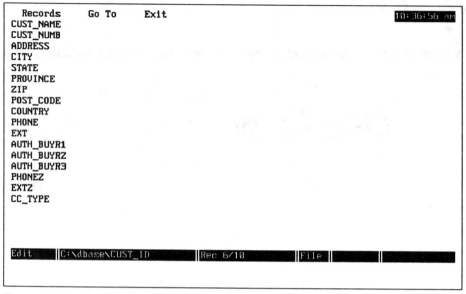

```
    Records      Go To      Exit                                10:36:56 am
  CUST_NAME
  CUST_NUMB
  ADDRESS
  CITY
  STATE
  PROVINCE
  ZIP
  POST_CODE
  COUNTRY
  PHONE
  EXT
  AUTH_BUYR1
  AUTH_BUYR2
  AUTH_BUYR3
  PHONEZ
  EXTZ
  CC_TYPE



 Edit    ┃C:\dbase\CUST_ID        ┃Rec 6/10        ┃File┃    ┃
```

Figure 6-1   Default Edit screen.

This screen is automatically generated by the system when you load a file that is selected from the Data panel. The current form does not apply any special filtering, validation, or picture functions to data that is input. (The system will accept default values. For example, characters will not be allowed in numeric fields, and values other than T or F will not be allowed in logical fields.)

> **Note** ⟩ If you've built a custom data entry or editing form, you should, of course, use that form.

Now, close the current form, by pressing **Esc**. Next, close the file by pressing **Enter** twice. The screen will again show no files selected, since no file is actively in use.

When a form (or label, report, or query) is selected, associated files are automatically selected. To see what is meant by this, move the cursor to the CUST_ID form in the Forms panel, and choose to edit the form by pressing **F2**. The form will be selected, and the related data file for which the form was designed to control input will also be selected.

When the CUST_ID form is selected, the screen should look like Figure 6-2.

In addition to the form itself, the design, filters, and other features of your designed form are in effect. Thus, with this form selected, all the components of your design will be implemented.

When you leave the form (through the Exit menu), the Control Center will have loaded the related data file and any other forms related to the data file.

Using the Forms panel to open an edit window provides an additional minor advantage. If you moved the highlight back to CUST_ID in the Data panel, and opened an edit window by pressing **F2**, you would load the last used data form (in this case, the

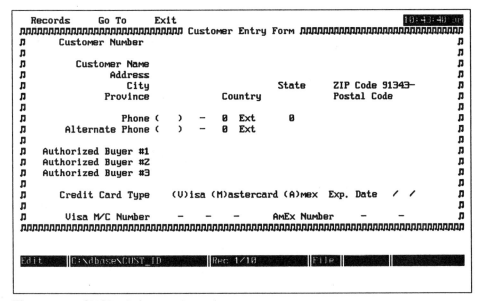

Figure 6-2 CUST_ID form selected.

CUST_ID form). All the features of the form will be in effect until you close the active file, or return to the Edit screen from the Query design screen.

If you've gone to the trouble of designing a data form that applies intelligence to the input of data, it is recommended that you take full advantage of the form by *only* selecting a data edit window from the Forms panel. The Data panel is more appropriately used to modify the data file and to append data to the file by importing it from other files. As a rule, once a form is designed, you should use the designed form, and not select the file from the Data panel.

To edit data or enter data into your data file, choose the desired form and press **F2** to open the form. In this case, open the CUST_ID form. The system will automatically place the customer number in the CUST_NUMB field. This happens because you included a special expression into the form that assigns a number that matches the record number to each new customer.

Type the first entry, *Sam's Records*. You'll see that the cursor is still on the Customer Name line. To move the cursor to the next field, press the **Enter** or **Tab** key. If the contents of a field match the length of the field, the cursor will automatically be advanced to the next field. You will see this when you type the *State* abbreviation.

Moving forward from field to field is easy. You just press the **Tab** or **Enter** key. You may also move to the next field by pressing the **F4** key or, if the desired field is one line down, using the **Down Arrow** key. Moving to a previous field is a bit more tricky. The **Up Arrow** key moves the cursor up one row at a time. **Shft-Tab** moves the cursor back one field at a time, although **Shft-Enter** still advances the cursor. The **F3** key will also move the cursor back one field at a time. The **F3** and **F4** keys also do something that the **Tab** and **Shft-Tab** keys and the **Enter** and **Up Arrow** and **Down Arrow** keys won't do. When you use **F3** or **F4** to move the cursor into a memo field, that field will be opened up, ready for editing.

As was shown in Chapter 5, the memo field contains text that can be edited by the data input operator, or by whoever is viewing the file (providing the *Permit edit If* clause permits it). However, before editing can happen, the memo window (or marker) must be expanded to the text edit window. Again, this can be done by using the **F3** or **F4** keys. A memo window can also be opened for editing by pressing the **Ctrl-Home** key combination.

Working with memo fields will be explored later. Essentially, when you expand a memo window, you are opening an editing window. In this window, if your setup permits an edit, you can add to, delete, or modify the contents of the text window. To close the window, you should use the Exit menu. (Although you can press the **Esc** key and confirm that you want to exit without making changes, it is best not to develop this habit because you *will* one day exit the menu window without saving changes that you want to retain.)

Once you've typed ***Sam's Records*** in the customer name field, press **Enter**, and the system will move the cursor to the address field. Type ***3344 Disk Drive*** **Enter** to fill in the address. Next, type ***Los Angeles*** **Enter**.

The next field, *State* is designed to accept two letters. If this field is skipped, by pressing **Esc**, you will be able to enter information in the province, country, and postal code fields. You will recall that in Chapter 5, you set the edit options for these fields to allow editing only if no state or ZIP code were entered. In this case, however, you want to enter a U.S. state. Type ***CA***.

Note >	The cursor moves to the ZIP code entry field as soon as the two-letter state identifier is entered. dBASE IV automatically advances the cursor to the next field if a preceding field is entirely filled with data.

The ZIP field will accept five or nine digits. Once you enter a digit into this field, you will be prevented from accessing the province, country, or postal code fields. Thus, users should be careful to begin entry in the ZIP code field only when such entry is appropriate.

The phone field automatically places the numbers in the data field in the order typed. Thus, the area code is followed by the phone number. You may wish to verify that the first two characters in the telephone prefix may be either letters or numbers, as was set in the template for the phone number fields.

The credit card type fields are quite interesting. First, only three entries are permitted: A, M, or V. Any other type of field entry will result in an error message. Once an acceptable value is typed, the system will move the cursor to the *Exp. Date* field. You *must* enter a date when the cursor is in this field. When the date is entered, the system compares this date to the current date, as stored in your computer's clock/calendar. If the date is later than the current date, the system lets you move to the next field. Otherwise, the system will beep and (if you've correctly set the edit options) will provide a useful error message. The first record, with the erroneous date, and the error message, is shown in Figure 6-3.

The cursor will be advanced to one of two fields. If you enter Credit Card Type **A**, the cursor will go to the *AmEx Number* field; if **M** or **V** is entered, the cursor goes to

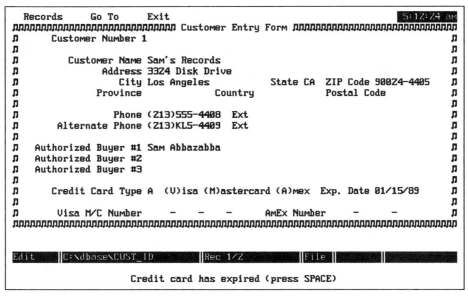

Figure 6-3   Record 1, with expiration date error shown.

Visa M/C Number. The system automatically accepts only numbers, and automatically inserts hyphens in the appropriate spot on the form. Once the numbers are entered, the system will advance to the next record, automatically assigning the next consecutive record number in the CUST_NUMB field.

> **Note** ⟩ The data, addresses, and phone numbers for the customers and buyers are all imaginary. Although the data may *look* real, it isn't.

Data Entry Using Browse

The Browse screen is a toggled option that is used primarily to display many records on the screen at once. It puts the data for a file on the screen in columnar format. Records are displayed in order from top to bottom, and, unless they have been sorted or are shown in indexed order, will be displayed in the order in which they were entered. Data for each field, in the order the fields appear in the database, are displayed on the Browse screen.

To switch from the Edit screen to the Browse screen (and back again), press **F2**. The Browse screen for this database (with data added) should look like Figure 6-4.

If record 1 (CUST_NUMB 1) is not shown in the browse screen, press the **Up Arrow** to bring the cursor to the top of the file. You should notice a few things about this form. First, the top line shows the names of the fields as they appear in your data file design. Although the Edit screen spelled out the words "Customer Number" and "Customer Name", the Browse screen only shows the field names you used when you defined your data file.

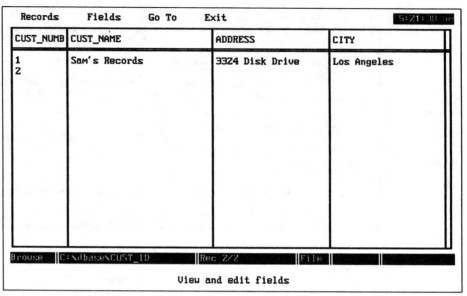

Figure 6-4   Browse screen for CUST_ID data file.

In addition, a new option is shown on the top menu bar. This option, Fields, allows you (or a data entry operator) to control the way that fields are displayed on the screen. In addition, you will be able to tell the system to allow you to edit a single field on multiple records using the *Freeze field* options. (These options will be explored shortly).

A quick trip through the first record shows some interesting features of the Browse menu. As you move from field to field (using the **F4** or **Tab** key), you will see the field on the left of the screen and its associated records scroll off the screen as the new fields appear on the right of the form. Move the cursor into the ZIP field. Next, press the **F4** or **Tab** key to move to the next legal field. The cursor will skip over the PROVINCE, COUNTRY, and POST_CODE fields, and stop in the PHONE field. This is the same as would happen in the Edit screen, with one significant exception. In the Edit mode, you can press **F3** or **Shft-Tab**, or use the **Up Arrow** to move to the previous field. The system will move the cursor to the previous editable field. In this case, the cursor would skip back over the POST_CODE, COUNTRY, and PROVINCE fields, moving the cursor back to ZIP.

An interesting thing happens when you toggle from Browse to Edit. The system keeps track of the field that the cursor is in when you switch modes. Although you would expect the cursor to move you into the same field for whichever mode you are in (for example, if you are in the PHONE_1 field in Browse, you should be in the PHONE_1 field when you toggle to Edit), this is not always the case. When moving from Browse to Edit, the cursor remains in the field it was editing when you were in Browse mode. However, if you move from Edit to Browse, the cursor may be placed into the field that was being viewed when you were last in the Browse mode. If you've saved a record and moved to the next, dBASE IV will keep the cursor in the same field in both Browse and Edit.

Returning to the Browse screen, you will find that the system automatically assigns the appropriate filters to the data that were set up when you designed your form. You can see this by changing the selection in the CC_TYPE field. If you enter **V**, the system will only allow you to enter a number in the CC_NUMB_VM field. Entering **A** will provide access only to the CC_NUMB_A field.

When you enter a date in the CC_EXP_DATE field, dBASE IV compares the date you enter with the current date, as stored on the system's clock. If the date is greater (or later than) the current date, the system allows you to advance to the CC_NUMB entry fields. If not, the system gives an error message and does not allow you to leave the entry field.

Browse/Edit Menus

The menus at the top line of the screen are essentially the same in both the Edit and Browse screens, with the exception of the Fields menu. The menus will be discussed in the order they are displayed on the Browse screen.

The Records Menu

The Records menu, shown in Figure 6-5, allows you to perform a number of changes to records in your database. Depending upon a number of variables, you may or may not be able to select all of the options available in this menu.

The first option, *Undo change to record*, is highlighted when you have made any changes to your record. When selected, the record will be restored to its original values.

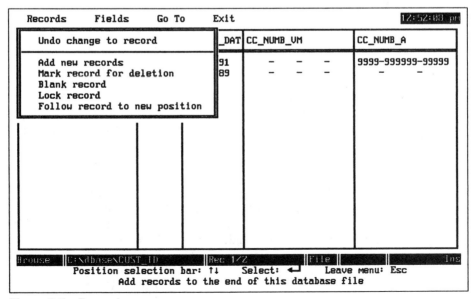

Figure 6-5 Records menu.

This option does not provide much security, however. dBASE IV automatically stores the values in each record whenever you move from one record to the next. Once you've moved from one record to another, the ability to undo any changes is lost, since dBASE IV considers the changes to a record to be final (and correct) whenever you move to another record.

In Browse mode, moving from one record to the next (and saving the changes in the record) is very easy to do. Pressing the **Up Arrow** or **Down Arrow** automatically saves the current record and moves you on to the next. In Edit mode, it is also easy to move from one record to another when you come to the end of a record and finish entering data in the last field, or if you are at the first field in a record and press **PgUp**, **Shft-Tab**, or the **Left Arrow**.

You should consider your data files unprotected while you are editing your files, since the *Undo change to record* option is only limited to changes made before you move from one record to another, and it is so easy to move from one record to another. Although *Undo change to record* is available, and can restore original values of a file, this feature becomes unavailable as soon as you move from one record to another.

Add new records is used to put the system into an Append mode. If you are at the end of your file and attempt to move to the next file, the system asks if you want to add more records. At this point, you can press **Y** to open a new, blank record.

However, if you have a very large file, and don't want to search to the end, choosing *Add new records* from anywhere in the data file will automatically move the cursor to the end of your database file, and bring you to a new, blank record. Again, the option may be of little use in a small file, since you can easily go to the end of your file and activate the append screen. However, for a large file, the option quickly moves to the end of your file and opens up a new, blank screen, ready for data input. (It should be noted that the screen may, technically, not be blank. If you have fields that are predefined, such as the automatically numbering CUST_NUMB field, or filled with values that carry over from the previous field, these values will already be inserted into your new record.)

The next option, *Mark record for deletion*, is used to identify a record as one that you wish to delete. To understand how this option works, it is important to understand how records are normally deleted. In order to delete a record, you must go into the data file design screen and select the option to delete marked records. A marked record is one that you have activated by selecting the *Mark record for deletion* option during viewing or editing. The system places a deletion mark into the file header information for the record, and when you select the *Delete marked records* option, removes the record from the file (and from the disk).

Records can also be marked for deletion using a query update process. For example, you may wish to delete from your customer list any customers who have not ordered in the last 18 months. By constructing a query that will mark all records in which the last order date was more than 18 months before today's date, and will update the file to reflect these inactive accounts, you can set up the stage for removal of these inactive customers. (You could, of course, have first created a query to select only the customers who have not ordered in more than 18 months, and created a new file that includes *only* those files. This way, when you delete the inactive customers from your *active* accounts list, you will still have the names of those customers whom you have deleted.)

Note〉 It is useful to remember that a marked record is not deleted until you tell the system to do so, from within organize menu.

Mark record for deletion is a toggled field. When the cursor is in a record that has been marked for deletion, the system will show *Clear deletion mark* as the option (instead of *Mark record for deletion*). By looking at this item, it is easy to tell whether or not a record has been marked for deletion. If it says *Mark record for deletion*, the record *has not* been marked; if the prompt says *Clear deletion mark*, the record *has* been marked for deletion.

Again, you may be able to design a "last check" query item that looks at the date of the last order and clears the deletion mark from any potentially inactive customers who have placed an order since your file was last updated. This query would then unmark those reactivated clients who should not now be deleted. When a record is marked for deletion, the system does not include it in sorts and other operations, and treats it as if it is not in the data file. In addition, the system puts the letters "Del" in the information line at the bottom right of the screen.

Blank record is an interesting option. It is used to delete all the information in the current record. Unlike marking a record for deletion, this leaves the record in the data file, but removes all the record's contents. Blanking a record is useful if you want to remove an obsolete record and replace it with a new one. However, if it's used instead of the *Mark record for deletion* option, you may end up with a large number of blank records cluttering up your database, since blanked records are not deleted, and remain as part of your database whether they contain data or not.

Lock record is available when you are using dBASE IV on a network. Normally, when you are working on a record, the system automatically locks the file. File locking prevents other users on the network from going into the record you are editing and making changes to it while you are also working on the record. Similarly, you will be locked out of records that others on the network are currently working on. The *Lock record* option is used to identify a file that you are working on as a locked record until you return to the file. This prevents others from modifying the record until you unlock it.

Follow record to new position is a command that is used when you are adding files to an indexed database. When you have defined indexed fields, the system will take each new record and place it in order in the data file's index.

On selecting *Follow record to new position*, your cursor will be placed in the location within the data file where the new record is placed. For example, if you add Abe's Records into your database, appending the new record to your file, the system will save the record, placing it in order, perhaps, between Aaron's Music Shop and Adam's Disco Dugout (if you set up the customer name as an indexed field).

When another entry, for Michael's Musical Mayhem, is added the cursor may then be located between Mark's Records and Milton Miltone's Rock Ranch. When you choose to Follow the record to its new position, then, the record is placed so that it can be viewed in indexed order, rather than being put into order by record number. This is useful if you are adding records from a presorted list.

In addition, if you are making changes to an existing record that will change its position in indexed order (for example, a name change from Abe's Records to Milton's Records), by setting the option to YES, the record will be moved to its new position in the data file. Setting the option to NO leaves the record in its previous indexed order. (You can rebuild an index from within the Organize menu, to be discussed in the next section.)

The Organize Menu

The Organize menu has been added to dBASE IV Version 1.1 at the request of many users of 1.0. This menu, previously only available from within the modify window for data files, allows you to modify your indexes, manage your indexes, unmark and erase your records, create new files with sorted fields, and design new index expressions. The menu is arguably the most useful in much of dBase.

The Organize menu is broken into two parts by a horizontal line. The bottom half of the menu is used to sort the attached database and to erase or unmark records. The top half is used for index management. This menu is also available from within the Data panel. The Organize menu will be discussed in fuller detail in Chapter 8.

The Fields Menu

The Fields menu, seen in Figure 6-6, is available only from within the Browse screen. The menu is not available from within Edit.

Lock fields on left is used to display nonadjacent fields on the screen at one time. For example, if you wanted to show the CUST_NUMB and the ZIP fields as adjacent fields, using the *Lock fields on left* option will allow you to do this.

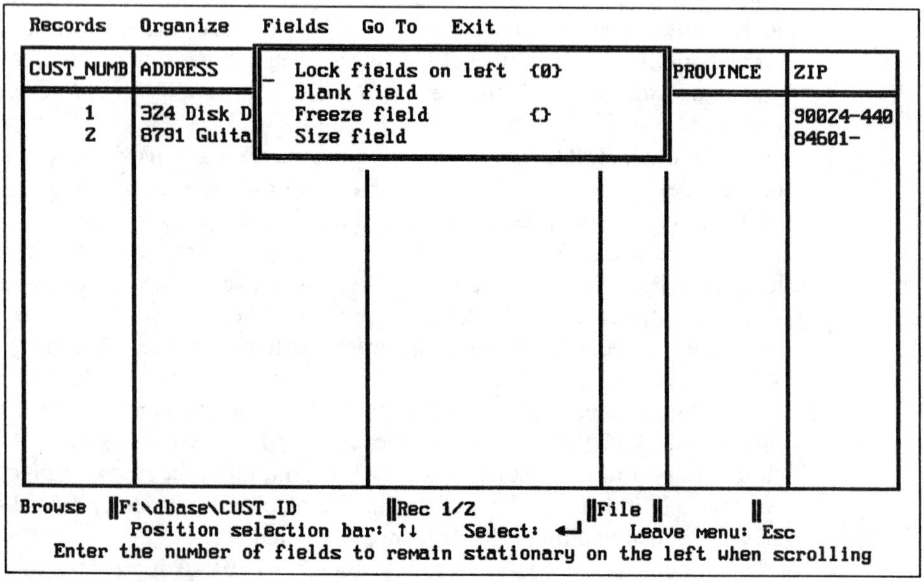

```
Records    Organize    Fields    Go To    Exit

 CUST_NUMB ADDRESS         Lock fields on left  {0}       PROVINCE  ZIP
                           Blank field
         1  324 Disk D     Freeze field         {}                  90024-440
         2  8791 Guita     Size field                               84601-




Browse   ||F:\dbase\CUST_ID        ||Rec 1/2      ||File ||       ||
            Position selection bar: ↑↓     Select: ↵    Leave menu: Esc
        Enter the number of fields to remain stationary on the left when scrolling
```

Figure 6-6 Fields menu.

When, in this example, you lock one field on the left, the first field, CUST_ NUMB will not scroll across the screen as you move from one field to the next (using **Tab** or **F3** or **Shft-Tab** or **F4**). So, when you press **Tab**, the cursor moves from CUST_ NAME to ADDRESS to CITY. The next time you press **Tab**, the CUST_NAME field scrolls to the left, off the screen, while the STATE, ZIP, and PROVINCE fields appear on screen. The CUST_NUMB field remains locked on the left of the screen, while the CUST_NAME field scrolls off the screen.

If CUST_NUMB was not a locked field, it would have scrolled off the screen before CUST_NAME did. You are free to lock any number of fields on the screen— limited, of course, by how many fields are visible on the screen. When you lock a field on the left, the field that is at the left of the screen is the first one locked. It does not have to be the first field in your file. You may scroll through the data file until the first record that you wish to lock is displayed.

The fields that appear to the left of the first locked fields cannot be displayed when fields are locked. Thus, if you lock the STATE field on the left, you can scroll through the records, but when you tab past the last field, the first available field (STATE) will be displayed on screen—all prior fields in the record will not be displayed or viewable. This may be useful when you wish only to show the last fields in a record.

There are other points to be made relative to locking fields on the left. Although you may use any field in a record to lock a field on, you can only lock adjacent fields. Assume, for example, that you wish to lock the first and third fields. You may try to lock the first field, tab across the screen until the second field scrolls to the left across the screen, moving the third field adjacent to the first, and then try to lock the first two fields on screen. Although this is a clever approach to displaying the two fields as adjacent fields, it doesn't work. If you wish to display the first and third fields in a data file, you must also lock the intermediate fields (the second field) onto the screen in order to achieve the display of the desired fields.

To select *Lock fields on left*, bring up the Fields menu and press **L** to select the option, or press **Enter** (since the cursor will normally be on this option when you open the Fields menu). The system will then prompt you for the number of fields to lock the record on. Type the number of fields to lock on, and press **Enter** to complete the selection). The fields can be unlocked by selecting the *Lock fields on left* and selecting **0** fields to lock on.

Blank Field This deletes the value entered into a field. This may be somewhat faster than holding down the **Del** key to clear out the value of a field from a record. This option only works on the current field and should be considered permanent, although *Undo changes to record* in the Records option menu can usually restore the value of a field (remember, however, that once you move the cursor up or down in the Browse menu, or to another record in Edit mode, your changes cannot be undone).

Freeze Field This is used to make a field the only editable field. The cursor is frozen inside of the field. Use of the **Tab, Shft-Tab, F3**, and **F4** keys only moves you to the previous or next record, staying within the frozen field. This is very useful if you are doing an update on the values in a single field. It saves you the trouble of locking fields or scrolling through a series of records to make changes in only one field.

One scenario demonstrating the immediate benefit of a mixture of locking fields and freezing a field would be to go through your database to update or validate expiration dates of credit cards. In this case, you may freeze the screen on CC_EXP _DAT, but the screen will not normally display the customer number or customer name, making it difficult to match the expiration date to the record, since the most important identifying information is at the front of your data file, where it isn't displayed.

The solution to this dilemma is to return the cursor to the front of your record by scrolling past the last field in your data file. This moves the cursor back to the first field, and again displays the beginning of your data file. From this position, you may lock the first two or three fields on the left, using the *Lock fields on left* option. This freezes the important identification information on the screen.

Next, reopen the Fields menu and select *Freeze field*. This is done by pressing **F** to freeze the field, or by moving the cursor to highlight *Freeze field* and pressing **Enter**. The screen will then prompt you for the name of the field that you wish to freeze (the system will prompt "Enter field name:"). Type the name of the field you wish to freeze (in this case, CC_EXP_DAT) and press **Enter**. The system will scroll the screen so that the frozen field is displayed on screen, while the locked fields remain unmoved. The screen, with the first two fields locked and the CC_EXP_DAT field frozen, looks like Figure 6-7. Additional records will be entered into this sample database shortly. A record may be unfrozen by reopening the Fields menu, selecting *Freeze field*, and typing a new field name or deleting the current field name, and pressing **Enter**.

Only one field at a time can be frozen. However, for certain types of updates, updating one field at a time may be faster than attempting to update two or three fields, since you can quickly scan your hardcopy records and update on a field by field

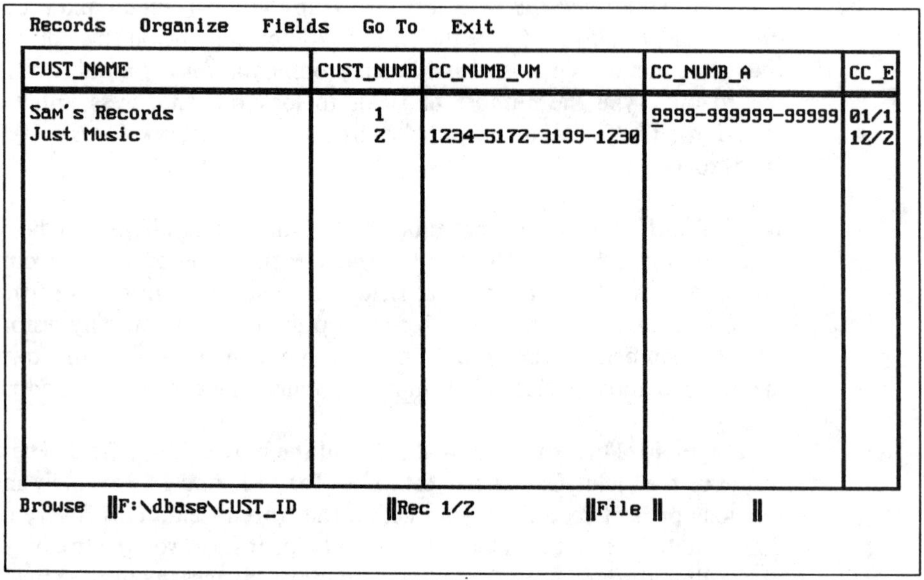

Records Organize Fields Go To Exit				
CUST_NAME	CUST_NUMB	CC_NUMB_VM	CC_NUMB_A	CC_E
Sam's Records	1		9999-999999-99999	01/1
Just Music	2	1234-5172-3199-1230		12/2

Browse ‖F:\dbase\CUST_ID   ‖Rec 1/2   ‖File ‖   ‖

Figure 6-7   Browse screen with records locked and frozen.

basis. When combined with the *Lock fields on left* option, the combined capabilities greatly simplify updating of all the records in a file.

The last option, *Size field*, is not available from within the Browse window. It can be used in the Labels panel and is designed to allow you to change the size of the window used to display the contents of a field. Pressing **Shft-F7** is a shortcut way of selecting *Size field*. When *Size field* has been selected, you can resize the field using the **Right Arrow** to make the field display window wider, and the **Left Arrow** to make the field display window smaller.

The Go To Menu

The Go To menu is a common menu that can be found in many of the panels within dBASE IV. It is used to quickly move to or locate a specific record. It is also used to find the first (or each) occurrence of a particular value in a field. The Go To menu looks like Figure 6-8.

Top Record This moves the cursor to the top record in your database file. If your file is not indexed, this selection would move the cursor to record 1. If you have put your record into indexed order, choosing *Top record* will bring the cursor to the first record in indexed order. You may also rapidly move to the top record by pressing the **Ctrl-PgUp** key combination.

Last Record This is essentially the converse of *Top record*. For an unindexed database, this command would move the cursor to the last record. For an indexed database, the

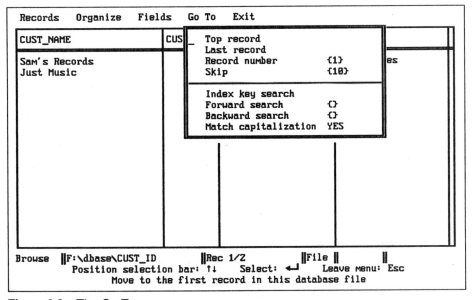

Figure 6-8   The Go To menu.

option would move the cursor to the last record in index order. Pressing **Ctrl-PgDn** would accomplish the same function.

Record Number This option allows you to move the cursor to a particular record number. This is useful for quickly moving to a desired position in your database. For example, in the CUST_ID database, you may have 5000 or more records, once all your customers are entered into the system. To move to the record for customer number 2801 using the **PgDn** or **Down Arrow** keys would take far longer than any data operator would want. For this kind of move, using the Go To menu's *Record number* option is virtually indispensable. To select this option, open the Go To window (by pressing **Alt-G**) and press **R** (for *R*ecord number). dBASE IV will prompt you for the number of the record that you are searching for. Type the number, press **Enter**, and dBASE IV will find the record, positioning the cursor in the same field it was in when you activated the option.

Skip This option allows you to jump a predetermined amount of records at a time. For example, assume that your database is sorted alphabetically by customer name. The database file has 5000 records in it, and you wish to find Murray's Music. Although the record can be more efficiently located using the search functions in dBASE IV, you can also rapidly find the general area where the desired file is by skipping 500 records at a time. Although you expect Murray's Music to be located somewhere near the middle of the data file, you can quickly get there by repeatedly skipping 500 records at a time, until you get close to the desired file. You can then reduce the number of records to skip, until you get close enough to the record to use the **PgUp** or **PgDn** keys.

The options at the bottom half of the Go To menu are used for defining and implementing searches through your database for records with fields matching your search criteria. It is important to understand how fields come into play during searches from the Go To menu.

When you select a search option, a window is opened asking for the text or value that you wish to search for. The records in your data file will be searched by the system. However, only the field where the cursor is positioned when you open the Go To window will be searched for.

For example, if you want to search for Murray's Music, the cursor must be positioned in the CUST_NAME field. Similarly, if you wish to find the first record in Santa Monica, you must first have the cursor positioned in the city field before opening the Go To menu.

The procedure for specifying a search field from within this menu is slightly different from that for specifying a query condition. In a forward, backward, or index key search, you may type the contents of a character field without enclosing the characters in quotation marks. When you design a query, as you will see later in this book, character fields must be enclosed in quotation marks, to indicate that the characters that appear within the quotation marks are characters, and not absolute values (such as numeric field entries).

Thus, to search for Murray's Music, you would open the appropriate search window by pressing the first letter of the search option, or by moving the cursor to the appropriate option and pressing **Enter**, and then type *Murray's Music*. From within a query, matching on the same store name would look like this: ''*Murray's Music*''.

Wildcards When you want to search for a particular value, like Murray's Music, specifying the search parameters is easy. You just type the complete name (or value) that you are looking for. However, if you are not sure of the exact store name (is it Murray's Music or Murray's Records, or is it even Murray, and not Murphy?) you may frequently have to search for inexact matches. Wouldn't it be nice to be able to find the first record that starts with Mur? In dBASE IV, you can easily search for inexact values using wildcard characters. A wildcard tells the system that *any* value in that character position should be considered a match.

There are two types of wildcards used in dBASE IV: the question mark ? and the star *. Each serves a slightly different function than the other.

The question mark tells dBASE IV to accept any value for a single character. For example, if you wanted to find a person named Smith, but were uncertain whether the name was Smith or Smyth, by telling dBASE IV to search to Sm?th, you would find the first occurrence of any name that matched the specification. It should be noted that in a forward search, using the ? wildcard, the first match would be located.

It should also be noted that *any* character can occupy the wildcard position—for example, dBASE IV would find Smath, Smeth, Smuth, or even Sm1th or any other variation, when the wildcard is specified. Specifying Sm??? would find the first record with a five-character name that started with the letters Sm. Further, repeated searching will turn up additional records (if any) of five-letter names starting with the two letters S and m.

Using the ? as a wildcard character also tells the system that only only a single character position is affected by the wildcard character. Thus, Sm??? tells dBASE IV to look for five-letter names, while Sm???? would tell dBASE IV to search for six-letter names.

The asterisk, or star *, tells the system to accept a match for all characters including and occurring after the star. For example, the search specification Sm* will match any Smith, Small, Smithfield, or other name matching the spec (the spec means to look for any record with a value in the specified field that begins with Sm.)

The * can also be used to accept any number of characters between a predetermined set of letters. For example, the query Sm*field would match Smithfield, Smallfield, Smeggeggyfield, or any other names beginning with *Sm* and ending with *field*. In summary, then, the asterisk * is a wildcard for any number of spaces, while the question mark ? is a wildcard for a single-character space.

Search Types There are three types of search available from within dBASE IV: *Forward search*, *Backward search*, and *Index key search*. The first two are always available from within the Edit or Browse menus, while *Index key search* is available when a database is displayed in indexed order.

A forward search searches the database from the current position in the database towards the end of the database. Thus, if you were editing record number 1000 in a 6000-record database file, dBASE IV would search through the records in increasing (record) order.

A backward search obviously searches for records having a lower record number. Thus, if you started at 1000, the next record checked would be 999, then 998, and so on. Remember, however, that any matches that occur before the point where your search begins in a forward search, and any records that occur after your search begins in a backward search, will not be found. Thus, unless you don't care about the portion of your data file that won't be covered by the search, you should start a forward search at the top record of your data file and a backward search from the end of your data file.

An index key search needs further explanation. When you set up a database file, you indicate which fields you want to be indexed on. When you add a record to the data file, dBASE IV automatically places the new record in its proper location in index order. Thus, if you index your database on customer name, the names will be in alphabetic order. When a data file is indexed, dBASE IV develops a list of records, with the record placed into order, based on the indexed field. In other words, the system makes a separate list of record numbers that corresponds to those records that appear in the desired order. When you search based on an indexed field, the system searches through the database using the index pointers, rather than searching through consecutively numbered records. For large data files, this can save considerable time, since the system is not required to scan through large portions of the database to find records in consecutive order. Indexing will be covered more thoroughly in Chapter 8.

The final option in the Go To menu is *Match capitalization*. This option tells dBASE IV whether it should look for exact matches of upper- and lowercase letters, or ignore the case of all letters when searching for a match. For example, a search instruction to find Murray's Records with *Match capitalization* set to NO would find MURRAY'S RECORDS, Murray's RECORDS, or any other record with the letters in the order of the example, regardless of which letters were uppercase and which were lowercase.

If you set *Match capitalization* to YES, the system will *only* find the records that exactly match the search specification. Thus, searching for Murray's Records with *Match capitalization* set to YES would only find Murray's Records, and would ignore MURRAY'S RECORDS, Murray's RECORDS, and any other record where the letters, but not the case, match the search specification.

In some databases, you may assign meaning to the use of case. In the current data file, for example, you may want to indicate which customers are headquarters offices, and which are franchises or branch stores. Although this can also be accomplished using a logical field (and would actually work more efficiently, since you can easily search for all records where a HQ Y/N entry is answered Y), you can differentiate the two types of locations by using all capital letters for headquarters offices, and mixed case for other locations.

In this way, if you are set to match capitalization, and only want to find a headquarters for Murray's Records, you would use MURRAY'S RECORDS as a search condition. Conversely, you could find the other locations, with *Match capitalization* set to YES, by searching for Murray's Records. *Match capitalization* makes an exact match of case, whether upper or lower.

Beginning a search is simple—press the first letter for the search type—**F** for Forward, **B** for Backward, **I** for Indexed (if available)—then type the search parameters. The search types can also be activated by moving the highlight on the GoTo menu to the search desired, and pressing **Enter**. The system will search in the desired direction, stopping when it reaches the first matching record.

To reactivate the search, in order to find the next matching instance, press **Shift-F4**. To find a previous match, press **Shift-F3**. The previous/next match searches can be used from any position in a database. However, you should be careful not to search for a previous match when you are at the beginning of your data file, or a next match when you are at the end. This is because, in early versions of dBASE IV, there would sometimes be significant delays when this was done.

Now that the menus have been discussed in detail, it's time to add some records. For ease of entry, return to the Edit menu (by pressing **F2**). This should bring you back to record number 1, Sam's Records. If not, use the **PgUp** key to move you up one screen at a time.

> **Note** If you have a large database, you may rapidly reach the first record by pressing the **Ctrl-PgUp** key combination. Similarly, to get to the last record, press **Ctrl-PgDn**.

With the cursor in record 1, for customer #1 (Sam's Records), you can again see how the completed record will look. Tab through the record, or press **PgDn** to move you to the next record. If you have already created a record 2, you will be brought into that record. Otherwise, when you move to the end of your last record, the screen will prompt you, asking if you want to create new records. Respond **Y** to the prompt, and a new record will be created for you.

The new record will already have a customer number inserted in the CUST_NUMB field, since you specified that this be done when you designed your form in Chapter 5. The rest of the fields should be blank. Next, enter the next set of records, in the order listed (to retain the correct record numbers):

CUSTOMER NAME:	Just Music
ADDRESS:	8791 Guitar Road
CITY:	Provo
STATE:	UT
ZIP CODE:	84601
PHONE:	801 555 8128
EXT:	225
ALTERNATE PHONE:	
EXT:	
CREDIT CARD TYPE:	V
EXP. DATE:	12/22/89
CARD NUMBER:	1234 5172 3199 1230

CUSTOMER NAME:	Discordant Discs
ADDRESS:	8911 Swamp Water Bl.
CITY:	Las Vegas
STATE:	NV
ZIP CODE:	89125
PHONE:	702 555 1234
EXT:	3322
ALTERNATE PHONE:	702 555 3322
EXT:	3322
CREDIT CARD TYPE:	A
EXP. DATE:	01/22/91
CARD NUMBER:	3724 999999 99999

CUSTOMER NAME: Other Vegas Music
ADDRESS: 8189 Albuquerque Rd
CITY: Las Vegas
STATE: NM
ZIP CODE: 87199
PHONE: 505 555 1892
EXT:
ALTERNATE PHONE:
EXT:
CREDIT CARD TYPE: V
EXP. DATE: 08/31/90
CARD NUMBER: 124-9912 9991 2221

CUSTOMER NAME: Where Else Audio
ADDRESS: 281 N.E. Southwest
CITY: Miami
STATE: FL
ZIP CODE: 33199
PHONE: 305 555 8911
EXT: 2881
ALTERNATE PHONE: 800 555 1219
EXT:
CREDIT CARD TYPE: V
EXP. DATE: 01/01/91
CARD NUMBER: 1299 2818 2222 2222

CUSTOMER NAME: The Musical Swamp
ADDRESS: 411 Pellagra Road
CITY: Clinton
STATE: IA
ZIP CODE: 52791
PHONE: 319 555 8299
EXT:
ALTERNATE PHONE:
EXT:
CREDIT CARD TYPE: M
EXP. DATE: 11/29/89
CARD NUMBER: 9912 8818 2811 9833

CUSTOMER NAME: The Singing Cow
ADDRESS: 7812 Bovine Blvd.
CITY: Trumbull
STATE: CT
ZIP CODE: 06611
PHONE: 203 555 2855
EXT: 7448

ALTERNATE PHONE:
EXT:
CREDIT CARD TYPE: M
EXP. DATE: 08/31/91
CARD NUMBER: 2855 7448 9999 9999

CUSTOMER NAME: Grandma's Disks & Tapes
ADDRESS: 1 Grandma Place
CITY: Grand Rapids
STATE: MI
ZIP CODE: 59409
PHONE: 616 555 6539
EXT:
ALTERNATE PHONE:
EXT:
CREDIT CARD TYPE: A
EXP. DATE: 11/11/90
CARD NUMBER: 3899 010101 00110

CUSTOMER NAME: The Music Source
ADDRESS: 98223 Polk Street
CITY: San Francisco
STATE: CA
ZIP CODE: 94105
PHONE: 415 555 7811
EXT: 44779
ALTERNATE PHONE:
EXT:
CREDIT CARD TYPE: V
EXP. DATE: 02/28/89
CARD NUMBER: 9999 1243 2299 9999

CUSTOMER NAME: DAT's CD
ADDRESS: 4280 Central #D4
CITY: Beverly Hills
STATE: CA
ZIP CODE: 90219
PHONE: 213 555 7424
EXT:
ALTERNATE PHONE:
EXT:
CREDIT CARD TYPE: A
EXP. DATE: 01/01/92
CARD NUMBER: 9981 929910 82991

Please note that all data in these records are entirely fictitious.

Once the ten records have been entered, return to the Control Center by pressing **Alt-E Enter** (confirming that you wish to exit, rather than transferring to Query Design). At this point it may be useful to see how the data is displayed in the ADDRESS screen. The cursor will still be in the SCREEN panel. Move the cursor to ADDRESS (or type **A** to select ADDRESS) and press **F2** to load the Edit screen.

When you open an Edit or Browse screen, dBASE IV automatically brings you into the field that was last edited. In this case, since you last entered customer number 10, this is the record that the system brings you into. Press **PgUp** five times to bring you to customer number 5, and then Exit to the Control Center.

Press **F2**, and you'll be brought back into record 5. The screen will look like Figure 6-9. In addition, you will see that dBASE IV only allows you to edit address information—the customer name and number fields don't allow editing. (Editing was locked out by setting *Editing allowed* in the *Edit options* screen of the Fields menu [by pressing **F5** from within a highlighted field] to NO). As stated in Chapter 5, this form can be useful for specific applications, such as address update, where it is not appropriate for changes to be made in customer name or number, and where additional information (such as credit card data) is not required.

If you switch to the Browse screen, by pressing **F2**, the cursor will be moved into the first field that may be edited, and will bring you into the current record, displayed in its present order. (Later, you'll see that indexing on the customer name puts the records out of numerical order.) You will also notice that prompts that you built into your screen design are displayed at the bottom of the Browse screen, as they are in the Edit screen. In addition, only the fields that can be edited will be shown in the Browse screen. Again, Exit from the current screen, returning to the Control Center.

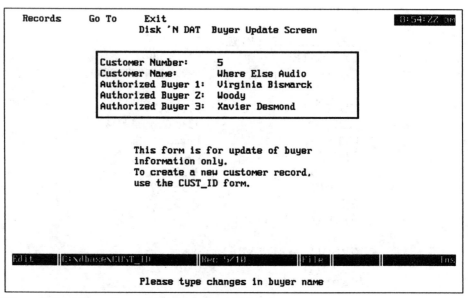

Figure 6-9   Buyer screen displays selected data.

You should now type the data for the BUYERS data file. To do this, return the cursor to the Data panel, select Buyers (by typing the first letters *BU* or moving the cursor to *Buyers* using the **Down Arrow** key) and press **F2** to open the Edit window. Next, add information for the following buyers:

CUST_NUMB: 1
BUYER_F_N: Sam
BUYER_L_N: Abbazabba
PHONE: 213 555 4408
EXTENSION:

CUST_NUMB: 2
BUYER_F_N: Jerome
BUYER_L_N: Justworthy
PHONE: 801 555 8128
EXTENSION: 225

CUST_NUMB: 2
BUYER_F_N: Martha
BUYER_L_N: Washington
PHONE: 801 555 8128
EXTENSION: 225

CUST_NUMB: 3
BUYER_F_N: Wally
BUYER_L_N: Wallace
PHONE: 702 555 1234
EXTENSION: 3322

CUST_NUMB: 3
BUYER_F_N: Amy
BUYER_L_N: Price
PHONE: 702 555 1234
EXTENSION: 3322

CUST_NUMB: 4
BUYER_F_N: Caroline
BUYER_L_N: Holt
PHONE: 505 555 1892
EXTENSION:

CUST_NUMB: 5
BUYER_F_N: Virginia
BUYER_L_N: Bismarck
PHONE: 305 555 8911
EXTENSION: 2881

CUST_NUMB: 5
BUYER_F_N: Woody
BUYER_L_N:
PHONE: 800 555 1219
EXTENSION:

CUST_NUMB: 5
BUYER_F_N: Xavier
BUYER_L_N: Desmond
PHONE: 800 555 1219
EXTENSION:

CUST_NUMB: 6
BUYER_F_N: Dusty
BUYER_L_N: Homburg
PHONE: 319 555 8299
EXTENSION:

CUST_NUMB: 7
BUYER_F_N: Bess
BUYER_L_N: Bullard
PHONE: 203 555 2855
EXTENSION: 7448

CUST_NUMB: 8
BUYER_F_N: Henrietta
BUYER_L_N: Goose
PHONE: 616 555 6539
EXTENSION:

CUST_NUMB: 8
BUYER_F_N: Charles
BUYER_L_N: Gosling
PHONE: 616 555 6539
EXTENSION:

CUST_NUMB: 8
BUYER_F_N: Thelma
BUYER_L_N: Drake
PHONE: 616 555 6539
EXTENSION:

CUST_NUMB: 9
BUYER_F_N: Slick
BUYER_L_N: Mitchell
PHONE: 415 555 7811
EXTENSION:

CUST_NUMB:	10
BUYER_F_N:	Megan
BUYER_L_N:	McYup
PHONE:	213 555 7424
EXTENSION:	

CUST_NUMB:	10
BUYER_F_N:	Ashley
BUYER_L_N:	Volvo
PHONE:	213 555 7424
EXTENSION:	

CUST_NUMB:	10
BUYER_F_N:	Brandon
BUYER_L_N:	Bonehead
PHONE:	213 555 7424
EXTENSION:	

Note It is a simple task to design an entry form that validates and formats your data for the BUYERS data file, and you may wish to develop such a form for this file.

Adding Records from Different Sources and Erasing Records

As you have seen, adding records to your database can be done from within a loaded screen design, simply by moving to the last record (by pressing **Ctrl-PgDn-PgDn** or by selecting *Add new records* from the Records menu). You have seen how to mark records for deletion from the data file, and how to unmark the records so that they aren't deleted.

However, there is more to dBASE IV than merely typing in new records. In some cases, you may want to bring in records that you created using a different database, spreadsheet, or word processor. Or you may want to add records to a master order data file that were entered by order entry operators using a number of computers. The process of adding records to your data file is called *appending* by dBASE IV. Files may be appended in a number of ways. The one way you've already seen is by typing records in at the end of your current data file.

The process of appending from other sources is performed from the *Modify structure/order* screen in the Forms panel. Move the cursor to the Forms panel, select CUST_ID, and press **Shft-F2** to quickly access the Modify screen. The opening screen, with your data structure displayed, looks like Figure 6-10.

The Organize menu will automatically be opened when you open the *Modify structure/order* screen. In Chapter 8, sorting and indexing will be covered. Unmarking and erasing marked records will be discussed shortly. Right now, the Append menu provides the area of interest. Move the cursor to the Append menu using the arrow keys.

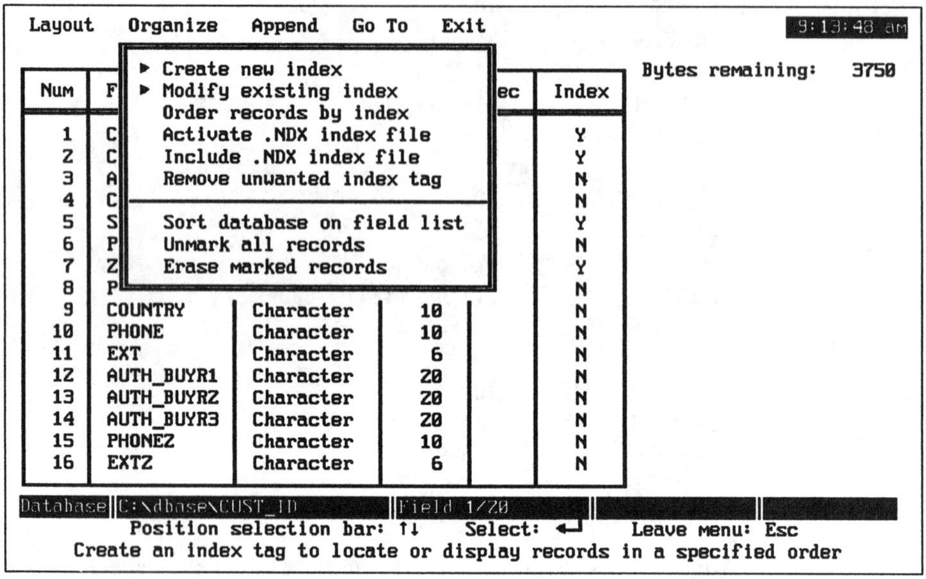

```
 Layout    Organize    Append    Go To    Exit                    9:13:48 am
┌─────────────────────────────────────────────────────────────────────────┐
│        ┌──────────────────────────────────┐                              │
│        │ ▶ Create new index               │        Bytes remaining:  3750│
│  Num   F│ ▶ Modify existing index         │ec │ Index │                  │
│        │   Order records by index         │   │       │                  │
│   1    C│   Activate .NDX index file       │   │   Y   │                  │
│   2    C│   Include .NDX index file        │   │   Y   │                  │
│   3    A│   Remove unwanted index tag      │   │   N   │                  │
│   4    C│                                  │   │   N   │                  │
│   5    S│   Sort database on field list    │   │   Y   │                  │
│   6    P│   Unmark all records             │   │   N   │                  │
│   7    Z│   Erase marked records           │   │   Y   │                  │
│   8    P└──────────────────────────────────┘   │   N   │                  │
│   9    COUNTRY       Character     10           │   N   │                  │
│  10    PHONE         Character     10           │   N   │                  │
│  11    EXT           Character      6           │   N   │                  │
│  12    AUTH_BUYR1    Character     20           │   N   │                  │
│  13    AUTH_BUYR2    Character     20           │   N   │                  │
│  14    AUTH_BUYR3    Character     20           │   N   │                  │
│  15    PHONE2        Character     10           │   N   │                  │
│  16    EXT2          Character      6           │   N   │                  │
│Database│C:\dbase\CUST_ID        │Field 1/20 │                             │
│      Position selection bar: ↑↓   Select: ⏎    Leave menu: Esc            │
│   Create an index tag to locate or display records in a specified order   │
└───────────────────────────────────────────────────────────────────────────┘
```

Figure 6-10   Modify structure/order opening screen.

The Append menu looks like Figure 6-11. It provides three options: *Enter records from keyboard*, *Append records from dBASE file*, and *Copy records from non-dBASE file*.

The first option, *Enter records from keyboard*, is essentially identical to what you've already done. Selecting the option brings you into the Edit screen, with the

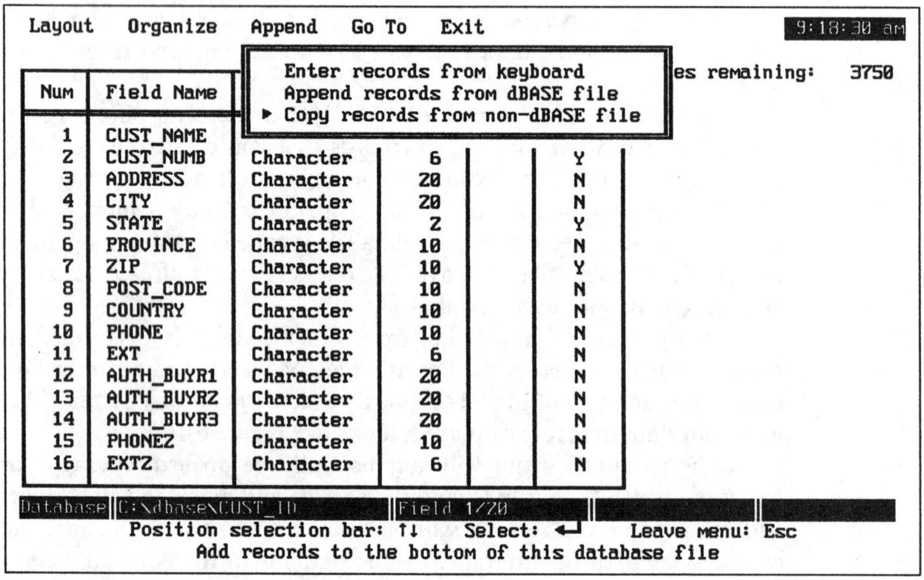

```
 Layout    Organize    Append    Go To    Exit                    9:18:30 am
┌─────────────────────────────────────────────────────────────────────────┐
│              ┌──────────────────────────────────────┐                     │
│              │   Enter records from keyboard         │es remaining:  3750 │
│  Num   Field │   Append records from dBASE file      │                    │
│              │ ▶ Copy records from non-dBASE file    │                    │
│   1    CUST_NAME                                                          │
│   2    CUST_NUMB    Character      6            │   Y   │                  │
│   3    ADDRESS      Character     20            │   N   │                  │
│   4    CITY         Character     20            │   N   │                  │
│   5    STATE        Character      2            │   Y   │                  │
│   6    PROVINCE     Character     10            │   N   │                  │
│   7    ZIP          Character     10            │   Y   │                  │
│   8    POST_CODE    Character     10            │   N   │                  │
│   9    COUNTRY      Character     10            │   N   │                  │
│  10    PHONE        Character     10            │   N   │                  │
│  11    EXT          Character      6            │   N   │                  │
│  12    AUTH_BUYR1   Character     20            │   N   │                  │
│  13    AUTH_BUYR2   Character     20            │   N   │                  │
│  14    AUTH_BUYR3   Character     20            │   N   │                  │
│  15    PHONE2       Character     10            │   N   │                  │
│  16    EXT2         Character      6            │   N   │                  │
│Database│C:\dbase\CUST_ID        │Field 1/20 │                             │
│      Position selection bar: ↑↓   Select: ⏎    Leave menu: Esc            │
│          Add records to the bottom of this database file                  │
└───────────────────────────────────────────────────────────────────────────┘
```

Figure 6-11   The Append menu.

currently active screen displayed. It is important to note that the currently active screen is displayed, since you (or a user who selects this option) may be allowed to add data that isn't filtered for accuracy.

A potential problem occurs when you have chosen to use a data file by selecting the file from within the Data panel. The Data panel is used to design your data file; the Forms, Reports, and Labels panels are used for adding the validation and display features that make the data useful, valuable, and most important, valid. Thus, if you had opened a file from within the Data panel, or had jumped into the Modify screen by selecting the file and pressing **Shft-F2**, then **F2** to go to the Browse/Edit screens, you would wind up with a screen that displays your data as it appears in your data design. The intelligence that the designed screens provide would not be available, and you could end up with invalid data.

Thus, before you select *Modify structure/order* (or press **Shft-F2** to move immediately into the Database design panel), you should be sure that you have selected the screen form that applies the proper filters and options to your data. To do this in the present example, exit from this screen (press **Alt-E-A** to return to the Control Center). Next, move the cursor back to the Forms panel, highlight CUST_ID (the form you wish to use), press **F2** to load the form, then exit back to the Control Center. Finally, return the cursor to the Data panel, again making sure that CUST_ID is highlighted, and press **Shft-F2**. You can now be sure that the features you implemented in your Forms design will be applied to data that you may add from the Append menu.

The example shown here points out a problem with appending data into a data screen that uses automatic features like the one implemented to automatically assign customer numbers to each new file as it is added to the data file. You will recall that in Chapter 5, you used a special picture function that automatically checked the CUST_ NUMB field to see if it contained a value, and inserted the record number if no value was found.

When you append data from another data file, you are unable to apply the data filters and special input functions that are available for manual input. The system will allow you to add new files—files that may possibly provide duplicate values for fields where a unique value is required. For example, the file that you are appending from may have a customer number 3. Your data file already has a customer number 3.

dBASE IV will allow you to add record 3 from your secondary data file, and will not be able to detect the duplication of numbers when you are adding it. Although the total number of records will be correct, it will not reflect the possibility of duplicate "unique" records.

You may, of course, append from a file that has no CUST_NUMB field, or lacks values in the CUST_NUMB field. However, with the current design, you are not able to edit the values in the CUST_NUMB field. Thus, to change or add numbers to the CUST NUMB field, you will have to open a different FORMS design or will have to close, and then reopen, the Data panel, without the CUST_ID Form screen activated.

The third option in the Append window, *Copy records from non-dBASE file*, will be discussed in the next chapter, which deals with the import and export of data. The final edit option to be discussed in this chapter is how to deal with marked records.

At the bottom of the Organize menu, two options are available that deal with the erasure of records in your data file. The last option, *Erase marked records*, is used to remove records from your database that you have marked for deletion from within the

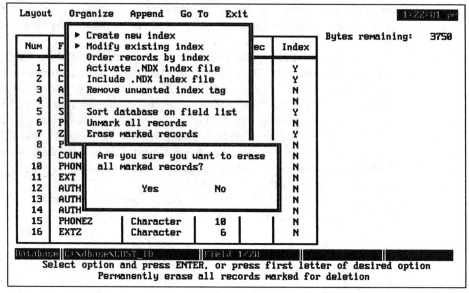

Figure 6-12   Last chance to cancel erasure of marked files.

Edit or Browse windows. You will recall that one of the options in the Records menu was a field that toggled between *Mark record for deletion* and *Clear deletion mark*.

A record may be marked for deletion for a number of reasons. You may have appended a number of duplicate records and want to remove the duplicates to streamline the database and to prevent the confusion that could result once changes are made to one of many duplicate files. Marking a record for deletion sets a special mark the system can read later that is used to indicate a record to be deleted.

From within the Query facility, you may also select records that meet certain conditions for deletion. For example, you may delete records of customers who have not ordered for more than 24 months. The actual deletions are performed from within the Organize menu. When you select *Erase marked records*, dBASE IV gives you one last chance to change your mind, popping a prompt on the screen, shown in Figure 6-12.

If you answer **Y**, dBASE IV will go through your file, erasing the marked records from the file, and will then reindex the file in the order you established when you designed it. Once erased, those records should be considered lost from the system and unrecoverable.

The other option, *Unmark all records*, is a convenient method of removing the erasure indicator from the records in your data file. This is a much faster and easier way to unmark records than attempting to do so on a record by record basis. Typically, your marked records will probably not be consecutively ordered in your data file. When you select the *Unmark all records* option, dBASE IV will automatically go through your entire file and delete the Erase mark from those records that you selected for deletion.

7

Import and Export

In Chapter 6, you were shown how to enter data and update your files. In this chapter, you'll see how to *import* and *export* your data. "import" and "export" are terms used to indicate *bringing in* data from other sources (other database programs, spreadsheets, word processors, or any character editors), or *sending out* data from dBASE IV to the numerous other programs that may be able to work with your data.

The meaning of the terms is obvious, and they are used relative to dBASE IV. For example, although you may be sharing data with Lotus 1-2-3, when you bring data from Lotus into dBASE IV you are *importing* it into dBASE IV. The data that has been imported into dBASE IV has been *exported* out of Lotus 1-2-3. The point here is that import or export is all relative; you import data into an application and export it out of an application.

In this chapter, "import" will mean bringing data into dBASE IV from another application. "export" will mean moving data from dBASE IV to another application.

The previous chapter showed how to append data from a dBASE IV data file. In a sense, you were importing from one data file into your currently active file. In that case, you brought the records in through the Append menu in the Modify Data design screen. In addition to importing via the Append menu, you may also import and export files through the Tools menu in the main Control Center screen.

Importing Files

There is a clear difference between the Import function in the Tools menu and importing via the Append menu. When records are imported using the Append menu, the data is inserted into a file that already has all required fields defined. The field names, field lengths, field types, and other field parameters are defined, and you are bringing in data that is supposed to match your predefined data file structure.

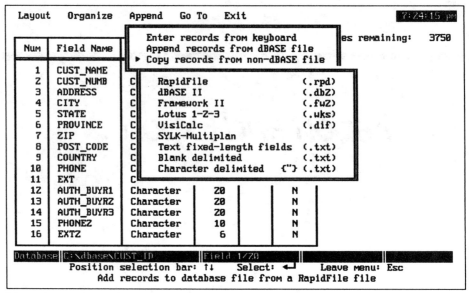

Figure 7-1   Import file sources for appending to a file.

As can be seen in Figure 7-1, data can be appended to your file from a wide range of data sources.

Importing from the Tools Menu

When you import using the Tools menu, you are bringing in an entire data file, rather than preformatted data. dBASE IV converts the data files that are imported through the Tools menu into a dBASE IV file with varying degrees of compatibility. Unlike importing to Append a file, importing from the Tools menu requires dBASE IV to create a new file structure. dBASE IV can understand and convert only a limited number of data sources. These sources are shown in Figure 7-2.

To import a data file via the Tools menu, open the Tools menu, select *Import* (by pressing **I** or moving the highlight to *Import* and pressing **Enter**), and select the source for the data file. Once your source type is selected, dBASE IV will bring up a panel showing your current disk structure and all files that match the file extension indicated next to the file type. The system is asking you to tell it which file you want to import. For example, in Figure 7-3, RapidFile was selected as the import source, and dBASE IV attempted to bring up all files with the .RPD extension.

Using methods shown earlier in this book, you may move to the appropriate drive or directory, and select the file that you wish to import. Once the file is selected, dBASE IV suggests a name for the dBASE IV file that will be created. This name will normally be the same as that of your source file, with a new extension (.DBF). The **.DBF** extension is the standard file extension for dBASE IV files.

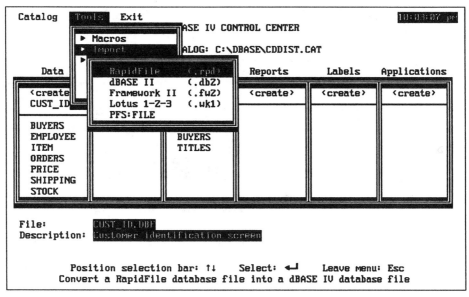

Figure 7-2   Data sources for complete file import via Tools menu.

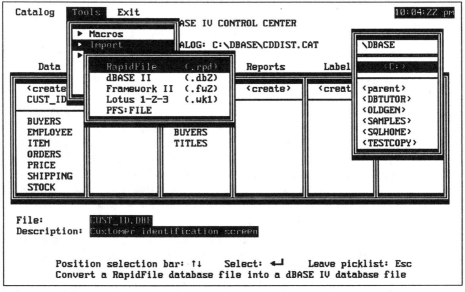

Figure 7-3   Import File selection panel looks for correct extension.

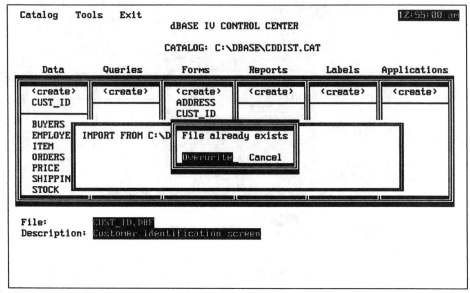

Figure 7-4   dBASE IV prompts when a duplicate target name is chosen.

Before saying Yes to the new name, you should be careful that it does not already match one in use in your current data directory. Although dBASE IV is designed to prevent duplication of filenames, it is prudent to not have to rely upon dBASE IV to trap an error of this type.

Once you have selected the source file, and chosen a name for the new dBASE IV file that is to be created from the imported file, the system will issue a command to import the data file. This command will be seen in a window on the screen. If the filename is already in use, the system will tell you that the target filename already exists. This prompt and the underlying import command are seen in Figure 7-4.

If you don't want to overwrite a target file, you have two basic options. From within DOS, or within the DOS shell accessible from the Tools menu, you can rename either the source file or the target file. In the example shown in Figure 7-4, a file named CUST_ID.RPD was to be imported, and would have produced a dBASE IV file called CUST_ID.DBF. The problem was that a file called CUST_ID.DBF was already on the directory. To resolve the conflict between filenames, you could have renamed the source (or imported) file to something like CUST_ID2.RPD, which would have created a file called CUST_ID2.DBF; or you could have renamed the conflicting dBASE IV file (possibly calling it CUST_ID2.DBF).

When a file is imported, it copies many of the fields and the related data. It also creates the basic data structure, creating a data record that is closely related to or (depending upon the source file type) identical to the original source file. Depending upon the source, however, not all data fields or field names will be copied over into the dBASE IV file. Thus, you should check the data file that is created during an import in order to see which fields lose their names or values. (You can use the Modify menu to rename fields so that they match those of the source file).

In order to import a dBASE II file, you must change the file extension of the data file from .DBF to .DB2. Unless the extension is changed, dBASE IV will be unable to recognize the file as a dBASE II file, and will try to treat it as a dBASE III or III + file, resulting in errors when the file is imported. You should also be careful not to overwrite your dBASE II source file when the file is imported. (Remember that your dBASE II file was originally a .DBF file, and that the new dBASE IV file is also a .DBF file.) In some cases, creating a new subdirectory on your disk for importing and exporting may be a good way to avoid the risk of corrupting or deleting files in your active dBASE directories.

Importing from the Append Menu

From within the Append menu in the Modify Data screen, you have somewhat different options. The menu shown in Figure 7-1 allows you to import data from a large number of PC applications, including spreadsheets, database programs, word processors, and text editors. Importing from the Tools menu is automatic, since dBASE IV is able to read the source data file and create a new data file structure with fields already defined and known delimiters. The number of applications whose data can be imported from within the Import menu in the Tools panel is limited to those applications with file structures that dBASE IV can readily understand.

The Append menu inside the Modify Data design screen is somewhat different in the way an imported file is created. More options are provided in the Append menu than in the Tools Import menu, but that is because in the Append menu, you have already defined a data structure into which the data will be inserted.

The top options in the menu box are the same as those in the Tools Import menu. dBASE IV knows the structure of these files and can easily add them at the end of your data file. The other options are different, relating to files that may be structured in a number of different ways. In order to append these files to the end of your data file, you must tell dBASE IV how each field is separated from the next, and how the file shows the end of each record.

In this case, you should be certain that your source file (containing the data to be imported) contains fields that appear in the same order as they are listed in the dBASE IV file. Although it is preferable to have field widths that match the widths of the comparable fields in dBASE IV, this is not essential in the last three file types, which use a special type of character to indicate the end of one data field and the beginning of another.

If your source files feature fields that are larger than those in dBASE IV, the data will either be ignored by dBASE IV and will not be imported into the dBASE IV file or, in the case of the text source file with fixed-length fields, will completely throw off the import process.

The last three file types, all of which require the *.txt* extension, are basically text files that are used as sources for your data. These files can be created by most word processors or text editors, and can often be created by other data management and spreadsheet programs. If you have performed "mailmerge" printing of documents from your word processor, you've probably worked with text fields that are delimited in one of the ways listed here. Or, if you've worked with data or spreadsheet applications that use their own file formats (and which are incompatible with dBASE), you may have had to generate data output referred to by names such as "ASCII" or "text" or "character."

The important thing with text files is that the fields must be in the same order as those in the dBASE IV file into which data will be imported, and must be properly delimited. A delimiter is a character that tells dBASE IV that one field has ended, and the next one begins. In each case, the carriage return character indicates the end of each record.

Text Fixed-Length Fields The first type of delimited file structure, *text fixed-length fields*, uses field length to indicate the end of one field and beginning of the next. In this case, there really is no delimiter. When data is appended from a text fixed-length file, dBASE IV counts the characters in the source file, and plugs the exact number of characters into the dBASE IV file. For example, if you were creating a simple database with a 10-character FIRST_NAME field, and a 15-character LAST_NAME field, the source file should have records that are 25 characters wide. When the data is imported, the first 10 characters will be automatically inserted into the FIRST_NAME field, and the next 15 will go into the LAST_NAME field, once you've told the system the field widths.

In most cases, the first names will not all be 10 characters long, nor will the last names all be 15 characters long. When the entry into a field is shorter than the field width that has been defined, in a fixed-length field data file, you must insert blank spaces after each field entry in order to provide the correct width for the import to work properly. An error in field length will result in part of a first name becoming part of a last name, or part of a last name becoming part of a first name, or part of one record becoming part of another record. (In our example, which required record lengths of 25 characters, a record having 24 characters will be imported, including the first character of the following record as the 25th character of the preceding record.)

Blank Delimited These records use the blank to indicate the end of one field and beginning of the next. If possible, text fixed-length or character delimited fields would be preferable as sources. Although blanks may work fine in most cases, when the system comes to a value that is two words (for example, Los Angeles or Santa Monica), dBASE IV will treat each word as a separate field. To import data from fields that include spaces, you should replace the blank character in the source file with a character other than the blank. For example, you can make Los Angeles into Los_Angeles or Santa Monica into Santa_Monica and overcome the problem. From inside dBASE IV, you can then edit the files and replace the underline characters with blanks.

Character Delimited These fields provide the most flexibility. An ASCII character, typically the comma, is used to tell the system that the data for your field has been completed. It is also used to indicate a blank field. When data is imported from a blank delimited field, all characters preceding a comma are read into the first field. When the comma is reached, all characters between the first comma and the second comma are read into the next field, and so on.

In records that use fields that don't always have data entered, the presence of a comma indicates that the system should move from one field to the next. For example, in a data structure that consists of LAST_NAME, MID_INIT (middle initial), and FIRST_NAME, a name without a middle initial would be listed in the source database as, say, Brownstein,,Mark. When the file is imported, it will read Brownstein into the LAST_NAME field, see the comma, and move on to the next field.

The second field is empty. When the system encounters the second comma, it skips to the third field, reading Mark into the FIRST_NAME data field. In many databases, fields may frequently be left empty. The comma provides the system with the ability to detect when each field's data has been completed, even if the field is left blank.

In addition to the comma, used as a delimiter, quotation marks or other ASCII characters can perform other functions for import. Character strings, such as those used for first name, last name, and street address, are usually surrounded by quotation marks, to indicate that the data is a character, rather than a numeric or logical string. The quotation mark is especially useful when a character string contains commas.

A law firm called Eenie, Meenie, Minie and Mo would cause dBASE IV to jump from field to field if there was no way to indicate that the commas were part of the field's data, rather than an end of field indicator. By storing the entry as ''Eenie, Meenie, Minie and Mo'', with quotation marks surrounding the text entry, dBASE IV knows that commas in the string between the quotation marks are to be treated as part of a single data field, rather than as an indication to move to the next field.

When such data is imported, the quotation marks are stripped out by dBASE IV, leaving only Eenie, Meenie, Minie and Mo as the contents of the data field. In the case of a name that includes quotation marks, a simple method tells dBASE IV to include the quotation marks as part of the character string.

The case where you want to use a name or other data field value that is normally surrounded by a quotation mark requires special handling. dBASE IV recognizes the second quotation mark as the end of the field value. Thus, the name Jay Danforth ''Dan'' Quayle would pose a problem to dBASE IV. If you were to write the text string as ''Jay Danforth ''Dan'' Quayle'', dBASE IV would read only Jay Danforth, stopping at the second quotation mark. A common method to work around this limitation is to use the single quotation mark ' to surround text that uses embedded quotation marks.

In case that you do not wish to use a quotation mark to enclose character strings, dBASE IV allows you to select the character used in your source file to accomplish the string definition function. The character can be changed by selecting *Character delimited* from the menu and pressing **Enter**, then scrolling through the ASCII table and selecting with the **Enter** key, or typing the appropriate character.

In a character delimited file, the comma separates fields or indicates empty fields. The carriage return character indicates the end of a record. This is the preferred method for importing, when one of the other, standard structures such as Lotus, RapidFile, or SYLK-Multiplan is not available.

The options at the top of the file format selection window assume that your source file uses the same structure as the file you are importing into. Care should be taken to see that this is so. When you append from these other data formats, the data is read from the source file and placed into fields that were defined when you designed the data file you are appending into. It is important to see that there is a consistency between the source file and the file being appended into.

To copy a dBASE II file so that it can be appended to dBASE IV, issue the following commands at the DOS prompt (you must exit dBASE IV or go to DOS from within the DOS panel of the Tools menu), substituting the name of the actual file for FILENAME.

COPY FILENAME.DBF FILENAME.DB2

You would, of course, use the directory and path information, if appropriate. It may also be wise to set up a different directory into which to save your converted .DB2 files. The directory may also be useful if you wish to export files from dBASE IV into dBASE II. Assuming that you had three directories, **dbase** (for dBASE IV files and the program), **dbase2** (containing the dBASE II program and files), and **dbcopy** (for files that will be moved between dBASE IV and dBASE II), the command to copy a dBASE II file called FILENAME to the temporary directory for Import into dBASE IV would look like this:

COPY C:\dbase2\filename.dbf c:\dbcopy\filename.db2

The intermediate directory will prove useful for storing files that will be imported into dBASE IV, as well as for files that were exported from dBASE IV for use in your dBASE II system. (Although it is probably unlikely that you'll continue to use dBASE II, once you've gotten dBASE IV, there may be a few users who are still working with dBASE II on old CP/M-based computer systems.)

The use of an intermediate directory for holding files that are being converted to or from, rather than doing conversions directly in your application's main file directory, is a method that may help to retain the integrity of your data. It is always prudent to make any changes to a *copy* of your original file, in case the change is not what is expected, or something happens during the conversion that damages your original files. In fact, the use of a temporary file to do your conversions into and out of is highly recommended when making conversions from any application into or out of dBASE IV.

In spite of the flexibility and wide range of source options provided by dBASE IV, in some instances the application that contains data you want to bring into a dBASE file cannot be put into a form that can be imported into dBASE IV. For example, some time management programs use their own data structures and are designed so that the data can't be exported. Although you can print out reports and other documents based on the data, you aren't able to read the data files into any other application or data management program.

Another possible scenario is one in which you want to get information from data on a mainframe. However, mainframe data is stored using a different coding scheme (PCs use a scheme called ASCII, while mainframes use something called EBCDIC). Although EBCDIC can be translated to ASCII, the data files on a mainframe may be much larger than the data that you actually want to import.

A product called Extract, from a company called Datatrope, can be used to create data files from such seemingly incompatible sources. In order to use Extract you must produce a report from your source application that is saved on disk as an ASCII file. In most cases, the source applications (including those on a mainframe) can produce an ASCII character stream that is intended for the printer, but can be saved to a disk. A saved ASCII character report can be read by Extract and converted into a .DBF or delimited file. Although Extract may be unable to produce database files from every type of output, the program does an impressive job with most reports and should be considered a valuable adjunct to dBASE IV in situations where you need to work with a data file, but are unable to get the source data file.

The *Append records from dBASE file* option allows you to add new records to an already existing data file. Many database systems frequently use this capability. In the case of order entry or file update, for example, you may have order takers, or update entry operators, or others, who are adding records on a daily basis. When a new order is taken, a new record is made for each item ordered. There may be little need to add the records to a much larger data file that contains all the orders for the last week, month, or year. In such a case, historical data and the ability for an order entry or data update clerk to find one of thousands of orders may not be required for the current task at hand, and loading an entire large database file so that records can be added would be a waste of disk space, and could wind up adding delays to the system, as dBASE IV attempts to reindex each new entry.

A daily order entry form (or other data update forms for real-time data entry) would be useful in such a situation. You may have many order takers, with each working on a version of the daily update file. At the end of the day, you can append the data records from each update station's daily order file to the main order data file, using the *Append records from dBASE file* option. When this option is selected, dBASE IV reads the data from matching fields, and plugs each record into a new database record.

The final option in the Append menu, *Enter records from keyboard* opens a data entry screen, bringing the cursor into a new record beyond the end of the existing data file. (In other words, this command brings the cursor to the bottom of the database and opens a new record to which you can then add your records.)

Exporting Files

Files are normally saved in standard dBASE IV format, and many other applications are able to read these files. However, there are some differences in the way a dBASE IV file is produced and the way that dBASE III and dBASE III+ files are written. Without getting into specifics, it should be pointed out that dBASE III and some compatible programs that are able to read dBASE III data files may have problems reading dBASE IV data files because of these differences, which are related to indexing capabilities and to memo fields in dBASE IV.

dBASE IV's ability to export data in a variety of formats can be quite valuable and provides significant flexibility for providing data that can be used by other programs. Export operations are set up from within the Export menu that is accessed from within the Tools menu. To open the Export menu, return the cursor to one of the

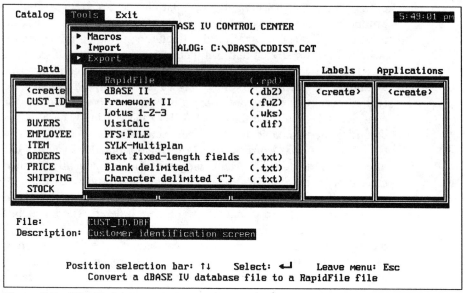

Figure 7-5   The Export menu.

panels and press **Alt-T** to bring up the Tools menu. From within the Tools menu, press **E** to select the Export menu. The Export menu looks like Figure 7-5.

The options are similar to those provided by the Append menu in the Database design screen, except that the options are for Export, rather than Import. A wider range of applications can be exported from the Tools panel than can be imported to it, since the files you are exporting already have a defined data structure and format. Converting these data files for export is a relatively simple task for dBASE IV, since the formats are already known to the system.

The first five target file options provide you with a default file extension for the exported file. When you select one of these export file options, dBASE IV opens a window for selecting the file that you wish to export. This can be seen in Figure 7-5. To select a file, move the cursor so that the file you wish to export is highlighted, or type the first letters of the data filename. In this screen, you can only select files in the currently active catalog for exporting. Thus, you will not be able to change drives or directories, since the catalog already handles the task of file selection.

Documents that have descriptions attached will also show the description in a file description window in the middle of the screen, directly below the Export option box. Once you have chosen a file to export, press **Enter**, and dBASE IV will export the file to the format you designated, with the exception of the last option, *Character delimited*.

For *Character delimited* exports, you must select the character that will be used to indicate the beginning and end of a character field. In most applications, the quotation marks ", with a hex value of 22, are the character used as a delimiter. Only in rare instances would you have to change the character delimiter. The use of the quotation mark (or another character) to delimit (mark the beginning and end of) a text field was discussed earlier in the section on importing data.

PFS: FILE data files use the same data extension as used by dBASE IV (.DBF). Inside of PFS:Professional File, import and export capabilities can convert dBASE IV files to PFS:Professional File, and export to dBASE IV files. However, during testing of the crossover capabilities between the two programs, there appeared to be incompatibilities. It is strongly suggested that, if you must make the transfers, they be tried on data files that have been thoroughly backed up, in case of changes made to either file that may make it unusable by dBASE IV or PFS:Professional File.

The three character-based export conversions that use the *.txt* file extension carry potential to cause a minor problem, if you will ever need to export to more than one format. When you select one of the three export formats, dBASE IV will create an export file that matches your parameters, and uses the *.txt* file extension.

When dBASE IV writes the new file, it uses the name of the source file, substituting the .txt extension for the .dbf in the original (source file), while also making the conversions required by the target mode. If a file has already been saved with the target name or extension, dBASE IV will issue a prompt, shown in Figure 7-6, that asks whether you want to overwrite the target file. If you answer *Yes* to the prompt, dBASE IV will export your file, deleting the file with the same name that has already been created.

Allowing the system to overwrite a file causes the new data to write over the original file. Once this is done, you will be unable to restore the data in the overwitten file. If you wish to export a file in more than one manner that creates a file with the *.txt*

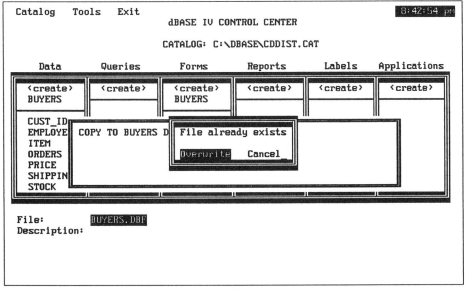

Figure 7-6   The system prompts to confirm overwriting exported file.

extension, you should take care to copy the exported files from the dBASE IV directory to the directory that your application is installed on, in order to avoid overwriting your file. If you want to overwrite your file, press **O** or press **Enter** to accept the default. To cancel an overwrite, press **C** to cancel the operation or move the highlight to *Cancel* and press **Enter**.

Conclusion

In this chapter, importing and exporting of data files has been discussed. In addition, a new program that allows the importing of data from applications that don't create data files which can be imported was also discussed. Future chapters will explore the functionalities provided by dBASE IV for analyzing, searching, reporting on, and creating applications using the data that you create or bring into dBASE IV.

8

Sorting and Indexing

The preceding chapter explored importing and exporting data files. Earlier, you designed a database, developed the data entry (which can also be used to view your data according to the screen design), and entered data into the application data files that will be used in this book.

In this chapter, you'll see two of the ways dBASE IV can manipulate the data and learn when you should use the Sort instead of the Index capabilities of dBASE IV.

Sorting versus Indexing

Although the concepts of Sorting and Indexing may seem very similar—both put the data into a predefined order—there are significant differences between the two, as far as dBASE IV and most other database management programs are concerned. Both Sorting and Indexing are accessed from within the Organize menu in the Edit, Browse, and Database Modify screens.

To see this menu, select CUST_ID and press **Shft-F2** to bring up the Modify data design screen. This also, by default, opens the Organize menu. The Organize menu is shown in Figure 8-1. (If the top half of the menu, which deals with indexing, appears to dominate this window, the reason is that indexing is much more frequently used by most users of dBASE IV than sorting is.)

Sorting and indexing are used to put your data into a desired order. When you create your data records, most entries will be relatively random. The records you will be putting into the system won't, of themselves, be automatically in alphabetic order or in order by state, ZIP code, or any other desired order, unless you are copying from a list that has already been put into order.

Although your data may be in your data files in a random order, it is usually much more useful when you are able to look at it as if it were entered in a specific order. In

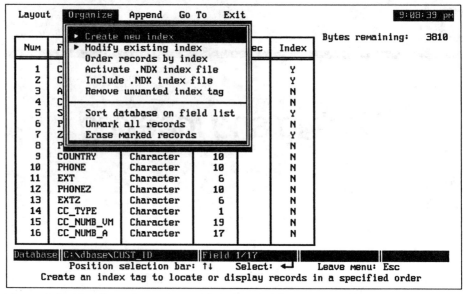

Figure 8-1 The Organize menu, with Index and Sort capabilities.

the CUST_ID data file, for example, it would be valuable to have all the customers listed in alphabetic order. In the TITLES data file, it would be of value to have the titles listed in alphabetic order. It may also be useful to have them listed by date of first release, or in order alphabetically by category.

You may also want to see your records sorted in ZIP code order. This type of ordering simplifies the assignment of routes to sales people, and can also save substantial amounts of money if you plan to send out bulk mailings, since the postal service offers a lower rate for mail that has been presorted by ZIP code. With dBASE IV, such lists are easily made.

Although sorting and indexing can provide you with a way to view your files in a particular order, there are significant differences between the two processes. The CUST_ID file will provide a basic model for the two processes. Sorting will be less frequently used than indexing, but will be discussed first, so that the rest of the chapter can explore indexing more fully.

Sorting

When you sort a data file, you are creating a new file that contains all the records, placed into order as defined in your sort definition. For example, if you wanted to create a data file that had all customers alphabetically listed, in order, by ZIP code, you could do this using the Sort command. Sorting will create a data file that has all the records in correct order, based on the order you define when you begin the sort.

This new data file can then be used for mailmerge letters or labels, and can be exported to other applications that need the files to be in a particular order. If you are creating a file that will be used by an application that is unable to do its own sorting, the dBASE IV Sort option will allow you to make such a presorted file.

To begin creating your sorted file, go to the Data panel and highlight CUST_ID. Press **Shft-F2** to open the Modify window. The Organize panel will be displayed. Move the cursor to *Sort database on field list* and press **Enter**, or press **S** to open the Sort definition window.

When first opened, the Sort definition screen looks like Figure 8-2.

At the left side of the window is a column labelled *Field order.* This column is used to set the order in which your files will be sorted. The number of fields that can be sorted on are limited only by the number of fields.

Sort order is hierarchical; that is, the first field will be the controlling sort field. If you want to sort on name and ZIP code, setting the name field first, followed by the ZIP code field, the system will produce records for the first name. Within that list, dBASE IV will put the records for each name in order by ZIP code. If you have six John Smiths, for example, such an ordered scheme will put all John Smiths into ZIP code order, then go on to the next name.

Note > Sorting by ZIP code first, and then by name will produce a more useful file. For each ZIP code, the sorted files will then be in order alphabetically.

In other words, sorting is performed in the order in which the sort fields are entered into the field order. In an actual application, all records in ZIP Code 10001 would be sorted, with the names put into alphabetic order. Next, all records in ZIP code 10002 (or the next valid value) would be sorted, with names put into alphabetic order, and so on.

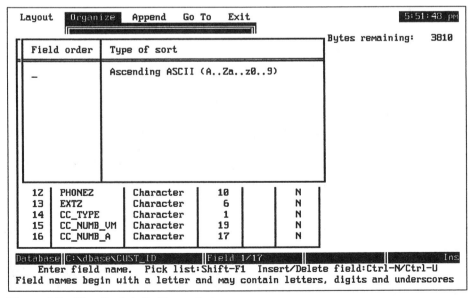

Figure 8-2 The Sort definition window.

Sort Types

There are four basic types of sort for text fields: *Ascending ASCII*, *Ascending Dictionary*, *Descending ASCII*, and *Descending Dictionary*. These sort types deal with the way text and numbers are ordered when sorted.

Earlier versions of dBASE could perform ascending and descending ASCII sorts, but were not able to perform a new form of sort, called a ''dictionary sort,'' that is included in dBASE IV. ASCII sorts are easier on the system to perform, since dBASE assigns strict numeric order to the ASCII characters.

An Ascending sort goes from **A** to **Z**, then from lowercase **a** to lowercase **z**, and finally from **0** through **9**. A descending sort goes from lowercase **z** to lowercase **a**, from uppercase **Z** through uppercase **A**, and from **9** through **0**.

Thus from the following list,

APPLE

apple

ZEBRA

zebra

an Ascending ASCII sort would put the field values in the following order:

APPLE

ZEBRA

apple

zebra

A Descending sort would work in opposite order:

zebra

apple

ZEBRA

APPLE

A dictionary sort, on the other hand, sorts numbers and letters in much the same way that a dictionary would sort them. Field values starting with capital letters would be sorted before those fields starting with lowercase letters, but lowercase characters would not be passed over while capital letters were being sorted.

In the preceding list, the sort order for an ascending sort would be as follows:

APPLE

apple

ZEBRA

zebra

A descending dictionary sort would work in the opposite direction, with lowercase characters sorted before their uppercase counterparts. A descending dictionary sort would run from zZ to zA and 9 to 0.

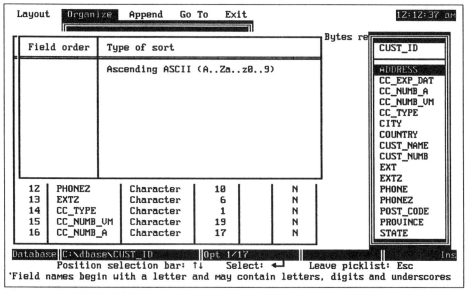

Figure 8-3   Field pick list.

The Example

To select a field to sort, type the name of the field in the *Field order* panel, or press **Shft-F1** to bring down a list of fields in the data file. A pick list showing all fields in the active database file will be shown in a window at the right side of the screen. The pick list for this data file looks like Figure 8-3.

Select ZIP, using one of the methods already discussed. The field name will be placed in the *Field order* panel. Press **Tab** to move to the *Type of sort* option panel. To see the four options for text, press the **Spacebar** to toggle through the options. When *Ascending Dictionary* is shown, press **Enter**. A new line will be added to the sort order list. Next, select the CUST_NAME field (using the pick list or by typing the name into the panel), and choose *Ascending Dictionary* sort for this field also. Press **Enter** to complete the selection. The cursor will move to the next line. Your screen, with sort parameters for the two fields that you will be sorting on defined, looks like Figure 8-4.

To finish specifying your sort criteria and to begin creation of a new file, press **Enter** when your cursor is positioned in a blank *Field order* panel. dBASE IV will pop a window on screen that asks you to name the new file that will be created. Type *custsort* to name the file. Press **Enter** to tell dBASE IV to begin sorting your file.

A new window will appear on screen, indicating that dBASE IV is sorting the file, and showing the progress made so far. *For a large data file, this can take a considerable amount of time.* When dBASE IV is finished sorting the file, a new window will appear on screen, asking for a description of the file. Type *Customers sorted by ZIP and name*. Press **Enter** to complete the sorting process.

At this point, you have created a sorted file based on the currently open data file. dBASE IV does not open the new, sorted file. The file that you used as the source for

Layout Organize Append Go To Exit
4:56:46 am
Bytes remaining: 3810
Field order | Type of sort
ZIP | Ascending Dictionary (Aa..Zz0..9)
CUST_NAME | Ascending Dictionary (Aa..Zz0..9)
Ascending ASCII (A..Za..z0..9)
12 PHONE2 Character 10 N
13 EXT2 Character 6 N
14 CC_TYPE Character 1 N
15 CC_NUMB_VM Character 19 N
16 CC_NUMB_A Character 17 N
Database C:\dbase\CUST_ID Ins
Enter field name. Pick list:Shift-F1 Insert/Delete field:Ctrl-N/Ctrl-U
Field names begin with a letter and may contain letters, digits and underscores

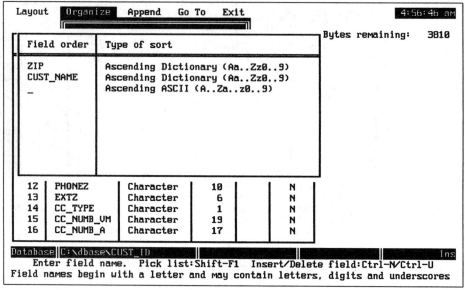

Figure 8-4 Sort parameters defined.

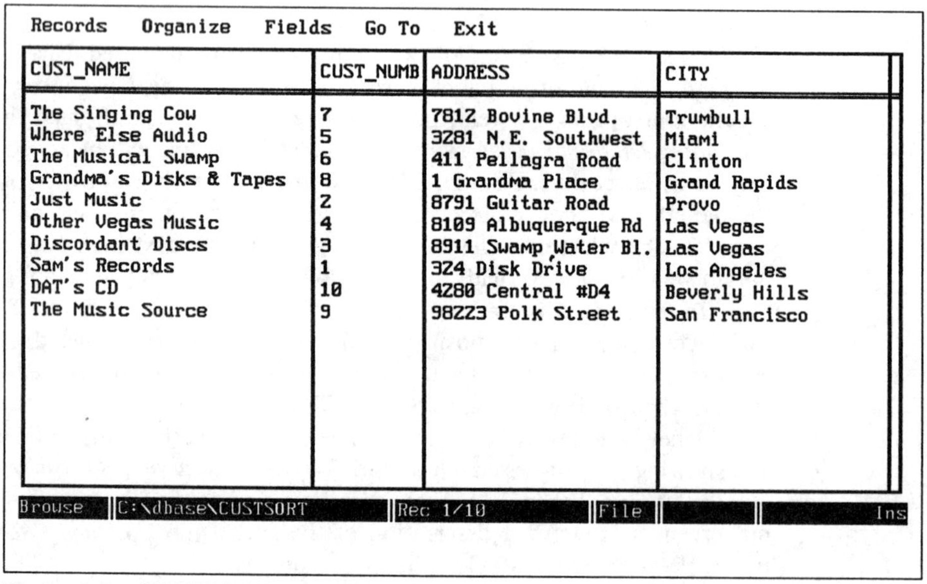

Records Organize Fields Go To Exit
CUST_NAME | CUST_NUMB | ADDRESS | CITY
The Singing Cow | 7 | 7812 Bovine Blvd. | Trumbull
Where Else Audio | 5 | 3281 N.E. Southwest | Miami
The Musical Swamp | 6 | 411 Pellagra Road | Clinton
Grandma's Disks & Tapes | 8 | 1 Grandma Place | Grand Rapids
Just Music | 2 | 8791 Guitar Road | Provo
Other Vegas Music | 4 | 8109 Albuquerque Rd | Las Vegas
Discordant Discs | 3 | 8911 Swamp Water Bl. | Las Vegas
Sam's Records | 1 | 324 Disk Drive | Los Angeles
DAT's CD | 10 | 4280 Central #D4 | Beverly Hills
The Music Source | 9 | 98223 Polk Street | San Francisco
Browse C:\dbase\CUSTSORT Rec 1/10 File Ins

Figure 8-5 CUSTSORT appearing in sorted order.

your new sorted file is still the open file. If you want to see, edit, or make any other use of the sorted file that you just created, you must first exit from the current screen and open the sorted file.

No changes have been made to the CUST_ID file. Press **F2** to bring up the Browse or Edit screen. If the Edit screen is shown, press **F2** a second time to go to the Browse screen. You may have to press **Ctrl-PgUp** to bring the cursor to the first record in the data file.

To see the new file that you've just created, Exit to the Control Center. The new file, CUSTSORT will appear in the Data panel. Select the CUSTSORT file, and press **F2** to bring up a Browse screen for the new file.

The Browse screen for CUSTSORT looks like Figure 8-5. Notice that the customer numbers are no longer in order. Instead of being displayed in the order in which they were created, the files are now displayed in order by ZIP code, with records within a ZIP code sorted.

To better show how sorting and indexing are performed on fields that have more than one matching record, add the following five records:

CUST_NAME:	Discordant Ducks
CUST_NUMB:	11
ADDRESS:	9911 Swamp Water Bl.
CITY:	Las Vegas
STATE:	NV
ZIP:	89125
PHONE:	7025551234
EXT:	3322
PHONE2:	
EXT2:	
CC_TYPE:	A
CC_NUMB_VM:	
CC_NUMB_A:	3724-999999-9999
CC_EXP_DAT:	01/22/91

CUST_NAME:	Nowhere Else Audio
CUST_NUMB:	12
ADDRESS:	4281 N.E. Southwest
CITY:	Miami
STATE:	FL
ZIP:	33199
PHONE:	3055558911
EXT:	2881
PHONE2:	8005551219
EXT2:	
CC_TYPE:	V
CC_NUMB_VM:	1299-2818-2222-2222
CC_NUMB_A:	
CC_EXP_DAT:	01/01/91

CUST_NAME: The Musical Slimepit
CUST_NUMB: 13
ADDRESS: 4121 Pellagra Road
CITY: Clinton
STATE: IA
ZIP: 52791
PHONE: 3195558299
EXT:
PHONE2:
EXT2:
CC_TYPE: M
CC_NUMB_VM: 9912-8188-2811-9833
CC_NUMB_A:
CC_EXP_DAT: 11-29-90

CUST_NAME: The Singing Frogs
CUST_NUMB: 14
ADDRESS: 7812 Provine Blvd.
CITY: Trumbull
STATE: CT
ZIP: 06611
PHONE: 2035552855
EXT: 7448
PHONE2:
EXT2:
CC_TYPE: M
CC_NUMB_VM: 2855-7448-9999-9999
CC_NUMB_A:
CC_EXP_DAT: 08/31/91

CUST_NAME: Grandpap's Disks and Tapes
CUST_NUMB: 15
ADDRESS: 21 Grandpa Place
CITY: Grand Rapids
STATE: MI
ZIP: 59409
PHONE: 6165556539
EXT:
PHONE2:
EXT2:
CC_TYPE: A
CC_NUMB_VM:
CC_NUMB_A: 3899-010101-00110
CC_EXP_DAT: 11/11/90

Open the Organize menu and sort the database with the same sort instructions that you used earlier. Activate the sort, naming the new, sorted file CUSTSRT2. The

```
 Records    Organize   Fields   Go To   Exit
┌──────────────────────────┬─────────┬─────────────┬─────┬─────────┬─────┐
│CUST_NAME                 │CUST_NUMB│CITY         │STATE│PROVINCE │ZIP  │
├──────────────────────────┼─────────┼─────────────┼─────┼─────────┼─────┤
│The Singing Cow           │7        │Trumbull     │CT   │         │0661 │
│The Singing Frogs         │14       │Trumbull     │CT   │         │0661 │
│Nohere Else Audio         │12       │Miami        │FL   │         │3319 │
│Where Else Audio          │5        │Miami        │FL   │         │3319 │
│The Musical Slimepit      │13       │Clinton      │IA   │         │5279 │
│The Musical Swamp         │6        │Clinton      │IA   │         │5279 │
│Grandma's Disks & Tapes   │8        │Grand Rapids │MI   │         │5940 │
│Grandpap's Disks & Tapes  │15       │Grand Rapids │MI   │         │5940 │
│Just Music                │2        │Provo        │UT   │         │8460 │
│Other Vegas Music         │4        │Las Vegas    │NM   │         │8719 │
│Discordant Discs          │3        │Las Vegas    │NV   │         │8912 │
│Discordant Ducks          │11       │Las Vegas    │NV   │         │8912 │
│Sam's Records             │1        │Los Angeles  │CA   │         │9002 │
│DAT's CD                  │10       │Beverly Hills│CA   │         │9021 │
│The Music Source          │9        │San Francisco│CA   │         │9410 │
│                          │         │             │     │         │     │
│                          │         │             │     │         │     │
└──────────────────────────┴─────────┴─────────────┴─────┴─────────┴─────┘
 Browse  C:\dbase\CUSTSRT2         Rec 1/15         File                Ins
```

Figure 8-6   CUSTSRT2 showing files within a ZIP code alphabetically sorted.

Browse screen for the new, sorted data file, with two fields locked on the left in order to show customer name, number, city, state, and part of the ZIP code, is shown in Figure 8-6.

Notice again in this figure that the records are not in order by customer number. Notice also that for records that have the same ZIP code, the names of the companies are displayed in alphabetic order (The Singing Cow appears before The Singing Frogs, for example). Further, it should be clear that ZIP codes, and not city names, are part of the sort. Near the bottom of the screen, three records are shown for stores in Las Vegas. These appear in ZIP code order. The two stores in Las Vegas, Nevada (both with the same ZIP code), are in order by name.

When creating your sort definition, you may also add or remove fields from the sort list. To delete a field from the list, move the cursor into the field to be removed and press **Ctrl-U**. The field will be removed from the list. To insert a new field between two existing fields, move the cursor into the line where you would like to add a sort instruction and press **Ctrl-N**. A blank line will be inserted. You may now add the field name and sort type instruction into the blank line.

So far, you've seen how a sorted data file is created. It is important to note that when you perform a sort operation, you are creating a new file, rather than just displaying your records in a particular order.

Indexing

Indexing is considerably different from sorting in a number of ways. The first, major difference between indexing and sorting is that when you index a file, you are not creating a new data file. Indexing provides you with a way to view your records in a particular order. Beyond merely viewing your records, you may switch from index to index, to view the records in a number of different orders. Indexing records is quite similar to indexing a book. When your data file is indexed, dBASE IV goes through your data file, and creates an index that tells it the order that each record is to take within that index.

When you use a data file that is in indexed order, dBASE IV reads the index and displays the records in order based on the index. If you were to display indexed items from this book, you would go to the index, and jump to the appropriate page for each indexed listing. dBASE IV displays records when it displays an index, based on the pointers in the index.

Earlier versions of dBASE IV were only able to produce indexes in ascending order. Although experienced programmers could get dBASE to produce an index in descending order, it was difficult. dBASE IV is now capable of producing ascending or descending index files without requiring the user to go through machinations required to do so.

From the Control Center, highlight CUST_ID and press **F2** to bring up the Browse/Edit screen. Go to the Browse screen, if this isn't already displayed. Your files should still be shown in order by customer number. Open the Organize menu by pressing **Alt-O**. You are provided with a range of options for managing your index or for creating a new index. To quickly see how indexing works, select *Order records by index*. When this option is selected, a window showing the index expressions created so far is displayed. The screen will look like Figure 8-7.

The first option, *Natural Order*, puts the records into the order in which they were created. This is the order in which they will be displayed when you first open your data file. You can also return your files to natural order by returning to the Control Center

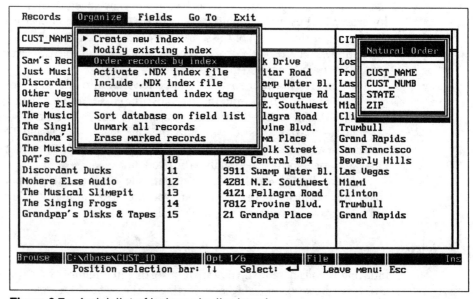

Figure 8-7 A pick list of indexes is displayed.

and activating any other data file. When you reopen your original data file, the records will again be shown in their natural order.

The Example

To see how an index works, select *ZIP* (but don't press **Enter** yet). When an index is selected, the index expression is displayed in a window to the left of the index pick window. This new window makes it easier to understand how your records will be displayed. Press **Enter** to activate the ZIP index. The Browse screen will look like Figure 8-8.

By reopening the Organize menu, you can select another index to display your records. The records, in order by customer name, are shown in Figure 8-9. If you've also activated this index, you've probably noticed that the change from ZIP order to CUST_NAME order occurred fairly quickly. This is because dBASE IV automatically updates your index each time you add a new record. The process of reading the index in order to get pointers to your records is not particularly time-consuming. However, for data files that are very large, and that have a large number of index expressions, there may be considerable delay between addition of records while each new record is placed into index order.

When you index by customer number, an interesting thing happens, as shown in Figure 8-10. You'll notice that the customer numbers are not in true numeric order. The record with customer number 1 is followed by the number with customer number 10. The number with customer number 2 follows the one with customer number 15. It can be correctly assumed that, if this were a large data file, the record with customer number 2 would follow that numbered 19, or 199, or 1999, and so on.

```
 Records    Organize    Fields    Go To    Exit
┌─────────────────────┬──────────┬──────────────────────┬──────────────────┐
│CUST_NAME            │CUST_NUMB │ADDRESS               │CITY              │
├─────────────────────┼──────────┼──────────────────────┼──────────────────┤
│The Singing Cow      │7         │7812 Bovine Blvd.     │Trumbull          │
│The Singing Frogs    │14        │7812 Provine Blvd.    │Trumbull          │
│Where Else Audio     │5         │3281 N.E. Southwest   │Miami             │
│Nohere Else Audio    │12        │4281 N.E. Southwest   │Miami             │
│The Musical Swamp    │6         │411 Pellagra Road     │Clinton           │
│The Musical Slimepit │13        │4121 Pellagra Road    │Clinton           │
│Grandma's Disks & Tapes│8       │1 Grandma Place       │Grand Rapids      │
│Grandpap's Disks & Tapes│15     │21 Grandpa Place      │Grand Rapids      │
│Just Music           │2         │8791 Guitar Road      │Provo             │
│Other Vegas Music    │4         │8109 Albuquerque Rd   │Las Vegas         │
│Discordant Discs     │3         │8911 Swamp Water Bl.  │Las Vegas         │
│Discordant Ducks     │11        │9911 Swamp Water Bl.  │Las Vegas         │
│Sam's Records        │1         │324 Disk Drive        │Los Angeles       │
│DAT's CD             │10        │4280 Central #D4      │Beverly Hills     │
│The Music Source     │9         │98223 Polk Street     │San Francisco     │
└─────────────────────┴──────────┴──────────────────────┴──────────────────┘
 Browse   C:\dbase\CUST_ID           Rec 7/15        File              Ins
```

Figure 8-8   Records in index order by ZIP code.

```
 Records   Organize   Fields   Go To   Exit
┌──────────────────────────┬───────────┬───────────────────┬─────────────────┐
│CUST_NAME                 │CUST_NUMB  │ADDRESS            │CITY             │
├──────────────────────────┼───────────┼───────────────────┼─────────────────┤
│DAT's CD                  │10         │4280 Central #D4   │Beverly Hills    │
│Discordant Discs          │3          │8911 Swamp Water Bl.│Las Vegas       │
│Discordant Ducks          │11         │9911 Swamp Water Bl.│Las Vegas       │
│Grandma's Disks & Tapes   │8          │1 Grandma Place    │Grand Rapids     │
│Grandpap's Disks & Tapes  │15         │21 Grandpa Place   │Grand Rapids     │
│Just Music                │2          │8791 Guitar Road   │Provo            │
│Nohere Else Audio         │12         │4281 N.E. Southwest│Miami            │
│Other Vegas Music         │4          │8109 Albuquerque Rd│Las Vegas        │
│Sam's Records             │1          │324 Disk Drive     │Los Angeles      │
│The Music Source          │9          │98223 Polk Street  │San Francisco    │
│The Musical Slimepit      │13         │4121 Pellagra Road │Clinton          │
│The Musical Swamp         │6          │411 Pellagra Road  │Clinton          │
│The Singing Cow           │7          │7812 Bovine Blvd.  │Trumbull         │
│The Singing Frogs         │14         │7812 Provine Blvd. │Trumbull         │
│Where Else Audio          │5          │3281 N.E. Southwest│Miami            │
│                          │           │                   │                 │
├──────────────────────────┴───────────┴───────────────────┴─────────────────┤
│Browse   C:\dbase\CUST_ID        Rec: 10/15      File              Ins        │
└─────────────────────────────────────────────────────────────────────────────┘
```

Figure 8-9 Records in index order by customer name.

```
 Records   Organize   Fields   Go To   Exit
┌──────────────────────────┬───────────┬───────────────────┬─────────────────┐
│CUST_NAME                 │CUST_NUMB  │ADDRESS            │CITY             │
├──────────────────────────┼───────────┼───────────────────┼─────────────────┤
│Sam's Records             │1          │324 Disk Drive     │Los Angeles      │
│DAT's CD                  │10         │4280 Central #D4   │Beverly Hills    │
│Discordant Ducks          │11         │9911 Swamp Water Bl.│Las Vegas       │
│Nohere Else Audio         │12         │4281 N.E. Southwest│Miami            │
│The Musical Slimepit      │13         │4121 Pellagra Road │Clinton          │
│The Singing Frogs         │14         │7812 Provine Blvd. │Trumbull         │
│Grandpap's Disks & Tapes  │15         │21 Grandpa Place   │Grand Rapids     │
│Just Music                │2          │8791 Guitar Road   │Provo            │
│Discordant Discs          │3          │8911 Swamp Water Bl.│Las Vegas       │
│Other Vegas Music         │4          │8109 Albuquerque Rd│Las Vegas        │
│Where Else Audio          │5          │3281 N.E. Southwest│Miami            │
│The Musical Swamp         │6          │411 Pellagra Road  │Clinton          │
│The Singing Cow           │7          │7812 Bovine Blvd.  │Trumbull         │
│Grandma's Disks & Tapes   │8          │1 Grandma Place    │Grand Rapids     │
│The Music Source          │9          │98223 Polk Street  │San Francisco    │
│                          │           │                   │                 │
├──────────────────────────┴───────────┴───────────────────┴─────────────────┤
│Browse   C:\dbase\CUST_ID        Rec: 1/15       File              Ins        │
└─────────────────────────────────────────────────────────────────────────────┘
```

Figure 8-10 Records in index order by customer number.

The reason that this happens is that the CUST_NUMB field is a character field, not a numeric one. When an index is created, dBASE IV looks at the value of the index fields one character at a time. Thus, any record whose customer number begins with a 1 would naturally occur before any record whose customer number begins with a 2. After the first character is indexed, the second character is similarly indexed. Since the first record, that for Sam's Records, doesn't have a character after the 1, it is placed in order before those records that do have a character following the 1. At this point, dBASE IV again puts records into order based on this second character (in this case, those records that start with 1 are put into order from 0 through 5). If you were working with letters instead of numeric characters, the process involved in creating the index would be obvious.

There is a way to work around this problem, however. Since dBASE IV creates its index by reading each character from left to right, the answer is to insert leading blanks or zeros before the number you use in the character field. You will recall that you set up a way to automatically create and assign a customer number. The method used did not add any leading zeros or spaces.

To enable a sort that is accurately indexed, you must modify the numeric data in your data files. In order to do this, open the Browse screen for your data and move the cursor into the field that is to be changed. Move the cursor to the first record. The cursor should be positioned on top of (or in front of) the first number in the field. Press the **Spacebar** so that the field value is moved to the right edge of the highlighted area that denotes the field width. (You may also add zeros instead of spaces to indicate the null values leading up to the record value.) Using this method, an index operation will correctly organize your records.

When you look at the Browse screen produced by displaying files in order by customer name, the process should become clear. Many of the records have store names that are very similar. Only where the two names become different, as in Discordant Discs and Discordant Ducks, where the difference follows the letter **D** in the second word of the name, does the index separate the two files. Perhaps even more obvious is the display of The Music Source before The Musical Slimepit, since the space following Music in The Music Source is a smaller-value character than the a in the word "Musical." By using indexes, your data can remain in the data files in its original order, yet you can view it in a variety of ways, depending upon the order that is appropriate at the time you wish to edit or review it.

In addition to viewing your data based on an already defined index, you can also create an index expression from within the Organize menu that combines index expressions or that applies special conditions. You can also modify existing index expressions. To modify an existing index, select *Modify existing index* from inside the Organize menu. This can be done by pressing **M**, or by moving the cursor so that *Modify existing index* is highlighted and pressing **Enter**.

The index selection window will be opened at the right of the screen, with the index expression displayed to its left. (The index selection window is shown in Figure 8-7.) Select ZIP, since this is the index that you will be modifying. An index expression editing window, as shown in Figure 8-11, will be opened.

When you choose to modify an existing index, you can change the index, storing

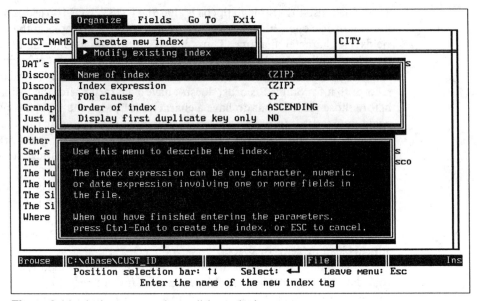

Figure 8-11   Index expression editing window.

the modified index by its original name, or you can modify an existing index, giving it a new name. While the process is similar to creating a new index, there are some times when it's easier to modify an existing index (since field names and relationships are already defined) than to pick all the necessary field names for creating a completely new index.

Select *Index expression* (by pressing **I**), and the brackets around the expression will disappear, signifying that you can edit the expression. If you want more space to edit the expression, pressing **F9** will open an editing window at the bottom of the screen.

> **Note** Indexing expressions are easy to write, when compared to expressions that can be created for report generation or query design. Index expressions are of the form **FIELD1 + FIELD2**, where fields 1 and 2 are the fields that you wish to index on, and the + establishes the order of index creation.

In the present example, you'll create an index that matches the one created when you sorted your data file by ZIP code and customer name. dBASE IV provides you with an expression builder, which can be accessed by pressing **Shft-F1**. The cursor should be placed after ZIP. Press **Right Arrow** to move the cursor into the Operator panel of the expression builder. Press the period key to move the highlight to + and press **Enter** (or just press +) to move the selection into the edit line. Since you still need to add a field to the expression, press **Shft-F1** again to bring up the expression builder window.

Press **Left Arrow** to move the cursor back into the Field name panel. CUST_ NAME, which is the first field in the data file, will be highlighted. Press **Enter** to select the field. The index expression, **ZIP + CUST_NAME** will be shown in the expression edit line. Press **Enter** to store your index expression.

The *For clause* option is a new addition to dBASE IV, Version 1.1. In Version 1.0 of dBASE IV, an index was created for an entire data file. If you wanted to show only the files for dealers in the state of California, for example, you would have to use the query processor to write a query that produces a file for only those records with **CA** entered into the state field. Using *FOR clause*, you can assign a condition that must be matched in order for a record to be included in an index. This is a very powerful addition that you'll see shortly.

Order of index gives you two options: Ascending ASCII or Descending ASCII. This type of ordering was described earlier in this chapter in the section on sorting. To toggle between Ascending and Descending, press the **Spacebar** or **Enter** key.

Display first duplicate key only is used to indicate that, in cases where a field value may be duplicated, only the first occurrence of such a value is built into the index. In an order file that may have dozens of orders for each customer, you may need just the first occurrence of each customer record if you are only interested in mailing addresses. Setting this to NO includes all records that match the For clause conditions in the indexed data file. This item may also be toggled between YES and NO using the **Spacebar** or **Enter** key.

Since the index is no longer merely a ZIP code index, you should rename it. Move the cursor to the *Name of index* line and press **Enter** (or simply press N) and add the word *NAME* to the index name. The new index name will be ZIPNAME, describing the index as one that indexes on ZIP and NAME. Press **Enter** to accept the new name. To save the new name and index parameters, press **Ctrl-End** to save the new index description. Once the description has been saved, the data files will be reindexed, and the Browse screen will display the files in the new index order, as shown in Figure 8-12.

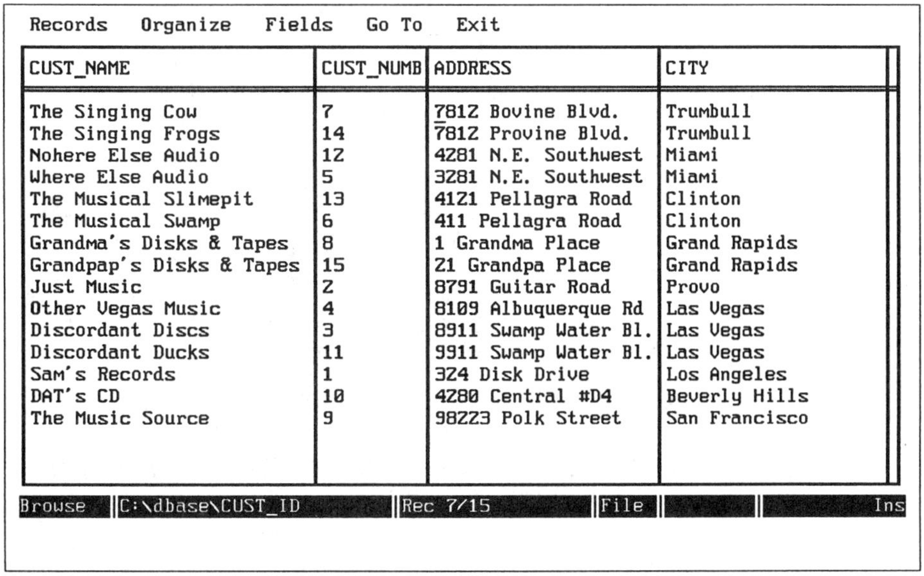

```
  Records   Organize   Fields   Go To   Exit

  CUST_NAME                    CUST_NUMB ADDRESS              CITY

  The Singing Cow              7         7812 Bovine Blvd.    Trumbull
  The Singing Frogs            14        7812 Provine Blvd.   Trumbull
  Nohere Else Audio            12        4281 N.E. Southwest  Miami
  Where Else Audio             5         3281 N.E. Southwest  Miami
  The Musical Slimepit         13        4121 Pellagra Road   Clinton
  The Musical Swamp            6         411 Pellagra Road    Clinton
  Grandma's Disks & Tapes      8         1 Grandma Place      Grand Rapids
  Grandpap's Disks & Tapes     15        21 Grandpa Place     Grand Rapids
  Just Music                   2         8791 Guitar Road     Provo
  Other Vegas Music            4         8109 Albuquerque Rd  Las Vegas
  Discordant Discs             3         8911 Swamp Water Bl. Las Vegas
  Discordant Ducks             11        9911 Swamp Water Bl. Las Vegas
  Sam's Records                1         324 Disk Drive       Los Angeles
  DAT's CD                     10        4280 Central #D4     Beverly Hills
  The Music Source             9         98223 Polk Street    San Francisco


  Browse   C:\dbase\CUST_ID          Rec 7/15         File              Ins
```

Figure 8-12   Files displayed indexed on ZIP and CUST_NAME.

When you rename a file that is modified by selecting the *Modify existing index* option, the new name will replace the existing index. dBASE IV does not add the new name and expression to the list of expressions already in use. Thus, if you want to create a new expression, you should do this by activating the *Create new index* option.

You should notice that the records in the current Browse screen are in the same order as those created when you sorted your data file. It can't be concluded, though, that all files sorted and indexed using the same definitions will always match. The reason that the assumption is flawed is because the sort was made using a dictionary sort, while indexing applies an ASCII sort parameter. Thus, an indexed file may put records into a different order than would a file that is created as a result of a dictionary sort.

In this next example, you'll apply a condition (*FOR clause*) to the index specification. Reopen the Organize window and again select *Modify existing index*. Choose ZIPNAME as the index you wish to modify, and press **Enter** to open the index description window.

In this index, you'll tell the system that you only want records for customers that are located in California. To begin, move the highlight to the *For clause* line and press **Enter** (or press F to bring up the edit line). The expression that you want to use is **STATE = "CA"**. The quotation marks around the state name indicate that dBASE IV should attempt to match the contents of the STATE field in each record to the text string CA. If the string matches, the record will be added to the index. If not, the record will not be indexed. The expression can be typed into the line, or can be created using the expression builder (opened by pressing **Shft-F1**). The value to check against must be

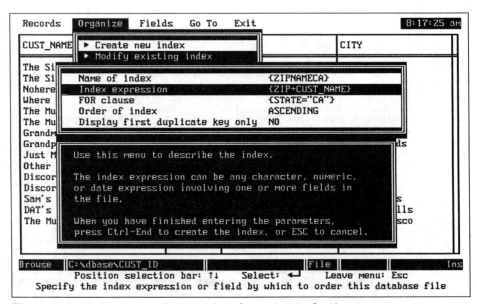

Figure 8-13   Index expression to select for stores in California.

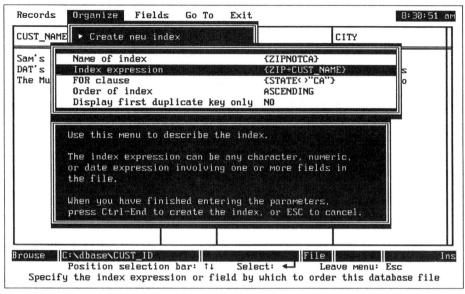

```
Records   Organize  Fields   Go To   Exit                    8:30:51 am
┌────────┐┌─────────────────────────────────────┐┌──────────────────┐
│CUST_NAME││ ▸ Create new index                  ││CITY              │
│        │├─────────────────────────────────────┤│                  │
│Sam's   ││ Name of index            {ZIPNOTCA}  ││                  │
│DAT's   ││ Index expression         {ZIP+CUST_NAME}          s      │
│The Mu  ││ FOR clause               {STATE<>"CA"}            o      │
│        ││ Order of index           ASCENDING   ││                  │
│        ││ Display first duplicate key only  NO ││                  │
│        │└─────────────────────────────────────┘│                  │
│        │┌──────────────────────────────────────────────────┐      │
│        ││ Use this menu to describe the index.             │      │
│        ││                                                  │      │
│        ││ The index expression can be any character, numeric,│    │
│        ││ or date expression involving one or more fields in │    │
│        ││ the file.                                        │      │
│        ││                                                  │      │
│        ││ When you have finished entering the parameters,  │      │
│        ││ press Ctrl-End to create the index, or ESC to cancel.│  │
│        │└──────────────────────────────────────────────────┘      │
│        │                                                          │
└────────┘                                                          │
 Browse  │C:\dbase\CUST_ID                     │File│           Ins │
        Position selection bar: ↑↓    Select: ◄┘    Leave menu: Esc
     Specify the index expression or field by which to order this database file
```

Figure 8-14   Index expression for states outside of California.

typed in by the user. Rename the new index expression ZIPNAMECA. The index expression looks like Figure 8-13.

It is important to consider that FOR clause conditions may draw from any field, and may also use date or mathematical calculations for providing the FOR condition. For example, you may want to index a list for all customers whose credit cards expire within 30 days, or who haven't ordered in more than 90 days. You may want to create an index on customers who have made at least one order of more than $10,000.

Now, create an index expression that indexes for all states other than California. Select *Create new index* from within the Organize menu. To tell the system that you want to select FOR all records whose state is not California, use the inequality marks < >. By themselves, the two marks, < (less than) and > (greater than), have their own meanings. When used as a pair, they mean "not equal to." The # key also means "not equal to."

The index expression to achieve our desired goal (indexing by ZIP code and customer name for those states outside of California) is shown in Figure 8-14. The Browse screen for records matching this index definition is shown in Figure 8-15.

FOR conditions can be strung together. For example, the following FOR condition, STATE = "CA".OR.STATE = "NV" tells dBASE IV to index only on records where the State field is matched by either CA or NV. The Browse screen showing the selected records is shown in Figure 8-16.

Increasingly complex indexing and FOR conditions can be created using dBASE IV. Expression building and extremely complex syntax will be discussed in more detail in future chapters.

```
Records   Organize   Fields   Go To   Exit
┌─────────────────────────┬──────────┬───────────────────┬──────────────┐
│CUST_NAME                │CUST_NUMB │ADDRESS            │CITY          │
├─────────────────────────┼──────────┼───────────────────┼──────────────┤
│The Singing Cow          │7         │7812 Bovine Blvd.  │Trumbull      │
│The Singing Frogs        │14        │7812 Provine Blvd. │Trumbull      │
│Nohere Else Audio        │12        │4281 N.E. Southwest│Miami         │
│Where Else Audio         │5         │3281 N.E. Southwest│Miami         │
│The Musical Slimepit     │13        │4121 Pellagra Road │Clinton       │
│The Musical Swamp        │6         │411 Pellagra Road  │Clinton       │
│Grandma's Disks & Tapes  │8         │1 Grandma Place    │Grand Rapids  │
│Grandpap's Disks & Tapes │15        │21 Grandpa Place   │Grand Rapids  │
│Just Music               │2         │8791 Guitar Road   │Provo         │
│Other Vegas Music        │4         │8109 Albuquerque Rd│Las Vegas     │
│Discordant Discs         │3         │8911 Swamp Water Bl│Las Vegas     │
│Discordant Ducks         │11        │9911 Swamp Water Bl│Las Vegas     │
│                         │          │                   │              │
│                         │          │                   │              │
│                         │          │                   │              │
├─────────────────────────┴──────────┴───────────────────┴──────────────┤
│Browse  ║C:\dbase\CUST_ID    ║Rec 7/15    ║File ║           ║      Ins   │
└────────────────────────────────────────────────────────────────────────┘
```

Figure 8-15   Browse screen for indexed records not matching Figure 8-14 setup.

```
Records   Organize   Fields   Go To   Exit
┌─────────────────────────┬──────────┬───────────────────┬──────────────┐
│CUST_NAME                │CUST_NUMB │ADDRESS            │CITY          │
├─────────────────────────┼──────────┼───────────────────┼──────────────┤
│Discordant Discs         │3         │8911 Swamp Water Bl│Las Vegas     │
│Discordant Ducks         │11        │9911 Swamp Water Bl│Las Vegas     │
│Sam's Records            │1         │324 Disk Drive     │Los Angeles   │
│DAT's CD                 │10        │4280 Central #D4   │Beverly Hills │
│The Music Source         │9         │98223 Polk Street  │San Francisco │
│                         │          │                   │              │
│                         │          │                   │              │
│                         │          │                   │              │
│                         │          │                   │              │
│                         │          │                   │              │
│                         │          │                   │              │
│                         │          │                   │              │
│                         │          │                   │              │
│                         │          │                   │              │
├─────────────────────────┴──────────┴───────────────────┴──────────────┤
│Browse  ║C:\dbase\CUST_ID    ║Rec 3/15    ║File ║           ║      Ins   │
└────────────────────────────────────────────────────────────────────────┘
```

Figure 8-16   Browse field for State = "CA" .OR. State = "NV."

.MDX and .NDX Files

dBASE IV's index management capabilities are among the most powerful in the industry. dBASE III, FoxPro, and most other microcomputer database management programs manage indexes slightly differently than does dBASE IV. In earlier versions of dBASE, you were allowed to design many index expressions, but you were not able to use them all at the same time. When a file was changed, the indexes that were not active were not updated to reflect the changes that were made to the files. This caused a potential problem, since the index no longer correctly related to the current state of the data file. dBASE IV has solved that problem, and automatically updates all indexes in an index catalog that is applied to your data file, as it changes.

As you've been shown, dBASE IV creates and manages a pick list of index statements (and indexes) for the data file that you are working with. At any time, you can bring up the Organize menu, select *Order records by index*, select an index to apply, and view or edit your data in index order, with the appropriate FOR condition filtering out the unmatched records, and the *Display first duplicate key only* option showing all matching records or just the first, based on how the index expression was written. To provide the index management capabilities included in dBASE IV, two types of files are created. The actual index expressions, which you've been working with in this chapter, are given the file extension .NDX. These expressions are stored as .NDX files, and can be called or modified either from within the Organize menu or from the dot prompt, when dBASE IV is used via the programmer's interface (from the dot prompt).

A second type of file, a multiple index file, is created when your data file is defined. This file, which carries the extension .MDX, contains a list of all the index file tags (which refer to the index files, but don't actually include the index data) that apply to the current data file. The .MDX multiple index file catalogs the index expressions that apply to your data files. Up to 49 different index expressions can be managed by each .MDX file.

The two options, *Activate .NDX index file* and *Include .NDX index file*, are used to select index files that will be available as part of your master index, or which will be used to maintain your data file as it is updated. The options are also used to tell dBASE IV which already saved index file should be automatically applied to your data file.

Activate .NDX index file brings up a list of index (.NDX) files. This list represents those .NDX files that you have included in your multiple index file using the *Include .NDX index file* option. When this option is selected, the system will update this index as records are added or deleted, and will display files in the order indicated by this index file specification. Further, when you activate an .NDX file, the index is not only updated as any changes are made to the data, it also provides the order in which your data will be displayed or viewed.

Include .NDX index file adds an index expression to your master index file. If, for example, you have written an index expression from inside the dot prompt, or want to use an index expression that was valuable to you when you used dBASE III, you can add the index to the master index list. This option is used to add a new index tag to your multiple index file.

The final index option on the Organize menu, *Remove unwanted index tag*, is used to remove an index expression from the index catalog that can be selected using

Modify existing index. When your index file has been selected, pressing **Enter** removes the index tag from the master index.

When you have put your file into an indexed order, it will remain in that order until you close the data file. When you reopen the data file, it will be in natural order until you tell dBASE IV to *Order records by index*.

Conclusion

In this chapter, you've seen how to use sorting and indexing to put your data into a desired order. Sorting creates new files, while indexing merely creates a file that is used to view the records in their index order.

The FOR option provides significant power, allowing you to define conditions that must be met in order for a file to be indexed (and viewed or modified).

Future chapters will discuss how to retrieve specific data from multiple data files, and how to create data files that can be used for such custom reports as order forms, invoices, and shipping manifests.

9

Simple Queries

Previous chapters laid the groundwork for designing your data files, for setting update entry forms, for indexing and sorting, and for moving data in and out of your data files. So far, you've been primarily concerned with getting data *into* your data files, and getting unprocessed data *out* of the data files, but not on analysis of the data. In future chapters, you will create reports and labels based on the data that is stored in one or more files. While the report and label design forms provide considerable flexibility and significant data management and summary capabilities, they don't provide the tools needed to pull together only the data fields that you want to use for your reports or labels.

Say, for example, that you want to print out an order form. This form would have the customer name and address; an order number; the item name, quantity, and price; subtotals; and totals for the amount ordered. A buyer's name may also be included on the form, as well as the name or code for the person who took the order. In order to produce such a form, you will have to extract data from the CUST_ID data file, the BUYERS data file, the TITLES data file, and perhaps additional data files. If you want to prepare this list with various fields sorted, the task will be further complicated. To create such a list, you would have to relate fields in many data files, and create a single data file that contained all the information necessary to create a complete form. The query processor in dBASE IV is well suited to massaging your data into a single file that is needed to produce your reports or labels.

In earlier versions of dBASE, special data files could be created, extracting the data from the multiple files that contained the specific information needed, but to do so required some fairly sophisticated coding. Data extraction expressions could become quite lengthy and may even have seemed somewhat convoluted, but experienced programmers and application developers learned to design such expressions. Some may even have come to enjoy the challenge, and the rewarding feeling that comes from having designed a complicated query that actually provided the desired result.

In dBASE IV, a better way to produce such data lists has been provided—let the computer do it for you. The Queries panel in the Control Center is your interface to the *Query by Example* facility of dBASE IV. Query by example is the name (and description) of an innovative approach to describing *how* your query will relate fields and extract data, and letting the system create the actual program instructions for extracting your data.

Queries can cover a broad range of complexity, ranging from the very simple (find all customers in Alaska) to the very complex (find all customers in Alaska who ordered less than $500 worth of rock albums or more than $1000 worth of classical albums between January 10 and January 20, and whose phone number doesn't end in "9").

Some simple lists can be created from a single data file through judicious use of the FOR condition applied to a carefully designed index. However, since most of your files contain a minimum number of data fields needed to manage a small portion of the information for a large application, you will need the abilities of dBASE IV's query processor to extract information from multiple data files.

In this chapter, you'll see the basics of query design using the Query by Example (QBE) panel in dBASE IV. Future chapters will cover more sophisticated queries that relate multiple files, include special conditions for including a file, and include calculated fields. Further, you'll see how queries can be used to create temporary files that can be used to create reports in addition to producing new files or updating old ones.

The Queries Panel

The Queries panel is used to provide access to dBASE IV's Query by Example technology. In this panel, as with the other panels in the Control Center, all queries that have been saved and stored in the current catalog are listed. When you activate a data file, related queries are moved into the top portion of the panel, so that they may be applied to the active data file.

Because the Query function is central to the importance of dBASE IV, since it provides you with the method of retrieving your data in a more consolidated and highly filtered form than any of the other panels can provide, the Queries panel is not the only access to the Query function. In fact, unless you have a query that you regularly run, you may find yourself using and designing queries less frequently from within the panel than from other screens.

The Query facility can be accessed from within the other panels in the Control Center. When the Exit menu in the Browse/Edit screens is opened from within the Data, Forms, Reports, and Labels panels it includes the *Transfer to Query Design* option. When this option is chosen, the Query design screen is opened, and you can begin defining your query.

To view the results of your query, pressing **F2** begins the query evaluation process and, if files are found that match your query specification, displays the results in either a Browse or Edit screen. There is a minor problem related to viewing the data produced by a query in an Edit screen.

When you bring up a browse screen from within the Query design screen, the view you will be given of your data will be the generic, opening screen with your files listed, but no data filters or picture or edit functions. Thus, if you were using a specially designed form to view and validate your data, and then went to the Query design menu, when you went back to your data, it would no longer be formatted as it was when you applied a screen format form to the data.

There is good reason for this, however. The query design process allows you to select the fields to display and to modify the order in which they'll be listed. It also allows you to add fields from other data files. Thus, applying a special form that is linked to a specific data file with specific fields would not be appropriate in the case of many of the queries produced by dBASE IV, so for consistency of operations, any format files that were applied to your data before transferring to the Query design screen are unlinked from your data files once a query is generated.

In addition to being able to transfer to query design from within Browse/Edit screens, you may also begin a query from inside the Queries panel in the Control Center. If a data file is open, the fields from that file will be automatically included in the structure for the query design.

With CUST_ID the active database, selecting < create > from the queries panel results in a screen that looks like Figure 9-1. Close the current Query design screen without saving the file, and close the CUST_ID.DBF file (by moving the cursor into the Data panel, pressing **Enter,** and choosing the *Close* option).

When you select *Add file to query,* the system will bring up a window with the names of the database files in your current directory. For the first example of query design, move the cursor into the Queries panel and select < create >. The screen will open with *Add file to query* active. Select CUST_ID.DBF as the file you wish to perform a query on. dBASE IV will create a *file skeleton,* with the fields listed at the

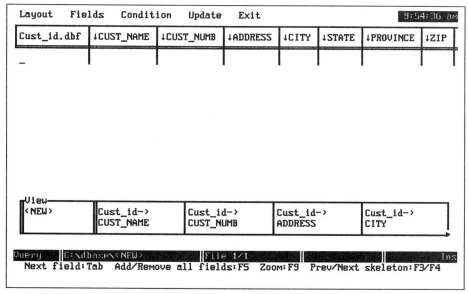

Figure 9-1 Query design screen, defaults for CUST_ID data file.

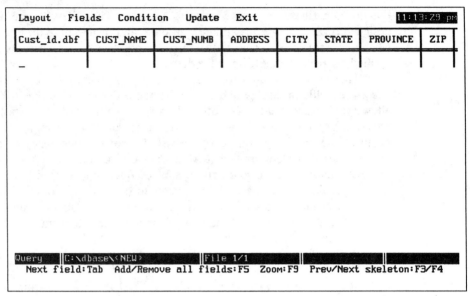

Figure 9-2   Query screen with file skeleton.

top of the screen. Note that each field name is only as wide as the number of characters taken up by the field name. You will soon see how adding data to a query definition can make the panel widen. Thus, the ZIP field is considerably smaller than the PROVINCE field. The screen with the file skeleton is seen in Figure 9-2.

The file skeleton shows the fields that are included in a data file. The box on the extreme left of the skeleton contains the name of the data file. To the right are the fields in the file design, in the order that they were included in the design. For now, exit the query design without saving it and return to the Control Center. The file CUST_ID should be shown as active in the Data panel. The cursor should still be in the Queries panel. Press **Enter** with the word <create> highlighted, and the Query design window will open.

At the bottom of the screen, a new set of boxes appears on the design screen. This set of boxes is called a *view skeleton*. You should notice that the file skeleton at the top of the screen has arrows to the left of each field name that point down to the *view skeleton*. This is no accident. The view skeleton provides the name of the fields (and the source data file) that will be included in the data file or view that is created using the query processor. The arrow next to the field name in the file skeleton indicates that the field is part of the view skeleton.

When a field is added to the skeleton, it is appended to the existing skeleton. That is, it is placed at the end of the skeleton. When you load the query processor when a data file is in use, the Query screen will automatically come up with all fields in their natural order in a view skeleton. As was shown earlier, simply adding a file to the query does not make any changes to the view skeleton. The Query with the File skeleton and View skeleton shown is seen in Figure 9–3.

You will be shown how to add, delete, and move files in the View skeleton later in this chapter. Now you will see how queries are written and how the process works.

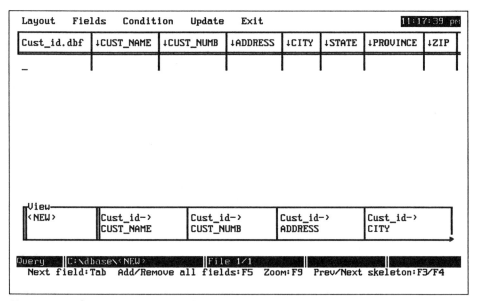

Figure 9-3   Query screen with File skeleton and View skeleton.

Creating a Query

When you create a query, you tell the system what values for your data you are looking for, and you also define relationships between data fields and between data files. Those records that match your query criteria can be copied to a new file, can be marked for deletion (or undeleted), can be used to replace records or add them to a data file, and can produce temporary files that can be browsed by the user.

To see how this works, start with a simple example. Move the cursor (using the **Tab** key) so that the highlight is under the word "CITY". Type "*Las Vegas*". Be sure to include the quotation marks, since CITY is a character field. Characters must be enclosed in quotation marks, single quotation marks, or brackets. You'll see more about how to use the three different character delimiters a little later in this chapter.

If you are using dBASE IV Version 1.1, you will see that the CITY panel widens as you type your value, since LAS VEGAS is wider than the field name. The fields to the right of CITY are pushed to the right as you add your data into the file skeleton.

You can execute the query by pressing the **F2** key, which will bring up a Browse or Edit screen showing only those records that match the query expression. Press **F2** to evaluate your data file, based on the current query. The Browse screen produced will look like Figure 9-4.

If the query was executed properly, you will see three records in your Browse screen. Scrolling through the records will show that you have two stores in Las Vegas, Nevada, and one store in Las Vegas, New Mexico. Suppose you only wanted to find the stores in Las Vegas, Nevada.

To create a new query that looks for records that match on CITY = "LAS VEGAS" and STATE = "NV", you should first return to the Query design screen. To do this, open the Exit menu (by pressing **Alt-E**) and select *Transfer to Query Design*.

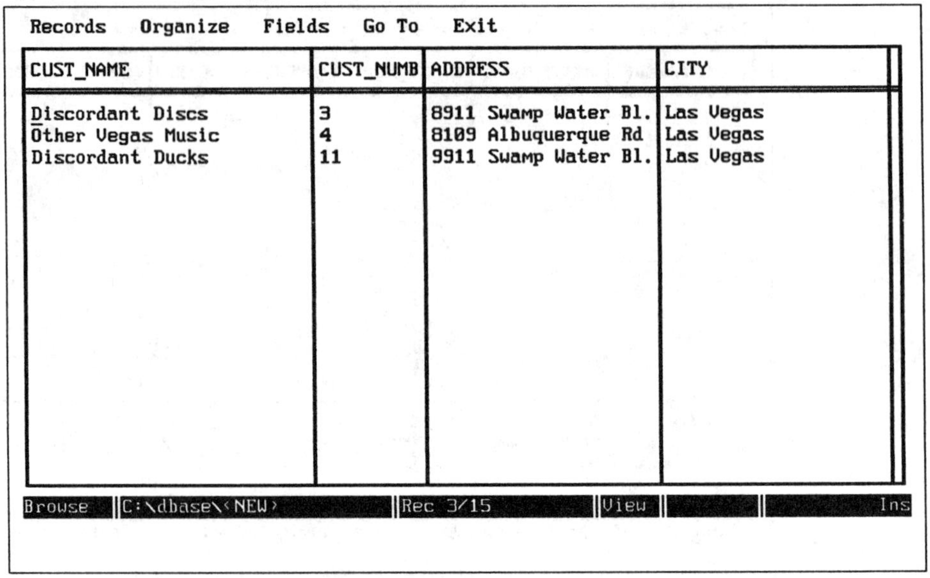

```
 ┌──────────────────────────────────────────────────────────────────────┐
 │   Records   Organize   Fields   Go To    Exit                          │
 │ ┌──────────────────────┬──────────┬───────────────────┬────────────┐  │
 │ │CUST_NAME             │CUST_NUMB │ADDRESS            │CITY        │   │
 │ ├──────────────────────┼──────────┼───────────────────┼────────────┤  │
 │ │Discordant Discs      │3         │8911 Swamp Water Bl.│Las Vegas  │   │
 │ │Other Vegas Music     │4         │8109 Albuquerque Rd │Las Vegas  │   │
 │ │Discordant Ducks      │11        │9911 Swamp Water Bl.│Las Vegas  │   │
 │ │                      │          │                   │            │   │
 │ │                      │          │                   │            │   │
 │ │                      │          │                   │            │   │
 │ │                      │          │                   │            │   │
 │ │                      │          │                   │            │   │
 │ │                      │          │                   │            │   │
 │ └──────────────────────┴──────────┴───────────────────┴────────────┘  │
 │ Browse   C:\dbase\<NEW>           Rec 3/15         View           Ins  │
 └──────────────────────────────────────────────────────────────────────┘
```

Figure 9-4   Results of query to find all stores in Las Vegas, Nevada.

When the system returns the cursor to the Query design panel, your highlight should still be in the CITY field. Press the **Tab** key so that the highlight is moved under STATE. Type *"NV"* (remembering to include the quotation marks).

Before processing this query, however, it is well to understand some of the logic involved in designing a query. If you press the **Down Arrow**, you will see that the panels can be extended downward. Each line allows you to add a new query condition. When you place more than one query statement on a single line, you are telling the system that *all* conditions on that line must match the record in order for the record to be selected. In this case, you are telling dBASE IV to find all records with the CITY value "LAS VEGAS" that also have the STATE value "NV". If you run this query, dBASE IV will select only two files, excluding the one for *Other Vegas Music* because the STATE value doesn't match the query condition. The results of this query are shown in Figure 9-4.

You may also enter more than one value inside a single field. Each value must be separated from the other values by a comma. You may want to use such a query description if you want to create a list of customers who ordered more than 12 and less than 48 copies of any item. In such a case, the expression $>12, <48$ in a QUANTITY field would produce the desired record. The comma in such an expression means AND. In the example given, the expression could mean "find all records whose quantity ordered was greater than 12 *and* less than 48."

Care should be taken in writing the expression, however, because dBASE IV will give you exactly what you've asked for. In this case, you'll get records of customers who ordered 13 or more, but 47 or less, units. If you really wanted to know who ordered 12 or more, or 48 or less, the expression could have been written $>=12, <=48$ ($>=$ means greater than or equal to, while $<=$ means less than or equal to). You could also have written $>11, <49$ and gotten the same result. However, this method would

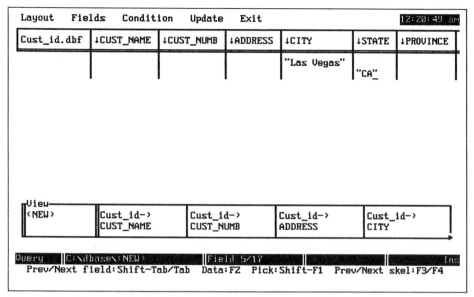

Figure 9-5   Query to find all stores in Las Vegas or California.

probably *not* work when you are using a field with noninteger values. Such a query would accept records whose values are 11.2 or 48.95, clearly not what you desire. Using the equality expressions < = and > = is a more exact means of stating the numeric expression.

> **Note** ▷ Returning to our example, it is well to remember that *all* conditions entered onto the same line *must be met* in order for a record to be selected by dBASE IV.

Placing conditions on a separate line means OR. For example, if you moved the query entry for STATE down to the next line, dBASE IV will select all records whose CITY field matches "LAS VEGAS", OR whose STATE field matches "NV". Thus, if you had customers located in other cities in Nevada, this query would select all Nevada cities. Further, it would select all customers in Las Vegas, regardless of what state Las Vegas happens to be in.

The query in Figure 9-5 selects all records that are in "LAS VEGAS" or in "CA". (If you left the value "NV" in the STATE field on the first line, you would have selected all stores in Las Vegas, Nevada, OR all stores in California. In this case, the first line did not have a state field entry, so the store in New Mexico is included in the Browse screen). Figure 9-6 shows the results of the query.

Sounds Like   In addition to exact matches, dBASE IV allows you to perform a number of inexact matches. *Sounds like* is an operator that performs a match to fields that contain values that sound like the expression typed in.

To use this operator, type *Sounds like*, followed by the phonetic character string you will be attempting to match. If you have forgotten how to spell Las Vegas, for example, you can find all records with cities that sound (to dBASE IV's SOUNDEX

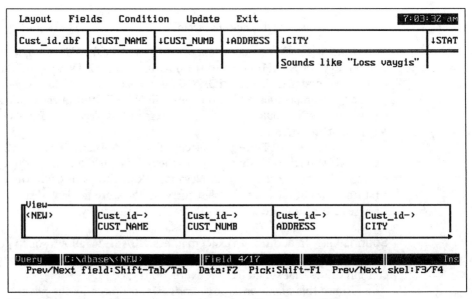

```
 Records    Organize    Fields    Go To    Exit
┌─────────────────────────┬─────────────┬──────────────────────┬──────────────────┐
│CUST_NAME                │CUST_NUMB│ADDRESS               │CITY              │
├─────────────────────────┼─────────────┼──────────────────────┼──────────────────┤
│Sam's Records            │1            │324 Disk Drive        │Los Angeles       │
│Discordant Discs         │3            │8911 Swamp Water Bl.  │Las Vegas         │
│Other Vegas Music        │4            │8109 Albuquerque Rd   │Las Vegas         │
│The Music Source         │9            │98223 Polk Street     │San Francisco     │
│DAT's CD                 │10           │4280 Central #D4      │Beverly Hills     │
│Discordant Ducks         │11           │9911 Swamp Water Bl.  │Las Vegas         │
│                         │             │                      │                  │
└─────────────────────────┴─────────────┴──────────────────────┴──────────────────┘
 Browse   C:\dbase\<NEW>              Rec 1/15          View                   Ins
```

Figure 9-6   Results of query to find all stores in Las Vegas or California.

```
 Layout    Fields    Condition    Update    Exit                        7:03:32 am
┌───────────┬──────────────┬──────────────┬─────────────┬──────────────────────────┬──────┐
│Cust_id.dbf│↓CUST_NAME    │↓CUST_NUMB    │↓ADDRESS     │↓CITY                     │↓STAT │
├───────────┼──────────────┼──────────────┼─────────────┼──────────────────────────┼──────┤
│           │              │              │             │Sounds like "Loss vaygis" │      │
│           │              │              │             │                          │      │
│           │              │              │             │                          │      │
│           │              │              │             │                          │      │
│           │              │              │             │                          │      │
│           │              │              │             │                          │      │
│           │              │              │             │                          │      │
│  View──────                                                                             │
│  <NEW>       Cust_id->     Cust_id->      Cust_id->     Cust_id->                 │
│              CUST_NAME      CUST_NUMB      ADDRESS       CITY                      │
└───────────────────────────────────────────────────────────────────────────────────────┘
 Query   C:\dbase\<NEW>              Field 4/17                                        Ins
  Prev/Next field:Shift-Tab/Tab   Data:F2   Pick:Shift-F1   Prev/Next skel:F3/F4
```

Figure 9-7   *Sounds like* matches based on the sound of the words.

processor, at least) like your phonetic approximation of the field being queried. In Figure 9-7, one such *Sounds like* query is displayed.

While the *Sounds like* operation selected all records that were located in Las Vegas, it also selected one in Los Angeles. Such queries are not exact and, unless the phonetic guess at a spelling is close to what dBASE IV wants to hear, not always successful. However, *Sounds like* is a powerful tool that can, and often does, find matches on records that may be otherwise extremely difficult to locate. In the case of LOSS VAYGIS, the correct value was displayed in the Browse screen, and can be used to replace the *Sounds like* expression with the exact spelling for the desired records.

In some cases, you may want to use *Sounds like* to locate records containing fields that sound similar but have slightly different spellings. Many foreign names, for example, may have been translated to English with slightly different spellings. Names may have a number of different spellings (BROWNSTEIN, BRAUNSTEIN, GUTIER-REZ, GUTIEREZ, GUTERREZ, and variations thereof). Of course, for this process to work, there must be some degree of similarity between the actual name and the guess that you've entered. Using Sounds like may be the most efficient way of finding all records whose last names sound like Brownstein or Gutierrez, regardless of the correct spellings.

Exact Another method of matching on inexact values is provided by dBASE IV. In this case, a program setting for dBASE IV is used. The setting, accessed from the Settings option in the Tools panel, is the *Exact* setting. The options menu that is used to turn *exact* on and off is shown in Figure 9-8. *Exact* is toggled on and off by moving the

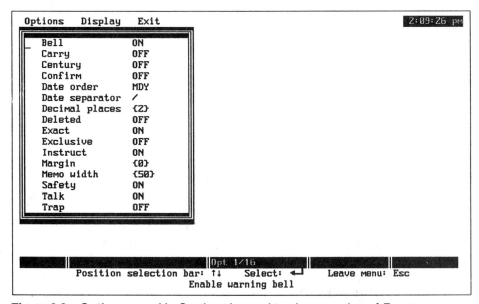

Figure 9-8 Options panel in *Settings* is used to change value of *Exact*.

highlight to the *Exact* option (by pressing **E** or moving the cursor down to highlight the option), and pressing the **Spacebar**. dBASE IV normally defaults to setting Exact OFF.

For the purposes of the next examples, set *Exact* OFF. When the value for *Exact* is OFF, select the Exit option (**Alt-E**) to return to the *Control Center*. Reopen <create> in the Queries panel, and you will again have a file and view skeleton displayed for the CUST_ID.DBF data file.

The difference with a query run with *Exact* set to ON is that all characters in the record must match all characters in the query parameter (with the exception of blanks that appear after the matching names or values). When Exact is set to OFF, the record is evaluated based on a match between the characters in the record and the characters in the query specification.

When *Exact* is ON, dBASE IV attempts to find an exact match between the expression provided and the field value. For example, if you want to find matches for the string "Los", only those records whose field is "Los" (and not Los Angeles, Los Alamitos, Lost and Found, or any other string that was not exactly Los) will be matched. Setting *Exact* OFF matches the characters from the beginning to the end of the match expression, and determines a match based on those characters matching. Any characters beyond the match string are ignored so any files that match the string specified will match, whether or not additional characters appear beyond the match expression. Thus, with *Exact* OFF, performing a match on "Los" would produce matches with Los, Los Angeles, Los Alamitos, Lost and Found, and any other string with the matching character string. Since dBASE IV is looking for an exact match, such values as Las Vegas and Long Beach would not match, since they don't match the expression.

The $ Character A very powerful query operator finds character strings that are part of a field value. The character $ placed in front of the query specification tells dBASE IV to look at the contents of a field and find all records where the character string is contained in the field. This is different from the use of the $ character in the rest of dBASE, where it means "contained in." In a query, the operator means that the field contains the string of characters.

To see how this works, the query shown in Figure 9-9 tells dBASE IV to find all records whose customer name includes the word "Music". As seen in Figure 9-10, all records in the data file containing the string Music have been selected. It is useful to note that the string can be part of a larger word, as in the word "Musical."

You could search for any string of characters. For example, if you wanted to search for all records for companies whose name begins with the letter M, you could use the expression **$' M'**. Note, however, that the space is used before the letter M to indicate that the character follows a space. However, placing a character after a space would not match any records whose first word begins with the desired letter, since the first character in a field is not a space, but a character.

Similarly, setting up a specification to find all words which end in a particular character or string of characters will only match all but the last word in a field, since field entries are usually concluded with a character, rather than a space. You may also use the $ expression to match text anywhere inside of a string of characters. For

Layout Fields Condition Update Exit
2:46:24 pm
Cust_id.dbf
↓CUST_NAME
↓CUST_NUMB
↓ADDRESS
↓CITY
↓STATE
↓PROVINCE
↓ZIP
$'Music'_
View
<NEW>
Cust_id-> CUST_NAME
Cust_id-> CUST_NUMB
Cust_id-> ADDRESS
Cust_id-> CITY
Query
C:\dbase\<NEW>
Field 1/17
Prev/Next field:Shift-Tab/Tab Data:F2 Pick:Shift-F1 Prev/Next skel:F3/F4

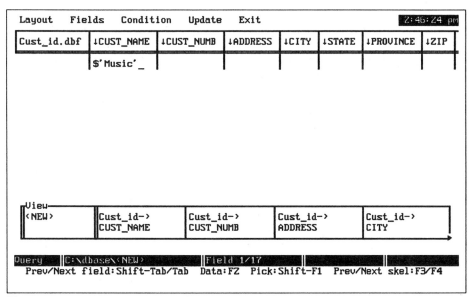

Figure 9-9 Query statement using ($) "Is Contained in."

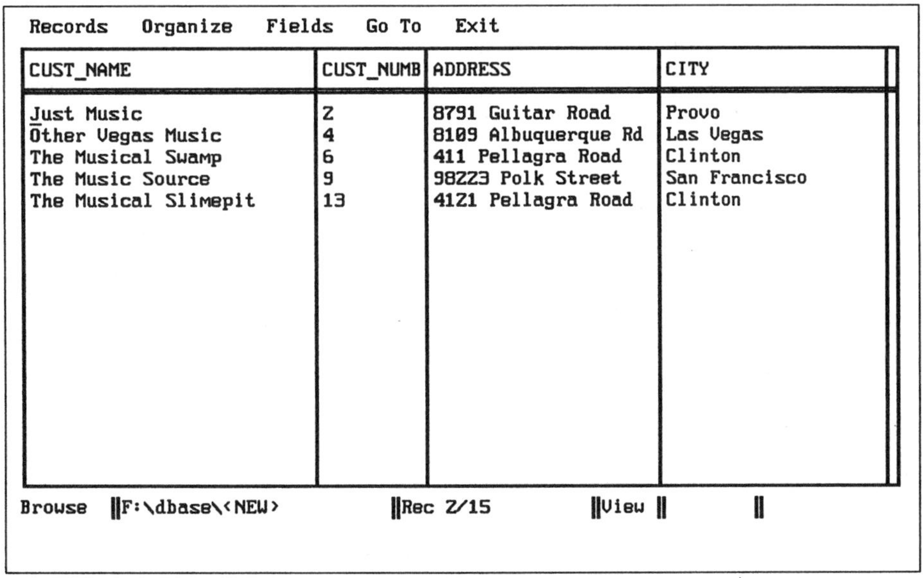

Records Organize Fields Go To Exit
CUST_NAME
CUST_NUMB
ADDRESS
CITY
Just Music 2 8791 Guitar Road Provo
Other Vegas Music 4 8109 Albuquerque Rd Las Vegas
The Musical Swamp 6 411 Pellagra Road Clinton
The Music Source 9 98223 Polk Street San Francisco
The Musical Slimepit 13 4121 Pellagra Road Clinton
Browse
F:\dbase\<NEW>
Rec 2/15
View

Figure 9-10 Results of query to find all customers with Music in name.

example, the expression **$'and'** would match records for such imaginary record stores as M*and*eville Canyon Music, Bob *and* Ray's Disks, and H*and*yman's CD Emporium. The $ parameter matches on case, however, so the string just listed wouldn't match *And*erson's Records, since Anderson's begins with an uppercase A, and the expression contained a lowercase a.

> Note⟩ One of the special strengths of dBASE IV is related to the $ parameter. In earlier versions of dBASE, you were unable to search memo fields to find text strings. dBASE IV, however, can look for records with matching character strings in memo fields.

Suppose you want to find all CD titles that are primarily Rap music. If you set up your data system so that the memo field in the TITLES data file is used for descriptions of the music included in the CD, you can create two query statements, which would appear on the memo field on two lines. The first line would find all records whose memo field contained the string *rap*. The expression for this is **$'rap'**. The second line would match for occurrences of the word with an initial uppercase character. This expression would be **$'Rap'**. By placing each expression on its own line, you are telling dBASE IV to find a match on the expressions on either line. This was discussed earlier in this chapter.

Delimiters There are three optional ways of beginning and ending character strings. These characters are the single quotation mark ', the double quotation mark'', and the brackets [ ]. Why three when one can do? Because one character won't always do. Suppose, for example, that you were attempting to match for a record that included a nickname. To find records for William ''Billy'' Boyd, you couldn't use an expression like **$''William ''Billy'' Boyd''**, because dBASE IV would consider the second occurrence of the character delimiter used (in this case the second occurrence of the '') as the end of the field description. Thus, the expression would match for all records with the string *William*, but might also detect an error, since it would be unable to interpret the rest of the expression, **Billy'' Boyd''**. If you were to use one of the other delimiters, however, the internal characters that would otherwise be seen as a delimiter would be regarded as characters that are part of a text string, rather than as a signal of the end of an expression.

The expressions **$ [William ''Billy'' Boyd]** and **$ 'William ''Billy'' Boyd'** would both result in locating the appropriate records. The important thing to remember when using any of the three characters to mark the beginning and end of a character field is that the characters at the beginning and end of a field must be the same, since dBASE IV identifies the first occurrence of the '', ', and [characters and considers any string of characters between that point and the matching '', ', or] to end the character string.

Describing the Output

The view skeleton tells dBASE IV in which fields, and in which order, the results of the query will appear. When you first load the query processor (if a file is in use), a view skeleton that matches the initial data file is automatically created as the view skeleton, shown at the bottom of the screen.

The view skeleton can include fields from any of the data files that are used to create the query. In the next chapter, you will see how queries can use data from a number of different data files. The view skeleton can accommodate data fields from any of the files.

The boxes in the view skeleton provide a substantial amount of information. The leftmost box shows the name of the view. So far, you have not saved any queries, so the name of the currently active view is <NEW>. At the right, the boxes show the name of the source data file, shown above the name of the field whose data will be displayed in the output data file or view.

In addition to the name of the source file and source field, each field box can also include a special name for a particular view. This is used when you have created a special field, such as one calculated by performing a mathematical function based on one or more fields (say, a Quantity times Price calculation for a new PTOTAL field) that does not exist in any of the source data files.

> **Note** As seen in all figures so far displayed in this chapter, the field skeleton, at the top of the screen, shows each field with an arrow pointing downward, located at the left of each field name. The arrow that points down indicates that the field is included in the view skeleton.

Any field can be added to, or removed from, the view skeleton. When a field is added to the view skeleton, it is placed at the end of the list of files in the view skeleton. Thus, if you were to add files to the skeleton, you should take care to add them in the order in which you want them to appear in the file that is produced by the query. Otherwise, the fields in the view skeleton must be reorganized (not a difficult task).

dBASE IV uses two methods to indicate if there are more data fields than can be shown in the width of the screen. Looking at the file skeleton, the right side of the skeleton will show a portion of the unseen field name. This is an indication that there are more fields on the current skeleton. This has been seen in all previous views of the Query design box so far.

Figure 9-11 shows the file skeleton with the highlight in the last field in the record. Note the closed box at the right side of the skeleton. Also, take note of the arrow pointing to the left in the first field visible on the screen. The arrow pointing to the left in the first screen in either the file or view skeletons indicates that there are more fields to the left of the ones shown on screen. In the view skeleton, an arrow at the bottom of the rightmost visible box indicates that there are additional fields on the right. To move quickly to the beginning of the file or view skeleton, press the **Home** key. To quickly move to the end of a file or view skeleton, press the **End** key.

Movement between file skeletons and to the view skeleton is also easily accomplished. The **F4** key moves the cursor down one step at a time. If you were preparing a query that had three or four different files in use, the **F4** key would move the cursor down, from the top of the screen to the bottom file skeleton. After the last file skeleton is reached, the **F4** key brings the cursor into the view skeleton. The **F3** key moves the cursor in the other direction, from the bottom of the screen to the top, one skeleton at a time. In addition, either key will cause the cursor to wrap around to the other end of the file skeleton.

Move the cursor into the view skeleton (by pressing **F3** or **F4**). The highlight

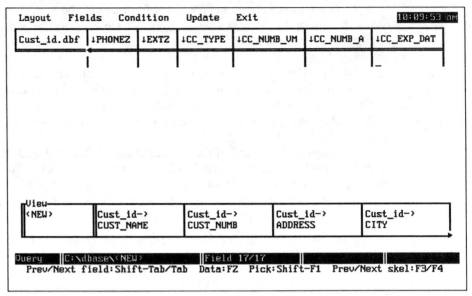

Figure 9-11 The last box on the File skeleton is closed.

should be above the first field, CUST_NAME. The bar at the top of the box serves a number of purposes. First, it indicates which field you have selected (this knowledge is useful if you want to move or remove a particular field). Second, it allows you to assign a different name or parameter to the data field. This is useful if, for example, you want to perform a calculation based on the field, or assign a condition to it. This will be explored in the next chapter.

Fields may be added to, or removed from, the view skeleton using the **F5** key. From within the view skeleton, you may remove a field by positioning the cursor on the field and pressing **F5**. Remove the CUST_ID field now.

> Note ⟩ Although fields can be removed from the view skeleton, it is considerably more efficient to do the field additions and deletions from the appropriate file skeleton. From within the file skeleton, fields may be added to or removed from the view skeleton.

For the next example, assume that you want to view only the customer name and address, and that credit and telephone information is not necessary. Further, assume that your data file contains no foreign companies. Thus, you want to remove all fields except those that specifically relate to address and company name. The fields can be removed by moving the cursor into them (using the **Tab** key) and pressing **F5**. When you press **F5**, dBASE IV again provides an animation showing the box moving into the view skeleton, grabbing the field, and pulling it back into the file skeleton. The **F5** key acts as a toggle. It not only removes a field, it can also place a removed field back into the view skeleton.

Remove all fields not related to name and address. Next, move the cursor into the

CUST_ID field and press **F5** to place the field back onto the view skeleton. You should notice the animation, showing the field being brought down and placed off-screen on the view skeleton.

> **Note** ⟩ When you press **F5** to remove a field, dBASE IV provides a brief graphical animation of the field moving from the view skeleton into the original file skeleton.

Move the cursor into the view skeleton and press **End**. You will see that the CUST_ID field is at the end of the skeleton, following the ZIP field. This is not where you want the field to appear when you create your new data file. Instead, you would like to have the CUST_ID field displayed as the first field in the data display. Thus, you must move the field from one spot in the view skeleton to another position.

> **Note** ⟩ Although the CUST_ID field may have been the first in the file skeleton, it is placed at the end of the view skeleton. Fields are placed on the view skeleton in the order in which they are selected.

Moving a Field in the View Skeleton

To move a field name (or names) in a view skeleton from one area to another, the field(s) to be moved must first be highlighted. To move a single field, position the highlight so that it is above the field to be moved, and press **F6**.

To move a range of fields, move the highlight to the first or last field to be moved and press **F6**. A box will be drawn around the field that the highlight was positioned on. This box is shown in Figure 9-12. To include additional fields in your Move operation,

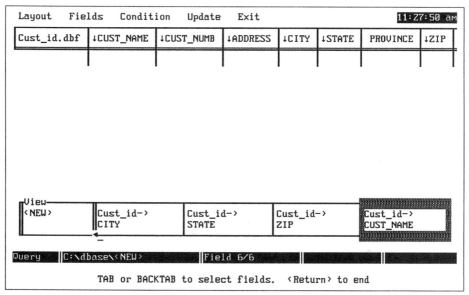

Figure 9-12   A box is drawn around a field that is highlighted.

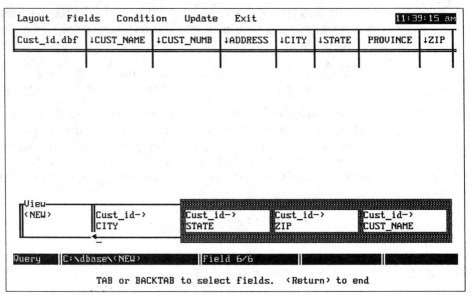

Figure 9-13   **Shft-Tab** extends the highlight to the left.

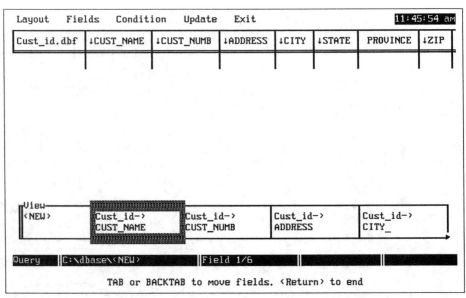

Figure 9-14   CUST_NAME field is placed in its desired position.

press the **Tab** key to extend your selection to the right, or the **Shft-Tab** key combination to move the selection to the fields to the left. Figure 9-13 shows the results of pressing **Shft-Tab** twice, to select the two additional fields to the left of the CUST_NAME field. Once you have highlighted the field(s) that you want to move, press **Enter** to complete your selection.

> **Note** ⟩ If you make a mistake marking your fields, these can be undone using the **Tab** or **Shft-Tab** keys.

The **F7** key is used to tell dBASE IV that you are moving the highlighted field(s) to another position on the file skeleton. To move the field(s), you may move the highlighted area above the cursor to the position where you want the highlighted field(s) to be inserted, then press **F7**, or you may press **F7** and move the highlighted field(s) as a complete block. It is recommended that you press **F7** to move the block of fields, because moving the highlight and then pressing **F7** may place the field after, rather than before, the location where it is to be inserted. As you move the field(s) (using the **Tab** or **Shft-Tab** keys), you will see the portion of the view skeleton that is visible, in the order in which the fields will appear if you were to complete your move operation at the current position.

> **Note** ⟩ The **Home** and **End** keys cannot be used during a Move operation.

When you have placed your field(s) in the location where you want them to appear, as shown in Figure 9-14, press **Enter** to complete the move.

Highlighted files may also be deleted, as a group, by pressing the **F5** key. In most cases, however, it may be faster and easier to move to the view skeleton and remove them from the skeleton by pressing the **F5** key as the cursor moves into each field.

You may move an entire data file structure (all fields in the structure) onto a view skeleton (or remove them from the skeleton), by moving the highlight into the data filename box (at the far left of the file skeleton), and pressing **F5**. This is perhaps the simplest way to add or remove fields into or out of a view skeleton. If you want to move most, but not all, of your data fields into the view skeleton, it may be more efficient to copy the entire data file's fields (using the method just outlined), and delete the fields you don't want in the view skeleton by using the **F5** key on each unwanted field.

To show how the view skeleton displays only those fields selected in the skeleton, remove the address information fields from the skeleton, leaving only the CUST_NAME and CUST_NUMB fields. The Browse screen showing only those fields selected in the view skeleton is shown in Figure 9-15.

The fields that are shown in the view skeleton are displayed in the Browse screen produced by a query or become part of a new data file that can be created by dBASE IV's query processor.

Pull-Down Menus

Many of the functions performed by the pull-down menus have been shown in this chapter. The function keys substantially speed up the operation of building a query.

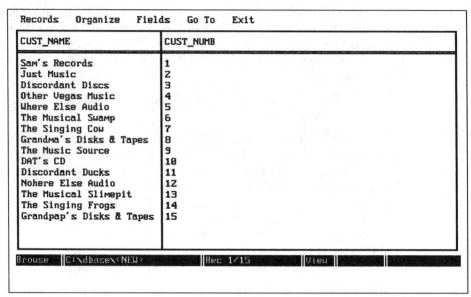

Figure 9-15   Browse screen created with View skeleton using two fields.

The Layout Menu

The Layout menu, seen in Figure 9-16, is used to control some of the functions of file selection and file creation. The options are as follows:

Add File to Query This option allows you to select from the files listed in your catalog a data file that is to be included in the query design. If you open the Queries <create> panel with no data file open, this option will automatically become the default. When you are relating the data across more than one file (or multiple versions of the same file, for certain types of queries), use this menu option to select and place another data file in the query design structure.

Remove File from Query This option is used to remove the highlighted data file from the query structure. Any fields from the removed file that are in the view skeleton will also be removed. Calculated fields can also be removed from the query definition by selecting this option.

Create Link by Pointing This option will be explored in further detail in the next chapter. When you are creating a query definition that uses more than one data file, the link between fields is used to establish *how* the data in each file is matched. For example, if you want to produce a file that generates invoices, you may have to use more than one data file. One file would have customer ID information, while another would have the actual customer order, but no identification other than the customer number.

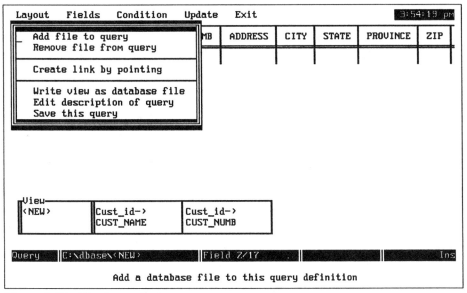

Figure 9-16   The Layout menu.

By defining a link in both the order data file and the CUST_ID data file that selected records having the *same* number in both data files, you would then have a link that would allow you to retrieve the customer name and address from the CUST_ID file, and also allow you to add in the details of the order. Linking two files, then, defines the field data that would allow you to find related data files so that other reports, labels, or queries can be created based on the linked files.

Write View as a Database File   This option is one of the most common results of a query. When a query is run, it is often to produce a data file that contains the specific data fields and results of linked records to produce a new data file. This file may be used to produce a report or to generate labels, or as a new data file that can be otherwise modified. The new data file will consist of the fields in the order and form defined in the view skeleton.

When this option is selected, dBASE IV will prompt you for a name for the new data file. If the name is not unique, you will also be prompted to confirm that you want to overwrite an existing data file or to give a new name to the new data file that you will be creating.

Edit Description of Query   This option is used to attach a query description to your saved query design. After you have saved your query definition, the name of the query and view will be shown on the screen.

Save This Query   This option is used to save a query definition. When you select this option, you are asked to name the query or to accept the current name, if it has already been previously saved.

The Fields Menu

The Fields menu allows you to perform some of the same functions (adding and deleting fields from the view skeleton) that have already been demonstrated. The menu options are as follows:

Add Field to View This option performs the same function as pressing the **F5** key. When the cursor is on a field that is not already in the view skeleton, this option will be available. If the field is already in the view skeleton, this option cannot be selected.

Remove Field from View This option is the complement of *Add field to view*. If the cursor is positioned on a field that is already part of the view skeleton, this option can be selected.

When taken in combination, the above options perform the same functions as the **F5** key. With the **F5** key, however, fields can be quickly added or removed from a view skeleton without the necessity of opening the Fields menu and selecting the desired option.

Edit Field Name This option is used to modify the name of a field as it appears on the view skeleton. This option can only be selected when the highlight is on a field box in the view skeleton. It is useful for creating a more descriptive field name than one already in use, and to provide an alias that can be used for condition boxes. This will be explored more fully in the next chapter.

Create Calculated Field This option is used to create a new field that includes calculations based on data in your data files. Using this option, you may create a field that does not naturally occur in any of the data files you are using.

Calculated fields can be created at any time. Unlike the previous option, a calculated field can be created whether the cursor is in a view skeleton or in a file skeleton. Examples of calculated fields will be provided in the next chapter.

Sort on This Field dBASE IV can sort the data in your records for all records that match your query specification. To use this option, you must first highlight the field that you want the sort to be performed on, and then select the *Sort on this field* option in the Fields window. When this option is selected, you are given a choice of four methods of sorting, as shown in Figure 9-17. These options were discussed in previous chapters.

When a sort type is selected, dBASE IV will insert a sort instruction and number in the field box in the file skeleton. The first part of the instruction is a code that defines which type of sort you want performed. The second part is a number that indicates the sort order. For example, if you selected an ascending sort, the first time this is used, dBASE IV will place the expression **Asc1** in the panel for the field to be sorted on. The second time this option is selected, **Asc2** will be inserted, and so on. The number following the sort instruction indicates what order the sort will be performed in. Chapter 8 discusses sort order.

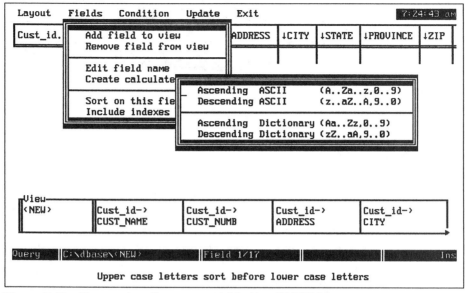

Figure 9-17   Four sort options are provided by dBASE IV.

Include Indexes This option is a toggled field. By selecting this option and pressing **Enter**, the option can be set ON or OFF.

When you create a new file, you may tell dBASE IV to attach multiple field indexes (or the indexes that were attached to a data file when it was created) that were created in one of the files in the query design screen to the new data file. The fields that are associated with the index will be shown with a # symbol to the left of the field name, to indicate that the field is included in an index expression that will be used by the new data file.

The Condition Menu

The Condition menu allows you specify conditions that are applied to your data to determine if the records should be included in a query's results. The condition box functions much like the *Permit edit if* function seen in the Forms panel. With the condition box, you can tell dBASE IV to look for specific conditions that match those required before a record can be included in a query.

For example, you can set a condition box to select all records whose total units purchased is greater than 50. When dBASE IV performs the query, it will first find records that match the condition(s) specified, then evaluate it based on the query expressions. The Condition menu options are as follows:

Add Condition Box This option is used to create or define a new condition box. Once the condition box has been added to the query design, you may move into or out of the

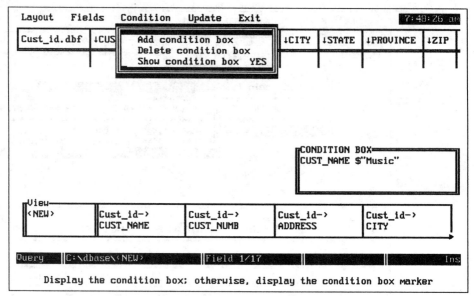

Figure 9-18   The conditon box and Condition menu.

box using the **F3** and **F4** keys. Only one condition box may be used in a query, although a condition expression may be quite complex. In the next chapter, the condition box will be explored further.

Delete Condition Box This option removes the condition box from the query. There are no keyboard shortcuts for removing the condition box. Care should be taken when this option is selected, since the condition box is removed without any additional confirmation that you want to do this. Thus, once you've removed a condition box, it's gone.

Show Condition Box This option allows you to tell dBASE IV to show the condition box on screen or to minimize it by reducing it to a single line. The condition box, seen in Figure 9-18 (along with the Condition menu), occupies a prime piece of screen real estate. This is especially important when you have two or more data files in the file skeleton. There are times when the condition box occupies more space than you want it to. You can always set *Show condition box* to YES when you want to evaluate or edit your conditions.

This option is toggled between YES and NO by selecting the option and pressing **Enter,** or by opening the Condition menu and pressing **S.** When this option is set to NO, the box is minimized, and a marker is placed above the view skeleton, as seen in Figure 9-19.

The Update Menu

The Update menu provides you with a different type of query management. dBASE IV can be used to perform two basic types of query. The first type, in which a new data file

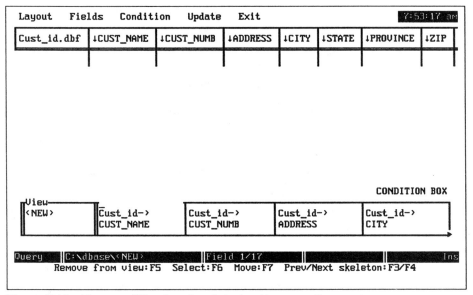

Figure 9-19 The condition box is minimized to a one-line marker.

or view is created, has already been shown. The second type of query operation is an update operation. It is used to modify (update) records in your data file. This menu can only be activated when there is no view skeleton (since you aren't creating a view).

A range of update options are available. These options are displayed by opening the *Specify update operation* option in the Update menu. The options available in the Update menu and from the *Specify update operation* option are as follows:

Perform the Update This option performs the update that has been defined by the *Specify update operation* options. The update operation selected is performed when this option is chosen.

This operation is performed on those records that match the query conditions defined in your query definition screen. For example, you can set a query to remove accounts that have not ordered in more than 365 days. By writing a query expression that finds the number of days since the last order, and selecting *Mark records for deletion*, you can have dBASE IV locate all records that match the query specification and perform the update operation.

Specify Update Operation This option opens a new panel that is used to specify which of four operations are to be performed on records that match your query specification. The query update options perform the following functions (some of which will be demonstrated in the following chapters):

Replace values in FILENAME.dbf. When this is selected, the word REPLACE is included in the query expression. In order to make use of this option, you must tell dBASE IV what you are replacing. The option is used to replace the contents of a field. For example, if you wish to replace the contents of the current ZIP field with a new definition that lists the five-digit ZIP and adds a hyphen in the ZIP field, you would type *WITH*

LEFT(ZIP,5) + "-", to tell dBASE IV to use the five leftmost characters in the ZIP field, and add the hyphen.

Append records to Filename.dbf is used to add new records to the first file in the query design.

Throughout this book, the situation has been described where many people are taking data in small data files that will be moved into a master data file. For example, an order entry system may have a daily order file that is updated when orders are received. If you have three order entry clerks, each one may use his or her own data file. At the end of the day (or whenever), you will want to combine the orders into a single data file (or add them to a weekly file or to a master file). By putting the files on the same query definition screen, the records can be appended by dBASE IV to the first file in the query design. Using the condition box, you may also select *which* records will be appended (added to the end) to your initial data file.

Mark records for deletion has been briefly described earlier. This option evaluates the records in your file(s) to see which ones match your query definition. Those that match are marked by dBASE IV.

> **Note** You should recall that marking a record for deletion does not immediately delete the record. In order to delete marked records, the Organize menu (available in Browse, Edit, and Database design screens) provides an option to remove marked records. (Marked records can be removed from within the dot prompt using the PACK command).

Unmark records in FILENAME.dbf removes the deletion mark from records that match the query definition. This option can be used to undo deletion marks for records that meet criteria that qualify them for not being deleted.

You may, for example, have marked for deletion all customers who have not ordered for more than 90 days. Before deleting the records, you may wish to unmark any customers who have placed orders after the last update operation was performed. If you have a large number of records marked for deletion and only expect a few to be unmarked, this option may be the best way to accomplish an unmarking process.

The Exit Menu

Finally, the Exit menu provides you with two options.

Save Changes and Exit This option saves your query definition. If you haven't yet assigned a name to your query, dBASE IV will ask for one.

Abandon Changes and Exit This option returns you to the Control Center without saving your changes. You will be prompted to confirm that you want to leave.

It should be pointed out that the Exit menu may be less frequently used than it is in other panels. From within the Layout menu, you can save your query by selecting *Save this query*. This performs almost the same function as the *Save changes and exit* option. In many cases, you will load or design a query, and transfer out to the Browse screen to view the data that has been selected or created by the query. If you attempt to exit from your Browse or Edit session while a query that has not been saved was in use, dBASE IV prompts you, asking if you want to save your query design.

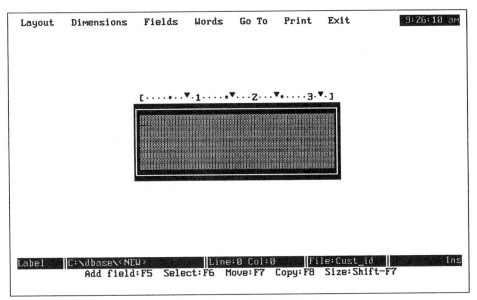

Figure 9-20   The Label design panel.

There is another way to produce a query. This will be used to create a report or label with a query that is used once and does not (necessarily) have to be saved. To quickly see how this is done, return to the Control Center and move the cursor into the Labels panel. <create> should be highlighted. Press **F2** to load the Label design panel. The screen will look like Figure 9-20.

Press **F5** to open the fields selection menu and select CUST_NAME. Press **Ctrl-End** to select the default settings for the field. Press **Enter** to move the cursor to the next line. Add ADDRESS to the second line of your form, and CITY, STATE, and ZIP_CODE on subsequent lines, selecting the standard defaults by pressing **Ctrl-End** for each one. Next, press **F2** to enter the Browse or Edit screen. Open the Exit window (by pressing **Alt-E** or **F10** and using the cursor arrows to open the window). The Exit menu provides you with three options, as seen in Figure 9-21.

Now, select *Transfer to Query Design*. Create a very simple query to select all stores with the string *Music* in their name. To this, move the cursor into the CUST_ NAME field, and type *$"Music"*. Next, remove the unnecessary fields from the view skeleton (by moving the cursor into the fields to be removed from the skeleton and pressing **F5**).

Now, press **F2** to return to Browse or Edit. The screen should show five records that include the string *Music* in their name. Open the Exit menu and you will be given the option of returning to Query Design or to Label Design. Select *Return to Label Design*, and the cursor will again be placed in the Label design panel. To see that labels will be produced only for those records selected by the query processor, open the Print menu, and select *View labels on screen*. dBASE IV will create the labels, according to your design, and print them on screen. The first screen of labels is shown in Figure 9-22.

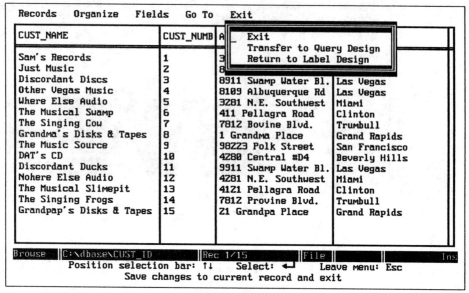

```
 Records   Organize   Fields   Go To   Exit
┌────────────────────────────┬────────────┬─────────────────────────┐
│ CUST_NAME                  │ CUST_NUMB  │A┌──────────────────────┐ │
│                            │            │ │  Exit                │ │
│ Sam's Records              │ 1          │3│  Transfer to Query Design │
│ Just Music                 │ 2          │8│  Return to Label Design   │
│ Discordant Discs           │ 3          │8911 Swamp Water Bl.│Las Vegas │
│ Other Vegas Music          │ 4          │8109 Albuquerque Rd │Las Vegas │
│ Where Else Audio           │ 5          │3281 N.E. Southwest │Miami     │
│ The Musical Swamp          │ 6          │411 Pellagra Road   │Clinton   │
│ The Singing Cow            │ 7          │7812 Bovine Blvd.   │Trumbull  │
│ Grandma's Disks & Tapes    │ 8          │1 Grandma Place     │Grand Rapids │
│ The Music Source           │ 9          │98223 Polk Street   │San Francisco │
│ DAT's CD                   │ 10         │4280 Central #D4    │Beverly Hills │
│ Discordant Ducks           │ 11         │9911 Swamp Water Bl.│Las Vegas │
│ Nohere Else Audio          │ 12         │4281 N.E. Southwest │Miami     │
│ The Musical Slimepit       │ 13         │4121 Pellagra Road  │Clinton   │
│ The Singing Frogs          │ 14         │7812 Provine Blvd.  │Trumbull  │
│ Grandpap's Disks & Tapes   │ 15         │21 Grandpa Place    │Grand Rapids │
│                            │            │                    │          │
│                            │            │                    │          │
└────────────────────────────┴────────────┴─────────────────────────┘
 Browse  │C:\dbase\CUST_ID      │Rec 1/15    │File│            Ins
        Position selection bar: ↑↓    Select: ↵    Leave menu: Esc
              Save changes to current record and exit
```

Figure 9-21   The Exit menu from within a design gives an extra option.

```
Just Music
8791 Guitar Road
Provo
UT
84601-

Other Vegas Music
8109 Albuquerque Rd
Las Vegas
NM
87199-

The Musical Swamp
411 Pellagra Road
Clinton
IA
52791-

The Music Source
98223 Polk Street
San Francisco
CA
94105-

_            Cancel viewing: ESC,  Continue viewing: SPACEBAR
```

Figure 9-22   First screen of labels produced using Query.

Note> You will notice that only those records that matched the query specification were displayed on screen. If you wanted, you could also have printed the labels with the same information.

In this example, you have designed your label, created a query to select your data files, and produced labels based on that data. Neither your query nor a new data file that includes the data produced by your query (and used to print your labels) was created or saved.

This process also works from within the Report design panel. When you exit either design surface, the system asks if you wish to save your query. At this point, if your query and label or report form works as desired, you may save both the query and the label or report design.

Conclusion

In this chapter, the basic elements of query design were explored. Subsequent chapters will explore additional features of dBASE IV's Queries panel, and show the power of the relational features of dBASE IV.

10

Query Design—Part Two

In Chapter 9, many of the basics of query design using dBASE IV were detailed. This chapter explores more advanced query functions, and concludes with a section on relational queries. You will build a variety of data files, add data to existing files, and create new files as needed to demonstrate the powers of dBASE IV's powerful query processing components.

The first part of the chapter is concerned with more complex queries—queries that use advanced features, queries using condition boxes, queries that create new fields, and others. The second part of the chapter deals with queries that draw data from multiple data files. Such queries are referred to as *relational queries*. Whether these can be called truly relational or not is moot: The fact is, queries of this type effectively produce records that call on the data in as many data files as are included in the query, and can produce reports combining data from a variety of sources. Substantial power is provided by the relational linking in dBase IV. For the purposes of this book, the abilities of dBASE IV to process queries based on linking data fields in different files will be referred to, and treated, as relational capabilities.

In addition to being performed on character fields, the queries can also be performed on numeric or logical fields. For logical fields, you may specify .T. or .F. for True or False (or Yes or No).

Numeric fields support the use of specific values or range of values. You are also able to use summary operators to find totals, averages, and other summary values for your numeric field(s). As is suggested by the previous sentence, you can perform calculations on more than one numeric field by creating a calculated field. Summary processes can also be performed on calculated fields. These topics will all be discussed shortly.

Simple Queries

Suppose you want to produce a list of records of all customers in states with borders on the Pacific Ocean. Although you can certainly use a series of lines with each state listed

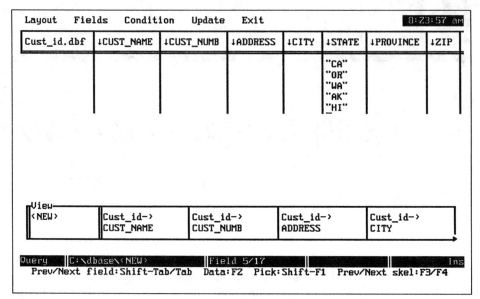

```
 Layout   Fields   Condition   Update   Exit                    8:23:57 am
┌──────────────┬───────────┬───────────┬──────────┬───────┬────────┬──────────┬──────┐
│ Cust_id.dbf  │↓CUST_NAME │↓CUST_NUMB │↓ADDRESS  │↓CITY  │↓STATE  │↓PROVINCE │↓ZIP  │
│              │           │           │          │       │ "CA"   │          │      │
│              │           │           │          │       │ "OR"   │          │      │
│              │           │           │          │       │ "WA"   │          │      │
│              │           │           │          │       │ "AK"   │          │      │
│              │           │           │          │       │ "HI"   │          │      │
│              │           │           │          │       │        │          │      │
│              │           │           │          │       │        │          │      │
│              │           │           │          │       │        │          │      │
│              │           │           │          │       │        │          │      │
│              │           │           │          │       │        │          │      │
│ ┌View────    │           │           │          │       │        │          │      │
│ │<NEW>       │ Cust_id-> │ Cust_id-> │ Cust_id->│ Cust_id->│      │          │      │
│ │            │ CUST_NAME │ CUST_NUMB │ ADDRESS  │ CITY  │        │          │   →  │
│                                                                                    │
 Query    C:\dbase\<NEW>              Field 5/17                              Ins
     Prev/Next field:Shift-Tab/Tab   Data:F2   Pick:Shift-F1   Prev/Next skel:F3/F4
```

Figure 10-1   Query to find customers in states bordering the Pacific.

on its own line in the query description, as shown in Figure 10-1, you can also define the range of ZIP codes that match those records you seek to locate.

With knowledge of the ZIP codes involved, the query could be written using a single line, with a single statement. Since all states bordering on the Pacific Ocean have ZIP codes beginning with the number 9 (90000 through 99999), using one of two query expressions, >**"89999"** (since the first integer greater than 89999 is 90000, and ZIP codes are integer values) or > = **"90000"** (since this is actually what you want to match on), will also produce the desired result. The expression(s) would, of course, be typed into the ZIP data column, as shown in Figure 10-2.

> **Note** In this example, the numeric values are placed inside quotation marks. This is done because the ZIP field is a character field, not a numeric one. In a character field, the numbers must be delimited in order for the expression to be valid.

The numbers inside a character field are not treated by dBASE IV as values that can be used for calculations. Although an equality statement like the one used in this example will be acted upon more or less appropriately, you aren't able to do processes like finding the average ZIP code for all orders. (This is not completely true. There are methods to convert a character field that contains numbers into a numeric field that can be used for numeric operations.) As was shown earlier, ordering records by numbers in a character field doesn't always work, since dBASE IV looks at the first character in a field to decide how to sort or index the record. Such a process on a character field that contains numbers would put record 1,000,000 before number 9 because the 1 in 1,000,000 appears (in a sort order) before 9.

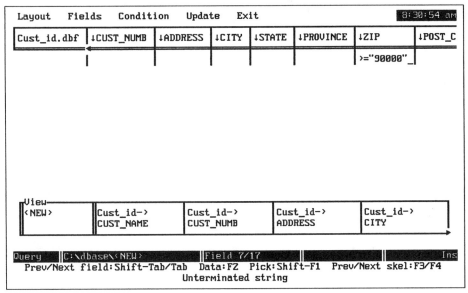

Figure 10-2   Query expression using numeric ZIP codes.

This problem can be avoided (as discussed in Chapter 8) by placing leading spaces or zeros before the number in a character field. The goal is to assure that your numbers are aligned with the right side of the data field. If the numbers used in character fields are right aligned, a query that sorts or indexes on the data field *will* correctly organize the data in your data file. To show that this works, the customer numbers in the CUST_ ID data file have been right aligned. *Include indexes* is set to Yes, and a sort on the CUST_NUMB field is selected, as shown in Figure 10-3. The resulting Browse screen is shown in Figure 10-4.

If you want to select only those records located in the state of California, and don't want to do it by setting a match for "CA" in the STATE field, you can also do this using the range of ZIP codes that are valid in the state. The expression $> = 90000, < = 95999$ will select all customers having ZIP codes valid for the state of California. *The entire expression must be typed on a single line with the two inequality expressions separated by a comma.*

Exclusion Queries

In the preceding query, you were shown two different ways to design a query for the same condition (you could have set a match on "CA" or a match on a range of ZIP codes). What if you want to find all customers who were *not* located in California?

dBASE IV provides you with an elegant method for writing such a query. The *not equal to* operators, $< >$, and #, can be used to find all records that do not match the value in the query expression. Thus, to find all customers not located in California, the

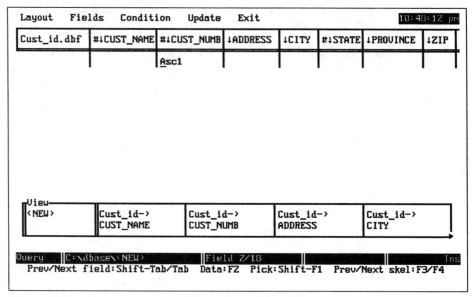

Figure 10-3 Ascending sort with numbers right aligned.

Records	Organize	Fields	Go To	Exit

CUST_NAME	CUST_NUMB	ADDRESS	CITY
Sam's Records	1	324 Disk Drive	Los Angeles
Just Music	2	8791 Guitar Road	Provo
Discordant Discs	3	8911 Swamp Water Bl.	Las Vegas
Other Vegas Music	4	8109 Albuquerque Rd	Las Vegas
Where Else Audio	5	3281 N.E. Southwest	Miami
The Musical Swamp	6	411 Pellagra Road	Clinton
The Singing Cow	7	7812 Bovine Blvd.	Trumbull
Grandma's Disks & Tapes	8	1 Grandma Place	Grand Rapids
The Music Source	9	98223 Polk Street	San Francisco
DAT's CD	10	4280 Central #D4	Beverly Hills
Discordant Ducks	11	9911 Swamp Water Bl.	Las Vegas
Nohere Else Audio	12	4281 N.E. Southwest	Miami
The Musical Slimepit	13	4121 Pellagra Road	Clinton
The Singing Frogs	14	7812 Provine Blvd.	Trumbull
Grandpap's Disks & Tapes	15	21 Grandpa Place	Grand Rapids

Browse   C:\dbase\<NEW>   Rec 1/15   View   Ins

Figure 10-4 Browse screen resulting from query in Figure 10-3.

expression #"**CA**" in the STATE field will provide you with the desired records. Remember, however, that the # (or < >) operator must appear before the query expression and that, in a character field, the characters in the expression must still be enclosed by single or double quotes or brackets.

Wildcard Searches Using LIKE

Up until now, you've used the query operator to match exact values or ranges of values, or, in the case of the **SOUNDS LIKE** and **$** operators, to find records that sound like a particular string or characters, or that contain a particular string of characters. However, for other types of matches, you have been required to type the exact text or value that you want to match on. The LIKE operator allows the use of wildcard characters.

Two wildcard characters are allowed in dBASE IV. The ? character indicates that any character can appear in the same position in an expression as the ? appears. For example, if you use the expression **LIKE SM?TH**, names such as SMITH, SMYTH, and even such weird names as SM2TH or SMXTH would also be selected by such an expression.

A wildcard tells dBASE IV to accept any character in that position (or to the end of the field). There are two types of wildcard that can be used in dBASE IV. The ? applies only to a single character position, with one ? used for each character position. When you use the ? wildcard character, you tell dBASE IV that any character in that position in the field is acceptable.

The * wildcard indicates that any character from that point on in a field is acceptable. Taking our earlier example, if we were to slightly modify the expression to **LIKE SM?TH***, SMYTH and SMITH, as well as SMITHFIELD, SMITHSON, SMYTHBURG, and any other combination of characters that match the definition screen would be included in the browse results. As shown earlier, the ? wildcard character allows a Y, an I, or any other character to be placed between the letters SM and TH. The * wildcard allowed the additional characters FIELD, SON, or BURG (or any other characters) to be used from the position of the * through to the end of the field.

Figure 10-5 defines a query to find all customers whose names begin with the word "The." Figure 10-6 shows all matching records.

Date Queries

In addition to the queries that can be performed on character fields, and the numeric summary and comparison queries that will be demonstrated later in this chapter, dBASE IV also has a fairly sophisticated date management capability. You can match for exact dates, compare dates in your data to the current date (or to any number of days before or after the current date), and define a range of dates to be matched in your data files.

To match to the current date, the comparison operator is **date( )**. The parentheses are required for the expression to be valid. To run a query to find all customers whose credit cards have expired (or whose expiration dates have not been updated), the query

Layout Fields Condition Update Exit
11:59:32 pm
Cust_id.dbf
↓CUST_NAME
↓CUST_NUMB
↓ADDRESS
↓CITY
↓STATE
↓PROVINCE
↓ZIP
Like "The*"
View
<NEW>
Cust_id-> CUST_NAME
Cust_id-> CUST_NUMB
Cust_id-> ADDRESS
Cust_id-> CITY
Query
C:\dbase\<NEW>
Field 1/17
Ins
Prev/Next field:Shift-Tab/Tab Data:F2 Pick:Shift-F1 Prev/Next skel:F3/F4

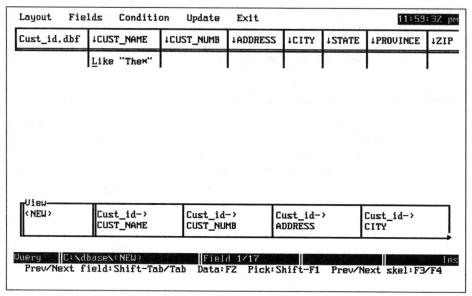

Figure 10-5 Query expression using the LIKE operator.

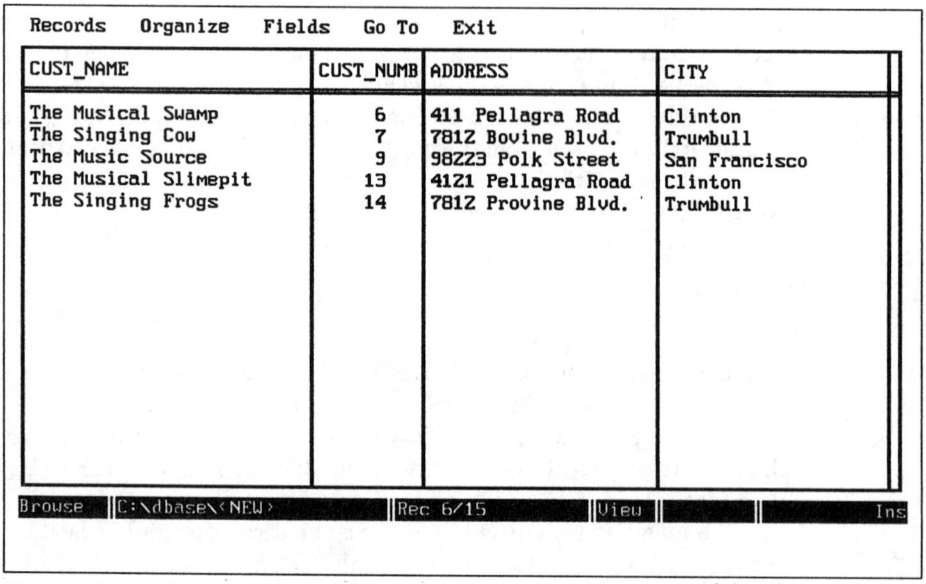

Records Organize Fields Go To Exit
CUST_NAME
CUST_NUMB
ADDRESS
CITY
The Musical Swamp 6 411 Pellagra Road Clinton
The Singing Cow 7 7812 Bovine Blvd. Trumbull
The Music Source 9 98223 Polk Street San Francisco
The Musical Slimepit 13 4121 Pellagra Road Clinton
The Singing Frogs 14 7812 Provine Blvd. Trumbull
Browse
C:\dbase\<NEW>
Rec 6/15
View
Ins

Figure 10-6 Browse screen showing results of query using LIKE.

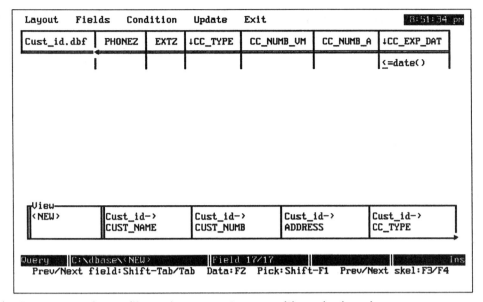

Figure 10-7 Query file to choose customers with expired cards.

in Figure 10-7, $< = $ **date( )**, can be used. When the query is run, it selects all records whose credit cards have expired on the day of the query.

Similarly, to find customers whose cards have expired, or will expire within the next 60 days, the query expression $< = $ **date( ) + 60** can be used. Such a file will produce a list that can be used for updating credit information, although in this case, a 15-day period may be more appropriate, since credit cards are often renewed only in the last week or two before they expire.

You may also search for, add to, or subtract from specific dates. To include a date in a query, the date must be enclosed by braces ({}). Thus, to find all customers whose credit cards expire more than six months from a particular date (say, 2-10-90), use the expression $> = $ **{02/10/90} + 182** (182 is approximately one half of 365, the number of days in a year). This expression will select all records with dates matching the specification.

To produce a list of records that match a range of dates, more than one date expression can be used in the same field. For example, to find records for all customers that have expired in the last 30 days, or that will expire in the next 30 days, use the expression $> = $ **date( )-30, $< = $ date( ) + 30**. The comma is required in the expression, making it an AND statement.

The FIND Expression

When you define a query and activate it, dBASE IV provides a list of records that match the query arguments. Only those records that match the query expression(s) are displayed. If, however, you want to retain all the data in your files, but to find the first

Layout Fields Condition Update Exit 9:35:37 pm
Cust_id.dbf ↓CUST_NAME ↓CUST_NUMB ↓ADDRESS ↓CITY ↓STATE ↓PROVINCE ↓ZIP
find >="5"
View
<NEW>
Cust_id-> CUST_NAME
Cust_id-> CUST_NUMB
Cust_id-> ADDRESS
Cust_id-> CITY
Query C:\dbase\<NEW> File 1/1 Ins
Next field:Tab Add/Remove all fields:F5 Zoom:F9 Prev/Next skeleton:F3/F4

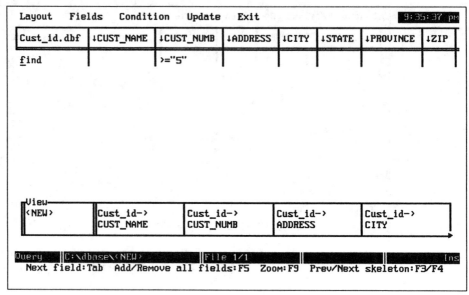

Figure 10-8 Query expression using FIND expression.

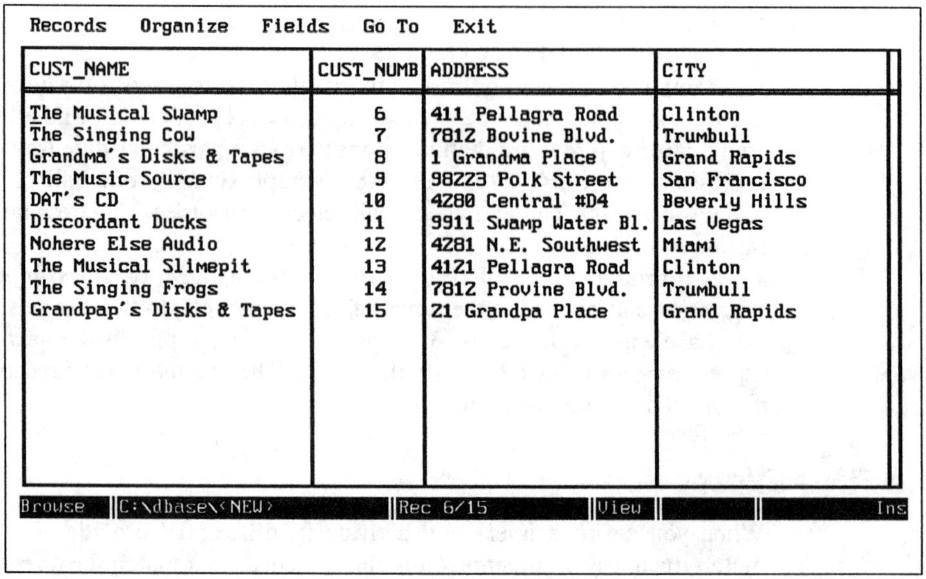

Records Organize Fields Go To Exit
CUST_NAME CUST_NUMB ADDRESS CITY
The Musical Swamp 6 411 Pellagra Road Clinton
The Singing Cow 7 7812 Bovine Blvd. Trumbull
Grandma's Disks & Tapes 8 1 Grandma Place Grand Rapids
The Music Source 9 98223 Polk Street San Francisco
DAT's CD 10 4280 Central #D4 Beverly Hills
Discordant Ducks 11 9911 Swamp Water Bl. Las Vegas
Nohere Else Audio 12 4281 N.E. Southwest Miami
The Musical Slimepit 13 4121 Pellagra Road Clinton
The Singing Frogs 14 7812 Provine Blvd. Trumbull
Grandpap's Disks & Tapes 15 21 Grandpa Place Grand Rapids
Browse C:\dbase\<NEW> Rec 6/15 View Ins

Figure 10-9 Browse screen resulting from query in Figure 10-8.

occurrence of a matching condition, a new operator can be used. In order to perform such a process, enter *Find* in the leftmost box on your file skeleton (the box with the data file name).

In the query expression shown in Figure 10-8, dBASE IV will look for all records whose customer number is greater than or equal to 5. The cursor will be positioned at record #6, the first record that matches the query condition. The Browse screen resulting from the query statement and the FIND expression is shown in Figure 10-9.

The LIKE expression can also be used when you want to view the contents of your data files without clearing out the query expression(s) in your query definition screen. Once you have found the field values you desire, you may use the Exit menu and the *Transfer to Query Design* option to return to the design screen. You can then make the changes to your query description that will produce the records that match your *Find* definition.

A More Complex Query

The query conditions already shown in this and the previous chapter demonstrate many of the options. As has been discussed, each option can be implemented by itself, or can be combined with other query expressions to form a more complex query. In the following query, for example, dBASE IV will be told to look for all customers whose names begin with the letters O through Z, and who are located in CA or NV. The query will be performed on the CUST_ID file.

A Range and OR Query

The query is actually two different types of query: a range query (selecting for customers whose names begin with letters between O and Z), and an OR query (the customers who fall within the range must also be located in CA or NV). This type of query can present a logical trap for some users, because it requires that the range expression be included on each line of the query.

The query expression in Figure 10-10 is incorrect. To understand why it is wrong, you must understand what the query, as it currently appears, is actually saying. The first line of the query expression clearly asks that dBASE IV find all records whose CUST_NAME begins with letters falling between (and including) O and Z; and for those records, find only those in the state of California. The second line, however, asks that ALL records that contain the value NV in the STATE field be found; without the range expression, this is exactly what dBASE IV will do. When the query is run, the results look like Figure 10-11 (definitely not what was desired).

The correct statement, which applies the range conditions to each of the two related queries, is shown in Figure 10-12. Note that the range expression has been included on each line. No Nevada customers were selected, since none with names starting with the letters defined were included in the data file.

It should also be noted that, had you wished to find all customers with names beginning with letters ranging from O through Z, *and* located in California, *or* you

Layout Fields Condition Update Exit
9:17:39 pm
Cust_id.dbf
↓CUST_NAME
CUST_NUMB
ADDRESS
CITY
↓STATE
PROVINCE
ZIP
>="0",<="Z"
"CA"
"NV"
View
<NEW>
Cust_id->
CUST_NAME
Cust_id->
STATE
Query
C:\dbase\<NEW>
Field 5/17
Ins
Prev/Next field:Shift-Tab/Tab Data:F2 Pick:Shift-F1 Prev/Next skel:F3/F4

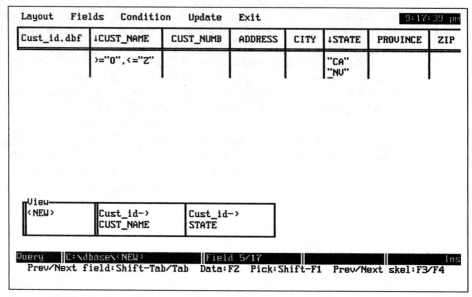

Figure 10-10 Incorrect query statement for range and OR expression.

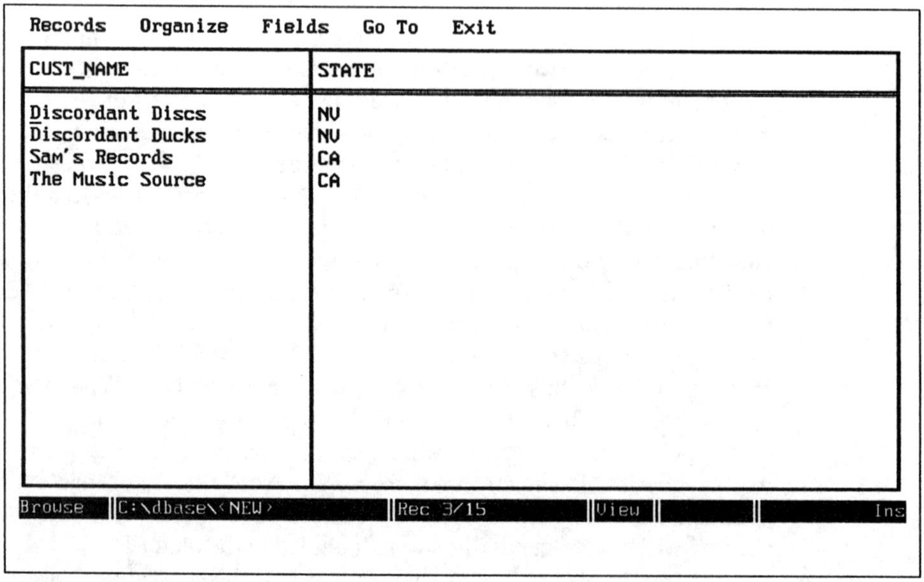

Records Organize Fields Go To Exit
CUST_NAME
STATE
Discordant Discs
NV
Discordant Ducks
NV
Sam's Records
CA
The Music Source
CA
Browse
C:\dbase\<NEW>
Rec 3/15
View
Ins

Figure 10-11 Incorrect query statement yields incorrect data.

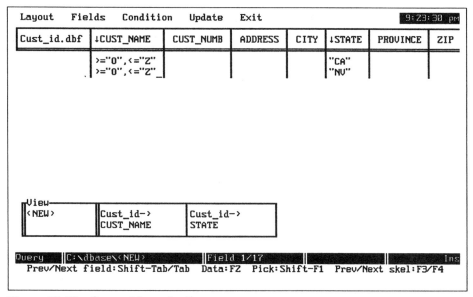

Figure 10-12   Correct form for the query.

wanted to find customers with names starting with letters ranging from A to L, you could easily have made such a request (using one expression on each line) as shown in Figure 10-13. The results of this query are the same as those in Figure 10-11 (only because *all* Nevada customers fell inside the range defined in the query).

When more than one condition is listed on the same line in a query, dBASE IV understands that *all* conditions on the line must match. When more than one condition is included in a single field definition, separated by a comma, dBASE IV understands the conditions to be additive (i.e., customer names must begin with letters O or greater *and* end with the letter Z or smaller).

Each line in a query is ORed into the query. Thus the condition in line one, OR the condition in line two, OR the condition in line three, and so on, must be matched by the data file or the record will not be included in the query results. Since each line is independent of the others, it is important to remember that if you want special conditions to be applied to more than one line, the condition must be placed on *each* line of the query definition where the condition is desired.

An Update Query

For the next query, you must add data to the PRICE data file. Open the PRICE file and, using the Browse screen, edit the prices as shown in Figure 10-14. Assume that your suppliers have implemented a price increase of $1.00 for each CD with a list price higher than $7.95. Although the current list of prices is small, in real applications, you may have hundreds or thousands of items that require updating. An update query,

Layout Fields Condition Update Exit
9:26:14 pm
Cust_id.dbf
↓CUST_NAME
CUST_NUMB
ADDRESS
CITY
↓STATE
PROVINCE
ZIP
>="O",<="Z"
>="A",<="L"
"CA"
"NV"
View
<NEW>
Cust_id->
CUST_NAME
Cust_id->
STATE
Query
C:\dbase\<NEW>
Field 1/17
Ins
Prev/Next field:Shift-Tab/Tab Data:F2 Pick:Shift-F1 Prev/Next skel:F3/F4

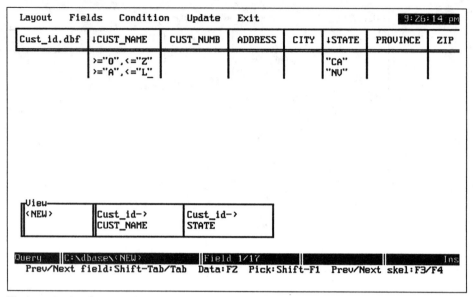

Figure 10-13 Query with a different range and state on each line.

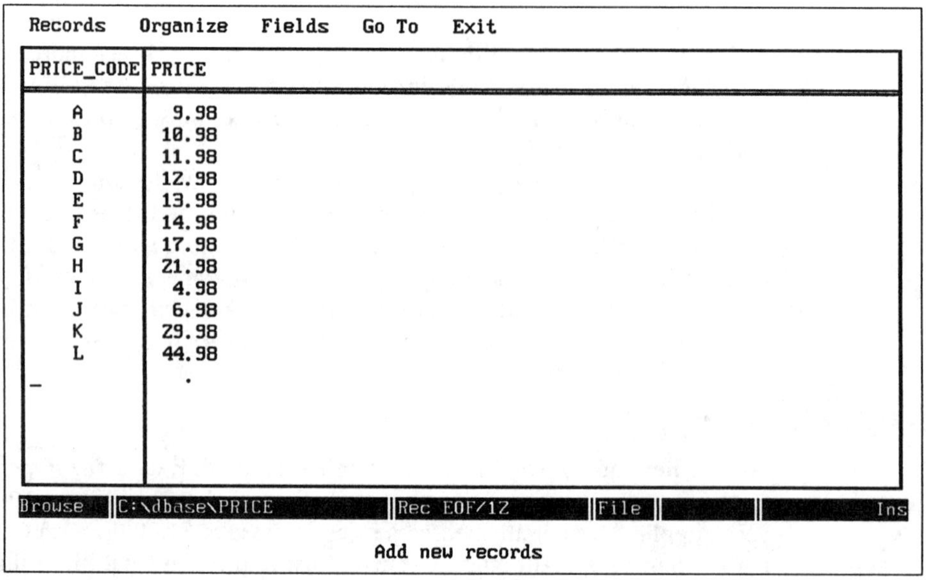

Records Organize Fields Go To Exit
PRICE_CODE
PRICE
A 9.98
B 10.98
C 11.98
D 12.98
E 13.98
F 14.98
G 17.98
H 21.98
I 4.98
J 6.98
K 29.98
L 44.98
Browse
C:\dbase\PRICE
Rec EOF/12
File
Ins
Add new records

Figure 10-14 List price data.

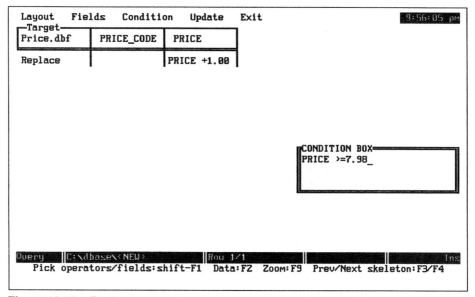

Figure 10-15   Replace query increases prices, applies condition.

along with a condition defining those records to be updated, can automatically update the data files. In this case, you wish to replace the current price with a new list price.

Open the Query menu and add the Price.dbf file, if it isn't already on the file skeleton. Make sure that the view skeleton (at the bottom of the screen) is not active—if it is, you will not be able to run your update query. To deactivate the view skeleton, move the cursor into the farthest box on the left in the view skeleton (from within the File skeleton, press **Home** to move the cursor to the first field, which is the filename) and press **F5** to move all fields out of the view skeleton.

Move the cursor into the PRICE field and open the Update menu (press **Alt-U** to open the menu box). Select *Specify update operation*. Next, select *Replace values in Price.dbf*, since this is the operation you will be performing. *Replace* will appear in the filename column. The highlight will be in the PRICE field. Type in the replacement expression, ***PRICE + 1.00.***

This part of the query will add $1.00 to the price of *all* records. To apply the increase only to those titles that are priced at $7.95 or above, you must open a condition box. Press **Alt-C** to open the Condition menu. Select *Add condition box* and a condition box will appear. Remember that the box can be opened to full screen width by pressing **F9** (and closed by pressing **F9** a second time). Enter the condition ***Price > = 7.98***. The complete replace query is shown in Figure 10-15.

When you have defined the conditions for your update, reopen the Update menu and select *Perform the update*. dBASE IV will perform the update, will indicate how many records have been replaced, and will also prompt to tell you how to view the changes. The query completion screen is shown in Figure 10-16.

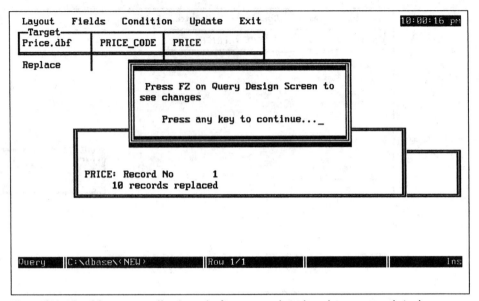

Figure 10-16 Messages displayed after an update has been completed.

A similar expression can be used to reverse the effects of your replace query. To undo what you have already done, set the replace expression to **WITH Price − 1.00**, and change the condition to **PRICE > = 8.98** (the current value of all titles previously priced at $7.98). Other mathematical expressions can also be used for the update. To increase prices by 6%, for example, the expression **WITH PRICE*1.06** can be used. Standard mathematical operators (+ , − ,*,/) can be applied to values to be replaced.

The update query is somewhat limited. For example, if you want to add $1.00 to all titles priced between $7.98 and $14.98, to add $2.00 to all titles currently $14.99 and above, and to add $0.50 to all titles under $7.97, three separate updates are required, since you can only do one replacement for each update.

The other update queries can be used to mark records for deletion or to unmark those selected for deletion. For example, if you want to delete all titles that sold for less than $6.95, a query like that shown in Figure 10-17 will achieve that purpose. Note that there is no need for a condition box, since you've defined the query condition in the Price field. When the update has been implemented, those records matching the definition will be marked for deletion, and may be deleted from within Browse or Edit by means of the Organize menu.

The mark update confirms that you do, indeed, want to mark the selected records for deletion. The fail-safe prompt, indicating the results of the update, is shown in Figure 10-18. To confirm that you want to mark records, press **Y Enter**. Pressing **F2** to bring up the Browse (or Edit) screens and opening the Records menu will allow you to see *Clear deletion mark* when the cursor is on those records that were marked for deletion by dBASE IV. These records can be unmarked using this menu option, or using an unmark query.

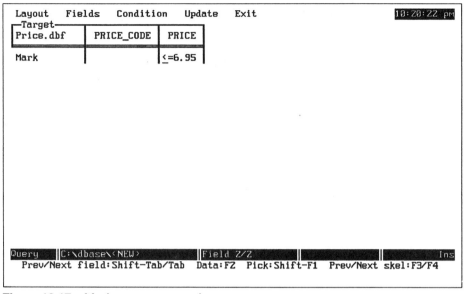

Figure 10-17   Mark query expression.

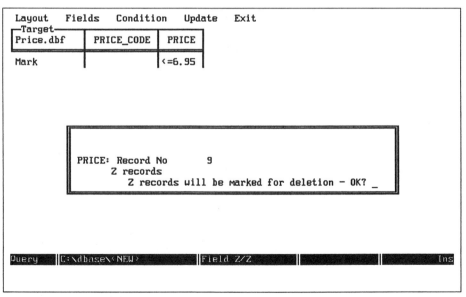

Figure 10-18   dBASE IV gives you a chance to change your mind.

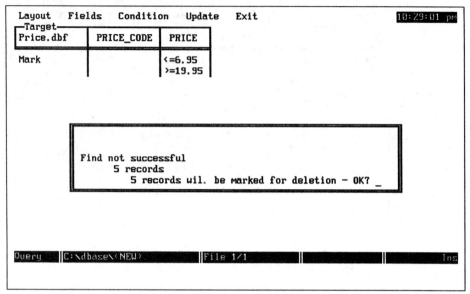

Figure 10-19   Updates can be performed on more than one definition.

With the expression currently active in the Query design screen, you can return to the query design (by selecting *Transfer to Query Design* from the Exit menu in Browse), and specify an Unmark operation from the *Specify update operation* menu. Performing the update will complete the operation. You can also perform an update on more than one query definition. In Figure 10-19, dBASE IV has been instructed to mark all records priced at $19.95 or higher, and all records priced at or below $6.95. When the query is run, five records are selected to be marked for deletion. Later in this chapter, you will see how append operations work.

Calculated Fields

A calculated field is one that has performed a mathematical operation on a numeric field. For example, if you wanted to show the list price, and the price including tax, a calculated field can be used. Suppose the sales tax rate in Los Angeles County is 6.75%. To calculate the price including tax, use the formula **PRICE *1.0675**.

A calculated field can be displayed in a Browse or Edit screen and can be included in a new file created by a query. To create a calculated field, open the Fields menu (press **Alt-F** to quickly open the menu), and select *Create calculated field*. A box will be opened on the screen. The top line is used for the first calculated field. After you've entered the formula for calculating the field value, the formula may be added to the view skeleton by pressing **F5**. dBASE IV prompts for a field name. Call this field LA_ TAX.

Additional calculated fields can be created, and will be added to the right of the current calculated field, by opening the Fields menu and pressing **C**. (Although you

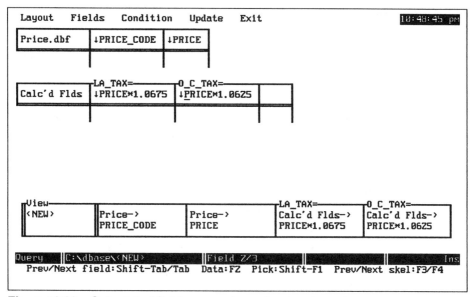

Figure 10-20   Calculated field expression using two tax rates.

can't move the cursor into the *Create calculated field* line, pressing **C** will add a new field box to the screen.

Suppose the sales tax rate for Orange County, California, is 6.25%. The expression for a query that results in a list of prices for both Los Angeles and Orange County is shown in Figure 10-20. Figure 10-21 shows the results of the query. It is interesting to

		Records	Organize	Fields	Go To	Exit	

PRICE_CODE	PRICE	LA_TAX	O_C_TAX
A	9.98	10.65	10.60
B	10.98	11.72	11.67
C	11.98	12.79	12.73
D	12.98	13.86	13.79
E	13.98	14.92	14.85
F	14.98	15.99	15.92
G	17.98	19.19	19.10
H	21.98	23.46	23.35
I	4.98	5.32	5.29
J	6.98	7.45	7.42
K	29.98	32.00	31.85
L	44.98	48.02	47.79
.		0.00	0.00

Browse   C:\dbase\<NEW>   Rec 1/13   View   Ins

Figure 10-21   Results of the query using calculated fields.

note that you may enter prices into the Price column, and the values will be automatically updated when you move the cursor out of the field (the values of the calculated fields cannot be edited).

Conditions for selecting records that are based on the value of the calculated fields can also be defined. For example, if you wanted to select only those records with a calculated field value for O_C_TAX of $15.00 or more, putting the expression > = **15.00** in the panel below the calculated field definition for O_C_TAX will result in a list of titles with list prices of $14.98 and higher. Multiple conditions can be applied to the values of calculated fields. (For example, ranges and OR expressions can be implemented).

Relational Queries (Links)

The last chapter and this one have provided many of the fundamentals of query design. However, the real power of dBASE IV is in relating files to produce new data files or logically new files (files that are created in memory, but not actually stored as a physically distinct file that can be read from or copied from the disk) that can be used for a wide range of reports or labels, or as sources of new composite data files.

When a relational query is defined, you are able to take data from many different data files and produce reports based on selected fields in each file. To make sense, of course, the data in one file must match that in another file, so that the two files can be related. A simple example of this can be shown using the data for the BUYERS data file, shown in Figure 10-22. This data file demonstrates that some customers have more than one buyer.

Records	Organize	Fields	Go To	Exit	

CUST_NUMB	BUYER_F_N	BUYER_L_N	PHONE	EXTENSION
1	Sam	Abbazabba	2135554408	
2	Jerome	Justworthy	8015558128	
2	Martha	Washington	8015558128	
3	Wally	Wallace	7025551234	3322
3	Amy	Price	7025553322	3322
4	Caroline	Holt	5055551892	
5	Virginia	Bismarck	3055558911	
5	Woody		8005551219	
5	Xavier	Diamond	8005551219	
6	Dusty	Homburg	3195558299	
7	Bess	Bullard	2035552855	7448
8	Henrietta	Goose	6165556539	
8	Charles	Gosling	6165556539	
8	Thelma	Drake	6165556539	
9	Slick	Mitchell	4155557811	
10	Megan	McYup	2135557424	
10	Ashley	Volvo	2135557424	

Browse	C:\dbase\BUYERS	Rec 1/18	File		Ins

Figure 10-22   Data for the BUYERS data files.

If you had wanted to create a single data file that listed more than one buyer, you would have wound up with a somewhat awkward design. Questions about how to add buyers, and how many buyers to include in your data design would have required answering during the design of the data file (or would require redesign at a later time to accommodate the extra fields). By creating a separate data file for buyers, you avoided the problem of designing a data file that has fields which may contain many values. To answer the question, "*Show me names of the customers and all the buyers for each store,*" a simple query can be designed.

The key to answering the question is to be able to match the stores to the buyers. The data for answering this query resides in two files: BUYERS.DBF and CUST_ID.DBF. When creating the answer to such a question, you must bring the required files onto your Query design screen. Close all data files in the Data panel, and open a new Query window (by moving the cursor to <create> and pressing **Enter**).

The *Add file to query* option in the Layout menu will prompt you to place a data file into the query design. Select the CUST_ID data file. Reopen the Layout menu and select *Add file to query*. Add the Buyers.dbf file to the query skeleton. You will notice that the CUST_NUMB field is included in the data structure for each data file. *This is no accident*.

The way to answer the question posed earlier is to tie the two files together. The means for creating this connection is by linking the two files, based on customer number. When a query is run, the data is extracted from the desired fields, based on linkages between the files.

There are a few ways to define a link. You may move the cursor into the field that you will be linking to another data file, select *Create link by pointing* from the Layout menu, move to the file and field to be linked to (**F3** moves you back one file, while **F4** moves forward one file), and press **Enter** to complete the link definition.

The first set of linked fields are labeled LINK1, the second link is labeled LINK2, and so forth. You aren't required to use the *Create link by pointing* option in order to link two fields. All that is required is that the character string used to name the link in one field is the same string as that used in the other. When the query is run, dBASE IV links the records, based on the matching values of the link expression. When dBASE IV creates a link, the first set of linked fields are named LINK1, the second is named LINK2, and so forth. As long as you use the same name for each of the two linked fields (such as Dan, Mark, Zelmo, or most other names), the linking will work. You should avoid using any operators (such as ASC1, which indicates an ascending sort) as strings for two fields to be linked on.

A simple demonstration of how this works should clarify the process. Define links on CUST_NUMB in both the CUST_ID.DBF and BUYERS.DBF data files. Once the links are defined, add the CUST_NAME, and CUST_NUMB fields from the CUST_ID.DBF file to the view skeleton (by moving the cursor into the fields and pressing **F5**). Press **F4** to move the cursor to the Buyers.dbf file and add BUYER_F_N and BUYER_L_N to the view skeleton. The completed query, including the links and the four fields to be viewed, is shown in Figure 10-23. Note that the view skeleton shows both the field name and the data file that the field is extracted from.

Press **F2** and the system will perform the query. The first screen with query results is shown in Figure 10-24. Note that all buyers are shown, with more than one buyer for

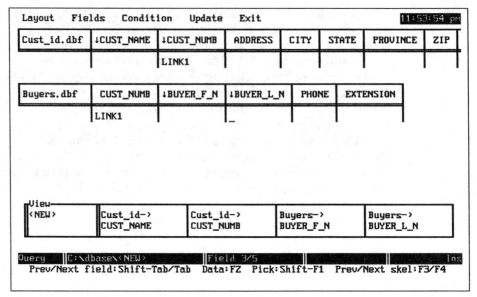

Figure 10-23 Query definition using linked fields.

Records	Organize	Fields	Go To	Exit		
CUST_NAME		**CUST_NUMB**	**BUYER_F_N**		**BUYER_L_N**	

CUST_NAME	CUST_NUMB	BUYER_F_N	BUYER_L_N
Sam's Records	1	Sam	Abbazabba
Just Music	2	Jerome	Justworthy
Just Music	2	Martha	Washington
Discordant Discs	3	Wally	Wallace
Discordant Discs	3	Amy	Price
Other Vegas Music	4	Caroline	Holt
Where Else Audio	5	Virginia	Bismarck
Where Else Audio	5	Woody	
Where Else Audio	5	Xavier	Diamond
The Musical Swamp	6	Dusty	Homburg
The Singing Cow	7	Bess	Bullard
Grandma's Disks & Tapes	8	Henrietta	Goose
Grandma's Disks & Tapes	8	Charles	Gosling
Grandma's Disks & Tapes	8	Thelma	Drake
The Music Source	9	Slick	Mitchell
DAT's CD	10	Megan	McYup
DAT's CD	10	Ashley	Volvo

Browse C:\dbase\<NEW>   Rec 1/18   View ReadOnly   Ins

Figure 10-24 Browse screen resulting from linked fields.

many of the customer companies. The simple link allows you to define which data fields will be displayed in your output file, and provides a method for relating the data in one file to another.

> Note⟩ In the information bar at the bottom of the screen, the displayed screen is ReadOnly. This means that you are not allowed to alter the value of any of the fields or records. Browse and Edit screens resulting from relational queries *cannot* be edited.

In this simple example, only one link was defined, and data was shown from two different data files. Future queries will demonstrate how additional links can be used, and will demonstrate additional query design and analysis capabilities.

O:O, O:M, and M:M

Although the heading for this section may sound something like a series of mantric incantations, the impression isn't completely correct. True, you could probably gain significant insights chanting O:O or O:M, or even trying to chant M:M, but you'd be much better off understanding the principles that the letters represent. The letters refer to the relationship between data files and the data in individual records.

One to One (O:O)

One to One (O:O) describes most basic, flat file databases. Examples of such commercially available databases include RapidFile, FrameWork II and III's data manager, PFS:Professional File, and Reflex. Also included in the list are the numerous telephone number data products, electronic Rolodex, menu filers, and other data or information management programs.

These programs assume that there is a one-to-one relationship between the data in each file and each record. Data structures for this type of relationship attempt to include all relevant fields for each record in a single record. A telephone list, for example, would include name, address, company name, and one or more telephone numbers. In theory, each record will contain all the information required to make a complete record.

In this type of design, a one-to-one relationship between each record and the data in the record is assumed. (Each person will have one address, each address will relate to one person, etc.). In cases where there may be a record for more than one family member living in the same house, the one-to-one relationship is still assumed to apply. If you want to look up records for Barbara Brownstein, her telephone number and address may be the same as that for Mark, Vonnie, and Charles Brownstein (and maybe even for her dogs, Misty and Lucky). But the important thing here is that the record is really keyed to the individual, and all the information needed to find her will be in a single record. However, stating that there is a 1:1 relationship implies relationality and linking, concepts that are not included or supported by flat file database systems. For the purposes of this book, 1:1 describes situations where such single links occur and a single data file will be able to contain all the relevant information needed for each new record.

One to Many (O:M)

Relational models can handle the many situations when there may be more than one value related to a single data field. For example, as shown earlier, each customer may have many buyers. The query used retrieved the names of all the buyers that serviced each customer. In this case, there was a one-to-many (one customer/many buyers) relationship at work.

O:M data designs are one of the powerful features of the relational data model. Although dBASE IV, and most so-called "relational" databases for microcomputers, aren't truly relational (that is, they don't meet the criteria for true relationality), their ability to link multiple data files and produce meaningful results provides substantial power to evaluate much more complex data structures than flat file database programs can. And, although it would be a case of overkill, dBASE IV can be used as a powerful flat file data manager.

The idea of O:M is one that takes considerable thought, especially for users who have done data management using flat file structures or flat file databases. If this applies to you, the discovery of true relational design and implementation may come as something of a revelation; it isn't necessarily a concept that simply comes to you.

Where in flat file management designs it is a distinct design goal to include *all* data fields that may possibly be necessary in a single design, the goal for relational, or linking, data structures is to minimize the number of fields in a design. Instead of building all the required fields into a single data file, the concept of *links* (common fields that are used during query design to connect the data in one data file with that in another) provides significant power to the user. The earlier example linked the CUST_ ID data file and the BUYERS data file using the common field, CUST_NO. Although each store had a unique customer number, many stores had more than one buyer. By linking on the unique customer number, all records in the BUYERS database were matched to the unique customer number, and each buyer with the matching customer number was added to the results of the query.

Many to Many (M:M)

In addition to O:O and O:M, another common situation can be handled by dBASE IV. This is the many-to-many (M:M) relationship. For example, if you are dealing with a chain of record stores, the chain may provide a more complicated situation. Assume, for example, that each buyer specializes in a particular type of music and that each buyer services the needs of many stores. As was seen earlier, each store may use many buyers. In fact, this would be the case for every store in the chain, since each store carries a variety of music types, and is thus serviced by a number of specialty buyers.

The situation is complicated. Each buyer buys for many stores, and each store uses many buyers. Simple O:M queries will result in a list of all stores that each buyer purchases for, or a list of all buyers who service a particular store. Methods of dealing with M:M relationships will be dealt with later in this chapter.

Creating an Order Processing File

You've seen how files can be related to produce new, logically combined data files that contain data from more than one file, and how calculated fields and condition boxes can assist in the design of a query. Before exploring esoterica, you will create queries that can be used to create an order processing data file and perform similar data tasks that are common to many businesses.

Adding to the TITLES File

First, add the following records to the TITLES data file:

TITLE	12 Greatest Hits
ARTIST	Patsy Cline
COMPOSER	
ID_NUMBER	MCAD-12
PRICE_CODE	C
FIRST_REL	
SPARS_CODE	AAD
CATEGORY	COUNTRY

TITLE	Symphony No. 6
ARTIST	Karajan, Berlin Phil.
COMPOSER	Beethoven
ID_NUMBER	DG 413932-2
PRICE_CODE	D
FIRST_REL	
SPARS_CODE	DDD
CATEGORY	CLASSICAL

TITLE	Abbey Road
ARTIST	The Beatles
COMPOSER	
ID_NUMBER	CCT-46446
PRICE_CODE	D
FIRST_REL	
SPARS_CODE	AAD
CATEGORY	Rock

TITLE	Rubber Soul
ARTIST	The Beatles
COMPOSER	
ID_NUMBER	CDP-46440
PRICE_CODE	D
FIRST_REL	
SPARS_CODE	AAD
CATEGORY	Rock

TITLE	Rock the House
ARTIST	DJ Jazzy Jeff
COMPOSER	
ID_NUMBER	026-2-J
PRICE_CODE	E
FIRST_REL	
SPARS_CODE	DDD
CATEGORY	Rap

TITLE	Live at Cook County Jail
ARTIST	B. B. King
COMPOSER	
ID_NUMBER	CAD-31080
PRICE_CODE	E
FIRST_REL	
SPARS_CODE	AAD
CATEGORY	Blues

TITLE	Live at Cook County Jail
ARTIST	B. B. King
COMPOSER	
ID_NUMBER	MCAD-31080
PRICE_CODE	E
FIRST_REL	
SPARS_CODE	AAD
CATEGORY	Blues

TITLE	Socialized Hate
ARTIST	Atrophy
COMPOSER	
ID_NUMBER	RRD-9518
PRICE_CODE	D
FIRST_REL	12/01/88
SPARS_CODE	ADD
CATEGORY	Metal

TITLE	King Kong Lives
ARTIST	John Scott
COMPOSER	
ID_NUMBER	MCAD-6203
PRICE_CODE	C
FIRST_REL	06/87
SPARS_CODE	ADD
CATEGORY	Soundtrack

These nine records use fictional pricing codes, and the descriptions may include other errors. In addition, the complete records on each of the nine titles have not been included in the example database to be queried. However, adequate information is included to demonstrate some of the features of the relational query designs that can be created using dBASE IV.

The item numbers used correspond to numbers assigned by their publishers. In many cases, it would be preferable to use a simpler, more consistent numbering scheme. In the case of compact disks, the industry catalogs titles using this scheme, and most customers would have access to master guides listing all available titles and their standard numbers.

While no easily acquired cross-index listing titles by number exists to simplify matching a stock number to a disk's title, such a listing could easily be generated once your titles database is built. In addition, most customers would know the title and artist for each item being ordered, and standard catalogs published by a number of companies will easily provide the standard numbers.

Modifying the Orders and Buyers Files

A few minor modifications to the orders data file and the buyers data file provide additional flexibility. Since a single buyer may be buying for more than one store, it is appropriate to assign a buyer number to each buyer. In this way, a list of stores that the buyer services, a list of titles that the buyer orders, and other queries that may have been made by a particular buyer for many stores, rather than for one specific store, can easily be written.

Assigning a number to a buyer need not be difficult or insulting. It can be as simple as the buyer's initials followed by a one- or two-digit code. The numbers may increment. For example, if two buyers were named Mark Brownstein and Michael Braverman, the first buyer would be given the number MB01, while the second would be given MB02.

dBASE IV can quite easily index the buyer numbers and print out a list of all buyers, making it easy to assign new numbers by simply referencing the list for each new buyer and seeing where the numbering scheme assigned the last buyer number. With the new field added to the BUYERS data file, the data structure looks like Figure 10-25.

Use the Layout menu to save the new data structure, then use the Browse/Edit screens to assign buyer numbers to the list of buyers already entered into the data file. In addition, if you have chosen to make the BUYER_NO field the only indexed field and have activated the index, the buyer names will be placed in index order once they have been completed and you have moved to another record. When this happens, it is easy to detect when there may be a duplication of buyer numbers.

Figure 10-26 shows the first screenful of buyers. The buyers are now shown in index order, placed in order by buyer number, and there are two buyers whose initials are BB. The first occurrence of a set of initials was for the record for Bess Bullard, and she became BB01.

This example can be extended even further, however. Since the customer number is no longer of particular relevance in the BUYERS data file (since one buyer may service many customers), it is probably wise to remove the CUST_NUMB field from

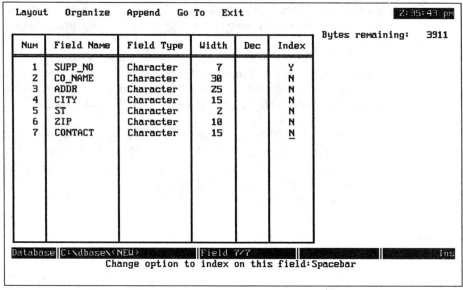

Figure 10-25   SUPPLIER data structure.

| Records | Organize | Fields | Go To | Exit | | 10:28:42 pm |

CUST_NUMB	BUYER_F_N	BUYER_L_N	PHONE	EXTENSION	BUYER_NO
3	Amy	Price	7025553322	3322	AP01
10	Ashley	Volvo	2135557424		AV01
7	Bess	Bullard	2035552855	7448	BB01
10	Brandon	Bonehead	2135557424		BB02
8	Charles	Gosling	6165556539		CG01
4	Caroline	Holt	5055551892		CH01
6	Dusty	Homburg	3195558299		DH01
8	Henrietta	Goose	6165556539		HG01
2	Jerome	Justworthy	8015558128		JJ01
10	Megan	McYup	2135557424		MM01
2	Martha	Washington	8015558128		MW01
1	Sam	Abbazabba	2135554408		SA01
9	Slick	Mitchell	4155557811		SM01
8	Thelma	Drake	6165556539		TD01
5	Virginia	Bismarck	3055558911		VB01
3	Wally	Wallace	7025551234	3322	WW01
5	Woody		8005551219		W_01

Browse   C:\dbase\BUYERS   Rec 5/18   File   Ins

Figure 10-26   First screen of buyers indexed by buyer number.

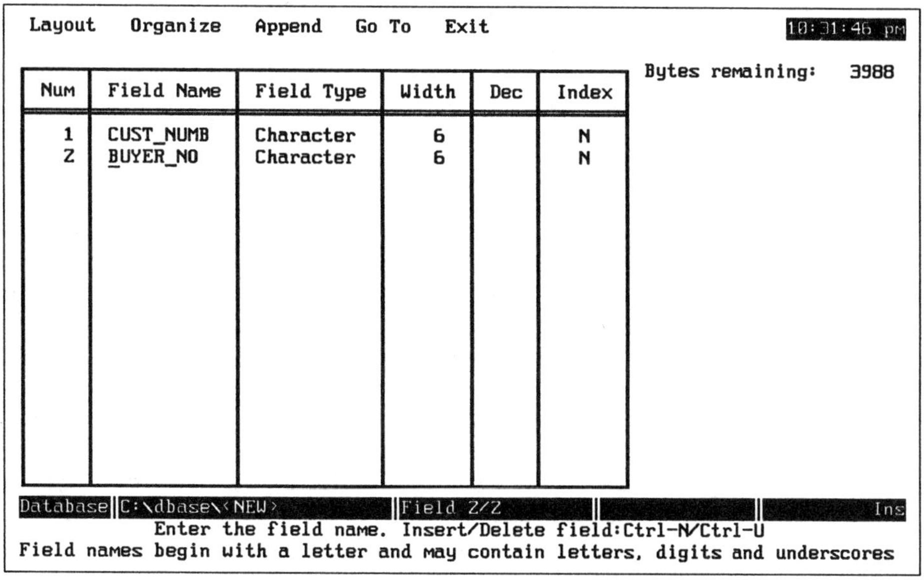

```
  Layout   Organize   Append   Go To   Exit              10:31:46 pm

                                                   Bytes remaining:   3988
  ┌─────┬──────────────┬─────────────┬───────┬─────┬───────┐
  │ Num │ Field Name   │ Field Type  │ Width │ Dec │ Index │
  ├─────┼──────────────┼─────────────┼───────┼─────┼───────┤
  │   1 │ CUST_NUMB    │ Character   │   6   │     │   N   │
  │   2 │ BUYER_NO     │ Character   │   6   │     │   N   │
  │     │              │             │       │     │       │
  │     │              │             │       │     │       │
  │     │              │             │       │     │       │
  │     │              │             │       │     │       │
  │     │              │             │       │     │       │
  │     │              │             │       │     │       │
  │     │              │             │       │     │       │
  │     │              │             │       │     │       │
  │     │              │             │       │     │       │
  └─────┴──────────────┴─────────────┴───────┴─────┴───────┘
  Database║C:\dbase\<NEW>              ║Field 2/2      ║         Ins
              Enter the field name. Insert/Delete field:Ctrl-N/Ctrl-U
  Field names begin with a letter and may contain letters, digits and underscores
```

Figure 10-27   CUSTBUYR data design.

the BUYERS data file. The buyers and customers can be matched through a *linkage database*. A linkage database provides a minimum number of fields; only those fields that are required to match the two parts of a *tuple* (a pair of related fields—in this case buyers and customers) are included. In this case, a new data file called CUSTBUYR is needed. The structure of this new data file is shown in Figure 10-27. Note that each record contains a single tuple, representing a combination of buyer number and customer number. This defines which buyers buy for which customers.

Creating Links

Creating two index expressions (one called LNKBYCUST and using the expression **CUST_NUMB + BUYERNO,** and the other called LNKBYBUYR and using the expression **BUYERNO + CUST_NUMB)** allows you to arrange your data in two ways. The LNKBYCUST will list all customers in order, with each assigned buyer occupying a separate line. LNKBYBUYR puts the data in order by buyer number and is useful for producing a list of customers each buyer services.

Using a CUSTBUYR data file, with its two fields, makes it simple to define which buyers serve which customers and which customers use which buyers. The linkage database makes M:M (many-to-many) data relationships manageable.

We can now prepare for a demonstration of how the linkage data file works by defining some new linkages. Add new records to this new data file according to the following data:

CUST_NUMB	BUYER_NO
2	SA01
6	SA01
7	VB01
9	VB01
3	BB02

Before defining the query for an order processing task, you can see how the linkage database simplifies data acquisition by designing queries that show which buyers service which customers and which customers use which buyers. Finally, to simplify the data structures, remove the CUST_NUMB field from the data structure for the BUYERS data file (ignore the prompts that you'll get when you try to exit after deleting the field; this time you really do want to delete a field and its related data). The linkage database renders this field unnecessary, as will be seen shortly.

To find which customers use which buyers, close all data files and <create> a new query. Add the CUST_ID file to the query. Next, from the Layout menu, add CUSTBUYR, the linkage data file to your query structure. Finally, add BUYERS to your query skeleton. Three File skeletons should be shown, with no View skeleton in view yet.

Next, we must define the links between the data files. This may be done by moving the cursor into the field(s) to be linked and typing a linkage word (referred to by Ashton-Tate as an *example variable*) or by using the *Create link by pointing* option in the Layout menu to indicate the linking fields. Links should be specified between the CUST_NUMB fields in the CUST_ID data file and the CUSTBUYR data file, and in

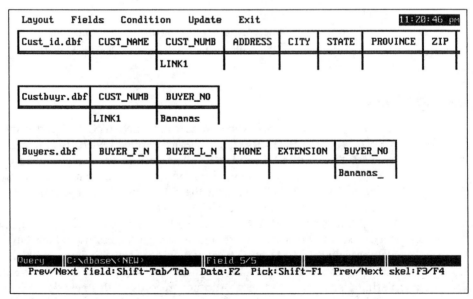

Figure 10-28 Query design showing linkages.

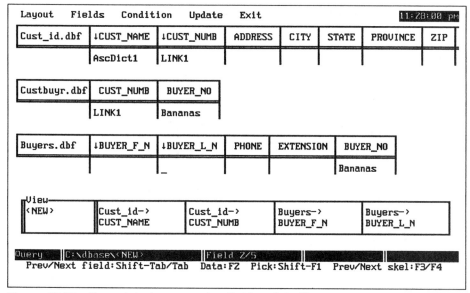

Figure 10-29 Completed query using linking data file.

the BUYER_NO field in the CUSTBUYR and BUYERS data files. Figure 10-28 shows the file skeletons with the links (one linking by LINK1, and the other linking somewhat more imaginatively, if not more descriptively).

Finally, create the view skeleton, telling dBASE IV how you want your results to be listed. First, move into the CUST_ID file skeleton (the **F4** key moves forward one skeleton at a time, while the **F3** moves back one at a time) and position the cursor in the CUST_NAME field. Press **F5** to move this field into the view skeleton. The name of the field and the name of the source data file will appear in a box in the view skeleton.

Since it would be useful to have the query results in alphabetic order by customer name, select *Sort on this field* in the Fields panel to tell dBASE IV to put your records in alphabetic order (in this example, an ascending dictionary sort was selected). Next, move the cursor to CUST NUMB and add that to the skeleton. Finally, move the cursor into the BUYERS data file and add BUYER_F_N and BUYER_L_N (first and last name) to the skeleton. You could, of course, add BUYER_NO, but you don't need to. The completed query design is shown in Figure 10-29.

Figure 10-30 shows the first screen of results of the query. In Figure 10-31, the first screen of results that would have been produced had the sort been done on buyer's last name, rather than on customer name, is shown. In both figures, it should be clear that many stores used multiple buyers, and that many buyers serviced multiple stores.

The linking data file is a very simple, elegant way to define links between data residing in different files, and avoids the impulse to obtain more information than necessary to link information. (For example, unless you have confidence in the simple linking data file, you may be tempted to add descriptive fields, such as CUST_NAME or BUYER_L_N to such a data file.)

```
 Records    Organize    Fields    Go To    Exit

 CUST_NAME                    CUST_NUMB  BUYER_F_N      BUYER_L_N

 DAT's CD                        10      Brandon        Bonehead
 DAT's CD                        10      Ashley         Volvo
 DAT's CD                        10      Megan          McYup
 Discordant Discs                 3      Brandon        Bonehead
 Discordant Discs                 3      Wally          Wallace
 Discordant Discs                 3      Amy            Price
 Grandma's Disks & Tapes          8      Henrietta      Goose
 Grandma's Disks & Tapes          8      Charles        Gosling
 Grandma's Disks & Tapes          8      Thelma         Drake
 Just Music                       2      Jerome         Justworthy
 Just Music                       2      Sam            Abbazabba
 Just Music                       2      Martha         Washington
 Other Vegas Music                4      Caroline       Holt
 Sam's Records                    1      Sam            Abbazabba
 The Music Source                 9      Slick          Mitchell
 The Music Source                 9      Virginia       Bismarck
 The Musical Swamp                6      Dusty          Homburg

 Browse   C:\dbase\<NEW>             Rec 1/23          View  ReadOnly
```

Figure 10-30 Results of query shown in Figure 10-29.

```
 Records    Organize    Fields    Go To    Exit

 CUST_NAME                    CUST_NUMB  BUYER_F_N      BUYER_L_N

 Where Else Audio                 5      Woody
 Sam's Records                    1      Sam            Abbazabba
 The Musical Swamp                6      Sam            Abbazabba
 Just Music                       2      Sam            Abbazabba
 The Music Source                 9      Virginia       Bismarck
 The Singing Cow                  7      Virginia       Bismarck
 Where Else Audio                 5      Virginia       Bismarck
 Discordant Discs                 3      Brandon        Bonehead
 DAT's CD                        10      Brandon        Bonehead
 The Singing Cow                  7      Bess           Bullard
 Where Else Audio                 5      Xavier         Diamond
 Grandma's Disks & Tapes          8      Thelma         Drake
 Grandma's Disks & Tapes          8      Henrietta      Goose
 Grandma's Disks & Tapes          8      Charles        Gosling
 Other Vegas Music                4      Caroline       Holt
 The Musical Swamp                6      Dusty          Homburg
 Just Music                       2      Jerome         Justworthy

 Browse   C:\dbase\<NEW>             Rec 1/23          View  ReadOnly
```

Figure 10-31 Results of query shown in Figure 10-29 sorted by buyer.

Figure 10-29 clearly shows that there are no common fields in the BUYERS or the CUST_ID data files, yet using the linking data file, data from both files was easily connected. Save the query, naming it CUSTBUYR.

Order Entry

Order entry using a standard form is a relatively simple task, once the relational links are understood. The ORDER form created earlier should be changed to be more consistent with the current data structure. The ORDER_BY field is replaced by the BUYER_NO field, since buyer numbers can be used instead of buyer names. Note that, had each store had *only one* buyer, the buyer name could have been assumed. Since there can be more than one buyer per store (and more than one store per buyer), both types of data are now necessary. In addition, a character field six characters wide can be used for the order taker's code number. Although the order takers all work for one company, it may be faster and more convenient to use a unique number for each employee, rather than attempting to use a potentially lengthy name.

The revised ORDERS data file looks like Figure 10-32. This data file requires that a separate form be completed for each item ordered. However, the form can be designed using a template that automatically copies the data in specific fields into the next record. Thus, when order entry is being performed, only the item number and quantities ordered need to be changed.

A custom form for order entry can easily be made using techniques demonstrated

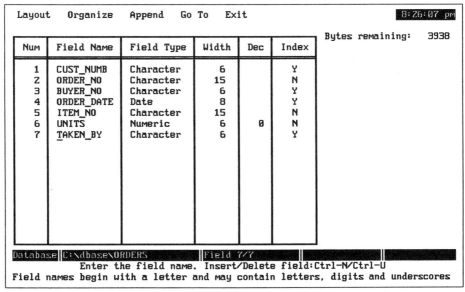

Num	Field Name	Field Type	Width	Dec	Index
1	CUST_NUMB	Character	6		Y
2	ORDER_NO	Character	15		N
3	BUYER_NO	Character	6		Y
4	ORDER_DATE	Date	8		Y
5	ITEM_NO	Character	15		N
6	UNITS	Numeric	6	0	N
7	TAKEN_BY	Character	6		Y

Layout   Organize   Append   Go To   Exit   8:26:07 pm

Bytes remaining: 3938

Database C:\dbase\ORDERS   Field 7/7
         Enter the field name. Insert/Delete field:Ctrl-N/Ctrl-U
Field names begin with a letter and may contain letters, digits and underscores

Figure 10-32   Revised ORDERS data file structure.

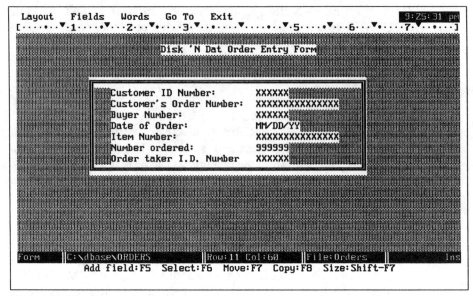

Figure 10-33 Sample order entry form.

earlier in this book. Such a form may look like the one in Figure 10-33, although you are free to design the most useful form for your specific requirements.

In order to see how the order entry data file can be used to link to data in other data files, you have to create some sample orders. Although the system can support thousands of orders, only a few are required to show some of the fundamentals of order entry and order processing. The following order information will be sufficient to demonstrate some of the order entry and relational capabilities that are built into dBASE IV. If you wish to see for yourself how these work, enter the following data:

CUST_NUMB	1
ORDER_NO	12345
BUYER_NO	SA01
ORDER_DATE	12/11/90
ITEM_NO	CDP-46446
UNITS	4
TAKEN_BY	MB
CUST_NUMB	1
ORDER_NO	12345
BUYER_NO	SA01
ORDER_DATE	12/11/90
ITEM_NO	1026-2-j
UNITS	12
TAKEN_BY	MB

CUST_NUMB	6
ORDER_NO	123
BUYER_NO	SA01
ORDER_DATE	12/11/90
ITEM_NO	1026-2-J
UNITS	6
TAKEN_BY	AAB

CUST_NUMB	6
ORDER_NO	981
BUYER_NO	DH01
ORDER_DATE	11/11/90
ITEM_NO	CDP-46446
UNITS	24
TAKEN_BY	AAB

Note that the first four data entry fields can be set to carry forward to the next record, so that the only numbers that must be entered for a new record are the item number and the quantity ordered. Similarly, the order taker can also be set as a carry forward field. This makes particular sense if each order taker has his or her own data entry terminal. In a nonnetworked user environment, each order taker can run a unique terminal, with the data files created each day (or after each four-hour shift) copied onto a disk that can be merged into the day's orders using an update query process.

Generating the Invoice

Even with the small number of orders in the sample database, an invoice or shipping form can be generated. The data screen shown in Figure 10-34 is an example of the complexity that can be achieved using the query processor in dBASE IV. In the figure, the name of the customer, date of order, and order number are shown. In addition, for each title ordered, the identification number, title, price, number of units, cost, and the cost with tax added are shown. To produce this data file requires five data fields in addition to two calculated fields—quite a complex dBASE IV program statement to try to write from scratch, but relatively easy to design using dBASE IV.

To reproduce this query, exit the order entry data file and close the file. Next, move the cursor into the Queries panel and select <create>. *Add file to query* will be the first option that you can select. The first file to add to your query is ORDERS.DBF. This is the data file that you just edited.

Next, reopen the Layout menu panel and select *Add file to query*. Add the Cust_id.dbf data file to the design. Now, define a link between both database files, linking on the CUST_NUMB field. This can be done by moving the cursor into the CUST_NUMB field in each data file and typing *LINK1* in each. Remember that you can move to the next data file in your skeleton by pressing **F4**, or you can move up a skeleton by pressing **F3**.

From within the Cust_id.dbf file skeleton, move the cursor to the CUST_NAME field and press **F5** to move the field name into the view skeleton. To set up the query so that it presents your data in order by customer name, type *Asc1* (or select *Sort on this*

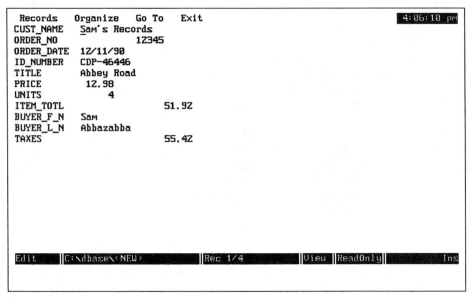

```
   Records   Organize   Go To   Exit                           4:06:10 pm
 CUST_NAME   Sam's Records
 ORDER_NO               12345
 ORDER_DATE  12/11/90
 ID_NUMBER   CDP-46446
 TITLE       Abbey Road
 PRICE       12.98
 UNITS           4
 ITEM_TOTL                      51.92
 BUYER_F_N   Sam
 BUYER_L_N   Abbazabba
 TAXES                          55.42




 Edit      C:\dbase\<NEW>              Rec 1/4        View ReadOnly          Ins
```

Figure 10-34   A complex order report produced by query.

field from the Fields menu). It may be preferable to sort by customer number. If so, define a sort for the CUST_NUMB field. The query so far reads the customer number from ORDERS.DBF, links to the CUST_ID file, and puts the customer name into the view skeleton. You've barely scratched the surface.

Next, return to the Orders.dbf data file and move the ORDER_NO and ORDER_ DATE fields into the view skeleton. (Useful, but not significant information.) Now you will indicate the title ID number and the title of each ordered item, followed by the price code. (The structure begins to gain in complexity.) To display the name of the title selected, you must link the ITEM_NO field in the Orders.dbf data file to the ID_ NUMBER field in the Titles.dbf file. Note that the field names don't match. But that is not important, as long as the link is defined and the data types and field lengths are the same in both linked files. After defining the link, move the ID_NUMBER field and TITLE field into the view skeleton. The query, as it appears so far, looks like Figure 10-35. Note that the TITLE data field is not shown on the view skeleton. It is on the skeleton, but off the screen.

Next, you want to retrieve price data for your order fulfillment form. The Orders.dbf file doesn't contain that data. Neither do the other files currently in the query design. The file that *does* contain the data is called Price.dbf. Add that data file to the skeleton. Next, define a link between PRICE_CODE in both the Titles.dbf and the PRICE field in the Price.dbf data file. This should be LINK3. Now, move PRICE onto the view skeleton. Next, from the Orders.dbf file, move UNITS onto the view skeleton. From within the Price.dbf file, open the Fields window (by typing **Alt-F**). Select *Create calculated field*. This will open a calculated field skeleton. Press *Shft-F1* to open the pick list. The fields in the Price.dbf data file are shown in the Field name pick list. Pick *Price* from the skeleton.

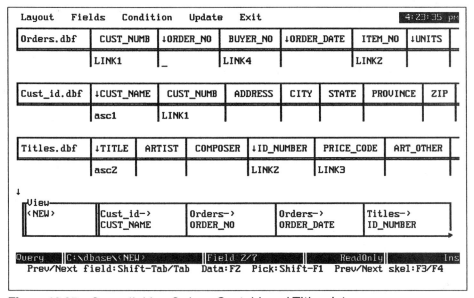

Figure 10-35   Query linking Orders, Cust_id, and Titles data.

Things get a little complicated here. You want to multiply the price times the number of units. Although it is easy to put the multiplication operator * into the calculated field that calculates the total, including tax, for each item total. To do this, the expression **PRICE*UNITS*1.0675** (assuming a tax rate of 6.75%) is used. This expression is written in a manner similar to that used for the first expression. However, you need only type the field names, rather than having to go to the file skeletons and jumping to the calculated field skeleton. Add the new calculated field, calling it TAXES (or some other name).

press **Shft-F1**. The fields in the Orders.dbf file should now be shown. Select UNITS and press **Enter**. The expression should be complete.

Now, move the expression onto the view skeleton. To do this, press **F5**. dBASE IV will ask for a name for the field. Call it ITEM_TOTL. The field will be moved into the view skeleton. At this point, it may be useful to see the results so far. Pressing **F2** will run the query, giving you results of the query as it currently stands. The calculated field should be displayed in the view screen created by the query. To return to query design, open the Exit menu and press **T** (for *Transfer to Query Design*).

The calculated field is quite an accomplishment. It is based on the price of a title selected in the orders data file, and retrieved from the price data file, and based on the number of units ordered in the Orders.dbf data file. Next, you can add another calculated field that calculates the total, including tax, for each item total. To do this, the expression **PRICE*UNITS*1.0675** (assuming a tax rate of 6.75%), is used. This expression is written in a manner similar to that used for the first expression. However, you need only type the field names, rather than having to go to the file skeletons and jumping to the calculated field skeleton. Add the new calculated field, calling it TAXES (or some other name).

The final step you want to take is to list the first and last names of the buyer who ordered the titles. Add Buyers.dbf to the skeleton, and define LINK4, linking on the BUYER_NO field in both Buyers.dbf and Orders.dbf. When you tell the system to write the view as a database file, a database file is created, using the data written to the view file. When this is done, an entirely new data file is created, using fields retrieved from the data files that make up the query design. In this particular design, a new record is created for each item ordered.

A report can be created that is used for billing the customer. This report can add the amounts of each buyer's daily orders, producing a total daily invoice for each customer.

As shown earlier in this chapter, the information in the various data files can be used to retrieve certain types of data. For example, if you wanted to retrieve only the orders made by Sam Abbazabba, putting the expression "SA01" in the BUYER_NO field in Buyers.dbf will produce a file containing only those orders placed by buyer number SA01 (Sam Abbazabba). In addition, conditions can be attached to your queries.

An Update Query

Update queries have been discussed earlier. This next example will create one. This example will use a master order file that is updated from the Orders.dbf data file. To easily create this new file, move the cursor into the Data panel, position the cursor on Orders.dbf, and press **Shft-F2** to load the modification screen. Once the design screen is opened, press **Esc** to close the Organize menu. Open the Layout menu and choose *Save this database file structure*, naming the new file structure Mstrordr.dbf (for master order). dBASE IV will create a new data file, including the data in Orders.dbf.

To show that the update query actually works, mark all the records in MSTRORDR for deletion, and delete them, using the Organize menu *Erase marked records* option. Finally, return to the *Control Center* and move the cursor into the Queries design panel. Select <create> to open the Query design screen. Add Mstrordr to the data structure, and then add Orders to the design.

In the current example, all files in ORDERS will be added to MSTRORDR, although you can make selections based on date, order entry operator, buyer, or other criteria. Open the Update menu, and open *Specify update operation*. Next, select *Append records to Orders.dbf*. The word *Append* will appear under the name of the file that you are appending from. When you reopen the Update panel, press **P** to select *Perform the update*. The update will be created, with records copied from ORDERS to MSTRORDR.

> **Note** ⟩ Update queries can be saved and reused as often as required. An append update can be used to consolidate records in a number of data files.

Conclusion

The next chapter, shows how to produce reports and labels based on the results of queries created by dBASE IV. When used with query output, powerful data management and analysis capabilities are possible.

11

Reports and Labels

In previous chapters, you've seen how to design your data file; how to enter, modify, and add data to your file; how to sort and index your data; and how to design and implement queries to retrieve the desired data from your data files. The data analysis power of dBASE IV is impressive. The last two chapters provided tools for producing new data files based on the data already created in your data file structures.

Impressive as dBASE IV's powers of analysis and extraction are, the data is of little value unless you can produce useful output. Two of the six panels in the Control Center are devoted to producing reports and labels. These are the two primary methods of presenting your data in a meaningful manner.

Reports and labels can be produced based on the data in a single data file; these panels are designed to produce on-screen or printed displays and summaries of the data already analyzed or processed. Reports and labels can be produced based on complex queries and other analyses; however, a report or label must use the data from a file that is produced by the output of a query, or from a query view. The reports and labels processors have little control over the data that is displayed.

Before useful work can be performed on your data, the data must be put into a form that produces meaningful output. To print an order invoice, for example, a query such as the one designed in the last chapter is required to collect all the relevant fields for inclusion in your invoice. Any field, with some exceptions to be noted later, that must be included in the data output must be in the single file or view that is used to build the report.

The terms *file* and *view* should be explained. Before you can open a report or label design panel, you must first select and activate a data file or a view. You should be familiar with data files—they were created in the Data panel, and could also have been created as the result of a query operation. In addition to pure data files, however, you can also select a query file and have the output from the query become the source data for your report or label. In this case, you are using a temporary file (the result of the query) as the source of data for the report or label. A *query view* defines the fields to be used and the relations between fields in the various data files, and instructs dBASE IV to produce a temporary data file based on the query view definition that is used in preparing your printed report.

There is a potential cost for using a view rather than a generated data file. If you are dealing with a complex query involving large data files or many linked files, a large amount of data is being managed by dBASE IV. This takes substantial amounts of system memory, both to perform the query analysis, and to store the temporary data that will be used as the basis for your report. Add to that the complexity of a report or label design and you may wind up pushing the system to its limits. Reading from a data file, on the other hand, is somewhat simpler, because the report or label generation can be performed using a static database, rather than one that requires frequent updating and continued analysis. The perspective that should be taken as regards reports and labels is that your data files should be created, and provide the necessary data for your report, *before* the report or label form is designed.

Somewhat complicating things is the ability to perform summary calculations and certain calculations based on existing data within a report. These operations include totals, averages, other summary functions, and certain calculations. With the exception of such summary operations, which are useful for many applications (such as providing a total bill for each vendor, based on a day's orders or on a single order number), the Reports panel design should not be thought of as creating or changing new fields. And aside from the summary information, the Reports panel *does not* create new fields and is unable to read data that is not already in the source data file or view.

Quick Reports

There are two ways to design a report. The faster is to position the cursor on a data file, a view file, or a query filename and press **Shft-F9**. The system will then create a simple report based on the data fields and related data for the selected data file. The second method of producing a report is to design the report and then run it. This method allows considerably more control over the data going into the report, how it is to be arranged, how it is to be analyzed, and how your report will look when it is printed out or displayed on screen.

The first method, pressing **Shft-F9** to automatically generate a report, produces a report that lists the fields across the top line of the report, with data for each field on lines below. This type of report is fine for data files using only a small number of fields. However, since each new field is added to the right of the previous fields, when a data file has fields whose total character count (including spaces between each field) exceeds 60 spaces, the additional fields may wrap to the next line. Reports printed for such data files are virtually unreadable, since the data for each record is printed onto more than one line. The first screen for a quick report based on the data in the CUST_ID data file demonstrates this problem, and is shown in Figure 11-1.

However, a quick report using the Buyers.dbf data file, and including fewer fields, results in a report that is quite readable and may be adequate without any modification. The first screen of an automatically created report based on Buyers.dbf is seen in Figure 11-2.

```
Page No.   1
03/06/90

CUST_NAME                    CUST_NUMB  ADDRESS                      CITY
   STATE   PROVINCE    ZIP         POST_CODE   COUNTRY      PHONE          EXT      PHO
NEZ        EXTZ    CC_TYPE  CC_NUMB_VM               CC_NUMB_A            CC_EXP_DAT

Sam's Records                    1         324 Disk Drive       Los Angeles
   CA                      90024-4405                              2135554408              213
KL54409          A                                     9999-999999-99999  01/15/91
Just Music                       2         8791 Guitar Road      Provo
   UT                      84601-                                  8015558128  225
                 U          1234-5172-3199-1230                                12/22/89
Discordant Discs                 3         8911 Swamp Water Bl.  Las Vegas
   NV                      89125-                                  7025551234  332Z      702
555332Z  332Z    A                                    3724-999999-99999  01/22/91
Other Vegas Music                4         8109 Albuquerque Rd   Las Vegas
   NM                      87199-                                  5055551892
                 U          1234-9912-9991-2221                                08/31/90
Where Else Audio                 5         3281 N.E. Southwest   Miami
   FL                      33199-                                  3055558911  2881      800
5551219          U          1299-2818-2222-2222                                01/01/91
The Musical Swamp                6         411 Pellagra Road     Clinton
   IA                      52791-                                  3195558299
_                         Cancel viewing: ESC,  Continue viewing: SPACEBAR
```

Figure 11-1   Cluttered report using data file with too many fields.

Thus, Quick Report (**Shft-F9**) is adequate for data files with few fields in their design, and which require no calculations or summary fields. For larger data structures, or those requiring calculations on individual values or on all values in a set, the Reports panel is the best way to create a useful report.

```
Page No.   1
03/06/90

BUYER_F_N         BUYER_L_N        PHONE        EXTENSION  BUYER_NO

Sam               Abbazabba        2135554408              SA01
Jerome            Justworthy       8015558128              JJ01
Martha            Washington       8015558128              MW01
Wally             Wallace          7025551234   332Z       WW01
Amy               Price            702555332Z   332Z       AP01
Caroline          Holt             5055551892              CH01
Virginia          Bismarck         3055558911              VB01
Woody                              8005551219              W_01
Xavier            Diamond          8005551219              XD01
Dusty             Homburg          3195558299              DH01
Bess              Bullard          2035552855   7448       BB01
Henrietta         Goose            6165556539              HG01
Charles           Gosling          6165556539              CG01
Thelma            Drake            6165556539              TD01
Slick             Mitchell         4155557811              SM01
Megan             McYup            2135557424              MM01
Ashley            Volvo            2135557424              AV01
Brandon           Bonehead         2135557424              BB0Z
                  Cancel viewing: ESC,  Continue viewing: SPACEBAR
_
```

Figure 11-2   Quick report based on Buyers. dbf.

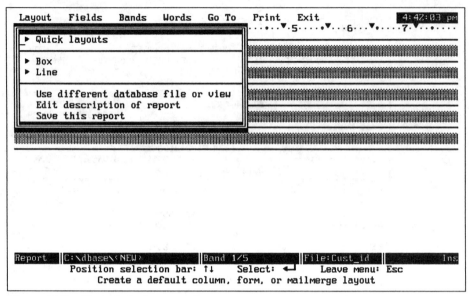

Figure 11-3 Report design opening screen.

The Labels design panel and the Reports design panel share a number of the same techniques and menu options. In addition, a number of similarities in design are shared with the Forms design panel. The Reports panel is more complex than the Labels panel, since it provides additional summary capabilities and the ability to group data together. The reporting functions feature more capability, since a report is inherently more complex than is a label. The Reports design panel will be discussed first, with the Labels panel rounding out this chapter.

Reports

In order to create a report, you must first have a data file or view active. In this case, you should move the cursor into the panel (either the Data panel, the Queries panel, or the Forms panel) and select the appropriate file. It should be noted that selecting a Forms design will load the related data file for reporting on. Once you have told the system which data file or query output file it is to use for creating the report, you may move the cursor into the Reports panel. Select <create> to open the Report design screen. The opening screen looks like Figure 11-3.

Quick Layouts

The screen opens with the Layout window opened, and *Quick layouts* highlighted. If you select *Quick layouts*, three layout choices are provided: *Columns layout*, *Form layout*, and *Mailmerge layout*. The first two layouts automatically insert the fields in your attached data file into a predesigned layout. Column layout produces a layout that

```
   Layout   Fields   Bands   Words   Go To   Print   Exit              3:13:44 pm
[·····•··▼·1·····•··▼···2···•·▼·····3·▼·•·····▼······•··▼·5·····•··▼···6··•▼·•·····7·▼·•·····
   Page       Header  Band─────────────────────────────────────────────────────────────

   Page No. 999
   MM/DD/YY

   CUST_NAME                    CUST_NUMB  ADDRESS                      CITY

   Report     Intro   Band──────────────────────────────────────────────────────────────
   Detail             Band──────────────────────────────────────────────────────────────
   XXXXXXXXXXXXXXXXXXXXXXXXXXX XXXXXXXXX XXXXXXXXXXXXXXXXXXXXXXX XXXXXXXXXXXXXXXXXXXX
   Report     Summary Band──────────────────────────────────────────────────────────────

   Page       Footer  Band──────────────────────────────────────────────────────────────



   Report   ‖F:\dbase\<NEW>        ‖Band 1/5          ‖File:Cust_id ‖          Ins
            Add field:F5  Select:F6  Move:F7  Copy:F8  Size:Shift-F7
```

Figure 11-4 Columnar report format for CUST_ID.

looks similar to a Browse screen. A quick column layout for the CUST_ID data file looks like Figure 11-4.

This is essentially the same report format as that produced using the Quick Report option from the Control Center. It is also subject to the same limitations. With a file such as Cust_id.dbf, the fields will scroll far beyond the right margin on the page. Unless you are using very small characters and extra wide paper, you will be unable to view or print meaningful results. For data files with a limited number of fields, the column layout is a useful method of presenting your data.

Note ⟩ In many cases, the column layout is the preferred method of preparing a report. Limiting the number of fields in order to match the width of your output capabilities (printer or screen) can produce practical, information-rich reports.

Form layout provides a record similar to that viewed in the Edit screen for the data file. When the form is printed, multiple records may be printed on each page, unless you design the report to start a new page for each unique value. The form layout is useful for listings of customers, titles, or other such information where you don't want to display large quantities of data in a columnar format.

Note ⟩ If you are printing onto adhesive-backed paper or Rolodex-type cards, the form layout is useful, although the Labels panel could probably provide more consistent output.

Mailmerge is probably the most different from the preceding layouts. *Mailmerge layout* allows you to create a shell document, inserting data from your data file. The mailmerge layout screen is shown in Figure 11-5.

Mailmerge output is treated differently from normal text output. In a mailmerge report, you may write boilerplate text, with data being brought in from your data files.

```
 Layout   Fields   Bands   Words   Go To   Print   Exit        5:10:46 pm
[·····•···▼·1·····▼···2··▼·····3·▼·•·····▼·•·····▼·5····▼···6···▼··▼···7·▼·•····
 Page      Header  Band─────────────────────────────────────────────────────────
 Report    Intro   Band─────────────────────────────────────────────────────────
 Detail            Band─────────────────────────────────────────────────────────
 ─



 Report    Summary Band─────────────────────────────────────────────────────────
 Page      Footer  Band─────────────────────────────────────────────────────────


 Report   ║C:\dbase\<NEW>          ║Line:0 Col:0   ║File:Cust_id ║         Ins
           Add field:F5   Select:F6   Move:F7   Copy:F8   Size:Shift-F7
            CUST_ID->CUST_NUMB   Type: Character   Width:   6   Decimal:   0
```

Figure 11-5   Mailmerge layout for Cust_id. dbf.

```
 Layout   Fields   Bands   Words   Go To   Print   Exit        9:28:30 pm
[·····•···▼·1·····▼···2··▼·····3·▼·•·····▼·•·····▼·5····▼···6···▼··▼···7·▼·•····
 Page      Header  Band─────────────────────────────────────────────────────────
 Report    Intro   Band─────────────────────────────────────────────────────────
 Detail            Band─────────────────────────────────────────────────────────

This is an excellent opportunity for XXXXXXXXXXXXXXXXXXXXXXXXXX to strike it rich
During the next 90 days, XXXXXXXXXXXXXXXXXXXXXXXXXX can purchase all of our $14.9
titles for only $1.98.             ─



 Report    Summary Band─────────────────────────────────────────────────────────
 Page      Footer  Band─────────────────────────────────────────────────────────


 Report   ║C:\dbase\<NEW>          ║Line:3 Col:33  ║File:Cust_id ║         Ins
           Add field:F5   Select:F6   Move:F7   Copy:F8   Size:Shift-F7
```

Figure 11-6   Mailmerge setup with trimmed fields.

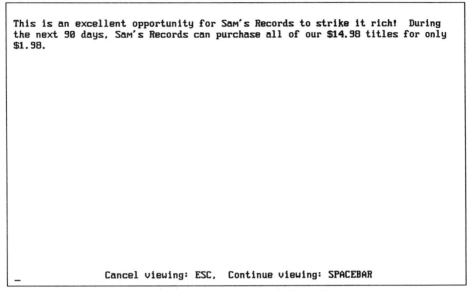

This is an excellent opportunity for Sam's Records to strike it rich! During the next 90 days, Sam's Records can purchase all of our $14.98 titles for only $1.98.

Cancel viewing: ESC,   Continue viewing: SPACEBAR

Figure 11-7   Mailmerge screen output for Sam's Records.

The amount of data in each data field may vary. For example, one company's name may be only five or six characters long, while another company's name contains 20 characters. If you insert the contents of a particular field into a record, and use a *Trim option* (to be discussed shortly), you can end up with different words at the right margin, depending upon the length of your data included on the line.

Mailmerge format allows your letter to automatically determine the end of each line, based on the number of characters included in the inserted fields. To see how this works, let's see what *Trim* means and how it functions.

In many data fields, the data entered into a field is often shorter than that which the field is defined to contain. When you select *Trim*, dBASE IV ignores the spaces beyond the last character in your field entry and places the next string of data or text immediately after it, separated by a space.

In Figure 11-6, a boilerplate paragraph is written that contains the field CUST_ NAME in the position of the Xs. The Xs indicate the complete width of the CUST_ NAME field. In both cases, the Trim option is set for each occurrence of the field.

Figures 11-7 and 11-8 show the screen output for two files—one for Sam's Records, the other for Other Vegas Music. Note that the line endings are significantly different in both files. The line endings are determined by the length of the data in the trimmed field.

In Figure 11-9, the Trim function is set to OFF. It should be clear that the untrimmed field for CUST_NAME allocates the entire width of the field, regardless of whether or not characters fill the entire field width.

In mailmerge mode, trimmed fields can be inserted into a text file created as part of your report. When dBASE IV determines the end of a line (based on the number of

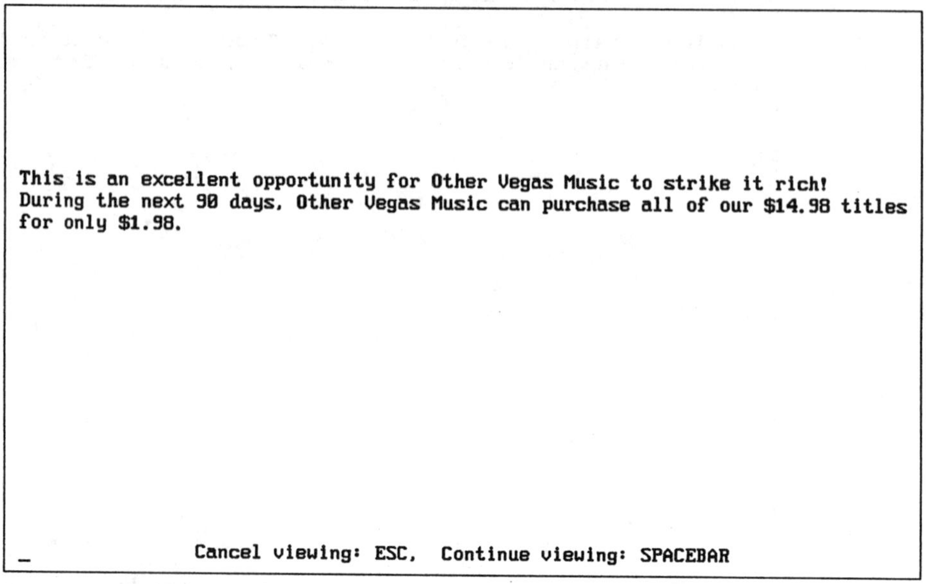

```
This is an excellent opportunity for Other Vegas Music to strike it rich!
During the next 90 days, Other Vegas Music can purchase all of our $14.98 titles
for only $1.98.




                     Cancel viewing: ESC,   Continue viewing: SPACEBAR
```

Figure 11-8   Mailmerge screen output for Other Vegas Music.

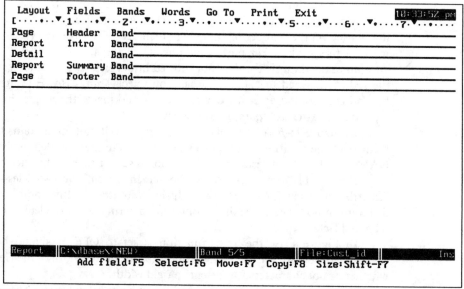

Figure 11-9   Report form with all bands closed.

characters of boilerplate plus trimmed text), it automatically wraps the cursor to the next line. In normal mode, there is no automatic wordwrap capability. A line can in principle run many thousands of characters wide. A hard return is required to move the cursor to the next line. Mailmerge recognizes the return character as a paragraph end marker. Any text that occurs between returns is automatically wrapped to the next line when the end of a defined line is reached.

> **Note** Mailmerge mode is useful for letters or documents that are designed to include data from your data files. In many businesses, a library of basic mailmerge forms can be used to produce standard letters that use variable information.

When setting up a mailmerge document, you must set the margins. To do this, select *Modify ruler* from the Words menu. This will bring the cursor into the ruler line at the top of the screen. The right bracket] is used to mark the right margin. A left bracket [marks the left margin. To set a tab, place an exclamation mark ! in the desired tab position. To delete an exising tab, press **Del** when the cursor is located on a tab position that you wish to remove.

To set an indentation point for a paragraph, place a pound (or number) sign # on the ruler line at the point where you wish the paragraph to indent. The indentation option only works in the Reports panel; it is not functional in the Labels or Forms panels. An option in the Words menu, *Enable automatic indent*, automatically indents the first line of each paragraph, placing the first character of the first line at the position defined in the ruler line, and wrapping all subsequent lines in the paragraph to the left margin. Once the ruler line settings are complete, pressing **Enter** returns the cursor to the position it was in when the Words menu was opened, and implements any format change that results from the modified ruler line.

When used in combination with the Words menu options (to be discussed more fully later), wordwrap mode provides significant flexibility and allows you to design and print custom letters, reports, and other documents that include the data from your data files.

Report Layout

Although you can select automatic, quick layouts, you can also design your own. In many cases, you may not want all the data fields placed into a report. Removing fields from a columnar report and adjusting the remaining fields is time-consuming and difficult.

The nature of the column layout is to place the field name in the Page Header band of the report, with corresponding data appearing in the Detail band. To remove a field, you must remove the field name from the Page Header band and the corresponding data field from the Detail band. This leaves a hole in your report form, because the data fields and field names to the right of the deleted field name and data are not automatically moved to the left to fill up spaces left by deleted field names and data.

> **Note** In many cases, it may be easiest to build your own report layout, placing the fields and field names into the bands where you believe they belong.

Bands The word "Bands" has been used so far without explanation. The use of bands in designing a report provides you with flexibility in data definition and data placement. The standard report form includes five bands: a Page Header band, a Report Intro band, a Detail band, a Report Summary band, and a Page Footer band.

Each band serves a slightly different purpose. The *Page Header* band includes text that is printed at the top of each page. In the quick layout for a columnar report, this includes the page number, date of the report, and the name of each field. The header band is useful for defining (or naming) the fields that are reported in the Detail band. The *Report Intro* band appears only once: at the beginning of the report. It can be placed either above the Page Header band on the first page, or below the header. The position of the Report Intro band is set by setting *Page heading in report intro* to YES or NO. It is used to describe the report or to give other information about the report. Depending upon your report design, the Report Intro band may belong either above or below the Page Header band, or not be needed at all.

The *Detail* band contains the actual data or other details that make up the report. In the columnar report, the actual data fields are included in the detail band.

The *Report Summary* band appears at the end of the report. It is designed to contain summary information based on the data in the Detail band. In a billing report, it may contain the totals of all orders for a particular date by a Single customer. This summary data can be used, then, as the amount due.

The *Page Footer* band is the final band in the basic design. It is used in much the same way as the Page Header band—to contain information such as report title, page number, or other identifying details.

It should be noted that bands are linked together in terms of position in a report. At the center of the band structure is the Detail band. Going one level out, you usually encounter the Report Intro band directly above the Detail band, and the Report Summary band directly below the Detail band. Going one level further out from the center, the Page Header band and the Page Footer band appear. If you have set *Page heading in report intro* to NO, the position of the Report Intro band and the Page Header band, and the position of the Page Footer band and the Report Summary band are switched.

Bands can be thought of as nested, with the Detail band being the central band in your report. Not all bands are needed in all reports. Bands can be opened and closed easily. A closed band does not print and contributes no data to your reports.

To open or close a band, move the cursor onto the band name and press **Enter**. If the band is open, it will be closed until you again press **Enter**. On the other hand, positioning the cursor on a closed band will open the band when you press **Enter**. Thus, with the cursor located on the band name, the **Enter** key toggles the band open and closed.

 When you move the cursor onto a band, the related band is also highlighted. The dual highlighting of all but the Detail band helps to remind you which bands are related, and how the nesting of the bands occurs.

Figure 11-9 shows a report with all bands closed. When a report based on this closed form is printed, no data, text, or field descriptions are printed. It is as if no report were specified. On the other hand, a form that includes all opened bands, seen in

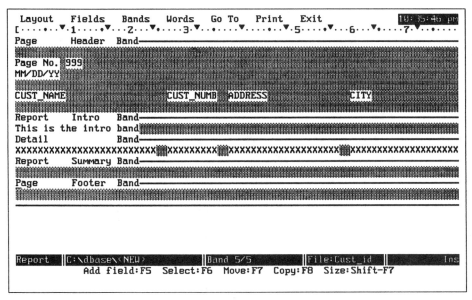

Figure 11-10   Report form with all bands opened.

Figure 11-10, will produce a report with the defined data from each band printed in its appropriate place. You can easily open all bands from within the Bands menu by selecting *Open all bands*.

It is possible that you may be able to use one basic report form design for more than one report. By placing header and footer text into the Intro and Summary bands, and switching between open header and footer and open intro and summary, two different basic reports can be made, the only change required being which bands are opened and which are closed. Text placement and editing are performed in much the same way as is done for form design. Text placement and editing are performed in much the same way as is done for form design. Text can be typed onto the screen, inside any of the bands. When the band is opened, the text will be printed.

Predefined Fields In addition, data field names and related data can be placed into any band (not just the summary bands). In fact, the page number and date shown in the quick layout for columnar reports use predefined fields that can be selected from the pick list that is opened when *Add field* or *Modify field* is selected from the Fields menu or the **F5** key is pressed. The available predefined fields are shown in the third column in Figure 11-11.

The four predefined fields are *Date*, *Time*, *Recno*, and *Pageno*. These functions print the date that the report is printed (or stored to disk), the time that the report is printed (or saved to disk), the record number of the current record, and the number of the current page of the report. Although Quick Layout places some of the predefined fields onto the report form, you may place the predefined fields at any position in your report.

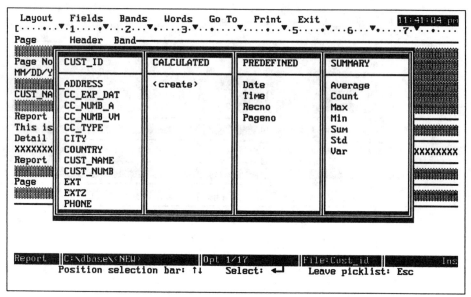

Figure 11-11 Predefined fields are shown in the fields pick list.

An Example Invoice Report

To demonstrate some of the powerful capabilities of the dBASE IV report panel, this chapter creates an invoice report. It begins by showing what the typical output from a report of this type will look like, and then designs the report form that was used to create the invoice. The first report, for Sam's Records, is shown in Figure 11-12.

The invoice clearly shows the date of the invoice (in this case, the date that the sample screen was produced), the company name, the name of the customer, and the title, price, and relevant totals for the order. At the bottom of the order, the total before taxes, the tax, and the grand total are all calculated. It should be clear that data from many different data files was included in the report. In addition, data that was not included in any of the data files was also included. Examples of the new data are the computed tax, the total for all sales, and the grand total. Furthermore, the date of the report was also a new addition to the report form.

The design of a report form such as the one used to create this example is relatively easy, once an understanding of the components of a report design is achieved. It is hoped that by the end of the section on reports, this understanding will enable you to prepare your own custom reports.

Before you can start your report, you must be certain that the required data is available. This data may be in the form of a data file that has been set up as a separate data file, that has been produced by running and saving a query, or that exists merely as a query view. A query view is a saved query definition. Such views are seen in the Queries panel in the Control Center. When selected, the query view is loaded, and the attached file(s) will serve as the source of data for your report. For the present report, a

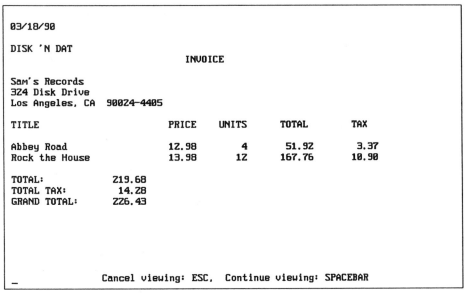

```
03/18/90

DISK 'N DAT
                              INVOICE

Sam's Records
324 Disk Drive
Los Angeles, CA   90024-4405

TITLE                     PRICE     UNITS     TOTAL       TAX

Abbey Road                12.98         4     51.92       3.37
Rock the House            13.98        12    167.76      10.90

TOTAL:          219.68
TOTAL TAX:       14.28
GRAND TOTAL:    226.43




                Cancel viewing: ESC,  Continue viewing: SPACEBAR
 _
```

Figure 11-12   Screen output for invoice.

query that produces the data fields shown in Figure 11-13 was created. This form is similar to the query designed in Chapter 10.

As already mentioned, a data file or query view definition must be activated before a report can be designed or run. In this example, a query view called ORDERS is

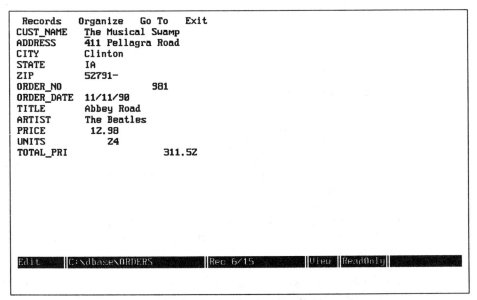

```
  Records    Organize    Go To    Exit
 CUST_NAME    The Musical Swamp
 ADDRESS      411 Pellagra Road
 CITY         Clinton
 STATE        IA
 ZIP          52791-
 ORDER_NO              981
 ORDER_DATE   11/11/90
 TITLE        Abbey Road
 ARTIST       The Beatles
 PRICE         12.98
 UNITS           24
 TOTAL_PRI                   311.52








 Edit     ║C:\dbase\ORDERS         ║Rec 6/15        ║View ║ReadOnly║
```

Figure 11-13   Fields used for inclusion in the current report.

being used. To use a view, the cursor is moved onto the name of the desired view, and the **Enter** key is pressed. This moves the query view above the line in the Queries panel that separates files in use or available for use from inactive files. In the case of a query view, only one view at a time may be in use (although you can <create> a query, but not go to report design until the query form is saved or a data file that is the result of the query has been created).

Designing the Form

Once you've told dBASE IV which data file or view you wish to use, you may next move the cursor into the Reports panel and select <create> to open the report design screen. The first option you have is *Quick layout*. In this case, you want to design your own form, and the quick layouts aren't satisfactory for the current type of report. The Page Header band is used to print your company name, the date of the invoice, and the description of the report at the top of each form. This use of the header band is practical if your company does not have a preprinted invoice.

If your company uses a preprinted invoice, but you wish to start printing at a point beyond where the company data and the word "INVOICE" appears on the form, you may enter blank lines into the header block to move the cursor down to the point where you want your actual report printing to begin.

Typically, placing six returns (assuming that you are printing using the standard line spacing of six lines per inch) will position the first line to be printed one inch below the top of the page. If you are using a laser printer, you should confirm that such a command actually places the first printable line one inch below the top—some printers may start counting the blank lines one inch below the first *printable* line on the page (laser printers typically are unable to print the top and bottom 0.2–0.5 inch of each page). Thus, a little trial and error may be required to determine the exact number of carriage returns (**Enter**) required to position the first line of your report onto the page.

In the example being built here, an invoice form that includes the date, company name, and a title for the form (INVOICE) will be created. The data included in the report comes from a query file called ORDERS.

Before starting the report design, the cursor is moved onto the name of the query to be used (in the Queries panel) or the data file (in the Data panel) that you will be using to provide the data fields to be used in producing your report. When the desired data file or query form is highlighted, press **Enter** to bring up the menu asking what you wish to do with the file. The cursor will be positioned over the words *Use file*. Press either **U** or **Enter** to tell dBASE IV that you want to use the file or view.

Next, move the cursor into the Reports panel and position it on <create>. Press **Enter** or **Shft-F2** to open the report design screen. The initial screen will show all five basic bands, with the Layout window open and *Quick layouts* highlighted. This report will not use the quick layouts, since you will be using group bands, and wish to place the fields in positions that aren't automatically produced using any of the quick layout formats.

A Page Header The first element you will be building is a page header. This header will be printed at the top of each page. Three fields are to be used.

With the cursor placed at the left margin on line 2, press **F5** to open the field selection menu. This menu could also have been opened by opening the Fields menu and selecting *Add field*. You will be placing the Date field, which is selected from the PREDEFINED panel in the field selection display, onto your form. To place the field onto your form, move the cursor onto *Date* and press **Enter**.

An options box will appear, allowing you to modify certain parameters related to the field. In the case of this field, you can only change two settings. If you wish, you may give the field a new name and you can tell the system to suppress repeated values. Selecting *Suppress repeated values* tells the system to print a value the first time it appears. In this case, if you tell dBASE IV to suppress repeated values, the first page of your report will have the current date, and all other pages will not.

This option is more useful for reports that only require a particular data value to be printed only once. For example, you may be attempting to prepare a report listing the names of cities where your company has active customers. If you have a successful business, it is quite possible that you may have many customers in each major city. However, for the purposes of such a city listing, you only need to list each city only once. If your list is properly sorted, dBASE IV can be instructed to suppress repeated values and add only *new* values for the desired field to the report.

In the case of the Date field, which will be printed at the top of each page (and which shouldn't change from report to report, unless you start printing your invoices a few minutes before midnight), and which is a field you want on top of each new invoice, you should leave *Suppress repeated values* set at NO.

The template that defines the order in which the day, month, and year will be displayed or printed is one that you cannot change from within the current menu. This template is read from defaults that can be changed from within the Options menu that is selected from the Settings option in the Tools menu. The Tools menu is one of three available at the top level of the Control Center.

The *Date order* option allows you to select the format for the order of month, day, year to be used in your report. In addition, the *Century* option is used to tell dBASE IV whether to use the last two numbers in the year (91) or the century (1991) in reports, labels, or screens that show the data. *Date Separator* allows you to define the character that is used to separate the month, day, and year from each other (there are three options; /, -, and .). Pressing **Enter** toggles between the three options. *Date order* is also toggled through using the Enter key. *Century* is set ON or OFF by pressing the **Enter** key. When you set the Date field onto your report, it will include the date based on the values for date order, century, and date separator selected from within the Options panel.

Once the field name and setting for *Suppress repeated values* are as desired, press **Ctrl-End** to set the field and place it onto your form. The cursor is moved down to line four, and the name of the company is typed in. Two lines further down, the word "INVOICE" is added. The word is highlighted and centered, using techniques shown in the chapter on Form design. With the header completed, the simple part (conceptually) has been created.

Defining the Fields to Include

The next step is to define the fields that you want to include on each invoice. This is where designing a report can get tricky. What you have to do is decide which data fields must be unique to each new store and to each new location, and what fields can be carried forward for an overall summary of *all* values in the report. This takes some thought, but after you explore the example and try a few reports on your own, the mechanism and reasoning should become fairly clear.

The Bands In this case, it may be useful to determine which fields you want included in the Detail band, and which fields should be treated as unique. When making such a determination, it is useful to consider the other types of reports that may be produced using the data in each Detail band.

Some explanation is in order here. The *Report Summary* band can be used to include summary fields that calculate totals, averages, and other values relating to the contents of *all* the data for each field in the Detail band. For example, if you produce 50 invoices, the Report Summary band can be used for calculating the total of *all* 50 customer orders.

> **Note** You should consider that you also wish to calculate totals for each customer's order. This total is not to be added to that for subsequent customers, and should be kept separate from the totals for orders from prior customers.

In order to produce summary reports, with a new report generated when the particular field value changes (for example, when CUST_ID changes), group bands are used. When you define a group band, dBASE IV groups the data in each band, based on the criteria you assign when you set up your group band. When you create a group band, two bands are created: a *group introduction band*, which is used to provide introductory information, field labels, and other information, and a *group summary band*, which can be used to total the values in the detail band. Figure 11-14 shows a group band that was inserted in your report, and shows how the group band surrounds the detail band.

In the example shown here, a number of text bands have been placed into the Group Intro band without any field labels attached. The fields used in the top three lines of the Intro band include the address information that will be used to identify the customer whose invoice is being prepared, as well as possibly providing a formatted address that can be used inside a window envelope for mailing the invoice. The fields include CUST_NAME, ADDRESS, CITY, STATE, and ZIP. Below the address fields, field descriptions are listed. The Group Intro band will print only the field descriptions when the report is printed; it has not been set up to print the contents of any record.

The Detail band, which appears directly below the *Group Intro* band, includes the data fields that are labelled in the Group Intro band. The detail band lists title, price per unit, and number of units, and includes two calculated fields: TOTAL and TAX. TOTAL represents the product of PRICE times UNITS. This field was created when the query that describes this data field was designed. However, TAX is a new field; the product of TOTAL_PRI (which represents PRICE*UNITS) and the tax rate. This example assumes a tax rate of 0.065. The field description and related calculations are seen in Figure 11-15.

In the example given so far, you've described the fields in the Group 1 Intro band, and placed the data from the relevant records and fields into the Detail band. The next step is to create a summary report based on the information in the Detail band. This is

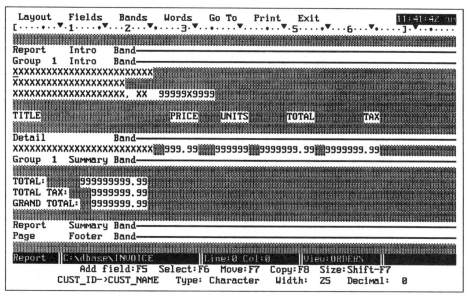

Figure 11-14 Group bands surround the Detail band.

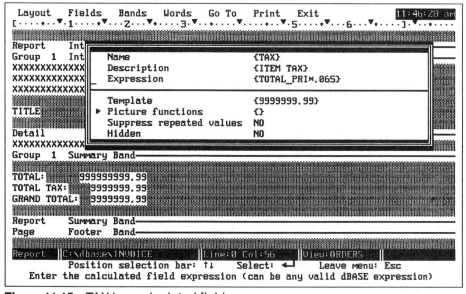

Figure 11-15 TAX is a calculated field.

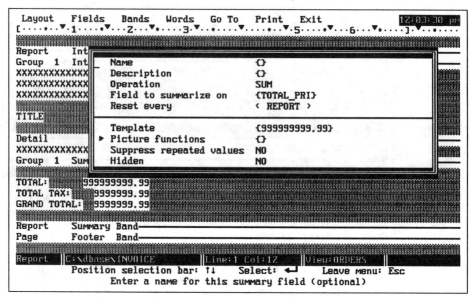

```
  Layout   Fields   Bands   Words   Go To   Print   Exit          12:03:30 pm
  [······▼·1·····▼···2··▼·····▼·····3·▼·····▼·····▼··5·····▼···6···▼····]·▼····
  ┌─────────────────────────────────────────────────────────────────────────┐
  │Report    Int │                                                           │
  │Group  1  Int │  Name                     {}                              │
  │XXXXXXXXXXXX  │  Description               {}                              │
  │XXXXXXXXXXXX  │  Operation                 SUM                             │
  │XXXXXXXXXXXX  │  Field to summarize on     {TOTAL_PRI}                     │
  │              │  Reset every             ‹ REPORT ›                        │
  │TITLE         │                                                           │
  │              │  Template                  {999999999.99}                 │
  │Detail        │ ▶ Picture functions        {}                             │
  │XXXXXXXXXXXX  │  Suppress repeated values  NO                             │
  │Group  1  Sum │  Hidden                    NO                             │
  │              └───────────────────────────────────────────────────────────┘
  │TOTAL:         999999999.99
  │TOTAL TAX:     9999999.99
  │GRAND TOTAL:   9999999.99
  │
  │Report    Summary Band─────────────────────────────────────────────────────
  │Page      Footer  Band─────────────────────────────────────────────────────
  │
  ┌Report │C:\dbase\INVOICE         │Line:1 Col:12  ││View:ORDERS   │
            Position selection bar: ↑↓    Select: ◄┘      Leave menu: Esc
                    Enter a name for this summary field (optional)
```

Figure 11-16   Group TOTAL for Group band.

done in the *Group Summary* band. New summary fields have been placed into the Summary band. These fields are labelled TOTAL, TOTAL TAX, and GRAND TOTAL (the sum of TOTAL and TOTAL TAX). The field description for TOTAL, seen in Figure 11-16, shows *Reset every* in the field setup menu.

This option allows you to tell dBASE IV which group of values you want to include in the summary. The options for this field allow you to begin the summary at zero when each new page, new report, or change in grouped field value is reached.

In Figure 11-17, the on-screen printout for the second record in an example file is shown. You will note that TOTAL is larger than GRAND TOTAL as displayed on the screen. GRAND TOTAL and TOTAL TAX correctly reflect the values in the detailed listing of titles ordered and prices attached to each item. The example shows a correct total; however, the total reflects the total of *all* records in the report. It includes those items ordered by other customers who were listed in previous invoices.

TOTAL TAX and GRAND TOTAL correctly reflect the totals only for the current customer, rather than for all orders, because the value of *Reset every* was set to change whenever the value of CUST_NAME (the group band field) changes. When the *Reset every* option is changed to CUST_NAME, the invoice correctly prints only the total for the current customer, as shown in Figure 11-18.

Three *Reset every* options are provided. If you choose to reset a value for every new report, report tells dBASE IV to keep a running total of all values in your report. This setting is most useful for report summaries, since it maintains a running total. A second option, Reset every *Page*, produces a new total for each page. This is useful for page by page subtotals.

To see a useful implementation of this option, you must back up a bit.

```
The Musical Swamp
411 Pellagra Road
Clinton, IA  52791-

TITLE                    PRICE    UNITS      TOTAL       TAX

Rock the House           13.98        6      83.88      5.45
Abbey Road               12.98       24     311.52     20.25

TOTAL:          615.08 `
TOTAL TAX:       25.70
GRAND TOTAL:    411.76




            Cancel viewing: ESC,  Continue viewing: SPACEBAR
_
```

Figure 11-17   TOTAL exceeds GRAND TOTAL because of incorrect reset.

```
The Musical Swamp
411 Pellagra Road
Clinton, IA  52791-

TITLE                    PRICE    UNITS      TOTAL       TAX

Rock the House           13.98        6      83.88      5.45
Abbey Road               12.98       24     311.52     20.25

TOTAL:          395.40
TOTAL TAX:       25.70
GRAND TOTAL:    411.76




            Cancel viewing: ESC,  Continue viewing: SPACEBAR
_
```

Figure 11-18   Correct reset setting results in correct data.

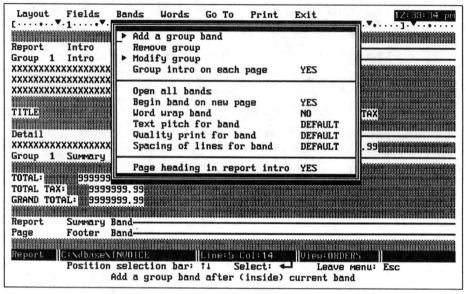

Figure 11-19   The Bands menu.

Adding a Band Group bands are used to tell dBASE IV how to combine data to be included in the band. You can easily add a band to a report form. To add a group band, move the cursor into the Detail band, and open the Bands menu. The Bands menu looks like Figure 11-19. The first option in the menu is *Add a group band*. When this is selected, you have three options: You may define a group based on a field value, an expression value, or a record count. The current report has defined a band based on the CUST_NAME field. When a field value is selected, a report is produced that contains all the selected data for that selected field. When the value of the field changes, a new record is produced. The current example produces a new invoice each time a new customer is encountered in the data file.

Nesting You can also use a technique referred to as *nesting*. A nested band is one that is placed inside of another group band. Nesting bands provides a number of benefits. For example, you may have a customer with stores in many cities. Preparing an invoice that is based only on changes in customer name will produce a report that combines *all* orders by *all* stores, regardless of their location.

In order to produce a report for the stores in each city, or at each location, you can use a second group band that produces a new report each time the address changes. For example, creating a second group band based on ZIP would create a new report for each store when the ZIP code for the store changes.

This is the way dBASE IV processes nested groups.

The innermost band value is processed first. If each value for a specific group band is used, dBASE IV then looks for the next outer band. Once a new value is encountered for the next band, dBASE IV then looks for the next level out.

Consider the following table of customer names and ZIP codes:

NAME	ZIP
Sam's Records	91304
Sam's Records	91305
Sam's Records	91306
Jim's CD Store	12345
Joe's Metal Pizzas	18200
Joe's Metal Pizzas	21221

If you nest groups, based on CUST_NAME and ZIP, and if you assume that the reports were already grouped by your query in the preceding order, invoices will be created in the same order. In other words, dBASE IV will produce a report based on orders whose CUST_ID fields match Sam's Records *and* also match the ZIP field 91304. When no more records match both values, dBASE IV goes to the next ZIP value for the CUST_ID field, Sam's Records. Thus, the next invoice will be for Sam's Records in ZIP code 91305. When no more Sam's Records in ZIP 91305 are encountered, dBASE IV looks for another Sam's Records, finding the one in ZIP 91306.

Once all ZIP values for Sam's Records have been encountered and processed, dBASE IV looks for the next CUST_ID value, finding Jim's CD Store. dBASE IV will prepare an invoice for the Jim's CD Store located in ZIP 12345, and look for another ZIP for Jim's CD Store. Finding no more nested values for Jim's CD Store, dBASE IV will then go to the next CUST_ID value and the first ZIP for that customer. In this case, the next group to be reported on is Joe's Metal Pizzas, in ZIP 18200. Once all Joe's Metal Pizzas in ZIP 18200 orders are processed, dBASE IV looks for the next new ZIP for Joe's Metal Pizzas, finds 21221, and makes invoices for that store. Once all Joe's Metal Pizzas in 21221 have been placed on the invoice (in the Detail band), dBASE IV will look for the next ZIP value for Joe's Metal Pizzas. Finding none, it will look for the next CUST_ID entry. Finding none, dBASE IV will then process a report summary (if a Report Summary band has been defined), and complete the preparation of the report.

In addition to grouping by customer name, city, ZIP code, or other similar parameters, you may also group by the number of records read into your report. Consider a business that routinely orders hundreds of titles for each store. It may be much simpler to reconcile a report and check the titles against stock deliveries (or perform other procedures) if you only list 10 or 15 titles on each page, and provide a subtotal for each page. Otherwise, you may produce a report with pages of titles ordered, but no easily reconcilable organization.

dBASE IV allows you to define a group band based on record count. When such a definition has been made, you are telling dBASE IV to build your band with *n* records, where *n* is the number of records you have defined as your group count. In the preceding example, if you further group each store by CUST_NAME, ZIP, and record count, you can then produce a report that lists only a preselected number of records on each page. A design that breaks the data into groups of 15 records per group is shown in Figure 11-20. Notice, at the bottom of the screen, the words "Group by 15" defining

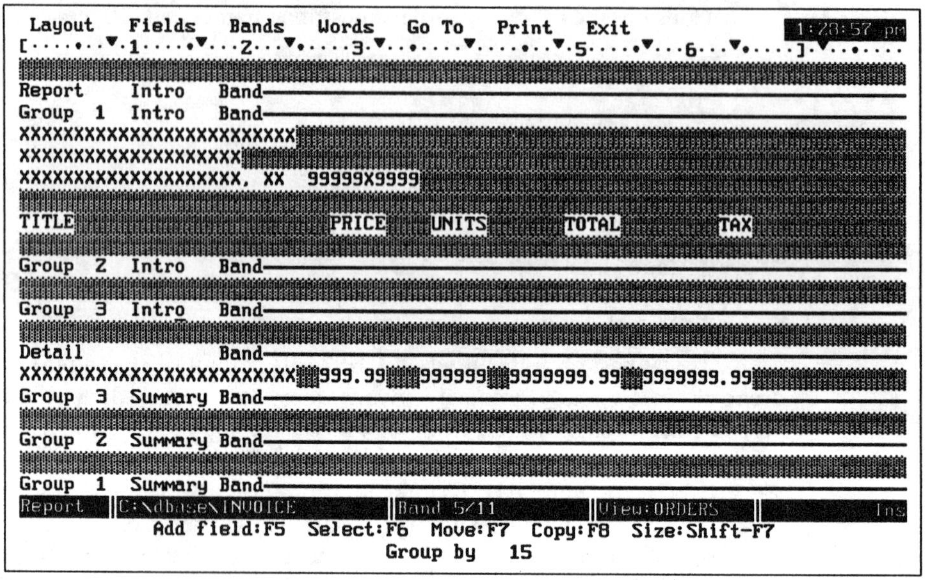

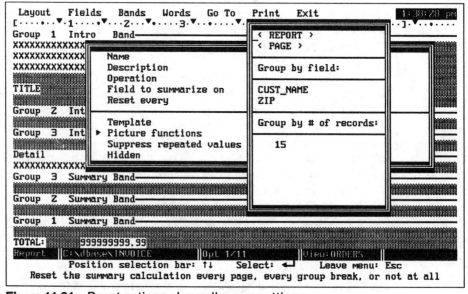

Figure 11-20   Report subgrouped by ZIP and groups of 15.

the type of grouping. With the current specification, a report with only 15 records per page, organized by ZIP and Customer name, will be produced.

A third option for grouping, *Expression value*, allows you to print reports only for those records that match a certain criterion. For example, if you want to produce reports only for those customers located in California, creating a GROUP BY expres-

Figure 11-21   Reset options show all group settings.

sion of {**STATE** = "**CA**"} will only report on those customers with the value of STATE equalling the string CA. By making the expression the outermost group band, processing speed will be greatest, since dBASE IV processes the bands from the outermost band inward. Thus, it will evaluate the expression and ignore all records that are not located in CA, subsequently processing the bands from the outer band inward. Although it may be somewhat confusing, considering that reports are produced from the inner band out, it is useful to remember that, as far as expressions are concerned, placing such filter items at the outermost band eliminates the otherwise essential processing that is required before the inner bands are reached.

The Reset Every Options Returning to the Summary band definition for Group summaries, you should be able to see how the *Reset every* option works. In Figure 11-21, the different types of grouping are displayed. You will note that there are more options on this screen, which relates to three different groups, than in Figure 11-20, which related to only a single group. This is what selecting each option will do with the current report:

<REPORT> will produce a summary that is based on *all* records in the report; it will provide a grand total (or whatever other type of summary option is selected) for all values in *all* invoices.

<PAGE> will calculate a new total for each page of records. This is useful for a page by page total of values.

CUST_NAME provides a total for each customer. In the case of Sam's Records, such a total (or other summary), will reflect orders for all Sam's Records stores in all locations—a chainwide total. It is useful to point out here that you may use this field in a Group 1 Summary band, shrinking the band (making it unavailable) when printing out an invoice for each store, and expanding the band (making it printable) when providing a master order to Sam's Records headquarters. Thus, one basic report form can be used to create two different types of customer report, merely by changing open bands. (A third type of report, the grand total of *all* customers, can be created by placing the *Reset every REPORT* parameter into a summary field in the Report Summary band.)

ZIP allows you to produce a summary based on each individual store (assuming that each store has a unique ZIP code). This type of invoice will go to the store that ordered the merchandise. It does not include data for other stores in the chain, since the value was reset when the new store became the one being reported on.

The final option, 15, is similar to the <PAGE> setting, if you have made a certain specific setting on the Bands menu. Otherwise, dBASE IV will provide a total of each block of 15 records in a report and reset after each 15 records.

Other Options in the Bands Menu Other options in the Bands menu should be explained, particularly in regards to the last item. The top half of the bands menu is relatively straightforward. It allows you to create a new group band, to delete a group band (although this can also be done by moving the cursor onto a band that you wish to delete, pressing **Del**, and answering the prompts from the system), to modify a group, and to put a group intro on each page. *Group intro on each page* gives you a choice of printing the contents of each group's introductory band on each page, or only on the first page of each report. In the case of the current report, you may wish to collapse the Group 3 band, and place the field identification materials into the Group 2 band. By telling dBASE IV to print the group intro for Band 2 on each page, you will produce a readable column heading for the fields shown in the Detail band.

Moving the field names from the Group 1 band into the Group 2 band allows you to tell dBASE IV not to print the customer name and address on each page, placing it instead only on page one of each invoice (by setting *Group intro on each page* to NO, for Group 1, and to YES for Group 2, which includes the field names). Thus, setting *Group intro on each page* to YES prints the intro on every page, while setting it to NO prints the intro only on the first page for each new group. This setting is toggled on and off by pressing **Enter**.

Open all bands is a quick way to open all bands. In many cases, you can use the same report design as the basis for many other reports. As has been discussed, by programming summaries for each band, as well as a report summary, you can create the basis for a variety of reports. Collapsing the report summary and Group 2 summary bands and leaving a Group 1 summary band open will allow you to produce a summary of invoices for each customer, including all locations. Collapsing the Group Summary bands, while leaving the Report Summary band open, can produce a summary report with totals (or other summary values) for the entire report—all detail items are reported. And collapsing all but the Group 2 band, as in this example, produces a separate summary for each location.

There may be times, however, when you want to rapidly open all bands—either for editing or for producing a report that includes *all* data. *Begin band on new page* tells dBASE IV whether or not you want to start each new group on a new page. If you are producing an invoice for each store, you probably want to set this to YES. In this case, whenever a new group value (such as a new customer name or a new ZIP) is encountered, a new report, starting on a new page, will be printed. On the other hand, if you are planning to run a report for all stores in a chain, you may prefer to list all locations continuously, without starting a new page for each new location.

Wordwrap band refers to bands that include data inside of text. In this case the information is meant as part of a paragraph or paragraphs, rather than as tabular data. For example, you may be developing a report that reads like a letter. In this type of report, you may write a paragraph (or paragraphs) that include the contents of one or more fields. A dunning letter may include a phrase like "According to our records, you still owe us TOTAL", where TOTAL is the amount still unpaid. Since the number of characters in such fields may not be constant, telling dBASE IV that the band is a wordwrap band instructs the system to end each line at a natural line break, rather than using fixed locations for line endings.

A report intro or group intro can be used as a wordwrap band, with details included, if needed. In addition, wordwrap or data bands can, of course, include both text and the contents of data fields. Text editing was covered earlier.

Text pitch for band allows you to select character size for the printed output.

This depends upon the characters supported by your printer, and upon the printer setup strings, if any, that have been entered into the printer setup (performed in the *Control of printer* menu of the Print panel). You may scroll through the options by pressing the **Spacebar**.

Quality print for band tells dBASE whether you want to print in draft mode, or in quality print mode. This applies primarily to dot matrix printers which may support both a high quality and a faster draft print mode.

In *Spacing of lines for band*, you can select single, double, or triple spacing by pressing the **Spacebar** until the desired setting is selected. The default for these print parameters is set in the Print panel.

Finally, *Page heading in report intro* tells dBASE IV whether or not you want the contents of the page heading band to be included in the report intro. When selected, the position of the Page Header band relative to the Report Intro band (and of the Page Summary band and Report Summary band) is switched. This was discussed earlier in this chapter.

Calculated and Summary Fields

It has been shown that you can create summary fields based on the data for a group band or for nested groups. As has been discussed, you can perform summary operations based on a number of options—new values for each new report, new field, or some other grouping criterion.

A variety of summary processes are available. Figure 11-22 shows the summary options that are available, without requiring special programming statements, from

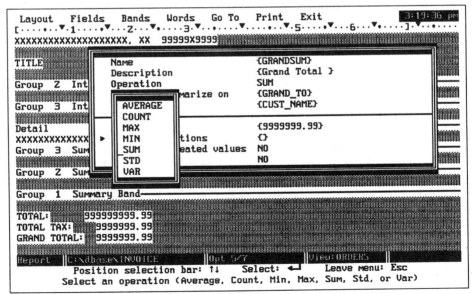

Figure 11-22 Summary options available.

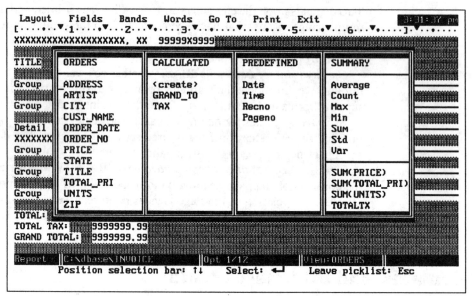

Figure 11-23 Field selection menu.

within dBASE IV. Most of the operations are relatively clear: AVERAGE totals the entries in the desired field and divides the total by the number of records, to find the average value for each record; COUNT keeps track of the number of records included in the report (it is the number that SUM is divided by to find an average); MAX and MIN return a single value—either the highest value for the designated field (the MAXimum), or the lowest value for the field (the MINimum value). SUM is the total of all values in the band/report (or whatever setting is used before the counter is set), while STD (standard deviation) and VAR (variance) are statistical measures that indicate the amount by which the values differ from an average value.

The summary operations relate to a particular field. The fields can be chosen from a pick list, which shows all available fields. In the example, you will note that fields that are nonnumeric appear in the pick list, in addition to calculated fields. dBASE IV only allows you to select numeric fields. The *Reset every* option, already explored, tells dBASE IV when to start the summary operation.

In addition to standard fields and summary fields, you can also create calculated fields. By moving the cursor into a blank area, you can open the Fields menu (by pressing **F5** or **Alt-F**). The menu appears like Figure 11-23. The menu shows all available fields, including those that have already been calculated.

The expression for a calculated field can include those already calculated. In addition, when you select a summary field, you can relate it to a calculated field (for example, summarize on a calculated field that adds tax to the total for each sale). Again, flexibility is provided by allowing you to define when to reset your summary value.

You can also use *hidden* fields. A hidden field is a field that is included in a report, and may be the basis of a summary operation, but is not printed or displayed on

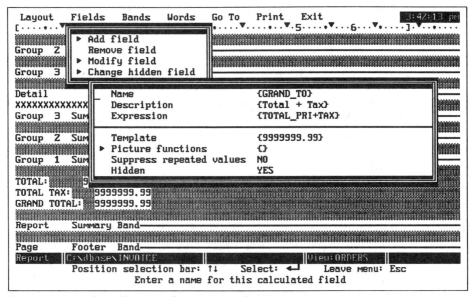

Figure 11-24   Specification for a hidden field.

the report. In this report, for example, a new field, GRAND_TO (for grand total) was created. The expression and description for this hidden field is shown in Figure 11-24.

The entry in the Group 1 summary band labelled GRAND TOTAL is actually a summary field, summarizing on the values within the group, for GRAND_TO, a field that is hidden to everything but the summary process. Hidden fields can be viewed or modified by accessing them using the *Change hidden field* option in the Fields menu. Fields can be made hidden from within the field setup menu.

You can also do multiple summaries on the same fields, achieving a different answer by changing the setting of the *Reset every* option. Thus, summarizing on GRAND_TO in the Group 1 summary band (with *Reset every* CUST_ID) provides a summary for each new customer, and doing the same summary operation on GRAND_ TO in the Report Summary band (with *Reset every* Report set) provides a total for all invoices.

The Words Menu

The Words menu, already touched on throughout this book, provides control over the appearance of the text in your report. The *Style* option allows you to change the appearance of the highlighted text. You can only change styles if your printer supports the changes, and if dBASE IV is set to produce the commands that produce the desired text attributes.

The *Position* option places the highlighted text at the left margin, right margin, or center of the screen. *Modify ruler* allows you to define the margins and tabs for your report. It was discussed earlier in this chapter. *Hide ruler* removes the ruler from the screen. This provides a slightly better view of the form than can be achieved with the ruler on the screen. Hiding the ruler only modifies the way that the screen appears; it does not affect the way that the report appears when it is printed.

Enable automatic indent tells dBASE IV to automatically indent the first line of each paragraph according to the first tab marker on the ruler line. This is designed primarily for use in wordwrap mode, when you desire your text to appear properly formatted (and correctly indented).

Add line inserts a line at the location of the cursor. This is approximately equivalent to pressing the **Enter** key. *Remove line* deletes a line at the cursor position. It is equivalent to the **Ctrl-Y** key combination. *Insert page break* places a special page break character onto your report form. This is useful when you are producing a letter that you want to break at the same spot each time it prints. When you are inserting data from fields into boilerplate text, the length of a page may vary, based on the amount of data taken from the associated fields. When a page break is inserted, you are telling dBASE IV to *always* start printing a new page following the break.

Finally, *Write/read text file* is used to save the text in your report so that it can be called into another report design. It can also be used to read saved text into a new report design. Being able to save text or to retrieve it from a file makes the use of dBASE IV for producing letters and other documents that require insertion of variable data an easy task.

The Go To Menu

The Go To menu is particularly useful in reports that include a large amount of text. When Go To is selected, the searches or movement to a particular line number are related only to the band that the cursor is currently positioned on.

In a band with only three or four lines, using the Go To menu is probably overkill. However, if a band includes a 400-line letter, being able to select *Go to line number* and type in a desired line number can be quite a time saver. In addition, forward or backward searches, with dBASE IV looking for particular characters, can also save significant time.

Replace is a useful addition to the forward and backward search. This provides some rudimentary word processing capabilities, allowing you to tell dBASE IV to both FIND a word or character string and REPLACE that string with a new word or character string. Say, for example, that you want to replace the string **Cheap bastard** with the string **Valued customer**. You can tell the system to search for **Cheap bastard** and make the replacement automatically.

Finally, *Match capitalization* tells whether you want an exact, case-sensitive match, or a case-insensitive match. If *Match capitalization* is set to NO, a search for **Cheap bastard** will match **cheap Bastard, cheap bastard,** and any other combination of the characters in the two words, regardless of which letters are capitalized. If *Match capitalization* is set to YES, dBASE IV will not match **cheap Bastard, cheap bastard, Cheap Bastard,** or any combination other than **Cheap bastard**.

The Print Menu

The Print menu provides a range of printer control options. *Begin printing* tells dBASE IV that your report is ready to print, and that all parameters and options are acceptable. *Eject page now* tells dBASE IV to send the command to your printer to spit out the current page, so that you can start printing on a clean page.

View report on screen is a useful option that you may find most valuable when you are designing your report. When you select that option—either by pressing **V** from within the Print menu, or by moving the cursor to *View report on screen* and pressing **Enter**—the report, as it is currently designed, will appear on screen. This is a useful method for previewing the final output of your report, and has been used to create a number of the figures used in this chapter.

The middle settings in the Print menu, *Use print form* { } and *Save settings to print form*, are closely related. When you have set your printer settings, using the options available at the bottom third of the Print menu, you will probably want to save the settings. In addition, you may have different printer settings for different types of documents (or may have settings for a draft printer, and different settings for a laser printer that is used for final output).

Having the ability to define printer settings only once for each type of printed document (or for each different printer) and then call them up from the named form saves you the trial and error that is often associated with designing a new printer setup.

> **Note** ⟩ It is good practice to save any new printer setup, giving it a unique name. In the future, when you are prepared to print another report, calling up a stored setup automatically activates the earlier settings.

The *Destination* option allows you to select the printer you will send the report to, as well as choosing to write your report directly to the printer, or to first write it to a file. There is an advantage to writing to a file. The advantage is this: If you have hundreds or thousands of reports to print, the speed at which dBASE IV can produce the reports will almost always be much greater than the speed at which the printer can print them. Thus, if you tell dBASE IV to print a large report to the printer, you may tie the printer up for many hours, and won't be able to do any additional work with dBASE IV or on the computer you are running dBASE IV on.

By writing to a disk, dBASE IV can finish producing the report in a considerably shorter time than it would if it wrote directly to the printer. Later on, you can issue the PRINT *filename* command, where *filename* is the name of the target file that dBASE IV wrote to. Thus, you can print the file during lunch, after work, or at some other time when the computer would otherwise not be needed or as important to current operations. (Doing so doesn't relieve *someone* from having to keep an eye on the printer to perform the necessary maintenance operations if paper should jam, a ribbon be used up, etc.)

If you print to a file, after selecting a desired printer, all necessary commands to talk to the printer (including formatting commands and other control codes) will be printed to the file. Such a file may not be easily readable, if you use a word processor to

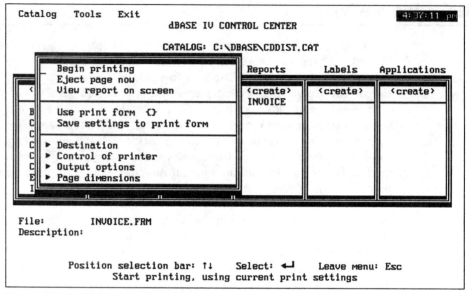

Figure 11-25   Print menu accessed from Control Center.

view the contents, but the commands should provide correct control of the targeted printer.

Echo to screen tells dBASE IV to show you the report while it is also being printed to the printer or to a file.

Control of printer allows you to set a variety of parameters that control the output of your report. The options are relatively self-explanatory, and are designed to support a wide range of printer types. Thus, *Quality print* truly applies only to dot matrix printers, as does *Wait between pages* (allowing you time to insert a new sheet of paper for the next page). *Advance page using* is also most closely related to the dot matrix printer, and tells dBASE IV whether or not a special form feed character is recognized by the printer or, if not, whether a sequence of line feeds are required to move the continuous paper to the beginning of the next page. *Printer control codes* are required by some printers to set up certain desired options, and to undo the changes after a print run is completed. These codes can be obtained from the owners' manual for your printer.

The *output options* are also self-explanatory. *Page dimensions* define to the system the length of the page, and the size of the left margin that you desire. In addition, this is where you set the default line spacing. Once the printer options have been set, you should consider saving them by selecting the *Save settings to print form* option and giving the print form a unique name.

Once the report is designed, you can save the form and exit. A compiled copy of the form is created, using the form template included with dBASE IV. You don't have to load a report form to print the form. You can also move the cursor into the Reports panel and highlight the report you wish to print. By pressing **Enter** (bringing up an

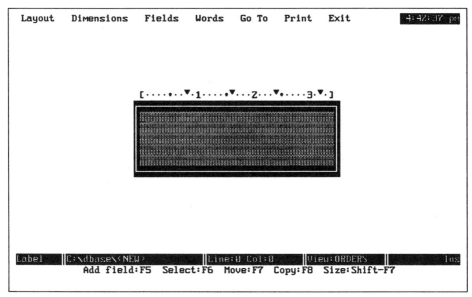

Figure 11-26   Opening Label design screen.

options screen) and then pressing **P** (for Print report), you will activate the Print menu. This menu is shown in Figure 11-25.

Labels

Labels are prepared in much the same way as are reports. However, since the purpose of labels is basically different, not usually requiring the same types of summary data, nor used for wordwrap text or large quantities of data, not all options available in the Reports panel are available in label design.

The opening screen for the Labels panel looks like Figure 11-26. Since there are many similarities between the Label design screen and both report and form design, only the important differences will be covered here.

The Layout menu allows you to select the database file or view. If a file or view is not active, you will be prompted to select one. The Dimensions menu is unique to the Labels design screen. Selecting *Predefined Size* displays a set of standard envelope and label formats. These options are shown in Figure 11-27.

The first three options are standard labels. The difference is in how many labels are arranged on the blank form. The first option assumes that only one label is printed across a horizontal line—this is a common format for dot matrix printers or other impact printers that provide tractor feeds. The second label format assumes that two labels on each line are printed; in this case, the blank is approximately 8 inches in width (7 inches for the two labels, plus approximately 1 inch for the tractor holes). The third format is designed for labels that print three per horizontal line.

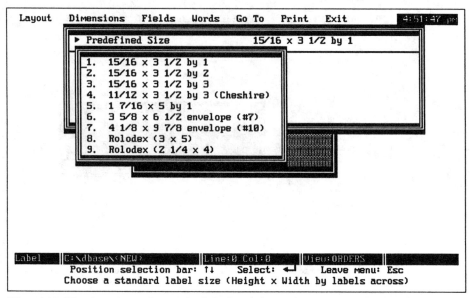

Figure 11-27   A variety of popular labels and envelopes are supported.

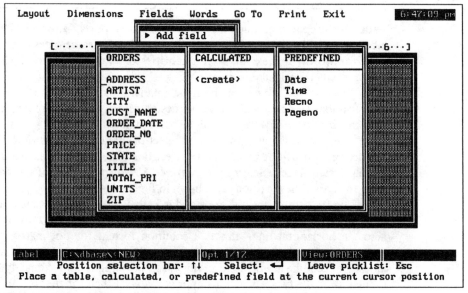

Figure 11-28   Available fields in the Label design screen.

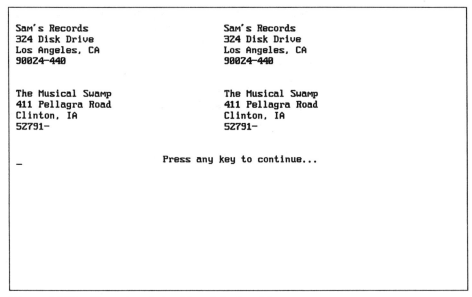

```
Sam's Records              Sam's Records
324 Disk Drive             324 Disk Drive
Los Angeles, CA            Los Angeles, CA
90024-440                  90024-440


The Musical Swamp          The Musical Swamp
411 Pellagra Road          411 Pellagra Road
Clinton, IA                Clinton, IA
52791-                     52791-


    _                Press any key to continue...
```

Figure 11-29   Sample printout two labels wide.

As the number of labels on a horizontal line increases, printing becomes more complicated, since dBASE IV must print the first line of one label, skip to the next label and print the first line of that label, then skip to the third label and print that first line, then return to the first label and print the second line, and so forth, until the three labels are completed.

Cheshire labels are a fairly common format that can be automatically placed onto envelopes by machine. In addition, formats for a larger label (designed primarily for mailing), two standard envelopes, and two standard Rolodex™ cards are supported. You can select a standard, predefined size for your label, or set the specific dimensions of your label by modifying the options in the Dimensions menu.

Custom settings are related to the size of the characters you are printing. For example, the predefined **15/16×3 1/2×1** label is shown to have a width of 35 characters. This assumes that you are using a print type that prints 10 characters per inch. If you are printing with a font that produces 12 characters per inch, you may have to change the width to 42 (3.5 times 12). The height measurement is the number of lines high your labels are, assuming the standard 6 lines per inch measurement of most printers. Other settings are also related to the size of the characters being printed, and assume that the printer prints 6 lines per inch. If you change the size of the type being used, you will probably have to change the settings for label width and spacing so that printing on the second or third labels (in forms two or more labels wide) can occur at the correct location.

Once a label or envelope dimension setting has been made and accepted (by pressing **Esc** after making your settings), dBASE IV will display a blank form the size and shape of your label, envelope, or card. The remaining menu options are basically the same as those used for report design. As with report design, you may combine text and field data. You may use fields from your source data file or view, may create calculated fields, and may use a limited number of predefined fields. Summary fields are not included in the available field types, although you may be able to define a formula as a calculated field expression that performs the same function. The available field options are shown in Figure 11-28.

Field selections default to automatically trimming the field values. When a value is trimmed, the space that is blank beyond the end of the field entry is not printed—instead, dBASE IV begins printing the next field. A screen sample of a label form supporting the printing of a label sheet two labels wide looks like Figure 11-29. Note that although you are viewing and printing three labels at a time, only the one label is shown (and designed) on your form.

It should be noted that each record prints two labels because two orders have been order entered for each customer. If you only want to print one label for each customer, you will have to do a sort or query on your data files to assure that only the first occurrence of each field value is put into your source data file.

Conclusion

Report and label design are two areas where the work that has gone into design of your data files and development of useful queries can pay off. The techniques shown in this chapter, and in earlier ones, provide you with the tools required to create your data files, evaluate your data, and last (but certainly not least important), to create useful reports and other output based on the data.

The remaining chapters in this book will explore methods for integrating the skills and components of the application already designed into complete applications, and will also demonstrate the methods for designing useful applications from scratch.

Fasten your seat belts!

12

Applications Generator

This chapter begins the discussion of probably one of the most exciting aspects of dBASE IV, the freshly revised and enhanced Applications Generator. Because this topic is so important, four chapters are devoted to investigating how to get the most out of the Applications Generator. Chapter 12 begins by illustrating the basics of applications design and methods of utilizing the Applications Generator to build complete and (most important) usable systems under dBASE IV. The stage is also set for a sample application to be constructed in later chapters. Building on this knowledge, Chapter 13 examines how to create a user interface, or menuing system, with which to tie the application together. Chapter 14 shows how to attach together the "objects" built in previous chapters of the book under one application. Finally, Chapter 15 goes one step further by showing how to create new objects from the Applications Generator and attach them to the application. In that chapter, some additional advanced topics that will make the application more contemporary are also discussed. Throughout these chapters, many techniques for deriving much of the power out of the dBASE IV Applications Generator are introduced. Both elegant solutions as well as pitfalls will be explored to make your trip through the Applications Generator a productive one.

 When referring to the Applications Generator, we will not distinguish between dBASE IV Versions 1.0 and 1.1, since there is little difference between the versions with respect to this area.

An Application Defined

An application program is a collection of objects, both dynamic and nondynamic in nature, tied together to form some cohesive whole to solve a business problem. Some examples of applications might be an accounting system, a legal office management system, a mail order processing system, or a church management system.

One can generally classify the *nondynamic* objects as database files, which hold the data; index files, which define one or possible multiple orderings of the databases; queries (QBE files), which define views; and filters and relations, which provide a linking mechanism for related databases. These objects are nondynamic because they do not take any action, but merely establish an environment for the application to process information. *Dynamic* objects can be grouped into several distinct groups: data entry screens (forms), printed output such as reports (report forms) and labels (label forms), lists, batch processes, and so on. These objects are dynamic, since they each carry out some operation. For example, a report form will utilize database, index, and query objects in order to provide printed results for questions the user may have posed. You should view all these items as "objects" in that they each perform some unique task for one common goal, to implement a system. Each object type must now be specifically defined.

Types of Objects

There are several types of objects available to you when putting together an application. Each object type plays its own specific role in implementing the application, with some object types playing a more important role than others. These next few chapters investigate all of the object types and include a sample of each in the final result. Now, all of the object types are briefly defined, in order to set the stage for later consideration.

Application Object This is the highest level of object and is the one that ties together the other objects that make up the application. In reality, it is the object that stores an application's name, its main menu, and the default database. In addition, this object normally serves as the sign-on screen with which the user is first presented when the application is begun.

Database and Index File Objects An application usually stores its information in one or more databases, whose orders are kept by one or more index files. More often than not, these databases will need to be linked according to key fields so that the information stored within may be viewed as coming from a single file, even though it is distributed across several databases.

Screen Form Objects A screen form object provides the vehicle by which new data may be entered and existing data may be edited in a database. Using the dBASE IV form design surface, you may define a rather sophisticated data entry screen, store its image, and then later call it up from an application.

Query Objects Query objects are really just QBE files that define database environments. Some of these environments may be complex, so storing them in a QBE file saves time. An example of an environment might be several databases, linked by common fields using indexes based on certain tags, with a filter condition in effect for the purpose of selecting only certain records. The query results may be displayed using a Browse window or any one of many other alternatives.

Report and Label Form Objects For printed output, both reports and labels may be designed using facilities available from the Control Center. The results of these designs are then saved to report and label form files, respectively. With a possible view in effect, you can produce printed output by using these objects.

List Objects A list object is physically just a pick list window that pops up when requested, presenting the user with a number of choices. There are three types of list objects. The most common type of list is a *file list*. This list is a window containing the names of a certain group of files. The user may be asked which query file to use, for example. Also available are *structure lists*. These present a series of database field names from which the user may choose. The last list type is the *value list*, which displays the values stored in a specific field of the current database.

Batch Process Objects A batch process object is one that defines a series of tasks to be performed. These tasks are then grouped in a single entity called a *batch process*. Examples of batch processes are a series of commands to delete certain records from a database and then perform a PACK operation, commands to print a series of reports, or a process to backup database files to an external device.

Code Segment Objects dBASE language code segment objects are a group of small dBASE programming statements (normally just a few lines, but possibly longer) that perform a function that cannot otherwise be done from the Application Generator or the Control Center. For example, you may wish to embed a code segment that defines certain SET variables as your application is running. For more extensive use of the dBASE language there are also *code objects* and *program objects*, which are examined in greater detail in Chapter 15.

What Is an Applications Generator?

An Applications Generator (often called an *ApGen* for short) is a piece of software that provides a platform for the design and definition of a complete application program. The term "application" denotes some final result such as a mail order management system that accepts orders, updates the inventory, prints invoices, and so on. When all of these component parts are tied together, the resulting system is called an *application*. Usually, an ApGen (there are several dBASE-based ApGens on the market) goes one step further and actually writes the computer programs in some target computer programming language required to implement the application. This is the case for the dBASE IV Applications Generator. The target language is the greatly enhanced (over dBASE III Plus) dBASE IV programming language.

The concept of an Applications Generator has been around for a long time, but its scope has always been somewhat limited by the inherent inability of these programs to address real system needs without ultimately requiring some programming. dBASE III Plus was a good example of this situation. It had an applications generator that did indeed build so-called "complete" applications, but these had such small-scale uses

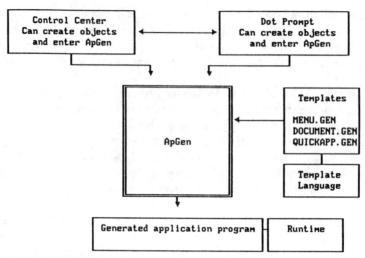

Figure 12-1   ApGen's integration into dBASE IV.

that they could not truly be classified as applications. Many wrote off using ApGen in dBase III Plus. This validates dBase IV's ApGen.

What dBASE IV has done is to allow the Applications Generator to tap into the storehouse of enhancements and new features available in dBASE IV and to wrap a slick, contemporary coating around them to produce a usable application. In fact, ApGen integrates nicely into the overall scheme of dBASE IV, as shown in Figure 12-1.

From the figure you can see the role both the Control Center and the dot prompt play in feeding ApGen with the objects it integrates into an application. From the Control Center you create objects in the usual fashion—for example, creating a new form or report object. From the dot prompt you can also create certain objects by issuing the proper command to do so (such as CREATE LABEL). It is also evident that the way ApGen builds applications is governed by several templates. This template philosophy allows the system developer to tailor how applications will be generated—a topic touched on again at the end of this chapter.

Once the final application has been built, it may be executed from the Control Center by running it from the Applications panel or from the dot prompt by entering: *DO <appname>* and pressing **Enter**. ApGen normally generates two dBASE program code files, named <appname>.PRG and <mainmenu>.PRG—where <appname> is the name you assign to the whole application and <mainmenu> is the name of the main menu of the application. There may be variations to this organization depending on your approach in building the application.

To run an ApGen-built application, dBASE IV must, of course, be present, though you can utilize the dBASE IV RunTime system, which will allow an application to run but will not allow the user any of the other features of dBASE IV. With the dBASE IV Professional Compiler (which is yet to be released), the application can be *compiled* (that is, translated into an .EXE file, which can run by itself without dBASE IV or the dBASE IV RunTime system).

The dBASE IV Applications Generator raises the threshold point at which programming must be undertaken to realize the goals of a particular application. Before, using dBASE III, programming would be required for even the simplest systems, but this is no longer the case. Moreover, the code actually generated is better in terms of readability, enhancability, and maintainability. The dBASE IV Applications Generator has taken the state of the art of automatically constructing complete applications one big step forward.

Analyzing the System

One of your first tasks as a nonprogramming system developer is to fully understand the requirements of the application you intend to define using the dBASE IV Applications Generator. Specifically, you need to determine what information must be present in order for the required output to be derived, how to best organize that information, and what the overall flavor of the application should be. Many times an existing system is in place and you must analyze it fully to understand its deficiencies as well as gain an appreciation for the goals of the new system. Sometimes the current system is a manual one, consisting of printed forms that are filled out by clerks and invoices that are prepared with a typewriter. Other times you begin with an existing automated system that has been deemed inadequate. Often, trying to "fix" an existing computerized system is more difficult than newly automating a manual one, since you are frequently burdened with poor or inflexible design decisions made by prior system designers. Using Figure 12-2 as a reference, a few basic areas of concern that anyone building a brand new application must consider are now defined.

A good way to begin analyzing the current system is to look first at all the possible forms of *output* that the system must be required to generate. Two general areas of

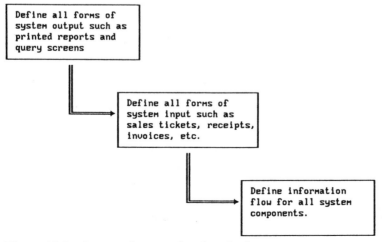

Figure 12-2 Approach to application design.

output need to be considered. First, printed output such as reports, invoices, statements, labels, and checks should be examined. Next, you should also examine visual displays such as query screens, which provide interactive support of user requirements. Once you have a firm notion of the desired output, you should have a pretty good understanding of the data requirements of the system—that is, the data required to produce the intended output. For example, if your customer statements are required to report an "aging analysis" (typically 30-60-90 days past due), then you know that an historical base for orders versus payments is needed.

To get another perspective on your new system, you should then consider the *inputs* of the system. These may take the form of manually prepared forms such as sales tickets, receipts, application forms, checks, order forms, and so on. The list is endless, since every business enterprise has its own collection of "forms" that it uses in everyday business operations. Some inputs, however, are not in the form of paper. For example, you might receive data electronically in the form of computer media (e.g., tapes, disks, CD-ROMs) or transmissions through data communication devices. Regardless of its form, by analyzing the input you will gain a feel for general size of the system, the databases to be used, and whether the inputs are satisfactory for the required output of the system.

The next, very important, area to determine is the *information flow* of the system. This is the way information comes into the system, the methods by which information is processed, and how the results are delivered to the user. Information flow is not always straightforward, since even in moderately complex systems data is often first placed in temporary files and then transferred to a permanent file once it is verified. A good example of this is an accounting system, where a transaction such as a customer invoice is placed in an invoice-posting journal, manually checked, and then posted to the accounts receivable database; once paid, it will then be posted to the general ledger database. Well-thought-out information flows can truly make or break a system, since issues such as usability, reliability, maintainability, and expandability are at stake.

While performing these system analysis tasks, you should always consider how the data of the system can be partitioned into database files and how it might need to be organized (indexed by what key fields). Moreover, you should try to get an idea of the structure of the whole system in terms of menus, data entry programs, query files, lists, and batch processes. Designing these items is what database and application design is all about and is the topic for our next discussion.

Application Design

This section defines several steps towards the goal of efficiently designing an application. These steps transcend the dBASE IV Applications Generator in that they are simply good system design philosophies. You should view application design as a process independent of language or environment.

In dBASE IV you have two basic approaches to application design. First, you may begin at the Control Center and individually define each of the objects—beginning with the databases and indexes, then the queries and screens, followed by the reports and labels. Each of these items may be defined and tested separately, but the underlying assumption should be that they will ultimately be tied together. This approach may initially seem attractive, since you have the freedom to float around creating objects at will. However, this approach also has one implied drawback—lack of structure. Since there is no overseeing structure, such as a menu of some kind, you may wind up creating objects that will not fit together well when you build the application.

The second approach is to go directly into the Applications Generator, define the encompassing structure first, and then selectively return to the Control Center to define each object. Sometimes you do not foresee the possibility of generating an application, in which case the first approach makes sense, but if you indeed intend to build an entire application, do consider the second approach. The inherent structure that will be gained will definitely provide benefit in the end result.

There is a third alternative that may be taken. This involves constructing the shell, menus, and so forth, first, and then going back to the Control Center to build each of the objects separately. This is a more "top-down" approach and is suitable for times when you wish to obtain a high-level perspective of the application before building and incorporating its component parts.

When designing an application, you normally begin by defining all the database objects to be used with the other objects of the system. As usual, you begin with creating the structure of each database by specifying all the fields and associated attributes (i.e., data type and length). In addition, you specify the indexes to be maintained by marking which fields are to be viewed as tags in the master index file for each database. Next, you create Query by Example files that define relationships between the databases. This is a very important task since it is the one that allows dBASE IV to be used in the way it was intended—that is, relationally. Other query files need to be defined also, but for the purpose of later screen displays, reports, and labels. For example, if the system is required to print a regional sales report for one of four regions, then a query file must exist to be able to select records for each of the regions. The application designer must think out all the possible ways the database(s) must be interrogated and build a query file to correspond to these ways. Query objects are a very important part of any database application.

Constructing the data entry screens is the next step in constructing an application, since now that you have all the databases and relationships set, you need a way to get data into the system. Generating adequate test data is another important phase of application development, since using data that is insufficient to demonstrate that an application is operating properly can yield an application that might not measure up to expectations.

Another important goal of the data entry screens should be to eliminate the possibility of bad data entering the system. For example, you would not want nonexistent customer codes, expired credit card dates, invalid state codes, and so on, to be entered. Data validation should be tight enough to weed out these kinds of things so that the output of the system will be more meaningful.

The next area that needs to be addressed pertains to the output of the system. Output may be in the form of reports, labels, or even visual displays of information.

dBASE IV allows the creation of several other types of objects that may be considered during the system design phase. Batch processes that perform a backup, reindex, or pack can be defined. Updates that could go through an inventory database and increase prices by 5% might be appropriate. Lists can be defined for other objects. They might take the form of lists of files, lists of fields, or lists of values. Also, you may you may wish to implement a dBASE code object that can be called in to perform this task.

Finally, you must design a menu structure, which will be the user interface, that will wrap around all the objects you have designed.

The Sample Application

Before the application is constructed, the system goals need to be trimmed down a bit (for pedagogical purposes only). In prior chapters, many databases and screen forms were defined. All these need not enter into the sample application that is about to be built, although they all could. Just to keep things more manageable, only the ORDERS, CUST_ID, TITLES, and EMPLOYEE databases will be considered. In fact, the structures of these databases will be modified slightly, again just to simplify the design. Please refer to Figures 12-3, 12-4, 12-5, and 12-6 for these structures. Briefly, what has taken place is that ORDERS now has all shipping information and TITLES has pricing (the PRICE field) and inventory (the NO_IN_STOC field) information. Both CUST_ID and EMPLOYEE remain unchanged and are provided here again for reference purposes.

Following is a complete collection of some of the objects created in previous chapters that are to be considered in our discussion of building a complete application:

Databases and Indexes

CUST_ID   the customer database
ORDERS   the orders database
EMPLOYEE   the employee database

Screen Forms

CUST_ID   customer data entry screen

Queries

QUERY9   view to relate ORDERS to CUST_ID and
              CUST_ID to STOCK; used with REPORT1
LABEL   view for selective label generation;
              relationally links ORDERS and CUST_ID;
              Used with LAB1

Report Forms

REPORT1   order list report
REPORT2   stock-by-supplier report

Labels

LAB1   customer mailing labels

```
 Layout   Organize   Append   Go To   Exit                    12:57:37 pm

                                              Bytes remaining:    3930
 ┌─────┬────────────┬────────────┬───────┬─────┬───────┐
 │ Num │ Field Name │ Field Type │ Width │ Dec │ Index │
 ├─────┼────────────┼────────────┼───────┼─────┼───────┤
 │  1  │ CUST_NUMB  │ Character  │   6   │     │   Y   │
 │  2  │ ORDER_NO   │ Character  │  15   │     │   Y   │
 │  3  │ ORDER_DATE │ Date       │   8   │     │   N   │
 │  4  │ ID_NUMBER  │ Character  │  10   │     │   Y   │
 │  5  │ TAKEN_BY   │ Character  │   8   │     │   Y   │
 │  6  │ NO_ORDERED │ Numeric    │   5   │  0  │   N   │
 │  7  │ NO_SHIPPED │ Numeric    │   5   │  0  │   N   │
 │  8  │ NO_BACKORD │ Numeric    │   5   │  0  │   N   │
 │  9  │ SHIP_DATE  │ Date       │   8   │     │   N   │
 │     │            │            │       │     │       │
 └─────┴────────────┴────────────┴───────┴─────┴───────┘
 Database C:\dbiv\sample\ORDERS     Field 1/9                  Num
            Enter the field name.  Insert/Delete field:Ctrl-N/Ctrl-U
 Field names begin with a letter and may contain letters, digits and underscores
```

Figure 12-3   ORDERS database structure for sample application.

```
 Layout   Organize   Append   Go To   Exit                    12:58:47 pm

                                              Bytes remaining:    3810
 ┌─────┬────────────┬────────────┬───────┬─────┬───────┐
 │ Num │ Field Name │ Field Type │ Width │ Dec │ Index │
 ├─────┼────────────┼────────────┼───────┼─────┼───────┤
 │  1  │ CUST_NAME  │ Character  │  25   │     │   Y   │
 │  2  │ CUST_NUMB  │ Character  │   6   │     │   Y   │
 │  3  │ ADDRESS    │ Character  │  20   │     │   N   │
 │  4  │ CITY       │ Character  │  20   │     │   N   │
 │  5  │ STATE      │ Character  │   2   │     │   Y   │
 │  6  │ PROVINCE   │ Character  │  10   │     │   N   │
 │  7  │ ZIP        │ Character  │  10   │     │   Y   │
 │  8  │ POST_CODE  │ Character  │  10   │     │   N   │
 │  9  │ COUNTRY    │ Character  │  10   │     │   N   │
 │ 10  │ PHONE      │ Character  │  10   │     │   N   │
 │ 11  │ EXT        │ Character  │   6   │     │   N   │
 │ 12  │ PHONE2     │ Character  │  10   │     │   N   │
 │ 13  │ EXT2       │ Character  │   6   │     │   N   │
 │ 14  │ CC_TYPE    │ Character  │   1   │     │   N   │
 │ 15  │ CC_NUMB_VM │ Character  │  19   │     │   N   │
 │ 16  │ CC_NUMB_A  │ Character  │  17   │     │   N   │
 └─────┴────────────┴────────────┴───────┴─────┴───────┘
 Database C:\dbiv\sample\CUST_ID    Field 1/17                 Num
            Enter the field name.  Insert/Delete field:Ctrl-N/Ctrl-U
 Field names begin with a letter and may contain letters, digits and underscores
```

Figure 12-4   CUST_ID database structure for sample application.

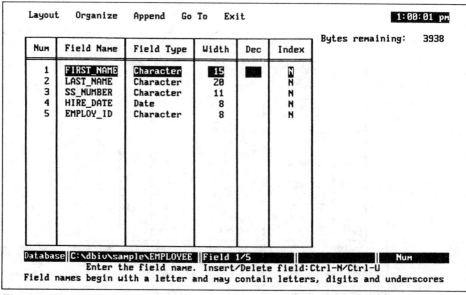

```
   Layout    Organize    Append    Go To    Exit                    12:59:30 pm

                                                          Bytes remaining:    3830
  ┌─────┬──────────────┬──────────────┬────────┬───────┬─────────┐
  │ Num │  Field Name  │  Field Type  │ Width  │  Dec  │  Index  │
  ├─────┼──────────────┼──────────────┼────────┼───────┼─────────┤
  │  1  │ TITLE        │ Character    │  25    │       │    Y    │
  │  2  │ ARTIST       │ Character    │  25    │       │    Y    │
  │  3  │ COMPOSER     │ Character    │  25    │       │    Y    │
  │  4  │ ID_NUMBER    │ Character    │  10    │       │    Y    │
  │  5  │ ART_OTHER    │ Memo         │  10    │       │    N    │
  │  6  │ PUBLISHER    │ Character    │  20    │       │    Y    │
  │  7  │ FIRST_REL    │ Date         │   8    │       │    N    │
  │  8  │ PLAY_TIME    │ Character    │   6    │       │    N    │
  │  9  │ SPARS_CODE   │ Character    │   3    │       │    Y    │
  │ 10  │ CATEGORY     │ Character    │  10    │       │    Y    │
  │ 11  │ PERFORMANC   │ Character    │   2    │       │    N    │
  │ 12  │ SOUND_QUAL   │ Character    │   2    │       │    N    │
  │ 13  │ TOTAL_QUAL   │ Character    │   2    │       │    N    │
  │ 14  │ COMMENTS     │ Memo         │  10    │       │    N    │
  │ 15  │ PRICE        │ Numeric      │   6    │   2   │    N    │
  │ 16  │ NO_IN_STOC   │ Numeric      │   6    │   0   │    N    │
  └─────┴──────────────┴──────────────┴────────┴───────┴─────────┘
  Database  C:\dbiv\sample\TITLES  Field 1/16                       Num
            Enter the field name.  Insert/Delete field:Ctrl-N/Ctrl-U
  Field names begin with a letter and may contain letters, digits and underscores
```

Figure 12-5   TITLES database structure for sample application.

```
   Layout    Organize    Append    Go To    Exit                     1:00:01 pm

                                                          Bytes remaining:    3938
  ┌─────┬──────────────┬──────────────┬────────┬───────┬─────────┐
  │ Num │  Field Name  │  Field Type  │ Width  │  Dec  │  Index  │
  ├─────┼──────────────┼──────────────┼────────┼───────┼─────────┤
  │  1  │ FIRST_NAME   │ Character    │  15    │       │    N    │
  │  2  │ LAST_NAME    │ Character    │  20    │       │    N    │
  │  3  │ SS_NUMBER    │ Character    │  11    │       │    N    │
  │  4  │ HIRE_DATE    │ Date         │   8    │       │    N    │
  │  5  │ EMPLOY_ID    │ Character    │   8    │       │    N    │
  │     │              │              │        │       │         │
  └─────┴──────────────┴──────────────┴────────┴───────┴─────────┘
  Database  C:\dbiv\sample\EMPLOYEE  Field 1/5                      Num
            Enter the field name.  Insert/Delete field:Ctrl-N/Ctrl-U
  Field names begin with a letter and may contain letters, digits and underscores
```

Figure 12-6   EMPLOYEE database structure for sample application.

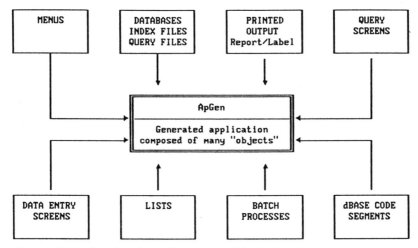

Figure 12-7 Applications Generator objects.

The Applications Generator provides other types of objects that help to bind together the application: menus, lists, batch processes, and dBASE IV programming language segments. Figure 12-7 depicts a way you may view how the applications generator treats objects when considering an overall application. The individual objects shown in this figure are addressed during a later discussion of application design and again in later ApGen chapters when you will actually construct these objects.

Starting Up ApGen

This section shows the basic ingredients in starting the development of any application. Whether you choose the first or second (or even third) approach to application design, these techniques are still valid. First, the high-level, application-oriented portions of the system are constructed. To start, select <create> from the Control Center Applications panel. You will immediately see the dialog box shown in Figure 12-8, which asks if you wish to begin the design of an application object, by selecting *Applications Generator*, or create (or modify) a dBASE language program, by selecting *dBASE program*. Selecting the latter option will get you into the integrated program text editor in dBASE IV, as shown in Figure 12-9, where you can enter or change a program written in the dBASE language. This option is normally not used by most nonprogramming system developers but is useful when preparing dBASE code to be embedded in an application (more about embedded code in Chapter 15). As a side note, this is the way Control Center users can invoke the MODIFY COMMAND dot prompt command. Notice the word *Program* in the current screen section of the status bar.

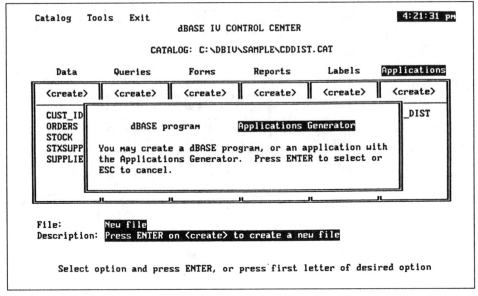

Figure 12-8 Entering the Applications Generator.

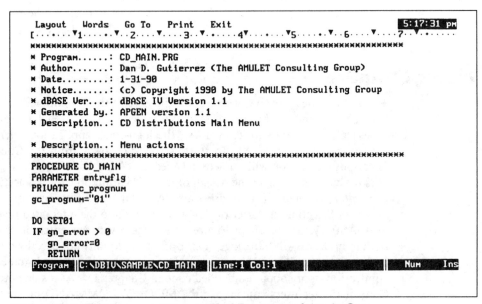

Figure 12-9 Creating or editing a dBASE program from ApGen.

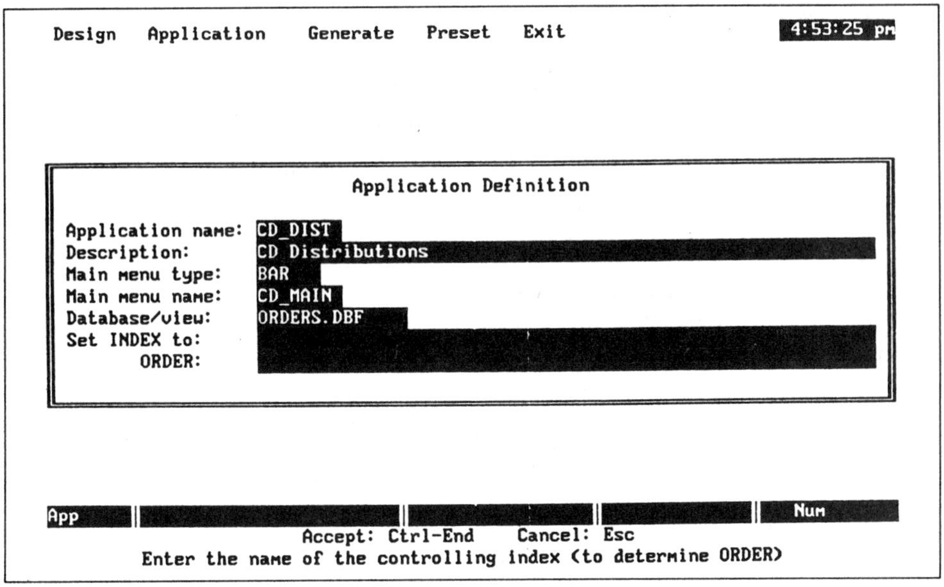

```
 Design   Application   Generate   Preset   Exit              4:53:25 pm



                           Application Definition
        Application name: CD_DIST
        Description:      CD Distributions
        Main menu type:   BAR
        Main menu name:   CD_MAIN
        Database/view:    ORDERS.DBF
        Set INDEX to:
               ORDER:




App                                                          Num
                     Accept: Ctrl-End     Cancel: Esc
            Enter the name of the controlling index (to determine ORDER)
```

Figure 12-10   Application Definition window.

Now, what happens when you select Applications Generator in this dialog box? The highest level of descriptive information for designing a new application is supplied in the Application Definition window, as shown in Figure 12-10. In this window, you must enter the following items.

Application Name This field contains the name you assign to represent the entire application. The name should be meaningful and obey the standard DOS filenaming conventions. dBASE IV will create a disk file with this name and an .APP extension. Later, when ApGen generates the program code, this name will also be assigned to one of the program files. This application name will then appear in the Applications panel in the Control Center. For our example, enter CD_DIST and press **Enter**.

At most times when providing information to ApGen, you may press **F1** to access context-sensitive help data that can assist you in entering the correct responses. The help provided if you were to press **F1** while positioned on the *Application name* field is shown in Figure 12-11. The help information in ApGen (and throughout dBASE IV) is generally excellent and should be utilized whenever necessary.

Description You may enter comments that briefly describe the purpose of the new application. These comments will automatically be inserted in the dBASE language program code and documentation that is generated by ApGen when the application is complete. For our sample application enter something like *CD Distributions* and then press **Enter**.

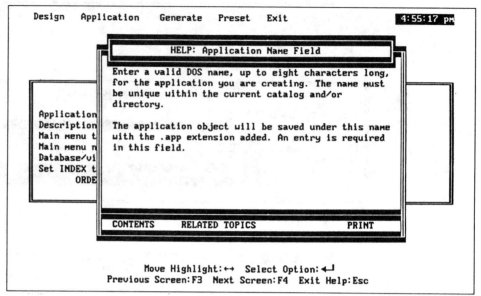

Figure 12-11 Context-Sensitive Help with ApGen.

Main Menu Type This field allows you to specify the type of menu object structure to use for the main menu of the application. This menu object will be the first the user sees when running your application. ApGen gives you three choices for the menu object. BAR, the default type, is a simple horizontal bar menu with a sliding highlight moving from option to option. POP-UP, by far the most popular as well as the most contemporary, is a vertical pull-down menu which can be standalone (a window with several selections organized in a vertical fashion) or attached to a horizontal bar menu. This is the type of menu used by dBASE IV. Last, BATCH can be used to invoke some processing sequence when the application is started and then, when the processing is complete, bring up a menu for further selections. You may cycle through each of these options by pressing the **Spacebar** several times. For this application, select *BAR* and then press **Enter**.

Main Menu Name This field requires a name to couple with the proper extension to identify the menu or batch process to be used to start your application. Depending on which menu object type is selected, a file is created with a .BAR filename extension, if the main menu is a horizontal bar menu; a .POP extension, if it is a pop-up menu; or a .BCH extension, if it is a batch process. Type in *CD_MAIN* and press **Enter**.

Database/View When an application with multiple databases is designed, there is usually one primary database or view that relates several databases in the system. This field allows you to enter the default database file or view for the application. Later, you may override this default and assign other databases or views for specific objects that you shall build. Here, type in *ORDERS.DBF* and press **Enter**. Note that this default will obviously need to be overridden when you are creating objects requiring access to the EMPLOYEE database. If you are uncertain as to what databases are available, you may press **Shft-F1** to select a database from a pick list directory window.

Set Index To This entry specifies what index or indexes to activate when the default database is in use. You may enter the name of any .MDX (dBASE IV master index) file or .NDX (dBASE III +) file or select one using **Shft-F1**. This function key will only display .NDX files, however. More than one index file may be entered by separating the names with commas. If you do not provide an entry here, the default .MDX file associated with the database will be used. While this default could be accepted for this sample application, you should type out the production master index filename for completeness, so type in *ORDERS.MDX* and press **Enter** here.

Order This field can be either of two possible entry types. A numeric value from 0 to 10 indicates the position an .NDX index file occupies in the list specified in the *Set INDEX to*: field. For example, if the hypothetical index files CUST_NUM, OR_DATE, and ITEM_NUM (named so as to indicate the key used in each) have been entered as the index files you wish to have active, you can specify a value here of 2 to have OR_DATE as the controlling index. Numeric values are only accepted when no .MDX file exists for the database. Remember, an .MDX file is automatically opened when the database it describes is opened. Alternately, a tag name may be specified corresponding to the tag in an .MDX file you wish to have act as the master (controlling) index. For the example, enter CUST_NUM as the tag name. Generally speaking, .NDX files are only useful in dBASE IV for temporary indexes for, say, generating a report. The more powerful .MDX index files are used more frequently, especially with the primary database of an application.

Note ⟩ Care should be taken when filling these three fields because ApGen does not do any checking to verify whether you have supplied filenames that actually exist.

Once you've entered all application definition parameters, press **Ctrl-End** to save your selections. You now see a screen resembling Figure 12-12, which shows the newly created application object on the ApGen design surface. This is the work environment with which the ApGen user must become very familiar.

The ApGen Design Surface

The ApGen design surface has several components. First, the *status bar* is located at the bottom of the screen. The status bar for ApGen contains, from left to right, the abbreviation *App* in the *current screen* section, the primary database path as specified in the Applications Definition dialog box (*C:\SAMPLE\ORDERS*) in the *current file* section, the cursor location, the application name as specified in the Applications Definition dialog box (*File:CD_DIST*) in the file supplying data section, and the usual toggle settings (Num lock and Insert).

The *navigation line* is located just under the status bar and is used to display information pertaining to current options for entry, such as which function keys are active and their purposes. The *message line* is the last line of the screen and is used for displaying context-sensitive descriptive phrases that prompt the user for correct data.

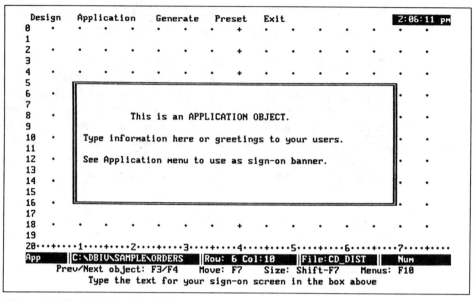

```
  Design   Application   Generate   Preset   Exit                    2:06:11 pm
0      ·        ·     ·      ·      ·      ·      +      ·      ·      ·      ·      ·
1
2      ·      ·      ·      ·      ·      ·      +      ·      ·      ·      ·      ·
3
4      ·      ·      ·      ·      ·      ·      +      ·      ·      ·      ·      ·
5
6      ·
7
8      ·                    This is an APPLICATION OBJECT.                  ·      ·
9
10     ·       Type information here or greetings to your users.
11
12     ·       See Application menu to use as sign-on banner.                ·
13
14     ·                                                                    ·      ·
15
16     ·                                                                           ·
17
18     ·      ·      ·      ·      ·      ·      +      ·      ·      ·      ·      ·
19
20···+····1····+····2····+····3····+····4····+····5····+····6····+····7····+····
App    ║C:\DBIV\SAMPLE\ORDERS ║Row: 6 Col:10 ║File:CD_DIST ║    Num
       Prev/Next object: F3/F4    Move: F7    Size: Shift-F7    Menus: F10
             Type the text for your sign-on screen in the box above
```

Figure 12-12   Application object on desktop.

At the very top of the screen is the ApGen *menu bar*—a horizontal bar with attached pull-down menus that allow you to select from the many options available to the ApGen developer. Each option has its own series of pull-down menus from which to choose. The menu bar shown in Figure 12-12 is the one displayed when an application is the current object. The selections seen here may change depending on the type of the currently selected object. There are similar menus for MENU, LIST, and BATCH objects, which are investigated in later chapters.

Underlying all of this is the *design surface*. The design surface is in essence a place for you to organize your thoughts when building your new application. You can strategically place the various pieces of the application, change your mind and move them around, and when satisfied, save the design surface and all the items you placed on it. Notice that ApGen puts alignment marks across the screen so that you may align objects in a pleasing manner.

At this junction in the design, you also see in Figure 12-12 an application object in the middle of the work surface. Normally, the application object is simply used as a sign-on screen to show the users of your application what software they are about to use. There is another ApGen option, discussed later, that will activate this use.

The application object can be moved and resized if needed by using the **F7** and **Shft-F7** keys, respectively. This would be a good idea for your sample application, since you might like to free up some space on the work surface. Press **Shft-F7** and then **Up Arrow** twice, followed by **Left Arrow** eight times. Notice that resizing involves moving the lower right corner of the window. Press **Enter** to accept the new size. Next, press **F7** and then **Right Arrow** five times, followed by **Enter**. This will reposition the new,

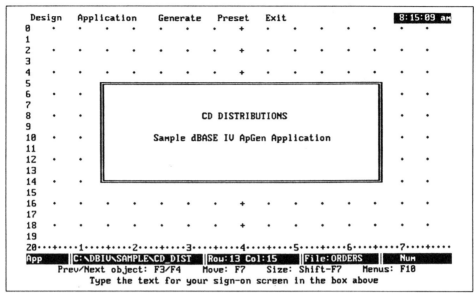

Figure 12-13   Sign-on banner for sample application.

smaller window in the center of the work surface. Now you may type in new text to customize your sign-on screen. To do this, you may press **Ctrl-Y** several times to delete the existing lines of text or simply type over them. The result should be something like what is shown in Figure 12-13.

To save the work done thus far, you have two options. Press **Ctrl-End** and ApGen will write the file CD_DIST.APP to the disk and then automatically return to the Control Center. On the other hand, if you wish to remain in ApGen, press **Alt-A** to get into the Application menu, select *Save current application definition*, and press **Enter**. This sequence will also save the application. Pressing **Esc** now will return you to the design surface.

In general, when working with ApGen you should save your work frequently. ApGen has so many features, embedded into so many menus, that it would be disheartening to lose your work just when you get the application exactly the way you want it.

The Application Menu

As mentioned in the preceding section, the ApGen menu bar changes dynamically, depending on the type of object selected. Currently, you are working with the highest-level object of an application: the application object. This being the case, there is a menu that is primarily directed towards further development of this type of object: the Application menu. Figure 12-14 shows the various selections available under this menu.

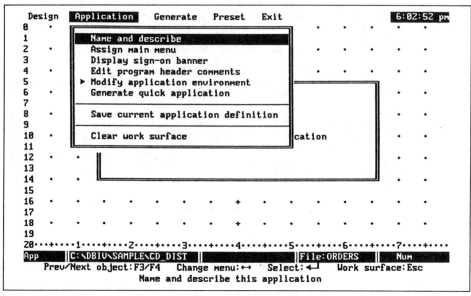

Figure 12-14   The Application menu.

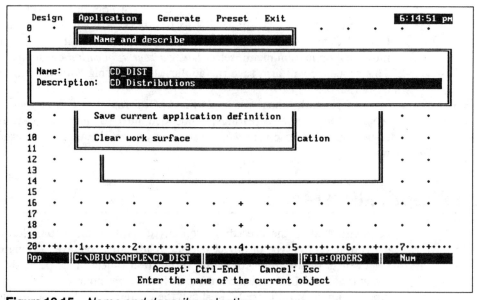

Figure 12-15   *Name and describe* selection.

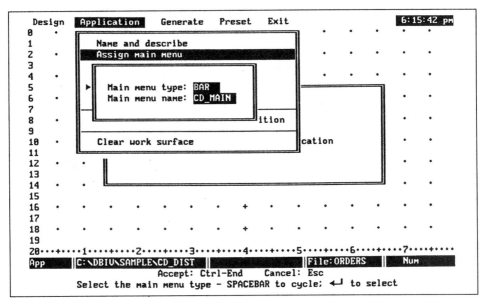

Figure 12-16 *Assign main menu* selection.

Name and Describe

This selection allows you to specify or modify the name of the application (the filename written by ApGen with the .APP extension) and provide a short description. Figure 12-15 shows the dialog box that appears when this item is selected. You can try it yourself by first pressing **Alt-A** to pull down the Application menu and then either highlighting *Name and describe* or pressing letter **N**. Notice that what appears is the same information you previously entered when in the Application Definition dialog box. ApGen will let you modify these initial selections, but does not present the whole Application Definition dialog box at once—you have to go into three separate boxes. The other boxes are discussed in later parts of this section.

Assign Main Menu

With this selection you may change the main menu type and name that were originally selected in the Application Definition dialog box. Figure 12-16 shows the dialog box that results. The value for the *Main menu type*: *field* may be changed by pressing the **Spacebar** to step through all the possibilities. For the *Main menu name*: *field*, you can type in a new name or press **Shft-F1** to view a pick list. You may press **Ctrl-End** to save any changes made.

Display Sign-On Banner

As mentioned before, you can have your application object automatically display when the application is first brought up. This is generally a good idea, because users new to

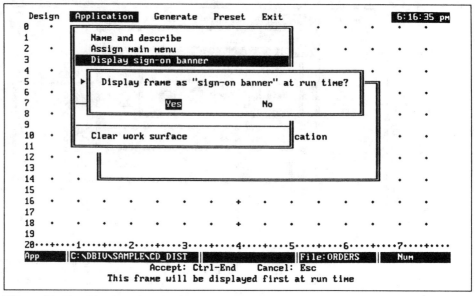

Figure 12-17 *Display sign-on banner selection.*

your software may feel welcome when greeted in this way. In addition, you might choose to provide some quick explanations or instructions in the application object that could benefit the first-time user. Figure 12-17 shows the dialog box for this selection. Simply press either **Y** or **N** followed by **Enter**. You will be returned to the Application menu.

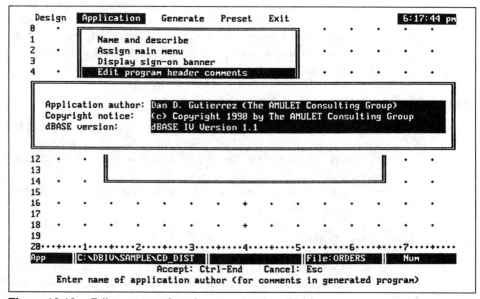

Figure 12-18 *Edit program header comments selection.*

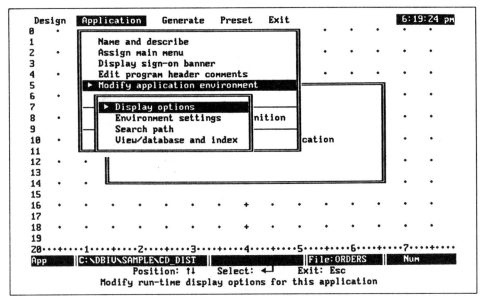

Figure 12-19 *Modify application environment* menu.

Edit Program Header Comments

When you eventually call upon ApGen to generate an application (as you will do in a later chapter), both the actual dBASE language program code and documentation are generated. This selection allows you to enter comments that will appear in both the code and documentation. The contents of these comments should be the name of the author of the application, a copyright notice, and the dBASE version used. See Figure 12-18 for a sample set of comments. You should enter your own information here; when done filling out the three lines, you can save the entries by pressing **Ctrl-End**, which will return you to the Application menu. You are not required to supply this information to ApGen, but responsible application developers should choose to do so.

The default comments inserted into this dialog box are the same as specified in the Preset menu's *Sign-on defaults* selection, which also supplies the Application object with its initial comments.

Modify Application Environment

This Application menu item is the only submenu selection available. The purpose of the options in this submenu is to allow the application developer to alter the defaults specified in the Preset menu and the Application Definition dialog box. Figure 12-19 shows how this submenu appears.

Display Options This selection is a submenu under the *Modify application environment* submenu. It enables the developer to customize how windows are to appear and the colors upon which the application is based. Figure 12-20 contains an example of the dialog box for this selection. First, you may alter the default, *Object border style*, which is *DOUBLE* (for a double-line frame around the object's window). You may

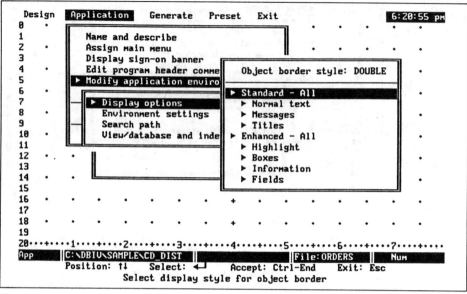

Figure 12-20 *Display options* selection.

browse through the other possible values for this item by pressing the **Spacebar**. The other values are: *SINGLE* for a single-line frame, *PANEL* for a wide frame, and *NONE* for no frame.

You may also specify the color scheme for the application in this submenu. The lower portion of the submenu is divided into two sections: *standard* display text and

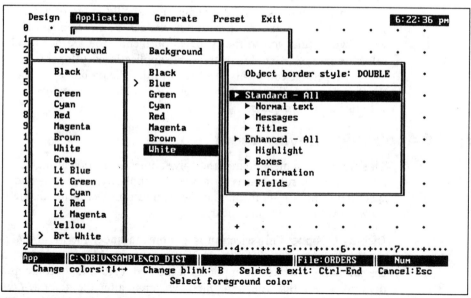

Figure 12-21 Color selection.

enhanced display text. With IBM and IBM-compatible personal computers, the display is normally partitioned in this manner. Standard text is information displayed on the screen as normal text, such as database records displayed as the result of a query; messages, such as unselected menu items and messages appearing on the navigation and message lines; and titles. Enhanced text, on the other hand, includes highlighted information, such as menu items that have been selected; boxes and object frames surrounding various objects; miscellaneous screen information, such as the clock, status bar, and error message box borders; and fields selected in full-screen data editing facilities like Browse.

To experiment with the multitude of color combinations possible, highlight one of the nine items on the submenu and press **Enter**. You will see another window, one very much like the one shown in Figure 12-21, which is divided up into a foreground section and a background section. If you have a color-based system, preferably EGA or VGA, you'll see a nice palette of colors from which to choose. To specify a color scheme for any one of the nine items, you must always define one color to be used as foreground and one for background. You can highlight a color and press **Enter** to select it. If you select a foreground color, you will then bounce over to the background side. You may bounce back and forth until you have selected the color combination you feel most comfortable with. You may even have various information blink on and off by pressing the letter **B** while the color palette window is on the screen. When you are done selecting colors, press **Ctrl-End** to save your color scheme. You can continue experimenting with the other items on the *Display options* submenu.

Environment Settings When this item is selected, a dialog box opens up that allows the developer to customize the way the application will operate by specifying ON/OFF values for the application runtime settings. Figure 12-22 shows this dialog box. To

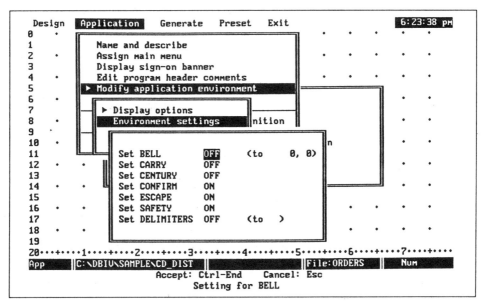

Figure 12-22 *Environment settings* selection.

toggle these options ON or OFF, simply press the **Spacebar**. The environment options shown are just a small subset of the many *Set* conditions available under dBASE IV. This subset was deemed the one most frequently needed when developing a typical application. You may tap into the power of the many other *Set* options by invoking them using the embedded dBASE code ApGen feature to be discussed later. The following are the environment options available on this screen:

Set BELL   This environment option specifies whether or not an audible signal should sound when the end of a data entry field has been reached. The default setting is ON, but should normally be turned OFF due to the excessive noise that results. Can you imagine a room full of data entry operators all beeping at the same time? There is a better way, as you will see, to make the entry operator notice the end of a data entry field.

If you decide to use the bell, you can customize the sound to your particular taste. As you can see in the dialog box, two numeric values are associated with the *Set BELL* option. The first dictates the frequency of the sound measured in hertz (cycles per second). The default value here is 512 hertz, although you may use values in the range from 19 to 10,000. For high-pitched sounds, use high values (600 to 6000). For low-pitched sounds, low values in the range 30 to 600 would make sense. The second numeric value is the duration of the sound measured in clock ticks, or about 0.0549 seconds each. The default is 2 ticks, although you may use a value from 2 to 19. As a reasonable application developer, you should not make the duration of the bell too long, as this will only serve to frustrate the user. A good combination is 400 and 2, which provides for an unobtrusive audible signal.

Be careful when entering these numeric values in ApGen because dBASE IV does not check for valid values. You will be allowed to enter, for example, 99,999 for frequency and 99 for ticks. When the application code is ultimately generated, an invalid SET BELL TO command is inserted into the code and will cause the program to abort.

Set Carry   This option determines whether to carry forward, during data entry, all previously entered field contents to the next (the current) record being entered. This may be useful when out of, say, 20 fields on a screen only 3 must be changed from one record to the next. If the records are very dissimilar from one another, then carrying forward data is annoying and actually proves to be less productive. The default is OFF for this setting, meaning information is not carried forward. When *Set CARRY* is turned ON, data for *all* fields is carried forward. You can specify only certain fields to carry forward from the dot prompt using the SET CARRY TO command, but not from ApGen.

Set Century   This option affects how dates are entered and displayed. When CENTURY is OFF, which is the default, only the year (i.e., 90) may be entered and displayed. The current century (twentieth century, now meaning 19) is assumed. If you prefer, CENTURY may be turned ON, in which case the century must be entered and displayed along with the year. For example, to enter October 27, 1955, with CENTURY OFF you would enter *10/27/55*; with CEN-TURY ON, you would enter *10/27/1955*. This option does not affect how dates are stored. Even though the date 10/27/2004 is ten characters long, the date still takes up only eight bytes in each record. Normally this option should be left OFF unless a majority of the dates you need to enter are in different centuries.

Set Confirm   Using CONFIRM ON is usually better than using BELL ON in that when the end of a data entry field is reached, the operator must press **Enter** to advance to the next field. BELL ON will alert you to the end of the field but will still let you go right past it and on to the next field. CONFIRM ON, on the other hand, makes you think about going on and will generally result in more reliable data. It does, however, require more keystrokes, namely the **Enter** key, but it is generally worthwhile. If CONFIRM is OFF, which is the default, when a character is entered into the last character position of an entry field, the cursor is automatically advanced to the first character position of the next entry field.

Set Escape   This environment option is used to enable (ON) and disable (OFF) the use of the **Esc** key to terminate the execution of an ApGen-generated-application. Since ApGen supposedly generates relatively bug-free program code, it is unlikely that the application will get into an "endless" loop or something equally terrible which would require the user to press **Esc**. It is therefore normally safe and often desirable for ESCAPE to be disabled. Set ESCAPE to OFF for the escape processing to have no effect. Remember that if ESCAPE is OFF and you for some reason do wish to abort the application, you must reboot your computer. With ESCAPE set to ON, pressing the ESCAPE key will cause an error box to pop up saying:

*** INTERRUPTED ***
Cancel, Ignore, Suspend? (C, I, or S)

Pressing **C** at this point will terminate the application and return control to the Control Center. If you press **I** then the application will continue as if **Esc** had not been pressed; **S** or suspend is normally used for program debugging purposes and is not directly applicable to ApGen-generated programs.

Set Safety   The SAFETY option determines whether or not the user is prompted each time a file is overwritten or deleted. For example, if you attempt to erase a database file from within a batch process and SAFETY is ON, which is the default, then the user will see a dialog box appear that asks if it is alright to delete the file:

File already exists

Overwrite Cancel

At this point the user may select *Overwrite* to proceed with the operation or *Cancel* to stop. If SAFETY is OFF, the user will not be prompted and the file, in this example, will be erased. Generally, during the development phase of an application, it might be a good idea to leave SAFETY to ON, since a new application may very well have some bugs in it that might be resolved with a prompt to the user. After an application is static and verified to be working properly, then the SAFETY prompt becomes an annoyance and should be turned OFF. In addition, it is generally not wise to give too much control to the user, especially over disk files, since mistakes are possible.

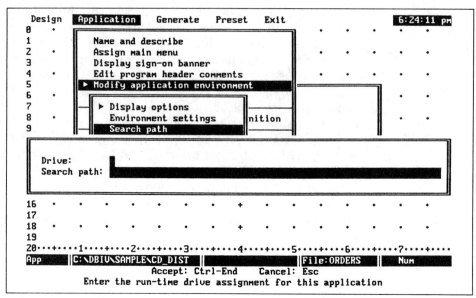

Figure 12-23 *Search path* selection.

Set Delimiters   This option allows the specification of special characters that surround all data entry fields (i.e., act as Delimiters) so that the user may easily determine the boundaries of the field. Normally, dBASE IV automatically delimits its fields using a "reverse video" scheme, where a data entry field appears as a highlighted box over a black background; when the user types in data, it appears as black-on-white text. Of course, color results may be achieved by using the SET COLOR command. Sometimes an alternate approach is desired. There the fields are outlined by special delimiting characters and when the user types data into a field, it appears as "normal video" text, that is, white-on-black text. To accept the dBASE IV standard of reverse video entry fields, set DELIMITERS to OFF. If you set DELIMITERS to ON, you can actually enter your own boundary characters in the field available. For example, if you want to use square brackets to delimit fields you would enter: [ ], where [would appear on the left of the field and] on the right. You may also specify just one delimiting character such as : and it will appear both on the left and right of all entry fields.

Search Path   Using this option you may specify both the default drive and path for the application. Figure 12-23 shows the dialog box and the two fields for these items. The *Drive:* field defines the drive letter (e.g., C:) on which all the applications objects can be found. You may use **Shft-F1** to choose a drive letter from a pick list. The **Search path:** field lets you specify a disk directory so that dBASE IV will search for objects when your application is running. If any object cannot be found, the default path, which is the one in which dBASE IV was started, will be searched.

Once you have completed the search path fields you must press **Ctrl-End** to save them and return to the Application menu.

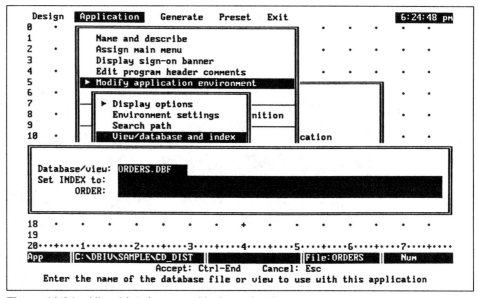

Figure 12-24 *View/database and index* selection.

View/Database and Index This selection from the *Modify application environment* menu allows you to change the selections originally made in the first dialog box that appeared when you began building the application. Please refer to the "Starting Up ApGen" earlier in this chapter. When you select this item you will notice that the fields will contain your previous responses to the fields *Database/view:*, *Set INDEX to:*, and *ORDER:*. Figure 12-24 shows these fields as they have been set.

Generate Quick Application

Often, the class of applications that you may wish to construct using ApGen involves very simple, single database applications that have only minimal requirements such as adding and editing records and maybe printing a simple report or set of labels. This class of applications is addressed by the *Generate quick application* item. The dialog box in Figure 12-25 shows the various fields that you must supply in order to build a quick application.

Database File This required field will initially contain the database file you specified when you first opened the application upon entering ApGen. You may change it now by entering another valid database filename or by pressing **Shft-F1** and selecting one from the pick list. You will notice that < create > is also an option in the pick list. If you choose < create > you may define a new database to be used by the quick application by transferring automatically to the Database design screen. From this latest capability you can begin to see that a quick application and its associated objects can be built from scratch from the *Generate quick application* selection.

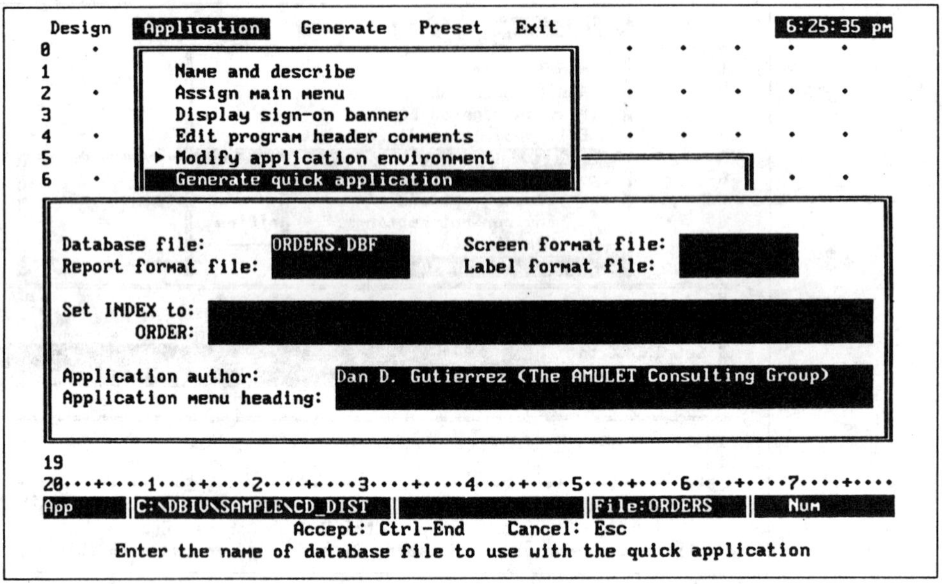

```
  Design   Application   Generate   Preset   Exit              6:25:35 pm
0    .
1    .      ┌──────────────────────────────────────┐  .   .   .   .   .
2    .      │    Name and describe                 │  .   .   .   .   .
3    .      │    Assign main menu                  │
4    .      │    Display sign-on banner            │  .   .   .   .   .
5    .      │    Edit program header comments      │
6    .      │  ► Modify application environment    │          .   .   .
            │    Generate quick application        │
   ┌────────┴──────────────────────────────────────┴─────────────────────┐
   │                                                                       │
   │  Database file:        ORDERS.DBF       Screen format file:           │
   │  Report format file:                    Label format file:            │
   │                                                                       │
   │  Set INDEX to:                                                        │
   │        ORDER:                                                         │
   │                                                                       │
   │  Application author:       Dan D. Gutierrez (The AMULET Consulting Group) │
   │  Application menu heading:                                            │
   │                                                                       │
19 └───────────────────────────────────────────────────────────────────────┘
20···+····1····+····2····+····3····+····4····+····5····+····6····+····7····+····
App    ║C:\DBIV\SAMPLE\CD_DIST ║            ║File:ORDERS ║   Num
              Accept: Ctrl-End        Cancel: Esc
        Enter the name of database file to use with the quick application
```

Figure 12-25   *Generate quick application* selection.

Screen Format File This optional field enables a screen format file to be invoked by the application for all append and edit operations. You may enter any valid screen format filename or press **Shft-F1** to pull down a pick list menu and choose one there. Notice that <create> is also an option in the pick list. If you choose <create> you may define a new screen format by transferring automatically to the screen format design screen. If you do not specify any screen format file then the new quick application will use the default screen arrangement for adding and editing records.

Report Format File This optional field allows a report form file to be used by the application for producing printed output. You may enter any valid report form filename or press **Shft-F1** to pull down a pick list menu and choose one there. Notice that <create> is also an option in the pick list. If you choose <create> you may construct a new report form by transferring automatically to the Report form design screen. If you do not supply a name here, the *Print Report* item will not be included on the application's main menu.

Label Format File This optional field lets you enter a label form filename to be used by the application for generating labels. You may enter any valid label form filename or press **Shft-F1** to pull down a pick list menu and choose one there. Notice that <create> is also an option in the pick list. If you choose <create> you may construct a new label form by transferring automatically to the Label form design screen. If you do not supply a name here, the *Mailing Labels* item will not be included on the application's main menu.

Set Index To This is an optional field that accepts the name of an index file other than the one specified when the application object was defined. Instead of typing an index filename, **Shft-F1** may be used to pick from a list of index files available. If multiple index files need to be active, then several files may be selected from the pick list by pressing **Enter** after each. If an entry is not supplied for this field then the *Reindex Database* option will not appear on the application's main menu.

Order In this field, enter an .NDX file order number or an .MDX file tag name to indicate the new controlling index. This field is only necessary if you wish to change the index order from what was specified when the application object was first defined. See "Starting Up ApGen" for a more detailed explanation.

Application Author This field contains the name of the person building the application. By default, you will see the name which was entered with the *Sign-on defaults* option in the Preset menu (which is discussed later). You may override the name previously entered here. The name will appear as a comment line in the dBASE program code and documentation generated by ApGen. No matter how simple the application, it is generally a good idea to include the author's name somewhere. Months down the road, when the application needs to be modified in some way, it is always nice to know who developed it.

Application Menu Heading The default name of the application that will appear on the menu created by ApGen is the application name specified when you first entered ApGen. If you prefer another, more detailed name, you may enter it here.

When you have finished supplying information for the *Generate quick application* dialog box, you must save it by pressing **Ctrl-End**.

Save Current Application Definition

This selection from the Application Menu enables you to save the current application object definition and continue work in ApGen. You should probably save periodically, especially if you've given much thought to your entries and don't wish to lose them in the event of a system failure. After you save the application definition you may enter into other areas of ApGen. It may be a good idea to save your newly defined application now. You will not be given any notification that the object was saved other than a very brief message in the status line.

Clear Work Surface

The *Clear work surface* option is available in all object menus. Generally, it allows you to clean off the various objects that may have accumulated on the work surface. All objects except the application object may be removed from the work surface. At our present position of application development, this option should have no effect since we only have the application object on the work surface.

The Preset Menu

As a regular ApGen user, you may specify the way your new applications will be generated by defining several parameters in the Preset menu. Of course, when you build a specific application, you may override any of these parameters. The Preset menu simply enables you to describe a starting point upon which all of your applications will be based.

Sign-On Defaults

Figure 12-26 shows the dialog box that appears when this item is selected from the Preset menu. Here you may define three pieces of information that will appear by default in the application's sign-on banner screen when the application is invoked by the user. You may enter any kind of text in these fields. The labelled field titles— *Application author*, *Copyright notice*, and *dBASE version*—only suggest one possibility. If you choose to enter other text, such as a greeting message to your users, then you can still have the author, copyright, and version information inserted into the application code and documentation by first selecting the Application menu and then the *Edit program header comments* option.

Once defined, this information will be automatically placed in the object itself each time you create a new application object. Note that if you change the information while an application is already loaded, it will not be reflected in the application object; all Preset menu parameters are for new, yet uncreated, applications only.

Finally, you must press **Ctrl-End** once you have provided entries for these fields in order to save them.

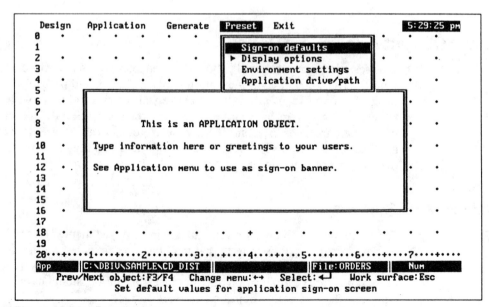

Figure 12-26   Preset menu.

Display Options

With this option you may define the color scheme of your applications. These definitions may later be changed in the *Display options* submenu, which is accessible from the Application menu previously discussed. Figure 12-20 shows the dialog box that appears for this option. Once you have provided entries for each field, you must press **Ctrl-End** to save them.

Environment Settings

Many times you may wish to establish an environment before your application begins to process data. This Preset menu option lets you define a few simple parameters that guide the way the application will operate. Basically, these definitions are automated uses of several SET commands that may be entered at the dot prompt or specified in a dBASE program code segment. Out of the universe of the many dBASE IV SET options, only the few most important are presented in the dialog box that appears for this option. You may later change the default environment parameters you define here by accessing the *Environment settings* dialog box, which is accessible from the Application menu. Figure 12-22 shows the dialog box that appears for this option. Once you have provided entries for each field, you must press **Ctrl-End** to save them.

Application Drive/Path

This option enables you to define the default disk drive letter and DOS pathname for your application. The defaults defined with this option may be later modified with the *Search path* dialog box that is accessible under the Application menu. Figure 12-23 shows the dialog box that appears for this option. Once you have provided entries for each field, you must press **Ctrl-End** to save them.

 You may notice from DOS or while in the Tools menu that a dBASE IV system file named DBASE2.RES can show different modification dates (kept by DOS to indicate the last time the file was altered) from time to time. This is the file that holds the settings from the Preset menu, so every time you change any of the fields just described, the date on this file will change. Realizing this is important to those using ApGen on a LAN, since *each* developer should have a copy of the file so as to not disturb the Preset menu defaults that may have been set by others.

Saving Your Work

Now that the application's top-level portions have been defined, it is a good idea to save all the work done thus far. From the ApGen main menu, choose *Exit*. This causes a selection window to appear, as shown in Figure 12-27. At this point you may choose *Save all changes and exit*, which in this case just saves the application object to disk. After saving, ApGen will return to the Control Center. In the next chapter, you will be

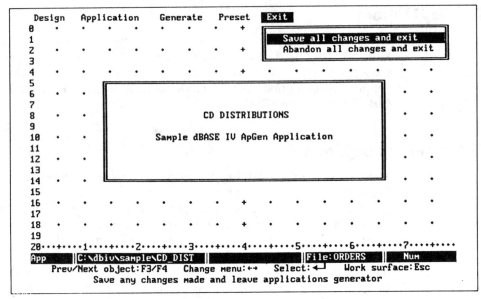

Figure 12-27 Exiting from ApGen.

attaching several other objects to the application, so saving will then have a broader effect than it does now. At this level of building the application you could achieve the same effect by selecting *Save current application definition* from the Application menu.

Alternately, you may choose *Abandon all changes and exit*, which will negate any work you have done in constructing the application. For safety, a dialog box will appear requesting you to confirm your decision to abandon your work. If you choose *Yes*, ApGen will abandon all changes (in our case, all new work) and return to the Control Center. If you choose *No*, you will be returned to the ApGen main menu without any affect to the application.

Your Future as a Nonprogramming Developer

Even after using the Applications Generator for a while and after building several complete applications yourself, you may still find that you really want more power at your grasp in order to build more sophisticated software. Fear not, because first of all, dBASE IV has a tremendously useful programming language underlying the Control Center operations, which will allow you to construct even the most involved applications. This is, however, a whole area of study in itself and is beyond the scope of this book, whose philosophy it is for you, the dBASE IV user, to do as much as you can without programming.

If you prefer, another alternative allows you to extend the functionality of the Applications Generator itself. This is yet another area of study, one which has become very popular as of late with application developers, called *template language programming*. Using this special purpose programming language (which is separate from though integrated with the dBASE IV programming language) you can actually modify, customize, and enhance the way ApGen produces application programs. This is due to the way the Applications Generator was designed. Ashton-Tate wanted to make the Applications Generator expandable, so they defined a way to make it operate according to somewhat of a script. If you decide you wish to change this script, you can do so. There is one hitch, however; you need the Developer's Edition of dBASE IV, because the Template Language is only available with that version.

One problem with using application generators in general is that the programs that result are usually much larger than needed to achieve the desired functionality. This is called "code bloat" and is often a consideration when using ApGen to build large systems. The situation is that ApGen, in an attempt to simplify the application development process, minimizes the amount of knowledge it requires from you about the application you wish to construct. Consequently, it doesn't know (or care), for example, if your application is a single-user or multiuser one, and therefore inserts program code to handle both environments. This is truly a waste, but the alternative would be for ApGen to ask more questions, and some cases would require some "artificial intelligence" in order to more accurately generate the program code.

Luckily, the dBASE IV Template Language provides for the capability to customize the ways in which ApGen generates code. You may, for example, bring up any of the dBASE IV ApGen template files, with a .COD extension, and insert your own program generation requirements. The applications you then get out of ApGen are completely tailored to *your* needs.

13

ApGen User Interface

Chapter 12 introduced the concepts underlying the dBASE IV Applications Generator (ApGen) and demonstrated how to initially define an application. This chapter takes you much deeper into the subject by actually constructing an entire application from scratch. As mentioned before, the nonprogramming application developer has two approaches for implementing an application. With one, existing "objects" may be tied together using the many user interface features of ApGen. With the other, the overall structure may be defined first and the objects created later, to fill in the application structure. The approach in the next several chapters is hybrid in nature.

In dBASE IV, especially when using the Control Center, most users experiment first: creating a couple of databases, painting a data entry screen, generating a sample report, and so forth. Only when several of these items have been built is an application conceptualized. At this point ApGen comes into play to connect the pieces and create a cohesive whole. This can be thought of as a "bottom-up" approach to application design. Because most dBASE IV users begin an application with an existing collection of objects, this method is described first.

For now, the goal is limited. First construct the user interface, or menus, under which you will attach these objects. Not to minimize the importance of the second approach, Chapter 15 is devoted to building an application using a "top-down" methodology by creating additional objects to attach to the application.

Building an Example Application

Begin with a global "snapshot" of proposed application, as shown in Figure 13-1. Here you see a structure containing the typical components of most systems. Many of the objects are defined in prior chapters, although some have yet to be built. Again, the plan of attack in implementing this system is to build the menus for the system, attach

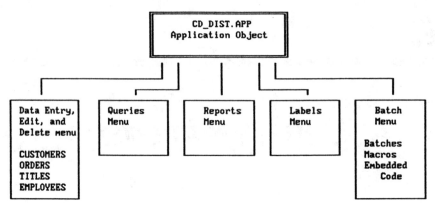

Figure 13-1   Proposed application structure.

all existing objects to these menus, and then build the additional objects you need and attach them also to the menus.

At this point, it is advisable to create a brand-new catalog in which to put only files that pertain to the sample application. This is generally a good idea when beginning to build new applications. Although dBASE III Plus also had the ability to maintain catalogs, dBASE IV does a better job with integrating catalogs into the Control Center. dBASE III Plus users commonly made separate hard disk directories for each application project and then copied disk files representing the various objects that the applications had in common from one directory to another. This was an acceptable approach, and still is with dBASE IV, but it creates the opportunity for duplicate files and requires a lot of switching directories. When using catalogs, you can choose to have only one application development directory on your hard disk if you wish, but utilize multiple catalogs to manage the multitude of files that must exist for each. There is no limit to the number of files that can be in a hard disk subdirectory, so you can include the files for many projects in a single development directory. Which-ever method you use, you should always refrain from depositing an application's files in the \DBASE directory. This is normally the directory in which you install dBASE IV, and if you pollute it with nonsystem files you'll experience trouble later on, especially if you need to reinstall dBASE IV or install a new release.

There is one disadvantage to using the catalog approach. When you want to back up all files dealing with a specific application to floppy disks, using the DOS BACKUP command becomes very difficult. BACKUP has no knowledge of dBASE IV catalogs and therefore is unable to distinguish a set of files in one catalog from those in another. You will eventually have to perform a backup (for example, to install your application on a client's or user's computer). So, if you foresee the need to transfer files for an application from one PC to another, it may be best to separate those files in a specific hard disk directory.

To create a new catalog, press **Alt-C** to pull down the Catalog menu and select *Use a different catalog*. A files list window appears, containing the names of any preexisting catalogs. Highlight the <create> option and press **Enter**. Now enter the

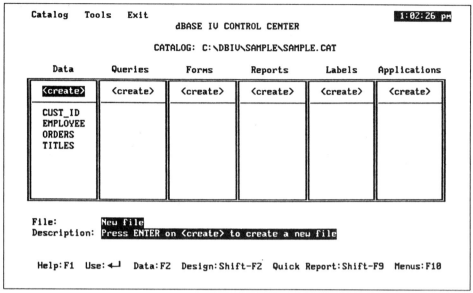

Figure 13-2   Database objects for sample application.

name of the new catalog (say, SAMPLE) in the dialog box that appears. You may also press **Alt-C** again, select *Edit description of catalog*, and enter *Sample dBASE IV ApGen Application* in the dialog box that appears. Now, with the Data panel highlighted so that only database files appear in the files list, press **Alt-C** once again and then select *Add a file to catalog*. A file pick list will pop up. Locate and highlight CUST_ID.DBF, then press **Enter**. You will be prompted to edit the description of the .DBF file. You may enter something like ***Customer database for sample application*** in the dialog box that appears. Notice that CUST_ID is now the only file listed in the Data panel. Continue this process for the other three files: ORDERS, TITLES, and EMPLOYEE. The order in which you select the files doesn't matter, since they will appear in the Data panel in alphabetical order. The resulting Control Center screen should be similar to the one shown in Figure 13-2. To complete the picture for now, you could also add the application object created in Chapter 12 to the new catalog. First move the highlight to the Applications panel, press **Alt-C**, select *Add file to catalog*, and select CD_DIST.APP from the files list. Now that you've set the stage for your new application, begin filling in the pieces. The first step is to design and create the main menu for the application.

Menu Differences

The Applications Generator menus are peculiar in that the options available to you will vary depending on the type of object being considered. For example, the menu descriptions in Chapter 12 are only valid if the current object is an *application*. Entirely different options will be shown if the current object is a *menu*, a *list*, or a *batch*. For example, when a menu is the current object, you will see two new menus listed, *Menu* and *Item*. Each of these new series of menus will be discussed in this and later chapters.

Bar Menus

The first order of business in building our complete application program is to create a governing structure into which all the component parts may fall. This structure is normally called a *main menu*. You can create a main menu for the application by pressing **Alt-D** while the application object is still showing. This will bring up the ApGen Design menu, shown in Figure 13-3.

This menu presents the opportunity to design several different types of objects. The object type you are concerned with at this time is the *Horizontal bar menu*. To select it, press **H**. You will immediately see a files list pop up. At this early stage, there should be no files representing horizontal menus listed in the box. If you had earlier experimented with this object type, you might see some remnants of these objects. There is one selection that should be displayed whether or not there are any horizontal menu objects present. This is the <create> selection, which is what is needed now. Make sure <create> is highlighted and press **Enter**. You will now see a dialog box like the one shown in Figure 13-4. In this box you are required to specify some basic information that describes the horizontal menu. There are three fields to fill in.

Name This is the name of the horizontal menu that will be used to reference the menu from within the generated application code. This is a required entry. Since this menu is

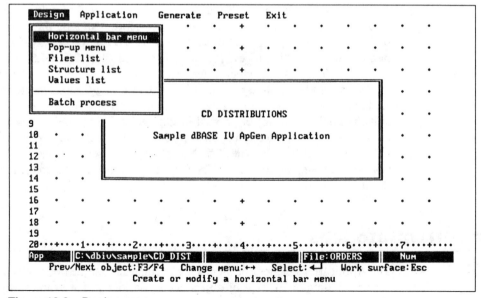

Figure 13-3 Design menu.

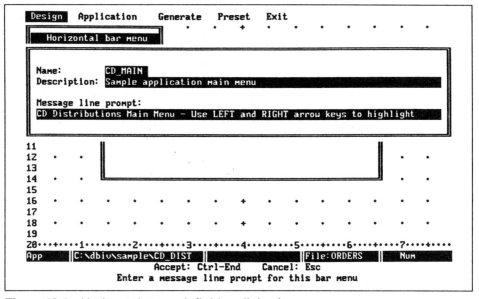

Figure 13-4   Horizontal menu definition dialog box.

the main menu of the application, it must also match the main menu name specified when you defined the application object. ApGen creates a file with this name and the .BAR extension. Enter *CD_DIST* and press **Enter**.

Description This field allows the entry of a simple, one-line verbal description of what the menu represents. It should be meaningful, since this description will show up in the program documentation that ApGen automatically generates. This is not a required entry, but it is good practice to be as complete as possible when creating a new application. Enter *Sample application main menu* and press **Enter.**

Message Line Prompt Enter here a single-line message that you want displayed whenever the menu is active. Since this is the main menu, this message will greet the user as the application is loaded and will remain on the screen whenever the user is viewing the main menu. This not a required entry, but again, it is good practice to supply one. Actually, this message may eventually not appear at all when the application is run, since there is a way to automatically pull down attached pop-up menus as they are highlighted on the bar menu. In this case, the messages assigned to the pop-ups will preempt this message. Enter *CD Distributions Main Menu - Use LEFT and RIGHT arrows to highlight*.

   Now, press **Ctrl-End** in order to save the entries in the dialog box. As you save your entries, notice that the ApGen menu selections on the top of the screen have changed. This is because a menu is now the "current object." You see the addition of the Menu and Item menus. These will be discussed in depth in the coming sections and chapters.

These entry fields may be altered at any time the menu is active (i.e., on the work surface and selected) by pressing **Alt-M** (bringing up the Menu menu, which will be discussed soon) and selecting *Name and describe*.

You should now see a double-line frame or window on the top of your screen with the cursor blinking at the leftmost position in the window. Here you enter the various option names that are to appear on the main menu. You cannot just begin typing, however. If you do, an error message indicating that text cannot be entered will result. Instead, you must declare where each menu option is to begin and end. Use the **F5** (Field) key for this purpose.

If you don't like the default position of the window, you can reposition it by using the **F7** (Move) key. If you do so, a dialog box will appear asking whether you wish to move the entire window or just the item. Select *Entire frame*, reposition the window with the arrow keys, and press **Enter** when done. **Shift-F7** (Size) is used to alter the dimensions of the window.

You may resize the window so as to have a vertical bar menu instead of a horizontal one. This kind of menu resembles a pop-up menu, but functions slightly differently. The main difference, and the primary reason to build a vertical bar, is to maintain the ability to attach pull-down menus to the bar menu. This allows you to have a collection of cascaded menus. Another difference is that even though the menu is vertical, you must still use the **Left** and **Right Arrow** keys to move from option to option.

The Main Menu

Now you can build the main menu. Press the **Spacebar** key a couple of times and then **F5**. Enter *Customer* and press **F5** again. Notice that as you type, your text is highlighted. Continue this pattern, entering all the options: *Orders, Titles, Employees, Queries, Reports, Labels, Batch,* and *Exit*. The completed horizontal main menu should appear as in Figure 13-5. If you are not satisfied with the spacing of the various options, simply position the cursor within the window and use the **Del** key to delete spaces or the **Ins** and **Spacebar** keys to insert spaces. There should be enough room in the window for all menu options.

When deciding what to name each option that is to appear on a menu of any type, you should always use names with unique first letters, as in the example. This is because when you run the application, the first letter of the option name may be used to select it. In the case of a bar menu, you may press the **Alt** key followed by the first letter of the option. If the menu is a pop-up (defined later in this chapter), type only the first letter. If there are duplicate first letters in the set of options, then the first option that starts with the first letter you type is selected. Clearly, an incorrect option might be selected. This may not be a serious situation here, since each option on the main menu will only open up another menu, but what if the option immediately began an update or information purge process? Unique first letters aid in avoiding this kind of problem.

One last thing to do for the main bar menu is to enter some help information in the event that the user presses **F1** (Help) while the menu is active. Press **Alt-M** to bring up the Menu menu (see Figure 13-6) and select *Write help text*. A large free-format

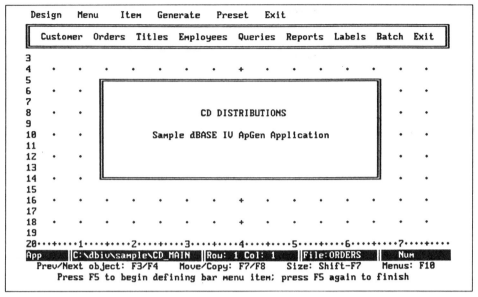

Figure 13-5   Completed horizontal bar menu.

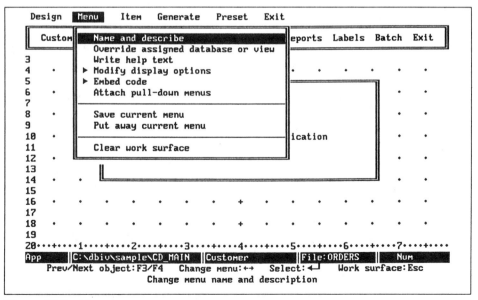

Figure 13-6   Menu menu.

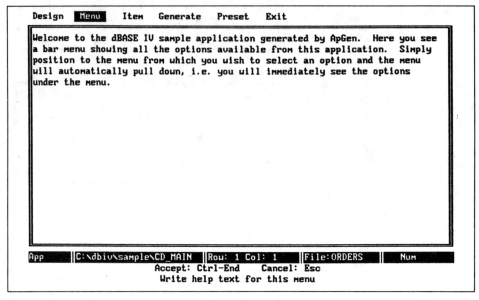

Figure 13-7 Main bar menu user help information.

dialog box opens up, and you may enter up to 19 lines of text. If you had previously entered help text, you could use this dialog box to modify it, too. When you are done entering the text, press **Ctrl-End** to save the text and return to the Menu menu. All help text for either bar or pop-up menus is actually stored in the .BAR and .POP files, respectively. See Figure 13-7 for an idea of the type of information to include in a help screen.

When you build a pop-up menu shortly, notice that the Menu menu for bar menus has one additional option on it, *Attach pull-down menus*, that does not appear for pop-up menus. All this option really does is force each pop-up menu that is tied to the main bar menu to automatically "pull down" (that is, display) for the user whenever the pop-up's option is highlighted on the bar menu. In the sample application, the pop-up menu for CUSTOMER database maintenance functions would automatically pull down when the CUSTOMER option is highlighted on the bar menu. As you press **Right Arrow** to move to the option labelled ORDERS, the pop-up menu for this option would appear. For unattached pull-down menus, the user presses **Alt** followed by the first letter of the option name or highlights the option and presses **Enter** just to see the pop-up menu associated with that option. When menus are attached, the **Alt** key has no effect at all. Therefore, when menus are attached, the only way to select an option in a pop-up is to use the **Left** and **Right Arrow** keys to select the menu, then use the **Up** and **Down Arrow** keys to highlight the option and press **Enter**.

> **Note** > dBASE IV displays attached pop-up menus more quickly than unattached ones. Moving from pop-up to pop-up can be annoying if the menus are unattached. You can see this by first generating the application with attached menus and then again without.

Now save the main bar menu by pressing **Alt-M** to bring up the Menu menu and selecting *Save current menu*. This will result in a message at the bottom of the screen saying that CD_MAIN.BAR is being saved. You are able to continue working after selecting this option. Selecting *Put away current menu* will also save the menu but will remove it from the work surface. For now let the main bar menu remain.

Pop-Up Menus

This section takes the next step towards constructing the user interface for your sample application. A series of pop-up style menus to be called from the main bar menu will be constructed. Pop-up menus for software applications have risen in popularity over the past several years, due to the demonstrated ease of use found with the Apple Macintosh user interface. Although they can be used alone, pop-up menus normally function in tandem with bar menus. For the sample application, a pop-up menu is needed for each option on the main bar menu (except for the Exit option, which must only return to the Control Center).

Begin by pressing **Alt-D** to pull down the Design menu. Highlight the *Pop-up menu* option, and you will see a dialog box identical to the one to define a bar menu. Fill in the *Name:* field with **CUSTOMER**. Use ***Pop-up menu for CUSTOMER database maintenance*** for the *Description:* field. For the *Message line prompt:* fill in ***Press UP and DOWN arrow to highlight then ENTER to select***. Figure 13-8 shows the resulting dialog box. Press **Ctrl-End** to save your entries.

At this point you will see an open window frame in the middle of the work surface, most likely overlapping the application object. Since you want to move the

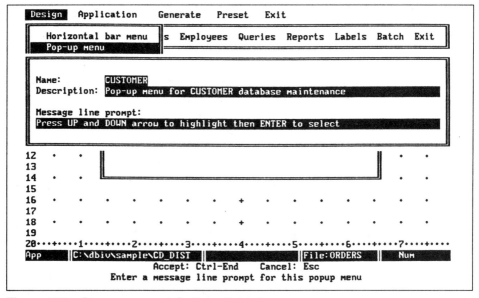

Figure 13-8   Pop-up menu definition dialog box.

window immediately to its appropriate place on the screen, press **F7** (Move), answer *Entire frame* to the dialog box prompt, and use the arrow keys to move the shadow of the window until the top of the pop-up menu is aligned with (actually overlapping) the bottom line of the main bar menu. Press **Enter** when you have moved the menu to a pleasing location and the window frame will move.

Entering Text Next, you need to enter the text of the menu inside the menu window. Since this menu is for maintenance functions relating to the CUSTOMER database, enter on separate lines: *Add a customer*, *Edit a customer*, and *Delete a customer*. You should generally left justify (i.e., begin typing on the left) each option title in the menu, although centering may also be appealing. Now add a dividing line using repeated hyphens or any other suitable character and then enter some information-only text, reminding the user to PACK a database having deleted records. This text is for reference only and cannot be selected as an option once the menu is functional. Actually, all the text that you enter in a pop-up menu initially is ''no-action text.'' For a line of text in a pop-up menu to relate to some action, an action must be assigned to it. The next chapter assigns actions to some of the lines listed in the pop-up menus built here, but some text is designated to remain ''no action text,'' since it appears in the menu for informational purposes only.

Editing Text While editing the menu text in a pop-up menu, you may use a couple of familiar editing keys. For example, to insert a blank line between two lines of menu text, you may press **Ctrl-N**. This does not enlarge the menu window frame; it just moves all the lines from where the cursor is positioned down one line. The **Ctrl-Y** key will delete a line of menu text. You can also move a menu item by moving the cursor to the line of the item, pressing the **F7** (Move) key, selecting *Item only*, and then moving the cursor to the desired location and pressing **Enter**.

One additional editing feature lets you move an item from one menu to another. To do this, position to the item you need to move, press **F7** (Move), and select *Item only* from the dialog box. Next, press either **F3** (Previous) or **F4** (Next) to switch to the desired menu object. You may bring up the Design menu to put the menu object on the work surface if it is not already there. Lastly, move to the position in the menu at which the item is to be moved and press **Enter**.

Notice that the menu window has more lines than you need and that the menu may be too wide for even your longest option description line. Press **Shft-F7** (Resize) and the arrow keys to make the window smaller, and then press **Enter** when satisfied. Figure 13-9 shows a completed pop-up menu.

Creating a Help Screen

The next order of business is to create a help screen with which the user may obtain useful information about the pop-up menu by pressing **F1** (Help). The help text may be displayed with **F1** any time the menu is selected. If no help text is entered for a menu and the user presses **F1**, then the message ''No help defined'' appears. As before with entering help information for the bar menu, press **Alt-M** and select *Write help text*.

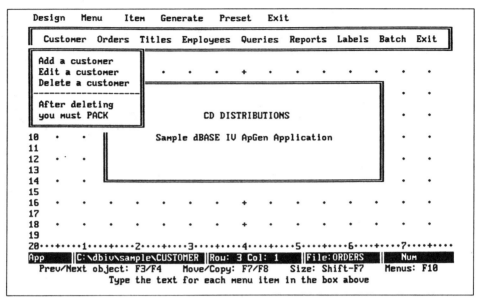

Figure 13-9   Completed pop-up menu.

When you built the application object for the sample application, you had to specify a default database for your system. You used the ORDERS database for this purpose, which means that in all portions of the application, ORDERS will be the database to use unless you override it. In the case of the sample pop-up you have just constructed, the primary database should not be ORDERS, but instead CUSTOMER, so press **Alt-M** and select *Override assigned database or view*, which results in the dialog box shown in Figure 13-10. Notice that the word *menu* is inserted in one of the fields on the screen, since other object types can have databases associated with them. The dialog here proceeds in two parts. The second part is conditional on the first.

For This Item You May Use Values Following this phrase you are asked to specify if the defaults, as displayed in the upper portion of the dialog box, are to be used for the menu. ABOVE, which means to accept the defaults, is the first choice. If you choose this option, you have nothing more to do.

Toggle further until you see ENTER BELOW once again. Press **Ctrl-End** and you will now be able to supply an alternate database. In the field labelled *Database/view:* enter CUSTOMER and press **Ctrl-End** again. Notice that the database shown in the you will see IN EFFECT AT RUN TIME. This option provides for the situation where you have a files list as one of the options on a pop-up menu to be used for selecting a database in further operations. With this option, the items that follow on the menu will use the database in use "at run time."

Toggle further until you see ENTER BELOW once again. Press **Ctrl-End** and you will now be able to supply an alternate database. In the field labelled *Database/view*: enter CUSTOMER and press **Ctrl-End** again. Notice that the database shown in the

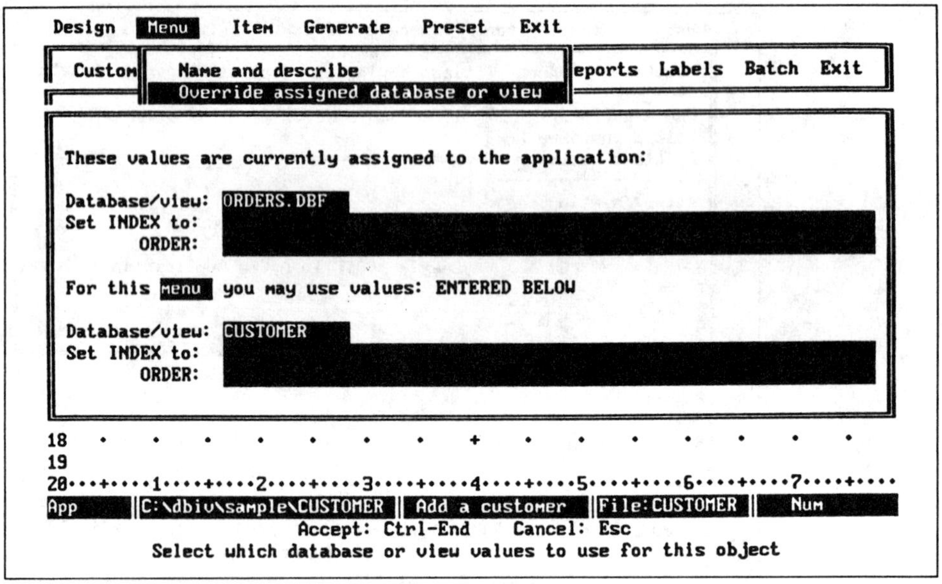

```
  Design  Menu    Item   Generate   Preset   Exit
┌──────────────────────────────────────────────────┐────────────────────────
│ Custom│  Name and describe                        │eports Labels  Batch  Exit
┌───────│  Override assigned database or view       │────────────────────────
│        └───────────────────────────────────────────────────────────────┐
│                                                                          │
│  These values are currently assigned to the application:                 │
│                                                                          │
│  Database/view: ███████████████                                          │
│  Set INDEX to:  ██████████████████████████████████████████████████████   │
│       ORDER:    ██████████████████████████████████████████████████████   │
│                                                                          │
│  For this ████ you may use values: ENTERED BELOW                         │
│                                                                          │
│  Database/view: ████████                                                 │
│  Set INDEX to:  ██████████████████████████████████████████████████████   │
│       ORDER:    ██████████████████████████████████████████████████████   │
│                                                                          │
└──────────────────────────────────────────────────────────────────────────┘
 18   ·    ·    ·    ·    ·    ·    ·    +    ·    ·    ·    ·    ·    ·
 19
 20···+····1····+····2····+····3····+····4····+····5····+····6····+····7····+····
 App    ││C:\dbiv\sample\CUSTOMER ││ Add a customer ││File:CUSTOMER ││  Num
                      Accept: Ctrl-End     Cancel: Esc
              Select which database or view values to use for this object
```

Figure 13-10   Overriding the default database.

status bar at the bottom of the screen has now changed from ORDERS to CUSTOMER. This is the intended effect.

> **Note** At this point it may be a good idea to save your work. Press **Alt-M** and select *Save current menu*, which saves the pop-up menu file CUSTOMER.POP to disk and allows you to continue work.

Completing the Menu Structure. To completely define the menu structure of your sample application, you must now get some more practice defining pop-up menus by defining one for each of the main bar menu options. Create, move, and resize a pop-up menu for each option. Build a help screen describing the function each pop-up serves. Remember to override the default database where necessary.

> **Note** One last touch you may wish to consider, especially if you are developing your application on a color system, is to add a color scheme to the menus. Press **Alt-M** and select *Modify display options*. This screen is identical to the one discussed in previous chapters. There is one difference, however. Instead of affecting the entire application's display options, this screen only affects the current object, in this case a menu. It may be interesting for you to experiment with thoughtful menu color schemes. If you know an interior decorator or fashion designer, you may wish to consult him or her.

You can also change the border of the pop-up menus to differentiate them from the main bar menu. From the *Modify display options* selection on the Menu menu, flip through the several *Object border style* settings until you see SINGLE. Press **Ctrl-End** to save the selection and return back to the Menu menu.

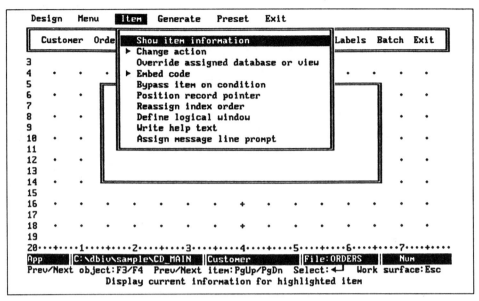

```
   Design    Menu    Item    Generate    Preset    Exit
 ╔═══════════════════════════════════════════════════════════════════════════╗
 ║  Customer  Orde║  Show item information           ║Labels  Batch  Exit ║
 ╟───────────────║ ► Change action                  ╟────────────────────╢
  3             ║   Override assigned database or view ║
  4    •    •    •║ ► Embed code                     ║      •    •    •    •
  5             ║   Bypass item on condition        ║
  6    •    •    ║   Position record pointer         ║           •    •
  7             ║   Reassign index order            ║
  8    •    •    ║   Define logical window           ║           •    •
  9             ║   Write help text                 ║
 10    •    •    ║   Assign message line prompt      ║           •    •
 11             ╚═══════════════════════════════════╝
 12    •    •                                                    •    •
 13
 14    •    •                                                    •    •
 15
 16    •    •    •    •    •    •    +    •    •    •    •    •    •
 17
 18    •    •    •    •    •    •    +    •    •    •    •    •    •
 19
 20···+····1····+····2····+····3····+····4····+····5····+····6····+····7····+····
 ╔App ══╗╔C:\dbiv\sample\CD_MAIN ══╗╔Customer══╗  ╔File:ORDERS══╗  ╔═ Num ═══╗
 Prev/Next object:F3/F4  Prev/Next item:PgUp/PgDn  Select:◄┘  Work surface:Esc
              Display current information for highlighted item
```

Figure 13-11   Item menu.

To save any color and border changes you made to the pop-up menus, press **Alt-M**, select *Put away current menu,* and choose *Save changes.*

Assigning Menus

You now have a main horizontal bar menu and several pop-up menus, but they are all separate objects. You must now connect up the pop-ups to the bar menu. To do this you have to use a function in the Item menu, which is shown in Figure 13-11. The idea is actually very simple. You begin with the main bar menu on the work surface, select each item on the menu individually, and assign to each a pop-up menu. When finished, you'll have a fully connected menu structure for your system, one you can generate the application for and actually play with.

Bring up the main bar menu to the work surface, if it is not already there, by pressing **Alt-M**, selecting *Horizontal bar menu,* and then picking CD_MAIN. With the menu on the screen, the cursor is positioned on the leftmost character position in the window frame. Press the **Right Arrow** key a few times until the word CUSTOMER becomes highlighted. You have just selected the first item on the main bar menu.

Now pull down the Item menu by pressing **Alt-I**. Select *Change item* and then *Open a menu*. A dialog box like the one shown in Figure 13-12 will appear. The first entry field is *Menu type:*. There are several possible values for this field; by pressing **Spacebar** several times you may see each one. The values are POP-UP, FILES, STRUC-TURE, VALUES, and BAR. We wish to choose POP-UP. Next, the field labelled *Menu name:* allows you to insert the filename of a previously created pop-up menu. This

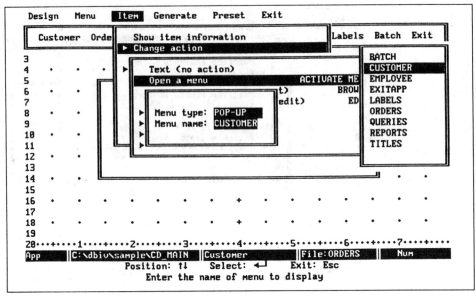

Figure 13-12 Assigning a menu to an option.

filename has a .POP extension. If you cannot remember what pop-up menus are defined, just press **Shft-F1** to obtain a file list. For now, select CUSTOMER. Now press **Ctrl-End** to save your selections and return to the Item menu.

You need to continue this process, moving the cursor to the right in the main bar menu, until you have visited each item and assigned a pop-up menu to that item. When you have finished assigning all the pop-up menus, you must save the .BAR menu file, which contains all of the assignments. Press **Alt-M**, select *Put away current menu* and choose *Save changes*.

Memory Constraints on the Design Surface

If you attempt to place too many menus on the ApGen design surface, you may experience difficulties (depending on the memory configuration of your development computer). For example, if you place the main bar menu plus four or five pop-up menus on the design surface when running on a typically configured PC (640K of RAM), a message will appear complaining of "insufficient memory." This is not an unreasonable limitation, since you rarely have occasion to need so many menus on the screen when designing an application. Remember, you are still in the design phase. You have not yet generated or run your application.

Generating the Application

Although your application is far from complete, you can at least test out the menu structure by "generating" the application as it stands now. This will provide you with a feel of how a program generated by dBASE IV ApGen functions and the steps involved in creating it.

The Generate Menu

Before using this menu, it would be a good idea to "put away" all the menus on the work surface and save any outstanding changes. This menu was omitted in the previous ApGen chapter because it made no sense to generate the application when the only object you had was the application object. Now, however, you have a menu structure. Press **Alt-G** to pull down the Generate menu as seen in Figure 13-13.

First select *Select template* to enter the name of the ApGen general purpose application writing template. Remember from the previous chapter that the dBASE IV ApGen is template driven, and exactly how it creates your new application depends on the operation of the template. Enter in this field the filename *MENU.GEN*, which is the standard ApGen template file that is provided with the product. Next, select *Display during generation* and choose *Yes*. When you request that the application program be displayed, a special window appears in the middle of the work surface. You will see a large amount of dBASE program code flash before your eyes. Even though the code generation process may take slightly longer with the display option on, it is always exciting for an application developer to see how quickly the code scrolls by as the program is automatically written. Finally, select *Begin generating* and just sit back and watch. The various programs, subprograms, and program structures are built before your eyes, and after a minute or so a message appears indicating that the generation is complete. Two new files are created, named CD_DIST.PRG and CD_MAIN.PRG, that contain all the program code. It is that simple.

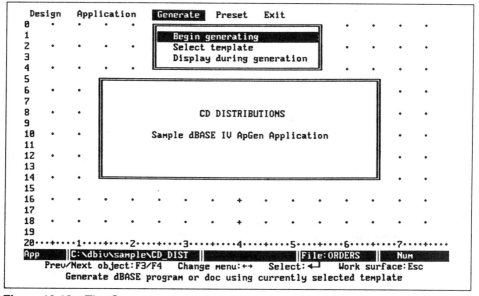

Figure 13-13   The Generate menu.

You should repeat this procedure using the DOCUMENT.GEN template. This time a special file, named CD_DIST.DOC, is generated containing complete program documentation that describes the application.

It may be instructional for you to print out both of the resulting files or go into the dBASE IV text editor to view them. To do the latter, return to the Control Center Applications panel and select <create>. When the dialog box appears, select dBASE program. This will activate the dBASE IV text editor. Now press **Alt-L** for the Layout menu and select *Modify a different program*. A dialog box will prompt you for the name of the program file you wish to load. Enter either *CD_DIST.PRG* or *CD_MAIN.PRG* and press **Enter**. After a few seconds to load the application program you will see the code on your screen. You can use the **PgUp** and **PgDn** keys to scroll through the program (both files are quite long) to get a feel for how much work you have saved using ApGen. After viewing the programs, press **Alt-E** to pull down the Exit menu, and select *Abandon changes and exit*. If you had loaded the CD_DIST.PRG program you could also select *Run program* here to begin execution at this time.

Note⟩ If you wish to change any of the menu objects you have created thus far, you will have to regenerate the application to put those changes in effect.

Running the Application

In order to run the application, exit from ApGen and return to the Control Center. From here, position to the Applications panel, highlight the application CD_DIST, and press **Enter**. You have two choices, *Run application* and *Modify application*, and you must pick the former. A dialog box will appear, asking if you are sure you want to run this application. Answer *Yes* to this prompt.

The first time a newly generated application begins to run you will briefly see a message at the bottom of the screen saying "Compiling," with numbers flashing by after it. These are program line numbers. This means dBASE IV is translating the ApGen-generated dBASE IV program code into what is called "pseudocode." Pseudocode is a more compact and optimized (for increased execution speed) form of the application program. It is the pseudocode that dBASE IV actually runs. Next, you will see the application object that you defined as the sign-on screen, and another message will appear saying "Press Enter to continue". Press the **Enter** key now and you will see yet another message saying "Loading . . . ." This indicates that the pseudocode form of the application is being loaded in dBASE IV's memory for execution.

If the application was built correctly, you should now see the main bar menu extended across the top of the screen with the Customer pop-up menu pulled down. You may press the **Left** and **Right Arrow** keys to move to different menu options. Since the pop-ups are attached, they should automatically pull down as you highlight each bar menu option. Note that as you move from item to item on the main menu, pressing **Enter** to select an option from any of the pop-up menus will have no effect. This is because you have not yet assigned an action to any of the menu items. Right now, the option names and the other descriptive text are considered to have the attribute *Text (no action)*. In order for a menu item to have something assigned to it you must dynamically do so. Assigning such actions is explored in the next chapter.

For now, you should terminate the application by pressing the **Escape** key. You will be prompted with ''Do you want to leave this application?'' and you must press **Y** to return to the Control Center.

Conclusion

This chapter has shown the power of the dBASE IV ApGen in generating a contemporary menu structure from which to build a complete application. The use of horizontal bar menus with attached pop-up menus makes for a very pleasing user interface. You now have a basis on which you may begin to assign actions to the menu options defined here. This is the task for Chapter 14.

14

Combining Objects in ApGen

This chapter takes steps towards completing the application whose user interface and global menu structure was defined in Chapter 13. In order to do this, all the existing objects needed as ingredients in the new application must be combined with the menu structure already established. In essence, the objects must be "attached" to the menus. Many types of objects come into play, and ApGen has many features that facilitate this process of attaching objects.

In order to assign actions to the various menu items in a menu structure, you must use the Item menu, which is available only if the current object is a menu, list, or batch. The Item menu and its many submenus form the basis for this chapter.

The Item Menu

The Item menu is shown in Figure 14-1. This menu is central to ApGen's ability to attach various objects to the global menu structure we constructed in the previous chapter. The second role the Item menu takes is its ability to customize an item's characteristics with regard to the overall application. For example, you may override the default database to be used in an item's function. You may also tailor the item's database scope (which records to consider), its ordering, its window attributes, and its user help information. The sections that follow and the next chapter define all the power underlying the Item menu, and also demonstrate how to use these various options in your sample application.

To use the Item menu, you must first make sure the item you want to describe is highlighted. At this point all the options available throughout the Item menu will be focused on this item. To move to another item, you may return to the menu containing the items and highlight another, or you may simply press **PgUp** or **PgDn** while the Item menu is pulled down.

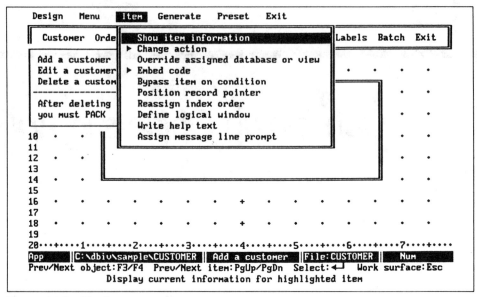

Figure 14-1 The Item menu.

Show Item Information

This option, the first selected from the Item menu, summarizes the options associated with the current object (see Figure 14-2). The object can be a menu, batch process, or list. This dialog box is informational only, in that it does not allow you to change any other information displayed. To modify any of the fields, you must select other options from the Item menu.

The only field with which you must be concerned is labelled OK. This field is truly misnamed. It seemingly indicates that you can edit the information and then OK its validity. This is not the case. You simply press **Enter** when you have finished reading the information and wish to return to the Item menu. Here are the various fields on the screen.

Object This field shows the name of the object. If the object is a menu, this will be the name of the .POP or .BAR file of the currently selected menu object. Other objects, such as batch processes and lists, are discussed in the next chapter.

Item This field contains the text used to identify the current item on the menu or batch process window. To change this field, you must retype the line of the menu in which these characters appear.

Current Database/View The database or view which has been tied to the current menu item is listed here. You may have specifically tied a database to the menu item by selecting *Override assigned database or view* from either the Item or Menu menus (which you would also use to modify this field). The difference between these two

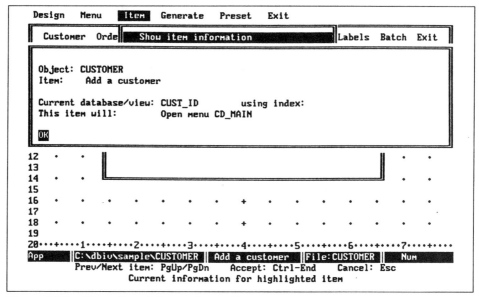

Figure 14-2 *Show item information* option.

dialog boxes will be discussed shortly. Alternately, the default database that was "inherited" from the application object is shown here.

Using index Any associated .NDX style index file, as specified in the *Override assigned database or view* option, is shown here. In this dialog box, you may have specifically entered an index file to describe the ordering of the overriding database or view.

This Item Will: This is an English phrase that is automatically given to the type of action the currently selected item will perform. ApGen has a series of these phrases it assigns depending on what is selected from the *Change action* submenu (in the Item menu). For your reference, all the possible phrases are listed here:

From the *Change action* menu

Display text (no action)

Open menu filename

Browse the database or view

Use form to edit database or view

From the *Display or print* menu (in the *Change action* menu)

Print report filename

Print labels filename

Display or list database records

From the *Perform file operation* menu (in the *Change action* menu)

Copy file filename to filename

Add records from filename

Copy records to filename

Substitute field values

Mark records for deletion

UNMARK records previously marked for deletion

Discard (delete from disk) marked records

Generate index filename

Reindex

Sort the database or view to filename

Import file (the import file is not shown in the phrase)

Export to file filename

From the *Run program* menu (in the *Change action* menu)

Do dBASE filename

Run batch filename

Insert dBASE code

Run program filename

Load/Call filename

Playback a macro filename

From the *Quit* menu (in the *Change action* menu)

Return to calling program

Quit to DOS

It is a good idea to use the *Show item information* dialog box to verify that each menu item has attached to it the intended attributes. For example, you can traverse the menu structure, highlight each option as you go, then select this dialog box to see if the correct database is being used or correct function is attached. This small step on your part now may save debugging your application, since ApGen does not do much checking as you build the pieces of your system. For example, if you attach a data entry form to a menu item, but fail to override the default database (to activate the database the screen needs to operate when the menu option is selected by the user), then the application will abort with an error message. If you peruse the *Show item information* display prior to running the application, this mistake may be discovered.

Try this with your sample application. Begin by putting the main bar menu, CD_ MAIN, on the work surface. Press **Alt-I**, select *Show item information*, and review the screen. Notice that the current object is CD_MAIN (the .BAR extension is assumed), the item is Customer, the current database is CUSTOMER.DBF, and the *This item will:* field value is **Open menu ORDERS** (the .POP extension is assumed). The Customer item on the main menu is automatically selected, because the cursor is first positioned over the leftmost item on the menu, here Customer. If you now move the cursor to the right so that Orders is highlighted and select again the *Show item information* dialog box, you'll find that the fields have changed.

Now bring the CUSTOMER pop-up menu to the work surface. The first menu item, *Add a customer*, should be highlighted. Press **Alt-I** again and bring up the *Show item information* dialog box. Now, see that the current object is CUSTOMER, the item is *Add a customer*, the database is CUSTOMER.DBF, and the *This item will:* field value is **Open menu CD_MAIN** (the .BAR extension is assumed). The only surprise is the last field. This is the default action, since you have not yet assigned an action to the menu item. You will soon change this.

Change Action

As mentioned before, the Item menu is instrumental to the use of ApGen, and it is primarily the *Change action* submenu that brings this power to the application developer. Here the various application objects may be defined and attached to menu items. Because of its importance, an entire section later in this chapter is devoted to describing the *Change action* menu's use.

Override Assigned Database or View

This option functions like the option with the same name in the Menu menu. Just as you can override the default database for the application to be used with a particular menu, you can do the same for other types of objects that are associated with menu options. If you have a simple single database application, you will never have to worry about using this option to specify an alternate database for a menu or menu item. In such a case, relying on the default database is satisfactory. However, if your application requires multiple, or even linked, databases, then this option shall be frequently used. In this latter case, you will sometimes rely on the default database, but at other times require a different database.

Utilizing the *Override assigned database or view* option from the Menu menu is appropriate if a particular database applies to all of the options of a specific menu. The sample application is a good example of this situation, in that all the Customer menu's options—namely Add, Edit, and Delete—pertain to the same database, CUSTOMER.DBF. If you decide to design the application in another manner, with an *Add records* menu providing options for adding customers, orders, titles, and employees, then you will not override the default database at the menu level, but will instead perform the override at the menu option level (using the Item menu option). Figure 14-3 shows the dialog box for this Item menu selection.

As before, the dialog box is driven by how you respond to the *For this item you may use values:* field. There are three possible values, which you may toggle through using the **Spacebar** key. They are: ABOVE, ENTERED BELOW, and IN EFFECT AT RUN TIME. Although both the correct database and .MDX index file tag name are already shown in the default (upper) portion of the screen, you still need to select

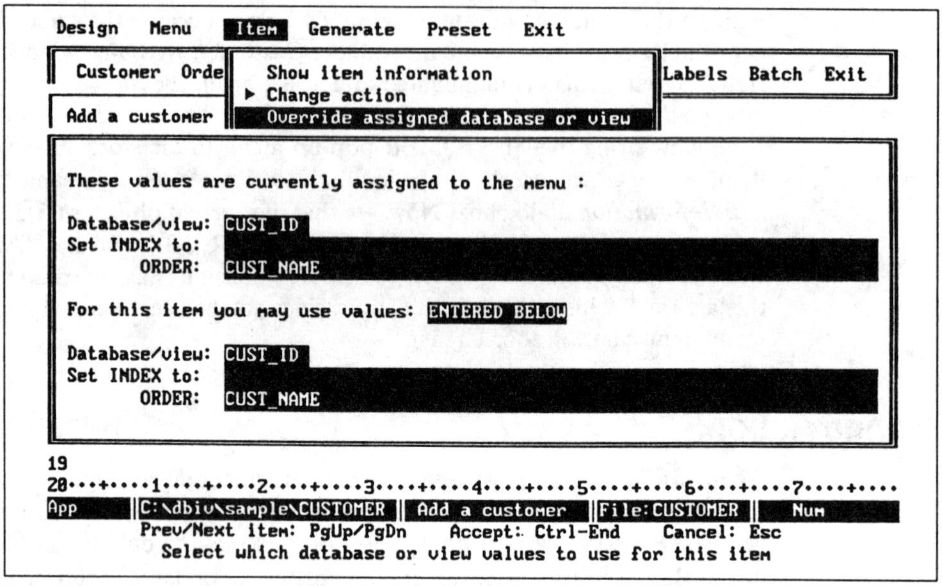

```
  Design   Menu   ▐Item▌  Generate   Preset   Exit
 ┌──────────────────┬───────────────────────────────┬──────────────────────┐
 │ Customer  Orde║     Show item information     ║Labels  Batch  Exit     │
 │                ║  ▶ Change action             ║                        │
 │Add a customer  ║   Override assigned database or view ║              │
 └────────────────┴───────────────────────────────┴────────────────────┘
 ┌──────────────────────────────────────────────────────────────────────┐
 │                                                                        │
 │ These values are currently assigned to the menu :                      │
 │                                                                        │
 │ Database/view: ▐CUST_ID                                              ▌ │
 │ Set INDEX to:                                                          │
 │       ORDER: ▐CUST_NAME                                              ▌ │
 │                                                                        │
 │ For this item you may use values: ▐ENTERED BELOW▌                      │
 │                                                                        │
 │ Database/view: ▐CUST_ID                                              ▌ │
 │ Set INDEX to:                                                          │
 │       ORDER: ▐CUST_NAME                                              ▌ │
 │                                                                        │
 └──────────────────────────────────────────────────────────────────────┘
 19
 20···+····1····+····2····+····3····+····4····+····5····+····6···+····7····+····
 App    ║C:\dbiv\sample\CUSTOMER ║ Add a customer ║File:CUSTOMER ║   Num
        Prev/Next item: PgUp/PgDn    Accept: Ctrl-End    Cancel: Esc
        Select which database or view values to use for this item
```

Figure 14-3 *Override assigned database or view* dialog box.

ENTERED BELOW and enter them again. This is an important distinction that ApGen makes and it has to do with a concept called "inheritance."

Inheritance says that all ApGen objects inherit attributes (databases, views, indexes, colors, etc.) from the application object. Moreover, items inherit the attributes of the object in which they appear, as is the case here. Abiding by these rules of inheritance, you would assume that the default database and index associated with the CUSTOMER pop-up menu (namely CUST_ID and CUST_NAME, respectively) will also be associated with the *Edit a customer* item in this menu, but this is not the case! There is an exception to the rules of inheritance when it comes to attached pull-down menus. If you attach pull-down menus, using the *Attach pull-down menus* option, the pull-down menus will inherit the attributes of the horizontal bar menu onto which they are attached. In this example, the database and index that were assigned to the CUSTOMER pop-up menu are overridden, and the database and index assigned to the CD_MAIN horizontal bar menu, namely ORDERS, will be used.

To rectify this problem of inheritance, you must either doubly assign the intended database and index, as is recommended, or not opt for attached pull-down menus. In general, attached pull-down menus are desirable, so this little extra step is well worth the trouble, as long as you understand why it is necessary.

Problems of inheritance, or misassigned databases, views, and indexes, can be difficult to diagnose once you run the completed application. Error dialog boxes will appear complaining of "variable not found". This usually results from an inheritance problem.

Shft-F1 (Pick) enables you to choose from a pick list when positioned in the database/view or index fields. If you enter a view name, you must specify the .QBE extension to distinguish it from a database name. If you wish to have a multiple file view active for a menu or menu item, then a multiple file view file must be specified. Embedded code segments, as discussed in the next chapter, may also suffice to set up the environment.

Normally, it does not matter in which order you override database/view defaults and attach actions to a menu item. However, if you plan to use the **Shft-F1** (Pick) key to choose fields to include in an edit, browse, list, or display object, then you should override the database/view first, so that the appropriate fields will be known and thus accessible.

Embed Code

The topic of embedding dBASE program code in an application is a powerful but more advanced topic and is therefore deferred to the next chapter.

Bypass Item on Condition

This option allows you to define a condition whereby the current item *cannot* be selected by the user. The current item may be an entire pop-up menu or an item in such a menu. The dialog box is shown in Figure 14-4. The condition is entered as any valid dBASE IV logical expression and may contain references to any appropriate built-in function. If the "value" of the logical expression is *True* (denoted **.T.** in dBASE IV notation), then the item will not be available to the user. Any logical expression can assume only one of two values (either **.T.** or **.F.**). A good example of a need for this

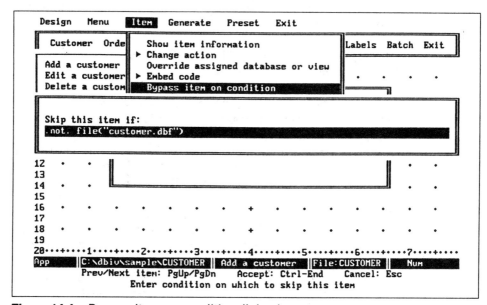

Figure 14-4 *Bypass item on condition* dialog box.

ability is to check for the existence of a database file, an index file, or even a .DBT file containing memo field data. You wouldn't want to proceed with a file operation if the required files were not present. Since hard disk environments have a tendency to inadvertently change over time, it is very desirable to provides such checks at runtime.

Now apply this capability to the sample application. With the Customer pop-up menu on the ApGen work surface and the *Add a customer* item highlighted, press **Alt-I** to access the Item menu. Next, select *Bypass item on condition* and fill into the dialog box the logical expression: *.NOT. FILE("CUSTOMER.DBF)*. This logical expression uses the FILE( ) built-in function, which determines the existence of a file on the disk. If the file exists, the function will return a **.T.** value and the **.NOT.** operator will reverse this value to **.F.** Since the item will be bypassed only if the logical expression evaluates to **.T.**, the item will still be available. In this case, we don't want the user to request the *Add a customer* item if the customer database is missing.

To save the entered condition you may press **Enter** or **Ctrl-End** and return to the Item menu. You must take care to construct the logical expression according to dBASE IV rules. No syntax checking is done in this dialog box, so if you make a mistake here, your application will likely abort when you run it.

Position Record Pointer

Certain operations that an application must perform require a method of positioning the database to a particular place before beginning the operation. For instance, you may wish for the user to select the record to edit prior to going to an Edit form, or you may wish the user to be able to restart a labels process at a specific zip code in the event of a paper jam. When a menu item is selected and this option is used, a dialog box automatically appears that gives several choices as to how to position in the database. The dialog box is seen in Figure 14-5. As you can see, four ways to position are provided, but you can only choose one.

Display Positioning Menu at Runtime? This option allows for the most flexible way to position before an operation. A small dialog box like the one in Figure 14-6 will appear when the user selects this menu item. Three ways of positioning are available. You can use the active index, shown on the top line of the screen, as the key for a *SEEK Record* type of search. If you highlight *SEEK Record* and press **Enter**, another entry box appears, which requests the user to enter the type of expression to be used in the search. A *1* means character, *2* means numeric, and *3* means date. You must be careful to select the type that matches the type of key used in the controlling index. If you don't, an error dialog box appears with a "Data type mismatch" message. If this happens, select *Ignore* to continue. Another field appears, in which you enter the value to look for (e.g., enter a *customer name*), and the operation is then performed. This is the fastest type of key value search because it uses the index file to locate the data.

If you wish to jump to a specific database record number you can select *GOTO Record* and a dialog box will appear allowing you to select TOP, BOTTOM, or RECORD #. If TOP is chosen, the database is positioned to the first record according to the controlling index. If BOTTOM is chosen, the database is positioned to the last

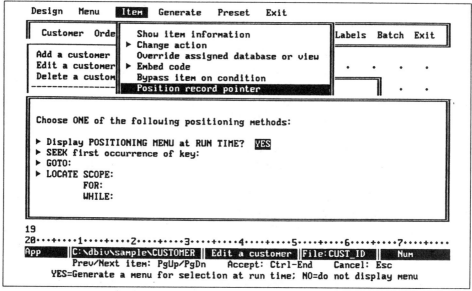

Figure 14-5 *Position record pointer* dialog box.

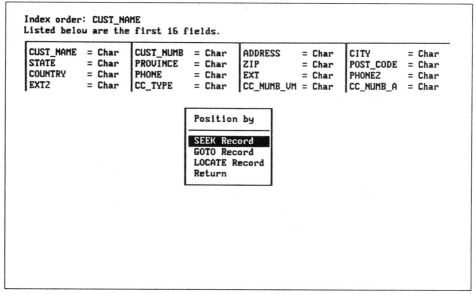

Figure 14-6 Record positioning during application execution.

record according to the controlling index. Finally, if RECORD # is chosen, an entry box appears that says *Record to GOTO*. You enter the record number; then the database is positioned and the operation performed. This dialog box also provides the maximum record number for the database. If a record number is entered that exceeds the maximum, a range violation message appears at the bottom of the screen saying "Range is 1 to 16 (press SPACE)" (assuming there are 16 records in the database). After this, you will be given another chance at entering a correct record number. This selection is of limited usefulness since it is unlikely a user will know a specific record number.

The last positioning selection is *LOCATE Record*. This option is the most flexible, in that you can search on a value for any field in the database, but it happens to be the slowest because it does not use the index file. For reference, the first 16 database fields are displayed on the screen. When this method is chosen, a special dialog box appears allowing you to enter the Scope (e.g., ALL, NEXT, and REST) of the search, a FOR clause (e.g., *city = "Los Angeles"*), and a WHILE clause (*country = ' '*). The database will be positioned to the first qualifying record and the operation performed. Notice the need for quotation marks around character literals.

> **Note** ⟩ If you select *Return*, no positioning is done and the operation specified for the menu item is performed starting at the beginning of the file.

Seek First Occurrence of Key This option lets you define a search key constant to be used whenever the menu item is selected. Depending on which controlling index is being used, this selection may or may not make sense. For example, if CUST_NAME is the controlling index, always positioning to a particular customer would generally not make sense. However, if ZIP is the controlling index and the menu item is labelled "West Coast Customers", then you might search for "90000".

GOTO Record You may enter TOP, BOTTOM, or a specific record number here to position the database. Again, it is unlikely that you will know a specific record number, though positioning to the TOP and BOTTOM of a database can occasionally be useful.

Locate Record The *SCOPE:*, *FOR:*, and *WHILE:* entry fields should be thought of as a group. You may specify the conditions whereby the database is positioned to begin the operation which is attached to the menu item.

Now, here is how to use the *Position record pointer* features with your sample application. For example, it makes sense to provide for record positioning capabilities with each of the edit and delete items on the pop-up database maintenance menus. Without any positioning, the user would have to page through all the records until the one needing editing or deleting came up. Instead, you will request that a *Position by* window appear at runtime for the user to first search the database for the record in question.

This brings up an important point concerning how much power an application developer should give to the user of the application. Using the *Position by* window has quite a bit of flexibility, but does require some dBASE expertise on the part of the user. For instance, the user must know the difference between the SEEK and LOCATE search operations. If LOCATE is chosen, the user must be capable of constructing dBASE logical expressions. This is often beyond the ability of casual computer users, many of which may be using your system.

If, for example, the user enters *CITY = LOS ANGELES*, the following in the FOR clause field, a "Variable not found" error dialog box results (because there are no quotation marks surrounding the literal value LOS ANGELES). The user is given a choice at this point to "Cancel, Ignore or Suspend". For a typical user, only the Ignore option makes sense, since the application will at least maintain control (in this case, control is passed to the Edit form as if nothing were wrong). There are alternatives whereby application developers can make things easier for the users. One such alternative involves pick lists, the other involves embedded dBASE language code—both topics for the next chapter.

Begin modifying the sample application by bringing up the CUSTOMER pop-up window and highlighting *Edit a customer*. Press **Alt-I** to pull down the Item menu, then select *Position record pointer*. You should be positioned at the first field, *Display POSITIONING MENU at RUNTIME?* Toggle the field's value by pressing the **Spacebar** until YES is displayed. Notice that only one of the four positioning methods can be selected in this dialog box. By toggling to YES, you've indirectly accepted this method, and you can no longer cursor down to any of the other methods. Press **Ctrl-End** to save your selection. Now press **PgDn** to move to *Delete a customer* and go through the same process again. Press **Alt-M** to get to the Menu menu, select *Put away current menu*, and save the changes. Repeat this entire process for each of the other pop-up menus—ORDERS, TITLES, and EMPLOYEES. You now have edit and delete screens that allow the user to first position to the record to edit or delete.

Reassign Index Order

This Item menu option allows you to specify an index file or tag for the action being defined. In the dialog box that appears, enter into the field labelled *Set ORDER to:* an .NDX filename, an order number (0 to 7), or an .MDX file tag name. This option differs from the *Set INDEX to:* and ORDER field in the *Override assigned database or view* option in that if the item you are defining will otherwise accept the default database or view, you can use this option to simply change the order. The more cumbersome alternative to using this option would be to override the assigned database and specify a different ordering.

Define Logical Window

This option enables your application to better control use of the screen by defining windows to display the results produced by the selected menu item. For example, if the menu item is to bring up a browse function, you can define a window of any size, at any screen position, that will contain the browse records. If you do not otherwise specify, the entire screen is used for each menu function. This full-screen approach is alright, but the multiwindow, layered (overlapping windows), or tiled (side-by-side windows) approach is much more contemporary.

When you select this option, a dialog box appears, as shown in Figure 14-7. First a window name must be selected and entered in the *Window NAME:* field. The name

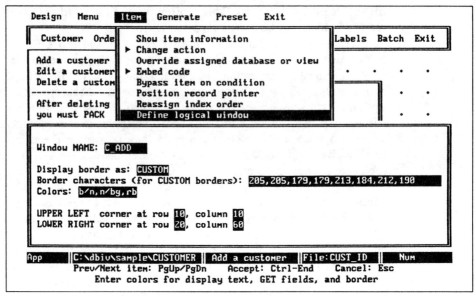

Figure 14-7   *Define logical window* dialog box.

selected should indicate the purpose of the window. Next, the type of border for the new window must be specified in the *Display border as:* field. This is a toggle field where the possible values are: SINGLE, DOUBLE, PANEL, CUSTOM, and NONE. Selecting SINGLE will produce a window with a single smooth graphics line around it; selecting DOUBLE produces a double line. PANEL is used with monochrome monitors, where the window's single-line border is displayed in reverse video. NONE is simply a window with no border displayed.

Finally, CUSTOM allows you to specify a custom window border, using special ASCII or graphics characters. This is the only selection for the *Display border as:* field for which you are able to fill in the *Border characters (for CUSTOM borders):* field. This field is used to define the characters to be used in a custom window border, and there are two ways to do this. First, you may specify a single character to be used throughout the border. For example, you could enter *[*]* to request that the asterisk be used as the border character. (The brackets are used as delimiters.) In addition, either the quotation mark or apostrophe could be used as delimiter characters. The second method of specifying a window border is somewhat more technical. You may specify a series of eight numeric ASCII character codes to identify the border characters to use. Each numeric ASCII code must be separated by a comma or blank space. To know what numbers to place in this field, you will need the aid of an ASCII code table, as found in the dBASE IV Language Reference manual. Moreover, the relative position of each ASCII value specified is significant, according to the following definition:

value 0:   Upper window border character

value 2:   Lower window border character

value 3:   Left window border character

value 4:   Right window border character

value 5:   Upper left window corner border character

value 6:   Upper right window corner border character

value 7:   Lower left window corner border character

value 8:   Lower right window corner border character

Therefore, an ASCII code sequence 205, 205, 179, 179, 213, 184, 212, 190 would result in a window with a double-line upper and lower border and a single-line left and right border. For your reference, you should look up each of these ASCII values to understand their visual effects.

Using the *Colors:* field, you may also define a particular color scheme for only the window just created. In this way, you may give your application a "personality" by assigning a specific color scheme for edit screens versus batch processes. The value you supply for this field is the familiar color string (such as *B/N,N/BG,RB*, which paints a window with blue on black standard video, black on cyan enhanced (highlighted) video, and a magenta border).

> **Note** This field may contain a maximum of 11 characters, which is not enough for many color code sequences.

The last four fields in the dialog box define the screen position of the window. First you fill in the *UPPER LEFT corner at:* field with the row and column number of the upper left coordinate of the window. Next, you fill in the *LOWER RIGHT corner at:* field with the row and column number of the lower right coordinate. This is enough to define the window's position. In determining the position of a window, care should be taken not to interfere with other screen components such as menus. Also, the window should be of a size commensurate with its function. For example, a Browse window should not be so small that the data cannot be viewed in tabular form. When completed, the selections in this dialog box may be saved by pressing **Ctrl-End**. You will return to the Item menu.

Not all menu item objects lend themselves to being driven from a window. Actually, some objects cannot be "scaled" down to be used inside a window. For example, a Browse operation works fine inside a window (even though the Browse window border overwrites the one you define). However, an Edit or Append operation with or without an Edit form cannot be performed inside a window. Instead, the full screen is automatically used regardless of whether you define your own window.

Right now, none of the objects in the sample application need to be run through a window, so the *Define logical window* feature will not be used until later.

Write Help Text

This option functions exactly like the option with the same name discussed in the section on creating menus. Basically, you may provide help information in the event the user presses the **F1** (Help) key while the menu item is selected. If you fail to define help information at the menu item level, then the help information defined for the menu will be displayed to the user when **F1** is used. If no help has been defined for the menu, the message "No help defined" is displayed.

With this option, a text entry window opens up, allowing you to enter up to 19 lines of text pertinent to the successful use of this menu item. To save the entered text, press **Ctrl-End** and return to the Item menu.

Assign Message Line Prompt

You may use this selection to define a single line of text that will display at the bottom of the screen as the user moves the highlight to this menu item. The message should simply state the basic function of the item and is used solely to remind the user of the function desired. If you fail to define a message line prompt at the menu item level, then any message line prompt defined for the menu will continue to display.

The Change Action Menu

Now we must turn our attention to probably the most powerful part of the dBASE IV ApGen, the *Change action* menu. From here you assign specific actions to the items appearing in the pop-up menus, actions that will be performed at runtime when the user selects the menu item. See Figure 14-8, which shows the options available under the *Change action* menu. This menu was used briefly in the last chapter in order to attach the pop-up menus to the main bar menu, but from this menu you may also attach many other objects, such as other menus, Browse windows, queries, reports, labels, various file operations, embedded code segments, and external programs.

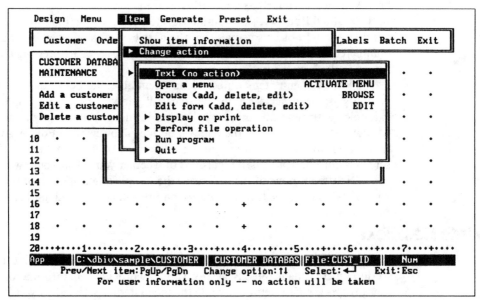

Figure 14-8 *Change action* menu.

Text (No Action)

This option is the default for all unassigned items on a menu. An item, in this sense, is simply a column (in the case of a bar menu) or row (in the case of a pop-up menu) appearing in a menu. Most items, even if they start off as "no action" items, will ultimately be assigned some function to perform. Some items, however, will remain "no action" items. These items may be simply viewed as descriptive text that helps the user understand the menu. The sample application has several "no action" items in each of the database maintenance menus. These items act as menu "titles" and will never have an action assigned to them.

Open a Menu

This option was used in the last chapter to assign the action of opening a pop-up menu to the items of the main bar menu. However, the name of this option is a bit of a misnomer, since you can do more than open menus with it—you may also open pick lists.

Figure 13-12 shows that this option requires you to specify the *menu type* and the *menu name*. The *Menu type:* field has five possible values—BAR, POP-UP, FILES, STRUCTURE, and VALUES. The first two are indeed menus, but the last three are all types of lists: files lists, structure (field) lists, and values lists. You may see each menu type by toggling through with the **Spacebar** key. Once the type has been selected, you may enter the menu or list name in the *Menu name:* field. If you don't know the name, press **Shft-F1** (Pick) to obtain a files list of only those objects with the appropriate type. Once you have selected the filename, press **Ctrl-End** to save the action.

The *Open a menu* option is very important. It is responsible for hooking together the various menu structures in an application. Without it, all you can achieve is a series of disconnected menus. In essence, it allows you to establish a global hierarchy for the application and define the flow of control that interrelates the menus. In addition, you can construct a cascading menu structure, where a menu will "open a menu," which will in turn "open a menu," and so on, just as ApGen itself does.

Browse (Add, Delete, Edit)

Browse allows you to invoke a Browse window. Since dBASE IV is considered a relationally oriented database system, it makes sense to view its databases as "tables." Tables are the basis for all relational systems. A Browse window promotes this perception, as it allows the user to view the databases in terms of rows and columns of data. In general, the Browse window in dBASE IV is very powerful, and ApGen lets your application take advantage of this power by providing the vehicle to include customized Browse windows in your application. Figure 14-9 shows the dialog box for defining a Browse window that will be included in an ApGen application. The various fields are now examined.

Fields This field allows you to specify which fields from the active database or view to include in the browse window. If you do not use this option, then all the fields from the

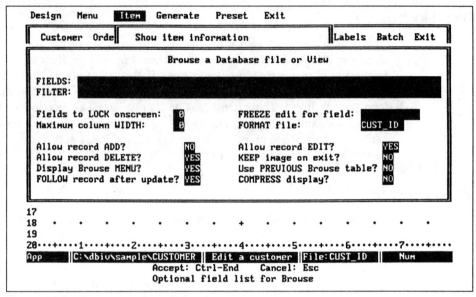

Figure 14-9   Browse action dialog box.

database will be used. You must separate each field entered by a comma. For example, you may want the Browse window to include only the customer number, customer name, and telephone number. You may also redefine the order of the fields as they would normally appear according to the database structure. For example, you may want the customer number to appear as the first field, although it is not the first field in the database. Just enter the fields you wish to include or press **Shft-F1** (Pick) to select them from a fields list. Using the pick list will place the fields in alphabetical order and with commas inserted. Notice that you may have to override the default database if it is not the one intended for this object.

Filter   With a filter expression, you may include and/or exclude only those records in the database or view that satisfy some kind of selection criteria. For example, you may wish to implement a Browse window that will only display records for West Coast customers. In this case, you would define a filter like: **STATE = "CA"**. As another example, you may wish to exclude all records that have been marked for deletion but have not been physically removed from the database. In this case, the filter expression would be **.NOT. DELETED( )**, which uses the built-in function for determining whether a record is deleted or not. The filter expression is any logical expression that ultimately evaluates to either True or False and may contain any of the available dBASE IV built-in functions. Due to the limited size of the FILTER field, only moderately complex filter expressions can be entered. If more sophisticated filters are required, you may have to use embedded code.

Alternately, you specify the name of a query file in this field. A query file is a file that was defined using the CREATE QUERY command in dBASE III+ and has a

.QRY extension. The filter expression found in this file is used in the same manner as if you specified it explicitly. You may not specify a Query by Example query file here, because the file will not be found (since a .QRY extension, not .QBE, is assumed). If you choose this option, you must precede the query filename with the keyword FILE. For example, to use a query file that was set up to extract only the phone numbers for West Coast customers, you would enter *FILE WCPHONE*.

Fields to Lock Onscreen You may use this option to keep one or more browse window field columns on the left side of the screen even during horizontal column-to-column scrolling. Specify a number here indicating the number of columns to lock. Normally only a few columns are frozen, since the screen is limited in size. A sample use might be with the CUST_ID database. You can lock the customer name field on the left so that it will remain visible while you pan to the right to see other field columns. The default for this field is 0, meaning that no field columns are to be locked.

Freeze Edit for Field This option enables you to specify a *single field* in which editing may take place while you are in a Browse window. The other fields in the browse window remain visible; however, you may not change their contents. For example, you may wish to allow the user to change only the PHONE field during the browse operation. Enter the name of the field or press **Shft-F1** (Pick) to select a field from a fields list. This is an optional field. Note that at runtime, the user may override any locked or frozen fields in the Browse window menu that are left accessible. You will see in a minute how you may disable this menu.

Maximum Column Width In order to assure that at least portions of all fields in a Browse window will fit on a single screen, you may wish to override the actual database field widths and specify a maximum width for all fields to appear. Note that if a field is longer than the maximum you enter here, the field can be scrolled within the space allotted. This means that if you cursor over to the rightmost end of the CUST_NAME field that has been limited to a length of 10, you may continue going to the right and the hidden characters will appear one by one. If a field length is smaller than the maximum, then its actual length will be used. This is an optional field.

Format File As you have seen in previous chapters, in a Browse window you may press **F2** (Data) to toggle between the tabular orientation that Browse provides and the Edit method of viewing and editing records. By specifying the name of a screen format file here, you dictate how the records will be displayed when the user toggles to Edit mode from a Browse window. Simply enter the name of a screen form file or press **Shft-F1** (Pick) to choose a name from a file list.

   If you specify a screen format file that uses fields from the database other than the ones you specified in the *FIELDS:* entry of this dialog box, then the latter will be ignored. Moreover, the entire screen is used for the Browse window even though a smaller window may have been defined using the *Define logical window* option from the Item menu.

Allow Record Add? In a normal Browse window, you may cursor down past the last record of the database and be asked whether you wish to add records. Sometimes you want the Browse window to be used for record modification only. In this instance, you must change the default setting for this field from YES to NO by pressing the **Spacebar. Spacebar.**

Allow Record Edit? The primary purpose of a Browse window is to provide the user with a table-oriented method of editing a database. Sometimes, however, you may wish to make available a "read-only" table to be used for reference purposes only. The user may view the table but not change any information in it. If this is desired then you must change the default YES for this field to NO by pressing the **Spacebar.**

Allow Record Delete? To complete the picture, you may also prohibit the user from deleting records in the database by changing the default YES for this field to NO by pressing the **Spacebar.** A completely "user-insulated" Browse window would prohibit APPEND, EDIT, and DELETE operations.

Keep Image on Exit? Normally, when you exit from a Browse window, the image of the window is automatically removed from the screen. If, however, you want the window to remain on the screen so that the user may reference its contents later, while in another object, you must override the default NO for this field and change it to YES by pressing the **Spacebar.**

Display Browse Menu? You may remove the user's runtime access to the Browse window menu by overriding the default YES for this option and changing it to NO by pressing the **Spacebar.** Without the menu, the user will have less control over the window's operation, but mishaps may be prevented. Many times, the user should only be able to "view" the data in the window, using just the simple record positioning keys such as **Up Arrow, Down Arrow, PgUp,** and **PgDn.** Giving users the added ability to lock and freeze fields, as well as positioning within the database, often complicates their perception of the overall system.

Use Previous Browse Table The idea behind this option is to preserve all the settings in effect for a previous Browse window definition dialog box for use with the currently activated Browse window. For example, if the application has a pop-up menu containing three browse window choices, *Browse Orders by Order Number, Browse Orders by Customer Number*, and *Browse Orders by ID Number*, you need to define all the settings only for the first Browse window. For the other two, just change this option from the default NO to YES. The other two Browse windows will now assume the characteristics of the first. The user must, however, always choose the *Browse Orders by Order Number* window first or else the other two will not have any settings to assume.

This option is also of limited usefulness due to how ApGen manages open files. The problem lies in the fact that the act of saving previous Browse window settings only works if the database that is the subject of the Browse remains open. If the database is closed after one Browse window and then reopened when another Browse window is invoked, all the settings from the previous window are lost. It just so happens that when you choose an option from a pop-up menu that involves a database other than the default database for the application, the database is opened as the option is invoked and closed when the option returns to the menu. Hence, all the settings are lost. This means that you should only use this option if the database or view to be used is the default. Even then, if you choose one option involving the default database and then another involving some other database, the settings will be lost if you again choose an option involving the default database.

Follow Record After Update? In the event that you allow the user to change database information, it is possible that a controlling index key value could be altered. If this happens, the default for this option, YES, causes the new key to be "followed" to its new position in the file. This is usually acceptable, but can occasionally be annoying, especially when you are reading down a list of records in ZIP code order and find one that was misentered and needs to be changed. If you change it, you will then be placed at the point of the database where the new key is placed. Instead, you probably wish to remain where you were. To disable the mechanism, toggle this option to NO by pressing the **Spacebar**.

Compress Display? A Browse window usually has the field names above the actual data with double-line boxes surrounding them. You may change the default NO for this option to YES by pressing the **Spacebar** in order to compress the Browse window slightly by having the field names displayed as part of a single-line border immediately surrounding the data. When optimal use of screen space is desired, the feature window makes sense.

Adding a Browse Window

You will now enhance your sample application to include a Browse window for each of the four databases, adding this function to each of the pop-up menus. Begin by bringing up the pop-up menu for the customer database. Press **Alt-D** to get the Design menu. Select *Pop-up menu* and highlight CUSTOMER. Press **Shft-F7** (Size) in order to lengthen the window by pressing **Down Arrow** one time and then **Enter**. Notice that an extra line has been added to the bottom of the pop-up menu. Position the highlight down the new line and enter *Browse customers*. To define the attributes of this new object, press **Alt-I** to get the Item menu. Select *Override assigned database or view* and toggle to ENTERED BELOW. In the field labelled *Database/view:* enter **CUST_ID** and for the *ORDER:* field enter *CUST_NAME*. Press **Ctrl-End** to save these responses. Select *Bypass item on condition* and in the field labelled *Skip this item if:* enter *.NOT. FILE("CUST_ID.DBF")* and press **Enter** to return to the Item menu. Select *Position record pointer*, toggle the *Display POSITIONING MENU at RUNTIME:* field to YES and press **Ctrl-End**. This will give the user the ability to first search for a customer name and have the database positioned before browsing. Next, select *Define logical window* in order to size down the Browse window. Toggle the *Display border as:* field to NONE, since a Browse window will override any borders you specify here. Enter *B/N,N/BG,RB* for the *Colors:* field so that the Browse window may be distinguished from the rest of the screen objects. Define the window's screen coordinates by entering

10 and 10 for the *UPPER LEFT corner row* and *column* positions respectively. Enter 20 and 60 for the *LOWER RIGHT corner row* and *column* positions. Press **Ctrl-End** to save these selections.

Select *Write help text* to define the help information that will appear when the user presses **F1** (Help). Enter the following text in the word processing window that appears:

> *Use this option to browse through EXISTING records in the customer database. Note that you may only browse the records. Use another option to add, edit, or delete records.*

Press **Ctrl-End** to save this help text.

Select *Assign message line prompt* and enter in the last line of the dialog box that appears:

> *Browse through EXISTING records in the customer database.*

Press **Ctrl-End** to save the new prompt message.

Finally, it is time to define the Browse window itself. Select the *Change action* menu and then *Browse (add, delete, edit)*. When in the *FIELDS:* field press **Shift-F1** (Pick) to select the fields to include in the Browse window. Alternately, you may type in the fields: *CUST_NUMB, CUST_NAME, CC_TYPE, CC_NUMBER_A, CC_ NUMBER_VM, CC_EXP_DAT*. Notice that the order of these fields is not the same as their actual order in the CUST_ID database. In the *FILTER:* field enter *NOT. DE-LETED( )* to eliminate all records marked for deletion from the records the user will see in the browse window. Specify *1* in the *Fields to LOCK onscreen:* field so that the CUST_NUMB field will remain on the screen as the user scrolls to the right to see additional fields. Specify 10 in the *Maximum column WIDTH:* field. (Due to the limited size of the Browse window you do not want the longer fields to dominate the display.) Override the default settings for *Allow record ADD?*, *Allow record EDIT?*, and *Allow record DELETE?* by toggling them to NO. This will ensure that the window will be used for Browse purposes only. No modification of the data may take place. Toggle the *Display Browse MENU:* field to NO so that the user may not access the special menu for browse windows. Finally, toggle the *COMPRESS display:* field to YES in order to optimize the use of screen space. Press **Ctrl-End** to save all these selections. Now you may press **Alt-M** to get the Menu menu and select *Put away current menu* and then *Save changes*.

In order to see the effect of defining a Browse window, you must again generate the whole application and run it from the Control Center. For completeness, you should add a Browse window to each of the other pop-up menus: ORDERS, TITLES, and EMPLOYEES.

Edit Form (Add, Delete, Edit)

Often a Browse window is not an appropriate instrument for data entry, since entering new data in tabular format can be somewhat unwieldy and unreliable (especially when one considers the lack of any data validity checking at the field level). Edit forms make more sense in these cases in light of the many data verification features available in the dBASE IV screen painter.

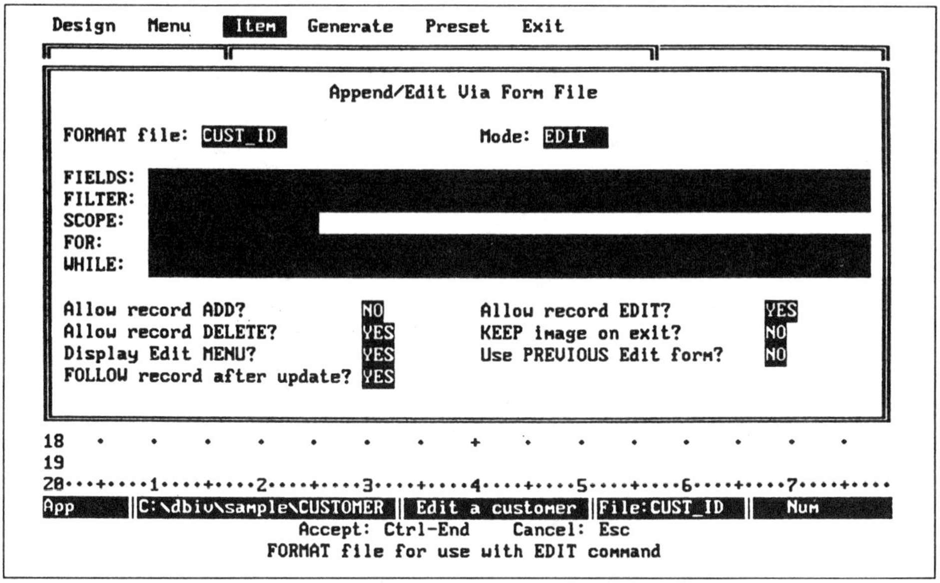

Figure 14-10   Edit form action dialog box.

You may choose to attach edit forms to perform the various maintenance functions your application requires for adding, editing, and deleting records in databases. When you select the Edit form object type, the dialog box in Figure 14-10 appears. The following is a description of the fields in this box.

Format File This field allows you to enter the name of a screen form file to be attached to the selected menu item. You may also press **Shft-F1** (Pick) to choose a form from a files pick list. If you wish, you may choose <create> to transfer to the form design screen to build a new Edit form. Creating new objects from ApGen will be examined in the next chapter. If you do not specify a screen form file here, but still attach this object type, the standard Edit form for dBASE IV will be used.

Mode This toggle field is used to determine the default editing mode upon entry to the Edit form object. The default APPEND may be changed to EDIT by pressing the **Spacebar**. At runtime, when the Edit mode is in effect, the first record of the database (or the first record according to an active index) will be displayed. You may of course modify this record or move to another record using the **PgUp** or **PgDn** keys. In Append mode, a blank record frame is initially displayed and the user may enter a new record or position to another record using the **PgUp** key. Even if **PgUp** is used immediately upon entry to the Edit form in Append mode, a blank record is still added to the database.

> Note Notice that when you toggle to APPEND, you cannot cursor down past the *FIELDS:* field.

Fields This field allows you to specify which fields from the active database or view to include in the Edit form object. If you do not use this option, then all the fields from the database will be used. You must separate each field entered with a comma. Just enter the fields you wish to include or press **Shft-F1** (Pick) to select them from a fields list. Using the pick list will place the fields in alphabetical order and with commas inserted. Notice that you may have to override the default database if it is not the one intended for this object. If you specify Append mode or if you specify Edit mode and use a form file, then the fields you enter here will be ignored.

Filter This field is only accessible for Edit mode. With a filter expression, you may include and/or exclude for editing only those records in the database or view that satisfy some kind of selection criteria. The filter expression is any logical expression that ultimately evaluates to either True or False and may contain any of the available dBASE IV built-in functions. Due to the limited size of the FILTER field, only moderately complex filter expressions may be entered. If more sophisticated filters are required, you may have to use embedded code.

Also, as mentioned earlier for the Browse window, you specify the name of a query file in this field. You may not specify a Query by Example query file here, because the file will not be found (since a .QRY extension, not .QBE, is assumed). If you choose this option, you must precede the query filename with the keyword FILE.

Scope You may use this option in Edit mode only to define the scope of the Edit operation (in other words, the number of records to consider).

For You may use this option in Edit mode only to specify the condition to be met for a record to be accessible in the Edit form object.

While You may use this option in Edit mode only to specify the condition that indicates when the editing of records should terminate.

Allow Record Add? When in Edit mode, you may indicate that new records may also be added by accepting the default YES for this field. Toggle the field value to NO, in order to inhibit appending records, by pressing the **Spacebar**.

Allow Record Edit? When in Edit mode, this option's default value, YES, will let the user modify the data in existing database records. Toggle the field value to NO, in order to inhibit any modification of existing records, by pressing the **Spacebar**.

Allow Record Delete? When in Edit mode, you may disable the user's ability to delete existing database records by accepting the default field value of YES. If you change the value to NO by pressing the **Spacebar**, then no records may be deleted.

Keep Image on Exit? This option's default of NO may be changed to allow the current Edit form's image to remain on the screen after the Edit form has been exited. This may prove useful, since after editing a record, you may want its contents to remain visible for reference purposes while you enter another area of the application.

Display Edit Menu? You may disable the display of the standard Edit form menu by changing the field's default value of YES to NO.

Use Previous Edit Form? The idea behind this option is to preserve all the settings in effect for a previous Edit form definition dialog box for use with the currently activated Edit form. The same restrictions and limitations exist with this option as with the *Use PREVIOUS Browse table?* option discussed earlier.

Follow Record After Update? The default YES for this option causes the database record pointer to "follow" a modified index key value to its new position in the file in the same manner as in a Browse window. The repositioning action occurs differently, however. In a Browse window, you simply move the cursor up or down and the record pointer is followed. In a screen form, you use **PgUp** or **PgDn** or cursor through the last field in the current record to initiate the action.

You have some very good applications of possible uses of the Edit form object with your sample application. Namely, each of the database maintenance functions in the CUSTOMER, ORDERS, TITLES, and EMPLOYEE pop-up menus should be implemented as Edit form objects. A few such objects will be constructed as an example.

Begin by bringing up one of the pop-up menus, say CUSTOMER, to the work surface. Now highlight one of the options. To start with, use *Add a customer*. Press **Alt-I** to pull down the Item menu and select *Override assigned database or view*. Remember from a previous discussion that due to "inheritance," you need to specify a new default database and ordering. In the dialog box that appears, toggle the *For this item you may use values:* field to ENTERED BELOW and enter *CUST_ID* in the *Database/view:* field and *CUST_NAME* in the *ORDER:* field. Press **Ctrl-End** to save your entries.

Now, from the Item menu, select *Change action* and then *Edit form (add, delete, edit)*. In the dialog box enter *CUST_ID* in the *FORMAT file:* field and accept the default value APPEND for the *Mode:* field. Since you cannot change the fields that define the Edit form environment when APPEND mode is specified, you must be satisfied with their results. Namely, the user may still edit and delete existing records even though only the ability to append records was requested. Press **Ctrl-End** to save the fields in this dialog box and return to the Item menu.

> Note⟩ To complete the picture for this menu item, as you should do for all menu items, select *Write help text* and *Assign message line prompt* in order to provide assistance to the user at runtime.

This completes the assignment of an Edit form object to a pop-up menu item. Next, you need to perform a similar assignment to both the Edit and Delete menu items. There are a few differences, which should be described now. From the Item menu, press **PgDn** to move to the *Edit a customer* menu item. First, override the assigned database as was done earlier. Next, select *Position record pointer* and in the dialog box toggle the *Display POSITIONING MENU at RUNTIME?* field to YES. Press **Ctrl-End** to save this selection. This will invoke the positioning menu at runtime whenever the user wishes to edit a record. Since the controlling index tag is CUST_

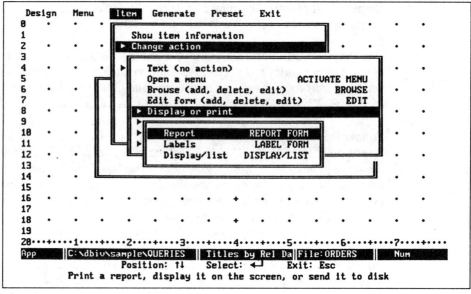

Figure 14-11 *Display or print* menu.

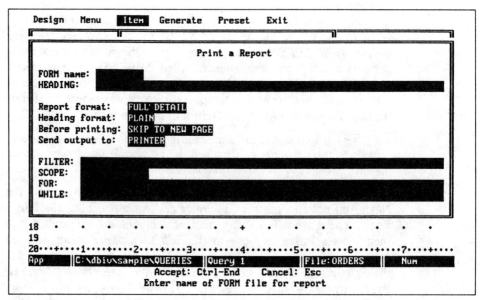

Figure 14-12 *Display or print* menu, Report dialog box.

NAME, the user will be able to search for a particular name, have the application retrieve the record, and then edit its contents. Last, attach an Edit form object to the menu item, but fill in the dialog box a bit differently. Enter *CUST_ID* in the *FORMAT file:* field as before. The *Mode:* field, however, should be EDIT. Specify a *FILTER:* field value of .NOT. DELETED( ) so that deleted records cannot be edited. Since this is an edit-only screen, toggle *Allow record ADD?* to NO, *Allow record EDIT?* to YES, and *Allow record DELETE?* to NO.

Repeat this process for *Delete a customer* menu, but for the Edit Form object dialog box fields set *Allow record ADD?* to NO, *Allow record EDIT?* to NO and *Allow record DELETE?* to YES. For this menu item, the user will position to a particular record at runtime and only be able to delete it.

Now take this procedure and apply it to the ORDERS, TITLES, and EM- PLOYEES pop-up menus. The result, in conjunction with the Browse windows at- tached to each menu earlier, will be complete maintenance menus for each of your application's four databases.

Display or Print This *Change action* menu option allows you to attach a report or label object to a menu item. In addition, for simple display-only queries you can also attach the output of a DISPLAY/LIST command to a menu item. When combined with a view file, this option provides the vehicle for constructing sophisticated query and reporting facilities that are accessible from an application. As you select this option, the menu shown in Figure 14-11 appears. Here you are requested to choose one of the three available output objects.

Report

When this option is selected from the *Display or print* menu, the dialog box shown in Figure 14-12 is displayed. Here you may fill in the various fields in order to define a report object. The first field, *FORM name:*, requests the name of a report form. This object may already have been created in the Control Center, in which case you can enter its name in this field or press **Shft-F1** (Pick) to choose a form from a files list, or the report form may be created at this time by selecting <create> from the files list. In the latter case, you will be automatically transferred to the report generator so that you may define the report. You may provide more flexibility by building a files list that would appear at runtime for the user to choose one of possibly many report forms. This process will be covered in the next chapter.

Heading This field allows you to enter a series of characters (without surrounding quotation marks) that will be printed on the first line of each report page. This heading is in addition to the heading you specify when defining the report. Be careful how you enter this heading information, since it will not be centered according to the length of the report's lines. Extra spaces may be needed to pad on the left so that the heading will appear centered.

Report Format This is a toggle field specifying the general format of the report. The default setting for this field is FULL DETAIL, which causes the report to print all detail line information in addition to subtotal and total lines. This means, for example, that if your report prints order information and groups the orders by customer, all the orders will be printed followed by the subtotal for each customer. Press the **Spacebar** to toggle to the other setting, SUMMARY ONLY, which causes only the subtotal and grand total information, not the detail lines, to be printed.

Heading Format This is a toggle field whose default setting, PLAIN, causes the report to be printed without both the date and page number on each printed page. Moreover, any text entered in the header and footer bands in the report definition will only print once, on the first page. Press the **Spacebar** to obtain the alternate setting, INCLUDE DATE AND PAGE, which prints the current date and page number as well as headers and footers on each report page. Note that if PLAIN is used, any text specified in the *HEADING:* field will not appear on the report.

Before Printing This field determines whether or not to perform an initial top of form command prior to printing the report. This is a toggle field whose default setting is SKIP TO NEW PAGE. The alternate setting, DO NOT EJECT, is obtained by pressing the **Spacebar** key. Although the default setting forces the printer to advance to the next page before printing the report, it is usually more advisable to simply begin printing the report where you have aligned the paper instead of wasting a blank sheet of paper each time. It makes more sense to perform an eject after the report is finished (which is automatically done regardless of the value of this setting), thus preparing the printer for the next report.

Send Output To This field allows you to customize the destination of the finished report. This toggle field has four possible settings. First, PRINTER directs the report output to the attached printer and is the default setting. The report is also echoed to the computer's screen. Second is DISK FILE, which directs the report to be written to a disk file as it is generated. The name of the output disk file is the same as the name report object specified in the *FORM name:* field with a .PRT extension. This is a very useful option because it affords the user the flexibility of printing the report whenever convenient by using the DOS PRINT command (i.e., printing the report disk file). You may also choose to send this report file to another computer via data communications.

The next setting is SCREEN, which directs the report to the user's screen only. This is appropriate for only the shortest of reports, as the user would not want to scroll through many pages of report output on the screen only. Lastly, the ASK AT RUN-TIME option causes a pop-up menu (one that you do not have to, or actually cannot, define) to appear at runtime for the user to decide where the report is to go. Since you cannot define this pop-up menu, you must be satisfied with its screen position. Specifically, you may not define a logical window for a report, label, or display/list object when this option is in effect unless the window is defined to be nearly the whole screen. This restriction is due to the fact that the pop-up menu will be displayed inside the logical window and the absolute positioning of this pop-up menu may not coincide with the window's border. Attempts to circumvent this situation may result in "Position out of window" error messages. Nevertheless, this last option should be used frequently since it gives the user the most flexibility. At runtime, the user has the following options to choose from:

CON: Console (your screen)

LPT1: Parallel port 1 (usually your primary printer)

LPT2: Parallel port 2 (secondary printer if any)

COM1: Serial port 1 (serial printer if any)

FILE

If the user selects the last option, FILE, the report will be written to a disk file named REPORT.TXT. This is the filename also used for the label and display/list objects. Since *Send output to:* is a toggle field, you can cycle through each setting by pressing the **Spacebar**.

The last group of fields on this dialog box—*FILTER:*, *SCOPE:*, *FOR:*, and *WHILE:*—determine what records will be considered in the report. Basically, these fields define the conditions whereby the current database or view is trimmed down to include only the data that is needed for the report. Since the field for specifying a filter condition is limited in length, you may need to combine it with a FOR condition or activate a view file containing the complex conditions by overriding the default database.

Many times, a display or print object needs only to process a portion of an indexed file or view. Using the SEEK option available in the *Position record pointer* option of the Item menu, you can position to the point in the file where processing is to begin. Then, with the use of the *WHILE:* field, you can continue processing until some condition changes. For example, if you need a customer list for only West Coast customers, you can SEEK on "90000" to position to the first occurrence of a West Coast zip code, then specify a WHILE condition such as **ZIP4> = "90000" .AND. .NOT. EOF( )**. Here, an equivalent FOR condition could also be constructed, but it would be much slower, since the records prior to those with ZIP field of "90000" would have to be searched through first. In a SEEK index search, the starting position would be found almost immediately.

If you plan to position the record pointer before processing a report, label, or display/list object, you should not also specify a filter condition. For a filter condition to begin selecting qualifying records, the record pointer needs to be positioned to the top of the database. Knowing this, ApGen includes in the application the required dBASE programming command go to the top of the database after a filter condition has been defined. Unfortunately, this action will nullify the effect of a record positioning action (e.g., SEEK, GOTO, and LOCATE). When all fields have been entered, press **Ctrl-End** to save the selections.

> **Note** A "work around" for this situation is to use the FOR field in place of a filter condition.

Now take a moment to add a report to the sample application. You want to attach a report form that was built in the earlier chapter on report creation. Place the Report pop-up menu on the work surface and highlight a menu item. Depending on what you named your Report menu items in the previous chapter, you may wish at this time to change the wording of the items, add descriptive text, or resize the window. Press **Alt-I** for the Item menu and select *Override assigned database or view*, toggle ENTERED BELOW, and enter the name of the database associated with the report form you intend to choose. Press **Ctrl-End** to save these changes.

Select *Change action*, *Display or print*, and then *Report*. In the *Print a report* dialog box, enter the report form name or press **Shft-F1** (Pick) to choose from a files list. If the name of the report form is not in the files list shown, you may have to exit ApGen in order to return to the Control Center to add the form to the catalog. Type in an appropriate heading in the *HEADING:* field. Set *Report format:* to FULL DE-TAIL, *Heading format:* to INCLUDE DATE AND PAGE, *Before printing:* to DO NOT EJECT, and *Send output to:* to PRINTER. These settings will produce a report acceptable for most purposes. Press **Ctrl-End** to save the settings.

Labels

When this option is selected from the *Display or print* menu, the dialog box shown in Figure 14-13 is displayed. Here, you may fill in the various fields in order to define a label object. The first field, *FORM name:*, requests the name of a label form. This object may have been already created in the Control Center, in which case you can enter its name in this field or press **Shft-F1** (Pick) to choose a form from a files list, or create the label form by selecting < create > from the files list. In the latter case, you will be automatically transferred to the label generator so that you may define the labels. You

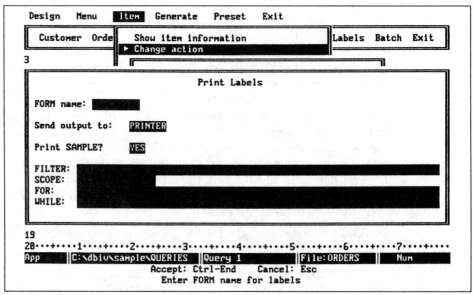

Figure 14-13   *Display or print* menu, Labels dialog box.

can provide the user more flexibility by building a files list that would appear at runtime for the user to choose one of possibly many label forms. This process is covered in the next chapter.

Send Output To This toggle field allows you to customize the destination of the finished set of labels. It has four possible settings. PRINTER directs the label output to the attached printer and is the default setting. The labels are also echoed to the computer's screen. DISK FILE directs the labels to be written to a disk file as they are generated. The name of the output disk file is the same as the name of the label object specified in the *FORM name:* field with a .PRT extension. This is a very useful option because it affords the user the flexibility of printing the labels whenever convenient by using the DOS PRINT command (i.e., printing the labels disk file).

The next setting is SCREEN, which directs the labels to the user's screen only. This would only be appropriate to first visually check the labels before you actually print them. Lastly, the ASK AT RUNTIME option causes a pop-up menu (one that you do not have to define) to appear at runtime for the user to decide where the labels are to go. This last option should be used frequently since it gives the user the most flexibility. At runtime, the user has the same options to choose from as with a report object. If the user selects the FILE option, the labels will be written to a disk file named LABEL.TXT. Since *Send output to:* is a toggle field, you may cycle through each setting by pressing the **Spacebar**.

Print Sample? This field is a YES/NO toggle with a default of YES. It causes a series of test labels to be printed before the actual labels. Accepting this default is usually a good idea, since the test labels will allow you to align the label forms on the printer. However, if you know you will not need these test labels, then you may press the **Spacebar** to select NO. At runtime, if this option is set to YES, one sample label is generated and then the user is prompted with the message "Do you want more samples?" At this time additional sample labels may be generated. Sample labels are generated even if the labels are being directed to the screen only or a disk file.

The last group of fields on this dialog box—*FILTER:*, *SCOPE:*, *FOR:*, and *WHILE:*— determine what records will be considered in the labels. Basically, these fields define the conditions whereby the current database or view is trimmed down to include only the data that is needed for the required set of labels. When all fields have been entered, press **Ctrl-End** to save the selections.

Take this opportunity to add labels to your sample application. Say you wish to attach a label form that was built in the earlier chapter concerning labels creation. Place the Labels pop-up menu on the work surface and highlight a menu item. As was suggested for the Report menu, depending on what you named your menu items in the previous chapter, you may wish at this time to change the wording of the label items, add descriptive text, or resize the window. Press **Alt-I** for the Item menu and select *Override assigned database or view*, toggle ENTERED BELOW, and enter the name of the database associated with the label form you intend to use. Press **Ctrl-End** to save these changes.

Select *Change action*, *Display or print*, and then *Labels*. In the *Print Labels* dialog box, enter the label form name or press **Shft-F1** (Pick) to choose from a files list.

If the name of the label form is not in the files list shown, you may have to exit ApGen in order to return to the Control Center to add the form to the catalog. Set *Send output to:* to PRINTER and *Print SAMPLE?* to YES. These settings will produce labels acceptable for most purposes. Press **Ctrl-End** to save the settings.

Display/List Database File Records

The last item available from the *Display or print* menu is *Display/List*. This simply allows you to attach the output of a Display or List command to a menu item, thus providing for a quick database querying mechanism. The dialog box for constructing a Display/List object is shown in Figure 14-14.

PAUSE at Full Page/Screen? This, the first field in the dialog box, determines whether or not the output resulting from the Display/List object will pause after each 20 lines so the user may view it. The default setting, YES, will cause the pause to occur. Pressing the **Spacebar** will toggle to the NO setting, causing the output to continue uninterrupted. If the output is directed to the screen, such a pause is mandatory. However, if the output is to be printed, no pause is necessary. The number of lines after which a pause occurs may vary if you define a logical window into which the output of a Display/List object is to be placed.

Send Output To This field defines the destination of the output of the Display/List object. It has four possible settings. First, PRINTER directs the Display/List output to the attached printer and is the default setting. The output is also echoed to the

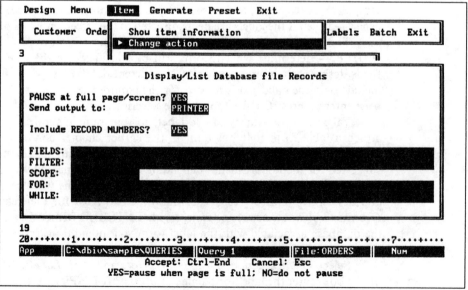

Figure 14-14   *Display or print* menu, Display/list dialog box.

computer's screen. Second is DISK FILE, which directs the output to be written to a disk file as it is generated. The name of the output disk file is always LIST.PRT. This is a very useful option because it affords the user the flexibility of printing the output whenever it is convenient by using the DOS PRINT command (i.e., printing the output disk file).

The next setting is SCREEN, which directs the output to the user's screen only. This is appropriate for only the shortest amount of output, as the user would not want to scroll through many screens of output on the screen only. Lastly, the ASK AT RUN-TIME option causes a pop-up menu (one that you do not have to define) to appear at runtime for the user to decide where the output is to go. This last option should be used frequently, since it gives the user the most flexibility. At runtime, the user has the same options to choose from as with both the report and label objects. If the user selects the FILE option, the labels will be written to a disk file named REPORT.TXT. Since *Send output to:* is a toggle field, you may cycle through each setting by pressing the **Spacebar**.

Include Record Numbers? This is a YES/NO toggle field whose default setting, YES, specifies that database record numbers should be included in the output resulting from a Display/List object. For most applications, however, the NO setting is more appropriate, since a typical user is rarely concerned with the physical record numbers associated with information in a database. Press the **Spacebar** to change the setting.

Fields This field determines which database field values to include in the Display/List object output. You may enter a set of fields or press **Shft-F1** (Pick) to choose them from a fields list. If you do not specify any fields, then all fields from the current database or view will be displayed.

The last group of fields on this dialog box—*FILTER:*, *SCOPE:*, *FOR:*, and *WHILE:*— determine what records will be considered in the Display/List object output. Basically, these fields define the conditions whereby the current database or view is trimmed down to include only the data that is needed for the required output. When all fields have been entered, press **Ctrl-End** to save the selections.

At this point, it would make sense to use a Display/Print object for one of the items in the sample application's Query menu. Begin by placing the Query pop-up menu on the work surface and resize the window in order to make room for another item by pressing **Shft-F7** (Size), **Down Arrow**, and then **Enter**. With the new line highlighted, type *Titles by artist*. Press **Alt-I** for the Item menu and select *Override assigned database or view*. Toggle to ENTERED BELOW and enter TITLES for the name of the database and ARTIST for the ordering. Press **Ctrl-End** to save. Set *PAUSE at full page/screen?* to YES, *Send output to:* to PRINTER, and *Include RECORD NUMBERS?* to NO. For the *FIELDS:* field, press **Shft-F1** (Pick) and select the ARTIST, FIRST_REL, and TITLE fields to be included in the query. Press **Ctrl-End** to save the contents of the dialog box.

This simple query will allow the user to quickly obtain a CD titles list arranged in order by artist's name. The operation could have been implemented as a Browse window, which would have given the user the ability to page forward and backward through the records. With this Display/Print object, records may only be viewed in the forward direction.

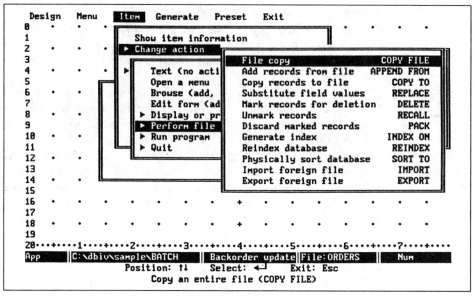

Figure 14-15   *Perform file operation* menu.

Perform File Operation

This *Change action* menu item contains a group of dot prompt commands, each of which may be attached to one of your application's menu items (see Figure 14-15). These dot prompt commands deal with various aspects of your database files. There are commands to manipulate records, make indexes, produce new databases, and provide import/export capabilities. In general, the options available for each file operation are limited when compared to the equivalent Control Center or dot prompt commands.

When a file operation object is selected by the user of your application, messages are displayed on the screen to indicate the success, progress, or failure of the operation. The underlying work surface is used for this purpose. If you wish to have a specific portion of the screen devoted to displaying these messages, then the *Define logical window* option from the Item menu should be used. Moreover, the message displayed and the progress statistics (which is the case when indexes are rebuilt) often confuse the user. A simple message like "Please wait for processing to complete" would be more appropriate. This can easily be done by embedding a few lines of dBASE code before and after the file operation.

Now, the use of each file operation object is thoroughly discussed.

File Copy   This file operation enables the application user to initiate the process of copying one disk file to another. The specific files that are copied must be entered in the dialog box that appears after selecting this option. Figure 14-16 shows this dialog box. First, the file to be copied is entered in the *COPY file:* field and then the destination file is entered in the *TO file:* field. For both selections, the **Shft-F1** (Pick) key may be used.

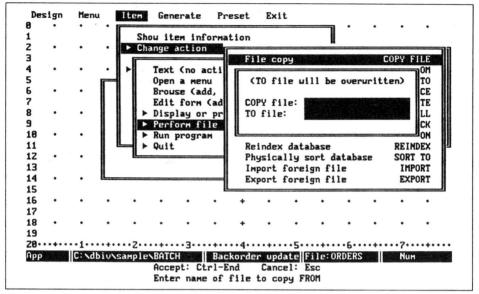

Figure 14-16 *File copy* option dialog box.

Since any type of file may be copied, the files list that appears will show all available filenames. Press **Ctrl-End** to save the entries in these two fields.

The note at the top of the dialog box stresses that the destination file, if it already exists, will be automatically overwritten. ApGen normally executes its generated applications with SET SAFETY (the dBASE feature to prompt the user whether existing files should be overwritten or not) OFF. This is so the user will not be annoyed with these prompt messages during the course of the application's operation. It is assumed that you, the application designer, have already considered the effects of automatically overwriting files.

Rather than specifying the exact filenames for the source and destination files in the copy operation, you may allow the user to choose them from a files list at runtime. This involves the use of a special type of object called a *list*, which will be thoroughly investigated in the next chapter.

There are many uses of the file copying capability, such as making a temporary backup copy of an important database immediately prior to a delicate update operation. If interrupted due to a hardware or power problem the operation would be impossible to restart, so the original database would have to be restored. Another impossible to restart, so the original database would have to be restored. Another use might be to make a period-end "snapshot" database right before a consolidation or purge operation. *File copy* is able to copy any file type, not just databases.

Add Records from File Many times you must take the data from several databases to produce a consolidated report. For example, if you receive daily sales databases from each of several store locations, you would want to combine them in order to produce

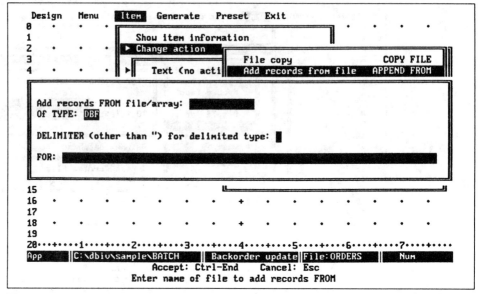

Figure 14-17 *Add records from file* option dialog box.

one master sales journal report for all stores. In this case, the *Add records from file* option may be used to append this information to an existing central sales database.

When you select this option, the dialog box shown in Figure 14-17 appears on the work surface. The first entry field is *Add records FROM file/array:*, which allows you to define the source of the new records. Here you may specify either a filename (normally a .DBF database file) or the name of an array. An array is a special kind of memory variable that may contain many different values, which are stored in what are called *elements*. Its application here is the ability to transfer the contents of the various array elements to corresponding fields in a new database record. Although crucial to effective dBASE programming, arrays are of limited usefulness without extensive use of embedded dBASE code to both declare and manipulate them. You may use **Shft-F1** (Pick) to select a file from which to obtain records.

The next field, *Of TYPE:*, is used to specify the type of data contained in the input file. The default is DBF, but other file types are possible, such as dBASE II, FW2 (Framework II), RPD (*RapidFile), DELIMITED, ARRAY,* SDF (System Data Format), DIF (VisiCalc), SYLK (MultiPlan), and WKS (Lotus 1-2-3 release 1A). You may toggle through these types by pressing the **Spacebar** while positioned in this field.

When you have chosen a database file with a .DBF extension in the previous field, then a DBF type is required here. If you specified an array name, then the ARRAY type is required here. The DELIMITED choice is normally used to append new data from an ASCII file where all character fields are enclosed between some delimiting character (most notably the quotation mark '') and where all the fields are separated by commas. SDF is where the data, also represented in ASCII form, is laid out according to fixed field widths, so that all incoming records are of equal length.

If you choose the DELIMITED file type, then you must enter a special delimiting character in the *DELIMITER (other than '') for delimited type:* field. This is a character that is to be used instead of the default quotation mark to define the beginning and ending of character fields.

The final field in the dialog box is labeled *FOR:*. The function of this field may not be immediately obvious since it would appear that the condition entered here applies to the source database (the file from which the new data is coming). This is not truly the case. When the FOR condition is used, a record in the source database is added to the receiving database only if the resulting record satisfies the FOR condition. Because the FOR condition is evaluated for the new record instead of for the source database record, the results may be somewhat surprising. Care must be taken when using this field.

Once you are done with each entry in the dialog box, press **Ctrl-End** to save the information.

Copy Records to File

For a variety of reasons, you may wish to create "subset" databases from the contents of a master database. For example, you might need to extract all the orders taken by a particular salesperson and place them in a separate database so that it may be sent to the branch office of the salesperson. To handle this situation, the *Copy records to file* option may be used to select the qualifying records and then write them to another database.

When you select this option, the dialog box shown in Figure 14-18 appears on the work surface. The first entry field is *Copy records TO file/array:*, which allows you to

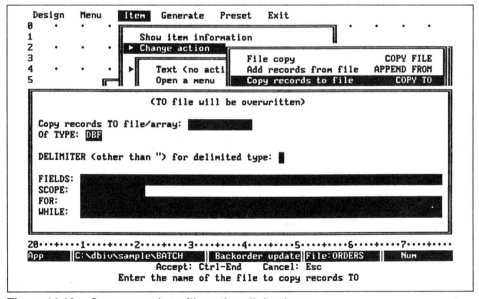

Figure 14-18 *Copy records to file* option dialog box.

define the destination of the new records. Here you may specify either a filename (normally a .DBF database file) or the name of an array. As mentioned before, an array is a special kind of memory variable that may contain many different values stored in what are called "elements." Its application here is the ability to transfer the contents of the various database fields to corresponding array elements. You may use **Shft-F1** (Pick) to select a file to which records will be written.

The next field, *Of TYPE:*, is used to specify the type of file to which the data will be written. The default is DBF, but, as before, other file types are possible, such as dBASE II, FW2 (Framework II), RPD (RapidFile), DELIMITED, ARRAY, SDF (System Data Format), DIF (VisiCalc), SYLK (MultiPlan), and WKS (Lotus 1-2-3 release 1A). You may toggle through these types by pressing the **Spacebar** while positioned in this field.

When you have chosen a database file with a .DBF extension in the previous field, then a DBF type is required here. If you specified an array name, then the ARRAY type is required here. The DELIMITED choice is normally used to write data to an ASCII file where all character fields are enclosed between some delimiting character (most notably the quotation mark ") and where all the fields are separated by commas. SDF is where the data, also written in ASCII form, is laid out according to fixed field widths, so that all outgoing records are of equal length.

If you choose the DELIMITED file type, then you must enter a special delimiting character in the *DELIMITER (other than ") for delimited type:* field. This is a character that is to be used instead of the default quotation mark to define the beginning and ending of character fields.

The *FIELDS:* field lets you choose the fields from each record that will be written to the output file. You may use **Shft-F1** (Pick) to select one or more fields from a fields list. If you leave this field empty, then all fields will be written.

The final three fields in the dialog box are *SCOPE:*, *FOR:*, and *WHILE:*. These define the conditions under which records in the source database shall be copied to the destination database. Along the lines of the example mentioned above, the FOR condition would be entered: *TAKEN_BY = "Darlene"*.

Once you are done with each entry in the dialog box, press **Ctrl-End** to save the information.

Substitute Field Values

This file operation implements a selective "global search and replace" of sorts. Up to five fields in each qualifying record from a database may be updated simultaneously using this option. Note that dBASE IV normally allows many more than five fields to be updated.

Reviewing the dialog box in Figure 14-19, which appears when this option is selected, you see the usual *SCOPE:*, *FOR:*, and *WHILE:* fields. These allow conditions to be set so that only qualifying records are updated. As a sample use, you may wish to replace the TAKEN_BY field for those ORDERS records taken by "Michelle" with a different salesperson's name. Here, the FOR condition would be *TAKEN_ BY = "Michelle"*.

In the lower part of the dialog box, up to five field names may be entered under

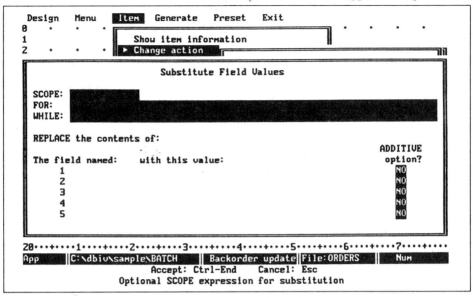

Figure 14-19 *Substitute field values* option dialog box.

the column labelled *The field named:*. Alternately, the fields may be chosen from the fields list window that results from pressing **Shft-F1** (Pick). To the right of the field names, under the column labelled *with this value:*, goes the replacement value, which may be a constant value or calculated expression. In the former case, you could enter *"Frederika"*. If you were doing an across-the-board price increase for all of your CDs in the TITLES database, you might require an expression like **PRICE*1.05** to get a 5% increase.

The last column is labelled *ADDITIVE option?* It is exclusively for memo fields. The default for this toggled field is NO. Changing the default to YES will cause the replacement character strings to be added to the end of the current value of the memo field.

Finally, press **Ctrl-End** to save these entries.

Mark Records for Deletion

This option allows you to define the conditions under which records in the current database should be marked for deletion. Remember that in dBASE IV, records that are deleted are not physically removed from the database immediately. They must be "packed" out during a separate process. A sample use of this file operation might be to delete all records from the ORDERS database that have a SHIP_DATE field one year or more before the current date.

The *SCOPE:*, *FOR:*, and *WHILE:* fields allow such conditions to be defined. Continuing the example, you would enter *SHIP_DATE<( )-365* in the *FOR:* condition field. Figure 14-20 shows the dialog box for this option. To save the conditions, press **Ctrl-End**.

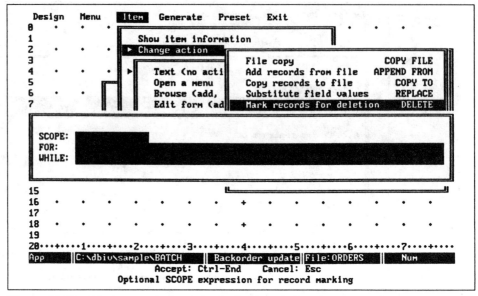

Figure 14-20 *Mark records for deletion* option dialog box.

When the user selects a menu item that is attached to a "delete" operation, the screen displays the message "Marking Records for Deletion", marks each qualifying record as deleted, and then displays how many records were marked.

Unmark Records

Until physically removed from the database, all records marked for deletion may be "recalled" back into an active status. This file operation does exactly that by selectively reversing a previous delete operation. This may prove useful (for example, if for some reason an historical report was mistakenly not run before the yearly purge described earlier). In this case, enter the value ALL for the *SCOPE:* field. This will scan through the database; when a deleted record is found, it will be returned to active use. Figure 14-21 shows the dialog box for *Unmark records* containing the *SCOPE:*, *FOR:*, and *WHILE:* fields. When the conditions for undeleting records have been entered, press **Ctrl-End** to save them.

When the user selects a menu item that is attached to a "recall" operation, the screen displays the message "Recalling Records Marked for Deletion", removes the deleted status for each qualifying record, and then displays how many records were recalled.

Discard Marked Records

This file operation will physically remove from the database any record that is currently marked for deletion. In dBASE terms, this is called a "pack" operation. Any active

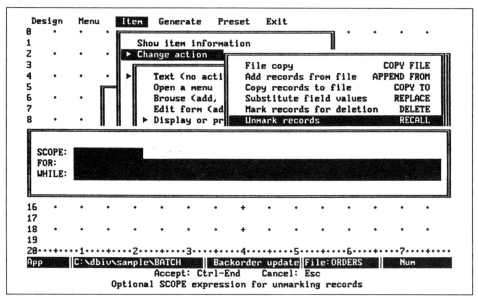

Figure 14-21 *Unmark records* option dialog box.

index files will automatically be updated to reflect the changes in the database. Most dBASE IV applications should have a "pack" selection in one of the utility menus. When the user selects a menu item that is attached to a pack operation, the screen displays the message "Looking for DELETED Records", purges deleted records, and then displays how many records were purged. In addition, messages tracking the progress of the index files being updated appear. The dialog box for this option is shown in Figure 14-22 and requires only that you acknowledge its selection by pressing **Enter** at the "OK" prompt.

Generate Index

For a special report, label, or query, it is often necessary to place the database containing the data into a particular order prior to the actual processing. For example, you may wish a report to be printed for all records in the TITLES database ordered by the date the CD was first released. This report would require the database to be ordered according to the FIRST_REL field. Upon inspecting the TITLES database structure, you notice that this field does not have a corresponding tag in the production .MDX file. You therefore need to create such an index before printing the report. You may define a menu item that is attached to an object that creates either a new tag in the .MDX file or a separate .NDX index file.

In either case, you must supply the following information in the dialog box that appears as shown in Figure 14-23. The first field, *Index KEY expression:*, should contain the field or expression to be used as the index key. In the case mentioned, this would simply be the FIRST_REL field. Next, you must decide whether the keys should

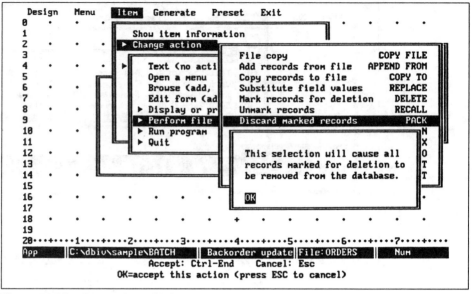

Figure 14-22   *Discard marked records* option dialog box.

be treated as unique or not. For example, if several titles were released on the same date, only the first would be found during a key search of the file.

The default for *Index first key occurrence only (UNIQUE)?* is NO, which is normally what you want, but may be changed to YES if only the first key occurrence is

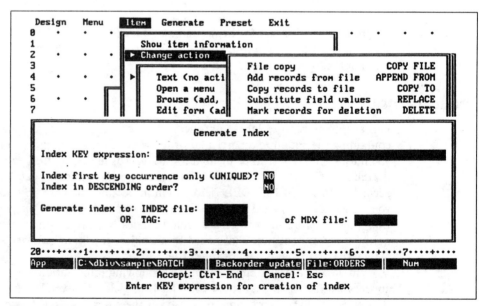

Figure 14-23   *Generate index* option dialog box.

to be kept. The default collating order is ascending. Therefore, the default value for the *Index in DESCENDING order:* field is NO. Specify the name of the .NDX index file in the *Generate index to: INDEX file* field, if that is the type of indexing scheme you wish to use. Otherwise, specify the tag name in the *OR TAG:* field and the .MDX multiple index filename in the *of MDX file:* field.

When done with these entries, press **Ctrl-End** to save all the selections. When the item is chosen by the user at runtime, the index file or tag will be created and the user may then go on to choose the report or other process that uses the new database order.

Reindex Database

This option allows a reindexing operation to be assigned to a menu item. This option is frequently needed to update a database file's associated index files. Reindexing in dBASE IV will rebuild all open .NDX and .MDX index files associated with the current database or view, including the tags inside .MDX files. Multiple index files (.MDX) are less likely to require such a regeneration, since they are tied to the database file they describe. If you use .NDX index files, however, then your application should contain a utility function in one of its menus to allow the user to periodically initiate the action in the event one of the indexes should get out of sync with the database.

The dialog box that appears for this option is shown in Figure 14-24 and requires only that you acknowledge that you have requested it by pressing **Enter** at the "OK" prompt.

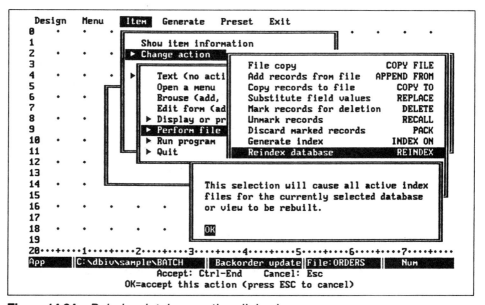

Figure 14-24 *Reindex database* option dialog box.

Physically Sort Database

Normally, getting a database in a certain "order" is achieved via index files in dBASE IV. In certain cases, however, a physical sort is preferred. For example, a sort can be faster overall than building an index file. So if your need for a particular sort sequence is only temporary, you might consider a sort instead of an index. The tradeoff is that you need extra disk space to accept the freshly sorted copy of the original database. Another example involves the efficiency of a frequently used index order which describes a database that is badly "out of order" with respect to that particular index. When this situation arises, the computer's hard disk heads are constantly moving great distances over the disk surface, trying to locate the next record. If the database were periodically sorted according to this frequently used index, the retrieval times would decrease.

The dialog box for this option is shown in Figure 14-25. The *TO file:* field accepts the name of a new .DBF file that will be written to contain the sorted copy of the original database. If this file already exists, it will be automatically overwritten. It is not allowable to request that a file be sorted to itself or to any other open file. Pressing **Shft-F1** (Pick) will yield a files list of all available .DBF files. The *SCOPE:*, *FOR:*, and *WHILE:* fields all work in the traditional ways to limit the number of records included in the sorted output database. Only those records that satisfy these three conditions will be included in the sort and thus written out to the specified file.

Next, you may define up to five fields which will be used as sort keys. You may enter the names of the database fields or press **Shft-F1** (Pick) to choose from a fields list. Associated with each field is a toggle field indicating whether the data is to be

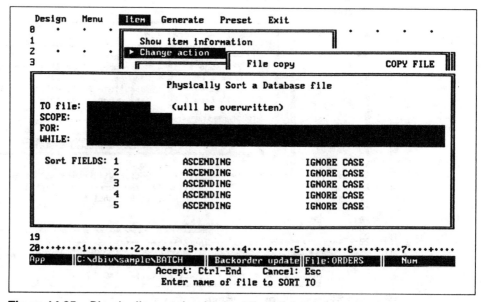

Figure 14-25 *Physically sort database* option dialog box.

sorted ASCENDING (the default) or DESCENDING. You may change from one to the other by pressing the **Spacebar** key. Lastly, since the case (upper- or lowercase letters) of each field may determine its sort sequence, you may request either to IGNORE CASE or USE CASE during the sort operation by pressing the **Spacebar**.

> **Note** Only five sort fields may be specified, even though the dBASE IV maximum is ten.

Import Foreign File

Contemporary software does not believe it exists in a vacuum. With all the different software available, it cannot afford to. dBASE IV accepts this reality by providing a method for "importing" foreign data, that is, data generated from other software and in non-dBASE format, to be copied into a dBASE style database file. This file operation can be attached as an object to a menu item in your application. The dialog box that appears is shown in Figure 14-26.

The *FROM file:* field accepts the name of the disk file containing the data to be imported. This can be any filename that contains data from any of the supported import file formats. You may type the filename or press **Shft-F1** (Pick) to choose a file from the current catalog. The next chapter shows how you can give the user the ability to choose a file from a files list at runtime.

The second field, *of type:*, is a toggle field that cycles through the various supported import file types. Press **Spacebar** to toggle to the type desired. The supported types are PFS, dBASE II, FW2, RPD, and WK1 (Lotus 1-2-3, other than release 1A). If the Lotus 1-2-3 release 1A .WKS format is needed, you must first

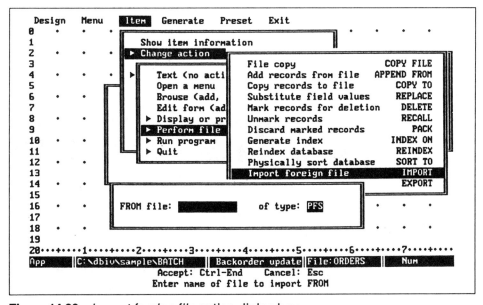

Figure 14-26   *Import foreign file* option dialog box.

convert to .WK1 format using the Lotus translation utility program. You should note that dBASE IV is downward-compatible with the entire dBASE III series of database products, so you do not need to import .DBF files created with these versions. Press **Ctrl-End** to save these entries.

The Import option is particularly useful for bringing in data from a Lotus 1-2-3 worksheet that is the result of calculations and is now in a form that is ready to be loaded into a database file. For example, Lotus 1-2-3 may have been used to prepare an optimal product pricing and discount schedule that is the result of several analytical factors. Once complete, the price list would need to be "imported" from Lotus 1-2-3 and placed in a PRICE database. The only requirement is that the worksheet be stored in tabular form that matches the structure of the receiving database file.

Export Foreign File

This option allows your application to prepare information from a dBASE IV database file to be used by another program. The list of supported export file types is less robust, as it lacks the Lotus 1-2-3 worksheet file type. The dialog box for this option is seen in Figure 14-27.

TO file: field accepts the name of the export (output) file to receive the converted data coming from the database. You may enter any valid DOS filename here or press **Shft-F1** (Pick) to choose an existing file in the current catalog to receive the data. Note that, as the warning in the dialog box indicates, the receiving file will be automatically overwritten. The next chapter shows how you can give the user the ability to choose a file from a files list at runtime.

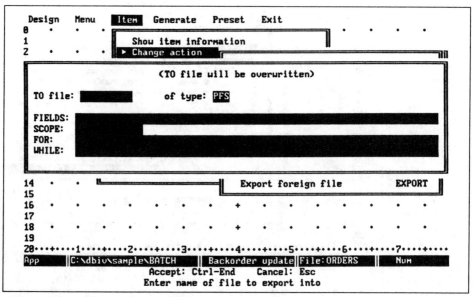

Figure 14-27   *Export foreign file* option dialog box.

The *of type:* field is a toggle field with which you may choose the export file type. The supported types are PFS, dBASE II, FW2, and RPD. Press the **Spacebar** key to cycle through the types. Note that Lotus 1-2-3 is not supported as an export file type. Notice also that dBASE III is not a supported export type. This is because you can directly access a dBASE IV file from dBASE III or III +. Of course, .MDX index files, which are specific to dBASE IV, cannot be referenced in dBASE III or III +.

The *FIELDS:* field allows only selected fields from the database to be exported. You may enter a series of fields or use **Shft-F1** (Pick) to choose them from a fields list. The *SCOPE:*, *FOR:*, and *WHILE:* fields allow you to specify the criteria that determine which records will be written to the export file.

> **Note** > Importing and exporting have become less important lately because many software packages now have the ability to convert their data to and from .DBF format (in fact, the .DBF format is somewhat of a standard now). This means that the *Add records from file* operation is more commonly used than the import feature and the *Copy records to file* is more commonly used than the export feature.

To sidetrack for just a moment, it might be useful to attach a file operation object to an item in the batch process menu. The operation you wish to attach is a simple one: perform a PACK on the ORDERS database to eliminate all records previously marked for deletion. Begin by placing the BATCH pop-up menu on the work surface. There is no need to override the default database since ORDERS is the default database for the application. Press **Alt-I** to pull down the Item menu and select *Change action.* Now select *Perform file operation* and choose the *Discard marked records* function. Acknowledge the ''OK'' prompt by pressing **Enter**. Since a PACK function will result in several messages being displayed on the screen, it is a good idea to define a logical window at a predetermined place on the screen to display the messages. Press **Alt-M** to move to the Menu menu, select *Put away current menu,* and then regenerate the application.

Run Program

With this *Change action* menu selection you may call programs that are entirely external to your ApGen-generated application. The programs may be small dBASE language code segments, entire dBASE language programs, a batch process (which is a sequence of dBASE commands), DOS programs that could have otherwise been run from the DOS prompt, or binary load files that are actually programs written in assembly language and dBASE IV macros (see Figure 14-28). The varied uses of this powerful feature are examined in the next chapter. The Run program menu is shown in Figure 14-28 and the Do dBASE program option dialog box is shown in Figure 14-29.

Quit

Once the user has finished utilizing the various items available from within the application, there must be one last item that provides for a way to leave or exit the application. This menu provides you with two methods of exiting an application. The only difference is what the user wishes to do after leaving. Figure 14-30 shows the Quit menu.

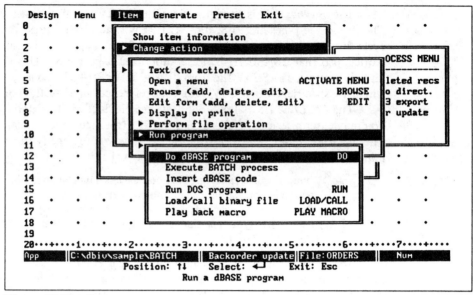

Figure 14-28 *Run program* menu.

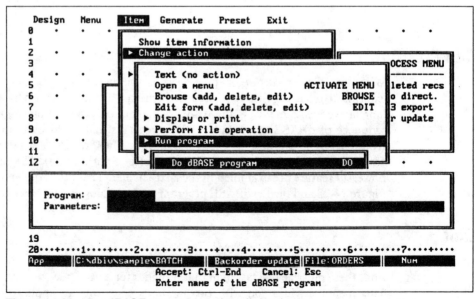

Figure 14-29 *Do dBASE program* option dialog box.

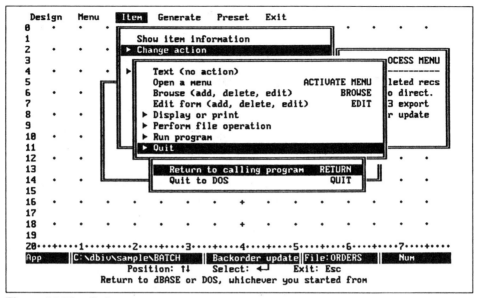

Figure 14-30   Quit menu.

Return to Calling Program When dealing with an ApGen application, the option to "return to calling program" simply means to return to the dBASE IV Control Center. This may be a good way to exit if the user decides to continue work outside the confines of the application. If you know the experience levels of your users ahead of time and they are familiar with the operation of dBASE from either the Control Center or Dot Prompt, then you may decide to include this alternative.

If your application was called from another menu program (possibly also generated by ApGen) whose job it is to organize multiple applications in a structured manner, then this option will return control to this program.

Quit to DOS An alternative to returning to dBASE after leaving an application is to go directly back to the PC's DOS prompt. You would choose this option if your users are inexperienced in using dBASE IV and would not benefit from being returned to the Control Center. In this case, control is most likely passed back, not actually to DOS but to some "user shell" like the one in DOS 4x.

Many applications provide both ways to exit. This is entirely possible and often a good idea since it provides more flexibility. For the more inexperienced users of the application, instructions may be given to not select the "Return to dBASE" option from the application's exit menu.

In our sample application, we want both methods of exiting the application to be available to the user. Place the quit pop-up menu on the work surface and use **Shft-F7**(Size) to expand the window to include one extra item line. The pop-up should now have two item lines. In the first line enter **Return to dBASE IV** and in the second enter **Return to DOS**. Highlight the first item and press **Alt-I**; select *Change action* and then *Quit*. Select the *Return to calling program* option and press **Enter**. Next, from the

Change action menu, press **PgDn** to move to the second item on the exit menu. Select *Quit*, then *Quit* to DOS and then press **Enter**. Put away the exit menu and regenerate the application.

More Ways to Run an Application

The previous chapter showed a simple way to run an application from the Control Center application panel. This method is acceptable if the user has experience in using dBASE IV. In the event that this is not the case, you may wish to "insulate" the user from dBASE and go directly into the application as dBASE IV is loaded. There are two ways to do this.

First, from the DOS prompt, you may reference a program to be run immediately after dBASE IV is loaded, without any user intervention. The only problem is to know the name of the program to run. The previous chapter noted that ApGen generates two programs: CD_DIST.PRG and CD_MAIN.PRG. It is CD_DIST.PRG that must be referenced while still in DOS. Remember that this is the name you gave the application early on during the application design process while filling out the dialog box for the application object. The DOS command is therefore:

DBASE CD_DIST Enter

The second method is to configure the dBASE IV environment so that the same program is automatically run each time dBASE is loaded. This is done through modifying the dBASE IV configuration file CONFIG.DB. In CONFIG.DB is a parameter called COMMAND, which tells dBASE what to enter immediately after it is loaded. Normally COMMAND is set to ASSIST, which brings up the Control Center. You may alter this default by placing the following command in your configuration file:

COMMAND = DO CD_DIST

This will run your application after dBASE IV is loaded, requiring you (or your user) to enter DBASE and then press the **Enter** key at the dot prompt. Now, even though dBASE is configured to bring the application automatically, you may override this COMMAND parameter setting by entering another program name from the DOS prompt after the DBASE command.

Conclusion

This chapter has investigated the majority of available objects that may be attached to menu items in your application. These in turn handle the majority of the requirements that your application may need to fill. You have filled out our sample application to a point at which it may be considered nearly complete, but you have yet to focus your attention on the more advanced uses of ApGen, which include building new objects such as databases, index files, entry forms, reports, and views. You also need to learn how to build batch processes and the various forms of list objects. Finally, you will take a small step toward using the dBASE programming language by including dBASE code segments and complete programs in your application.

15

ApGen—Advanced Features

This chapter completes the discussion of the dBASE IV Applications Generator. It covers the "top-down" approach to systems design by showing how to build additional objects and connect them to an existing application. To illustrate this, a new feature in the sample application is conceived and implemented, and a special method of linking up databases in dBASE IV is demonstrated. In addition, batch processes that the application can use to perform unattended oriented updates are constructed. Files, structure, and values lists are used, to show how important this capability is to the application developer. Also shown is how an application may extend itself even further by calling on external programs and program segments to gain more flexibility. These programs may be of many types: small portions of dBASE language code, entire dBASE language programs, DOS commands, and even programs written in other programming languages such as C or Basic.

The chapter then looks at generating an application, both the program code and system documentation. The last step is to package the application as a somewhat "standalone" system by not requiring dBASE IV to be present in order for the application to execute. For this, the dBASE IV RunTime system, which is included in the Developer's Edition, is investigated.

Top-Down Application Design

As described in earlier chapters, a very valid approach to constructing a new application is to first build its structure in the form of a menuing system, but without any objects actually existing. This approach is often a motivating one, since you can immediately visualize the application as it is being built, and fill in the blanks as you go. Up to now, however, the concentration has been on connecting up existing objects to the application's shell. To illustrate the new "top-down" approach involves building several new objects as you attempt to define each menu item requiring these objects.

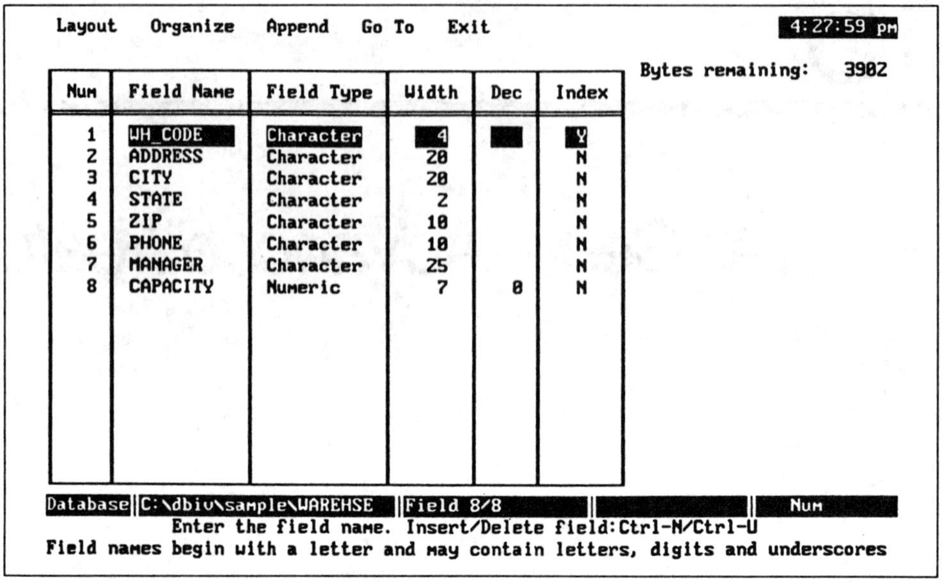

```
    Layout    Organize    Append    Go To    Exit                4:27:59 PM

                                                        Bytes remaining:    3902
  ┌─────┬────────────┬────────────┬───────┬───────┬───────┐
  │ Num │ Field Name │ Field Type │ Width │  Dec  │ Index │
  ├─────┼────────────┼────────────┼───────┼───────┼───────┤
  │  1  │ WH_CODE    │ Character  │   4   │       │   Y   │
  │  2  │ ADDRESS    │ Character  │  20   │       │   N   │
  │  3  │ CITY       │ Character  │  20   │       │   N   │
  │  4  │ STATE      │ Character  │   2   │       │   N   │
  │  5  │ ZIP        │ Character  │  10   │       │   N   │
  │  6  │ PHONE      │ Character  │  10   │       │   N   │
  │  7  │ MANAGER    │ Character  │  25   │       │   N   │
  │  8  │ CAPACITY   │ Numeric    │   7   │   0   │   N   │
  │     │            │            │       │       │       │
  │     │            │            │       │       │       │
  └─────┴────────────┴────────────┴───────┴───────┴───────┘
  Database C:\dbiv\sample\WAREHSE    Field 8/8                        Num
              Enter the field name. Insert/Delete field:Ctrl-N/Ctrl-U
       Field names begin with a letter and may contain letters, digits and underscores
```

Figure 15-1   Structure of WAREHSE.DBF.

Say you want to give your sample application a new feature. You want to add the capability for the CD distribution company to store its inventory in several warehouses. To implement this, you need to create another database, WAREHSE.DBF, which must contain information describing the specific warehouse facility (e.g., warehouse code, address, phone number, manager's name, capacity, etc.). Figure 15-1 shows the specific structure of this database. Each warehouse will stock only certain CD titles, and some titles may be stocked in several warehouses. In other words, warehouse A may stock many titles and title B may be found in many warehouses. This is a classic *many-to-many relationship* in database design, one that is very common in real-world business situations. Note further that the field named NO_IN_STOC in the TITLES database must be removed, since you now are concerned with not only the total quantity in stock for a particular title but also the quantity in stock at each warehouse.

In order to solve the many-to-many problem presented here, you need to create yet another database, TW_LINK.DBF, which will contain the "intersection" of the titles and warehouses. The structure of this database is shown in Figure 15-2. The first field contains the title ID number, that is, the same information stored in the ID_NUMBER field in the TITLES database. The second field contains the warehouse code as stored in the WH_CODE field in the WAREHSE database. The final field contains the number in stock for the specific title in the specific warehouse. For example, one record in this new database might say that there are 12 copies of CD ART-103948 in warehouse WH01. This means that inventory information for a title may be easily obtained by searching for all TW_LINK records containing the ID number for the CD in question and summing the NO_IN_STOC field values. Similarly, inventory information for an entire warehouse may be obtained by searching for all records containing the warehouse code in question. The last query, however, would only give you a bulk

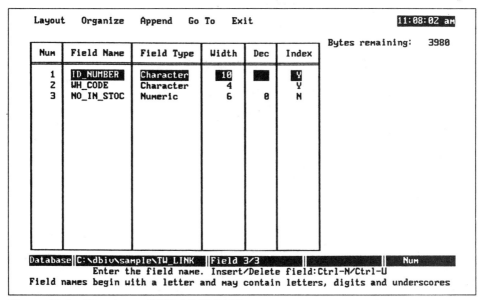

Figure 15-2   Structure of TW_LINK.DBF.

CD total regardless of title. dBASE IV's Query by Example can handle this structure and these types of queries easily.

Building New Database Objects

To begin, you need to build the additional databases. Instead of returning to the Control Center, you can create them right in ApGen. Following the top-down approach, you must first modify the structure of the application. From the ApGen worksurface, press **Alt-D** to pull down the Design menu and select *Pop-up menu*. From the pick list, choose the TITLES menu. You should now see the menu you created in Chapter 13. In order to add new options to this menu, you need to enlarge it. Press **Shft-F7** (Size), press **Down Arrow** three times, and then press **Enter**. Move the highlight down to the first blank line and enter a series of hyphens to act as a separator between the old options and the ones you are about to add. Next, move down again and enter *Inventory maint.* on this line and *Warehouse maint.* on another. The revised menu should look like the one shown in Figure 15-3.

Now, with the highlight placed over the warehouse maintenance option, press **Alt-I** to access the Item menu. Select *Override assigned database or view*, toggle to ENTERED BELOW, and press **Enter**. You should be positioned in the *Database/view:* field, so press **Shft-F1** (Pick) to see the list of available databases. On the pick list, you will notice that < create > is also an option. This is how you can use ApGen in a top-down manner, since you can create new database objects directly from within ApGen. Select < create > and you will automatically be transferred to the Database design screen just as if you were in the Control Center. Fill in the field names, types, lengths,

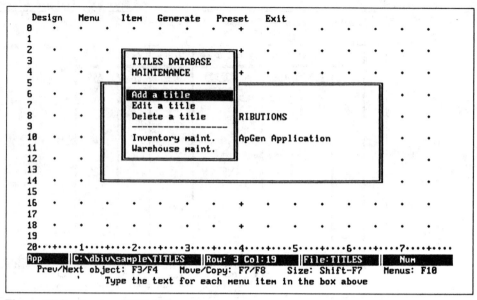

Figure 15-3   Revised TITLES pop-up menu.

and indexes according to Figure 15-1, and then press **Alt-E** to save the structure. When prompted with ''Save as'', enter *WAREHSE* and press **Enter**.

You have just created a database object, this time from within ApGen. Notice that when you save the database structure, you are not returned to where you came from. You are placed inside the TITLES pop-up menu on the ApGen work surface, not the Item menu. You will witness throughout ApGen that it occasionally loses its place when used in a top-down manner. This is not a problem, since you can easily return to where you were by repeating the preceding process to get to the *Override assigned database or view* dialog box. This time, from the *Database/view:* field, when you press **Shft-F1** to see the available databases, WAREHSE.DBF appears. Select this database and enter WH_CODE in the ORDER field.

To complete the definition for this menu item, perform the following steps. First, you must assign an object to the menu item. In this case, you could define a new screen form object to attach to the item; instead, simply use a Browse window. Do this in the familiar manner, by selecting *Change action* from the Item menu and then selecting *Browse*. In the Browse window object dialog box you may accept all of the defaults or customize the Browse according to your desires. Furthermore, you can scale down the Browse object and place it in a logical window. Also, do not forget to define a message-line prompt and write some help information for the user. Now, press **Alt-M** to pull down the Menu menu and select *Save current menu*. Press **Escape** to return to the TITLES pop-up menu.

Move the highlight up one menu item to the *Inventory maint.* option and press **Alt-I** to access the Item menu again. You wish to repeat the process of creating a new database object to associate with a new menu option. This time, you need to create the many-to-many linkage database, as previously discussed. The structure of this database was shown in Figure 15-2. For purposes that will become clear later, you need to define two additional index tags in the multiple index file for this new database—namely, a tag named TXW using the index expression **WH_CODE + ID_NUMBER** and another named WXT using the expression **ID_NUMBER + WH_CODE**. You can build these tags from the Organize menu from within database design. They will enable you to look at both sides of the many-to-many relationship.

Building New Query Objects

The way you will finish creating this database differs from the way you created WAREHSE.DBF because you also need to build new query objects, a process that must be done at this point. The method with which you will access QBE from inside ApGen is a somewhat tricky and undocumented path. After you have entered the fields for the linkage database, press **Alt-L** to pull down the Layout menu. Highlight and select the *Save this database file structure* option; when prompted, save the structure to TW_ LINK.DBF and then press **Enter**. Now that the structure is saved, press **Alt-A** to pull down the Append menu and select the *Enter records from keyboard* option. This will place you in a generic Edit form for the new database, although you do not wish to actually add any records at this time. The next step is to press **Alt-E** for the Exit menu and notice that there is a third option this time, *Transfer to Query Design*. This is your entry point to Query-by-Example.

Basically, you have to build your new query objects now, because this is your only chance to enter Query by Example. First, you had to save the new database structure so that you could enter records. Next, you had to pretend to want to add new records so that you could enter QBE. It is a long way around, but for top-down ApGen developers, this is the only path into designing a new query object. In any case, select the *Transfer to Query Design* option in order to enter the Query design screen.

The first thing you see once you are in QBE should resemble Figure 15-4. Here, the file skeleton for TW_LINK.DBF and a view skeleton containing each field from the database are automatically deposited on the design surface by QBE. Although a more intuitive arrangement of the files might serve your purposes, here you need to make use of what you have. You also need the two other databases that will be part of the many-to-many relationship you are about to define. Begin by pressing Alt-L to pull down the Layout menu, and select *Add file to query* and then TITLES.DBF from the files list. A new file skeleton is added to the Query design screen. Repeat this process to add a file skeleton for the WAREHSE.DBF too. The Query design screen should now be fully populated with three file skeletons and one view skeleton. You are now ready to establish the relationships between the databases.

Start by positioning to the TW_LINK file skeleton using **F3** (Previous) or **F4** (Next). Highlight the ID_NUMBER field using the **Tab** or **Back-Tab** keys. Press **Alt-L** and select *Create link by pointing*. This will insert the word LINK1 under the ID_ NUMBER field name in the file skeleton. This is a special name called an "example variable" that is used by QBE to relate databases. You can also enter example variables manually, which may be a better idea since you can use more meaningful names. To complete the link, press **F4** (Next) to get to the TITLES file skeleton, highlight the ID_

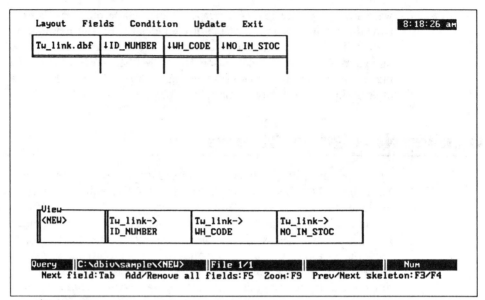

Figure 15-4 Initial new query object design.

NUMBER field, and press **Enter**. Notice that LINK1 appears here also. Now you must link the TW_LINK and WAREHSE databases. Repeat the preceding process by linking the databases using the WH_CODE field in each database as the linking field. For the second link, the example variable LINK2 is used in the related file skeletons. The next order of business involves advising QBE which database to use as the controlling database. In this case, the controlling database must be TW_LINK. Position to the TW_LINK file skeleton's ID_NUMBER field, and with the keyboard in Insert mode, enter the word *EVERY* before the LINK1 example variable. In the relationships set by QBE when the query is saved, the keyword EVERY will cause TW_LINK to be the center.

Now attend to the order in which the records will be accessed in the relationship. This is needed because there is no way from within QBE to select or activate a specific index tag from the .MDX file of a file skeleton. Whenever there are relationships between databases, however, the orderings of the databases involved are of extreme importance. The primary order—that is, the order of TW_LINK—must be by ID_ NUMBER. Therefore, highlight once again the ID_NUMBER field in the TW_LINK file skeleton and press **Alt-F** to bring down the Files menu. From here, select *Sort on this field* and then *Ascending ASCII*. The sort label Asc1 will be placed under the ID_ NUMBER field, to the right of EVERY LINK1, separated by a comma. Finally, perform this same process for the ID_NUMBER field of the TITLES skeleton and the WH_CODE field of the WAREHSE file skeleton. At this point the many-to-many relationship has been set.

The next step is to build the view skeleton so that only the desired fields from each of the three databases will appear in the query results. Press **F4** (Next) until you are positioned on the view skeleton. Highlight the leftmost field, TW_LINK->ID_NUM-

BER, press **F6** (Select), extend the selection to the right in order to encompass all three fields in the view skeleton, and then press **Enter**. Press **F5** (Field) to remove the fields from the view skeleton. This is necessary since you want to build the view skeleton manually. In particular, the order of the fields in the view skeleton is important when the user views the query results.

Now you may select pertinent fields from each database. Begin by moving to the TITLES file skeleton, position first to the ID_NUMBER field and press **F5**, then position to the TITLE field and press **F5**. The two fields from the TITLES database should now be in the view skeleton. Next, move to the WAREHSE database, position to the WH_CODE field, and press **F5**. Finally, move to the TW_LINK database, position to the NO_IN_STOC field, and press **F5**. The resulting Query design screen should resemble the one shown in Figure 15-5.

Now that the query is defined, it is time to save the file. There are two options here: You may press **Alt-E** to pull down the Exit menu in order to save the query, or you may press **Alt-L** for the Layout menu and select *Save this query*. The latter approach is useful if you need to define more than one query, since you may save the current query, define another, and then save that to another query file. In the case of your sample application, you could decide to define the Warehouses by Title orientation of the many-to-many relationship. (The opposite view, Titles by Warehouse, is left for you to complete on your own.) This second query, TXW, will actually be used in the upcoming section dealing with reports.

Whether you define more than one query or not, you eventually will need to exit QBE. When you do exit, a prompt appears for the name of the query file to be created with a .QBE extension. For the current query, enter *WXT*, indicating the Warehouses

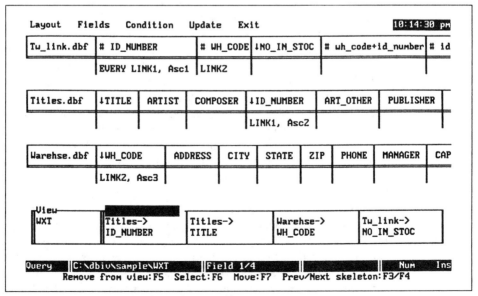

Figure 15-5   Completed new query object design.

by Title orientation. As you exit Query Design, notice that you are not returned to ApGen. This is a shortcoming of utilizing ApGen in a top-down manner—it cannot remember where you started. So, from the Control Center, move to the Application panel and press **Shft-F2** to return to the ApGen work surface. Notice that ApGen did remember that the TITLES pop-up menu was on the work surface at the time you left to enter QBE, so it is automatically brought up again.

Building New Screen Form Objects

As with the first new database object you created, you need to attach TW_LINK to a menu option. Override the assigned database for the Inventory maintenance option (*Inventory maint.*) in the same manner as before. You also need to attach an action to the menu item. From the Item menu, select *Change action* and then choose *Edit form* as the object type. You will now see how it is possible to create a new data entry screen form from within ApGen. Once in the Edit form dialog box, and while the cursor is in the *FORMAT file*: field, press **Shft-F1** (Pick) and view the file list that appears. Select the <create> item in this pick list and you will automatically be transferred to the Screen Design utility, normally only accessible from the Control Center.

Once inside Screen Design, the Layout menu is open and the *Use different database file or view* option is highlighted. Since you transferred here from ApGen, no actual database file was previously opened, so you must do so now. Press **Enter**, and from the file list that appears, select TW_LINK.DBF. You will be returned to the screen design work surface, but first you need to go back to the Layout menu. Press **Alt-L** and then select *Quick Layout*. As discussed in a.previous chapter, this will produce a generic screen, but after some massaging, it should resemble Figure 15-6. Once you have finished designing the new screen object, press **Alt-E** for the Exit menu, select *Save changes and exit*, and then for *Save as*: enter *TW_LINK*.

This will place you back in ApGen (actually in the TITLES pop-up menu). Return back to the Edit form dialog box and this time from the file list for the *FORMAT file*: field select the newly created TW_LINK form. You may choose to accept all the defaults for the Edit form dialog box, but you should probably toggle the *Mode*: field to Edit so that records may be edited as well as added. Save the Edit form object by pressing **Ctrl-End**. After writing a message-line prompt and entering help text, go to the Menu menu, put away the current menu, and save your changes.

Do not forget to modify the TITLES database. Remember, you added a field to TW_LINK that will contain the number of copies of a specific title stocked in a specific warehouse. This being the case, you no longer need this field in the TITLES database. Obviously, this will require you to modify the structure of the database. Unfortunately, this need illustrates one deficiency in ApGen—its inability to modify an existing object, such as a database, view, screen form, report, and so on. You can create these objects, but cannot modify them once they are created. Consequently, you must temporarily exit ApGen and return to the Control Center, position to the Data Panel, highlight TITLES, and press **Shft-F2** (Design). Delete the NO_IN_STOC field, save the structure, and then return to ApGen. Any screen forms for the TITLES database that reference this field must also be modified; but again, this must be done from the Control Center.

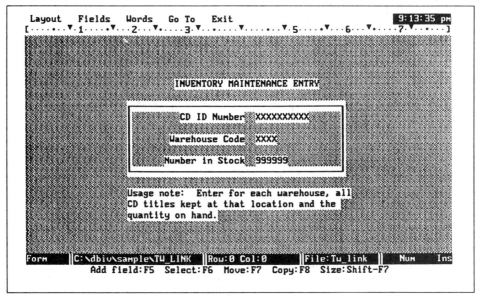

Figure 15-6   New data entry screen object for TW_LINK database.

Building New Display/List Objects

Now it is time to use the WXT.QBE file previously created. From the ApGen work surface, press **Alt-D** to pull down the Design menu and select *Pop-up menu*. From the pick list, choose the QUERIES menu. You should now see the menu you created in Chapter 13. In order to add new options to this menu, you need to enlarge it. Press **Shft-F7** (Size), press **Down Arrow** enough times to make room for two more options, and then press **Enter**. Move down to the first blank item and enter *Titles by Warehouse* on this line and *Warehouses by Title* on another. The revised menu should look like the one shown in Figure 15-7.

Highlight the *Warehouses by Title* option, press **Alt-I** for the Item menu, and then select *Override assigned database or view*. Toggle the field setting to ENTERED BELOW and press **Shft-F1** (Pick) to bring up the file list.

> **Note** In the files pick list, both .DBF and .QBE files are listed. This is because query files represent "logical databases" consisting of relationships between "physical databases."

Highlight and select WXT.QBE and press **Ctrl-End** to save. Now select *Change action* from the Item menu, select *Display or print*, and then select *Display/List*. Inside the Display/List dialog box, specify SCREEN for the *Send output to:* field and NO for the *Include RECORD NUMBERS?* field. Press **Ctrl-End** to save. Press **Alt-M** and select *Put away current menu* and *Save changes*.

The query pop-up is now removed from the ApGen work surface, although you could have defined another Display/List object for the other many-to-many orientation

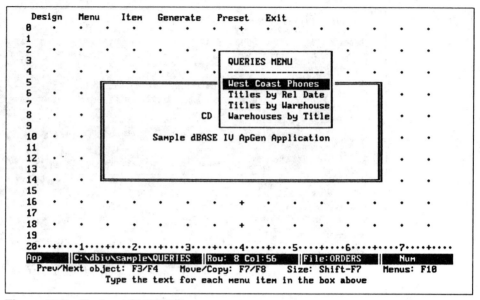

Figure 15-7 Revised QUERIES pop-up menu.

using the TXW.QBE query file. Once you generate the final application and select this query menu item, you should see query results similar in nature to the results shown in Figure 15-8. Here, the display is organized primarily by ID_NUMBER (CD identification number) and within ID_NUMBER, the detail lines are organized by WH_CODE (warehouse code). The orderings selected do not dictate that the detail lines should be in CD title order.

If your query results do not match those shown in Figure 15-8, then the .QBE file must have been defined slightly differently. The most likely problem would be in the manner in which the databases are related. You will see that when linking up databases in QBE, the *order of the link* is dictated by QBE in interesting ways. This means that if you want to link WAREHSE.DBF to TW_LINK to TITLE, in that order, you may, in fact, get the opposite order. The order in which you deposit the file skeletons on the query design surface does not matter, and the way you define the example variables also has no effect. Using the EVERY keyword adjacent to the example variables will help out this situation.

The precise results of defining a multiple database view with QBE may be determined by looking at the generated .QBE file. This requires a knowledge of programming, however, and is the subject of a later section of this chapter. Moreover, you may modify the .QBE file to better suit your requirements. One problem with the implementation of dBASE IV Query by Example is that, unlike most other design surfaces, it is not controlled by an underlying template that defines how the QBE program code is to be generated. Ashton-Tate is in the process of making QBE template-driven (in fact, future QBE templates will generate SQL code in addition) in a future release of the product, but until then you must get what you can out of a limited situation.

```
                                                 Ins    Num     ReadOnly
                ID_NUMBER  TITLE                 WH_CODE NO_IN_STOC
                CAR-1002-1 Cary in Venice        1002         7
                DAR-0049-0 Darlene Out in Mexico 1001         1
                JIM-4000-1 Jimbo Appears in Nihon 1003       21
                KIN-2330-0 The King Family       1002        10
                KIN-2330-0 The King Family       1005        11
                MAR-5550-1 Martin Goes Out       1004        16
                MAR-6559-5 Victoria: Live in L.A. 1001       45
                MAR-6559-5 Victoria: Live in L.A. 1002       40
                MAR-6559-5 Victoria: Live in L.A. 1004       23
                MIC-4490-1 Victoria in the Clouds 1003       19
                NAT-2293-0 Nathan's Best Hits    1005         9
                RRY-1101-1 Paul in Concert       1004         4
                Press any key to continue...
```

Figure 15-8   Query results for Warehouse by Title relationship.

Building New Report Objects

Report objects may also be defined and incorporated into an application directly from within ApGen. To illustrate this capability, you will build a new report that requires the second QBE file, TXW.QBE, that was suggested in a prior section of this chapter. Remember, this query file establishes an environment for processing CD titles by Warehouse. The result of this query (the report in the current example) would be a list showing all of the titles stored at each warehouse. Instead of just displaying this information, as in the last section, a report form will be defined so the user can get a printed copy of the list.

Begin by pulling down the Design menu by pressing **Alt-D**, and once again select *Pop-up menu*. From the pick list, choose *REPORTS*. You should now see the menu you created in a previous chapter. Enlarge the menu window to accommodate another item. In the available slot, enter **Titles by Warehouse Report**. The revised menu should look like the one shown in Figure 15-9.

Now highlight the new item, press **Alt-I** for the Item menu, and then select *Change action* followed by *Display or print* and *Report*. Once inside the Print a Report dialog box, press **Shft-F1** (Pick) in the first field, which is labelled *FORM name:*. Although you may see various report form names in the list, you should select <create>. This is your entrance to the Report Design surface from within ApGen. You should be automatically transferred to report design, but it is quite possible that no database is currently open for which a report is to be defined. In this event, a small dialog box will appear, requesting the name of a database filename. This situation actually presents a problem, because this dialog box incorrectly accepts .DBF file-

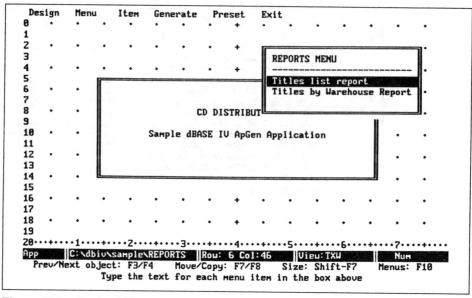

Figure 15-9 Revised Reports menu.

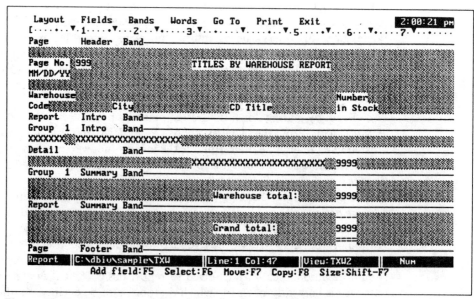

Figure 15-10 New report object: Titles by Warehouse Report.

names, not .QBE filenames. If you enter the name of a .QBE file, dBASE IV will respond with an error message claiming that the name of the file entered is not that of a .DBF file, which is quite true. Unfortunately, for this report you do not wish to use a .DBF file. Using **Shft-F1**, you can see, will only present .DBF files.

Luckily, there is a work-around for this limitation. Simply enter the name of a database file, say *TW_LINK.DBF*, and then proceed to the report design surface. Once there, you will see that the Layout menu is already pulled down for you. Immediately select *Use different database file or view* in order to remedy the problem. The key word in the title of this Layout menu option is the "view." Press **Shft-F1** to obtain a list of available files and now both .DBF and .QBE files are listed. It is not known why the previous dialog box would not accept QBE filenames. Select the file TXW.QBE.

Now start designing your new report. Begin by pressing **Alt-L** to get the Layout menu; then select *Quick layouts* and *Column Layout*. This will get you going with a simple columnar report containing all the fields in the environment dictated by the TXW.QBE view file. However, you need to modify the report's structure slightly before proceeding.

As usual when building a new report, the default column titles (database field names) should be changed to more meaningful English phrases. Next, it would make sense for this report to include a Group band, based on the field value for the WH_ CODE field of the TXW.QBE view. This will cause a report break for each unique warehouse code. Also, the values for both the WH_CODE and CITY fields should be moved to the Group band from the Detail band. This way the warehouse-specific fields will appear only once on the report instead of being repeated for each title. Finally, a new field should be added to the Group summary band to print the stock total for each particular warehouse. To do this, position to the Group summary band and move the cursor to the column in which the new field's value is to appear on the report. Press **Alt-F** to pull down the Fields menu and highlight the Sum option in the SUMMARY column of the field definition screen. In the dialog box that appears, fill in *WH_SUM* for the *Name*: field, *WH group summary* for the *Description:* field, *NO_IN_STOC* for the *Field to summarize on:* field, and alter the default *Template:* field value to *9999*. You may complete the report by adding any kind of cosmetic niceties that might strike your fancy. The Titles by Warehouse Report should now resemble the report design shown in Figure 15-10.

Now that you are happy with the definition of the new report, press **Alt-E** for the Exit menu and select *Save changes and exit*. Next, you will be asked to name the new report. Enter *TXW* in response to this prompt. At this instant, control is transferred back to the ApGen design surface with the REPORTS menu displayed.

Now you must attach the newly created report form to your application. With the Titles by Warehouse item highlighted in the REPORTS menu, press **Alt-I** for the Item menu, select *Change action*, *Display or print*, and *Report*. You were here once before, just prior to building your new report, but ApGen forgot where to return you. No matter, though; press **Shft-F1** in the *FORM name*: field of the Print a Report dialog box. From the list, choose TXW. Continue by toggling the *Heading format:* field to INCLUDE DATE AND PAGE, toggling the *Before printing:* field to DO NOT EJECT, and then pressing **Ctrl-End** to save the application object.

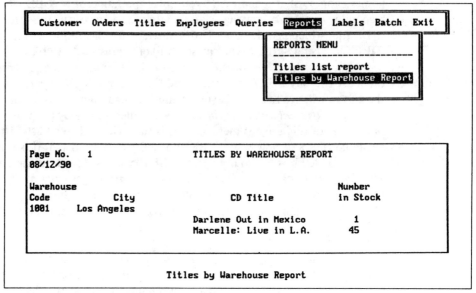

Figure 15-11   Titles by Warehouse Report running in window.

Again, from the Item menu, select *Override assigned database or view* and toggle the *For this item you may use values:* field to ENTERED BELOW. Press **Shft-F1** for the *Database/view:* field and select TXW.QBE. The last ingredient for our new report might be the addition of a logical window in which to display the report's results.

> **Note** This is a common ApGen technique used to combat the fact that a report takes over the screen when it prints, since the output is also echoed to the screen. By routing the report to a window, you can preserve the contents of the application's screen, such as the horizontal bar menu.

From the Item menu, select *Define logical window* and for the *Window NAME:* field, enter ***REP_WIN***, and define the window's screen coordinates. (Use 12,0 for the upper left corner and 20,79 for the lower right corner.) You'll find that a window of this size adequately provides a porthole of sorts with which you may view the report on the screen as it prints on the printer. If you generate the application at this point, run the program, and select this new report, you should see something similar to the results shown in Figure 15-11. Notice how the report scrolls entirely within the borders of the logical window, thus preserving the horizontal bar menu as well as the Reports pop-up menu. Once the report is completed, both on the screen and in printed form, the window and its contents are cleared from the application screen.

List Objects

Another class of objects available to include in an application is the *list*. Lists are special objects that drastically improve the user interface of an application by providing a vehicle whereby users may use the "point-and-shoot" method of choosing between a multitude of possible items. In system development terms, such technology is called a *pick list*. Consider the user wishing to print a regional sales report, where all the valid regions are coded and reside in a special database called REGION.DBF. With a pick list, the user is presented with a window containing the contents of the region database, and can highlight an entry in the window and have the report act on it—namely, print the sales report for only the region selected.

Now consider the case where a user wishes to customize the amount of information appearing on a Query screen. With a pick list, the user is presented with a series of database fields from the database or view that represents the source of data for the query. All the user has to do is highlight one or more fields to be included and then execute the query with the selected fields. Finally, consider the user who needs to export a daily transaction file to a spreadsheet program for analytical processing. Again, with a pick list, the user only has to highlight the file to export and then have the application process the request.

Each of these example requirements identifies one of the three types of list objects available in ApGen:

Values lists are used to display the values contained in a specific fields in the currently active database or view.

Structure lists are used to display the fields in the currently active database or view.

Files lists are used to display all files that match a specified file search pattern.

The next three sections of this chapter deal with examining all types of list objects. In doing so, you will add various features to your sample application that will make your users' lives a bit more pleasant, and will also expand the flexibility of the application.

Values Lists As described earlier, a values list adds the capability of inserting a pop-up pick-list window before an object is executed, allowing the user to choose a value of a predetermined database on which the operation of the object is to be based. The ease of use afforded the application using values lists (as well as list objects in general) is considerable. Pick lists are an important ingredient in any contemporary user interface.

To illustrate the use and implementation of values lists, add one such object to your sample application. Specifically, you must identify an existing object that would benefit from the addition of a values list. The QUERIES menu is a good place to start, since queries, by definition, require input from the user to determine the query's scope of processing. What better method of selection than a pop-up window containing the values from which to choose?

Begin by clearing the application design surface from any remaining objects and then press **Alt-D** to access the Design menu. Continue by selecting *Pop-up menu*, then choose *QUERIES* and press **Enter** to place the pop-up on the design surface. Highlight the menu option *Warehouses by Title*. With this option highlighted, press **Alt-I** to access the Item menu and select *Change action*. You previously defined an action for this menu option, but now you want to modify it. Select *Open a menu* here, and in the

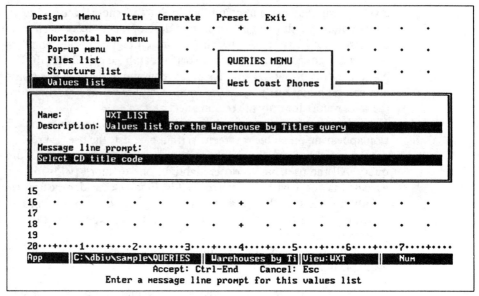

Figure 15-12 Dialog box for defining a list object.

dialog box that appears, toggle the *Menu type:* field to VALUES and enter *WXT_LIST* for the *Menu name:* field.

What you have done here is to redefine the object immediately attached to the menu option. Before, it was simply a Display/List object; now you are about to attach a list object. Whenever the user selects a menu option with a list object attached, the list object springs into action, displaying whatever you have arranged to have displayed inside a pop-up window. You will arrange to have a list of CD title codes placed in the window from which the user will choose. It should be noted at this point that a list object, especially a values list, should seldom be attached directly to a horizontal bar menu with attached pull-down menus, because lists tend to be rather slow in producing their results. You will see what this means when you actually generate the sample application at the end of this section. If a list object is attached to a horizontal bar menu, the user may get frustrated pressing **Left** and **Right Arrow** keys to move from option to option. Each time the user positions to a horizontal bar menu option with an attached list object, a period of time must pass for the object to display its results. This period of time is normally too great for most users to tolerate.

Next, press **Alt-D** to access the Design menu again. This time select the *Values list* option and then <create>. For each list object created, regardless of its type (i.e. values, structure, or files), the dialog box shown in Figure 15-12 must be filled out. The *Name:* field will allow you to identify the list object whenever you request, via **Shft-F1** (Pick), a list of such objects in appropriate places in ApGen. The *Description:* field is used during the system documentation generation process. The *Message line prompt:* field will appear whenever the user selects the menu option to which the list object is attached. Some thoughtful message should be entered here to help the user understand what is being selected. Press **Ctrl-End** to save the contents of the dialog box.

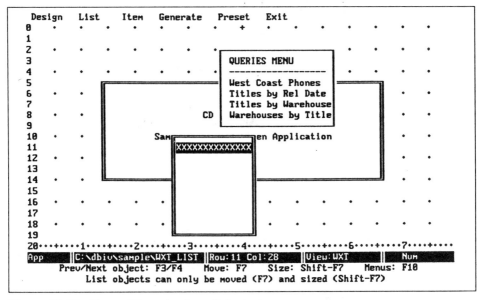

Figure 15-13   Repositioned values list window.

At this point the new list object window should appear on the application design surface, albeit likely in the wrong place. You may use the **F7** (Move) and **Shft-F7** (Size) keys to position the window to a place of your liking. The default width of the window is 14 characters. If the contents of the field is to contain values for a database field whose length is greater than 14, then you may widen the window. However, you are unable to shrink the window to less than the default width. The repositioned list object window should appear as in Figure 15-13.

Notice now that a new menu is listed on the top of the application design surface. The List menu, a special menu for list objects, is now activated since such an object is currently active on the design surface. Press **Alt-L** to access the List menu. The menu should be as shown in Figure 15-14.

The first thing that needs to be done for a values list object is to define the database or view to supply the data to be displayed inside the list window. In our case, we wish to activate the TITLES database, since it will provide the desired list of all CD title codes. Select the *Override assigned database or view* option from the List menu and toggle the *For this list you may use values:* field to ENTERED BELOW. For the *Database/view:* field that becomes accessible, enter *TITLES.DBF* and then **Ctrl-End**.

Next, select the *Identify field values in list* menu option. In the small dialog box that appears, enter the field name ID_NUMBER in the *Field to list values for:* field. Pressing **Enter** after this value will return you to the List menu. You could also use **Shft-F1** (Pick) to select a field name from a pick list. It is the function of this List menu option to tell the values list object which database/view field will supply the data for the window.

Before putting away the list object, the most important detail is still left to be settled: what should be done *after* the user has selected a value from the pick list. To

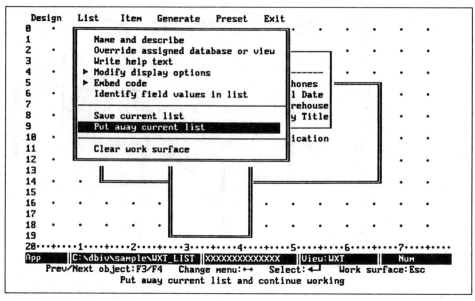

Figure 15-14 List menu.

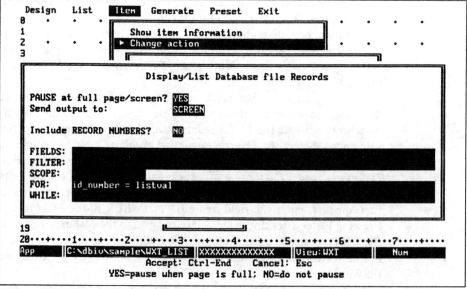

Figure 15-15 Specifying a FOR condition using the LISTVAL variable.

settle this, press **Alt-I** to access the Item menu once again, select *Change action*, *Display or print*, and finally Display/List. This sequence lets you to attach a Display/List object to the list object. Complete the Display/List dialog box as shown in Figure 15-15. The entry in the *FOR:* field needs some explanation.

List objects in general utilize a special internal ApGen memory variable named LISTVAL to capture the item selected by the user from a list object. In a values list, this item will be the value of the database/view field, but the item could also be a field name or filename if the other list types are used. This item must be captured so that it may be used later by the attached object. In this case, the object is a Display/List object, hence the scope for the query will be only those records where the key field (the ID_NUMBER field) is equal to the item (value in this case) chosen by the user. The logical expression shown in the *FOR:* field in Figure 15-15, **id_number = listval** says to consider only records where the answer is True for this expression.

Still from the Item menu, select *Override assigned database or view* using the view file WXT.QBE. Now press **Alt-L** to access the List menu, and select *Put away current list* and save changes. Saving a values list object will create a disk file with a .VAL extension. Notice that the QUERIES pop-up menu is still on the application design surface, though it is hidden by the application object. Press **F3** (Previous) to shuffle the objects, making the QUERIES menu come up on top. Now press **Alt-M** to access the Menu menu, select *Put away current menu*, and save the changes.

> **Note** You should probably save the application at this point, but before you do, regenerate the application so that when you return to the Control Center you can run it to see the result of the changes previously made. Figure 15-16 shows the values list that appears when the Warehouses by Title item is chosen from the QUERIES menu.

There are many other uses for values lists in an application. For example, you may precede a record edit operation with a pick list containing key field values with which the user may properly identify records. Once a key value is selected, the appropriate record is retrieved and displayed on the screen to accept changes. When a values list is used in this manner, however, you must be sure to select the *Position record pointer* option from the Item menu when defining the object that is to be attached to the list object. In the dialog box for this option, you must enter *LISTVAL* in the *SEEK first occurrence of key:* field if the database or view being used is ordered by the field used in the list object. If such an index is not available, you must enter *ID_NUMBER = LISTVAL*, for example, in the *LOCATE SCOPE:* field. Either method will suffice to position the record pointer at the proper place prior to the edit operation. After the edit is complete (i.e., after the user presses **Ctrl-End**, **Ctrl-W**, or **Esc**), the values list will again appear, waiting for another selection. Pressing **Esc** at this point, while in a list object, you will return back to the original menu (a pop-up or horizontal bar menu).

> **Note** As mentioned before in this section, the performance of list objects is somewhat less than desirable. In preparing the materials for this book, I ran the sample application on a fairly fast PC using dBASE IV 1.1 with database files containing relatively few records. It took at least 10 seconds for the values list to actually pop up after the item was selected from the menu. This observation is mentioned here as a caution only.

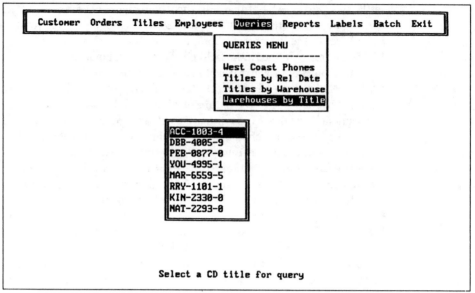

Figure 15-16   Values list selection at runtime.

It is important to mention as a side note at this time that the value placed in LISTVAL is always in character format regardless of the type of the value in the pick list. This means, for example, that if you use a date field in a pick list, the user-selected date will be returned in character, not date, format. Such a transformation affects how the *Position record pointer* option is handled. In this case, if you simply enter LIST-VAL in the *SEEK first occurrence of key:* field as before, an error message, "Data type mismatch", will occur. This is because the index tag is a date type but the value in LISTVAL is character. To rectify this situation, enter ***CTOD(LISTVAL)*** instead. CTOD( ) is a built-in dBASE IV function to perform a character to date conversion.

As an extension of this notion of using the LISTVAL variable to position to a point in a database, you can also use it to specify an upper bound on the processing that is to occur. For example, using the CUST_ID (Customer) database defined in Chapter 12, you could define a Display/List object attached to a values list object that prompts the user for a city name. As in the preceding example, you could position to the correct point in the file by entering LISTVAL in the *SEEK first occurrence of key:* field and then specify the logical expression ***CITY = LISTVAL*** in the *WHILE:* field. In essence, this says to start processing at the first occurrence of the CITY field value selected by the user and then continue processing for all subsequent like values.

One problem that will undoubtedly arise in the last example is many occurrences of the same city in the CUST_ID database, especially if there are many customers and the database is large. It is conceivable that hundreds of customers might have city field values of Los Angeles alone. Unfortunately, each occurrence of Los Angeles will appear in the values list object. To combat this difficultly, you can create a new .MDX tag for the city field using the *Display first duplicate key only* option when creating a new index tag in the database design screen. Then, when overriding the database for the values list object as just discussed, you simply specify the new tag in the *ORDER:* field of the dialog box that appears. This way, only unique CITY field values will appear in the values list window.

There is one final detail to consider in this situation. The unique index tag used for the values list is not needed for the actual processing of the Display/List object; in fact, it must *not* be used to obtain the desired results of the query. In this case, you would select *Reassign index order* on the Item menu when defining the object that is to be attached to the values list. This will cause the index to switch from the unique tag to the nonunique tag between the time when the user selects a value and when the query is processed. A similar technique was defined in the first part of this section, whereby different databases can be active during the values list operation and the operation of the attached object (in this case, a Display/List object).

One last example involves the use of a values list to prompt the user for some key word or phrase and then use it to scan through a memo field. For example, using the TITLES database's COMMENTS field (which is a memo field), the values list would need to be based on another, as yet undefined, database containing a series of comment codes—that is, codes that might appear within the COMMENTS field of TITLES. Once the user selects a specific code, the query processing would be based on a value of LISTVAL $ COMMENTS in the *FOR:* field.

> **Note** The $ operator is a special one that checks for the value contained in the memory variable on the left somewhere in the database field on the right. dBASE IV string functions such as the $ operator may be used on memo fields.

Structure Lists The second type of list object is the structure list. A structure list activates a pick list comprised of field names that are part of the current database or view. A structure list is constructed like a values list, and is attached to other ApGen objects in like manner. A good example of the usefulness of this type of list is enabling the user to select precisely which fields to include in the results of a query or report. A browse object could even be altered to include only those fields that are necessary at the moment. Often, the ApGen developer cannot foresee all possible field requirements an end-user may deem necessary when the system is being designed. A structure list is an easy alternative that gives the user the responsibility of choosing the content of the output of an ApGen object.

To define a structure list, you must follow the same procedure as when building a values list. You begin with opening up a pop-up menu item into a structure list. Then you actually create the list object, and finish by attaching it to an ApGen object. In your sample application, you will do exactly this by creating a new, very unique kind of query.

Begin by placing the QUERIES menu on the ApGen design surface, by pressing **Alt-D** to access the Design menu, selecting *Pop-up menu*, and then choosing QUERIES from the pick list. You will most likely have to resize (**Shft-F7**) the pop-up menu to make room for another item. After the empty space is available, move the highlight down to the area and enter *Orders (selective fields)* as the name of the new item. Now press **Alt-I** to access the Item menu, select *Change action*, and *Open a menu*, and then toggle the *Menu type:* field to STRUCTURE. Now enter the name of the list object to be created, *OR_LIST*, into the *Menu name:* field. There is no need to alter the assigned

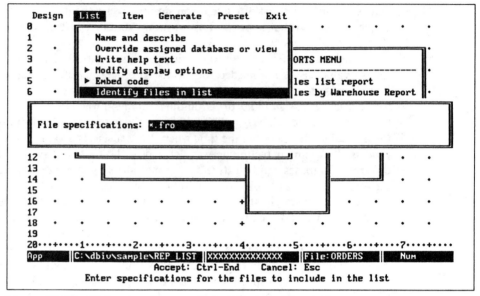

Figure 15-17   Dialog box for specifying file selection pattern.

database while in the Item menu since the default is ORDERS.DBF, which is just what you want. Leave the QUERIES menu on the design surface until you've created and correctly positioned the new list object.

To build a structure list, press **Alt-D** to access the Design menu again and select *Structure list*. In the pick list that appears, you should not see any lists of this type. In any case, select <create> and fill in the resulting dialog box. Enter *OR_LIST* in the *Name:* field. The name of the list entered here must match the one entered earlier. Complete the *Description:* and *Message line prompt:* fields and press **Ctrl-End**. The new list object should now be visible. You will most likely have to move (**F7**) the list to just under the lower right corner of the QUERIES pop-up menu.

> **Note** You will not have to resize the list, since it will only contain field names that are limited to 10 characters. Remember that the default width of a list is 14 characters.

Press **Alt-L** to access the List menu. This menu will differ from the List menu associated with the other two types of list objects in a single way, the *Identify fields in list* item. Select this item to enter all the fields to be included in the pick list with which the user is presented at runtime. Figure 15-17 depicts the dialog box that appears. Notice that you may press **Shft-F1** (Pick) to select these fields from a pick list. Only those fields in the current database or view will be shown in this pick list. If you wish to have all fields available to the user, simply leave this dialog box blank. Of course, in sensitive applications, such as employee files that may include salary fields, certain fields may be appropriately omitted.

It is now time to attach an ApGen object to the structure list under construction. Press **Alt-I** to access the Item menu, select *Change action*, *Display or print*, and then *Display/List*. In the Display/List dialog box, toggle the *Send output to:* field to

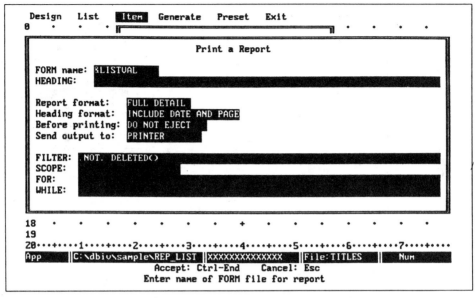

Figure 15-18   Dialog box for generic report selection and printing.

SCREEN and the *Include RECORD NUMBERS?* field to NO. Most important, however, enter *&LISTVAL* in the *FIELDS:* field. This entry will ensure that only the fields selected by the user from the structure list will be included in query results. Remember that LISTVAL is the special variable that contains the user selections from a list object and that the & is necessary to tell ApGen to use what is stored inside of LISTVAL and not LISTVAL itself. An error message claiming "Variable not found" will result if the & is omitted.

Instead of using only the user-selected fields, you could have combined a set of default fields with user-selected ones by entering, for example, *ORDER_NO, &LISTVAL*. Here, the field ORDER_NO will always be included in the query in addition to the ones selected by the user. Press **Ctrl-End** to save the dialog box entries and then put away both the list object and the QUERIES pop-up menu. Saving a structure list object will create a disk file with an .STR extension.

Figure 15-18 shows how a structure list object looks at runtime. Notice that as in the example, fields may be chosen in any order from the pick list. After all the fields required have been selected, simply press either **Left Arrow** or **Right Arrow** to initiate the query. The query results are shown in Figure 15-19 (a logical window was defined to contain the query results).

As mentioned before, it is possible to attach a list object to a horizontal bar menu item. If the structure list type is used, a slight problem arises. No matter what database the list uses (via overriding the assigned database), only the fields from the default database assigned to the bar menu will appear in the pick list at runtime. Moreover, even if you choose the default database as the subject of the structure list, the fields entered in the *Identify fields in list* dialog box will be ignored and instead all fields will be displayed.

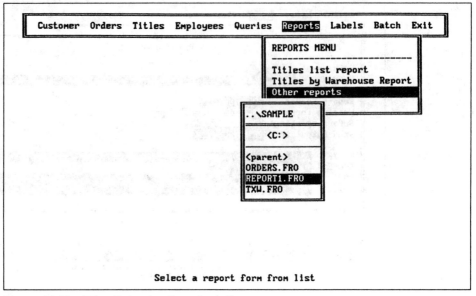

Figure 15-19 Files list selection at runtime.

Files Lists The final type of list object, the files list, is perhaps the most important from a top-down application design point of view. It is always the philosophy of the top-down system designer to start at the highest level of the system (namely the menu structures) and then attach additional objects to these structures. (Remember, this is the subject of this chapter.) As an extension of this methodology, it would be helpful to allow new reports, conceived of in the future, to be attached to the application. Normally, when new objects are constructed, the application must be "opened up" by modifying the items available on the menus and then attaching the objects to them. With the help of files lists, however, new report objects may be built and automatically attached to the application without touching the application itself.

The purpose of a files list is to enable the user to select an item on, say, a pop-up menu and have a list of possible filename choices appear in a window. Just as in previous list types, the user may scroll through the choices, highlight one, and then press **Enter** to select it. The underlying function of the selected object will then activate. For example, if the list of filenames in the files list reflects report forms, then once a report form is selected, the report will initiate and print. The objects displayed in the files list window should all be of the same type; however, complete flexibility is given in that the normal DOS wildcard specifications may be used to determine just what files will actually appear. (More about this concept a bit later.)

Possibly the most powerful ramification of the files list object is the ability to include a completely open-ended menu item—called, for example, "Other Reports"—in the application structure. Attached to this menu item will be a file list, displaying all report form files. If at a later time a new report form is built, all that need be done is to make sure the new form resides in the application directory so that it may be found when the files list object is selected. Think of files lists used in this manner as a porthole to future requirements, especially if the user is sophisticated enough to build his or her own reports. Of course, this concept of *open-ended applications* can be extended to include not only report forms, but also screen forms, label forms, and much, much more.

Now, begin constructing a files list by modifying your sample application to include a REPORTS menu item called *Other reports*. For additional experience, you might consider undertaking a parallel project of including an *Other labels* item, too. Press **Alt-D** to access the Design menu and select *Pop-up menu*; then choose REPORTS from the pick list. The REPORTS menu may need to be lengthened, using **Shft-F7** (Size), in order for additional items to be added. Add the new item, *Other reports*, to the menu. This will be your porthole. Now, while the new item is still highlighted, press **Alt-I** to access the Item menu, and select *Change action* and *Open a menu*. Here, toggle the *Menu type:* field to FILES and then enter REP_LIST in the *Menu name:* field. **Ctrl-End** will save these selections.

Now that you have established the link between the pop-up menu item and the files list object, you must actually create the object. Press **Alt-D** to access the Design menu; select *Files list* and then < create >. The dialog box that appears should resemble the one shown in Figure 15-12. Fill in the *Name:* field with ***REP_LIST*** and the *Description:* and *Message line prompt:* fields with appropriate values. An empty list window will now appear on the application design surface. It will probably be necessary to use **F7** (Move) to position the window to a more logical place. (See Figure 15-13 for reference.)

It is now time to define the contents of the files list object. Press **Alt-L** to access the List menu. The menu should appear similar to the one in Figure 15-14, the menu that appeared during the creation of the values list object. The one difference is the *Identify files in list* item. Choosing the item will result in the dialog box shown in Figure 15-20. This is where the file selection specification is entered. As shown, enter ****.FRO*** in the *File specifications:* field. The standard DOS filename wildcard characters are available here to define groups of files to be considered for inclusion in the file list. It is important to understand which file extensions must be specified here in order to include the appropriate files. For example, the .FRO extension is used in the example to include all "compiled" report forms. The .LBO extension would be used for label forms, and .FMO for screen forms. Of course, .DBF would be used for all database files.

It may be necessary to also choose the *Override assigned database of view* item from the List menu. This enables a primary database or view file to be specified for the report objects accessible through the new files list object. In this example, use the TITLES.DBF database. This presents a very real problem in accessing form files from a file list. If the user selects, for example, a screen form from a file list, but it does not match the currently assigned database or view, the application will abort with an error message complaining "Variable not found". To avoid this type of problem, the file specification should be narrowed somewhat to include only form files for a particular database or view. For example, **T_*.FRO** might indicate that only compiled report forms beginning with the prefix **T_** be included in the file list. Via such "object naming conventions" you can circumvent potential problems.

Finally, it is necessary to attach an ApGen object to the files list object. For our

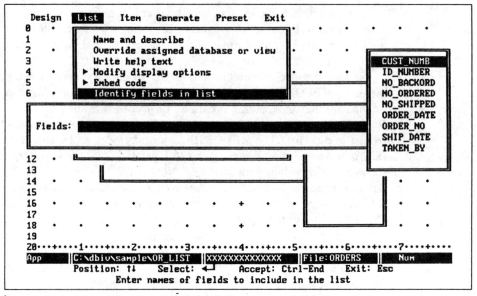

Figure 15-20   Specifying a fields list for a structure list object.

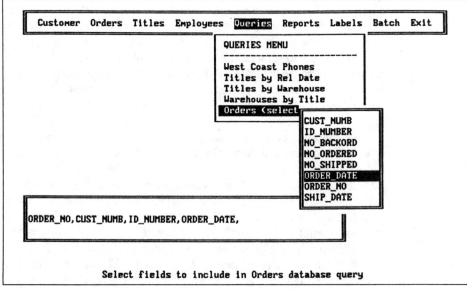

Figure 15-21   Selecting fields from a structure list at runtime.

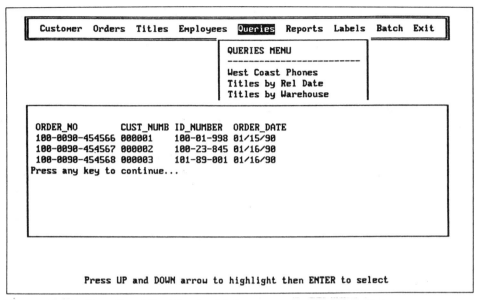

Figure 15-22   Results of the Display/List query using structure list.

example, it would make sense to use a generic report object. Press **Alt-I** to access the Item menu, and select *Change action*, *Display or print*, and then *Report*. In the Print a Report dialog box enter *&LISTVAL* in the *FORM name:* field and fill in the rest of the fields per Figure 15-21. It is necessary here to precede LISTVAL with the ampersand **&** character. The & means that a macro substitution is to occur—that is, the character value found inside the memory variable named LISTVAL is to be used as entry data for the field in question. Remembering that the item the user selected from the pick list is temporarily stored in LISTVAL (in the case of a files list the value will be a filename), you see that a filename will substitute for LISTVAL. This is so the application will access the proper Report form file, not a Report form named LISTVAL. In fact, if the & were left out, the application would abort with an error message claiming that the file was not found. Wrap up the files list definition by pressing **Alt-L** and selecting *Put away current list*. Saving a file structure list will create a disk file with a .FIL extension. Press **F3** (Previous) to bring back the REPORTS menu to the top on the design surface and then **Alt-M** to access the Menu menu, selecting *Put away current menu* and saving the changes.

If you now regenerate the application with the files list object attached to the REPORTS menu, the results may look similar to those shown in Figure 15-22. The various entries in the files list need some explanation. In the top portion of the list window, the current hard disk directory is shown (or at least as much of it as possible is shown, since pathnames can be quite long). Directly underneath is the current drive letter. The entry labelled < parent > indicates that you may actually change the directory in your search for a qualifying filename. Selecting < parent > will move up the hard disk directory hierarchy. No matter which directory is current, only those files in that directory that match the file specifications will appear on the lower portion of the file list window. Selecting any of the Report forms (in our example) itemized in the file list will result in the report being generated. After the report is complete, control is returned back to the file list.

Batch Process Objects

Defining batch process objects in ApGen is the closest thing there is in the dBASE IV ApGen to programming without actually programming. A batch process can be simply defined as being some cohesive series of operations (e.g., replacing values in records, deleting records, copying records, packing databases, etc.) whose end results when performed together achieve some desired goal. For example, you may wish to define a sequence of operations that will selectively delete all records with a back order quantity exceeding 10, move the records to a different file, and then pack the original file. Unlike changing an assigned action to a pop-up menu item in the *Perform file operations* menu, you need more than a single operation. Batch files give you this ability to group together a collection of operations under one name. You may assign a batch process to any menu item in the system. Generally, you build a separate pop-up menu for the system to contain all the batch processes in the system, although this organization is not a hard-and-fast rule, since you may decide it is more appropriate to deposit a few batch files in several of the other menus of the application.

In order to define a batch process object the following three steps should be followed:

1. Assign and name a batch process object to a pop-up menu item.
2. Create a batch process object with multiple steps defined. If there is only one step, there is no need to use a batch process; instead, simply use the *Perform file operations* menu.
3. Assign an action to each step in the batch process object.

To illustrate this procedure, you will define a batch process object for your sample application. The goal of the batch process is to decrement all the back order quantity fields by five and then pack the orders database. Begin by pressing **Alt-D** to access the Design menu, select *Pop-up menu*, and then select BATCH from the pick list. Depending on how you chose to establish this menu, you may need to add an item labelled "Backorder update". Making sure this item is highlighted, press **Alt-I** to access the Item menu, select *Change action*, *Run program*, and then *Execute BATCH process*. Figure 15-23 shows the state of menus as you enter the name of the batch process in the field called *Batch name:*. Next, press **Alt-D** again and select *Batch process*. Since this is the first time this option has been selected from the Design menu there should be no existing batch process objects in the pick list, so choose <create>.

A small window containing descriptions of the various steps in the batch process will appear. The items entered here are descriptive only, similar in nature to the item titles entered in a pop-up menu, and like their pop-up counterparts, all of the items are assigned to other ApGen objects. You will see how to attach these objects in a moment.

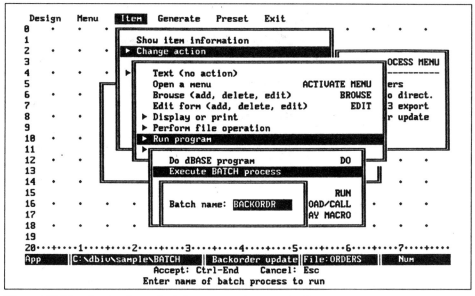

Figure 15-23 Assigning a batch process to a menu item.

Right now, you may need to resize the window to reduce it to two items in length. In the space for the two items enter *Update back order quantities* and *PACK orders database*, respectively.

To attach objects to these two batch process steps begin by highlighting the first of the two and press **Alt-I** to access the Item menu, select *Change action* and *Perform file operations*, and then choose *REPLACE*. In the REPLACE dialog box, as you saw in the last chapter, enter ALL for the *SCOPE:* of the operation. In the first *field named* entry, type *NO_BACKORD*, and in the first *with this value* entry, type *NO_BACKORD-5*. This operation will go through all the order database records and decrement the quantity back ordered by five. Next, press **PgDn** to point to the second step in the batch and repeat the procedure of selecting a file operation. This time, however, choose PACK. Since both of these operations for the batch operate on the default database, ORDERS, there is no need to override the assigned database. Also, at runtime, a batch process will run, displaying any dBASE messages that pertain to the particular operations being performed. For example, during a PACK, dBASE will display the progress of the operation, including when the index tags are being rebuilt. It would make sense to enclose these messages inside a logical window located just below the pop-up menus. This is not possible, however, since a batch process will always use the entire screen. The final step in creating a batch process object is to access the Batch menu by pressing **Alt-B**. Figure 15-24 shows this menu. Choose *Put away current batch process* to save the batch just created. Finally, also save the BATCH pop-up menu.

Often situations require that multiple database relations be active while a batch process is executed in order to perform the desired task. You may, of course, override the assigned database or view for each step in the batch process, but a separate QBE file would be necessary and possibly used only in this one remote part of the application.

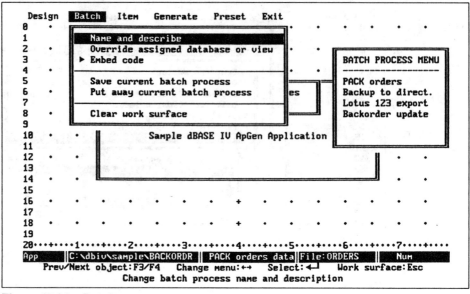

Figure 15-24   Batch process menu.

Consequently, it may be wiser to embed some dBASE code necessary to establish the relation instead. You may have noticed that the *Embed code* option was available in the Batch menu. This is, however, a topic for the next section.

Program Objects

The ultimate extension available through ApGen is the ability to create dBASE language code sections as objects and attach them to an application. The ability was alluded to in several places in preceding chapters. It is now time to take a brief look at this feature's underlying capabilities.

Writing dBASE programs is somwhat outside the scope of this book, which is a guide for the nonprogramming application developer. To do the subject proper justice would require an in-depth examination of the dBASE programming language. This will not be done, but some simple techniques on which you may capitalize with the help of the dBASE IV manuals or possibly other sources will be illustrated. A firm knowledge of the syntax of dBASE IV command structures is necessary. These commands are not just the ones recognized at the dot prompt either, but entail many ''programming only'' commands.

This situation brings to light two points about ApGen. First, ApGen can be used as the vehicle with which the nonprogramming developer can get a taste of programming in a small way. Then, as the experience level grows, more and more sophisticated endeavors may be undertaken, but still from within the framework of ApGen. Second, and equally alluring, is the potential for seasoned professional dBASE programmers to utilize ApGen as the starting place for creating complex systems.

With the ability to embed dBASE code segments inside an application, ApGen could potentially be the cure-all for many of the professional developer's problems. It is a difficult (not to mention an often extremely costly) task to begin a new application from scratch. With ApGen to provide a starting point, yielding the user interface of the application as well as many of the other components of a typical system, all that need be done to finish the job is to use the dBASE language to fill in the gaps. Some complicated processes still need to be written in the dBASE language, but focusing on these portions and leaving the rest to ApGen provides an economically feasible path towards more efficient application development.

Now take a look at how this important ApGen interface works. The *Run program* menu appearing on the *Change action* option of the Item menu is the way ApGen allows an application to attach to dBASE programming. You saw this menu once before, in the discussion of batch process objects, but now your attention will be entirely on programming. There is one other entrance through which programming may be used—in the *Embed code* option, also on the Item menu. In order to become comfortable with the subject, begin with this method first.

Embedded Code

Selecting the *Embed code* option will produce a submenu requesting a choice between *Before* and *After*. These indicate the positioning the embedded dBASE code segment will take with reference to the object being assigned. As a simple example of how this might be useful, consider the process of assigning a report object to a menu item. Say the report requires a multiple database environment with a relation established between the files. The method described in this book for performing this task was to create a Query by Example file to set up the environment. It is well known that the dBASE code generated by QBE is far from optimal, so in order to optimize the application for speed, you decide to write equivalent dot prompt commands to open the files and indexes and build the links. These commands can be placed in the application as an embedded code segment to be executed before the object being assigned. Furthermore, additional commands may be placed in another code segment to be executed after the object completes. In this example, the "before" segment will establish the environment instead of a QBE file, the report object will print a report, and then the "after" segment will return the environment to its state prior to the use of the object.

Functionally, it works something like this. You select *Before* and the text editor opens up, allowing entry of up to 19 lines of dBASE code. Here you type in the commands just as you would at the dot prompt. It may be prudent to document the code segment with descriptive phrases that explain how the program does what it does. ApGen will not examine the contents of this screen, but will blindly place it in the application at the position indicated. If you type nonsense here, errors will not be detected until you attempt to run the application. See Figure 15-25 for a sample code segment to establish the environment defined in the TXW.QBE view file built earlier in this chapter. There is one obvious difference between the embedded dBASE code and the code in the Query by Example file—namely, the quantity of program statements required to perform exactly the same task. It is usually the case that manual programs are shorter than the equivalent automatically generated ones. In addition, the code

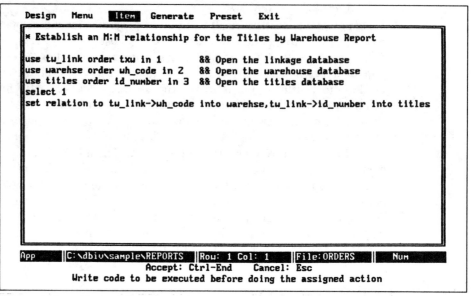

```
  Design   Menu   [Item]  Generate   Preset   Exit

* Establish an M:M relationship for the Titles by Warehouse Report

use tu_link order txu in 1       && Open the linkage database
use warehse order wh_code in 2   && Open the warehouse database
use titles order id_number in 3  && Open the titles database
select 1
set relation to tu_link->wh_code into warehse,tu_link->id_number into titles
```

```
App    ||C:\dbiv\sample\REPORTS ||Row: 1 Col: 1  ||File:ORDERS  ||   Num
                  Accept: Ctrl-End     Cancel: Esc
          Write code to be executed before doing the assigned action
```

Figure 15-25   Embedded code example to set up an M:M relationship.

shown in Figure 15-25 cannot be generated by QBE. This form of the SET RELATION command, which defines two links at once, is not possible from within QBE. Instead, QBE generates an equivalent, though much larger, program. For these reasons, using embedded code segments often improves an application's efficiency.

Since this example deals with the file environment required for the successful operation of an ApGen object, you should override the assigned database or view in the Item menu and select *IN EFFECT AT RUNTIME*. This means that ApGen will not make any assumptions or enforce any defaults concerning what files are open as the object begins to run.

> **Note** The code entered into ApGen code segments is simply inserted into the application at the appropriate place. You can examine the placement by viewing the generated ApGen code in the dBASE IV text editor and searching for the statements.

Another example of an embedded code segment that often makes sense for commercial software is a mechanism to create a "demo version" of the application. Such a demo version can be a real boon to product marketing, since the intended audience may play with a live, working version of the program. The only difference between the demo and the production version is that the former is limited or crippled in some way. The most common way of limiting the demo version is to restrict the number of database records allowed to be stored in the main database. In the sample application it would be appropriate to limit the TITLES database to only 200 records (this may sound too generous, but the application is intended for operations carrying thousands of titles). Figure 15-26 depicts the code segment that implements this restriction. Actually, the example goes a bit further by placing a date limit, after which the system is rendered useless.

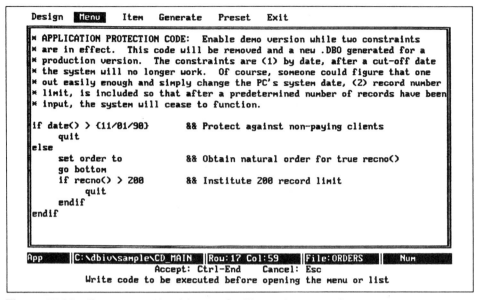

```
  Design  Menu   Item   Generate   Preset   Exit

 * APPLICATION PROTECTION CODE:  Enable demo version while two constraints
 * are in effect.  This code will be removed and a new .DBO generated for a
 * production version.  The constraints are (1) by date, after a cut-off date
 * the system will no longer work.  Of course, someone could figure that one
 * out easily enough and simply change the PC's system date, (2) record number
 * limit, is included so that after a predetermined number of records have been
 * input, the system will cease to function.

if date() > {11/01/90}          && Protect against non-paying clients
     quit
else
     set order to              && Obtain natural order for true recno()
     go bottom
     if recno() > 200          && Institute 200 record limit
          quit
     endif
endif
```

```
App      C:\dbiv\sample\CD_MAIN    Row:17 Col:59    File:ORDERS    Num
                 Accept: Ctrl-End     Cancel: Esc
            Write code to be executed before opening the menu or list
```

Figure 15-26   Program code object to facilitate demo versions.

Here is a quick look at what is involved. The first portion of the code object (those lines beginning with an asterisk) are only program comments and have no bearing whatsoever on the operation of the code. The code begins later, with the IF statement that first compares the current system to the cutoff date. If the current date has passed the last day on which the demo is authorized, then the application will stop. However, if the date check is passed, another check is performed. Next, the code object determines how many records are in the default database (ORDERS.DBF), and if the maximum has been exceeded, the application will again stop.

The placement of this code segment is important. You insert it as embedded code before the main horizontal bar menu. Simply place the bar menu on the application design surface and pull down the Menu menu. Select *Embed code* and *Before*, and then enter the dBASE code. Its placement here will keep the user from proceeding to any other part of the system if the constraints have been violated.

A third example of embedded code is the implementation of a security scheme whereby a code segment is inserted before each pop-up menu option (or just the sensitive ones) to prompt the user for a password and compare it to entries stored in a special password database. In this way different passwords could be assigned for each portion of the application, so only certain users could perform maintenance (e.g., add new titles) on the databases.

A final example of using the embedded code feature of ApGen is to provide for date range selection criteria for reports. Reports often need to be date-driven—that is to say, only data falling between two end points will be included on the report. Figure 15-27 shows a code segment that is embedded before a report object.

The code defines two memory variables, which can be thought of as temporary storage areas for information. In this case, the memory variable named **mstartdate** will

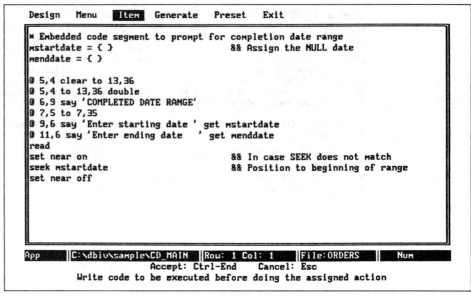

Figure 15-27   Code segment to provide for a date range prompt window.

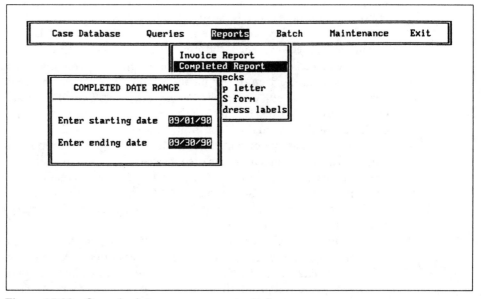

Figure 15-28   Sample date range prompt window.

hold the lower date value and **menddate** will hold the upper value. The report object will have to be modified slightly to take advantage of this new feature. In the *WHILE:* field of the Print a Report dialog box, enter, for example, *ORDER_DATE < = MENDDATE*. This condition will allow the report to include all records up to the specified ending date. The code segment, with its SEEK command, is responsible for making sure the report begins at the right place. Now, when the user selects this option from the Reports menu of the application, a small window appears, as shown in Figure 15-28. After the user enters the dates, the report proceeds as usual, being displayed in a presized window.

Code Objects

A similar approach to interfacing dBASE code to the application is to define code objects. Instead of writing a piece of dBASE code to prefix or suffix another ApGen object, you can have dBASE code represent an object itself. These entities are called ''code objects.''

What can be done inside a code object depends upon your imagination and programming experience. Any task not ordinarily performed or provided for inside ApGen may be defined in a code object. The only restriction is the same 19-line limit in program length as with embedded code segments. As mentioned before with embedded code, care must be taken to make the actions performed in a code object unobtrusive when the the application is operated. Often this can be quite a challenge.

> Note To attach a code object to a menu item, you must go through the *Change action* menu, select *Run program*, and then select *Insert dBASE code*. At this point, the code window opens up, allowing the entry of the dBASE program statements.

Program Objects

Program objects are identical to code objects, the only difference being in the length of the dBASE code allowable. As was stated earlier, there is a 19-line limit for code objects and embedded code segments. With program objects, there is no such limit. This is because the dBASE program code is placed in a file external to the ApGen-generated code that is called when the user selects the pop-up menu item to which the file is attached.

To create a program object, you must return back to the Control Center's Applications panel, select < create >, and choose *dBASE program*. This will get you into the dBASE IV program editor. From here, press **Alt-L** to access the Layout menu and select *Modify a different program*. In the dialog box that appears, enter the name of the program object you wish to create. All program object files must end in,a .PRG extension. Now you can begin to enter the dBASE code for the object. When done entering the program, press **Alt-E** to access the Exit menu and select *Save changes and exit*. Back at the Control Center you can reenter ApGen and attach the new program object to a menu item.

> Note It might be good practice to test out the code first, before handing it over to ApGen. It is generally easier to debug a small program object outside of ApGen.

An alternate way to gain access to the program editor is from the Tools menu at the Control Center level. Press **Alt-T**, select *DOS utilities*, then press **Alt-O** to gain access to the Operations menu, and select *Edit*. Actually, the editor will load the contents of the file you happened to be positioned on prior to selecting *Edit*. Do not worry about what you may see on the editor's screen, just press **Alt-L** to access the Layout menu. From here select *Modify a different program* and then proceed in the same manner as just described.

To attach a program object to a menu item, you select basically the same options as when attaching a batch process object—that is, you go through the *Change action* menu, select *Run program*, and then select *Do dBASE program*. In the dialog box that appears (see Figure 14-29), the name of the .PRG program object must be entered along with any required program parameters. The concept of parameters involves a method of writing dBASE programs in a modular fashion. (This topic is left up to you for further investigation.)

Other Program Objects

Three final classes of programs may be attached to an application. The first enables ordinary DOS commands (including batch files) and/or executable programs (written in C, for example) to be run from the ApGen-generated code. There are occasions when this is necessary. For example, you may wish to call up a communications program to access a remote information service, download some data, and then return to the application to process the data. Care must be taken, however, to ensure that enough memory is available to load the DOS program over dBASE IV and your application. These objects may be attached by selecting the *Run DOS program* option from the *Run program* menu.

Binary files (most often written in assembler language) are another class of object that may be attached to an application. Again, there may be reasons to dive into the depths of machine language, but they are few and far between. The *Load/call binary file* option of the *Run program* menu facilitates this linkage.

The final class of objects are keystroke macros. The concept of macros was pioneered by products like Lotus 1-2-3, which allow a sequence of keystrokes to be "remembered" and then saved in a special disk file. dBASE IV has provisions for managing macros (available in the Tools menu). Through ApGen, you may access saved macro files by selecting the *Play back macro* option from the *Run program* menu. This activates a previously created and saved macro when the user selects the application menu option to which it is attached.

Generating a Complete Application

Having ApGen generate the application is the final step towards completing your application. You saw how to do this briefly in Chapter 13, but now the technique will be formalized. Basically, there are two forms of generation with an ApGen system. The first involves the generation of the dBASE language code for the program. As was seen earlier, usually two main program files, containing many different smaller programs, are built. The first goes by the name entered in the application object when the application was first conceived. Your sample application goes by the name CD_DIST, so the program generated is called CD_DIST.PRG. The second program file is named CD_MAIN.PRG and is the set of programs that actually handle the bulk of the processing of the application. These relate to the horizontal bar menu that was used as the main menu of the application. This is the normal organization of an ApGen application; however, it is conceivable to have others.

Unfortunately, the two program files for the sample application are too massive (due to all the features included by this time) to list here. It is a very good idea to print out these two programs and try to get a conceptual idea of how the program is structured. If you should desire to learn dBASE IV programming, studying ApGen code is a good place to begin. ApGen code may have some useful techniques to strive for as well as bad coding styles to avoid.

Figure 15-29 shows the Generate menu with the *Select template* dialog box open. Here you may enter the name of the production templates provided with dBASE IV—MENU.GEN, or DOCUMENT.GEN—which are used to generate the dBASE program code and system documentation respectively. It is the job of MENU.GEN, to generate the .PRG program files that constitute the application. DOCUMENT.GEN, on the other hand, generates CD_DIST.DOC (for our example), which contains useful system documentation. Other templates may be written, or the production templates may be modified to create a library of templates. For this, however, the Developer's Edition of dBASE IV is needed since the template compiler is not included with the Standard Edition.

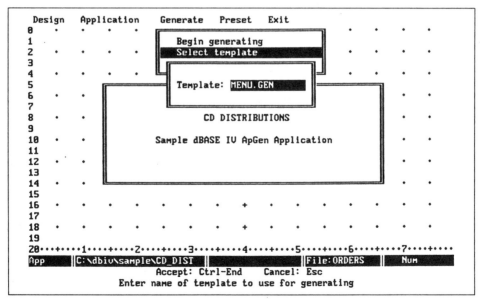

Figure 15-29 Specifying the code-generation template.

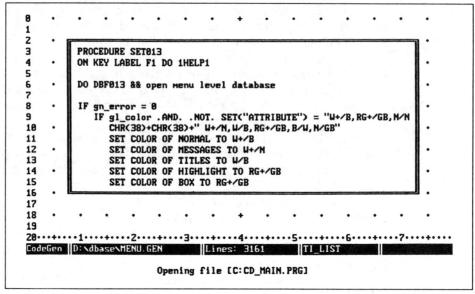

```
 0    ·     ·     ·     ·     ·     +     ·     ·     ·     ·     ·
 1
 2    ·                                                             ·
 3        PROCEDURE SET013
 4    ·   ON KEY LABEL F1 DO 1HELP1                                 ·
 5
 6    ·   DO DBF013 && open menu level database                     ·
 7
 8    ·   IF gn_error = 0                                           ·
 9          IF gl_color .AND. .NOT. SET("ATTRIBUTE") = "W+/B,RG+/GB,N/N
10    ·        CHR(38)+CHR(38)+" W+/N,W/B,RG+/GB,B/W,N/GB"           ·
11             SET COLOR OF NORMAL TO W+/B
12    ·        SET COLOR OF MESSAGES TO W+/N                         ·
13             SET COLOR OF TITLES TO W/B
14    ·        SET COLOR OF HIGHLIGHT TO RG+/GB                      ·
15             SET COLOR OF BOX TO RG+/GB
16    ·                                                             ·
17
18    ·     ·     ·     ·     ·     +     ·     ·     ·     ·     ·
19
20····+····1····+····2····+····3····+····4····+····5····+····6····+····7····+····
CodeGen ||D:\dbase\MENU.GEN        ||Lines: 3161    ||TI_LIST        ||
```

Opening file [C:CD_MAIN.PRG]

Figure 15-30   Code generation window.

The last option on the Generate menu is *Display during generation?* Here you answer either YES or NO, depending on whether you want the resulting program code and/or documention to be displayed in a special window as it is being generated. Figure 15-30 shows a sample code generation window and Figure 15-31 illustrates a documentation generation window. Remember that although it is appealing to see the application being built, the process is slower, since ApGen must display all results on the screen as well as write them to the disk.

The Generate menu option that initiates the generation process is *Begin generating*. If you have specified that the results be displayed during generation, then a window appears as the process proceeds. If the display feature is turned off, however, the only evidence that the application or documentation is being generated is an autoincrementing line number field in the status bar at the bottom of the screen. When generation is complete, a message appears, requesting that any key be pressed. The amount of time required to generate an application varies depending on how many objects are included and the speed of the PC used for development. (The sample application for this book took just under four minutes with the display option turned off.)

There is a single difference in the generation process of program code and documentation. When DOCUMENT.GEN is active, an additional prompt occurs after *Begin generating* is selected. The message "Do you have an IBM graphics compatible printer (Y/N)?" appears. The answer entered will define the style of documentation generated. If YES is specified then smooth line graphics characters are used in the .DOC text file. In Figure 15-31 the EMPLOYEE pop-up menu is represented using graphics characters. If NO is specified, a series of nongraphics characters are used. This option is necessary for older and less full-featured printers (including daisy-wheel letter-quality printers) that do not support graphics characters.

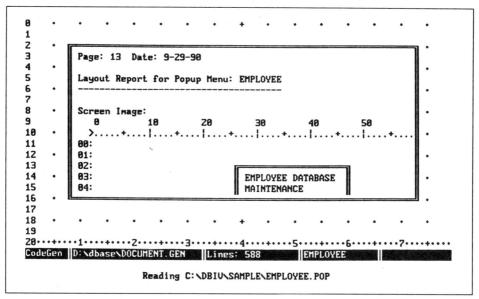

Figure 15-31   Documentation generation window.

DOS Environment Variables

Several special DOS environment variables may be used in conjunction with ApGen to produce certain results. These variables, new with dBASE IV 1.1, are established outside of dBASE IV while you are at the DOS level. The DOS SET command is used to define values for the variables. It may be prudent to modify your AUTOEXEC.BAT batch file to include the SETs. The first variable is DTL_NOGEN. When you issue the DOS command, SET DTL_NOGEN = ON, the dBASE IV code generation function is turned off. This means that when you save objects that normally result in dBASE language code, such as screen forms and reports, the code generation step is not performed. This may be useful at some point if you are designing and saving a series of similar objects and do not wish to wait for the compilation of each. Of course, you would eventually have to compile the objects before the application could run properly. You may get an error message when this variable is set ON, since the compilation step proceeds as normal, only to find that the .FMO (for example) does not exist. This condition should be ignored.

Another environment variable is DBTMP (and TMP), which controls the placement of all the temporary files created by dBASE IV. dBASE IV is notorious for creating a multitude of temporary files during its processing of various application objects. If you do not specify where to put them, these files will be deposited in the directory that contains the DBASE.EXE file (the main dBASE IV executable file—the one you call at the DOS prompt when you first load the program). This means that over time, the dBASE directory on your hard disk will become littered with many temporary files, and it may be difficult to weed them out from the necessary files in the same directory. By issuing the command SET DBTMP = C:\TEMP, at the DOS prompt you will route all the files to this directory. Then, you may periodically visit this directory and erase all files found.

The last environment variable that needs to be examined is called DBHEAP. The setting of this variable may be crucial to the performance of your application. DBHEAP is a variable that instructs dBASE IV (and the RunTime version) how to utilize the amount of free memory above the approximately 450K required by dBASE IV. This memory may be used for memory variables or overlay swapping. Memory variables are distinguished from database fields in that both hold information, but while database fields reside on the disk, memory variables live in the PC's RAM memory only for the duration of the application's execution. Once the application is ended, the memory variables disappear. An ApGen application uses many such memory variables, but not excessively. Overlay swapping pertains to the action of pulling required portions of the dBASE IV program from the hard disk into RAM so that you will be able to use certain features. dBASE IV is such a large program that it cannot all fit into RAM at the same time.

Therefore, you issue the command SET DBHEAP = N (where N is the ratio of the amount of free memory allocated to memory variables over the amount allocated to overlay swapping and may range from 0 to 100) at the DOS prompt. A high value indicates more memory for memory variable usage and a low value indicates more memory for overlay swapping. Low values normally increase the application's performance. One area in which performance needs to be addressed is with values list objects, which are notoriously slow when there is a reasonably large number of records in the database. Often the time interval between when the user selects a menu option that is attached to a values list and when the pick list appears can be minutes. This kind of response time is unreasonable. Setting DBHEAP to a low value, say N = 5, will produce a noticeable speedup.

One last recommendation concerning the performance of an ApGen application is to investigate the use of dBASE IV 1.1's new memory caching utility, Dbcache. This program is supplied along with dBASE IV to take advantage of any expanded or extended memory that might exist on the development PC. If you have this type of additional memory, Dbcache will use it to often dramatically increase performance.

The dBASE IV RunTime Module

The RunTime module is a part of the dBASE IV Developer's Edition that may be viewed as basically a compromise, albeit a powerful one. RunTime has many of the benefits of a dBASE language compiler (which is to be discussed in the next and last section of this chapter). It allows the nonprogramming application developer to "pseudocompile" the programs that ApGen generates into a single cohesive unit, and then allows the application to be run without dBASE IV present on the target computer system. This approach has many advantages. For instance, numerous disk files, representing the various objects that comprise the application, need not be present, since they are embedded in with single-user applications. A significant portion of any ApGen application (often referred to as "code bloat") is involved with multiuser processing. There are techniques to modify the template programs to avoid multiuser code.

The following files must be available to a RunTime application when it executes. As you will see in a moment, there is a provision when building a RunTime system to automatically copy these files to the target subdirectory.

RUNTIME.EXE

RUNTIME.OVL

RUNTIME.RES

The first two files are very large, which makes it impossible to have a RunTime application reside on a single floppy diskette for distribution. You will see in a later section how this can be handled.

The RunTime Utilities

Two programs that constitute the RunTime preparation software combine with the set of library files mentioned earlier that allow the software to be executed once it has been prepared. The first program is the BUILD utility, whose job it is to use dBASE IV to compile the program files generated by ApGen (those with the file extension of .PRG) into an intermediate form. If you remember, dBASE IV automatically compiles other application objects into their compiled counterparts. Report forms (.FRM files) are compiled into .FRO files. Screen forms (.FMT files) are compiled into .FMO files. Label forms (.LBL files) are compiled into .LBO files. The result of BUILD is one or more .DBO files, which contain the compiled dBASE program code representing the aforementioned objects. All the associated files of an application may then be combined into a single compiled output file with a .DBO extension using the DBLINK utility. DBLINK may be automatically called from BUILD if requested to do so.

There is a tradeoff as to whether to have a single or multiple compiled files that comprise an application. The case for a single file is such that with only one file, the chance that a file might become missing, causing the application to fail, will not exist, since all files are combined together. The case for multiple files is that if only one file containing an application object needs to be changed, it is not necessary to regenerate the whole application.

The BUILD Utility

The first step in producing a RunTime version of an ApGen application is to load the BUILD utility. To do this, exit dBASE IV and return to the DOS prompt. All the RunTime files just mentioned must reside in this directory. Presumably the directory is \DBASE; if it is not, issue the appropriate DOS command to attach to the hard disk directory in which the RunTime files have been placed. In either case, enter the command BUILD at the DOS prompt. Attempting to issue the command RUN BUILD from the dot prompt will result in an "Insufficient memory" error message. The BUILD utility will load the screen, which should resemble Figure 15-32 without the dialog box. As you can see, BUILD has three pop-up menus attached to a horizontal bar menu: *Build*, *Options*, and *Exit*. The Build menu is automatically pulled down as you enter BUILD.

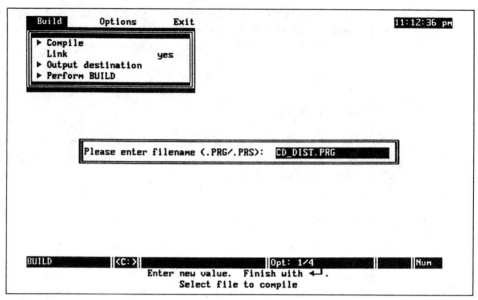

```
  Build       Options       Exit                        11:12:36 pm
 ┌──────────────────────────────────┐
 │ ► Compile                         │
 │   Link                 yes        │
 │ ► Output destination              │
 │ ► Perform BUILD                   │
 └──────────────────────────────────┘




         ┌─────────────────────────────────────────────────┐
         │Please enter filename (.PRG/.PRS):  CD_DIST.PRG   │
         └─────────────────────────────────────────────────┘







 ┌BUILD──────┐ ┌<C:>┐                    ┌Opt: 1/4┐      ┌Num┐
              Enter new value.  Finish with ↵ .
              Select file to compile
```

Figure 15-32 BUILD utility menu and Compile dialog box.

The BUILD Menu

This menu is the primary menu for the BUILD utility. It allows you to specify various parameters dealing with how the build operation is to proceed. The menu items found in this menu are now described.

Compile Selecting this option yields the dialog box shown in Figure 15-32. Here you specify the name of the main program module of the application. This is the name you specified when the application object was first defined in ApGen. To check the name, if you have forgotten what it was, get out of BUILD, load dBASE IV, and enter the application design surface. With the application object as the currently selected object on the surface, press **Alt-A** to access the Application menu and select *Name and describe.* In the dialog box that appears, you should recognize the name of the application in the *Name:* field. Remember this name for use in the BUILD utility.

Link This is a toggle field, defaulting to YES, which provides the linkage to the DBLINK utility following the compilation of the application files. For normal use, simply accept the default, and when the BUILD operation is complete, DBLINK will be called upon to finish the task by combining all the objects into a single .DBO file. Pressing the **Spacebar** will change the value of the field to NO.

Output Destination Selecting this field yields a dialog box allowing you to specify the output destination of the build process results (i.e., all files produced in relation to producing a RunTime application). It is generally a good idea to create a separate hard disk directory to act as a repository for these files. For example, if your development directory (the one in which ApGen was used to store all of the application's objects) is \SAMPLE, then the BUILD output directory could be \SAMPLE\BUILD. In this way, after the build operation is complete, you need only copy the files found in this new directory to the target machine (more about this subject a bit later).

Perform Build When this option is selected, the BUILD process is initiated with the indicated parameters. Normally, the process of producing a RunTime application takes only a few minutes, depending on the size of the application. Remember, you may use RunTime to generate non-ApGen applications, using the dBASE programming language, which can be quite large.

The Options Menu

The various options available in this menu interact with the BUILD utility in order to allow you to customize the way your RunTime application is produced. The Options menu is shown in Figure 15-33, and each item is described here.

Default Program File Extension This toggle field, defaulting to the value .PRG, is only used when SQL programs are to be compiled with RunTime. Most of the time, the default value is the one required. Press the **Spacebar** to toggle to the value .PRS, which is required for SQL programs.

Search for New Functions This is another toggle field, with a default value of *no*. This option normally only pertains to non-ApGen applications built by dBASE pro-

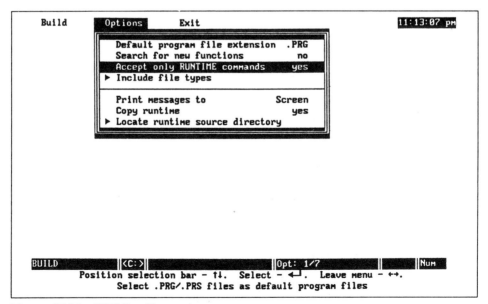

Figure 15-33   BUILD utility options menu.

grammers, but may be applicable if you have specified any UDFs (*User-Defined Functions*) in any dBASE language embedded code segment or code object, or any program object that is called by your application. Basically, if you press the **Spacebar** to switch to *yes*, BUILD will attempt to resolve duplicate UDF names. Duplicate names could arise if you should reference a UDF that happens to have the same name as a dBASE IV built-in function. For most pure ApGen applications the default value is satisfactory.

Accept Only Runtime Commands The default for this field is *yes*, which indicates that an error message should result if a command not supported in the runtime version of dBASE IV is encountered in the application being processed by BUILD. Such occurrences are unlikely when processing an ApGen-generated application; nevertheless, the default should be accepted. You may press the **Spacebar** to toggle the *no* value. The following dBASE IV commands are not supported in a RunTime system:

ASSIST
COMPILE
CREATE or MODIFY FILE
CREATE or MODIFY LABEL
CREATE or MODIFY QUERY
CREATE or MODIFY REPORT
CREATE or MODIFY SCREEN
CREATE or MODIFY STRUCTURE
CREATE or MODIFY VIEW
DEBUG
HELP
HISTORY
LIST or DISPLAY HISTORY
SET
MODIFY COMMAND or FILE
RESUME
SET DEBUG
SET DOHISTORY
SET ECHO
SET HISTORY
SET INSTRUCT
SET SQL
SET STEP
SET TRAP
SUSPEND

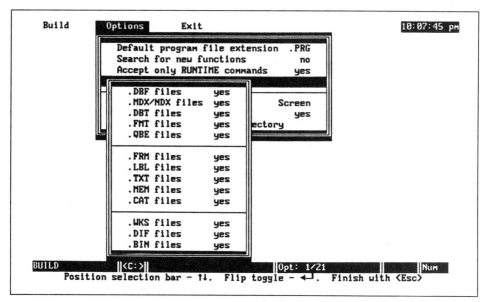

Figure 15-34   BUILD utility *Include file types* pick list.

Include file types Selecting this option results in the pick-list window shown in Figure 15-34. Here, various dBASE IV file types (as identified by their file extensions) are listed with either a *yes* or *no* indicator next to each. The default is *yes* for all files types except for .COM/.EXE files. The file types specified are to be included in the copy operation that completes the RunTime application.

Print Messages To The user of the BUILD utility has the option of where to send the information and error messages resulting from the BUILD process. The default destination is *Screen*. Use the **Spacebar** to toggle between the other possible settings: *Printer*, *File* (all messages are written to a file named BUILD.TXT), and off (which suppresses all messages).

Copy Runtime This is a toggle field, whose default value is *yes*, that determines whether the RunTime files RUNTIME.EXE, RUNTIME.OVL, and RUNTIME.RES should be copied to the target directory. Accepting the default is normally wise, since the files deposited in the output directory will be those required for successful execution of the RunTime application. There is the drawback, however, that quite a bit of extra space on the hard disk is taken up by having duplicate copies of the large RunTime files.

Locate Runtime Source Directory Choose this option to specify a pathname with which BUILD may find the RunTime files. Take care in specifying the pathname, especially if the source directory is on a different drive than the target directory.

Exit Menu

This menu has but one option, *Exit to DOS*. Choose this option immediately after selecting the *Perform BUILD* item from the Build menu. How to now run the application using the RunTime system is described next.

Executing a RunTime Application

Now it is time to execute the new standalone application produced by the BUILD and DBLINK utility programs. While at the DOS prompt and still attached to the BUILD directory, enter *RUNTIME* <appname> where <appname> is once again the primary name of your application as specified in the Compile option of the Build menu. No extension need be entered here, though the default is .DBO. If you prefer, you may do a slight sidestep here to eliminate the specification of the application name all together. If you simply enter *RUNTIME* at the DOS prompt, the RunTime system will assume an application name of DBRUNCMD.DBO. If you had renamed your application main program before compiling it to this special name, and then had BUILD produce a RunTime application with this name, you would not need to specify any name when calling RUNTIME.

Distribution

In order to distribute the application to the target machine you will need to copy the files from the output directory of the BUILD utility to one or more floppy disks. If you are using high-density diskettes (1.44 MB), you may choose to simply copy the contents to one or more diskettes, depending on the size of your application and database files. Usually, however, due to the size of the files involved, the DOS BACKUP command is necessary. For example, issue the following command from the DOS prompt:

BACKUP C:\SAMPLE\BUILD*.* A:

This will copy the BUILD directory contents to multiple floppy disks. Make sure that the DOS version of your development machine is the same as that of the target machine if you use the BACKUP command. The backup format of DOS 3.2 and below is not compatible with DOS 3.3 and above. This means that if you are doing development on a PC, using MS-DOS 4.0 and wish to distribute the dBASE IV RunTime software to a PC running MS-DOS 3.1, the RESTORE command necessary on the target PC will not execute properly. It will not suffice to copy over a DOS 4.0 RESTORE command to the target PC, since the command will respond with "Incorrect DOS version" when executed. The PC must be booted with the correct DOS version.

the BUILD directory into a single .ARC or .ZIP file. To do this, however, you need a special archiving utility program to shrink and then combine all the files into a single, smaller file. This program may be obtained through the public domain on various BBS (*B*ulletin *B*oard *S*ystem) computers and on-line services such as CompuServe.

The dBASE IV Professional Compiler

Now that the concept of a RunTime environment as a means of distribution for a dBASE IV application is well understood, the concept of a dBASE language compiler is the logical next step. dBASE language compiler products have been around for quite a long time, beginning with the dBIII Compiler from Wordtech Systems. Wordtech was the first company to produce a program to translate a computer program written in the dBASE language to a standalone, executable file with an .EXE extension. Later, Nantucket Corporation produced another compiler, called Clipper, which in the past few years has become the favorite among serious dBASE language application developers. Bear in mind, Ashton-Tate has never produced a compiler for the computer language it originated.

There has been an announcement, however, that a compiler project is in the works by Ashton-Tate, though it is being developed by Apex Software Corporation. The product, called the dBASE IV Professional Compiler, was only going into preliminary beta testing as this book was being finished. The likely shipping date for the product will not be until 1991. The compiler's goals are ambitious, which says a lot about why it is taking so long to complete. The compiler is attempting to enable the translation of "most" dBASE IV language constructs into an executable form. This is a monumental task, since the dBASE IV language is rather robust, but dBASE IV compatibility is a primary goal of the Professional Compiler. Another company that is committed to bringing out a dBASE IV compatible compiler is Wordtech Systems, with their Arago Quicksilver compiler. The announced release date of this product is mid-1991, which seems to indicate that theirs will most likely beat the Ashton-Tate product out the door.

What Is a Compiler?

A compiler is a computer program that takes as input a computer program written in some common programming language such as dBASE and outputs an executable, .EXE file. If you are familiar with DOS jargon, an .EXE file is a program file whose name can be entered from the DOS prompt (the only other file type for which you can do this is a .COM file), resulting in the execution of the program. In dBASE terms, this is to say that a compiled dBASE application may be run from the DOS prompt by just typing in the application's name, without dBASE even present.

A given compiler is generally limited to translating statements and commands for a specific programming language. Moreover, many compilers specialize further, accommodating only certain dialects of the language. For example, the Clipper compiler only recognizes a subset of the dBASE III language standard in its translation capabilities, but then adds a significant number of additional features, making it qualify as a dBASE language dialect. The Ashton-Tate Professional Compiler will translate only dBASE IV specific commands and statements (although many of the features of the competing products such as Clipper, Quicksilver, and FoxPro are now in dBASE IV).

As a nonprogramming application developer, you should perhaps view a compiler in a more specialized way. A compiler will take the dBASE program code generated by

ApGen, as well as all the associated objects—such as screens, reports, windows, and menus—and combine them all into a single .EXE file that you may run from the DOS prompt. The only objects not included in an executable file are databases and their index files (since these are dynamic in nature, as they change in size and content).

If you have the Developer's Edition, and were to try to generate a RunTime version of your ApGen application as described in the previous section, you would notice that several quite large files had to accompany the resulting .DBO file in order for the application to run. Compiling the application would alleviate this requirement. The only files necessary to run a compiled version of the application would be the .EXE file and any .DBF and .MDX files. One special goal of the Professional Compiler is to minimize the size of the resulting .EXE file. This is good, given the limited memory in DOS-based PCs.

Benefits of Compiled Applications

The benefits of compiled applications are many, though most pertain to the overall professional "look and feel" of the finished product. In a sense, compiling dBASE applications normalizes them so as to fit into the same genre of PC-based application software. After an application is compiled, there is no reason to be able to identify it as one developed in a dBASE environment versus one done in an ordinary high-level language such as C or Basic.

One nature of compiled programs in general is that they execute much faster than their interpreted counterparts. (Remember, when you run an application inside of dBASE it is done so interpretively.) This is even true of RunTime versions of an application, since using RunTime is just a matter of packaging. Applications wrapped around a runtime interpreter are still interpretive in nature, except that the production interpreter, such as dBASE IV, need not be present; instead, the runtime version of dBASE IV is substituted. Compiled applications are optimized for speed over interpreted versions since they are translated directly into .EXE executable files. This is another primary goal of the Professional Compiler: to maximize performance.

Another benefit of compiled applications concerns size. The disk files related to a compiled application are smaller than their RunTime equivalents. Consider the total number of bytes involved in distributing a RunTime version of an ApGen application. A conservative estimate would be well over 1 MB. The compiled equivalent is usually much smaller, normally under 640K. This relates directly to the number of diskettes that your application must occupy in the distribution process. The fewer the number of diskettes involved in distributing an application software package the better, even though the application might only be going to a couple of branch offices of a large corporation.

A third benefit is security. With a compiler, the application is translated directly into an .EXE file, which is virtually unreadable by the recipient. This means that your application is protected from prying eyes that may want to learn your techniques of software development. This is less important when using ApGen to guide the development tasks, but even then you may depend heavily on the embedded dBASE language code segments, and revealing the code in these areas of the application could be viewed as a breach of propriety. There are utility products on the market that will reverse-engineer a RunTime version of an application into working dBASE language source code (program statements). At the time of this writing, only the dBASE III+ RunTime was supported, but it is certain that a version for deciphering dBASE IV RunTime modules will appear soon enough. There is no product, however, that will take an .EXE compiled form and yield source code.

Final Directions

Now that you have finished this book, the question of where to go naturally arises. The Control Center represents a large portion of dBASE IV's functionality, but this is by no means the end of the story. The next logical step is to enlist the aid of add-on products that provide even more functionality without the need for programming. Ashton-Tate has made available (in a "work-in-progress form") a very powerful add-on called the Control Center Booster. This utility enhances several design surfaces, including the forms designer and QBE. For serious Control Center use this utility is a must.

Even with a full complement of add-ons, the Control Center has its limits, and at some point programming must be considered. This may come in steps. First, you could get a dose of programming using the interface inside ApGen for creating and attaching embedded code segments and code objects. Later you could try your hand at writing complete program objects and call them from ApGen. At this point, complete programming tasks may be undertaken. Bear in mind, however, that even seasoned dBASE programming developers can gain usefulness out of the various dBASE IV design surfaces, in particular ApGen. ApGen can certainly provide for the applications structure. As a programmer, you could then fill in the blanks by writing various program modules. Many professional developers overlook ApGen in this respect.

As a last step, you must realize that ApGen is customizable. As with most of the design surfaces, ApGen is driven by templates written by Ashton-Tate, but completely modifiable by anyone possessing the Developer's Edition, which contains the template compiler. This is truly the ultimate in application development—to use an application generator that is tailored to your specific needs. With this, there is no limit to what you can achieve.

Index